American LITERATURE
for Christian Schools®

Raymond A. St. John

BJU PRESS
GREENVILLE, SOUTH CAROLINA

NOTE: The fact that materials produced by other publishers may be referred to in this volume does not constitute an endorsement of the content or theological position of materials produced by such publishers. Any references and ancillary materials are listed as an aid to the student or the teacher and in an attempt to maintain the accepted academic standards of the publishing industry.

AMERICAN LITERATURE for Christian Schools®
Second Edition

Raymond A. St. John, Ph.D.

Coordinating Writer	**Designer**	**Composition**	**Project Coordinator**
Greta Forman	Duane Nichols	Kelley Moore	Richard Ayers
Editor	**Cover**	**Photo Acquisition**	
Nathan M. Huffstutler	Joseph Tyrpak	Tara Swaney	
	Duane Nichols		

Produced in cooperation with the Bob Jones University Division of English Language and Literature of the College of Arts and Science, the School of Religion, and Bob Jones Academy.

for Christian Schools is a registered trademark of Bob Jones University Press.

© 2003 Bob Jones University Press
Greenville, South Carolina 29614

First Edition © 1981 Bob Jones University Press
Second Edition © 1991 Bob Jones University Press

ISBN 1-59166-438-1

15   14   13   12   11   10   9   8   7   6   5   4   3   2   1

Introduction

AMERICAN LITERATURE for Christian Schools® tells the story of the writing done in the United States from its beginnings until the present. It covers key events, major literary movements, and principal players of a dynamic heritage that was born four centuries ago and remains today a vital expression of the heart and soul of the American people. Like other anthologies it showcases as fully as possible the rich variety and impressive appeal of the literature produced in this nation.

But the book does more. It tells the story of a culture that has shifted from essential agreement with the truth of God's Word to almost universal rejection of that truth. At times the change, as reflected in the literature, has been virtually glacial in its pace, hardly discernible to those of its day. At other times the change has been dramatic, apparent even to casual observers.

To understand the values of our society and culture today, we must know our past. The textbook provides a traditional but still useful means of identifying, arranging, and storing ideas. As you will notice, this account of American literature has been partitioned into four major phases: Early American Literature (1607-1820), American Romanticism (1820-65), American Realism and Naturalism (1865-1914), and Modern American Literature (1914-present).

What writers say (their themes) and how they express themselves (their styles) are powerfully dependent upon their times. Most writers, in fact, are affected more deeply by their times than they often realize. In this text we will look at historical events and trends before examining the works themselves. Since this work assumes a Christian reader with a Christian worldview, we will maintain a genuinely Christian perspective throughout. We will examine all writings in the light of Scripture—especially when we study authors whose philosophies contradict the Word of God. It is the prayer of the author that this textbook will further enable you to be discerning and Christlike in your approach not only to American literature but to life itself.

Early American Literature

3 LITERATURE OF REVOLUTION

American Romanticism

An Era of Optimism 138

7 TRANSCENDENTAL PESSIMISTS

American Realism and Naturalism

8 REGIONALISTS

9 MASTERS OF REALISM

10 NATURALISTS

11 ANTI-NATURALISTS

Modern American Literature

13 MODERN AMERICAN PROSE

1

PART ONE

The Washington Family: Edward Savage; National Gallery of Art, Washington; Andrew W. Mellon Collection.

An Era of Change

Hardly anyone today wants to be called a Puritan. To many people the name *Puritan* suggests grim judgmentalism—a rigid, repressive prudery that once darkened American thought but is now thankfully outgrown. Although this Puritan stereotype has been discredited by historians, the myth lives on.

The truth is that Puritanism has been much more central in American life than is commonly supposed. The Puritans gave America not only a doctrinal system but also an idea of how life should be lived. Puritan theology lost its hold on American thought within two hundred years. However, the Puritan view of life—the work ethic, the goal-centeredness, the subservience of pleasure to duty—has survived, even among many who despise its religious foundation.

Two Puritan themes are strongly apparent in the literature of the early period. The first is this country's role as idealistic leader and practical innovator. The Puritans set high goals and devised means for reaching them; their efforts would command the attention of all peoples. In 1629 while sailing to Massachusetts, Governor John Winthrop urged the other Puritans aboard ship not to forget that their attempt to establish a religious state in the New World would be observed carefully by the rest of the world. "We shall be as a city upon a hill, the eyes of all people . . . upon us." These words were prophetic, for the rest of the world since Puritan times has carefully watched this country's political, religious, and social developments.

The second Puritan theme is the Christian's attitude toward the world. In his history of Plymouth Plantation, Governor William Bradford described how the Pilgrims, who were actually Separatists rather than Puritans, shared the Puritan view of the alluring, hostile world that had tried to destroy them and their testimony: "So they left that goodly and pleasant city [Leyden, Netherlands], which had been their resting place near twelve years; but they knew they were pilgrims, and looked not much on those things, but lifted up their eyes to the heavens, their dearest country, and quieted their spirits." Few writers have better summarized the faith of Christians, who while *in* the world are not to be *of* the world. The theme of America as

an idealistic leader and practical innovator persisted in American literature well beyond the early period. Regrettably, however, the idea of Americans as Christian pilgrims in the world appears only rarely after 1750.

The division known as Early American Literature spans over 200 years. This period is important not only because of its considerable length but also because of its influence on the character of the developing nation. In order to appreciate the literature of our first writers, therefore, we must understand something of the key developments during their time.

During these centuries, American writers were affected by changes occurring in three major areas. First, the population of the country, while constantly expanding, changed from essentially immigrant to distinctively American. Second, the principles that governed decisions made by men in power shifted from religious to secular and materialistic. Third, the political system of the country underwent a radical modification from colonial dependence on and subservience to England to proud independence as the United States of America.

EUROPEAN TO AMERICAN: THE SOCIAL CHANGE

The Early Immigrants

Most of our early colonists were immigrants from England. In 1607 the first permanent English settlement began at Jamestown, Virginia. Here the small band of poorly organized Englishmen confidently expected to become wealthy merely by picking up the gold and pearls they thought awaited them. Had Captain John Smith not organized and directed them, the Jamestown planting would probably have failed like the ill-fated settlements of Roanoke Island.

In 1620, thirteen years after Jamestown's founding, the first permanent English settlers arrived in New England. The 102 colonists aboard the *Mayflower* were greeted by a barren, wintry wilderness and hostile savages. By the spring of 1621, more than half the original settlers were dead. What sustained these Pilgrims through the hardships of their first years in New England was their will to succeed and their confidence in God's providential care.

In the 1630s the struggling colony at Plymouth was surpassed by the Massachusetts Bay Colony, which had experienced an influx of relatively wealthy and influential Puritans. The first group of them, unlike the Pilgrims, embarked for the New World in a fleet of ships. From 1630 to 1640, during what is called the Great Migration, some twenty thousand people sailed to Massachusetts, hastened by political and religious events in England. During the period immediately before the English Civil War (1642-1646), many dissenters came to the New World because of especially severe repression by the Church of England.

Immigration slackened during the Commonwealth period in England when the Puritans seized political control and stopped the persecutions. However, it dramatically increased in 1660, when the monarchy was restored. This year marked the beginning of the second major Puritan migration. Reacting against the stern Puritan rule during the preceding decade, Parliament passed a series of harsh, repressive acts against nonconformists. Until the Toleration Act of 1689 somewhat eased conditions for Puritans, these laws caused thousands more to flee to the New World.

Religious reasons for immigration The main motive behind these migrations to New England was religious. Many colonists came because of religious persecution. In chapter 2 of his history of Plymouth, Governor Bradford movingly describes the severe oppression endured by just one small band of English dissenters: those who settled Plymouth. Because they were Separatists (members of independent congregations that had left the Church of England for conscience' sake), their practice of worship was especially hated by leaders of the state church. These dissenters were betrayed and imprisoned, had their property confiscated, and finally were forced to flee illegally to the Netherlands. For many later dissenters, this persecution took another form. They were forbidden to preach from pulpits, to teach in schools or colleges, and to hold political office.

Other colonists sailed to the New World because they wanted to put their religious ideals into operation. The Massachusetts Puritans wanted to follow what they believed the Bible taught in doctrine and church government. Beyond that, they wished to establish a state governed by religious principles. They believed that their government should be theocratic (governed by God) rather than democratic (governed by the people). Since the Bible describes only one form of government specifically ordained by God, the theocratic government of Israel, the Puritans took it as their model.

Secular reasons for immigration Colonists also came to the New World because of nonreligious motives. Some came for adventure, some to help England challenge Spain's claims to the American continent, and some to gain personal independence and wealth. The last of these motives, self-realization and advancement, gave rise to the American Dream. Many immigrants believed that in the New World they could free themselves from the class restrictions of European societies and rise by their own abilities to positions of affluence and prestige. The dream was so strong that hundreds even sold themselves into bondage as indentured servants in order to repay the cost of their passage to the colonies.

What made these seventeenth-century immigrants so valuable to the emerging nation is that they brought with them the culture of their homeland. As they struggled to construct their "city upon a hill" in the wilderness, they built their new society upon the rich cultural values which they had brought from England.

The Transitional Colonists

With the coming of the eighteenth century, however, colonists became noticeably less European. Since many colonials were by this time second-, third-, or even fourth-generation residents, they felt few ties to England. Increasingly, these home-bred citizens recognized they were no longer merely transplanted Europeans. In New England the transitional colonist took on a special identity, that of the "Yankee." This sturdy New England type was characterized by homespun wisdom, practical ingenuity, and a shrewd business sense.

Meanwhile, as more Europeans flocked to the New World, the colonial population lost its distinctively English identity. Large numbers of Dutch, French Huguenot, German, and Scottish immigrants helped shape the national spirit as they pushed westward into the wilderness. But since most of these new immigrants were Protestant and most sought the liberty which had been denied them in their homelands, they carried on the spirit of the first immigrants.

The Americans

The product of these developments was described in 1782 by a Frenchman who had himself immigrated to New York. In his *Letters from an American Farmer,* J. Hector St. John de Crèvecoeur gives a stirring answer to the question, "What then is the American, this new man?"

> He is either an European, or the descendant of an European, hence that strange mixture of blood which you will find in no other country. I could point out to you a family whose grandfather was an Englishman, whose wife was Dutch, whose son married a French woman, and whose present four sons have now four wives of different nations. *He* is an American, who, leaving behind him all his ancient prejudices and manners, receives new ones from the new mode of life he has embraced, the new government he obeys, and the new rank he holds. He becomes an American by being received in the broad lap of our great *Alma Mater.* Here individuals of all nations are melted into a new race of men, whose labors and posterity will one day cause great changes in the world. Americans are the western pilgrims, who are carrying along with them that great mass of arts, sciences, vigor, and industry which began long since in the east; they will finish the great circle. The Americans were once scattered all over Europe; here they are incorporated into one of the finest systems of population which has ever appeared, and [one] which will hereafter become distinct by the power of the different climates they inhabit. The American ought therefore to love this country much better than that wherein either he or his forefathers were born. . . . The American is a new man, who acts upon new principles; he must therefore entertain new ideas, and form new opinions.

Crèvecoeur strikes several major themes developed by later writers: the United States as a melting pot of nationalities, Americans as the "western pilgrims" who will accomplish great things for mankind, the American as the "new man" who is forward-looking and experimental.

PURITANISM TO DEISM: THE RELIGIOUS CHANGE

The Essence of Puritanism

Because most of the first New England colonists embraced Puritan ideals, Puritanism has formed the main current in the development of American values. The Puritan movement began in England during the reign of Elizabeth I (1558-1603). It

sought to complete the English Reformation by purifying the Church of England of all non-Scriptural elements retained from Roman Catholicism. The movement produced two major dissident groups: those who tried to reform the Church of England (the Puritans) and those who broke altogether with the Church of England (the Separatists). These groups, in addition to Presbyterians, Baptists, and some other dissenting groups, composed English nonconformity. During the seventeenth century, as Puritanism grew into a potent political force, the meaning of the term *Puritan* broadened to include virtually all English Protestants other than those supporting the Anglican church.

The religious identities of the first colonies reflected the major factions within English Protestantism. Virginia was Anglican; Plymouth Plantation, Separatist; Massachusetts Bay, Puritan (in the narrower, original sense). However, in spite of differences over church government and the ordinances, these Protestant groups held basically to the same body of doctrine, the historic beliefs of the Protestant church.

The religious thought of seventeenth-century New England was extensively shaped by the works of John Calvin (1509-1564), especially his *Institutes*. Many Christians today do not concur with all of Calvin's emphases. In fact, many Puritans would not have accepted the modern oversimplification of historic Calvinism, the so-called Five Points. These Five Points, however, can help to show how Puritan writers, especially the later ones, believed God deals with mankind. The first of these is *total depravity:* because of Adam's fall, all men are totally wicked and spiritually disabled and deserve punishment in hell. The second is *unconditional election:* since God has chosen, or "elected," certain ones to be saved on no merits of their own, none can by good works or faith bring to pass their salvation. The third is *limited atonement:* Christ's death atones only for the sins of the elect, not for those of the entire human race. The fourth is *irresistible grace:* no elect will ultimately refuse God's grace; if chosen, the sinner will be drawn to salvation in spite of himself. Fifth is *the perseverance of the saints:* those chosen by God cannot fall from His grace into damnation.

The Puritans believed that the Scriptures set forth a total plan for man's existence on earth. Therefore, in the Massachusetts Bay Colony, they formed a government based on God's plan for Israel in the Old Testament. Their government combined civil and religious authority under the same magistrates. Persons guilty of moral infractions were punished by the state. In his journal of Massachusetts Bay, Governor Winthrop records some of the punishments for acts condemned in the Bible. A man and a woman found guilty of adultery were executed. A merchant convicted of selling his goods at exorbitant prices was publicly censured and required to make restitution. The founders of Massachusetts Bay were attempting to create a theocracy.

The Causes of Puritanism's Decline

Theocracy lasted only a short while in the Massachusetts Bay Colony. By 1660, thirty years after the colony's founding, spiritual fervor had declined throughout the colonies. With material prosperity had come worldly interests and goals. Secular values were replacing religious ones. As a result, church membership had fallen. Since church membership was the foundation of society, the whole theocratic principle was at risk. At first, the Puritan ministers tried to preach the colonists back to their first fervor. Then, having failed, they compromised by drafting what became known as the Halfway Covenant.

The Halfway Covenant Prior to 1662 a prospective church member had to give a detailed public testimony, a profession of his salvation through faith in Christ, before he could qualify for church membership. Those who were either unwilling or unable to give this testimony could attend church (in fact, were required by law to do so in many settlements) but could not vote or participate in the ordinances of the church (baptism and communion). By 1662, however, many second-generation colonists were not members because they had not given the required public testimony. Alarmed at declining church membership, ministers allowed children of full members to come "halfway" into the church without the public testimony. That is, they could be baptized but could enjoy none of the other special benefits. By 1700 many ministers went beyond even the Halfway Covenant and allowed church attenders with good standing in the community to participate in the Lord's Supper without the required public testimony. Like most religious compromises, the Halfway Covenant was not only ineffective, but also ultimately contributed to the problem of declining interest in the church.

The Revivals of the Eighteenth Century

For seventy years after the creation of the Halfway Covenant, religious interest continued to slacken. Then, in the 1730s, New England experienced the outbreak of the first major American revival. It began in Jonathan Edwards's church at Northampton, Massachusetts, then spread to other parts of New England. During the 1740s, as the movement gained strength, it came to be called the Great Awakening. Through the preaching of English evangelist George Whitefield and others, thousands in New England were converted. These itinerant preachers, barred from most pulpits, often conducted their meetings outdoors. The revival spread without the support and sympathy of the established churches, and two results followed their refusal to participate. First, the parish ministers lost influence among the people in religious matters, and vital religion became individualistic. Second, denominations such as the Baptist, Methodist, and Presbyterian became powerful competition for the Congregational church, which up to this time had been the most influential ecclesiastical power.

The next major revival, the Second Awakening, came fifty years later, in the early decades after the Revolutionary War. This movement had a special impact on the frontier regions and helped make the Methodist and Baptist denominations the two largest religious groups in the nation. The Second Awakening also produced the camp meeting, a spiritually powerful institution of American religious life until the end of the nineteenth century.

The Rise of Deism

While these two revivals were slowing religious decline, deism was furthering it. An outgrowth of eighteenth-century rationalism, deism maintained that the solution to the problems of man lies in his reason, not in supernatural revelation, the Bible. Popular in colonial colleges and among the intellectuals of the day, this enemy of true faith was adopted by many colonial leaders.

Beliefs of deism The rise of deism revealed how far the eighteenth century, or Age of Reason, had drifted from the Biblical truth of Puritanism. Deists believed, first, that although God is all-powerful and controls the world He created, He does not personally intervene in the operation of it. They described God by such terms as the "Great First Cause" and the "Clock-winder." Deists believed, second, that man is not a flawed, fallen creature but a being who can by his own works please God. Deists believed, third, that man's good on earth will be rewarded in a future life and that his evil will be punished, although they were unsure exactly how and where the future judgment will take place. They believed, fourth, that man can become better through education; in fact, education can help man eradicate evil from the world. Deists, finally, distrusted all existing systems and institutions of religion.

The deistic emphases on reason and man's inherent rights influenced the key political documents written during the last quarter of the eighteenth century. The belief that man has failed God through sin was replaced by the man-centered tenets of deism. For all practical purposes, the last major spokesman for Puritanism disappeared in 1758 with the death of Jonathan Edwards. Edwards had perpetuated the spirit of Puritanism, if not its entire body of thought. After his death, the Puritan influence lingered only in the secular, vaguely ethical form apparent in the writings of Benjamin Franklin and Nathaniel Hawthorne.

COLONIES TO NATION: THE POLITICAL CHANGE

Political Foundations

The Early American period was also a time of profound political change. At first, political rights were severely limited for most people. Political power resided almost exclusively in the hands of those authorizing and financing new settlements. In fact, only male property holders who were church members had the right to vote in most colonies. Women, slaves, indentured servants, and tenant farmers were excluded, as well as frequently all who were not members of the state church.

In the early seventeenth century there emerged a document of great importance for future political developments: the Mayflower Compact (1620). Since the Pilgrims and other passengers aboard the *Mayflower* had landed north of the territory granted to the company sponsoring their settlement, they were beyond England's colonial jurisdiction. The adult males aboard the ship, however, voluntarily agreed to surrender their individual rights in order to establish a government for the colony. Their agreement to establish government by compact no doubt developed from the Separatist position on church polity, or form of government. Under Separatist theory, churches could be created and governed only by agreement of the members, not from some outside source.

This action by the Pilgrims set a significant precedent for the eighteenth-century framers of the Constitution, our most important national document. They based their new plan of government on the current political theory that the authority of the state rests upon the consent of the governed. In another way, this action prepared the way for the revolutionary era. The early colonists believed that all political authority derives finally from God, not from a king. They regarded their elected representatives, as well as other governmental agents, as vice-regents of God, who hold their offices at His pleasure.

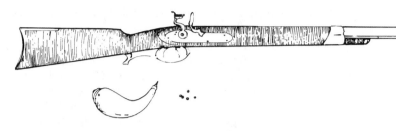

Colonial Unrest

What made the source of authority an important issue in the eighteenth century was England's determination to restrict freedom in the colonies. Since England neglected to intervene when the early settlers first began assuming rights of self-determination, she encountered aggressive colonial resistance when she later tried to impose controls. She found it difficult to turn back the political clock. By 1752 the king had annulled the original charters except for those of the proprietary colonies of Maryland, Pennsylvania, and Delaware and the charter colonies of Rhode Island and Connecticut. The remaining colonies were royal colonies directly under the control of the king. While the king grudgingly allowed the colonists to elect legislative bodies to represent their interests, those who actually held the power were the colonial governors and councils, appointees of the king.

Economic issues The political rift with England widened during the middle part of the eighteenth century as English policy shifted to a stricter enforcement of revenue on trade with the colonies. It mattered little to the colonials that they were not being taxed as greatly as their relatives in England or that on certain products the English were paying taxes not collected in the colonies. Colonies began to rally behind the cry "no taxation without representation." Economic and political issues merged as the colonists increasingly felt their lack of political freedom.

After the Peace of Paris (1763) ended the French and Indian War, English colonial policy became particularly offensive to the colonists. First, the treaty restricted further settlement west of the Allegheny Mountains. It reserved the land lying between this mountain range and the Mississippi River as a giant hunting preserve for Indian tribes. Second, the war had left England saddled with a huge debt for its military action against the French and their Indian allies. The colonists were rigidly unwilling to help assume payment of this debt. On the other side, George III (1760-1820) and key policymakers made no attempt to pacify the politically restless colonies but enforced policies that widened the breach. In the final decade before the Revolutionary War, England's acts convinced many influential colonists that the best—in fact, the only—course of action for the colonies was political separation from England.

American Independence

America officially announced her independence in 1776 and made this independence permanent by military victory over England in 1783. The new country soon learned, however, that military success was only the beginning. America now stood among the nations of the world as a political unit, but it had not yet learned how to function effectively as a nation. There was quarreling among the colonies, each of which regarded itself as a sovereign state. The new country needed a strong constitution to unify all the states if it was to survive. In 1787, after long weeks of fierce debates, the Second Constitutional Convention worked out a detailed plan protecting the rights of both the majority and the minority. With the ratification of the Constitution in 1789, the country was ready to step forward under President George Washington, the brilliant general who had engineered the colonial victory in the Revolutionary War.

By 1820 the United States was a recognized world power. It had more than doubled its size with the Louisiana Purchase (1803) and had demonstrated its naval strength in its victory over England in the War of 1812. The fledgling country seemed ready to provide mature leadership among the nations of the world. It was time, many believed, for the birth of a distinctively American literature.

IMITATION TO MATURITY: THE LITERARY CHANGE

Literary Form

Before a distinctly American literature could exist, early writers had to cast off their childlike dependence on English literature. Since literature grows out of personal experience, it is only natural that the first writers in America should reflect their English backgrounds. Isolated from British authors and often from each other, colonial writers tended to imitate the popular, respected forms they had known during their formative years in England or had read, if they were born in this country, during their educational preparation. This tendency caused early American writers to lag nearly a whole generation behind their English contemporaries. Accordingly poets such as Anne Bradstreet and Edward Taylor imitated forms already out of favor in England.

It was not until after the Revolutionary War that the time lag began to disappear and the first consciously American voices began to speak through the literature. With the emergence of a national consciousness appeared also the first signs of a truly national literature. The full flowering of American literature would not come until the Romantic Age, but the soil was prepared during America's first literary period.

Subject Matter

Colonial literature quite naturally reflected the interests and concerns of its writers. Since America was founded in adversity, it is not surprising that the earliest authors wrote mostly of the threatening features of their environment. We read of the rigors of the climate and the hostility of the wilderness, of attacks by warring Indians, and of clashes over religious and political issues. Once the colonists had established permanent settlements in the wilderness, the subject matter became predominantly religious. Writers wrote either for personal stimulation (Edward Taylor and, at times, Samuel Sewall) or for public instruction (Jonathan Edwards). As the eighteenth century neared its end, the subject matter reflected the revolutionary attitudes sweeping the colonies. Writers' concerns became almost totally secular. Typical are the writings of Benjamin Franklin and Thomas Jefferson.

World View

This secularization of subject matter reflects a changing world view. When a seventeenth-century writer such as William Bradford viewed an event in nature, he tried to understand the spiritual significance of that event. For example, when the Puritan clergyman Cotton Mather had witnessed the effects of a severe hailstorm on the nearly completed house of Boston merchant and jurist Samuel Sewall, he prayed that God would help those present to remember the frailty of their bodies as they contemplated the broken panes of glass. He saw a spiritual lesson in the facts of nature. Later writers did not interpret spiritually what they saw but tried instead to describe it with scientific accuracy.

Literary Purpose

In early America the primary purpose of literature was instruction. For the Puritan writer the goal of this instruction was religious improvement. Virtually all Puritan literature, even the poetry, is frankly didactic (intended to instruct). In the eighteenth century, literature still served didactic purposes, even in forms new to America such as the novel and satire. The difference, of course, is that the eighteenth-century literary purpose was generally secular instruction rather than religious. Benjamin Franklin taught the secular virtues of Prudence (discretion), Frugality (thrift), and Industry (diligence). It was not until the early nineteenth century, with the appearance of Washington Irving (1783-1859), that a major American writer aimed primarily at entertainment.

Plain Style

Early American literature is uniform not only in purpose but also in style. The early Puritan writers sought to express their ideas with the utmost plainness. Their desire for plainness resulted partly from a rejection of the ornate writing popular in early seventeenth-century England. The English writers preferred an ornate style which displayed their use of scholarly allusions, flights of imagination, and fancy rhetorical devices. The Puritans, however, viewed such ornateness as self-glorifying and distracting. They preferred, instead, a style which directed attention to the message rather than to the writer, a style characterized by clarity, simplicity of word choice and organization, scarcity of elaborate figurative expression, and naturalness.

Because Puritans deliberately cultivated a prose that was religious in content, didactic in purpose, and plain in style, their writing has suffered badly at the hands of critics who have preferred secular subject matter, ambiguity of purpose, and complexity of style. One standard charge against Puritan writers is that their writing is merely an extension of their preaching and therefore lacks artistry. What this criticism ignores is that the Puritan, while carefully avoiding ornateness, was true to the artistic requirements of the plain style. This style, in fact, was soon to come into vogue in eighteenth-century England during the Neoclassic era. The Neoclassic writers' concern for restraint and decorum reflects the Puritan plain style. Not until the Romantic era did writers again prefer an ornate rather than a plain writing style.

The legacy of the Puritan writers is an impressive one for the American who delights in the birth and growth of his country and for the Christian whose beliefs enable him to sympathize with Puritan experiences and goals. As these practical men addressed themselves to practical issues through practical literary forms, they left a record of their approach to life—a tough-minded individualism that challenges modern sentimental or pessimistic views of man and his world. It is a pleasure to begin the study of American literature with writings that teach what Christians have always believed.

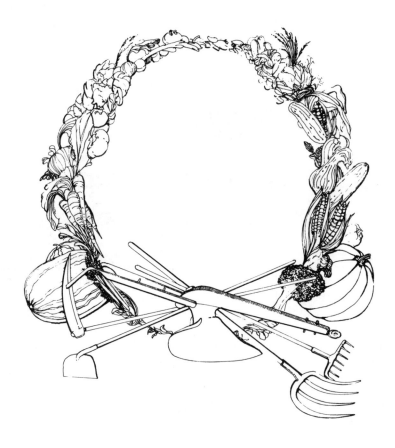

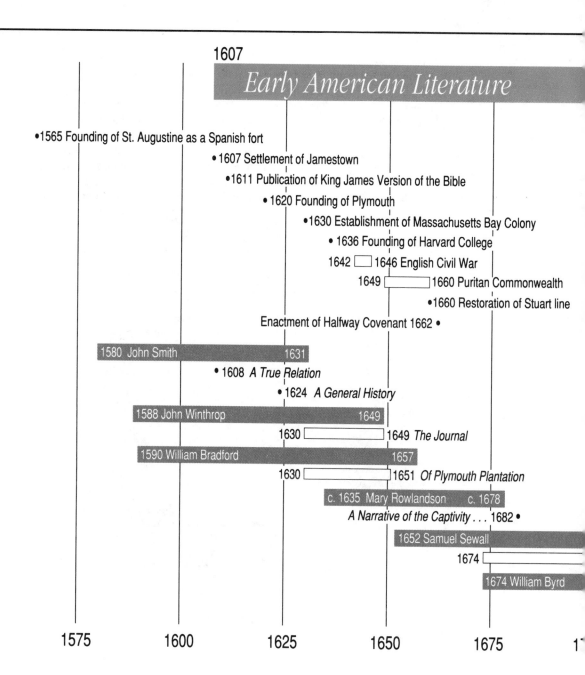

1607

Early American Literature

•1565 Founding of St. Augustine as a Spanish fort

• 1607 Settlement of Jamestown

• 1611 Publication of King James Version of the Bible

• 1620 Founding of Plymouth

•1630 Establishment of Massachusetts Bay Colony

• 1636 Founding of Harvard College

1642 ☐ 1646 English Civil War

1649 ☐ 1660 Puritan Commonwealth

•1660 Restoration of Stuart line

Enactment of Halfway Covenant 1662 •

1580 John Smith   1631

• 1608 *A True Relation*

• 1624 *A General History*

1588 John Winthrop   1649

1630 ☐ 1649 *The Journal*

1590 William Bradford   1657

1630 ☐ 1651 *Of Plymouth Plantation*

c. 1635 Mary Rowlandson   c. 1678

A Narrative of the Captivity . . . 1682 •

1652 Samuel Sewall

1674 ☐

1674 William Byrd

1575   1600   1625   1650   1675   1

1820

1 *Literature of Settlement*

1730

1729 *The Diary*

1744

• 1728 *The History of the Dividing Line*

John Smith   1580-1631

Few men have undergone the hardships endured by Captain John Smith. During an incredibly busy and useful life, Smith found time to write the earliest significant accounts of the Virginia and New England settlements.

During the first phase of Smith's adventurous life (1580-1606), he served as a foot soldier for the English in the Scottish Lowlands; traveled extensively throughout Europe; fought against the Turks, who captured him and sold him as a slave; and escaped from his masters to live as a pirate along the coast of North Africa before returning to England. Back in his homeland he entered the second phase of his life (1606-9). Catching the fever for colonization, he invested his money in the Virginia Company and sailed to the New World. On his arrival he was appointed to the governing council of Virginia and even served for a year as its governor. But despite his success, Smith continued to skirt disaster. He had been imprisoned for mutiny aboard the ship bound for Virginia. Later, after being captured by Indians, he was nearly put to death. Then he almost lost his life at the hands of a small but influential faction of colonists. This group insisted on Smith's execution as repayment for the lives of men who, while under his command, had been killed by Indians. It was largely because of his successful leadership and diplomacy that Jamestown escaped destruction from within by the bickering, jealousy, and laziness of its own men and from without by the hostile Indians led by the crafty Powhatan. Seriously injured by an explosion in 1609, Smith returned to England, never again to visit Jamestown. In the last phase of his life (1610-31), Smith promoted the settlement of New England. His explorations of its coast, his carefully drawn maps, his glowing description of the fruitfulness of the land and fishing waters, his advice to the Pilgrims and later New England colonists–all showed his belief in the promise of the New World. He died in England in 1631, the embodiment of the Renaissance adventurer.

Three of Smith's books and pamphlets have significance for American literature. In *A True Relation of Such Occurrences and Accidents of Note as Hath Happened in Virginia Since the First Planting of That Colony* (1608), Smith gives an eyewitness account of the early, difficult months in Jamestown. His testimony is undercut, critics claim, by his tendency to use his account for self-praise and self-justification. In *A Description of New England* (1616), Smith reports the result of his 1614 exploration of the New England coast. His maps from this exploration guided the Pilgrims, who arrived in 1620, and his description of the fertility of the land and sea helped attract numerous colonists to the New World. In *A General History of Virginia, New England, and the Summer Isles*

(1624), he expands much of the information from the earlier works. The famous account of Pocahontas's saving his life does not appear in the 1608 record but does in the 1624 version. This fact has led some critics and historians to discount the story and claim that the legend was created by Smith's fertile imagination because he needed money and because no one could dispute it since Pocahontas had died. However, since his accounts are usually supported by the testimony of his contemporaries and since the Indians had the custom of giving a captive to whichever tribe member desired him, Smith's tale may be much more than just a romantic invention.

It is interesting that Smith's motivation for colonizing the New World was not only to gain wealth and territory for England but also to evangelize the savages. Moreover, in his records of the Jamestown planting, Smith writes that Pocahontas's untiring efforts to save the struggling colony were but second to God's providential intervention on behalf of the new venture. Thus, the first writer in America establishes a firm precedent in American literature for recognition of God's hand in the directing and preserving of the new country.

A General History

A General History *(1624) is an expansion of* A True Relation *(1608), Smith's first account of Jamestown's founding. In the* History *this account takes on an apologetic quality; that is, it becomes a defense of Smith's actions and a vindication of his beliefs. While recording the events, Smith often points out the weakness in the poorly conceived plans of others and justifies his own actions.*

After explaining in Chapter 1 how the Virginia Company had come into being and how the 105 pioneers were ill prepared for the hardships they faced in Virginia, Smith tells how he was suspected of treason and put under guard. He conducted himself so well, he reports, that he won the majority of the colonists to his side and was acquitted.

The second chapter opens with the colonists faring very poorly after the ships had returned to England. Rather than work, the men preferred to bicker among themselves and search for the gold and pearls they thought would be lying on top of the ground. The leaders could not get the colonists to attend to the essentials of settlement: building houses, planting food crops, organizing the defenses, and so forth. After nearly starving, they were surprised by the changed attitude of the Indians, who unaccountably started bringing food to the colonists. When the Indians' hospitality ceased, Smith led a party of armed men to obtain food by force, if necessary. As winter approached, flocks of migrating waterfowl amply supplied the Jamestown colonists with food.

from Chapter Two

But our comedies never endured long without a tragedy, some idle exceptions being muttered against Captain Smith for not discovering the head of the Chickahominy River, and being taxed* by the Council to be too slow in so worthy an attempt. The next voyage he proceeded so far that with much labor by cutting of trees asunder* he made his passage; but when his barge could pass no farther, he left her in a broad bay out of danger of shot, commanding none should go ashore till his return: himself with two English and two savages went up higher in a canoe; but he was not long absent, but his men went ashore, whose want of government gave both occasion and opportunity to the savages to surprise one George Cassen, whom they slew and much failed not to have cut off the boat and all the rest.

taxed: accused
asunder: apart

Smith little dreaming of that accident, being got to the marshes at the river's head, twenty miles in the desert, had his two men slain (as is supposed) sleeping by the canoe, whilst himself by fowling sought them victual: who finding he was beset with 200 savages, two of them he slew, still* defending himself with the aid of a savage his guide, whom he bound to his arm with his garters and used him as a buckler,* yet he was shot in his thigh a little and had many arrows that stuck in his clothes but no great hurt, till at last they took him prisoner.

still: always
buckler: shield

When this news came to Jamestown, much was their sorrow for his loss, few expecting what ensued.*

ensued: occurred afterward

Six or seven weeks those barbarians kept him prisoner, many strange triumphs and conjurations* they made of him, yet he so demeaned* himself amongst them as he not only diverted* them from surprising the fort but procured* his own liberty, and got himself and his company such estimation amongst them that those savages admired him more than their own *Quiyoughkasoucks.* . . .

conjurations: magic spells
demeaned: conducted
diverted: distracted
procured: acquired

At last they brought him to *Meronocomoco,** where was Powhatan their Emperor. Here more than two hundred of those grim courtiers* stood wondering at him as* he had been a monster; till Powhatan and his train had put themselves in their greatest braveries.* Before a fire upon a seat like a bedstead, he sat covered with a great robe made of *rarowcun** skins and all the tails hanging by. On either hand did sit a young wench* of 16 or 18 years, and along on each side of the house two rows of men, and behind them as many women, with all their heads and shoulders painted red; many of their heads bedecked* with the white down of birds, but everyone with something and a great chain of white beads about their necks.

Meronocomoco: sometimes Werowocómoco: i.e., "chief's town"
grim courtiers: attendant members of Powhatan's court
as: as if
braveries: showy attire; finery
rarowcun: raccoon
wench: young woman
bedecked: adorned

At his entrance before the King, all the people gave a great shout. The Queen of *Appomattoc* was appointed to bring him water to wash his hands, and another brought him a bunch of feathers instead of a towel to dry them; having feasted him after their best barbarous manner they could, a long consultation was held, but the conclusion was, two great stones were brought before Powhatan: then as many as could laid hands on him, dragged him to them, and thereon laid his head, and being ready with their clubs, to beat out his brains, Pocahontas the King's dearest daughter, when no entreaty* could prevail, got his head in her arms, and laid her own upon his to save him from death; whereat the Emperor was contented he should live to make him hatchets and her bells, beads, and copper. . . .

---

entreaty: petition, appeal

Two days after, Powhatan, having disguised himself in the most fearfullest manner he could, caused Captain Smith to be brought forth to a great house in the woods and there upon a mat by the fire to be left alone. Not long after, from behind a mat that divided the house, was made the most dolefullest* noise he ever heard; then Powhatan more like a devil than a man, with some two hundred more as black as himself, came unto him and told him now they were friends and presently* he should go to Jamestown to send him two great guns and a grindstone, for which he would give him the country of *Capahowasick* and forever esteem* him as his son Nantaquaus.

---

dolefullest: most mournful
presently: shortly, soon
esteem: regard

So to Jamestown with 12 guides Powhatan sent him. That night they quartered* in the woods, he still expecting (as he had done all this long time of his imprisonment) every hour to be put to one death or another, for all their feasting. But almighty God (by his divine providence*) had mollified* the hearts of those stern barbarians with compassion. The next morning betimes* they came to the fort, where Smith having used the savages with what kindness he could, he

showed Rawhunt, Powhatan's trusty servant, two demi-culverings* and a millstone to carry [to] Powhatan: they found them somewhat too heavy; but when they did see him discharge them, being loaded with stones, among the boughs of a great tree loaded with icicles, the ice and branches came so tumbling down that the poor savages ran away half dead with fear. But at last we regained some conference* with them and gave them such toys* and sent to Powhatan, his women, and children such presents as gave them in general full content.

---

quartered: camped
providence: care
mollified: softened
betimes: early
demi-culverings: small cannons
conference: were able to talk with them again
toys: trinkets

Now in Jamestown they were all in combustion,* the strongest preparing once more to run away with the pinnace;* which, with the hazard of his life, with saker, falcon,* and musket shot, Smith forced now the third time to stay or sink.

---

combustion: confusion
pinnace: small schooner-rigged vessel
saker, falcon: two types of cannon

Some no better than they should be had plotted with the President* the next day to have put him to death by the Levitical law* for the lives of Robinson and Emry,* pretending the fault was his that had led them to their ends; but he quickly took such an order* with such lawyers that he laid them by the heels till he sent some of them prisoners to England.

President: John Ratcliffe, appointed head of the governing council
Levitical law: Leviticus 24:17
Robinson and Emry: colonists killed on Smith's expedition
took . . . order: gained such control of the situation

Now every once in four or five days, Pocahontas with her attendants brought him so much provision that saved many of their lives, that else for all this had starved with hunger. . . .

His relation of the plenty he had seen, especially at *Werowocómoco,* and of the state and bounty of Powhatan (which till that time was unknown) so revived their dead spirits (especially the love of Pocahontas) as all men's fear was abandoned.

Thus you may see what difficulties still crossed any good endeavor; and the good success of the business being thus oft brought to the very period of destruction, yet you see by what strange means God hath still delivered it.

from A Description of New England

After returning to England in 1609, Smith directed his energy toward promoting the settling of New England. In 1614 he explored the coast of New England, drawing maps that later settlers would use. His praise of the bounty of the area and his vision of what men could accomplish in the New World are the earliest extended statement of the American Dream.

In the month of April, 1614, with two ships from London, of a few merchants, I chanced to arrive in New England, a part of America. . . : our plot was there to take whales and make trials of a mine of gold and copper. If those failed, fish and furs was then our refuge, to make ourselves savers* howsoever. . . .

---
savers: salvagers

Whilest the sailors fished, myself with eight or nine others of them that might best be spared, ranging the coast in a small boat, we got for trifles* near 1100 beaver skins, 100 martin skins, and near as many otters, and most of them within the distance of twenty leagues. . . .

---
trifles: articles of little value

Now because I have been so often asked such strange questions, of the goodness and greatness of those spacious tracts of land, how they can be thus long unknown, or not possessed by the Spaniard, and many such like demands, I entreat* your pardons if I chance to be too plain or tedious* in relating my knowledge for plain men's satisfaction. . . .

---
entreat: earnestly request
tedious: boring

I have had six or seven several plots* of those northern parts, so unlike each other and most so differing from any true proportion or resemblance of the country as they did me no more good than so much waste paper though they cost me more. It may be it was not my chance to see the best, but at least* others may be deceived as I was or through dangerous ignorance hazard themselves as I did, I have drawn a map from point to point, isle to isle, and harbor to harbor with the soundings, sands, rocks, and landmarks as I passed close aboard the shore in a little boat, although there be many things to be observed which the haste of other affairs did cause me to omit. For being sent more to get present commodities* than knowledge by discovering for any future good, I had not power to search as I would: yet it will serve to direct any that should go that ways to safe harbors and the savages' habitations. What merchandise and commodities for their labor they may find, this following discourse shall plainly demonstrate. . . .

---
several plots: different maps
at least: lest
commodities: articles of trade

It is not a work for everyone, to manage such an affair as makes a discovery and plants a colony. It requires all the best parts of art, judgment, courage, honesty, constancy, diligence, and industry, to do but near well. Some are more proper for one thing than another and therein are to be employed: and nothing breeds more confusion than misplacing and misemploying men in their undertakings. . . .

Who can desire more content that hath small means but only his merit to advance his fortunes than to tread and plant that ground he hath purchased by the hazard of his life? If he have but the taste of virtue and magnanimity,* what to such a mind can be more pleasant than planting and building a foundation for his posterity,* got from the rude* earth by God's blessing and his own industry without prejudice* to any? If he have any grain of faith or zeal in religion, what can he do less hurtful to any or more agreeable to God than to seek to convert those poor savages to know Christ and humanity, whose labors with discretion* will triply requite* thy charge and pain? What so truly suits with honor and honesty as the discovering things unknown, erecting towns, peopling countries, informing the ignorant, reforming things unjust, teaching virtue; and gain to our native mother country a kingdom to attend her, find employment for those that are idle, because they know not what to do; so far from wronging any as to cause posterity to remember thee and, remembering thee, ever honor that remembrance with praise? . . .

magnanimity: generosity
posterity: descendants
rude: uncultivated
prejudice: injury
discretion: prudence
requite: repay

My purpose is not to persuade children from their parents, men from their wives, nor servants from their masters, only such as with free consent may be spared; but that each parish or village in city or country that will but apparel their father-less children of thirteen or fourteen years of age or young married people that have small wealth to live on, here by their labor may live exceeding well: provided always, that first there be a sufficient power to command them, houses to receive them, means to defend them, and meet* provisions for them; for any place may be overlaid,* and it is most necessary to have a fortress . . . and sufficient masters (as, carpenters, masons, fishers, gardeners, husbandmen, sawyers, smiths, spinsters, tailors, weavers, and such like) . . . to take ten, twelve, or twenty, or as there is for apprentices. The masters by this may quickly grow rich; these may learn their trades themselves to do the like, to a general and an incredible benefit for King, and country, master, and servant. . . .

meet: suitable
overlaid: overburdened, overpopulated

Religion above all things should move us (especially the clergy), if we are religious, to show our faith by our works* in converting those poor savages to the knowledge of God, seeing what pains the Spaniards take to bring them to their adulterated* faith. Honor might move the gentry,* the valiant, and industrious; and the hope and assurance of wealth, all, if we were that we would seem and be accounted. Or be we so far inferior to other nations, or our spirits so far dejected from our ancient predecessors, or our minds too set upon spoil,* piracy, and such villainy, as to serve the Portuguese, Spaniard, Dutch, French, or Turk (as to the cost of Europe too many do) rather than our God, our King, and our country, and ourselves, excusing our idleness and our base complaints by want of employment, when here is such choice of all sorts, and for all degrees, in the planting and discovering these north parts of America?

faith . . . works: James 2:18
adulterated: impure, corrupted: i.e., Roman Catholicism
gentry: lesser nobility
spoil: plunder seized by violence

For Thought and Discussion

1. What do you learn about the character of the writer from the first sentence in *A General History?* In formulating your answer, consider the following:
   a. In what person does he refer to himself? Why?
   b. How do his fellow colonists, particularly members of the Council, regard him?
   c. What does his action reveal about his attitude toward his fellow colonists? Consider such words and phrases as *idle exceptions, muttered, taxed.*
   d. Why does he use the terms *comedies* and *tragedy?*
2. What effect might your analysis of the character of the writer have on your reaction to the account he gives?
3. God's providential care for His children is a recurring theme in seventeenth-century literature. Identify two sentences in which Smith expresses this theme.
4. In *A Description of New England* what spiritual motive does Smith give in paragraph 6 for the colonization of New England? In what paragraph does he support this point by further development?
5. Where in the final paragraph does Smith arrange his arguments in descending order of importance? Why?
6. Which does Smith emphasize, spiritual or material motives for colonization? How does he achieve this emphasis?

William Byrd II   1674-1744

William Byrd II typifies the eighteenth-century Southern aristocrat, the American version of the English cavalier. Nearly one hundred years after the founding of Jamestown, Byrd inherited Westover on the James River, a 26,000-acre plantation that he had enlarged to 180,000 acres by the time of his death. His writing shows the difference between the preoccupations of the Southern colonial leaders and those of the Northern leaders such as his Massachusetts contemporary Samuel Sewall.

Byrd was born to wealth and power. Educated in England and the Netherlands, he was appointed to the Virginia House of Burgesses in his early adulthood. Upon his return to Virginia following his father's death in 1704, having served as London agent for the colony, he was appointed auditor and receiver-general of Virginia in 1706. From 1715 to 1726 he again lived in London as agent for Virginia. While in England, he socialized with some of the most influential people, continued his reading and translation of the classics, studied current science, was admitted to the

Royal Society (an English scientific academy founded in 1660), and even participated in the exciting literary world by helping write a play. He returned to Virginia in 1726 and concerned himself thereafter with the colony's social, economic, and political matters. By the time of his death, Byrd had amassed not only a huge estate but also a library of some 3,600 volumes, second in size only to that of Cotton Mather (1663-1728), Boston's leading minister.

Although Byrd wrote throughout his lifetime, he did not seek or even desire publication; for a person in his social position usually wrote for just a few close friends. In the works that have been preserved, Byrd gives an invaluable picture of colonial life. In his private diary he used a method of shorthand not deciphered until the early 1940s. The parts thus far discovered (recounting the years 1709-12, 1717-21, and 1730-41) reveal that Byrd recorded all facets of his daily life: his translations from the Greek and Latin classics, his shadow-boxing program of calisthenics ("danced my dance"), his main dishes during the day, his business and recreation, even his prayers or lack of prayer at bedtime. He omitted virtually nothing, not even quarrels with his wife, punishment of slaves, fits of temper, lustful thoughts, or dreams. In three long narratives Byrd details the experience of the survey party commissioned to settle the boundary dispute between Virginia and North Carolina, records his investigation of the cost of iron manufacture and his journey to the mines, and recounts his surveying a 20,000-acre tract of land at the junction of the Dan and Irvine rivers. Often Byrd spices these accounts with anecdotes, penetrating observations on his fellowmen, and detailed information about the land and Indian customs. His polished, direct style makes these narratives of colonial travel enjoyable today.

Byrd's conventional attitude toward religion appears everywhere in his writings. Because he fears that the inhabitants of the Dismal Swamp are irreligious, he insists that an Anglican chaplain accompany the surveying party to christen children, perform marriages, and conduct services for the backcountry people. In his diary his high-church Anglican background seems to keep religion somewhat at a distance from his personal life. Byrd, like most other eighteenth-century writers, was preoccupied not with spiritual matters but with the affairs of this world.

from **The Secret Diary** (1709)

March 25

I rose at 6 o'clock and read two chapters in Hebrew and 200 verses in Homer's* *Odyssey*. I said my prayers and ate milk for breakfast. I danced my dance. The Doctor went to Williamsburg.* I wrote a letter to England. Parson Ware sent to me for a pint of canary,* he being sick with the gripes* with the New England rum, which I sent him, notwithstanding I have but a little, because I should be glad if I were in his condition to receive such a kindness from another. Mrs. J-f-r-y was sick again today. I ate nothing but hash of beef. In the afternoon I took a nap, contrary to custom. I settled my accounts. In the evening we walked about the plantation. I said my prayers, I had good thoughts, good health, and good humor all day, thanks to God Almighty.

Homer: Greek epic poet of the ninth century B.C., traditional author
    of the *Iliad* and the *Odyssey*
Williamsburg: capital of Virginia 1699-1776
canary: white wine from Canary Islands off N. Africa
gripes: pain in the bowels

April 24

I rose at 6 o'clock and said my prayers very shortly. We breakfasted about 10 o'clock and I ate nothing but bread and butter and sack.* We rode to Jamestown Church, where Mr. Commissary preached. When church was done I gave 10 shillings to the poor. Nothing could hinder me from sleeping at church, though I took a great deal of pains against it. We rode home to Colonel Ludwell's again where we dined and I ate fish and asparagus. In the afternoon we took a walk and saw the carcasses of 50 cows which had been burnt in a house belonging to Colonel Ludwell. Mr. W-l-s ran two races and beat John Custis and Mr. [Hawkins]. He likewise jumped over the fence which was a very great jump. Colonel Carter returned to town with Mr. Harrison and we stayed and ate syllabub* for supper. I neglected to say my prayers. I had good thoughts, good humor, and good health, thanks be to God Almighty.

sack: wine
syllabub: dish of milk or cream with wine or cider

April 27

I rose at 6 o'clock and read two books in Homer and a chapter in Hebrew. I said my prayers and ate milk for breakfast. I wrote a letter to my wife by Will Randolph. I did abundance of business. My sister Custis came to town on her way to Major Burwell's. I went to wait on her at Mr. Bland's, where came abundance of other ladies. I stayed with them two hours. My brother and sister Custis went away. I paid several of the Council their money. I agreed with Captain C-l to give him bills for money at five guineas per cent. I went to dinner where I ate nothing but mutton hash. After dinner we played at cricket and then went to whist* and I lost 30 shillings. I went home about 11 o'clock. I had good health, good thoughts, and good humor all day, thanks be to God Almighty.

whist: card game

May 6

I rose about 6 o'clock and Colonel Ludwell, Nat Harrison, Mr. Edwards and myself played at cricket, and I won a bit. Then we played at whist and I won. About 10 o'clock we went to breakfast and I ate some boiled rice. Then Colonel Ludwell went to Jamestown court and then we played at [l-n-s-n-t] and I lost £4, most of which Nat Harrison won. In the afternoon Colonel Ludwell returned and brought us the bad news that Captain Morgan had lost his ship in Margate Roads by a storm as likewise had several others. My loss was very great in this ship where I had seven hogsheads of skins and 60 hogsheads of heavy tobacco. The Lord gives and the Lord has taken away–blessed be the name of the Lord.* In the evening Mr. Clayton and Mr. Robinson came and confirmed the same bad news. However I ate a

good supper of mutton and asparagus. Then we went to dance away from sorrow. I had good health, good thoughts, and good humor, notwithstanding my misfortune, thanks be to God Almighty.

The Lord gives . . . name of the Lord: Job 1:21

from The History of the Dividing Line

Byrd was appointed in 1728 as one of the commissioners to survey the eastern part of the boundary between Virginia and North Carolina. He kept a journal of his observations and of the surveying party's experiences in striking the line through the Dismal Swamp, where the settlers had grown uneasy about which colony they owed allegiance to. The prejudices of the upper-class Virginian become evident especially in his observations of the backcountry people living near the boundary line.

March 23

There is one remarkable part of the Dismal, lying to the south of the line, that has few or no trees growing on it, but contains a large tract of tall reeds. These being green all the year round, and waving with every wind, have procur'd* it the name of the Green Sea.

procur'd: gained

We are not yet acquainted with the precise extent of the Dismal, the whole having never been survey'd; but it may be computed at a medium to be about 30 miles long and 10 miles broad, tho' where the line crost it, 'twas completely 15 miles wide. But it seems to grow narrower towards the north, or at least does so in many places. The exhalations* that continually rise from this vast body of mire and nastiness infect the air for many miles round, and render it very unwholesome for the bordering inhabitants. It makes them liable to agues,* pleurisies,* and many other distempers,* that kill abundance of people, and make the rest look no better than ghosts. It would require a great sum of money to drain it, but the public treasure could not be better bestow'd, than to preserve the lives of his Majesty's liege* people, and at the same time render so great a tract of swamp very profitable, besides the advantage of making a

channel to transport by water-carriage goods from Albemarle Sound into Nansimond and Elizabeth Rivers, in Virginia.

exhalations: vapors
agues: fevers with or without chills
pleurisies: inflammation of the lungs
distempers: illnesses
liege: owing allegiance

March 24

This being Sunday, we had a numerous congregation, which flockt to our quarters from all the adjacent country. The news that our surveyors were come out of the Dismal, increas'd the number very much, because it would give them an opportunity of guessing, at least, whereabouts the line would cut, whereby they might form some judgment whether they belong'd to Virginia or Carolina. Those who had taken up land within the disputed bounds were in great pain lest it should be found to lie in Virginia; because this being done contrary to an express order of that government, the Patentees* had great reason to fear they should in that case have lost their land. But their apprehensions were now at an end, when they understood that all the territory which had been controverted* was like to be left in Carolina. . . .

Patentees: landholders
controverted: disputed

March 25

Surely there is no place in the world where the inhabitants live with less labor than in N. Carolina. It approaches nearer to the description of Lubberland* than any other, by the great felicity* of the climate, the easiness of raising provisions, and the slothfulness of the people.

Lubberland: mythical land of ease
felicity: bliss

Indian corn is of so great increase, that a little pains will subsist a very large family with bread, and then they may have meat without any pains at all, by the help of the low grounds, and the great variety of mast that grows on the high-land. The men, for their parts, just like the Indians, impose all the work upon the poor women. They make their wives rise out of their beds early in the morning, at the same time that they lie and snore, till the sun has run one third of his course, and disperst all the unwholesome damps.* Then, after stretching and yawning for half an hour, they light their pipes, and, under the protection of a cloud of smoke, venture out into the open air; tho', if it happens to be never so little cold, they quickly return shivering into the chimney corner. When the weather is mild, they stand leaning with both their arms upon the corn-field fence, and gravely consider whether they had best go and take a small heat at the hough:* but generally find reasons to put it off till another time.

unwholesome damps: vapors, mists
hough: hoe

Thus they loiter away their lives, like Solomon's sluggard,* with their arms across, and at the winding up of the year scarcely have bread to eat.

Solomon's sluggard: Proverbs 6:6, 9-11

To speak the truth, 'tis a thorough aversion* to labor that makes people file off to N. Carolina, where plenty and a warm sun confirm them in their disposition to laziness for their whole lives.

aversion: dislike, opposition

For Thought and Discussion

1. What sentence recurs in each diary entry? What is the effect of such repetition? Does the content seem more sincere or less sincere as a result of the repetition?
2. What activities does Byrd engage in on Sunday? Which of them might the Puritans have disapproved of? What is his single "good deed" for the day?
3. Does Byrd's account of his daily life coincide with what you might have imagined the life of a wealthy, powerful colonist to have been like? Explain your answer.
4. How does the content of *The History of the Dividing Line* differ from that of *The Secret Diary?*
5. The two works also differ in style. Analyze these differences in style by answering the following questions.
   a. Which work employs passages of description?
   b. Which is more detailed?
   c. For what audience is each intended?
   d. Describe the tone of each work.
   e. How does the sentence style of the two works differ?
6. What prejudices does Byrd reveal in *The History of the Dividing Line?* Do you believe that most Americans today are as narrowly loyal to their own region or state as Byrd was? Why or why not?

William Bradford
1590-1657

Because of the clarity and vigor of William Bradford's style, nearly every American knows the details of the establishing of the *second* English colony in this country. With elegant simplicity Bradford pictures the suffering and triumphs of the struggling band of Pilgrims.

Bradford's life was inseparably linked to the Pilgrims. Orphaned early in life, as a teen-ager he joined the Separatist congregation at Scrooby, England, and then emigrated with it to the Netherlands in 1609. Since Separatists rejected the ceremonies, organization, and even the Thirty-Nine Articles of the Established Church (statements that all Anglican ministers had to agree to), their religious practice was illegal. Consequently, they were subject to persecution by the authorities and their property was liable for seizure. For twelve years this group stayed in exile until it became evident that they were losing their youth to the corruption of the Dutch society and that they were having no moral influence on their neighbors. Moreover, they were slowly sinking into poverty despite their hard work. After an ill-fated start, they sailed aboard the *Mayflower* for the New World. Their sixty-five-day voyage finally put them off the coast of New England, not of Virginia as they had planned. The first winter nearly destroyed the colony. More than half of the 102 original settlers died during that winter, among them Governor John Carver. Bradford was elected to succeed Carver and from 1622 to 1656 served as governor of the colony except for five years, when he acted as assistant. His generosity of spirit and genuine spirituality greatly assisted the colony's struggle for survival. Although he was Plymouth Plantation's chief legal, judicial, and executive counselor, colonial affairs never totally occupied his attention. In his last years he studied Hebrew so that he might better understand the Old Testament.

Bradford's foremost literary work is his history entitled *Of Plymouth Plantation*. He began writing it in 1630 at the start of the Great Migration to Massachusetts Bay. Perhaps he feared that the small colony of Plymouth would be eclipsed one day by its much more powerful sister colony. Whatever his reason, he movingly describes the difficulties overcome by the Pilgrims both before and after their arrival in the New World. Bradford saw God's hand guiding and protecting the Pilgrims; in fact, providential care is his most insistent theme. His style displays the best characteristics of the Puritan plain style: simple yet dignified; concrete, vivid, and dramatic. His is one of the most readable histories of early America.

This man's life and writing reveal a Christian serving God in the confidence of His calling, willing to suffer in order to carry out what he believes to be God's will. His example encourages all Christians to rely on God's providential care.

Of Plymouth Plantation

And first of the occasion and inducements* thereunto; the which, that I may truly unfold, I must begin at the very root and rise of the same.* The which I shall endeavour to manifest in a plain style, with singular regard unto the simple truth in all things; at least as near as my slender judgment can attain the same.

inducements: incentives, in the sense of causes
root . . . same: Bradford begins his history with a brief account of the Reformation in England.

from Chapter Seven

So they left that goodly and pleasant city, which had been their resting place near twelve years; but they knew they were pilgrims,* and looked not much on those things, but lifted up their eyes to the heavens, their dearest country, and quieted their spirits. . . .

pilgrims: The name Pilgrim was first applied to these colonists in 1793. Plymouth itself disappeared as a separate political entity in 1691, when it was absorbed by Massachusetts Bay.

from Chapter Nine

These troubles being blown over, and now all being compact together in one ship,* they put to sea again with a prosperous wind, which continued divers* days together, which was some encouragement unto them; yet, according to the usual manner, many were afflicted with seasickness. And I may not omit here a special work of God's providence. There was a proud and very profane young man, one of the seamen, of a lusty,* able body, which made him the more haughty; he would alway be contemning the poor people in their sickness and cursing them daily with grievous execrations;* and did not let to tell* them that he hoped to help to cast half of them overboard* before they came to their journey's end, and to make merry with what they had; and if he were by any gently reproved, he would curse and swear most bitterly. But it pleased God before they came half seas over, to smite this young man with a grievous disease, of which he died in a desperate manner, and so was himself the first that was thrown overboard. Thus his curses light on his own head, and it was an astonishment to all his fellows for they noted it to be the just hand of God upon him. . . .

These . . . ship: They had started their voyage in two ships, but the Speedwell proved unseaworthy.
divers: several
lusty: strong
execrations: denunciations
let to tell: stop telling
cast . . . overboard: bury them at sea

In sundry* of these storms the winds were so fierce and the seas so high, as they could not bear a knot of sail but were forced to hull* for divers days together. And in one of them, as they thus lay at hull in a mighty storm, a lusty young man called John Howland, coming upon some occasion above the gratings, was with a seele* of the ship, thrown into sea; but it pleased God that he caught hold of the topsail halyards* which hung overboard and ran out at length. Yet he held his hold (though he was sundry fathoms under water) till he was hauled up by the same rope to the brim of the water, and then with a boat hook and other means got into the ship again and his life saved. And though he was something ill with it, yet he lived many years after and became a profitable member both in church and commonwealth. . . .

sundry: several
to hull: to shorten sail and drift with the wind
seele: roll
halyards: ropes for hoisting sails

Being thus arrived in a good harbor, and brought safe to land, they fell upon their knees and blessed the God of Heaven who had brought them over the vast and furious ocean, and delivered them from all the perils and miseries thereof, again to set their feet on the firm and stable earth, their proper element. And no marvel if they were thus joyful, seeing wise Seneca* was so affected with sailing a few miles on the coast of his own Italy, as he affirmed, that he had rather remain twenty years on his way by land than pass by sea to any place in a short time, so tedious and dreadful was the same unto him.

Seneca: Roman writer living about the time of Christ

But here I cannot but stay and make a pause, and stand half amazed at this poor people's present condition; and so I think will the reader, too, when he well considers the same. Being thus passed the vast ocean, and a sea of troubles before in their preparation (as may be remembered by that which went before), they had now no friends to welcome them nor inns to entertain or refresh their weatherbeaten bodies; no houses or much less towns to repair to, to seek for succour. It is recorded in Scripture* as a mercy to the Apostle and his shipwrecked company that the barbarians showed them no small kindness in refreshing them, but these savage barbarians, when they met with them (as after will appear) were readier to fill their sides full of arrows than otherwise. And for the season it was winter, and they that know the winters of that country know them to be sharp and violent, and subject to cruel and fierce storms, dangerous to travel to known places, much more to search an unknown coast. Besides, what could

they see but a hideous and desolate wilderness, full of wild beasts and wild men—and what multitudes there might be of them they knew not. Neither could they, as it were, go up to the top of Pisgah* to view from this wilderness a more goodly country to feed their hopes; for which way soever they turned their eyes (save upward to the heavens) they could have little solace or content in respect of any outward objects. For summer being done, all things stand upon them with a weather-beaten face, and the whole country, full of woods and thickets, represented a wild and savage hue. If they looked behind them, there was the mighty ocean which they had passed and was now as a main bar and gulf to separate them from all the civil parts of the world. If it be said they had a ship to succour them, it is true; but what heard they daily from the master and company? But that with speed they should look out a place (with their shallop*) where they would be, at some near distance; for the season was such as he would not stir from thence till a safe harbor was discovered by them, where they would be, and he might go without danger; and that victuals consumed apace* but he must and would keep sufficient for themselves and their return. Yea, it was muttered by some that if they got not a place in time, they would turn them and their goods ashore and leave them. Let it also be considered what weak hopes of supply and succour they left behind them, that might bear up their minds in this sad condition and trials they were under; and they could not but be very small. It is true, indeed, the affections and love of their brethren at Leyden was cordial and entire towards them, but they had little power to help them or themselves; and how the case stood between them and the merchants at their coming away hath already been declared.

It . . . Scripture: Acts 28:2
go . . . Pisgah: Deuteronomy 34:1
shallop: small, open boat
apace: rapidly

What could now sustain them but the Spirit of God and His grace? May not and ought not the children of these fathers rightly say: "Our fathers were Englishmen which came over this great ocean, and were ready to perish in this wilderness; but they cried unto the Lord, and He heard their voice and looked on their adversity,"* etc. "Let them therefore praise the Lord, because He is good: and His mercies endure forever." "Yea, let them which have been redeemed of the Lord, shew how He hath delivered them from the hand of the oppressor. When they wandered in the desert of wilderness out of the way, and found no city to dwell in, both hungry and thirsty, their soul was overwhelmed in them. Let them confess before the Lord His lovingkindness and His wonderful works before the sons of men."*

Our . . . adversity: Deuteronomy 26:7
Let . . . men: Psalm 107:1, 2, 4, 8; Bradford used the Geneva Bible

from Chapter Eleven

I shall a little return back, and begin with a combination made by them before they came ashore; being the first foundation of their government in this place. Occasioned partly by the discontented and mutinous speeches that some of the strangers* amongst them had let fall from them in the ship: That when they came ashore they would use their own liberty, for none had power to command them, the patent they had being for Virginia and not for New England, which belonged to another government, with which the Virginia Company had nothing to do. And partly that such an act by them done, this their condition considered, might be as firm as any patent, and in some respects more sure.

---

strangers: those not Separatists; over half of the original colonists

The form was as followeth:

IN THE NAME OF GOD, AMEN.

We whose names are underwritten, the loyal subjects of our dread Sovereign Lord King James, by the Grace of God of Great Britain, France, and Ireland King, Defender of the Faith, etc.

Having undertaken, for the Glory of God and advancement of the Christian Faith and Honour of our King and Country, a Voyage to plant the First colony in the Northern Parts of Virginia, do by these presents solemnly and mutually in the presence of God and one of another, Covenant and Combine ourselves together into a Civil Body Politic, for our better ordering and preservation and futherance of the ends aforesaid; and by virtue hereof to enact, constitute and frame such just and equal Laws, Ordinances, Acts, Constitutions and Offices, from time to time, as shall be thought most meet and convenient for the general good of the Colony, unto which we promise all due submission and obedience. In witness whereof we have hereunder subscribed our names at Cape Cod, the 11th of November, in the year of the reign of our Sovereign Lord King James, of England, France and Ireland the eighteenth, and of Scotland the fifty-fourth. Anno Domini* 1620.

Anno Domini: Lat., in the year of our Lord

To every thing

under the heaven.

there is a season and

a time to every purpose

After this they chose, or rather confirmed, Mr. John Carver (a man godly and well approved amongst them) their Governor for that year. And after they had provided a place for their goods, or common store (which were long in unlading for want of boats, foulness of the winter weather and sickness of divers) and begun some small cottages for their habitation; as time would admit, they met and consulted of laws and order, both for their civil and military government as the necessity of their condition did require, still* adding thereunto as urgent occasion in several times, and as cases did require.

---

still: continually

In these hard and difficult beginnings they found some discontents and murmurings arise amongst some, and mutinous speeches and carriages* in other; but they were soon quelled* and overcome by the wisdom, patience, and just and equal carriage of things, by the Governor and better part, which clave faithfully together in the main.

---

carriages: conduct
quelled: quieted

But that which was most sad and lamentable was, that in two or three months' time half of their company died, especially in January and February, being the depth of winter, and wanting houses and other comforts; being infected with the scurvy and other diseases which this long voyage and their inaccommodate* condition had brought upon them. So as there died some times two or three of a day in the foresaid time, that of 100 and odd persons, scarce fifty remained. And of these, in the time of most distress, there was but six or seven sound persons who to their great commendations, be it spoken, spared no pains night nor day, but with abundance of toil and hazard of their own health, fetched them wood, made them fires, dressed them meat, made their beds, washed their loathsome clothes, clothed and unclothed them. In a word, did all the homely and necessary offices for them which dainty and queasy stomachs cannot endure to hear named; and all this willingly and cheerfully, without any grudging in the least, showing herein their true love unto their friends and brethren; a rare example and worthy to be remembered. Two of these seven were Mr. William Brewster, their reverend Elder, and Myles Standish, their Captain and military commander, unto whom myself and many others were much beholden in our low and sick condition. And yet the Lord so upheld these persons as in this general calamity they were not at all infected either with sickness or lameness. . . .

---

inaccommodate: unfavorable

All this while the Indians came skulking about them, and would sometimes show themselves aloof* off, but when any approached near them, they would run away; and once they stole away their tools where they had been at work and were gone to dinner. But about the 16th of March, a certain Indian came boldly amongst them and spoke to them in broken English, which they could well understand but marveled at it. At length they understood by discourse with him, that he was not of these parts, but belonged to the eastern parts where some English ships came to fish, with whom he was acquainted and could name sundry of them by their names, amongst whom he had got his language. He became profitable to them in acquainting them with many things concerning the state of the country in the east parts where he lived, which was afterwards profitable unto them; as also of the people here, of their names, number and strength, of their situation and distance from this place, and who was chief amongst them. His name was Samoset. He told them also of another Indian whose name was Squanto,* a native of this place, who had been in England and could speak better English than himself.

---

aloof: from hidden positions at a distance
Squanto: captured by an English captain who intended to sell him into slavery

Being, after some time of entertainment and gifts dismissed, a while after he came again, and five more with him, and they brought again all the tools that were stolen away before and made way for the coming of their great Sachem,* called Massasoit. Who, about four or five days after, came with the chief of his friends and other attendance, with the aforesaid Squanto. With whom, after friendly entertainment and some gifts given him, they made a peace with him (which hath now continued this 24 years*) in these terms:

Sachem: chief
which . . . years: Bradford wrote this passage no earlier than 1644.

1. That neither he nor any of his should injure or do hurt to any of their people.

2. That if any of his did hurt to any of theirs, he should send the offender that they might punish him.

3. That if anything were taken away from any of theirs, he should cause it to be restored; and they should do the like to his.

4. If any did unjustly war against him, they would aid him; if any did war against them, he should aid them.

5. He should send to his neighbours confederates to certify them of this, that they might not wrong them, but might be likewise comprised in the conditions of peace.

6. That when their men came to them, they should leave their bows and arrows behind them.

After these things he returned to his place called Sowams, some 40 miles from this place, but Squanto continued with them and was their interpreter and was a special instrument sent of God for their good beyond their expectation. He directed them how to set their corn, where to take fish, and to procure other commodities, and was also their pilot to bring them to unknown places for their profit, and never left them till he died. He was a native of this place, and scarce any left alive besides himself.* He was carried away with divers others by one Hunt, a master of a ship, who thought to sell them for slaves in Spain. But he got away for England and was entertained by a merchant in London, and employed to Newfoundland and other parts, and lastly brought hither into these parts by one Mr. Dermer, a gentleman employed by Sir Ferdinando Gorges and others for discovery and other designs in these parts. . . .

He . . . himself: Squanto was apparently the sole survivor of his tribe, which had been killed off in the pestilence of 1617.

But to return. The spring now approaching, it pleased God the mortality began to cease amongst them, and the sick and lame recovered apace, which put as it were new life into them, though they had borne their sad affliction with much patience and contentedness as I think any people could do. But it was the Lord which upheld them, and had beforehand prepared them; many having long borne the yoke, yea from their youth.*

many . . . youth: cf. Lamentations 3:27

from Chapter Twelve

Afterwards* they (as many as were able) began to plant their corn, in which service Squanto stood them in great stead, showing them both the manner how to set it, and after how to dress and tend it. Also he told them, except they got fish and set with it in these old grounds it would come to nothing. And he showed them that in the middle of April they should have store enough come up the brook by which they began to build, and taught them how to take it, and where to get other provisions necessary for them. All which they found true by trial and experience. Some English seed they sowed, as wheat and pease,* but it came not to good, either by the badness of the seed or lateness of the season or both, or some other defect. . . .

Afterwards: 1621
pease: peas

They began now to gather in the small harvest* they had, and to fit up their houses and dwellings against winter, being all well recovered in health and strength and had all things in good plenty. For as some were thus employed in affairs abroad, others were exercised in fishing, about cod and bass and other fish, of which they took good store, of which every family had their portion. All the summer there was no want; and now began to come in store of fowl, as winter approached, of which this place did abound when they came first (but afterwards decreased by degrees). And besides waterfowl there was great store of wild turkeys, of which they took many, besides venison, etc. Besides they had about a peck a* meal a week to a person, or now since harvest, Indian corn to that proportion. Which made many afterwards write so largely of their plenty here to their friends in England, which were not feigned* but true reports.

harvest: the first Thanksgiving
a: of
feigned: fictitious, imaginary

For Thought and Discussion

1. In *Of Plymouth Plantation,* Chapter 9, what ironic occurrence at sea does Bradford describe? What Scriptural teaching does Bradford draw from this event?

2. In which paragraph does Bradford allude to both the Christian theme of God's providence and the Roman Stoic philosopher, Seneca, whose philosophy runs counter to Christianity? Why does Bradford place these allusions side by side? What is the effect of his doing so?

3. List several difficulties encountered by the colonists on their arrival in the New World. What recourse did these people have in their troubles?

4. According to Bradford, who among the colonists began to murmur and complain? What argument did these same people use to reject the claims of government over them?

5. What event brings about the turning point in the colonists' fortunes? Why is this event ironic? Whom does Bradford credit with bringing about this event?

John Winthrop   1588-1649

The *Journal* of John Winthrop is the record of Massachusetts Bay's first two decades of existence. In keeping with his training as a lawyer, Winthrop gives his account in an emotionless, impersonal style that focuses on the religious policies of the colony as they affected its political and social matters.

Born to a prosperous upper middle-class family, Winthrop accepted Puritan religious and political values early. As conditions in England grew less tolerable for Puritans, Winthrop, with a number of other well-established men, decided to emigrate to the New World. After banding together in 1628 and securing a charter from the king in 1629, these men organized a government for the colony and elected Winthrop their governor. In 1630 the first wave of colonists arrived at Massachusetts Bay. Whereas the Pilgrims ten years earlier had arrived in New England in a single ship, the first Puritans landed at Boston Harbor in four ships. Quickly mushrooming in size, the Bay Colony almost immediately assumed the dominant position in New England. Winthrop was the foremost administrative officer of the colony, serving as either governor or deputy governor for all but seven years until his death in 1649.

Winthrop's *Journal,* kept intermittently during his New England years, concentrates on the trials and triumphs of the Puritans, detailing God's providential care for the colonists. It sets forth without apology the rigorous Puritan punishment for sin. Since the Massachusetts colonists sought to establish a theocratic, not democratic, form of government, they took the laws God laid down in Leviticus as the basis for their law. For example, those guilty of adultery were executed. Hawthorne may very well have derived inspiration for *The Scarlet Letter* from Winthrop's account of Mary Latham, a young woman who confessed to adultery and, with her partner, who also confessed, was put to death. The *Journal* also illustrates the role of the Puritan historian, who not only recorded the most minute facts but also interpreted them for their underlying spiritual significance. In his letters Winthrop's writing displays what has been called the "human side" of Puritan literature.

Described by Cotton Mather as the American Nehemiah, Winthrop nobly led his people by his example of piety and discipline, his exercise of wisdom, and his application of inflexible principle. His record of early Puritan life in Massachusetts Bay shows his support of social and doctrinal purity, both in theory and in practice.

from **Journal**

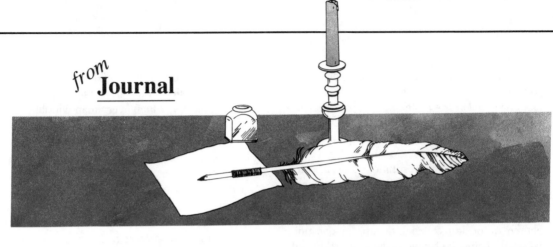

July 5, 1632

At Watertown there was (in the view of divers* witnesses) a great combat between a mouse and a snake; and, after a long fight, the mouse prevailed and killed the snake. The pastor of Boston, Mr. Wilson, a very sincere, holy man, hearing of it, gave this interpretation: That the snake was the devil; the mouse was a poor contemptible people, which God had brought hither, which should overcome Satan here, and dispossess him of his kingdom. Upon the same occasion, he told the governor, that, before he was resolved to come into this country, he dreamed he was here, and that he saw a church arise out of the earth, which grew up and became a marvelous goodly church.

divers: several

November, 1639

At a general court holden at Boston, great complaint was made of the oppression used in the country in sale of foreign commodities; and Mr. Robert Keayne, who kept a shop in Boston, was notoriously above others observed and complained of; and, being convented,* he was charged with many particulars; in some, for taking above six-pence in the shilling profit;* in some above eight-pence; and, in some small things, above two for one; and being hereof convict (as appears by the records), he was fined £200. . . . For the cry of the country was so great against oppression, and some of the elders and

magistrates had declared such detestation* of the corrupt practice of this man (which was the more observable, because he was wealthy and sold dearer* than most other tradesmen, and for that he was of ill report for the like covetous practice in England, that incensed* the deputies very much against him). And sure the course was very evil, especial circumstances considered: 1. He being an ancient professor* of the gospel; 2. A man of eminent parts; 3. Wealthy, and having but one child; 4. Having come over for conscience's sake, and for the advancement of the gospel here; 5. Having been formerly dealt with and admonished, both by private friends and also by some of the magistrates and elders, and having promised reformation; being a member of a church and commonwealth now in their infancy and under the curious* observation of all churches and civil states in the world. These added much aggravation* to his sin in the judgment of all men of understanding. Yet most of the magistrates (though they discerned of the offense clothed with all these circumstances) would have been more moderate in their censure:* 1. Because there was no law in force to limit or direct men in point of profit in their trade; 2. Because it is the common practice, in all countries, for men to make use of advantages for raising the prices of their commodities; 3. Because (though he were chiefly aimed at, yet) he was not alone in his fault; 4. Because all men through the country, in sale of cattle, corn, labor, etc., were guilty of the like excess in prices; 5. Because a certain rule could not be found out for an equal rate between buyer and seller, though much labor had been bestowed in it, and divers laws had been made, which, upon experience, were repealed, as being neither safe nor equal; Lastly, and especially, the law of God appoints no other punishment but double restitution; and, in some cases, as where the offender freely confesseth, and brings his offering, only half added to the principal. After the court had censured him, the church of Boston called him also in question, where (as before he had done in the court) he did, with tears, acknowledge and bewail his covetous and corrupt heart, yet making some excuse for many of the particulars, which were charged upon him, as partly by pretense of ignorance of the true price of some wares, and chiefly by being misled by some false principles. . . .

---

convented: brought before the assembly
above . . . profit: 12 pence = shilling; thus 50 per cent profit
detestation: dislike, abhorrence
dearer: at higher prices
incensed: angered
professor: one who professes
curious: close, careful
aggravation: intensity: i.e., made his sin much worse
censure: reproof

The rules for trading were these:

1. A man may not sell above the current price, i.e., such a price as is usual in the time and place, and as another (who knows the worth of the commodity) would give for it, if he had occasion to use it; as that is called current money, which every man will take, etc.

2. When a man loseth in his commodity for want of skill, etc., he must look at it as his own fault or cross, and therefore must not lay it upon another.

3. Where a man loseth by casualty of sea, or, etc., it is a loss cast upon himself by providence, and he may not ease himself of it by casting it upon another; for so a man should seem to provide against all providences, etc., that he should never lose; but where there is a scarcity of the commodity, there men may raise their price; for now it is a hand of God upon the commodity, and not the person.

4. A man may not ask any more for his commodity than his selling price, as Ephron to Abraham, the land is worth thus much.*

A . . . much: Genesis 23:15-16

The cause being debated by the church, some were earnest to have him excommunicated;* but the most thought an admonition would be sufficient. . . .

---

excommunicated: a cutting off from sacraments, privileges, or fellowship of the church

---

In 1645 Winthrop was accused of having exceeded his authority as deputy governor and was brought to trial. The court, after lengthy and bitter debate, acquitted him of the charge. Winthrop then made these remarks, which he recorded in the Journal, *on liberty as perceived under the Massachusetts theocracy.*

Concerning liberty, I observe a great mistake in the country about that. There is a twofold liberty, natural (I mean as our nature is now corrupt) and civil or federal. The first is common to man with beasts and other creatures. By this, man, as he stands in relation to man simply, hath liberty to do what he lists; it is a liberty to evil as well as to good. This liberty is incompatible and inconsistent with authority, and cannot endure the least restraint of the most just authority. The exercise and maintaining of this liberty makes men grow more evil, and in time to be worse than brute beasts. . . . This is that great enemy of truth and peace, that wild beast, which all the ordinances of God are bent against, to restrain and subdue it.

The other kind of liberty I call civil or federal; it may also be termed moral in reference to the covenant between God and man in the moral law and the politic covenants and constitutions amongst men themselves. This liberty is the proper end and object of authority, and cannot subsist without it; and it is a liberty to that only which is good, just, and honest. This liberty you are to stand for, with the hazard (not only of your goods, but) of your lives, if need be. Whatsoever crosseth this is not authority but a distemper* thereof. This liberty is maintained and exercised in a way of subjection to authority; it is of the same kind of liberty wherewith Christ hath made us free. The woman's own choice makes such a man her husband; yet being so chosen, he is her lord, and she is to be subject to him, yet in a way of liberty, not of bondage; and a true wife accounts her subjection her honor and freedom, and would not think her condition safe and free but in her subjection to her husband's authority. Such is the liberty of the church under the authority of Christ, her king and husband; his yoke is so easy and sweet to her as a bride's ornaments; and if through forwardness* or wantonness,* etc., she shake it off, at any time, she is at no rest in her spirit until she take it up again; and whether her lord smiles upon her and embraceth her in his arms, or whether he frowns, or rebukes, or smites her, she apprehends the sweetness of his love in all, and is refreshed, supported, and instructed by every such dispensation* of his authority over her. On the other side, ye know who they are that complain of this yoke and say, let us break their bands, etc., we will not have this man to rule over us. Even so, brethren, it will be between you and your magistrates. If you stand for your natural corrupt liberties, and will do what is good in your own eyes, you will not endure the least weight of authority, but will murmur and oppose and be always striving to shake off that yoke; but if you will be satisfied to enjoy such civil and lawful liberties, such as Christ allows you, then will you quietly and cheerfully submit unto that authority which is set over you, in all the administrations of it, for your good. Wherein, if we fail at any time, we hope we shall be willing (by God's assistance) to harken to good advice from any of you, or in any other way of God; so shall your liberties be preserved, in upholding the honor and power of authority amongst you.

distemper: disturbance, disorder
forwardness: disobedience
wantonness: looseness, as in a moral sense
dispensation: dispensing, giving forth

Letter from Boston, November 29, 1630

My sweet wife,–The blessing of the Almighty be upon thee and thine forever.

There is a ship arrived at Plimouth, some thirty miles from us, which came from London the 10th of August, and was twelve weeks at sea in such tempests as she spent all her masts;* yet, of sixty passengers, she lost but one. All the rest (through the Lord's great mercy) are safe and in health. Edy of Boxted, who came in her, told me, a fortnight* since, that he had many letters in the ship for me; but I hear not yet of them, which makes me now (having opportunity to send to Plimouth) to write these few lines to thee, lest the ship should be gone before I have received my letters, and can return answer to them.

spent . . . masts: used up all her spare masts
fortnight: fourteen days

Thou shalt understand by this, how it is with us since I wrote last, (for this [is] the third or fourth letter I have written to thee since I came hither,) that thou mayest see the goodness of the Lord towards me, that, when so many have died and many yet languish,* myself and my children are yet living and in health. Yet I have lost twelve of my family, viz.* Waters and his wife and two of his children: Mr. Gager and his man: Smith of Buxall and his wife and two children: the wife of Taylor of Haverill and their child; my son H. makes the twelve. And, besides many other of less note, as Jeff. Ruggle of Sudbury, and divers others of that town, (about twenty,) the Lord hath stripped us of some principal persons, Mr. Johnson and his lady, Mr. Rossiter, Mrs. Phillips and others unknown to thee. We conceive that this disease grew from ill diet at sea and proved infectious.

languish: become weak
viz.: namely

I write not this to discourage thee but to warn thee and others to provide well for the sea and, by God's help, the passage will be safe and easy, how long soever. Be careful (I entreat thee) to observe the directions in my former letters; and I trust that that God who hath so graciously preserved and blessed us hitherto will bring us to see the faces of each other with abundance of joy.

My dear wife, we are here in a paradise. Though we have not beef and mutton etc., yet (God be praised) we want them not; our Indian corn answers for all. Yet here is fowl and fish in great plenty.

I will here break off, because I hope to receive letters from thee soon and to have opportunity of writing more largely. I will say nothing of my love to thee, and of my longing desires towards thee. Thou knowest my heart. Neither can I mention salutations to my good friends, other than in general. In my next, I hope to supply all. Now the Lord, our good God, be with thee and all my children and company with thee. Grace and peace be with you all. So I kiss my sweet wife and all my dear children, and bless you in the Lord. Farewell.

Thy faithful husband, Jo. Winthrop
Boston in Massachusetts, November 29, 1630.

Thou must excuse my not writing to my son John and other of my friends at this time; for I defer* it till I receive my letters.

defer: delay

For Thought and Discussion

1. Who does Winthrop imply are "a poor contemptible people" whom God brought to the New World for the purpose of overcoming Satan and "dispossess[ing] him of his kingdom"? Who is Satan in this context? What is "his kingdom"? *Puritans are the poor contemptible*

2. Who, in November 1639, was charged by the assembly in Boston with selling imported goods at an illegally high rate of profit? What reasons does Winthrop cite for the accused's high degree of accountability for his "evil" practice? What reasons does he cite to suggest that the assembly should show leniency toward the accused? Why do you suppose Winthrop presents both sets of arguments? *Robert Keayne* *selling for higher profit not a law* *because everyone a christian*

3. According to colonial trading policy, under what circumstances may a man raise his prices for a commodity? Under what circumstances may he not raise them? How does Winthrop justify this distinction? *Being hone* *when a person lose lack of sk* *when there's not a lot of fore*

4. How does Winthrop's diction in his "Letter from Boston" contrast to that in the *Journal* selection? *letter has more error*

5. Analyze the structure of paragraph three of the letter.
   a. What is its major idea? *goodnest*
   b. What specifics does the writer include to support this idea? *ppl around are dy*
   c. How is the final sentence in the paragraph related to the topic sentence? *the disease grew*

Mary Rowlandson
c. 1635-c. 1711

Mary Rowlandson's account of her Indian captivity was one of the most popular seventeenth century American books. It is also one of the most representative works of that century in its picture of the dangers confronting the colonists, their attitude toward the Indian, and their reliance on the Bible in times of adversity.

Relatively little is known about Mary Rowlandson except from the details she gives of her captivity by the Indians during King Philip's War (1675-76). The daughter of John White, a prosperous settler in Lancaster, Massachusetts, she married in 1656 a Congregational minister, Joseph Rowlandson. Her life drastically changed on February 10, 1676, when the Narragansett Indians attacked Lancaster. The Rowlandson garrison, one of six fortified houses into which the local settlers retreated at times of Indian attack, was the only one that fell to the Indians. After witnessing death all around her, she and her critically wounded daughter were taken captive. After eleven weeks and five days among the Indians, she was ransomed and reunited with her husband and their two surviving children.

Mrs. Rowlandson's account is the first and most notable of the more than one hundred existing Indian-captivity narratives. She records in realistic detail the suffering and abuse she experienced. During the twenty "removes" of her captivity, she witnessed the killing of many captured infants. She agonized as her wounded daughter lingered on for nine days of excruciating pain before she finally died. While viewing the Indians as agents of Satan, barbaric in their cruelty, she nevertheless records their occasional acts of pity to her. She notes that they endured the same hardships that their captives endured. Her simple, unpretentious description, often understated, implants the circumstances poignantly in the reader's mind.

The story is told as a vindication of the writer's confidence in God's providence. The title indicates her main theme: *The Sovereignty and Goodness of God, Together with the Faithfulness of His Promises Displayed; Being a Narrative of the Captivity and Restoration of Mrs. Mary Rowlandson.* The work's simplicity and pathos are well balanced by the simple truth that leads her to reflect at the end of her book: "we must rely on God himself, and our whole dependence must be upon him. . . . I have learned to look beyond present and smaller troubles, and to be quieted under them, as Moses said, Exod. 14.13. 'Stand still and see the salvation of the Lord.'"

from A Narrative of the Captivity and Restoration of Mrs. Mary Rowlandson

Mrs. Rowlandson tells a story of the horror often experienced along the New England frontier after the middle of the seventeenth century. As the white man continued encroaching on Indian land, the Indians grew steadily more alarmed. King Philip was the first Indian chief to consolidate the New England tribes and lead a unified attack against the colonists. Mrs. Rowlandson was captured during one of the more successful raids by Philip's plundering band.

This excerpt, unlike the other accounts appearing thus far in your text, has been reproduced using the original spelling, punctuation, and capitalization.

On the tenth of February 1676, Came the Indians with great numbers upon Lancaster: Their first coming was about Sunrising; hearing the noise of some Guns, we looked out; several Houses were burning, and the Smoke ascending to Heaven. There were five persons taken in one house, the Father, and the Mother and a sucking Child, they knockt on the head; the other two they took and carried away alive. Their were two others, who being out of the Garison upon some occasion were set upon; one was knockt on the head, the other escaped: Another their was who running along was shot and wounded, and fell down; he begged of them his life, promising them Money (as they told me) but they would not hearken to him but knockt him in the head, and stript him naked, and split open his Bowels. Another seeing many of the Indians about his Barn, ventured and went out, but was quickly shot down. There were three others belonging to the same Garison who were killed; the Indians getting up upon the roof of the Barn, had advantage to shoot down upon them over their Fortification. Thus these murtherous wretches went on, burning, and destroying before them.

At length they came and beset our own house, and quickly it was the dolefullest day that ever mine eyes saw. The House stood upon the edg of a hill; some of the Indians got behind the hill,

others into the Barn, and others behind any thing that could shelter them; from all which places they shot against the House, so that the Bullets seemed to fly like hail; and quickly they wounded one man among us, then another, and then a third, About two hours (according to my observation, in that amazing time) they had been about the house before they prevailed to fire it (which they did with Flax and Hemp, which they brought out of the Barn, and there being no defence about the House, only two Flankers at two opposite corners and one of them not finished) they fired it once and one ventured out and quenched it, but they quickly fired it again, and that took. Now is the dreadful hour come, that I have often heard of (in time of War, as it was the case of others) but now mine eyes see it. Some in our house were fighting for their lives, others wallowing in their blood, the House on fire over our heads, and the bloody Heathen ready to knock us on the head, if we stirred out. Now might we hear Mothers and Children crying out for themselves, and one another, Lord, What shall we do? Then I took my Children (and one of my sisters, hers) to go forth and leave the house: but as soon as we came to the dore and appeared, the Indians shot so thick that the bulletts rattled against the House, as if one had taken an handfull of stones and threw them, so that we were fain to give back. We had six stout Dogs belonging to our Garison, but none of them would stir, though another time, if any Indian had come to the door, they were ready to fly upon him and tear him down. The Lord hereby would make us the more to acknowledge his hand, and to see that our help is always in him. But out we must go, the fire increasing, and coming along behind us, roaring, and the Indians gaping before us with their Guns, Spears and Hatchets to devour us. No sooner were we out of the House, but my Brother in Law (being before wounded, in defending the house, in or near the throat) fell down dead, wherat the Indians scornfully shouted, and hallowed, and were presently upon him, stripping his cloaths, the bulletts flying thick, one went through my side, and the same (as would seem) through the bowels and hand of my dear Child in my arms. One of my elder Sisters Children, named William, had then his Leg broken, which the Indians perceiving, they knockt him on head. Thus were we butchered by those merciless Heathen, standing amazed, with the blood running down to our heels. My eldest Sister being yet in the House, and seeing those wofull sights, the Infidels haling Mothers one way, and Children another, and some wallowing in their blood: and her elder Son telling her that her Son William was dead, and my self was wounded, she said, And, Lord, let me dy with them; which was no sooner said, but she was struck with a Bullet, and fell down dead over the threshold. I hope she is reaping the fruit of her good labours, being faithful to the service of God in her place. In her younger years she lay under much trouble upon spiritual accounts, till it pleased God to make that precious Scripture take hold of her heart, 2 Cor. 12.9. *And he said unto me, my Grace is sufficient for thee.* More then twenty years after I have heard her tell how sweet and comfortable that place was to her. But to return: The Indians laid hold of us, pulling me one way, and the Children another, and said, Come go along with us; I told them they would kill me: they answered, If I were willing to go along with them, they would not hurt me.

Oh the dolefull sight that now was to behold at this House! *Come, behold the works of the Lord, what dissolations he has made in the Earth.* Of thirty seven persons who were in this one House, none escaped either present death, or a bitter captivity, save only one, who might say as he, Job 1.15, *And I only am escaped alone to tell the News.* There were twelve killed, some shot, some stab'd with their Spears, some knock'd down with their Hatchets. When we are in prosperity, Oh the little that we think of such dreadfull sights, and to see our dear Friends, and Relations ly bleeding out their heart-blood upon the ground. There was one who was chopt into the head with a Hatchet, and stripped naked, and yet was crawling up and down. It is a solemn sight to see so many Christians lying in their blood, some here, and some there, like a company of Sheep torn by Wolves, All of them stript naked by a company of hell-hounds, roaring, singing, ranting and insulting, as if they would have torn our very hearts out; yet the Lord by his Almighty power preserved a number of us from death, for there were twenty-four of us taken alive and carried Captive.

I had often before this said, that if the Indians should come, I should chuse rather to be killed by them then taken alive but when it came to the tryal my mind changed; their glittering weapons so daunted my spirit, that I chose rather to go along with those (as I may say) ravenous Beasts, then that moment to end my dayes; and that I may the better declare what happened to me during that grievous Captivity, I shall particularly speak of the severall Removes we had up and down the Wilderness.

The First Remove

Now away we must go with those Barbarous Creatures, with our bodies wounded and bleeding, and our hearts no less than our bodies. About a mile we went that night, up upon a hill within sight of the Town, where they intended to lodge. There was hard by a vacant house (deserted by the English before, for fear of the Indians). I asked them whither I might not lodge in the house that night to which they answered, what will you love English men still? this was the dolefullest night that ever my eyes saw. Oh the roaring, and singing and danceing, and yelling of those black creatures in the night, which made the place a lively resemblance of hell. And as miserable was the wast* that was there made, of Horses, Cattle, Sheep, Swine, Calves, Lambs, Roasting Pigs, and Fowl (which they had plundered in the Town) some roasting, some lying and burning, and some boyling to feed our merciless Enemies; who were joyful enough though we were disconsolate. To add to the dolefulness of the former day, and the dismalness of the present night: my thoughts ran upon my losses and sad bereaved condition. All was gone, my Husband gone (at least separated from me, he being in the Bay; and to add to my grief, the Indians told me they would kill him as he came homeward) my Children gone, my Relations and Friends gone, our house and home and all our comforts within door, and without, all was gone, (except my life) and I knew not but the next moment that might go too. There remained nothing to me but one poor wounded Babe, and it seemed at present worse than death that it was in such a pitiful condition, bespeaking Compassion, and I had no refreshing for it, nor suitable things to revive it. . . .

wast: devastation

The Second Remove

But now, the next morning, I must turn my back upon the Town, and travel with them into the vast and desolate Wilderness, I knew not whither. It is not my tongue, or pen can express the sorrows of my heart, and bitterness of my spirit, that I had at this departure: but God was with me, in a wonderfull manner, carrying me along, and bearing up my spirit, that it did not quite fail. One of the Indians carried my poor wounded Babe upon a horse, it went moaning all along, I shall dy, I shall dy. I went on foot after it, with sorrow that cannot be exprest. At length I took it off the horse, and carried it in my arms till my strength failed, and I fell down with it: Then they set me upon a horse with my wounded Child in my lap, and there being no furniture* upon the horse back, as we were going down a steep hill, we both fell over the horses head, at which they like inhumane creatures laught, and rejoyced to see it, though I thought we should there have ended our dayes, as overcome with so many difficulties. But the Lord renewed my strength still, and carried me along, that I might see more of his Power; yea, so much that I could never have thought of, had I not experienced it.

furniture: riding equipment: viz., saddle

After this it quickly began to snow, and when night came on, they stopt: and now down I must sit in the snow, by a little fire, and a few boughs behind me, with my sick Child in my lap; and calling much for water, being now (through the wound) fallen into a violent Fever. My own wound also growing so stiff, that I could scarce sit down or rise up, yet so it must be, that I must sit all this cold winter night upon the cold snowy ground, with my sick Child in my armes, looking that every hour would be the last of its life; and having no Christian friend near me, either to comfort or help me. Oh, I may see the wonderfull power of God, that my spirit did not utterly sink under my affliction: still the Lord upheld me with his gracious and mercifull Spirit, and we were both alive to see the light of the next morning.

The Third Remove

I sat much alone with a poor wounded Child in my lap, which moaned night and day, having nothing to revive the body, or cheer the spirits of her, but in stead of that, sometimes one Indian would come and tell me one hour, that your Master will knock your Child in the head, and then a second, and then a third, your Master will quickly knock your Child in the head.

This was the comfort I had from them, miserable comforters are ye all, as he said.* Thus nine dayes I sat upon my knees, with my Babe in my lap, till my flesh was raw again; my Child being even ready to depart this sorrowfull world, they bade me carry it out to another Wigwam (I suppose because they would not be troubled with such spectacles) Whither I went with a very heavy heart, and down I sat with the picture of death in my lap. About two houres in the night, my sweet Babe like a Lambe departed this life, on Feb. 18, 1676. It being about six yeares, and five months old. It was nine dayes from the first wounding, in this miserable condition, without any refreshing of one nature or other, except a little cold water. I cannot, but take notice, how at another time I could not bear to be in the room where any dead person was, but now the case is changed; I must and could ly down by my dead Babe, side by side all the night after. I have thought since of the wonderfull goodness of God to me, in preserving me in the use of my reason and senses, in that distressed time, that I did not use wicked and violent means to end my own miserable life. In the morning, when they understood that my child was dead they sent for me home to my Masters Wigwam: (by my Master in this writing, must be understood Quanopin, who was a Saggamore, and married King Philips* wives Sister; not that he first took me, but I was sold to him by another Narrhaganset Indian, who took me when first I came out of the Garison). I went to take up my dead child in my arms to carry it with me, but they bid me let it alone: there was no resisting, but goe I must and leave it. When I had been at my masters wigwam, I took the first opportunity I could get, to go look after my dead child: when I came I askt them what they had done with it? then they told me it was upon the hill: then they went and shewed me where it was, where I saw the ground was newly digged, and there they told me they had buried it: There I left that Child in the Wilderness, and must commit it, and my self also in this Wildernesscondition, to him who is above all.

Miserable . . . all: Job 16:2
King Philips: chief of the Wampanoag tribe who led King Philip's
    War, the most severe Indian war in New England history.

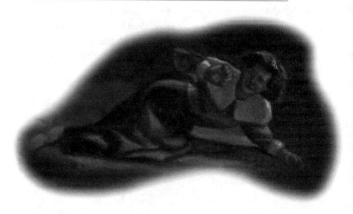

Mary Rowlandson's captivity ended when several prominent Boston citizens paid a ransom of twenty pounds for her release. Her son was released for seven pounds, paid by several unknown persons. Her daughter simply walked away from the Indians to safety.

For Thought and Discussion

1. What details in the first paragraph establish the reliability of the writer as narrator of the events she describes?

2. In which sentence does Rowlandson first refer to the Lord's hand in these affairs? What theme does she incorporate in her narrative at this point?

3. At what point does Rowlandson first employ disparaging diction to refer to the Indians?

4. How does her diction up to this point in the narrative differ from John Smith's in *A General History?* What effect does her diction have on her credibility?

5. What spiritual theme does Rowlandson finally emphasize? Point out the sentences in which she states this theme. How do her Biblical allusions support this theme?

Samuel Sewall   1652-1730

Samuel Sewall's *Diary* was a private record, not intended for publication. Combining details of his private and public life, it displays intimately and candidly what Sewall did and thought. While it shows the lingering form of Puritanism, it also reveals the growing spirit of materialism among the colonists. The *Diary* thus reflects a condition the mid-seventeenth-century preachers feared: that the Puritan colonists would allow encroaching worldliness to affect their attitudes and goals.

Sewall, who received a divinity degree from Harvard College in 1671, settled into a business and public career. His career was no doubt helped by his marriage to Hannah Hull, daughter of the wealthiest man in the colony. Although untrained in the legal profession, Sewall was appointed to numerous offices. He became a judge in 1692 at the notorious Salem witchcraft trials. He later, however, publicly renounced his participation in these trials. He served as chief justice of the Bay Colony from 1718 to 1728. Known as the first Yankee, Sewall was a prototype of the American businessman. While spending much of his life in public service, he accumulated worldly goods during a time when a person's materialistic success was regarded by many as a sign of God's favor. He died in 1730, apparently the richest man in Massachusetts.

Sewall's literary reputation rests primarily on his *Diary,* which covers the years 1674 to 1729 except for an eight-year gap. Because he did not intend publication, he left his record unpolished. What he chose to include gives insight both into contemporary colonial life and into his values. Like Byrd, his Virginia contemporary, Sewall records the minute details of his life, including his travels, his domestic affairs, his courtship of eligible widows (like many other New England men, he outlived two wives and many of his children), and his intimate thoughts and feelings. In the following *Diary* selections, Sewall views the world in such a way that natural objects take on spiritual significance. Like the Puritan historian, Sewall sought to reveal the meaning that lay behind natural occurrences. In doing so, he displayed the continuing Puritan concern for the soul's relationship to God, the ever-present reality of death, the uncertainty of existence.

Sewall's *Diary* illustrates both the spiritual and the materialistic concerns of the contemporary Puritan mind: the desire to keep a careful record of one's life so as to measure spiritual growth and the desire to keep careful account of materialistic advances. This conflict between spiritual and materialistic values mirrors, to a great extent, the change in the New England temper, a condition Jonathan Edwards and others tried to counteract by recalling New England to full-hearted service of God.

from The Diary

April 29, 1695

The morning is very warm and sunshiny; in the afternoon there is thunder and lightning, and about 2 p.m. a very extraordinary storm of hail, so that the ground was made white with it, as with the blossoms when fallen; 'twas as big as pistol and musket bullets; it broke of the glass of the new house about 480 quarrels* of the front; of Mr. Sergeant's about as much; Col. Shrimpton, Major General, Gov. Bradstreet, New Meeting-house, Mr. Willard, &c. Mr. Cotton Mather dined with us, and was with me in the new kitchen when this was; he had just been mentioning that more ministers' houses than others proportionably had been smitten with lightning; enquiring what the meaning of God should be in it. Many hailstones broke through the glass and flew to the middle of the room, or farther; people afterward gazed upon the house to see its ruins. I got Mr. Mather to pray with us after this awful providence; he told God

He had broken the brittle part of our house, and pray'd that we might be ready for the time when our clay tabernacles* should be broken. 'Twas a sorrowful thing to me to see the house so far undone again before 'twas finish'd.

---

quarrels: squares
clay tabernacles: II Corinthians 5:1-4

December 21, 1696

A very great snow is on the ground. I go in the morn to Mr. Willard, to entreat him to choose his own time to come and pray with little Sarah; he comes a little before night, and prays very fully and well. Mr. Mather, the President, had pray'd with her in the time of the Court's sitting.

December 22, 1696

Being catechising day, I give Mr. Willard a note to pray for my daughter publicly, which he did.

. . . This day I remove poor little Sarah into my bed-chamber, where about break of day, Dec. 23, she gives up the ghost in Nurse Cowell's

arms. Born, Nov. 21, 1694. Neither I nor my wife were by, Nurse not expecting so sudden a change and having promis'd to call us. I thought of Christ's Words, "Could you not watch with me one hour!"* and would fain have sat up with her; but fear of my wife's illness . . . made me to lodge with her in the new hall, where was call'd by Jane's cry to take notice of my dead daughter. Nurse did long and pathetically ask our pardon that she had not call'd us, and said she was surpris'd. Thus this very fair day is rendered foul to us by reason of the general sorrow and tears in the family. Master Chiever was here the evening before; I desir'd him to pray for my daughter. The chapter read in course on Dec. 23 morning was Deut. 22, which made me sadly reflect that I had not been so thoroughly tender of my daughter nor so effectually careful of her defence and preservation as I should have been. The good Lord pity and pardon and help for the future as to those God has still left me.

December 25, 1696

We bury our little daughter. In the chamber, Joseph in course reads Ecclesiastes 3rd "a time to be born and a time to die"; Elisabeth, Rev. 22; Hannah, the 38th Psalm. I speak to each, as God helped, to our mutual comfort I hope. I order'd Sam. to read the 102nd Psalm. Elisha Cooke, Edw. Hutchinson, John Baily, and Josia Willard bear my little daughter to the tomb.

Note. 'Twas wholly dry, and I went at noon to see in what order things were set; and there I was entertain'd with a view of, and converse with, the coffins of my dear Father Hull, Mother Hull, Cousin Quinsey, and my six children: for the little posthumous* was now took up and set in upon that that stands on John's: so are three, one upon another twice, on the bench at the end. My mother lies on a lower bench, at the end, with head to her husband's head; and I order'd little Sarah to be set on her Grandmother's feet. 'Twas an awful yet pleasing treat;* having said "The Lord knows who shall be brought hither next," I came away.

posthumous: dead child: i.e., Sarah
treat: treatment: i.e., act of God

January 26, 1697

I lodged at Charlestown, at Mrs. Shephard's, who tells me Mr. Harvard built that house. I lay in the chamber next the street. As I lay awake past midnight, in my meditation I was affected to consider how long ago God had made provision for my comfortable lodging that night; seeing that was Mr. Harvard's house. And that led me to think of heaven, the house not made with hands, which God for many thousands of years has been storing with the richest furniture (saints that are from time to time placed there), and that I had some hopes of being entertain'd in that magnificent convenient palace, every way fitted and furnished. These thoughts were very refreshing to me.

from **Phaenomena**

Like many other prominent Puritans, Sewall studied the Bible extensively. Biblical prophecy and its fulfillment especially appealed to him. This brief excerpt from a 1697 pamphlet on the meaning of the book of Revelation (he predicts, incidentally, that the seat of the New Jerusalem will be New England) reveals Sewall's acute observation and love of the world around him.

As long as *Plum Island* shall faithfully keep the commanded post, notwithstanding all the hectoring words, and hard blows of the proud and boisterous ocean; as long as any salmon or sturgeon shall swim in the streams of *Merrimack* or any perch or pickerel in *Crane-Pond;* as long as the seafowl shall know the time of their coming and not neglect seasonally to visit the places of their acquaintance; as long as any cattle shall be fed with the grass growing in the meadows, which do humbly bow down themselves before *Turkey Hill;* as long as any sheep shall walk upon *Old Town Hills,* and shall from thence pleasantly look down upon the river *Parker* and the fruitful *Marshes* lying beneath; as long as any free and harmless doves shall find a white oak or other tree within the township to perch or feed or build a careless nest upon and shall voluntarily present themselves to perform the office of gleaners after barley harvest; as long as Nature shall not grow old and dote but shall constantly remember to give the rows of Indian corn their education, by pairs: So long shall Christians be born there; and, being first made meet, shall from thence be translated, to be made partakers of the Inheritance of the Saints in Light.*

Inheritance . . . Light: Colossians 1:12

For Thought and Discussion

1. What does Sewall mean by "this awful providence" in the April 29, 1695, entry? Did the word *awful* have a different connotation in 1695 than it does today?
2. Look at Deuteronomy 22:1-8, especially verse 8. Why does Sewall use the allusion in the December 21, 1696, entry?
3. Notice that the excerpt from *Phaenomena* consists of only one long sentence. Where does Sewall complete the extended comparison that begins with the word *As?*
4. Paraphrase the excerpt from *Phaenomena* in one brief sentence.

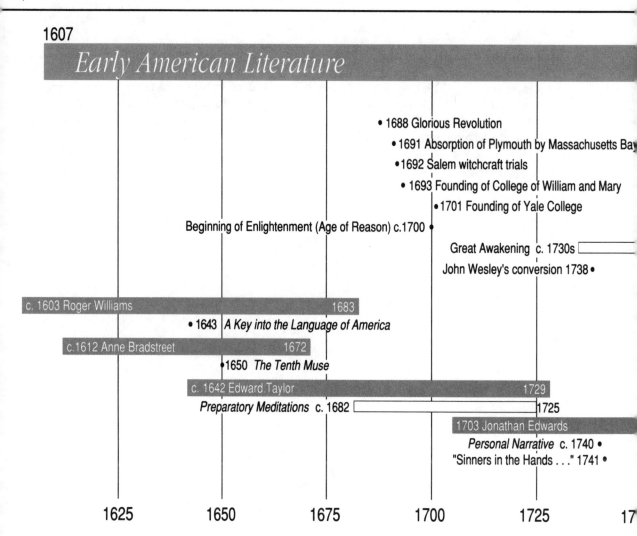

1820

2 Literature of Religious Experience

0   1775   1800

The Bay Psalm Book

The Puritans sang only the Psalms in their churches. Since they could not sing them in Hebrew, the language of the Old Testament, they had to have English translations. They believed, however, that the English collections already in use by the early seventeenth century took too many liberties with the original wording. So the Massachusetts Puritans authorized thirty of their ministers to translate the Psalms into English verse suitable for singing. (All the selections here can be sung to the tune of "Amazing Grace.")

The translators were instructed to make their English versions literal renderings of the original, adding only **rhyme** *and* **meter.** *They were not to embellish the Psalms with their own flights of imagination: "God's altar needs not our polishings," the preface states. Because the translators differed in poetic ability, the translations vary drastically in literary quality.*

The Bay Psalm Book was the first book printed in this country. It enjoyed great popularity here; in fact, the 1651 edition remained in common use in New England churches for nearly 150 years.

Psalm One

O blessed man, that in th' advice
   of wicked doeth not walk:
nor stand in sinners' way, nor sit
   in chair of scornful folk.

But in the law of Jehovah,   5
   is his longing delight:
and in his law doth meditate,
   by day and also by night.

And he shall be like to a tree
   planted by water-rivers: 10
that in his season yields his fruit,
   and his leaf never withers.

And all he doth, shall prosper well,
   the wicked are not so:
but they are like unto the chaff,   15
   which wind drives to and fro.

Therefore shall not ungodly men,
   rise to stand in the doom,
nor shall the sinners with the just,
   in their assembly come.   20

For of the righteous men, the Lord
   acknowledgeth the way:
but the way of ungodly men,
   shall utterly decay.

Psalm Twenty-three

The Lord to me a shepherd is,
Want therefore shall not I.
He in the folds of tender-grass,
Doth cause me down to lie:

To waters calm me gently leads   5
Restore my soul doth He:

He doth in paths of righteousness:
For His name's sake lead me.

Yea though in valley of death's shade
I walk, none ill I'll fear: 10
Because Thou art with me, Thy rod,
And staff my comfort are.

For me a table Thou hast spread,
   In presence of my foes:
Thou dost anoint my head with oil,   15
   My cup it overflows.

Goodness and mercy surely shall
   All my days follow me:
And in the Lord's house I shall dwell
   So long as days shall be.   20

Psalm 23 (Geneva Bible)

    The so-called Puritan Bible was the Geneva Bible (1560), translated by English exiles in Geneva, Switzerland. What particularly endeared the translation to the Puritans was its marginal notes, which took on a more and more Calvinistic flavor as new editions appeared. The Genevan translation, the first Bible to divide its contents into verses, strongly influenced the King James Version (1611).

The Lord is my shepherd, I shall not want.
He maketh me to rest in green pasture and
   leadeth me by the still waters.
He restoreth my soul, and leadeth me in the
   paths of righteousness for his name's sake.   5
Yea, though I should walk through the valley of the
   shadow of death, I will fear no evil; for thou
   art with me; thy rod and thy staff, they comfort me.
Thou dost prepare a table before me in the sight
   of mine adversaries; thou dost anoint mine head with   10
   oil, and my cup runneth over.
Doubtless kindness and mercy shall follow me all the
   days of my life, and I shall remain a long season
   in the house of the Lord.

For Thought and Discussion

1. Which three lines of "Psalm 1" are not written in either eight or six syllables? Write lines of your own with regular meter to substitute for these irregular lines.
2. Although the first English Bible in this country was likely the Genevan, does the translation of Psalm 23 in *The Bay Psalm Book* show more agreement with it or with the KJV?

Roger Williams c. 1603-1683

Roger Williams was accused of many heresies during his lifetime. Today he is generally regarded not as a heretic but as a thinker ahead of his time. In particular, his belief in the separation of church and state, a principle that struck at the heart of the Massachusetts theocracy, has been influential among later religious and political conservatives.

Except for Anne Hutchinson, no immigrant in the 1630s so troubled Massachusetts Bay as did Roger Williams. The son of a London tailor, Williams showed such early promise that the famous English jurist Sir Edward Coke (1552-1634) helped sponsor his education. After graduation from Cambridge in 1627, Williams was ordained to the ministry. In 1631 he immigrated to Boston, where he was asked to serve as teacher for the Boston church during the absence of its regular teacher, the Reverend John Wilson. Williams refused the call, however, because of his strong leanings toward Separatism. He declared that he could not pastor any church still maintaining ties with the Church of England. His decision, of course, created a disturbance in the colony, for the Massachusetts leaders feared that such a position might cause English authorities to revoke the charter. This disturbance proved to be only the first of a series of clashes with the religious and political leaders of the colony.

For four turbulent years, Williams continued preaching what the Massachusetts authorities regarded as seditious doctrine. Finally, an order for his arrest and deportation to England was issued. Williams fled the Bay Colony in January, 1636. Traveling southward to what is now Rhode Island, an area not yet covered by any of the king's grants, Williams negotiated with the Indians for a tract of land. (According to Williams, the legal owner of New England was not the king, who granted land to whomever he chose, but the Indians who lived there.)

After successfully securing a charter for the new colony in 1643, Williams had to renegotiate the charter in 1651 because an influential faction within the colony had secured an annulment. In 1654 the new charter was finally accepted by all the settlements in Rhode Island. From 1654 to 1657 Williams served as president of the new colony, both then and later protecting it from Massachusetts Bay's attempts to absorb it. Although remaining outside any formal church for the last four decades of his life, Williams continued to preach among the Indians. He died in poverty in his eighty-first year, respected by his foes for manifesting sweetness of temper and spirit even while engaged in religious and political controversy.

A voice calling for greater, but not total, toleration in a fundamentally intolerant age, Williams has been reverenced by later Americans as both a Baptist and a democratic hero. As Baptist hero, however, his credentials are uncertain. In 1639 he founded what is sometimes considered the first Baptist church in the New World, but four months later he resigned as pastor of the newly formed church, stating that his beliefs had changed. After this point in his life, Williams was a Seeker, one who believed all Christian churches to be in various stages of apostasy.

As democratic hero Williams deserves praise, for he established Rhode Island upon principles of religious liberty. He put into practice the important new theory of the separation of church and state. In fact, his difficulties with Massachusetts Bay arose largely because of his refusal to accept the union of church and state. The church, he believed, should not be subject to the authority of the state; moreover, the church should have authority only over church members, not over the entire community. In other words, he regarded the church's authority as limited to spiritual matters. It is no wonder that Williams was banished from the Bay Colony, for his position threatened the very core of the theocracy, which held that laws, schools, political structures, and so forth, should be established by church and state together.

Surely the American tradition of the separation of church and state is greatly indebted to Roger Williams. It is based on the principle of liberty of conscience. Williams would not have contended that separation exempts the church, as a physical institution, from all political jurisdiction. In his letter to the people of Providence (1655), he makes clear that religious conviction does not free a person from the normal obligations of citizenship. Rather, the principle of separation of church and state protects the church's *religious* conviction and operations from governmental interference and restrains the government, on the other hand, from establishing a state religion or favoring a particular form of religion over others.

Williams's religio-political debates with Massachusetts Bay–especially his pamphlet controversy with Reverend John Cotton, one of the foremost spokesmen for the Massachusetts theocracy–usually places Williams's work in the tradition of controversial prose. Yet he also wrote poetry. In *A Key into the Language of America* (1643), a book written to introduce the Narragansett Indian language to English-speaking people, Williams interspersed several poems treating his travels among and reactions to the Indians. His sympathetic attitude toward the Indians was similar to the romantic view of the Indian that became popular a hundred years after Williams's death. His poetry also, like his prose, reminds readers that when God evaluates mankind, He examines the individual, not the community.

from Letter to the Town of Providence, January 1655, on the Limits of Freedom

There goes many a ship to sea, with many hundred souls in one ship, whose weal and woe* is common, and is a true picture of a commonwealth or a human combination or society. It hath fallen out sometimes that both Papists* and Protestants, Jews and Turks, may be embarked in one ship; upon which supposal I affirm, that all the liberty of conscience that ever I pleaded for, turns upon these two hinges–that none of the Papists, Protestants, Jews, or Turks, be forced to come to the ship's prayers or worship, nor compelled from their own particular prayers or worship, if they practise any. I further add, that I never denied that, notwithstanding this liberty, the commander of this ship ought to command the ship's course, yet, and also command that justice, peace, and sobriety, be kept and practised, both among the seamen and all the passengers. If any of the sea-men refuse to perform their services, or passengers to pay their freight; if any refuse to help, in person or pursue, toward the common charges or defence; if any refuse to obey the common laws and orders of the ship, concerning their common peace or preservation; if any shall mutiny and rise up against their commanders and officers; if any should preach or write that there ought to be no commanders or officers, because all are equal in Christ, therefore no masters nor officers, no laws nor orders, nor corrections, nor punishments;–I say, I never denied, but in such cases, whatever is pretended, the commander or commanders may judge, resist, compel, and punish such transgressors, according to their deserts* and merits.

weal and woe: prosperity and misfortune
Papists: Roman Catholics
deserts: deserved punishment

A Key into the Language of America

They See God's Wonders

They see God's wonders that are call'd
    Through dreadful seas to pass,
In tearing winds and roaring seas,
    And calms as smooth as glass.*

I have in Europe's ships, oft been
    In King of terror's hand;   5
When all have cri'd, ''Now, now we sink,''
    Yet God brought safe to land.

Alone 'mongst Indians in canoes,
    Sometime o're-turn'd I have been*   10
Half inch from death, in ocean deep,
    God's wonders I have seen.

And . . . glass: Psalm 107:23-30

I have been: pronounced *I've been* for the sake of the meter

Boast Not Proud English

Boast not proud English, of thy birth and blood,
    Thy brother Indian is by birth as good.
Of one blood God made him, and thee and all.
    As wise, as fair, as strong, as personal.*

By nature, wrath's his portion, thine, no more   5
    Till grace his soul and thine in Christ restore.
Make sure thy second birth, else thou shalt see
    Heaven ope* to Indians wild, but shut to thee.

personal: having qualities of a person: i.e., the Indian is not different from the Englishman (cf. the view of the Indian as animal or demon)

ope: open

The Courteous Pagan

The courteous pagan shall condemn
    Uncourteous Englishmen,
Who* live like foxes, bears, and wolves,
    Or lion in his den.

Who: refers to *pagan*

Let none sing blessings to their souls,   5
    For that they courteous are:
The wild barbarians with no more
    Than nature, go so far;

If nature's sons both wild and tame,*
    Humane and courteous be: 10
How ill becomes it sons of God
    To want* humanity?

sons . . . tame: pagan and civilized men

want: lack

For Thought and Discussion

1. What two principles constitute "liberty of conscience," according to Williams?
2. Which of these two principles suggests that Williams believed in separation of church and state?
3. How does this view of the relationship of religion to government differ from the Puritans'? What did the Puritans claim as the Biblical basis for their view?
4. How does the view of the Indians conveyed by Williams differ from that implied by the Puritan writers whose selections you have read in this text? According to Williams, what is the only means by which Indian and Englishman may truly be united? Who needs restoration in Christ–Indian or Englishman?
5. What, according to Williams's speaker, constitutes "God's wonders"? What do we usually mean when we refer to "God's wonders" today?

Anne Bradstreet
c. 1612-1672

Somehow while caring for her husband (an important leader in Massachusetts Bay), her eight children, and her household, Anne Bradstreet found time to become the first colonist to write a sizable body of verse. Her best poems, like those of Roger Williams, grew out of her New England experience. Written in clear, unadorned style, they illustrate the human dimension of Puritan literature.

Born in England and married at sixteen to Simon Bradstreet, Anne Bradstreet sailed to New England in the first wave of the Great Migration to set up housekeeping in the Massachusetts wilderness. It must have been difficult for a young woman accustomed to a relatively easy life in England to adapt herself to the rigors of the New England frontier. Often she had to manage the household and growing family alone because her husband was frequently separated from her by colonial business.

In 1650, without her knowledge, a collection of her poems was published in London under the extravagant title *The Tenth Muse Lately Sprung Up in America*. The Reverend John Woodbridge, her brother-in-law, was evidently the instigator. Although such prominent New Englanders as Nathaniel Ward and Cotton Mather praised the book, it also elicited some negative comments from those who charged that the poetess should spend her time with a needle rather than with a pen. Six years after her death, a Boston printer published an enlarged, corrected edition of her poetry, entitled *Several Poems Compiled with Great Variety of Wit and Learning*. A copy of this volume was the only collection of English verse in the library of Edward Taylor, who is now recognized as our foremost colonial poet.

The poetry of Bradstreet's two books of verse is, for the most part, conventional imitation of such English Renaissance poets as Edmund Spenser and Sir Philip Sidney and the French poet Guillaume du Bartas. Among the more appealing of her public poems are ''The Author to Her Book'' (a poem prefacing her second volume of poetry) and ''Contemplations.'' It is, however, the private poems unpublished during her lifetime that have been most favorably regarded by readers since her time. Avoiding much of the artificiality of the poetry popular in her day and even of her published verse, they speak of such frontier hardships as the burning of her house in 1666 and the death of grandchildren. Some, addressed to her husband, express the intense love and happiness, amidst these sorrows and hardships, of this devout Puritan writer. The last poem written in her own hand, ''As Weary Pilgrim,'' represents the poet as weary of life and longing for death.

Bradstreet's poetry displays not only the technical skill of a talented seventeenth-century colonial woman but also her sincere desire to understand God's working in the world and her life. Against the backdrop of her domestic joys and sorrows, one may see the Puritan mind exploring but also accepting God's ways.

from Contemplations

The Puritans did not ignore nature, for they believed that the creation reveals the Creator. This poem shows Bradstreet musing on a scene in nature (what is the time of day and season of the year?), casting her gaze on a "stately oak" (l. 15), and then lifting her attention steadily upward: from oak (l. 15) to sun (l. 22) to Creator (l. 40).

1

Some time now past in the autumnal tide,
When Phoebus* wanted but one hour to bed,
The trees all richly clad, yet void of pride,
Where gilded* o'er by his rich golden head.
Their leaves and fruits seemed painted, but was true,   5
Of green, of red, of yellow, mixed hue;
Rapt* were my senses at this delectable* view.

2

I wist* not what to wish, yet sure thought I,
If so much excellence abide below,
How excellent is He that dwells on high,   10
Whose power and beauty by His works we know?
Sure He is goodness, wisdom, glory, light,
That hath this under world so richly dight;*
More heaven than earth was here, no winter and no night.

Phoebus: poetic name for the sun (Phoebus is Apollo, god of the sun and brother of Phoebe-Cynthia-Di-ana, goddess of the moon.)
gilded: coated with gold, adorned
Rapt: charmed/*delectable:* delightful

wist: knew

dight: adorned, dressed

3

Then on a stately oak I cast mine eye,   15
Whose ruffling top the clouds seemed to aspire;*
How long since thou wast in thine infancy?
Thy strength, and stature, more thy years admire,
Hath hundred winters past since thou wast born?
Or thousand since thou brakest thy shell of horn?   20
If so, all these as nought,* eternity doth scorn.

aspire: seemed to mount up to the clouds

nought: nothing

4

Then higher on the glistering Sun I gazed,
Whose beams was shaded by the leavie tree;
The more I looked, the more I grew amazed,
And softly said, ''What glory's like to thee,   25
Soul of this world, this universe's eye,
No wonder some made thee a deity;
Had I not better known, alas, the same had I.

5

Thou as a bridegroom from thy chamber rushes,
And as a strong man, joys to run a race;*   30   *Thou . . . race:* Psalm
The morn doth usher thee with smiles and blushes;   19:4-5
The Earth reflects her glances in thy face.
Birds, insects, animals with vegative,*   *vegative:* plant life
Thy heat from death and dullness doth revive,
And in the darksome womb of fruitful nature dive.   35

7

Art thou so full of glory that no eye
Hath strength thy shining rays once to behold?
And is thy splendid throne erect so high,
As to approach it, can no earthly mould?*   *mould:* ground: i.e.,
How full of glory then must thy Creator be,   40   man (see Gen. 2:7)
Who gave this bright light luster unto thee?
Admired,* adored for ever, be that Majesty.   *Admired:* wondered at

8

Silent alone, where none or* saw, or heard,   *or:* either
In pathless paths I lead my wandering feet,
My humble Eyes to lofty Skyes I rear'd   45
To sing some Song, my mazed* Muse* thought meet.*   *mazed:* amazed/*Muse:*
My great Creator I would magnifie,   goddess of poetic in-
That nature had, thus decked liberally: spiration/*meet:* fit
But Ah, and Ah, again, my imbecility!

On My Dear Grandchild Simon Bradstreet Who Died on 16 November 1669 Being But a Month and One Day Old

No sooner come, but gone, and fal'n asleep,
Acquaintance short, yet parting caus'd us weep,
Three flours,* two scarcely blown,* the last i' th' bud,
Cropt* by th' Almighties hand; yet is he good,
With dreadful awe before him let's be mute,   5
Such was his will, but why, let's not dispute,
With humble hearts and mouths put in the dust,
Let's say he's merciful as well as just.
He will return, and make up all our losses,
And smile again, after our bitter crosses.   10
Go pretty babe, go rest with Sisters twain*
Among the blest in endless joyes remain.

flours: flowers, i.e., Samuel Bradstreet's deceased children: Elizabeth, Anne, and Simon/*blown:* begun blooming/*Cropt:* picked

twain: two

Here Follows Some Verses upon the Burning of Our House July 10th, 1666. Copied Out of a Loose Paper

In silent night when rest I took
For sorrow near I did not look.
I wakened was with thund'ring noise
And piteous shrieks of dreadful voice.
That fearful sound of "Fire!" and "Fire!"   5
Let no man know is my desire.

I, starting* up, the light did spy,*   *starting:* jumping/*spy:*
And to my God my heart did cry   see
To strengthen me in my distress
And not to leave me succorless.*   10   *succorless:* helpless
Then, coming out, beheld a space*   *a space:* for a while
The flame consume my dwelling place.

And when I could no longer look,
I blest His name that gave and took,
That laid my goods now in the dust.   15
Yea, so it was, and so 'twas just.
It was His own, it was not mine,
Far be it that I should repine.*   *repine:* murmur,
                                                              complain

He might of all justly bereft*   *justly bereft:* might
But yet sufficient for us left.   20   justly have deprived
When by the ruins oft I past   us of all
My sorrowing eyes aside did cast,
And here and there the places spy
Where oft I sat and long did lie:

Here stood that trunk, and there that chest,   25
There lay that store I counted best.
My pleasant things in ashes lie,
And them behold no more shall I.
Under my roof no guest shall sit,
Nor at thy table eat a bit.   30

No pleasant tale shall e'er be told,
Nor things recounted done of old.
No candle e'er shall shine in thee,
Nor bridegroom's voice e'er heard shall be.
In silence ever shall thou lie,   35
Adieu,* Adieu, all's vanity.*

Adieu: farewell/all's vanity: Ecclesiastes 1:2

Then straight* I 'gin my heart to chide,*
And did thy wealth on earth abide?
Didst fix thy hope on mold'ring* dust?
The arm of flesh didst make thy trust.*   40
Raise up thy thoughts above the sky
That dunghill mists away may fly.

straight: at once/chide: scold

mold'ring: crumbling

The . . . trust: II Chronicles 32:8

Thou hast an house on high erect,
Framed by that mighty Architect,
With glory richly furnished,   45
Stands permanent though this be fled.
It's purchased and paid for too
By Him who hath enough to do.

A price so vast as is unknown
Yet by His gift is made thine own;   50
There's wealth enough, I need no more,
Farewell, my pelf,* farewell my store.
The world no longer let me love,
My hope and treasure lies above.

pelf: treasure pile

To My Dear and Loving Husband

If ever two were one, then surely we.
If ever man were loved by wife, then thee;
If ever wife was happy in a man,
Compare with me, ye women, if you can.
I prize thy love more than whole mines of gold   5
Or all the riches that the East doth hold.
My love is such that rivers cannot quench,
Nor ought* but love from thee, give recompense.*
Thy love is such I can no way repay.
The heavens reward thee manifold,* I pray.   10
Then while we live, in love let's so persever*
That when we live no more, we may live ever.

ought: anything/recompense: repayment

manifold: much

persever: accent on second syllable: per se ver

As Weary Pilgrim

As weary pilgrim, now at rest
    Hugs with delight his silent nest
His wasted limbes, now lye full soft
    That myrie* steps, have troden oft
Blesses himself, to think upon   5
    His dangers past, and travailes* done
The burning sun no more shall heat
    Nor stormy raines, on him shall beat.
The bryars and thornes no more shall scratch
    Nor hungry wolves at him shall catch   10
He erring pathes no more shall tread
    Nor wild fruits eate, in stead of bread,
For waters cold he doth not long
    For thirst no more shall parch his tongue
No rugged stones his feet shall gaule*   15
    Nor stumps nor rocks cause him to fall
All cares and feares, he bids farwell
    And meanes in safity now to dwell.
A pilgrim I, on earth, perplext
    With sinns with cares and sorrows vext   20
By age and paines brought to decay
    And my Clay house mouldring away
Oh how I long to be at rest
    And soare on high among the blest.
This body shall in silence sleep   25
    Mine eyes no more shall ever weep
No fainting fits shall me assaile*
    Nor grinding paines my body fraile
With cares and fears ne'r cumbred* be
    Nor losses know, nor sorrowes see   30
What tho my flesh shall there* consume
    It is the bed Christ did perfume
And when a few yeares shall be gone
    This mortall shall be cloth'd upon
A Corrupt Carcasse downe it lyes   35
    A glorious body it shall rise
In weaknes and dishonour sowne
    In power 'tis rais'd by Christ alone*
Then soule and body shall unite
    And of their maker have the sight   40

myrie: miry

travailes: labors, hardships

gaule: gall: injure, make sore

assaile: attack violently

cumbred: troubled, hindered

there: in the grave

'tis . . . alone: I Corinthians 15:52-55

Such lasting joyes shall there behold
    As eare ne'r heard nor tongue e'er told
Lord make me ready for that day
    Then Come deare bridgrome Come away.

from Meditations Divine and Moral

The Puritans' belief in the value of meditation runs throughout their literature. While Edward Taylor illustrates the poetic form of meditation, Anne Bradstreet, in the following prose excerpts, also illustrates the importance Puritans placed on private communion with the Lord.

For my dear son, Simon Bradstreet:

                 March 20, 1664

    Parents perpetuate their lives in their posterity, and their manners* in their* imitation. Children do naturally rather follow the failings than the virtues of their predecessors, but I am persuaded better things of you. You once desired me to leave something for you in writing that you might look upon when you should see me no more. I could think of nothing more fit for you, nor of more ease to myself, than these short meditations following.* Such as they are I bequeath to you: small legacies are accepted by true friends, much more by dutiful children. I have avoided encroaching upon others' conceptions,* because I would leave you nothing but mine own, though in value they fall short of all in this kind, yet I presume they will be better prized* by you for the author's sake. The Lord bless you with grace here, and crown you with glory hereafter, that I may meet you with rejoicing at that great day of appearing, which is the continual prayer of

           your affectionate mother, A.B.

manners: morals
their: their children's
following: 77 in number
I . . . conceptions: She included only meditations written by herself.
better prized: highly prized

IX

Sweet words are like honey, a little may refresh, but too much gluts the stomach.

X

Diverse children have their different natures; some are like flesh which nothing but salt will keep from putrefaction;* some again like tender fruits that are best preserved with sugar: those parents are wise that can fit their nurture according to their nature.

putrefaction: spoiling

XII

Authority without wisdom is like a heavy axe without an edge, fitter to bruise than polish.

XXXVII

Wickedness comes to its height by degrees. He that dares say of a little sin, "Is it not a little one?" will ere long say of a greater, "Tush,* God regards it not!"

Tush: an exclamation of disparagement

For Thought and Discussion

1. Notice the function of the pivotal word *yet* in line 4 of "On My Dear Grandchild Simon Bradstreet." First summarize the point made in the portion of the poem that precedes this word; next, summarize the point made in the portion that follows it. For which of these two points does Bradstreet offer more support? Why?

2. What spiritual truth does Bradstreet learn from the burning of her house? What specific lines convey this spiritual theme?

3. Discuss Bradstreet's use of pronouns in "To My Dear and Loving Husband." Who are the *we* and *thee* of lines 1 and 2? Whom does Bradstreet address directly in lines 3 and 4? At what point does Bradstreet return to the first and second person address? What effect does Bradstreet's selection of pronouns have on the tone of her poem?

4. At what point in "As Weary Pilgrim" does the persona depict a longed-for physical death? At what point in the poem does the persona, by means of Scriptural allusion, seem to contradict this longing for physical death? Why?

5. What is the significance of the final word in the poem "As Weary Pilgrim"? Does it add to or detract from the meaning of the poem? Why do you suppose Bradstreet chose to employ *away* in this context?

Edward Taylor c. 1642-1729

For over two hundred years after his death in 1729, Edward Taylor's poetry was unknown to the world because of the writer's strange request that his heirs preserve it but not publish it. In 1937 Thomas H. Johnson discovered a manuscript collection of Taylor's poems in the archives of Yale Library and two years later published a generous selection of them. Once published, these poems caused critics to reevaluate many of their conclusions about early American poetry. In particular, Taylor's poetry disproved the notion that a Puritan could not create excellent poetry from Biblical materials and personal religious experience.

Like many other seventeenth-century colonists, Taylor was an adult when he sailed to New England. Religious persecution, specifically the Act of Uniformity of 1662, forced him to leave England. This act, one of a series of laws intended to suppress the Puritan influence, required clergymen and schoolmasters to accept the Anglican prayer book and thus acknowledge the authority of the Established Church. Rather than violate his religious convictions, Taylor sailed for New England. On arriving in Boston in 1668, he enrolled in Harvard College, where he earned academic distinction. After his graduation in 1671, he was invited to organize a church in Westfield, Massachusetts, a frontier settlement a hundred miles west of Boston.

While pastoring the Westfield church for nearly fifty years, Taylor served as the town physician and organized the village's defenses against the Indians (notably during King Philip's War, 1675-76). By 1682, with the Indians less of a threat, his family settled, and his ministry well established, this frontier minister began writing poems of devotion to God. He continued this practice until 1725, when he became too feeble to do much more than long for death to release him for heaven.

Taylor's best poetry appears in his two major collections: *Preparatory Meditations Before My Approach to the Lord's Supper, Chiefly upon the Doctrine Preached upon the Day of Administration* and *God's Determinations Touching His Elect, and the Elect's Combat in Their Conversion and Coming up to God in Christ Together with the Comfortable Effects Thereof.* The *Preparatory Meditations* includes 215 poetic meditations written at somewhat regular two-to-four-month intervals from 1682 to 1725. The purpose of these meditations was to prepare Taylor spiritually for preaching the sermon preceding the Lord's Supper. Without spiritual preparation the participant, it was thought, could not receive God's blessing from his partaking of communion. Accordingly, these poems focus on the person of Christ and His atonement for fallen mankind. *God's Determinations,* Taylor's other major collection, is a sequence of thirty-five poems tracing spiritual redemption from man's fall in the Garden of Eden and resulting condemnation to the Christian's conversion and spiritual growth through fellowship with other believers.

The major themes and dominant tone of Taylor's poetry derive from the recognition that he is a sinner totally unworthy of God's love and that his only hope for salvation is in Christ. The atmosphere of personal intimacy and spiritual fervency that surrounds the poems springs from their function as expressions of the poet's private communion with his Lord.

Preparatory Meditations

Meditation 1.1

Taylor's poetry offers rich rewards for the Christian reader willing to give close attention. Its spelling and capitalization differ from modern practice; in fact, most writers prior to the nineteenth century followed their individual preferences for spelling and capitalization. Taylor's sentence structure is often inverted or suspended. But a thoughtful reading aloud can overcome these difficulties. When the first four lines of this poem are unraveled, for instance, they read like this: "What love is this of thine that cannot be confined in thine infinity, O Lord, unless it see Infinity [God] and Finity [Man] conjoined in thy very Person." Taylor says thus that God's love is so great that only Christ can hold it.

Moreover, because this poem is a meditation, Taylor approaches his subject from a very personal, subjective angle. He visualizes the incarnation as a marriage between God and man. He sees a flood of love overflowing heaven, earth, and even hell.

Because its **themes** *appear throughout the series of meditations, this poem serves as a prologue for those that follow. Also, Taylor's plea in this poem for the breath of divine love on the near-lifeless embers of his heart is analogous to the conventional prayer for poetic inspiration—the invocation to the Muse—that traditionally begins a poetic work of great magnitude. Taylor is acknowledging that the source of his poetic, as well as spiritual, strength is God.*

What love is this of thine, that Cannot bee
  In thine Infinity, O Lord, Confinde,
Unless it in thy very Person see,
  Infinity, and Finity Conjoyn'd?*
  What[!] hath thy Godhead, as not satisfide[,]   5   *Conjoyn'd:* joined to-
  Marri'de our Manhood, making it its Bride?   gether: i.e., the
                                                    incarnation

Oh, Matchless Love! filling Heaven to the brim!
  O're running it: all running o're beside
This World! Nay Overflowing Hell; wherein
  For thine Elect, there rose a mighty Tide!   10
  That there our Veans* might through thy Person bleed,
  To quench those flames,* that else would on us feed.   *Veans:* veins
                                             flames: hell's flames

Oh! that thy Love might overflow my Heart!
  To fire the same with Love: for Love I would.
But oh! my streight'ned* Breast! my Lifeless Sparke!   15   *streight'ned:* re-
  My Fireless Flame! What Chilly Love, and Cold?   strained, hampered
  In measure small! In Manner Chilly! See.   (helpless to respond)
  Lord blow the Coal: Thy Love Enflame in mee.

The Experience

This meditation is unlike most of Taylor's other meditations. First, it is one of only five titled meditations; the others are numbered. Second, it refers to an actual experience. While administering the Lord's Supper to his congregation, he received special insight into the meaning of the incarnation (stanza 2). This spiritual awareness made him feel especially close to God. Weeks later, however, the intense feeling had faded. The final stanza points out his awareness of the difference between what he felt during the intense spiritual experience and what he felt when he wrote the poem.

Oh! that I always breath'd in such an aire,
    As I suckt in, feeding on sweet Content!
Disht up unto my Soul ev'n in that pray're
    Pour'de out to God over last Sacrament.*   *last Sacrament:* Lord's
    What Beam of Light wrapt up my sight to finde   5   Supper
    Me neerer God than ere Came in my minde?

Most strange it was! But yet more strange that shine
    Which filld my Soul then to the brim to spy
My Nature with thy Nature all Divine
    Together joyn'd in Him thats Thou, and I.   10
    Flesh of my Flesh, Bone of my Bone.* There's run   *Flesh . . . Bone:* cf.
    Thy Godhead, and my Manhood in thy Son.   Genesis 2:23

Oh! that that Flame which thou didst on me Cast
    Might me enflame, and Lighten ery* where.   *ery:* every
Then Heaven to me would be less at last   15
    So much of heaven I should have while here.
    Oh! Sweet though Short! Ile not forget the same.
    My neerness, Lord, to thee did me Enflame.

I'le Claim my Right: Give place, ye Angells Bright.
    Ye further from the Godhead stande than I.   20
My nature is your Lord; and doth Unite
    Better than Yours unto the Deity.
    Gods Throne is first and mine is next: to you
    Onely the place of Waiting-men is due.

Oh! that my Heart, thy Golden Harp might bee   25
    Well tun'd by Glorious Grace, that e'ry string
Screw'd to the highest pitch, might unto thee
    All Praises wrapt in sweetest Musick bring.
    I praise thee, Lord, and better praise thee would
    If what I had, my heart might ever hold.   30

Meditation 1.6

In Taylor's day and before, poets often developed a poem with a **conceit** *(a striking, often elaborate, comparison carried out in considerable detail). The comparison in the opening line ("Am I thy Gold?") dominates the rest of the meditation. In stanza 2 he develops the* **metaphor** *of coinage. The poet now considers himself a golden coin. An angel (l. 12) was an English coin of Taylor's day, bearing the imprint of the archangel Michael slaying the dragon. The poet prays for his soul to be made God's plate (coin, usually silver but here gold). The final two lines collect the* **imagery** *of the preceding parts of the poem, especially echoing lines 1-2; he wants to be God's money and wants God to be his hoard; he wants to be a coin (an angel) and wants God to be his Lord.*

"Image" (ll. 10, 11, 13) is richly allusive. It refers to the defacing of God's image in man by the fall and its restoration through redemption. It also suggests the image and superscription of Caesar on the coin referred to by Christ (see Matt. 22:20-21). Finally, it suggests the Christian's being changed into Christ's image (see II Cor. 3:18).

Am I thy Gold? Or Purse, Lord, for thy Wealth;
    Whether in mine, or mint refinde for thee?
Ime counted so, but count me o're thyselfe,
    Lest gold washt face, and brass in Heart I bee.
    I Feare my Touchstone* touches when I try   5
    Mee, and my Counted Gold too overly.

Am I new minted by thy Stamp indeed?
    Mine Eyes are dim; I cannot clearly see.
Be thou my Spectacles that I may read
    Thine Image, and Inscription stampt on mee.   10
    If thy bright Image do upon me stand
    I am a Golden Angell in thy hand.

Lord, make my Soule thy Plate: thine Image bright
    Within the Circle of the same enfoile.
And on its brims in golden Letters write   15
    Thy Superscription in an Holy style.
    Then I shall be thy Money, thou my Hord:
    Let me thy Angell bee, bee thou my Lord.

Touchstone: a black, flintlike stone used to test the purity of gold or silver by the streak left on the stone by the metal

Huswifery

In this poetic prayer, Taylor, in accordance with Puritan practice, fashions a garment from humble material. Each stanza develops a different part of the process: stanza 1, making the thread on the spinning wheel; stanza 2, weaving the cloth on the loom; stanza 3, finishing the garment.

It is not, however, an ordinary garment. It is a wedding garment–the garment without which no guest can be admitted to the wedding supper of the Lamb.

Make me, O Lord, thy Spining Wheele compleate.
  Thy Holy Worde my Distaff* make for mee.
Make mine Affections thy Swift Flyers* neate
  And make my Soule thy holy Spoole to bee.
  My Conversation make to be thy Reele   5
  And reele the yarn thereon spun of thy Wheele.

Make me thy Loome then, knit therein this Twine:
  And make thy Holy Spirit, Lord, winde quills:*
Then weave the Web thyselfe. The yarn is fine.
  Thine Ordinances make my Fulling Mills.*   10
  Then dy the same in Heavenly Colours Choice,
  All pinkt* with Varnisht Flowers of Paradise.

Then cloath therewith mine Understanding, Will,
  Affections, Judgment, Conscience, Memory
My Words, and Actions,* that their shine may fill   15
  My wayes with glory and thee glorify.
  Then mine apparell shall display before yee
  That I am Cloathd in Holy robes for glory.

Distaff: implement for holding a bunch of wool or flax
Swift Flyers: revolving arms

quills: spindles on which yarn is wound

Fulling Mills: used to shrink and thicken cloth by moistening, heating, and pressing
pinkt: perforated with ornamental patterns

Note that Taylor covers all parts of a person with the garment.

God's Determinations

The Preface

In "The Preface" to God's Determinations, *Taylor describes God's creation by means of striking* **metaphors** *drawn from man's acts of creation (11. 1-18). In this section appears probably the most striking poetic line of early American literature: "Who in this Bowling Alley bowld the Sun?" The representation of God as a bowler hurling a gigantic bowling ball (the sun) into the alley of space shows the nature of Taylor's imagination: he delighted in unusual combinations of ideas. (Note that this series of questions, recalling Job 38-41, is designed to evoke awe and self-humiliation.)*

Taylor also describes the creation and sin of man, whose condition changes in the poem from a gemlike beauty (his period of innocence) to a worthless state (his total depravity caused by the fall). Taylor reveals here his tendency toward ingenious wordplay, **paradoxes,** *and other intellectual poetic devices of the seventeenth century.*

This poem is the preface to a thirty-five-poem history of redeemed man from the creation of Adam to the believer's entrance into heaven. The stages of this story include the fall (in Adam's sin all men for all time fell), man's attempt to flee from God after the fall, man's capture by God and his acceptance of salvation, Satan's attacks against the elect, the Christian's education through the teaching of a saint (a mature Christian), and finally the Christian's entrance into church fellowship, which in turn prepares him for heaven.

Infinity,* when all things it beheld
In Nothing, and of Nothing all did build,
Upon what Base was Fixt the Lath*, wherein
He turn'd this Globe, and riggalld* it so trim?
Who blew the Bellows of his Furnace Vast?   5
Or held the Mould wherein the world was Cast?
Who laid its Corner Stone? Or whose Command?
Where stand the Pillars upon which it stands?
Who Lac'de* and Fillitted* the earth so fine,
With Rivers like green Ribbons Smaragdine?*   10
Who made the Sea's its Selvedge,* and it locks*
Like a Quilt Ball within a Silver Box?
Who Spread its Canopy? Or Curtains Spun?
Who in this Bowling Alley bowld the Sun?
Who made it always when it rises set   15
To go at once both down, and up to get?
Who th' Curtain rods made for this Tapistry?
Who hung the twinckling Lanthorns in the Sky?

Infinity: God

Lath: a thin strip of wood nailed to framing as a support for shingles or tiles
riggalled: grooved

Lac'de: laced
Fillitted: ribboned
green . . . Smaragdine: green gemstone
Selvedge: border/*it locks:* locks it

Who? who did this? or who is he? Why, know
Its Onely Might Almighty this did doe.   20
His hand hath made this noble worke which Stands
His Glorious Handywork not made by hands.
Who spake all things from nothing; and with ease
Can speake all things to nothing, if he please.
Whose Little finger at his pleasure Can   25
Out mete ten thousand worlds with halfe a Span:
Whose Might Almighty can by half a looks
Root up the rocks and rock the hills by th' roots.*
Can take this mighty World up in his hande,
And shake it like a Squitchen* or a Wand.*   30
Whose single Frown will make the Heavens shake
Like as an aspen leafe the Winde makes quake.

Note ingenious play on words root *and* rock.

Squitchen: stick?/ *Wand:* cane

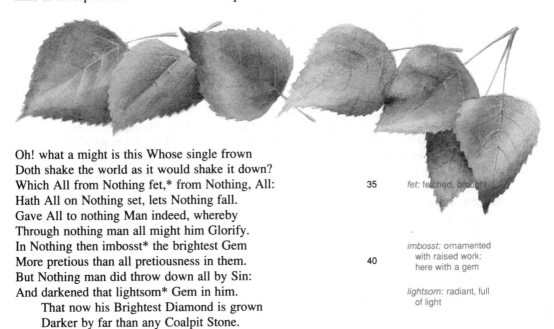

Oh! what a might is this Whose single frown
Doth shake the world as it would shake it down?
Which All from Nothing fet,* from Nothing, All: 35
Hath All on Nothing set, lets Nothing fall.
Gave All to nothing Man indeed, whereby
Through nothing man all might him Glorify.
In Nothing then imbosst* the brightest Gem
More pretious than all pretiousness in them.   40
But Nothing man did throw down all by Sin:
And darkened that lightsom* Gem in him.
    That now his Brightest Diamond is grown
    Darker by far than any Coalpit Stone.

fet: fetched, brought

imbosst: ornamented with raised work: here with a gem

lightsom: radiant, full of light

For Thought and Discussion

1. What spiritual experience does Taylor describe in ''The Experience''?
2. Analyze Taylor's extended metaphor in the final stanza of ''The Experience.''
   To what object does the speaker of the poem desire that his heart might be
   compared? What qualities does he already have in common with this object?
   In what ways does he desire to be more like this object? Why?

3. What is the central comparison introduced in line 1 of "Meditation 1.6"? List the ways in which Taylor develops the comparison in the poem as a whole. Are such comparisons appropriate for religious poetry? Why or why not?

4. In *Treatise Concerning the Lord's Supper,* Taylor writes that in order to participate in the Lord's Supper one must have a "wedden garment," or "the robe of evangelical righteousness[:] It's such a web that only the gospel markets afford; it's such a web that is only wove in the looms of the gospel, nay, and a richer web and better huswifery it gets not up." In what ways does this quotation from Taylor help to clarify the purpose and theme of "Huswifery"? For what purpose does the speaker pray for "Holy robes"?

Jonathan Edwards
1703-1758

Literary critics have had a hard time placing Jonathan Edwards in the history of American thought. Some have viewed him as reactionary–the last American Puritan, who tried to impose seventeenth-century religious standards on the more worldly eighteenth century. Others have described him as anticipatory–the first of America's great thinkers, especially in his analysis of the religious mind. Still others have seen him as transitional–a writer who held the same beliefs as the Puritans but attempted to analyze and defend these beliefs by all available means, including philosophy and scientific observation. Of all the ways of viewing Edwards, Christians have the most illuminating because they can understand and appreciate his Biblical approach to the needs of man.

Preparation, evangelism, exile–these three terms briefly describe the stages of Edwards's life. Under the private tutoring of his minister-father and afterwards at Yale College, Edwards distinguished himself as a student. When not yet a teenager, he wrote a highly respected essay on balloon spiders entitled "Of Insects." At seventeen he graduated with honors from Yale; four years later he received his master's degree. After preaching at a Presbyterian church in New York City for about nine months, Edwards returned to Yale to serve as a tutor from 1724 to 1726. The most important event during these preparatory years was his conversion. He had been greatly troubled for several years about spiritual matters and was converted evidently about the age of eighteen.

In 1726 Edwards entered the second phase of his life, his ministry of nearly twenty-four years at Northampton, Massachusetts. Edwards first became assistant to his maternal grandfather, Solomon Stoddard, the most widely respected minister west of Boston. The next year he married Sarah Pierrepont. Upon Stoddard's death in 1729, Edwards became minister of the Congregational church. As a result of his intense preaching, the apathetic congregation became troubled about spiritual matters. By 1735 religion had become the most important topic of conversation in the prospering town, and "souls," noted Edwards, "did, as it were, come by flocks to Jesus Christ." As revival spread to other parts of New England, Edwards grew concerned about distinguishing true religious experience from false. In the decade from 1736 to 1746, he published four works that investigate the Holy Spirit's work in persons' lives. In 1741, during the height of the Great Awakening, Edwards preached at Enfield, Connecticut, his famous sermon "Sinners in the Hands of an Angry God."

As spiritual fervor in his own church cooled, various people in the community began to oppose his ministry. A primary cause of their discontent was his attempt to reinstate the Puritan practice of requiring a candidate for church membership to give full, public testimony of how God had worked in his life and brought him to conversion. This testimony had been essential to church membership until the Halfway Covenant had allowed those living moral lives to get "halfway" into a church without offering the evidence of public testimony. They could be baptized but not partake of the Lord's Supper. What seemed to some to be merely a reactionary standard was actually the result of Edwards's desire to distinguish between the true and false religious experiences. Eventually dissatisfaction with Edwards's ministry became so great that finally he offered to resign his pastorate, choosing not to lead a group out of the church. The feeling in Northampton, however, was such that the church officials refused his offer. In 1750, however, the church council voted to dismiss him.

After this experience at Northampton, Edwards entered a new phase of ministry. Moving his family to Stockbridge, Massachusetts, from which he directed missionary activity among the Indians, he wrote the two works regarded as his greatest: *Freedom of the Will* (1754) and *The Great Doctrine of Original Sin Defended* (1758). God thus turned a seeming failure in Edwards's ministry into the most productive period of his life. In 1757 he received an invitation to become president of the College of New Jersey, now Princeton. When he arrived in January 1758 to assume his duties, he found the town in the grip of a smallpox epidemic. Though inoculated upon his arrival, he was physically too weak to resist the disease. He died on March 22, 1758.

Edwards's biographical works–the *Diary,* a record primarily of the period from 1722 to 1724, and *Personal Narrative,* an autobiographical account of his spiritual life–show the intense care with which he examined the mind and heart. In his sermons, images of nature and physical forces combine with the Puritan plain style and organization to produce forceful pulpit persuasion. His personal writings, such as the brief description of Sarah Pierrepont and the notebook collection entitled *Images or Shadows of Divine Things,* reveal Edwards's belief in the unity of the natural and spiritual worlds. For Edwards, only religious vision gives meaning to mankind and the world. The main theme of his writings is that religious knowledge must be in the heart, not just in the head.

The spiritual insight Edwards's works provide for a reader sympathetic to his experience and goals is unparalleled by that of any other American writer. His vision of man's corrupt nature was to influence later writers like Nathaniel Hawthorne and Herman Melville who, like Edwards, saw mankind as incapable of achieving its dreams or even its potential. Unlike Edwards, however, these later writers would fail to provide the Biblical answer for the terrible problem of man's fallen nature.

Sarah Pierrepont

Edwards was a college student at Yale when he wrote this brief description of Sarah Pierrepont. The girl, whom he had not yet met, was obviously not an average thirteen-year-old–then or now. Four years later he married her, and together they reared a large family of eight daughters and three sons.

They say there is a young lady in [New Haven] who is beloved of that Great Being, who made and rules the world, and that there are certain seasons in which this Great Being, in some way or other invisible, comes to her and fills her mind with exceeding sweet delight, and that she hardly cares for any thing, except to meditate on him–that she expects after a while to be received up where he is, to be raised up out of the world and caught up into heaven; being assured that he loves her too well to let her remain at a distance from him always. There she is to dwell with him, and to be ravished with his love and delight forever. Therefore, if you present all the world before her, with the richest of its treasures, she disregards it and cares not for it, and is unmindful of any pain or affliction. She has a strange sweetness in her mind, and singular purity in her affections; is most just and conscientious in all her conduct; and you could not persuade her to do any thing wrong or sinful, if you would give her all the world, lest she should offend this Great Being. She is of a wonderful sweetness, calmness and universal benevolence of mind; especially after this Great God has manifested himself to her mind. She will sometimes go about from place to place, singing sweetly; and seems to be always full of joy and pleasure; and no one knows for what. She loves to be alone, walking in the fields and groves, and seems to have some one invisible always conversing with her.

from The Diary

"While at New York," Edwards wrote in Personal Narrative, *"I sometimes was much affected with reflections on my past life, considering how late it was before I began to be truly religious and how wickedly I had lived till then, and once so as to weep abundantly and for a considerable time together."*

January 12

In the morning. I have this day solemnly renewed my . . . self-dedication. . . . I have been before God and have given myself, all that I am and have, to God, so that I am not, in any respect, my own. I can challenge no right in this understanding, this will, these affections, which are in me. Neither have I any right to this body or any of its members—no right to this tongue, these hands, these feet; no right to these senses, these eyes, these ears, this smell, or this taste. I have given myself clear away, and have not retained any thing as my own. I gave myself to God in my baptism, and I have been this morning to him and told him that I gave myself *wholly* to him. I have given every power to him, so that for the future I'll challenge no right in myself, in no respect whatever. I have expressly promised him, and I do now promise Almighty God, that by his grace, I will not. I have this morning told him that I did take Him for my whole portion and felicity, looking on nothing else as any part of my happiness, nor acting as if it were; and his Law for the constant rule of my obedience; and would fight, with all my might, against the world, the flesh, and the devil, to the end of my life; and that I did believe in Jesus Christ, and did receive him as a Prince and Saviour; and that I would adhere to the faith and obedience of the Gospel, however hazardous and difficult the confession and practice of it may be; and that I did receive the blessed Spirit, as my Teacher, Sanctifier, and only Comforter, and cherish all his motions to enlighten, purify, confirm, comfort, and assist me. This, I have done; and I pray God, for the sake of Christ, to look upon it as a self-dedication, and to receive me now as entirely his own, and to deal with me, in all respects, as such, whether he afflicts me, or prospers me, or whatever he pleases to do with me, who am his. Now, henceforth, I am not to act, in any respect, as my own.—I shall act as my own, if I ever make use of any of my powers to any thing that is not to the glory of God and do not make the glorifying of him my whole and entire business:—if I murmur in the least at affliction; if I grieve at the prosperity of others; if I am in any way uncharitable; if I am angry because of injuries; if I revenge them, if I do any thing purely to please myself, or if I avoid any thing for the sake of my own ease; if I omit any thing because it is great self-denial; if I trust to myself; if I take any of the praise of any good that I do, or that God doth by me; or if I am in any way proud.

from **Personal Narrative**

In Personal Narrative, *Edwards records the "ebb and flow" of his early Christian life. Since this work is his spiritual autobiography, written nearly twenty years after his conversion, it recounts his journey from conviction of sin to despair and finally to assurance of salvation.*

I had a variety of concerns and exercises about my soul from my childhood, but had two more remarkable seasons of awakening before I met with that change by which I was brought to those new dispositions* and that new sense of things that I have since had. The first time was when I was a boy, some years before I went to college, at a time of remarkable awakening in my father's congregation. I was then very much affected for many months and concerned about the things of religion and my soul's salvation, and was abundant in duties. I used to pray five times a day in secret and to spend much time in religious talk with other boys, and used to meet with them to pray together. I experienced I know not what kind of delight in religion. My mind was much engaged in it and had much self-righteous pleasure, and it was my delight to abound in religious duties. I with some of my school-mates joined together and built a booth in the swamp, in a very retired spot, for a place of prayer. And besides, I had particular secret places of my own in the woods where I used to retire by myself, and was from time to time much affected. My affections seemed to be lively and easily moved, and I seemed to be in my element when engaged in religious duties. And I am ready to think, many are deceived with such affections and such a kind of delight as I then had in religion, and mistake it for grace.

dispositions: tendencies

But in process of time, my convictions and affections wore off; and I entirely lost all those affections and delights, and left off secret prayer, at least as to any constant performance of it, and returned like a dog to his vomit,* and went on in the ways of sin. Indeed I was at times very uneasy, especially towards the latter part of my time at college, when it pleased God to seize me with a pleurisy,* in which he brought me nigh to the grave and shook me over the pit of hell. And yet, it was not long after my recovery before I fell again into my old ways of sin. But God would not suffer me to go on with any quietness; I had great and violent inward struggles, till, after many conflicts with wicked inclinations, repeated resolutions, and bonds that I laid myself under by a kind of vows to God, I was brought wholly to break off all former wicked ways and all ways of known outward sin, and to apply myself to seek salvation, and practice many religious duties, but without that kind of affection and delight which I had formerly experienced. My concern now wrought* more by inward struggles, and conflicts, and self-reflections. I made seeking my salvation the main business of my life. . . .

returned . . . vomit: Proverbs 26:11
pleurisy: inflammation of the lungs
wrought: worked

Often since I lived in this town, I have had very affecting views of my own sinfulness and vileness, very frequently to such a degree as to hold me in a kind of loud weeping, sometimes for a considerable time together, so that I have often been forced to shut myself up. I have had a vastly greater sense of my own wickedness and the badness of my own heart than ever I had before my conversion. It has often appeared to me that if God should mark iniquity against me I should appear the very worst of all mankind, of all that have been since the beginning of the world to this time, and that I should have by far the lowest place in hell. When others that have come to talk with me about their soul concerns have expressed the sense they have had of their own wickedness by saying that it seemed to them that they were as bad as the Devil himself, I thought their expressions seemed exceeding faint and feeble to represent my wickedness.

My wickedness, as I am in myself, has long appeared to me perfectly ineffable* and swallowing up all thought and imagination, like an infinite deluge or mountains over my head. I know not how to express better what my sins appear to me to be than by heaping infinite upon infinite and multiplying infinite by infinite. Very often for these many years, these expressions are in my mind and in my mouth, "Infinite upon infinite–Infinite upon infinite!" When I look into my heart and take a view of my wickedness, it looks like an abyss* infinitely deeper than hell. And it appears to me that were it not for free grace, exalted and raised up to the infinite height of all the fulness and glory of the great Jehovah, and the arm of His power and grace stretched forth in all the majesty of His power and in all the glory of His sovereignty, I should appear sunk down in my sins below hell itself, far beyond the sight of everything but the eye of sovereign grace, that can pierce even down to such a depth. And yet it seems to me that my conviction of sin is exceeding and faint; it is enough to amaze me that I have no more sense of my sin. I know certainly that I have very little sense of my sinfulness. When I have had turns of weeping and crying for my sins, I thought I knew at the time that my repentance was nothing to my sin.

Ineffable: unutterable
abyss: bottomless gulf

from Sinners in the Hands of an Angry God

This is the most famous sermon in American history. Edwards preached it on July 8, 1741, at Enfield, Connecticut, during the height of the Great Awakening. The people in the audience were largely church members, many of whom were unconverted because the Halfway Covenant had relaxed membership requirements. The sermon's organization follows rigorously the three-part Puritan structure: discussion of the Biblical text, development of the doctrine, uses of the doctrine (i.e., application to the hearers). The effect of the sermon was so great, according to eyewitnesses, that weeping and prayers drowned out Edwards's voice. Several times he had to request the audience to keep silent so that he could continue.

Deut. 32:35. *Their foot shall slide in due time.*

The expression that I have chosen for my text, *their foot shall slide in due time,* seems to imply the following things relating to the punishment and destruction that these wicked Israelites were exposed to.

1. That they were always exposed to *destruction;* as one that stands or walks in slippery places is always exposed to fall. . . .

2. It implies, that they were always exposed to sudden, unexpected destruction. . . .

3. Another thing implied is, that they are liable to fall of *themselves,* without being thrown down by the hand of another; as he that stands or walks on slippery ground needs nothing but his own weight to throw him down.

4. That the reason why they are not fallen already, and do not fall now, is only that God's appointed time is not come. . . .

The observation from the words that I would now insist upon is this.

There is nothing that keeps wicked men at any one moment out of hell, but the mere pleasure of God. *

There . . . God: This sentence expresses the doctrine developed in the middle section of the sermon. It is also a kind of thesis for the entire sermon, determining the choice of text, supported by the reasons that follow it, and then, having been proved, applied to the needs of his audience.

By the *mere* pleasure of God, I mean his *sovereign* pleasure, his arbitrary will, restrained by no obligation, hindered by no manner of difficulty, any more than if nothing else but God's mere will had in the least degree, or in any respect whatsoever, any hand in the preservation of wicked men one moment.

The truth of this observation may appear by the following considerations.

1. There is no want of *power* in God to cast wicked men into hell at any moment. Men's hands cannot be strong when God rises up: the strongest have no power to resist him, nor can any deliver out of his hands.

He is not only able to cast wicked men into hell, but he can most easily do it. Sometimes an earthly prince meets with a great deal of difficulty to subdue a rebel that has found means to fortify himself and has made himself strong by the number of his followers. But it is not so with God. There is no fortress that is any defence against the power of God. Though hand join in hand, and vast multitudes of God's enemies combine and associate themselves, they are easily broken in pieces: they are as great heaps of light chaff before the whirlwind, or large quantities of dry stubble before devouring flames. We find it easy to tread on and crush a worm that we see crawling on the earth; so it is easy for us to cut or singe a slender thread that any thing hangs by; thus easy is it for God, when he pleases, to cast his enemies down to hell. What are we that we should think to stand before him, at whose rebuke the earth trembles, and before whom the rocks are thrown down!

2. They *deserve* to be cast into hell; so that divine justice never stands in the way, it makes no objection against God's using his power at any moment to destroy them. Yea, on the contrary, justice calls aloud for an infinite punishment of their sins. . . .

3. They are already under a sentence of *condemnation* to hell. They do not only justly deserve to be cast down thither, but the sentence of the law of God, that eternal and immutable rule of righteousness that God has fixed between him and mankind, is gone out against them, and stands against them; so that they are bound over already to hell: John iii.18, "He that believeth not is condemned already." So that every unconverted man properly belongs to hell; that is his place; from thence he is—John viii.23, "Ye are from beneath"—and thither he is bound; it is the place that justice, and God's word, and the sentence of his unchangeable law, assign to him.

4. They are now the objects of that very same *anger* and wrath of God that is expressed in the torments of hell: and the reason why they do not go down to hell at each moment is not because God, in whose power they are, is not then very angry with them, as angry as he is with many of those miserable creatures that he is now tormenting in hell and do there feel and bear the fierceness of his wrath. Yea, God is a great deal more angry with great numbers that are now on earth—yea, doubtless, with many that are now in this congregation that, it may be, are at ease and quiet—than he is with many of those that are now in the flames of hell.

So that it is not because God is unmindful of their wickedness and does not resent it that he does not loose his hand and cut them off. God is not altogether such a one as themselves,* though they may imagine him to be so. The wrath of God burns against them; their damnation does not slumber; the pit is prepared; the fire is made ready; the furnace is now hot, ready to receive them; the flames do now rage and glow. The glittering sword is whet* and held over them, and the pit hath opened its mouth under them.

God . . . themselves: Psalms 50:21
whet: sharpened

5. The *devil* stands ready to fall upon them, and seize them as his own, at what moment God shall permit him. They belong to him; he has their souls in his possession, and under his dominion. The Scripture represents them as his goods, Luke xi.21. The devils watch them; they are ever by them, at their right hand; they stand waiting for them, like greedy hungry lions that see their prey, and expect to have it, but are for the present kept back; if God should withdraw his hand, by which they are restrained, they would in one moment fly upon their poor souls. The old serpent is gaping for them; hell opens its mouth wide to receive them; and if God should permit it, they would be hastily swallowed up and lost.

6. There are in the souls of wicked men those hellish *principles* reigning, that would presently kindle and flame out into hell-fire, if it were not for God's restraints. There is laid in the very nature of carnal men a foundation for the torments of hell: there are those corrupt principles in reigning power in them and in full possession of them that are the beginnings of hell-fire. These principles are active and powerful, exceeding violent in their nature, and if it were not for the restraining hand of God upon them, they would soon break out, they would flame out after the same manner as the same corruptions, the same enmity,* does in the hearts of damned souls, and would beget the same torments in them* as they do in them.* . . . The corruption of the heart of man is a thing that is immoderate and boundless in its fury; and while wicked men live here, it is like fire pent up by God's restraints, whereas if it were let loose, it would set on fire the course of nature; and as the heart is now a sink of sin, so, if sin was not restrained, it would immediately turn the soul into a fiery oven, or a furnace of fire and brimstone.

enmity: antagonism
them: the living wicked people
them: those already in hell

7. It is no security to wicked men for one moment that there are no visible means of death at hand. It is no security to a natural man that he is now in health, and that he does not see which way he should now immediately go out of the world by any accident, and that there is no visible danger in any respect in his circumstances. . . . Unconverted men walk over the pit of hell on a rotten covering, and there are innumerable places in this covering so weak that they will not bear their weight, and these places are not seen.

8. Natural men's prudence and care to preserve their own lives, or the care of others to preserve them, do not secure them a moment. . . . There is this clear evidence that men's own wisdom is no security to them from death; that if it were otherwise we should see some difference between the wise and politic men of the world, and others, with regard to their liableness to early and unexpected death; but how is it in fact? Eccles. ii.16, "How dieth the wise man? Even as the fool."

9. All wicked men's pains and *contrivance* they use to escape hell, while they continue to reject Christ, and so remain wicked men, do not secure them from hell one moment. Almost every natural man that hears of hell, flatters himself that he shall escape it; he depends upon himself for his own security; he flatters himself in what he has done, in what he is now doing, or what he intends to do; every one lays out matters in his own mind how he shall avoid damnation, and flatters himself that he contrives well for himself, and that his schemes will not fail. They hear indeed that there are but few saved, and that the bigger part of men that have died heretofore are gone to hell; but each one imagines that he lays out matters better for his own escape than others have done: he does not intend to come to that place of torment; he says within himself that he intends to take care*

that shall be effectual,* and to order matters so for himself as not to fail. . . .

care: i.e., precautions
effectual: effective

10. God has laid himself under *no obligation,* by any promise, to keep any natural man out of hell one moment. . . .

So that, whatever some have imagined and pretended about promises made to natural men's earnest seeking and knocking, it is plain and manifest, that whatever pains a natural man takes in religion, whatever prayers he makes, till he believes in Christ, God is under no manner of obligation to keep him a moment from eternal destruction.

So that thus it is, that natural men are held in the hand of God, over the pit of hell; they have deserved the fiery pit, and are already sentenced to it; and God is dreadfully provoked, his anger is as great towards them as to those that are actually suffering the executions of the fierceness of his wrath in hell, and they have done nothing in the least to appease or abate that anger, neither is God in the least bound by any promise to hold them up one moment; the devil is waiting for them, hell is gaping for them, the flames gather and flash about them and would fain lay hold on them and swallow them up; the fire pent up in their own hearts is struggling to break out; and they have no interest in any Mediator, there are no means within reach that can be any security to them. In short, they have no refuge, nothing to take hold of; all that preserves them every moment is the mere arbitrary will and uncovenanted, unobliged forbearance of an incensed God.

Application

The use of this awful* subject may be of awakening unconverted persons in this congregation. This that you have heard is the case of every one of you that are out of Christ. That world of misery, that lake of burning brimstone, is extended abroad under you. There is the dreadful pit of the glowing flames of the wrath of God;

there is hell's wide gaping mouth open; and you have nothing to stand upon, nor any thing to take hold of. There is nothing between you and hell but the air; it is only the power and mere pleasure of God that holds you up.

awful: awesome, dreadful

You probably are not sensible* of this; you find you are kept out of hell but do not see the hand of God in it, but look at* other things, as the good state of your bodily constitution,* your care of your own life, and the means you use for your own preservation. But indeed these things are nothing; if God should withdraw his hand, they would avail no more to keep you from falling than the thin air to hold up a person that is suspended in it.

sensible: conscious
look at: look to: i.e., attribute your safety to
bodily constitution: physical makeup

Your wickedness makes you as it were heavy as lead, and to tend downwards with great weight and pressure towards hell; and if God should let you go, you would immediately sink and swiftly descend and plunge into the bottomless gulf, and your healthy constitution, and your own care and prudence and best contrivance and all your righteousness would have no more influence to uphold you and keep you out of hell than a spider's web would have to stop a falling rock. Were it not that so is the sovereign pleasure of God, the earth would not bear you one moment, for you are a burden to it; the creation groans with you; the creature* is made subject to the bondage of your corruption, not willingly; the sun does not willingly shine upon you to give you light to serve sin and Satan; the earth does not willingly yield her increase to satisfy your lusts, nor is it willingly a stage for your wickedness to be acted upon; the air does not willingly serve you for breath to maintain the flame of life in your vitals,* while you spend your life in the service of God's enemies. God's creatures are good, and were made for men to serve God with, and do not willingly subserve to any other purpose, and groan when they are abused to purposes so directly contrary to their nature and end. And the world would spew you out, were it not for the sovereign hand of him who hath subjected it in hope. There are the black clouds of God's wrath now hanging directly over your heads, full of the dreadful storm, and big with thunder; and were it not for the restraining hand of God, it would immediately burst forth upon you. The sovereign pleasure of God, for the present, stays his rough winds;* otherwise it would come with fury, and your destruction would come like a whirlwind, and you would be like the chaff of the summer threshing floor.

creature: creation; see Romans 8:19-22
vitals: vital organs
The . . . winds: Isaiah 27:8

The wrath of God is like great waters that are dammed for the present; they increase more and more, and rise higher and higher, till an outlet is given; and the longer the stream is stopped, the more rapid and mighty is its course when once it is let loose. It is true that judgment against your evil works has not been executed hitherto; the floods of God's vengeance have been withheld; but your guilt in the mean time is constantly increasing, and you are every day treasuring up more wrath;* the waters are continually rising, and waxing more and more mighty; and there is nothing but the mere pleasure of God that holds the waters back that are unwilling to be stopped and press hard to go forward. If God should only withdraw his hand from the floodgate, it would immediately fly open, and the fiery floods of the fierceness and wrath of God would rush forth with inconceivable fury, and would come upon you with omnipotent power; and if your strength were ten thousand times greater than it is, yea, ten thousand times greater than the strength of the stoutest, sturdiest devil in hell, it would be nothing to withstand or endure it.

you . . . wrath: Romans 2:5

The bow of God's wrath is bent, and the arrow made ready on the string, and justice bends the arrow at your heart, and strains the bow, and it is nothing but the mere pleasure of God, and that of an angry God, without any promise or obligation at all, that keeps the arrow one moment from being made drunk with your blood.

Thus are all you that never passed under a great change of heart by the mighty power of the Spirit of God upon your souls; all that were never born again, and made new creatures, and raised from being dead in sin, to a state of new and before altogether unexperienced light and life, (however you may have reformed your life in many things, and may have had religious affections, and may keep up a form of religion in your families and closets, and in the houses of God, and may be strict in it) you are thus in the hands of an angry God; it is nothing but his mere pleasure that keeps you from being this moment swallowed up in everlasting destruction.

However unconvinced you may now be of the truth of what you hear, by and by you will be fully convinced of it. Those that are gone from being in the like circumstances with you, see that it was so with them; for destruction came suddenly upon most of them; when they expected nothing of it, and while they were saying, Peace and safety, now they see that those things that they depended on for peace and safety were nothing but thin air and empty shadows.

The God that holds you over the pit of hell, much as one holds a spider or some loathsome insect over the fire, abhors you, and is dreadfully provoked: his wrath towards you burns like fire; he looks upon you as worthy of nothing else but to be cast into the fire; he is of purer eyes than to bear to have you in his sight; you are ten thousand times more abominable in his eyes than the most hateful and venomous serpent is in ours. You have offended him infinitely more than ever a stubborn rebel did his prince: and yet it is nothing but his hand that holds you from falling into the fire every moment; it is to be ascribed to nothing else that you did not go to hell the last night, that you was suffered to awake again in this world after you closed your eyes to sleep; and there is no other reason to be given why you have not dropped into hell since you arose in the morning but that God's hand has held you up; there is no other reason to be given why you have not gone to hell, since you have sat here in the house of God provoking his pure eyes by your sinful wicked manner of attending his solemn worship; yea, there is nothing else that is to be given as a reason why you do not this very moment drop down into hell.

O sinner! consider the fearful danger you are in: it is a great furnace of wrath, a wide and bottomless pit, full of the fire of wrath, that you are held over in the hand of that God, whose wrath is provoked and incensed as much against you as against many of the damned in hell: you hang by a slender thread with the flames of divine wrath flashing about it and ready every moment to singe it and burn it asunder; and you have no interest in any Mediator, and nothing to lay hold of to save yourself, nothing to keep off the flames of wrath, nothing of your own, nothing that you ever have done, nothing that you can do, to induce God to spare you one moment. . . . It would be dreadful to suffer this fierceness and wrath of Almighty God one moment, but you must suffer it to all eternity. There will be no end to this exquisite horrible misery. When you look forward, you shall see a long forever, a boundless duration before you, which will swallow up your thoughts and amaze your soul; and you will absolutely despair of ever having any deliverance, any end, any mitigation,* any rest at all. You will know certainly that you must wear out long ages, millions of millions of ages, in wrestling and conflicting with this almighty merciless vengeance; and then when you have so done, when so many ages have actually been spent by you in this manner, you will know that all is but a point to what remains. So that your punishment will indeed be

infinite. Oh, who can express what the state of a soul in such circumstances is! All that we can possibly say about it gives but a very feeble, faint representation of it; it is inexpressible and inconceivable: For "who knows the power of God's anger?"

mitigation: moderation of the severity

How dreadful is the state of those that are daily and hourly in the danger of this great wrath and infinite misery! But this is the dismal case of every soul in this congregation that has not been born again, however moral and strict, sober and religious, they may otherwise be. Oh that you would consider it, whether you be young or old! There is reason to think that there are many in this congregation now hearing this discourse that will actually be the subjects of this very misery to all eternity. We know not who they are or in what seats they sit or what thoughts they now have. It may be they are now at ease and hear all these things without much disturbance and are now flattering themselves that they are not the persons, promising themselves that they shall escape. If we knew that there was one person, and but one, in the whole congregation that was to be the subject of this misery, what an awful thing would it be to think of! If we knew who it was, what an awful sight would it be to see such a person! How might all the rest of the congregation lift up a lamentable and bitter cry over him! But, alas! instead of one, how many is it likely will remember this discourse in hell? And it would be a wonder if some that are now present should not be in hell in a very short time, even before this year is out. And it would be no wonder if some persons that now sit here in some seats of this meeting-house, in health, quiet and secure, should be there before tomorrow morning. Those of you that finally continue in a natural condition, that shall keep out of hell longest, will be there in a little time! your damnation does not slumber; it will come swiftly and, in all probability, very suddenly upon many of you. You have reason to wonder that you are not already in hell. It is doubtless the case of some whom you have seen and known, that never deserved hell more than you, and that heretofore appeared as likely to have been now alive as you. Their case is past all hope; they are crying in extreme misery and perfect despair; but here you are in the land of the living and in the house of God and have an opportunity to obtain salvation. What would not those poor damned hopeless souls give for one day's opportunity such as you now enjoy!

And now you have an extraordinary opportunity, a day wherein Christ has thrown the door of mercy wide open, and stands in calling and crying with a loud voice to poor sinners; a day wherein many are flocking to him, and pressing into the kingdom of God. Many are daily coming from the east, west, north and south; many that were very lately in the same miserable condition that you are in are now in a happy state, with their hearts filled with love to him who has loved them and washed them from their sins in his own blood, and rejoicing in hope of the glory of God. How awful is it to be left behind at such a day! To see so many others feasting while you are pining and perishing! To see so many rejoicing and singing for joy of heart while you have cause to mourn for sorrow of heart, and howl for vexation of spirit! How can you rest one moment in such a condition? . . .

Are there not many here who have lived long in the world, and are not to this day born again? and so are aliens from the commonwealth of Israel,* and have done nothing ever since they have lived but treasure up wrath against the day of wrath? Oh, sirs, your case, in an especial manner, is extremely dangerous. Your guilt and hardness of heart is extremely great. Do you not see how generally persons of your years are passed over and left, in the present remarkable and wonderful dispensation of God's mercy? You had need to consider yourselves, and awake thoroughly out of sleep.* You cannot bear the fierceness and wrath of the infinite God.

aliens from the commonwealth of Israel: Eph. 2:12
awake thoroughly out of sleep: Rom. 13:11

And you, young men, and young women, will you neglect this precious season which you now enjoy, when so many others of your age are renouncing all youthful vanities and flocking to Christ? You especially have now an extraordinary opportunity; but if you neglect it, it will soon be with you as with those persons who spent all the precious days of youth in sin and are now come to such a dreadful pass in blindness and hardness.

And you, children, who are unconverted, do not you know that you are going down to hell, to bear the dreadful wrath of that God who is now angry with you every day and every night? Will you be content to be the children of the devil, when so many other children in the land are converted and are become the holy and happy children of the King of kings?

And let every one that is yet of Christ and hanging over the pit of hell, whether they be old men and women, or middle aged, or young people, or little children, now hearken to the loud calls of God's word and providence. This acceptable year of the Lord, a day of such great favors to some, will doubtless be a day of as remarkable vengeance to others. Men's hearts harden, and their guilt increases apace* at such a day as this, if they neglect their souls; and never was there so great danger of such persons being given up to hardness of heart and blindness of mind. God seems now to be hastily gathering in his elect in all parts of the land; and probably the greater part of adult persons that ever shall be saved will be brought in now in a little time, and that it will be as it was on the great out-pouring of the Spirit upon the Jews in the apostles' days; the election will obtain, and rest will be blinded. If this should be the case with you, you will eternally curse this day, and will curse the day that ever you was born, to see such a season of the pouring out of God's Spirit, and will wish that you had died and gone to hell before you had seen it. Now undoubtedly it is, as it was in the days of John the Baptist, the axe is in an extraordinary manner laid at the root of the trees, that every tree which brings not forth good fruit may be hewn down and cast into the fire.*

apace: rapidly
forth good . . . the fire: Luke 3:9

Therefore, let every one that is out of Christ, now awake and fly from the wrath to come. The wrath of Almighty God is now undoubtedly hanging over a great part of this congregation: Let every one fly out of Sodom: "Haste and escape for your lives, look not behind you, escape to the mountain, lest you be consumed."*

Haste and escape . . . be consumed: Gen. 19:17

For Thought and Discussion

1. Edwards's account of Sarah Pierrepont focuses not on her physical beauty or on her accomplishments or on her personality. What does the account tell us about her? What does it tell us about Edwards?

2. What spiritual experience is the subject of the January 12 entry from Edwards's diary? List the elements of the negative catalogue which concludes this entry. (Edwards writes, "I am *not* to act" in what ways?)

3. In the third paragraph of the "application" section of "Sinners in the Hands of an Angry God," Edwards employs four metaphors. Identify these metaphors and tell which one Edwards develops most fully.

4. At what point in this sermon does Edwards begin to address his audience in the second person pronoun *you?* Why do you think he adopts this strategy?

5. At what point in the sermon does he call on his hearers to take specific action on the basis of his message? Into what groups does Edwards subdivide the congregation? How does he tailor his final appeal to each of these groups?

Early American Literature

3 Literature of Revolution

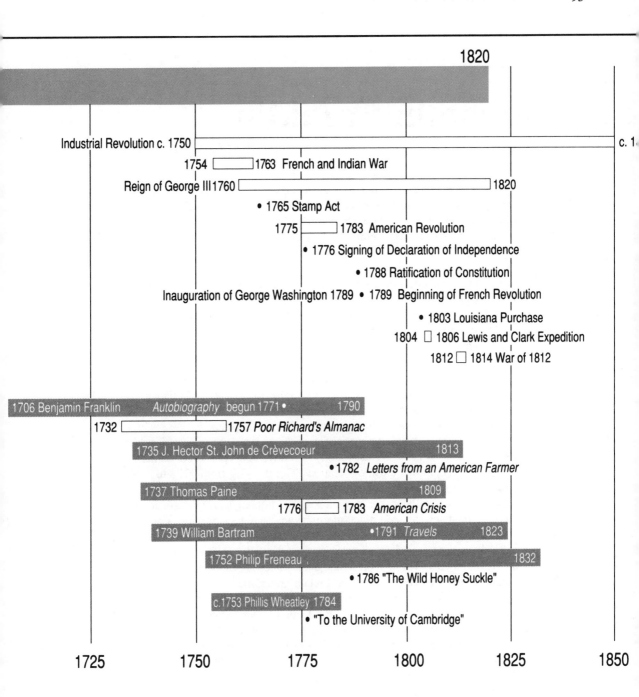

1820

Industrial Revolution c. 1750   c. 1

1754   1763   French and Indian War

Reign of George III 1760   1820

• 1765 Stamp Act

1775   1783   American Revolution

• 1776 Signing of Declaration of Independence

• 1788 Ratification of Constitution

Inauguration of George Washington 1789 •   1789   Beginning of French Revolution

• 1803 Louisiana Purchase

1804 ☐ 1806 Lewis and Clark Expedition

1812 ☐ 1814 War of 1812

1706 Benjamin Franklin   *Autobiography*   begun 1771 •   1790

1732   1757 *Poor Richard's Almanac*

1735 J. Hector St. John de Crèvecoeur   1813

•1782   *Letters from an American Farmer*

1737 Thomas Paine   1809

1776   1783   *American Crisis*

1739 William Bartram   •1791 *Travels*   1823

1752 Philip Freneau   1832

• 1786 "The Wild Honey Suckle"

c.1753 Phillis Wheatley 1784

• "To the University of Cambridge"

1725   1750   1775   1800   1825   1850

Benjamin Franklin
1706-1790

No American has better personified the American Dream than Benjamin Franklin, whose efforts brought him from poverty and insignificance to wealth and power. In the American environment, where one's accomplishments were far more important than one's ancestry, Franklin epitomized what the Renaissance term *virtu* implied: "great vigor combined with extraordinary ability crowned with striking success."

Franklin's life spanned almost the entire eighteenth century. He was born in Boston in 1706, just three years after Jonathan Edwards. Franklin's father intended the young lad to go into the ministry, but economic pressures on the family forced the boy to leave school. He was then apprenticed to his older half-brother James, who was a printer. In 1722 Franklin anonymously published in James's newspaper, *New England Courant,* a series of fourteen essays known as *The Do-Good Papers.* Encouraged by their popularity, the sixteen-year-old writer soon grew restless under the terms of his apprenticeship and ran away. He eventually arrived in Philadelphia, a bustling, rapidly growing trade center that was to become, by the start of the Revolutionary War, the second largest city in the British Empire.

In Philadelphia, through shrewd management of his time and talents, Franklin gained useful friends, became independently wealthy, and sponsored numerous community projects. From his close associations with this city from 1723 to 1757, Franklin made his mark on the colonies. It is this middle period of his life that Franklin recounts most fully in the *Autobiography.* Although he was a scientist, inventor, educator, statesman, and much more, he was first and foremost a printer.

The last portion of Franklin's life was dedicated to his country. For nearly twenty years he served as the chief colonial representative in England. During the Revolutionary War he represented the colonies in France, where his diplomatic finesse helped persuade the French government to support the colonists' struggle against England. Following his remarkably successful diplomatic career, Franklin returned to the United States, where he served as president of the executive council of Pennsylvania and helped draft the Constitution. In the eyes of both the world and his countrymen, Franklin embodied the spirit of the new nation. His death in 1790 was mourned by the entire nation.

Throughout his long, illustrious life, Franklin wrote scores of works, all revealing him as a child of his age. To the virtues of the Puritan plain style—simplicity, utility, didacticism—he added the elegance and wit of the polished conversation of his own age. ''The Way to Wealth'' (1757), the most popular work of the century, mirrors Franklin's ideals. This essay, which compiles the pithy maxims of the *Almanac,* dispenses with all fanciness of sentence structure and diction. The work is the ''sermon'' that Father Abraham, a country farmer, delivers to a group of people waiting to spend money at an auction. The maxims woven through the essay illustrate the secular virtues Franklin most wanted to teach his countrymen: Industry (diligence), Frugality (thrift), and Prudence (discretion). Thus, both utility and didacticism characterize Franklin's attempt to encourage his countrymen to handle wisely their money and time.

In the *Autobiography,* his only long piece, Franklin taught by the model of his life how the reader can achieve success. Like his Puritan forefathers he stressed right living as the means to happiness. But while stressing the virtues praised in ''The Way to Wealth,'' Franklin encouraged broad religious toleration. Because he held no personal beliefs, he was willing to accept any religion just as long as it made good citizens out of its converts. Although intimately acquainted with the evangelist George Whitefield, Franklin never admitted his own need for salvation. Instead, he tried to reach moral perfection through a rigorous program of self-discipline. He confessed with some candor, however, that the task was more difficult than he had imagined because he found more faults in himself than he had suspected.

Franklin's writings clearly depict how far the nation had shifted from its Puritan foundation. The Puritan examination of the world began with God; Franklin's began with man. For Franklin the natural and spiritual worlds were not united as they had been for the Puritans and for Edwards. Because Franklin's world extended only to the limits of the knowledge he could gain through his five senses, his concerns were social, scientific, economic, and political, not religious. Yet, as we have seen, Franklin was not totally cut off from the previous century. He has been called an ''ungodly Puritan'' because he retained Puritan values (such as hard work) without embracing Puritan theology. Franklin was never concerned with serving God or preparing for heaven. His focus was to serve himself and his fellowmen and to achieve earthly happiness. Franklin's emphases thus typify the new materialism becoming all too dominant in American life.

from The Autobiography

The Autobiography *of Benjamin Franklin began as a letter to his son but broadened into a letter to the world. In 1771, while a colonial agent in England, he started writing his memoirs for his son, William Franklin, who was then the forty-year-old royal governor of New Jersey. Interrupted by the Revolutionary War, Franklin did not return to the* Autobiography *until 1784. By this time he was estranged from his son because of political differences. Hereafter in the* Autobiography *Franklin's audience broadens to include any young man setting out to make his way in the world. The last two periods of composition were in 1788 and 1789. Unfortunately, because Franklin got no further in the story of his life than 1758, we do not have his account of his years of public service.*

[Reasons for Writing His Memoirs]

Dear Son: I have ever had a pleasure in obtaining any little anecdotes of my ancestors. You may remember the inquiries I made among the remains of my relations when you were with me in England, and the journey I undertook for that purpose. Now imagining it may be equally agreeable to you to know the circumstances of *my* life, many of which you are yet unacquainted with, and expecting a week's uninterrupted leisure in my present country retirement, I sit down to write them for you. To which I have besides* some other inducements.* Having emerged from the poverty and obscurity in which I was born and bred to a state of affluence and some degree of reputation in the world, and having gone so far through life with a considerable share of felicity,* the conducing* means I made use of, which with the blessing of God so well succeeded, my posterity may like to know, as they may find some of them suitable to their own situations and therefore fit to be imitated.

besides: also
inducements: incentives
felicity: happiness
conducing: contributing

That felicity, when I reflected on it, has induced me sometimes to say that were it offered to my choice I should have no objection to a repetition of the same life from its beginning, only

asking the advantages authors have in a second edition to correct some faults of the first. So would I, if I might, besides correcting the faults, change some sinister* accidents and events of it for others more favorable. But though this were denied, I should still accept the offer. However, since such a repetition is not to be expected, the next thing most like living one's life over again seems to be a *recollection* of that life and, to make that recollection as durable as possible, the putting it down in writing.

sinister: underhanded

Hereby, too, I shall indulge the inclination so natural in old men to be talking of themselves and their own past actions; and I shall indulge it without being troublesome to others, who, through respect to age, might think themselves obliged to give me a hearing, since this may be read or not as any one pleases. And lastly (I may as well confess it, since my denial of it will be believed by nobody), perhaps I shall a good deal gratify my own *vanity.* Indeed, I scarce ever heard or saw the introductory words, "Without vanity I may say," etc., but some vain thing immediately followed. Most people dislike vanity in others, whatever share they have of it themselves; but I give it fair quarter* wherever I meet with it, being persuaded that it is often productive of good to the possessor and to others that are within his sphere of action; and therefore, in many cases, it would not be quite absurd if a man were to thank God for his vanity among the other comforts of life. . . .

fair quarter: merciful consideration

[Becoming a Printer]

From a child I was fond of reading, and all the little money that came into my hands was ever laid out in books. . . .

This bookish inclination at length determined my father to make me a printer, though he had already one son (James) of that profession. In 1717 my brother James returned from England with a press and letters to set up his business in Boston. I liked it* much better than that of my father,* but still had a hankering for the sea. To prevent the apprehended* effect of such an inclination, my father was impatient to have me bound* to my brother. I stood out* some time, but at last was persuaded, and signed the indentures* when I was yet but twelve years old. I was to serve as an apprentice till I was twenty-one years of age, only I was to be allowed journey-man's wages* during the last year. In a little time I made great proficiency in the business and became a useful hand to my brother. I now had access to better books. An acquaintance with the apprentices of booksellers enabled me sometimes to borrow a small one, which I was careful to return soon and clean. Often I sat up in my room reading the greatest part of the night, when the book was borrowed in the evening and to be returned early in the morning, lest it should be missed or wanted.

it: James's business
that . . . father: candlemaking
apprehended: expected
bound: contracted: i.e., apprenticed
stood out: held out
indentures: contracts
journey-man's wages: earnings of one who has completed his apprenticeship

[Learning to Write]

As prose writing has been of great use to me in the course of my life, and was a principal means of my advancement, I shall tell you how . . . I acquired what little ability I have in that way.

There was another bookish lad in the town, John Collins by name, with whom I was intimately acquainted. We sometimes disputed; and very fond we were of argument, and very desirous of confuting one another, which disputatious turn, by the way, is apt to become a very bad habit, making people often extremely disagreeable in company by the contradiction that is necessary to bring it into practice; and thence, besides souring and spoiling the conversation, is productive of disgusts and, perhaps, enmities where you may have occasion for friendship. I had caught it by reading my father's books of dispute about religion. Persons of good sense, I have since observed, seldom fall into it, except lawyers, university men, and men of all sorts that have been bred at Edinburgh.

A question was once, somehow or other, started between Collins and me of the propriety of educating the female sex in learning, and their abilities for study. He was of opinion that it was improper, and that they were naturally unequal to it. I took the contrary side, perhaps a little for dispute's sake. He was naturally more eloquent, had a ready plenty of words, and sometimes, as I thought, bore me down more by his fluency than by the strength of his reasons. As we parted without settling the point, and were not to see one another again for some time, I sat down to put my arguments in writing, which I copied fair* and sent to him. He answered, and I replied. Three or four letters of a side had passed, when my father happened to find my papers and read them. Without entering into the discussion, he took occasion to talk to me about the manner of my writing; observed that, though I had the advantage of my antagonist in correct spelling and pointing* (which I owed to the printing-house), I fell far short in elegance of expression, in method, and in perspicuity,* of which he convinced me by several instances. I saw the justice of his remarks, and thence grew more attentive to the *manner* in writing, and determined to endeavour at improvement.

fair: legibly
pointing: punctuation
perspicuity: clarity

About this time I met with an odd volume of the *Spectator*.* It was the third. I had never before seen any of them. I bought it, read it over and over, and was much delighted with it. I thought the writing excellent, and wished, if possible, to imitate it. With that view I took some of the papers, and, making short hints of the sentiment in each sentence, laid them by a few days, and then, without looking at the book, tried to complete the papers again by expressing each hinted sentiment at length, and as fully as it had been expressed before, in any suitable words that should come to hand. Then I compared my *Spectator* with the original, discovered some of my faults, and corrected them. But I found I wanted* a stock of words, or a readiness in recollecting and using them, which I thought I should have acquired before that time if I had gone on making verses; since the continual occasion for words of the same import, but of different length to suit the measure, or of different sound for the rhyme, would have laid me under a constant necessity of searching for variety and also have tended to fix that variety in my mind and make me master of it. Therefore, I took some of the tales and turned them into verse; and, after a time, when I had pretty well forgotten the prose, turned them back again. I also sometimes jumbled my collections of hints into confusion, and after some weeks endeavored to reduce them into the best order, before I began to form the full sentences and complete the paper. This was to teach me method in the arrangement of thoughts. By comparing my work afterwards with the original, I discovered many faults and amended them; but I sometimes had the pleasure of fancying that in certain particulars of small import I had been lucky enough to improve the method or the language, and this encouraged me to think I might possibly in time come to be a tolerable English writer, of which I was extremely ambitious.

Spectator: English periodical written in the 1710s by Joseph Addison and Richard Steele
wanted: lacked

[First Entrance to Philadelphia]

I have been the more particular in this description of my journey, and shall be so of my first entry into that city, that you may in your mind compare such unlikely beginnings with the figure I have since made there. I was in my working dress, my best clothes being to come round by sea. I was dirty from my journey; my pockets were stuffed out with shirts and stockings; I knew no soul nor where to look for lodging. I was fatigued with traveling, rowing, and want of rest; I was very hungry; and my whole stock of cash consisted of a Dutch dollar and about a shilling in copper. The latter I gave the people of the boat for my passage, who at first refused it, on account of my rowing; but I insisted on their taking it, a man being sometimes more generous when he has but a little money than when he has plenty, perhaps through fear of being thought to have but little.

Then I walked up the street, gazing about, till near the markethouse I met a boy with bread. I had made many a meal on bread, and, inquiring where he got it, I went immediately to the baker's he directed me to, in Second Street, and asked for biscuit, intending such as we had in Boston; but they, it seems, were not made in Philadelphia. Then I asked for a three-penny loaf, and was told they had none such. So, not considering or knowing the difference of money, and the greater cheapness nor the names of his bread, I bade him give me three-penny-worth of any sort. He gave me, accordingly three great puffy rolls. I was surprised at the quantity, but took it, and, having no room in my pockets, walked off with a roll under each arm, and eating the other. Thus I went up Market Street as far as Fourth Street, passing by the door of Mr. Read, my future wife's father; when she, standing at the door, saw me, and thought I made, as I certainly did, a most awkward, ridiculous appearance.

[Religious Views]

I had been religiously educated as a Presbyterian; and though some of the dogmas of that persuasion, such as *the eternal decrees of God, election, reprobation, etc.,* appeared to me unintelligible, others doubtful, and I early absented myself from the public assemblies of the sect, Sunday being my studying day, I never was without some religious principles. I never doubted, for instance, the existence of the Deity; that he made the world, and governed it by his Providence; that the most acceptable service of God was the doing good to man; that our souls are immortal; and that all crime will be punished, and virtue rewarded, either here or hereafter. These I esteemed the essentials of every religion; and, being to be found in all the religions we had in our country, I respected them all, though with different degrees of respect, as I found them more or less mixed with other articles, which, without any tendency to inspire, promote, or confirm morality, served principally to divide us, and make us unfriendly to one another. This respect to all, with an opinion that the worst had some good effects, induced me to avoid all discourse that might tend to lessen the good opinion another might have of his own religion; and as our province increased in people, and new places of worship were continually wanted, and generally erected by voluntary contribution, my mite* for such purpose, whatever might be the sect, was never refused.*

---

mite: small contribution, from Luke 21:1-4
was . . . refused: i.e., he never refused the request of any for his
  contribution

Though I seldom attended any public worship, I had still an opinion of its propriety, and of its utility when rightly conducted, and I regularly paid my annual subscription* for the support of the only Presbyterian minister or meeting we had in Philadelphia. He used to visit me sometimes as a friend, and admonish me to attend his administrations,* and I was now and then prevailed on to do so, once for five Sundays successively.

subscription: sum of money
administrations: church services

[Plan for Moral Perfection]

It was about this time I conceived the bold and arduous project of arriving at moral perfection. I wished to live without committing any fault at any time; I would conquer all that either natural inclination, custom, or company might lead me into. As I knew, or thought I knew, what was right and wrong, I did not see why I might not always do the one and avoid the other. But I soon found I had undertaken a task of more difficulty than I had imagined. While my care was employed in guarding against one fault, I was often surprised by another; habit took the advantage of inattention; inclination was sometimes too strong for reason. I concluded, at length, that the mere speculative conviction that it was our interest to be completely virtuous was not sufficient to prevent our slipping; and that the contrary habits must be broken, and good ones acquired and established, before we can have any dependence on a steady, uniform rectitude* of conduct. For this purpose I therefore contrived* the following method.

rectitude: uprightness
contrived: devised

In the various enumerations of the moral virtues I had met with in my reading, I found the catalogue more or less numerous, as different writers included more or fewer ideas under the same name. Temperance, for example, was by some confined to eating and drinking, while by others it was extended to mean the moderating of every other pleasure, appetite, inclination, or passion, bodily or mental, even to our avarice* and ambition. I proposed to myself, for the sake of clearness, to use rather more names, with fewer ideas annexed* to each, than a few names with more ideas; and I included under thirteen names of virtues all that at that time occurred to me as

necessary or desirable, and annexed to each a short precept, which fully expressed the extent I gave to its meaning.

avarice: greed
annexed: added

These names of virtues, with the precepts were:

1. Temperance.
   Eat not to dullness; drink not to elevation.
2. Silence.
   Speak not but what may benefit others or yourself; avoid trifling conversation.
3. Order.
   Let all your things have their places; let each part of your business have its time.
4. Resolution.
   Resolve to perform what you ought; perform without fail what you resolve.
5. Frugality.
   Make no expense but to do good to others or yourself; i.e., waste nothing.
6. Industry.
   Lose no time; be always employed in something useful; cut off all unnecessary actions.
7. Sincerity.
   Use no hurtful deceit; think innocently and justly, and, if you speak, speak accordingly.
8. Justice.
   Wrong none by doing injuries, or omitting the benefits that are your duty.
9. Moderation.
   Avoid extremes; forbear resenting injuries so much as you think they deserve.
10. Cleanliness.
    Tolerate no uncleanliness in body, clothes, or habitation.
11. Tranquillity.
    Be not disturbed at trifles, or at accidents common or unavoidable.
12. Chastity.
    Rarely use venery but for health or offspring, never to dullness, weakness, or the injury of your own or another's peace or reputation.

13. Humility.

    Imitate Jesus and Socrates.

My intention being to acquire the *habitude* of all these virtues, I judged it would be well not to distract my attention by attempting the whole at once, but to fix it on one of them at a time; and, when I should be master of that, then to proceed to another, and so on, till I should have gone through the thirteen. . . .

I made a little book, in which I allotted a page for each of the virtues. I ruled each page with red ink, so as to have seven columns, one for each day of the week, marking each column with a letter for the day. I crossed these columns with thirteen red lines, marking the beginning of each line with the first letter of one of the virtues, on which line, and in its proper column, I might mark, by a little black spot, every fault I found upon examination to have been committed respecting that virtue upon that day.

I determined to give a week's strict attention to each of the virtues successively. Thus, in the first week, my great guard was to avoid every the least offense against *Temperance,* leaving the other virtues to their ordinary chance, only marking every evening the faults of the day. Thus, if in the first week I could keep my first line, marked T, clear of spots, I supposed the habit of that virtue so much strengthened, and its opposite weaken'd, that I might venture extending my attention to include the next, and for the following week keep both lines clear of spots. Proceeding thus to the last, I could go thro' a course complete in thirteen weeks, and four courses in a year. And like him who, having a garden to weed, does not attempt to eradicate all the bad herbs at once, which would exceed his reach and his strength, but works on one of the beds at a time, and, having accomplished the first, proceeds to a second, so I should have, I hoped, the encouraging pleasure of seeing on my pages the progress I made in virtue, by clearing successively my lines of their spots, till in the end, by a number of

TEMPERANCE Eat Not To Dullness Drink Not To Elevation							
	S.	M.	T.	W.	T.	F.	S.
T.							
S.	•	•		•		•	
O.	••	•	•			•	•	•
R.						•	
F.		•				•	
I.			•				
S.							
J.							
M.							
C.							
T.							
C.							
H.							

courses, I should be happy in viewing a clean book, after a thirteen weeks' daily examination.

    This my little book had for its motto these lines from Addison's *Cato:*

Here will I hold. If there's a power above us
(And that there is, all nature cries aloud
Thro' all her works), He must delight in
   virtue;
And that which He delights in must be happy.

    Another from the Proverbs of Solomon, speaking of wisdom or virtue:

Length of days is in her right hand, and in her left hand riches and honour. Her ways are ways of pleasantness, and all her paths are peace.–iii. 16, 17.

    And conceiving God to be the fountain of wisdom, I thought it right and necessary to solicit his assistance for obtaining it; to this end I formed the following little prayer, which was prefixed to my tables of examination, for daily use.

O powerful Goodness! bountiful Father! merciful Guide! Increase in me that wisdom which discovers my truest interest. Strengthen my resolutions to perform what that wisdom dictates. Accept my kind offices to thy other children as the only return in my power for thy continual favours to me.

I used also sometimes a little prayer which I took from Thomson's *Poems,* viz.:

Father of light and life, thou Good Supreme!
O teach me what is good; teach me Thyself!
Save me from folly, vanity, and vice,
From every low pursuit; and fill my soul
With knowledge, conscious peace, and virtue
    pure;
Sacred, substantial, never-fading bliss!

The precept of *Order* requiring that *every part my business should have its allotted time,* one page in my little book contained the following scheme of employment for the twenty-four hours of a natural day.

I entered upon the execution of this plan for self-examination, and continued it with occasional intermissions for some time. I was surprised to find myself so much fuller of faults than I had imagined; but I had the satisfaction of seeing them diminish. To avoid the trouble of renewing now and then my little book, which, by scraping out the marks on the paper of old faults to make room for new ones in a new course, became full of holes, I transferred my tables and precepts to the ivory leaves of a memorandum book, on which the lines were drawn with red ink, that made a durable stain, and on those lines I marked my faults with a black-lead pencil, which marks I could easily wipe out with a wet sponge. After a while I went thro' one course only in a year, and afterward only one in several years, till at length I omitted them entirely, being employed in voyages and business abroad, with a multiplicity of

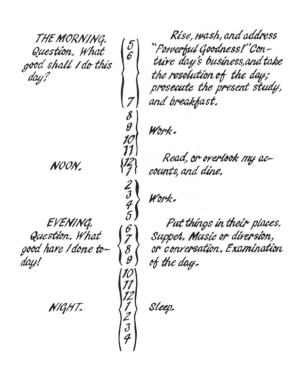

THE MORNING. Question. What good shall I do this day?	5 6 7	Rise, wash, and address "Powerful Goodness!" Contrive day's business, and take the resolution of the day; prosecute the present study, and breakfast.
	8 9 10 11	Work.
NOON.	12 1	Read, or overlook my accounts, and dine.
	2 3 4 5	Work.
EVENING. Question. What good have I done today?	6 7 8 9	Put things in their places. Supper. Music or diversion, or conversation. Examination of the day.
NIGHT.	10 11 12 1 2 3 4	Sleep.

affairs that interfered; but I always carried my little book with me. . . .

It will be remarked that, tho' my scheme was not wholly without religion, there was in it no mark of any of the distinguishing tenets of any particular sect. I had purposely avoided them; for, being fully persuaded of the utility and excellence of my method, and that it might be serviceable to people in all religions, and intending some time or other to publish it, I would not have any thing in it that should prejudice any one, of any sect, against it. I purposed writing a little comment on each virtue, in which I would have shown the advantages of possessing it, and the mischiefs attending its opposite vice; and I should have called my book *The Art of Virtue,* because it would have shown the means of obtaining virtue, which would have distinguished it from the mere exhortation to be good, that does not instruct and indicate the means, but is like the apostle's man of verbal charity, who only, without showing to the naked and hungry how or where they might get clothes or victuals, exhorted them to be fed and clothed.—James ii. 15, 16. . . .

In this piece it was my design to explain and enforce this doctrine, that vicious actions are not hurtful because they are forbidden, but forbidden because they are hurtful, the nature of man alone considered; that it was, therefore, every one's interest to be virtuous who wished to be happy even in this world; and I should, from this circumstance, . . . have endeavored to convince young persons that no qualities were so likely to make a poor man's fortune as those of probity and integrity.

My list of virtues contained at first but twelve; but a Quaker friend having kindly informed me that I was generally thought proud; that my pride showed itself frequently in conversation; that I was not content with being in the right when discussing any point but was overbearing and rather insolent,* of which he convinced me by mentioning several instances; I determined endeavoring to cure myself, if I could, of this vice or folly among the rest, and I added *Humility* to my list, giving an extensive meaning to the word.

insolent: disrespectful

I cannot boast of much success in acquiring the *reality* of this virtue, but I had a good deal with regard to the *appearance* of it. . . . The modest way in which I proposed my opinions procured them a readier reception and less contradiction; I had less mortification when I was found to be in the wrong, and I more easily prevailed with others to give up their mistakes and join with me when I happened to be in the right.

[Evangelist George Whitefield]

In 1739 arrived among us from Ireland the Reverend Mr. Whitefield, who had made himself remarkable there as an itinerant preacher. He was at first permitted to preach in some of our church-es; but the clergy, taking a dislike to him, soon refused him their pulpits, and he was obliged to preach in the fields. The multitudes of all sects and denominations that attended his sermons were enormous, and it was matter of speculation to me, who was one of the number, to observe the extraordinary influence of his oratory on his hearers, and how much they admired and respected him, notwithstanding his common abuse of them by assuring them they were naturally *half beasts and half devils.** It was wonderful to see the change soon made in the manners of our inhabitants. From being thoughtless or indifferent about religion, it seemed as if all the world were growing religious, so that one could not walk through the town in an evening without hearing psalms sung in different families of every street. . . .

naturally . . . devils: i.e., totally depraved

I happened soon after to attend one of his sermons, in the course of which I perceived he intended to finish with a collection, and I silently resolved he should get nothing from me. I had in my pocket a handful of copper money, three or four silver dollars, and five pistoles* in gold. As he proceeded I began to soften, and concluded to give the coppers. Another stroke of his oratory made me ashamed of that, and determined me to give the silver; and he finished so admirably, that I emptied my pocket wholly into the collector's dish, gold and all. . . .

pistoles: Spanish (or other European) gold coins

Some of Mr. Whitefield's enemies affected to suppose* that he would apply these collections to his own private emolument;* but I, who was intimately acquainted with him (being employed in printing his sermons and journals, etc.), never had the least suspicion of his integrity, but am to this day decidedly of opinion that he was in all his conduct a perfectly *honest man;* and methinks my testimony in his favor ought to have the more weight as we had no religious connection. He used, indeed, sometimes to pray for my conversion, but never had the satisfaction of believing that his prayers were heard. Ours was a mere civil friendship, sincere on both sides, and lasted to his death. . . .

affected . . . suppose: were inclined to believe
emolument: income

The last time I saw Mr. Whitefield was in London, when he consulted me about his Orphan House concern and his purpose of appropriating* it to the establishment of a college.

appropriating: setting something apart for

He had a loud and clear voice, and articulated his words and sentences so perfectly that he might be heard and understood at a great distance, especially as his auditories,* however numerous, observed the most exact silence. He preached one evening from the top of the Courthouse steps, which are in the middle of Market Street and on the west side of Second Street, which crosses it at right angles. Both streets were filled with his hearers to a considerable distance. Being among the hindmost in Market Street, I had the curiosity to learn how far he could be heard, by retiring backwards down the street towards the river; and I found his voice distinct till I came near Front Street, when some noise in that street obscured it. Imagining then a semi-circle, of which my distance should be the radius, and that it were filled

with auditors, to each of whom I allowed two square feet, I computed that he might well be heard by more than thirty thousand. This reconciled me to the newspaper accounts of his having preached to twenty-five thousand people in the fields, and to the ancient histories of generals haranguing whole armies, of which I had sometimes doubted.

auditories: hearers

By hearing him often, I came to distinguish easily between sermons newly composed and those which he had often preached in the course of his travels. His delivery of the latter was so improved by frequent repetitions that every accent, every emphasis, every modulation* of voice, was so perfectly well turned and well placed that, without being interested* in the subject, one could not help being pleased with the discourse, a pleasure of much the same kind with that received from an excellent piece of music. This is an advantage itinerant preachers have over those who are stationary, as the latter cannot well improve their delivery of a sermon by so many rehearsals.

modulation: adjustment
interested: personally engaged

from The Way to Wealth

For twenty-five years (1732-57) Franklin taught his countrymen when to plant their crops and how to live successfully. His vehicle of instruction was a most unlikely work, Poor Richard's Almanac. *In 1757, while sailing to England to take up duties as colonial agent, he wrote this essay, liberally sprinkling it with the maxims that had enlivened his almanacs. Always concerned about his fellow men, Franklin here stresses the secular values he thought his countrymen most needed for success in the world. This work became the best seller of the eighteenth century. It has since been translated into fifteen languages and reprinted over four hundred times.*

I have heard that nothing gives an author so great pleasure as to find his works respectfully quoted by other learned authors. This pleasure I have seldom enjoyed; for though I have been, if I may say it without vanity, an *eminent author* of almanacks annually now a full quarter of a century, my brother authors in the same way, for what reason I know not, have ever been very sparing in their applauses, and no author has taken the least notice of me, so that did not my writings produce me some solid *pudding,* the great deficiency of *praise* would have quite discouraged me.

I concluded at length that the people were the best judges of my merit; for they buy my works; and besides, in my rambles where I am not personally known, I have frequently heard one or other of my adages repeated, with *as Poor Richard says* at the end on 't; this gave me some satisfaction, as it showed not only that my instructions were regarded but discovered likewise some respect for my authority; and I own that to encourage the practice of remembering and repeating those wise sentences, I have sometimes *quoted myself* with great gravity.

Judge, then, how much I must have been gratified by an incident I am going to relate to you. I stopped my horse lately where a great number of people were collected at a vendue* of merchant goods. The hour of sale not being come, they were conversing on the badness of the times and one of the company called to a plain clean old man with white locks, "Pray, Father Abraham, what think you of the times? Won't these heavy taxes quite ruin the country? How shall we be ever able to pay them? What would you advise us to?" Father Abraham stood up, and replied, "If you'd have my advise, I'll give it to you in short, for *A word to the wise is enough,* and *Many words won't fill a bushel,* as Poor Richard says." They joined in desiring him to speak his mind, and gathering round him, he proceeded as follows:

vendue: an auction

"Friends," says he, "and neighbours, the taxes are indeed very heavy, and if those laid on by the government were the only ones we had to pay, we might more easily discharge them; but we have many others, and much more grievous to some of us. We are taxed twice as much by our idleness, three times as much by our pride, and four times as much by our folly; and from these taxes the commissioners cannot ease or deliver us by allowing an abatement. However, let us hearken to good advice, and something may be done for us; *God helps them that help themselves,* as Poor Richard says, in his Almanack of 1733.

"It would be thought a hard government that should tax its people one-tenth part of their time, to be employed in its service. But idleness taxes many of us much more, if we reckon all that is spent in absolute sloth, or doing of nothing, with that which is spent in idle employments or amusements that amount to nothing. Sloth, by bringing on diseases, absolutely shortens life. *Sloth, like* rust, consumes faster than labour wears; while the used key is always bright, as Poor Richard says. But dost thou love life, then do not squander time, for that's the stuff life is made of, as Poor Richard says. How much more than is necessary do we spend in sleep, forgetting that *The sleeping fox catches no poultry*, and that *There will be sleeping enough in the grave*, as Poor Richard says.

"*If time be of all things the most precious, wasting time must be*, as Poor Richard says, *the greatest prodigality;** since, as he elsewhere tells us, Lost time is never found again; and what we call time enough, always proves little enough. Let us then up and be doing, and doing to the purpose; so by diligence shall we do more with less perplexity. Sloth makes all things difficult, but industry all easy, as Poor Richard says; and He that riseth late must trot all day, and shall scarce overtake his business at night; while Laziness travels so slowly, that poverty soon overtakes him,* as we read in Poor Richard, who adds, *Drive thy business, let not that drive thee; and Early to bed, and early to rise, makes a man healthy, wealthy, and wise.*

---

prodigality: wastefulness

"So what signifies wishing and hoping for better times? We may make these times better, if we bestir ourselves. *Industry need not wish*, as Poor Richard says, *and he that lives upon hope will die fasting. There are no gains without pains; then help hands, for I have no lands*, or if I have, they are smartly taxed. And, as Poor Richard likewise observes, *He that hath a trade hath an estate; and he that hath a calling, hath an office of profit and honour;* but then the trade must be worked at, and the calling well followed, or neither the estate nor the office will enable us to pay our taxes. If we are industrious, we shall never starve; for as Poor Richard says, *At the working man's house hunger looks in but dares not enter.* Nor will the bailiff or the constable enter, for *industry pays debts, while despair encreaseth them*, says Poor Richard. What though you have

Now views the awful Throne of antient Night,
Then mounts exulting to the Realms of Light ;
Now launches to the Deep, now ftems the Shore,
An Ocean fcarce contains the wild Uproar.
　Whate'er of Life replenifhes the Flood,
Or walks the Earth, or warbles thro' the Wood,
In Nature's various Wants to thee complains,
The Hand, which gave the Life, the Life fuftains.
　　　　　　　　　　　　　　　　　　To

		Remark, days, &c	⊙ rif	⊙ fet	D pl.	Afpects, &c.
1	3	PHILIP & JACOB.	5 7	6 53	♈ 22	♂ rife 2 30
2	4	*Rain and*	5 6	6 54	♉ 5	♀ fet 10 28
3	5	Day inc. 4 40	5 5	6 55	18	☽ w ☿ ✳ ♄ ♂
4	6	*gufts*	5 3	6 57	♊ 2	If you would
5	7	*in fome*	5 2	6 58	16	☽ with ♀ *reap*
6	G	2 paft Eafter.	5 1	6 59	♋ 0	♂ ⊙ ☿ *Praife*
7	2	*places, with*	5 0	7 0	14	☽ with ♃ *you*
8	3	*thunder,*	4 59	7 1	28	7*s fet 7 56
9	4	Day 14 4 long.	4 58	7 2	♌ 13	*muft fow the*
10	5	*then fine*	4 57	7 3	27	Sirius fet 8 27
11	6	*growing*	4 56	7 4	♍ 11	✳ ♂ ☿ *Seeds.*
12	7	*weather,*	4 56	7 4	25	♄ rife 10 28
13	G	3 paft Eafter.	4 55	7 5	♎ 9	✳ ♃ ☿ *Gentle*
14	2	*pleafant,*	4 54	7 6	23	♃ fet 10 49
15	3	*with*	4 53	7 7	♏ 6	♂ rife 2 3
16	4	Day inc. 5 6	4 52	7 8	19	*Words and*
17	5	*wind and*	4 51	7 9	♐ 2	♀ fet 9 46
18	6	*flying*	4 50	7 10	15	*ufeful Deeds.*
19	7	*clouds,*	4 49	7 11	28	Ignorance *leads*
20	G	4 paft Eafter.	4 48	7 12	♑ 10	⊙ in ♊ ☾ ☽ ♄
21	2	*follow'd*	4 47	7 13	22	*Men into a*
22	3	Days 14 28 long.	4 46	7 14	♒ 4	*Party, and*
23	4	*by heat,*	4 45	7 15	16	Shame *keeps*
24	5	*then*	4 44	7 16	28	*them from get-*
25	6	*rain and*	4 44	7 16	♓ 10	*ting out again.*
26		*thunder,*	4 43	7 17	22	☽ with ♂
27	G	Rogation Sunday.	4 42	7 18	♈ 4	♄ rife 9 26
28	2	Day inc. 5 26	4 42	7 18	17	♃ fet 10 6
29	3	K. Cha. refto.	4 41	7 19	♉ 0	♂ rife 1 32
30	4	*pleafant.*	4 41	7 19	13	☽ with ☿ *Hafte*
31	5	Afcenfion Day.	4 40	7 20	2	*makes Wafte.*

found no treasure nor has any rich relation left you a legacy, *Diligence is the mother of good-luck*, as Poor Richard says, *and God gives all things to industry. Then plough deep, while sluggards sleep, and you shall have corn to sell and to keep*, says Poor Dick. Work while it is called to-day, for you know not how much you may be hindered to-morrow, which makes Poor Richard say, *One to-day is worth two to-morrows*, and farther, *Have you somewhat to do to-morrow, do it to-day.* If you were a servant, would you not be ashamed that a good master should catch you idle? Are you then your own master, *Be ashamed to catch yourself idle*, as Poor Dick says. . . .

"This doctrine, my friends, is reason and wisdom; but after all, do not depend too much upon your own industry, and frugality, and prudence, though excellent things, for they may all be blasted without the blessing of Heaven; and therefore, ask that blessing humbly, and be not uncharitable to those that at present seem to want it, but comfort and help them. Remember, Job suffered, and was afterwards prosperous.

"And now to conclude, *Experience keeps a dear school, but fools will learn in no other, and scarce in that;* for it is true, *We may give advice, but we cannot give conduct,* as Poor Richard says. However, remember this, *They that won't be counselled, can't be helped,* as Poor Richard says: and farther, that, *If you will not hear reason, she'll surely rap your knuckles.*"

Thus the old gentleman ended his harangue. The people heard it, and approved the doctrine, and immediately practiced the contrary, just as if it had been a common sermon; for the vendue opened, and they began to buy extravagantly, notwithstanding his cautions and their own fear of taxes. I found the good man had thoroughly studied my Almanacks, and digested all I had dropt on these topics during the course of five and twenty years. The frequent mention he made of me must have tired any one else, but my vanity was wonderfully delighted with it, though I was conscious that not a tenth part of the wisdom was my own, which he ascribed to me, but rather the gleanings I had made of the sense of all ages and nations. However, I resolved to be the better for the echo of it; and though I had at first determined to buy stuff for a new coat, I went away resolved to wear my old one a little longer. Reader, if thou wilt do the same, thy profit will be as great as mine. I am, as ever, thine to serve thee,

RICHARD SAUNDERS

from Exporting of Felons to the Colonies

Enraged at the British practice of exporting convicts from Great Britain's prisons to help settle the colonies, Franklin wrote this counterproposal. Although this essay lacks the satiric power of Franklin at his best, it is nevertheless a fair representative of his political satire. The essay appeared in the Pennsylvania Gazette *on May 9, 1751.*

To the Printers of the Gazette

By a Passage in one of your late Papers, I understand that the Government at home will not suffer our mistaken Assemblies to make any Law for preventing or discouraging the Importation of Convicts from Great Britain, for this kind Reason, *'That such Laws are against the Public Utility, as they tend to prevent the* IMPROVEMENT *and* WELL PEOPLING *of the Colonies.'*

Such a tender *parental* Concern in our *Mother Country* for the *Welfare* of her *Children,* calls aloud for the highest *Returns* of Gratitude and Duty. This every one must be sensible of. But 'tis said, that in our present Circumstances it is absolutely impossible for us to make *such** as are adequate to the Favour. I own it; but nevertheless let us do our Endeavour. 'Tis something to show a grateful Disposition.

such: i.e., such "Returns of Gratitude and Duty"

In some of the uninhabited Parts of these Provinces, there are Numbers of these venomous Reptiles we call RATTLE-SNAKES, Felons-convict from the Beginning of the World. These, whenever we meet with them, we put to Death, by Virtue of an old Law, *Thou shalt bruise his Head.** But as this is a sanguinary* Law, and may seem too cruel; and as however mischievous those Creatures are with us, they may possibly change their Natures if they were to change the Climate; I would humbly propose, that this general Sentence of *Death* be changed for *Transportation.*

Thou . . . Head: Genesis 3:15
sanguinary: bloodthirsty

In the Spring of the Year, when they first creep out of their Holes, they are feeble, heavy, slow, and easily taken; and if a small Bounty were allowed *per* Head, some Thousands might be collected annually and *transported* to *Britain.* There I would propose to have them carefully distributed in *St. James's Park,* in the *Spring-Gardens* and other Places of Pleasure about *London;* in the Gardens of all the Nobility and Gentry throughout the Nation; but particularly in the Gardens of the *Prime Ministers,* the *Lords of Trade* and *Members of Parliament;* for to them we are *most particularly* obliged.

There is no human Scheme so perfect but some Inconveniencies may be objected to it. Yet when the Conveniencies far exceed, the Scheme is judged rational, and fit to be executed. Thus Inconveniencies have been objected to that *good* and *wise* Act of Parliament by virtue of which all the *Newgates** and *Dungeons* in *Britain* are emptied into the Colonies. It has been said that these Thieves and Villains introduced among us spoil the Morals of Youth in the Neighbourhoods that entertain them, and perpetrate many horrid Crimes. But let not *private Interests* obstruct *public* Utility. Our *Mother* knows what is best for us.

What is a little *Housebreaking, Shoplifting,* or *Highway Robbing;* what is a *Son* now and then *corrupted* and *hanged,* a Daughter *debauched** and *poxed,** a Wife *stabbed,* a Husband's *Throat cut,* or a Child's *Brains beat out* with an Axe, compared with this 'IMPROVEMENT and WELL PEOPLING of the Colonies!'

Newgates: i.e., Newgate, a famous London prison
debauched: corrupted
poxed: given syphilis

Thus it may perhaps be objected to my Scheme, that the *Rattle-Snake* is a mischievous Creature, and that his changing his Nature with the Clime is a mere Supposition, not yet confirmed by sufficient Facts. What then? Is not Example more prevalent than Precept? And may not the honest rough British Gentry, by a Familiarity with these Reptiles, learn to *creep,* and to *insinuate,** and to *slaver,** and to *wriggle* into Place (and perhaps to *poison* such as stand in their Way), Qualities of no small Advantage to Courtiers! In comparison of which 'IMPROVEMENT and PUBLICK UTILITY,' what is a *Child* now and then killed by their venomous Bite, . . . or even a favourite *Lap Dog?*

insinuate: use devious means
slaver: drool

I would only add, that this exporting of Felons to the Colonies may be considered as a *Trade,* as well as in the Light of a *Favour,* now [that] all Commerce implies Returns. Justice requires them. There can be no Trade without them. And *Rattle-Snakes* seem the most *suitable Returns* for the *Human Serpents* sent us by our *Mother* Country. In this, however, as in every other Branch of Trade, she will have the Advantage of us. She will reap *equal* Benefits without equal risk of the Inconveniencies and Dangers. For the *Rattle-Snake* gives Warning before he attempts his Mischief, which the Convict does not. I am

Yours, &c.
Americanus [Franklin's pen name]

Letter to Ezra Stiles

Just one month before his death, Franklin explained his religious views in this letter to the president of Yale College. His comments reveal both his deistic creed and his pragmatic attitude toward other religions.

You desire to know something of my Religion. It is the first time I have been questioned upon it. But I cannot take your Curiosity amiss, and shall endeavour in a few Words to gratify it. Here is my Creed. I believe in one God, Creator of the Universe. That he governs it by his Providence. That he ought to be worshipped. That the most acceptable Service we render to him is doing good to his other Children. That the soul of Man is immortal, and will be treated with Justice in another Life respecting its Conduct in this. These I take to be the fundamental Principles of all sound Religion, and I regard them as you do in whatever Sect I meet with them.

As to Jesus of Nazareth, my Opinion of whom you particularly desire, I think the System of Morals and his Religion, as he left them to us, the best the World ever saw or is likely to see; but I apprehend it has received various corrupting Changes, and I have, with most of the present Dissenters* in England, some Doubts as to his Divinity; tho' it is a question I do not dogmatize upon, having never studied it, and think it needless to busy myself with it now, when I expect soon an Opportunity of knowing the Truth with less Trouble. I see no harm, however, in its being believed, if that Belief has the good Consequence, as probably it has, of making his Doctrines more respected and better observed; especially as I do not perceive, that the Supreme takes it amiss, by distinguishing the Unbelievers in his Government of the World with any peculiar Marks of his Displeasure.

Dissenters: Deists

For Thought and Discussion

1. In the first paragraph of the *Autobiography*, Franklin says that he has "emerged from . . . poverty and obscurity" to achieve what three goals? What advice does he therefore intend to record for "posterity"?

2. Is the success which Franklin attributes to himself material or spiritual? Why do you suppose Franklin is called "the Father of the great American Dream"?

3. What is the purpose of Franklin's account of his arrival in Philadelphia? Why do you suppose readers find this account one of the most interesting portions of the work?

4. At what point in Franklin's paragraph on his religious views (pp. 99-100) does he depart from the teachings of orthodox Christianity? Why is this statement Biblically unsound? Does Franklin take into account man's sinfulness in his religious views? If Franklin had been asked, "What is the chief duty of man?" what do you think his answer might have been?

5. For what reason does Franklin wish "to be completely virtuous"? (See p. 100, column A and p.105, column A.) In what ways does Franklin's philosophy of morality conflict with Biblical teaching concerning morality? Consider both the motivation and the method for achieving morality advanced by Franklin and by the New Testament.

Thomas Paine   1737-1809

Thomas Paine was one of the most prominent Americans of the Revolutionary War period. The foremost political pamphleteer of his day, he more than anyone else was responsible for uniting the colonists in the fight for independence from England. After he published *The Age of Reason,* however, his reputation plummeted because of his support of the radical revolution in France and his advocacy of radical Deism.

Paine spent the first half of his life in England and the last half about equally in America and France. In 1774 Paine met Benjamin Franklin. Evidently recognizing the thirty-seven-year-old man's potential, Franklin encouraged Paine to immigrate to the colonies. Prior to this point in his life, Paine had experienced a series of failures. He had tried his father's trade, corset-making; had served the English government in collecting excise taxes and watching for smugglers (a post from which he was dismissed because of his dishonesty, then reinstated, then dismissed again, probably for trying to unionize his fellow excisemen); had tried open-air preaching to Methodists; and had failed in business. Even his personal ties to England had been severed, for his second marriage (his first wife had died) had resulted in separation.

After his arrival in Philadelphia with letters of introduction from Franklin, Paine became editor of the *Pennsylvania Magazine* and supported a number of liberal causes. At first he seemed to have no interest in the colonies' political controversy with England. In January 1776 he finally entered the political debate with his influential pamphlet *Common Sense,* a tract that persuaded many previously uncommitted colonists to unite in seeking political independence. His four-part argument made two important points: that the breach with England could not be healed and that the American colonies ought to declare their independence from the mother country. In the summer of 1776, Paine enlisted in the Continental army. In December of that year–immediately after the defeat of Washington's army at Long Island, the first major battle of the war–Paine wrote the first and most famous of *The American Crisis* papers. So compelling was his persuasion that Washington ordered the pamphlet read aloud to all the units of the army. During the next seven years of the war, Paine wrote fifteen more pamphlets in this series, each of them designed to boost the colonial soldiers' morale following a major crisis. After the war ended, Paine received almost no compensation for his services and for a time seemed unsure about where he should direct his energy next.

In 1787 Paine found another cause and thus began the last stage of his life. Having sailed to France to publicize an iron bridge he had invented, he became engaged in defending the French Revolution. He wrote *The Rights of Man* to answer Edmund Burke's *Reflections on the Late Revolution in France* (1790), a devastating attack upon the French Revolution from a solidly conservative position. Since Paine's tract encouraged the English people to revolt against their monarch and the hereditary ruling class, Paine was declared a traitor in England and burned in effigy. After 1793 Paine began losing sympathy for the French movement because of its violent radicalism. He was soon imprisoned for his opposition and nearly executed. During this imprisonment he wrote much of *The Age of Reason,* his attack on all forms of religion, especially Christianity. This rationalistic, Deistic work cost him his popular support and made his return to the United States in 1802 less than happy. Until his death in 1809, he lived near New Rochelle on a small farm belatedly given him in 1784 by New York as compensation for his Revolutionary War service.

Paine excelled in making concepts understandable to the common man. In fact, his fiery political writing was successful primarily because he took current ideas and expressed them so that they caught the public sentiment. The beautiful cadence of the sentences that open the first *Crisis* paper, the vehemence of its attack against the enemies of the Revolution, the strength of its strongly emotional appeals–all these qualities characterize Paine's propagandistic writing. Critics agree that his genius lies in style rather than thought, however.

Paine's fervency, however, had made some readers mistakenly assume that his early writing expressed what he actually believed. His later works refute that assumption. They show, in particular, that the religious appeals carefully woven throughout his political writing were purposefully designed to influence an audience with conservative religious beliefs when Paine's own beliefs were, instead, radically Deistic. Because of the extent of his writing on political and religious matters, Paine served as a major spokesman for the new rationalism entering American literature. As valuable as his work was in the cause of American independence, we must remember to evaluate the whole of his achievement, not just a part. Paine's career, in fact, is a reminder that great personal gifts can serve unworthy as well as worthy endeavors.

from The American Crisis, No. 1

In the fall of 1776, the American cause seemed doomed to failure. In recent months Washington's troops had seen reversal after reversal. By January 1, 1777, the terms of enlistment of most of the soldiers would reach their end. Because only failure had marked the American struggle, even the master diplomat Franklin had been unable to secure desperately needed assistance from the French government.

On December 19, 1776, Paine penned his first Crisis *paper, writing it—according to legend—on a drumhead. In his call to the soldiers to continue the fight, in his representations of George III as only an extraordinary criminal and the Tories as submissive cowards, and in his appeals to the divine rightness of the cause, Paine struck just the right psychological note. On Christmas Day, 1776, Washington's 2400 men crossed the Delaware River to Trenton, New Jersey. Their bold attack surprised the camp of Hessian mercenaries drunkenly celebrating the holiday season and brought the colonials their first taste of success.*

This selection reveals Paine's mastery of the tools of persuasion. Notice, for instance, his use of scorn to intimidate his opposition (those either neutral or sympathetic to the king) in such epithets as "the summer soldier and the sunshine patriot." Also notice his frequent appeals to Christian revelation, in which he did not actually believe.

These are the times that try men's souls. The summer soldier and the sunshine patriot will, in this crisis, shrink from the service of their country; but he that stands it *now,* deserves the love and thanks of man and woman. Tyranny, like hell, is not easily conquered; yet we have this consolation with us, that the harder the conflict, the more glorious the triumph. What we obtain too cheap, we esteem too lightly: it is dearness only that gives every thing its value. Heaven knows how to put a proper price upon its goods; and it would be strange indeed if so celestial an article as FREEDOM should not be highly rated. Britain, with an army to enforce her tyranny, has declared that she has a right (*not only to TAX*) but "to BIND *us in* ALL CASES WHATSOEVER,"* and if being *bound in that manner,* is not slavery, then is there not such a thing as slavery upon earth. Even the expression is impious; for so unlimited a power can belong only to God.

to . . . WHATSOEVER: from the British Declaratory Act of Parliament of February 1776

I have as little superstition in me as any man living, but my secret opinion has ever been, and still is, that God Almighty will not give up a people to military destruction, or leave them unsupportedly to perish, who have so earnestly and so repeatedly sought to avoid the calamities of war, by every decent method which wisdom could invent. Neither have I so much of the infidel in me, as to suppose that He has relinquished the government of the world, and given us up to the care of devils; and as I do not, I cannot see on what grounds the king of Britain can look up to heaven for help against us: a common murderer, a highwayman, or a house-breaker, has as good a pretence* as he. . . .

pretence: pretended claim

I shall not now attempt to give all the particulars of our retreat to the Delaware; suffice it for the present to say, that both officers and men, though greatly harassed and fatigued, frequently without rest, covering, or provision, the inevitable consequences of a long retreat, bore it with a manly and martial spirit. All their wishes centred in one, which was, that the country would turn out and help them to drive the enemy back. Voltaire has remarked that king William never appeared to full advantage but in difficulties and in action; the same remark may be made on General Washington, for the character fits him. There is a natural firmness in some minds which cannot be unlocked by trifles, but which, when unlocked, discovers a cabinet of fortitude;* and I reckon it among those kind of public blessings, which we do not immediately see, that God hath blessed him with uninterrupted health, and given him a mind that can even flourish upon care.

---

fortitude: strength

I shall conclude this paper with some miscellaneous remarks on the state of our affairs; and shall begin with asking the following question, Why is it that the enemy have left the New-England provinces, and made these middle ones the seat of war? The answer is easy: New-England is not infested with tories,* and we are. I have been tender in raising the cry against these men, and used numberless arguments to show them their danger, but it will not do to sacrifice a world either to their folly or their baseness. The period is now arrived, in which either they or we must change our sentiments, or one or both must fall. And what is a tory? . . . I should not be afraid to go with a hundred whigs against a thousand tories, were they to attempt to get into arms. Every tory is a coward; for servile, slavish, self-interested fear is the foundation of toryism; and a man under such influence, though he may be cruel, never can be brave.

---

tories: colonists favoring England's side during the Revolutionary War

But, before the line of irrecoverable separation be drawn between us, let us reason the matter together: Your conduct* is an invitation to the enemy, yet not one in a thousand of you has heart enough to join him. Howe is as much deceived by you as the American cause is injured by you. He expects you will all take up arms, and flock to his standard, with muskets on your shoulders. Your opinions are of no use to him, unless you support him personally, for 'tis soldiers, and not tories, that he wants.

Your conduct: i.e., that of the uncommitted colonists

America did not, nor does not, want* force; but she wanted a proper application of that force. Wisdom is not the purchase of a day, and it is no wonder that we should err at the first setting off. From an excess of tenderness, we were unwilling to raise an army, and trusted our cause to the temporary defence of a well-meaning militia. A summer's experience has now taught us better; yet with those troops, while they were collected, we were able to set bounds to the progress of the enemy, and, thank God! they are again assembling. I always considered militia as the best troops in the world for a sudden exertion, but they will not do for a long campaign. Howe, it is probable, will make an attempt on this city; should he fail on this side of the Delaware, he is ruined: if he succeeds, our cause is not ruined. He stakes all on his side against a part on ours; admitting he succeeds, the consequence will be, that armies from both ends of the continent will march to assist their suffering friends in the middle states; for he cannot go everywhere, it is impossible. I consider Howe as the greatest enemy the tories have; he is bringing a war into their country which, had it not been for him and partly for themselves, they had been clear of. Should he now be expelled, I wish with all the devotion of a Christian that the names of whig and tory may never more be mentioned; but should the tories give him encouragement to come, or assistance if he come, I as sincerely wish that our next year's arms may expel them from the continent and the congress appropriate their possessions to the relief of those who have suffered in well-doing. A single successful battle next year will settle the whole. America could carry on a two years war by the confiscation of the property of disaffected* persons, and be made happy by their expulsion. Say not that this is revenge, call it rather the soft resentment of a suffering people, who, having no object in view but the *good of all,* have staked their *own all* upon a seemingly doubtful event. Yet it is folly to argue against determined hardness; eloquence may strike the ear, and the language of sorrow draw forth the tear of compassion, but nothing can reach the heart that is steeled with prejudice.

want: lack
disaffected: disloyal

Quitting this class of men, I turn with the warm ardor of a friend to those who have nobly stood, and are yet determined to stand the matter out. I call not upon a few but upon all, not on *this* state or *that* state but on *every* state: up and help us; lay your shoulders to the wheel; better have too much force than too little, when so great an object is at stake. Let it be told to the future world that in the depth of winter, when nothing but hope and virtue could survive, that the city and the country, alarmed at one common danger, came forth to meet and to repulse it. Say not that thousands are gone, turn out your tens of thousands; throw not the burden of the day upon Providence, but *"show your faith by your works,"** that God may bless you. It matters not where you live, or what rank of life you hold, the evil or the blessing will reach you all. The far and the near, the home counties and the back, the rich and the poor, will suffer or rejoice alike. The heart that feels not now, is dead; the blood of his children will curse his cowardice who shrinks back at a time when a little might have saved the whole and made *them* happy. I love the man that can smile in trouble, that can gather strength from distress and grow brave by reflection. 'Tis the business of little minds to shrink; but he whose heart is firm, and whose conscience approves his conduct, will pursue his principles unto death. My

own line of reasoning is to myself as straight and clear as a ray of light. Not all the treasures of the world, so far as I believe, could have induced me to support an offensive war, for I think it murder; but if a thief breaks into my house, burns and destroys my property, and kills or threatens to kill me, or those that are in it, and to *"bind me in all cases whatsoever"* to his absolute will, am I to suffer it? What signifies it to me whether he who does it is a king or a common man; my country-man or not my countryman; whether it be done by an individual villain, or an army of them? If we reason to the root of things we shall find no difference; neither can any just cause be assigned why we should punish in the one case and pardon in the other. Let them call me rebel, and welcome, I feel no concern from it; but I should suffer the misery of devils were I to make a whore of my soul by swearing allegiance to one whose char-acter is that of a sottish,* stupid, stubborn, worth-less, brutish man. I conceive likewise a horrid idea in receiving mercy from a being, who at the last day shall be shrieking to the rocks and moun-tains to cover him, and fleeing with terror from the orphan, the widow, and the slain of America.

show . . . works: James 2:18
sottish: drunken

There are cases which cannot be overdone by language, and this is one. There are persons, too, who see not the full extent of the evil which threatens them; they solace themselves with hopes that the enemy, if he succeed, will be mer-ciful. It is the madness of folly to expect mercy from those who have refused to do justice; and even mercy, where conquest is the object, is only a trick of war; the cunning of the fox is as mur-derous as the violence of the wolf, and we ought to guard equally against both. Howe's first object is, partly by threats and partly by promises, to terrify or seduce the people to deliver up their arms and receive mercy. The ministry recom-mended the same plan to Gage,* and this is what the tories call making their peace, *"a peace which*

*passeth all understanding"** indeed! A peace which would be the immediate forerunner of a worse ruin than any we have yet thought of. Ye men of Pennsylvania, do reason upon these things! Were the back counties to give up their arms, they would fall an easy prey to the Indians, who are all armed: this perhaps is what some tories would not be sorry for. Were the home counties to deliver up their arms, they would be exposed to the resentment of the back counties, who would then have it in their power to chastise their defection at pleasure. And were any one state to give up its arms, *that* state must be gar-risoned by all Howe's army of Britons and Hes-sians to preserve it from the anger of the rest. Mutual fear is the principal link in the chain of mutual love, and woe be to that state that breaks the compact. Howe is mercifully inviting you to barbarous destruction, and men must be either rogues or fools that will not see it. I dwell not upon the vapours of imagination: I bring reason to your ears, and, in language as plain as A, B, C, hold up truth to your eyes.

Gage: British general and former governor of Massachusetts
a . . . understanding: Philippians 4:7; notice Paine's ironic construc-tion of this phrase so as to denote a foolish peace

I thank God that I fear not. I see no real cause for fear. I know our situation well, and can see the way out of it. While our army was collected, Howe dared not risk a battle; and it is no credit to him that he decamped from the White Plains, and waited a mean opportunity to ravage the def-enceless Jerseys; but it is great credit to us that with a handful of men we sustained an orderly retreat for near an hundred miles, brought off our ammunition, all our field pieces, the greatest part of our stores, and had four rivers to pass. None can say that our retreat was precipitate,* for we were near three weeks in performing it, that the country might have time to come in. Twice we marched back to meet the enemy, and remained out till dark. The sign of fear was not seen in our camp, and had not some of the cowardly and disaffected inhabitants spread false alarms through the country, the Jerseys had never been ravaged. Once more we are again collected and collecting; our new army at both ends of the continent is recruiting fast, and we shall be able to open the next campaign with sixty thousand men, well armed and clothed. This is our situation, and who will may know it. By perseverance and fortitude we have the prospect of a glorious issue; by cowardice and submission, the sad choice of a variety of evils—a ravaged country—a depopulated city—habitations without safety, and slavery without hope—our homes turned into barracks and bawdyhouses for Hessians, and a future race to provide for, whose fathers we shall doubt of. Look on this picture and weep over it! and if there yet remains one thoughtless wretch who believes it not, let him suffer it unlamented.

precipitate: hasty

Benjamin Franklin's popular cartoon (1754) visualized John Dickinson's appeal to the Thirteen Colonies: "By uniting we stand, by dividing we fall." Colonial newspapers continued reprinting the cartoon until the Constitution was ratified.

The Age of Reason

In this work Paine attacks Christianity and defends Deism. It is here that his real beliefs surface. Although this work was published during America's second major revival and was thus providentially hindered from having much immediate effect, it has been influential since. Its arguments, however shallow and naive they appear on thoughtful consideration, have been tirelessly repeated by unbelievers up to the present. Paine's position anticipates modern religious liberalism, which is Unitarianism in Christian guise. The difference is that in Paine's writing the unbelief is blatantly aggressive.

Chapter One: The Author's Profession of Faith

It has been my intention, for several years past, to publish my thoughts upon religion; I am well aware of the difficulties that attend the subject, and from that consideration, had reserved it to a more advanced period of life. I intended it to be the last offering I should make to my fellow-citizens of all nations, and that at a time when the purity of the motive that induced me to it could not admit of a question,* even by those who might disapprove the work. . . .

admit . . . question: be legitimately questioned

As several of my colleagues, and others of my fellow-citizens of France, have given me the example of making their voluntary and individual profession of faith, I also will make mine; and I do this with all that sincerity and frankness with which the mind of man communicates with itself.

I believe in one God, and no more; and I hope for happiness beyond this life.

I believe in the equality of man, and I believe that religious duties consist in doing justice, loving mercy, and endeavouring to make our fellow-creatures happy.

But, lest it should be supposed that I believe many other things in addition to these, I shall, in the progress of this work, declare the things I do not believe, and my reasons for not believing them.

I do not believe in the creed professed by the Jewish church, by the Roman church, by the Greek church, by the Turkish church, by the Protestant church, nor by any church that I know of. My own mind is my own church.

All national institutions of churches, whether Jewish, Christian, or Turkish, appear to me no other than human inventions set up to terrify and enslave mankind, and monopolize power and profit.

I do not mean by this declaration to condemn those who believe otherwise; they have the same right to their belief as I have to mine. But it is necessary to the happiness of man, that he be mentally faithful to himself. Infidelity does not consist in believing, or in disbelieving; it consists in professing to believe what he does not believe. . . .

Soon after I had published the pamphlet *Common Sense,* in America, I saw the exceeding probability that a revolution in the system of government would be followed by a revolution in the system of religion. The adulterous connection of church and state, wherever it had taken place, whether Jewish, Christian, or Turkish, had so effectually prohibited, by pains and penalties, every discussion upon established creeds, and upon first principles of religion, that until the system of government should be changed, those subjects could not be brought fairly and openly before the world; but that whenever this should be done, a revolu-

tion in the system of religion would follow. Human inventions and priest-craft would be detected; and man would return to the pure, unmixed, and unadulterated* belief of one God, and no more.

unadulterated: uncontaminated

from Chapter Three: Concerning the Character of Jesus Christ, and His History

Nothing that is here said can apply, even with the most distant disrespect, to the *real* character of Jesus Christ. He was a virtuous and an amiable man. The morality that he preached and practised was of the most benevolent kind; and though similar systems of morality had been preached by Confucius, and by some of the Greek philosophers, many years before, by the Quakers since, and by many good men in all ages, it has not been exceeded by any.

Jesus Christ wrote no account of himself, of his birth, parentage, or anything else.* Not a line of what is called the New Testament is of his writing. The history of him is altogether the work of other people; and as to the account given of his resurrection and ascension, it was the necessary counterpart to the story of his birth. His historians, having brought him into the world in a supernatural manner, were obliged to take him out again in the same manner, or the first part of the story must have fallen to the ground.

Christ . . . else: cf. II Peter 1:16-18; I John 1: 1-3, 5:20

The wretched contrivance* with which this latter part is told, exceeds everything that went before it. The first part, that of the miraculous conception, was not a thing that admitted of* publicity; and therefore the tellers of this part of the story had this advantage, that though they might not be credited, they could not be detected. They could not be expected to prove it, because it was not one of those things that admitted of proof, and it was impossible that the person of whom it was told could prove it himself.

contrivance: trick
that . . . of: by nature allowed

But the resurrection of a dead person from the grave, and his ascension through the air, is a thing very different, as to the evidence it admits of, to the invisible conception of a child in the womb. The resurrection and ascension, supposing them to have taken place, admitted of public and ocular* demonstration, like that of the ascension of a balloon, or the sun at noon day, to all Jerusalem at least. A thing which everybody is required to believe, requires that the proof and evidence of it should be equal to all, and universal; and as the public visibility of this last related act was the only evidence that could give sanction to the former part, the whole of it falls to the ground, because that evidence never was given. Instead of this, a small number of persons, not more than eight or nine, are introduced as proxies* for the whole world, to say they saw it, and all the rest of the world are called upon to believe it. But it appears that Thomas did not believe the resurrection; and, as they say, would not believe without having ocular and manual demonstration himself. *So neither will I;* and the reason is equally as good for me, and for every person, as for Thomas.*

ocular: pertaining to the eye
proxies: delegates
So . . . Thomas: cf. John 20:24-29; I Peter 1: 8-9; II Peter 1:19-21; II Timothy 3:14-15

For Thought and Discussion

1. What is Paine's purpose for writing *The American Crisis, No. 1?* In which sentences does Paine state this purpose?

2. Summarize Paine's argument in paragraph 7 that the colonial soldiers in the Revolutionary War are not rebels. To what does Paine compare his "own line of reasoning"? To what does he compare "an offensive war"? To what does he compare the Revolutionary War?

3. Paine's tone in *The American Crisis* tracts might best be described as one of emotional fervor. How does he establish this tone in the first paragraph of *No. 1?* What strongly negative words does he use? To whom or what do these negative words refer?

4. Notice the following statement from a letter by Paine to Silas Deane: "The mind of a living public . . . feels first and reasons afterwards." In light of this statement and your analysis of Paine's tone, how do you think he expected his readers to respond to his tract?

5. Why do you think the first two sentences of *The American Crisis, No. 1* have become famous? What makes them inspirational and memorable?

6. In one brief sentence in Chapter 1 in *The Age of Reason,* Paine sums up the philosophy of rationalism, the theory that the only valid basis for man's belief or action is his own reason. Specify the sentence in which Paine identifies his "church."

William Bartram 1739-1823

William Bartram reflects the eighteenth century's new attitude toward nature. He did not, like earlier writers, focus upon unusual occurrences or fabulous creatures. Nor was he, like them, concerned primarily with the spiritual significance of the natural realm. Instead, he described what he actually observed, writing in a style characterized by scientific objectivity more than that of his American predecessors.

From youth, William Bartram showed an interest in nature. This interest was no doubt encouraged by his father (the first native American botanist), who in 1765 had been appointed Botanist to the King. In 1773 William Bartram began the trek that secured his fame. The full title of his account of the four-year expedition reveals its geographical extent: *Travels Through North and South Carolina, Georgia, East and West Florida, the Cherokee Country, the Extensive Territories of the Muscagulgees, or Creek Confederacy, and the Country of the Choctaws*. Bartram published this work in 1791, fourteen years after finishing the exploration. Contemporary British writers like William Wordsworth and Samuel Taylor Coleridge found inspiration and materials for their own writing in Bartram's rich description.

The *Travels* combines first-person narration of Bartram's experiences with scientific description of portions of the Southeast. The account of Bartram's battles with the Florida alligators shows his narrative skill. The frequent digressions upon nesting habits, Indian customs, native plants and animals, even local settlers, reveal the writer's scientific interest in the world around him. Bartram's work also shows the encroachment of romantic attitudes into American literature, especially in his sentimental and idealized portraits of the Indians.

Throughout his writing Bartram views God as an active and benevolent force in nature. Although such a view was conventional, Bartram does imply a role for Providence that goes beyond the standard Deistic conception of God as the great Clock-winder or First Cause. Even though he does not express the atheistic view of nature prevalent a century later, nowhere does he reflect the Biblical view of God and nature expressed by the earliest American writers. His work thus represents the new spirit of scientific observation rising in the late eighteenth century.

from **Travels**

The evening was temperately cool and calm. The crocodiles began to roar and appear in uncommon numbers along the shores and in the river. I fixed my camp in an open plain, near the upmost projection of the promontory,* under the shelter of a large live oak, which stood on the highest part of the ground and but a few yards from my boat. From this open, high situation, I had a free prospect of the river, which was a matter of no trivial consideration to me, having good reason to dread the subtle attacks of the alligators, who were crowding about my harbour. Having collected a good quantity of wood for the purpose of keeping up a light and smoke during the night, I began to think of preparing my supper, when, upon examining my stores, I found but a scanty provision. I thereupon determined, as the most expeditious* way of supplying my necessities, to take my bob and try for some trout. About one hundred yards above my harbour, began a cove or bay of the river, out of which opened a large lagoon. The mouth or entrance from the river to it was narrow, but the waters soon after spread and formed a little lake, extending into the marshes, its entrance and shores within I observed to be verged* with floating lawns of the Pistia* and Nymphea* and other aquatic plants; these I knew were excellent haunts for trout.

---

promontory: land jutting out into water
expeditious: fastest
verged: edged
Pistia: water lettuce
Nymphea: water lily

The verges and islets of the lagoon were elegantly embellished with flowering plants and shrubs; the laughing coots* with wings half spread were tripping over the little coves and hiding themselves in the tufts of grass; young broods of the painted summer teal,* skimming the still surface of the waters, and following the watchful parent unconscious of danger, were frequently surprised by the voracious* trout, and he in turn, as often by the subtle, greedy alligator. Behold him rushing forth from the flags and reeds. His enormous body swells. His plaited tail brandished* high, floats upon the lake. The waters like a cataract* descend from his opening jaws. Clouds of smoke issue from his dilated* nostrils.

The earth trembles with his thunder. When immediately from the opposite coast of the lagoon, emerges from the deep his rival champion. They suddenly dart upon each other. The boiling surface of the lake marks their rapid course, and a terrific conflict commences. They now sink to the bottom folded together in horrid wreaths. The water becomes thick and discoloured. Again they rise, their jaws clap together, re-echoing through the deep surrounding forests. Again they sink, when the contest ends at the muddy bottom of the lake, and the vanquished makes a hazardous escape, hiding himself in the muddy turbulent waters and sedge* on a distant shore. The proud victor exulting returns to the place of action. The shores and forests resound his dreadful roar, together with the triumphing shouts of the plaited trives* around, witnesses of the horrid combat.

laughing coots: black marsh fowl
teal: river ducks
voracious: all-devouring
brandished: waved menacingly
cataract: waterfall
dilated: enlarged
sedge: marsh plants
trives: i.e., groups of alligators

My apprehensions were highly alarmed after being a spectator of so dreadful a battle. It was obvious that every delay would but tend to increase my dangers and difficulties, as the sun was near setting, and the alligators gathered around my harbour from all quarters. From these considerations I concluded to be expeditious* in my trip to the lagoon, in order to take some fish. Not thinking it prudent to take my fusee* with me, lest I might lose it overboard in case of a battle, which I had every reason to dread before my return, I therefore furnished myself with a club for my defence, went on board, and penetrating the first line of those which surrounded my harbour, they gave way; but being pursued by several very large ones, I kept strictly on the watch, and paddled with all my might towards the entrance of the lagoon, hoping to be sheltered there from the multitude of my assailants; but ere I had half-

way reached the place, I was attacked on all sides, several endeavouring to overset the canoe.

expeditious: i.e., decided to be swift
fusee: firelock: i.e., gun

My situation now became precarious to the last degree. Two very large ones attacked me closely, at the same instant, rushing up with their heads and part of their bodies above the water, roaring terribly and belching floods of water over me. They struck their jaws together so close to my ears as almost to stun me, and I expected every moment to be dragged out of the boat and instantly devoured, but I applied my weapons so effectually about me, though at random, that I was so successful as to beat them off a little; when, finding that they designed* to renew the battle, I made for the shore, as the only means left me for my preservation, for, by keeping close to it, I should have my enemies on one side of me only, whereas I was before surrounded by them, and there was a probability, if pushed to the last extremity, of saving myself by jumping out of the canoe on shore, as it is easy to outwalk them on land, although comparatively as swift as lightning in the water. I found this last expedient* alone could fully answer my expectations, for as soon as I gained the shore they drew off and kept aloof. This was a happy relief, as my confidence was in some degree, recovered by it.

designed: purposed
last expedient: means of accomplishment (here, of escape)

On recollecting myself, I discovered that I had almost reached the entrance of the lagoon, and determined to venture in, if possible to take a few fish and then return to my harbour while daylight continued; for I could now, with caution and resolution, make my way with safety along shore. Indeed there was no other way to regain my camp without leaving my boat and making my retreat through the marshes and reeds, which, if I could even effect,* would have been in a manner throwing myself away, for then there would have been no hopes of ever recovering my bark and returning in safety to any settlements of men. I accordingly proceeded and made good my entrance into the lagoon, though not without opposition from the alligators, who formed a line across the entrance but did not pursue me into it; nor was I molested by any there, though there were some very large ones in a cove at the upper end. I soon caught more trout than I had present occasion for, and the air was too hot and sultry* to admit of* their being kept for many hours, even though salted or barbecued. I now prepared for my return to camp, which I succeeded in with but little trouble, by keeping close to the shore. Yet I was opposed upon re-entering the river out of the lagoon, and pursued near to my landing (though not closely attacked) particularly by an old daring one, about twelve feet in length, who kept close after me, and when I stepped on shore and turned about, in order to draw up my canoe, he rushed up near my feet and lay there for some time, looking me in the face, his head and shoulders out of water. I resolved he should pay for his temerity,* and having a heavy load in my fusee, I ran to my camp, and returning with my piece, found him with his foot on the gunwale* of the boat, in search of fish. On my coming up he withdrew sullenly and slowly into the water, but soon returned and placed himself in his former position, looking at me and seeming neither fearful or any way disturbed. I soon dispatched* him by lodging the contents of my gun in his head.

effect: bring to pass
sultry: sweltering
admit of: allow
temerity: boldness
gunwale: upper edge
dispatched: killed

[I] then proceeded to cleanse and prepare my fish for supper, and accordingly took them out of the boat, laid them down on the sand close to the water, and began to scale them, when, raising my head, I saw before me, through the clear water, the head and shoulders of a very large alligator, moving slowly towards me. I instantly stepped back, when, with a sweep of his tail, he brushed off several of my fish. It was certainly most providential that I looked up at that instant, as the monster would probably, in less than a minute, have seized and dragged me into the river. This incredible boldness of the animal disturbed me greatly, supposing there could now be no reasonable safety for me during the night but by keeping continually on the watch.

I therefore, as soon as I had prepared the fish, proceeded to secure myself and effects* in the best manner I could. In the first place, I hauled my bark upon the shore, almost clear out of the water, to prevent their oversetting or sinking her. After this every moveable was taken out and carried to my camp, which was but a few yards off. Then ranging some dry wood in such order as was the most convenient, [I] cleared the ground round about it, that there might be no impediment* in my way in case of an attack in the night either from the water or the land; for I discovered by this time that this small isthmus, from its remote situation and fruitfulness, was resorted to by bears and wolves. Having prepared myself in the best manner I could, I charged* my gun and proceeded to reconnoitre* my camp and the adjacent grounds; when I discovered that the peninsula and grove, at the distance of about two hundred yards from my encampment, on the land side, were invested* by a cypress swamp, covered with water, which below was joined to the shore of the little lake and above to the marshes surrounding the lagoon, so that I was confined to an islet exceedingly circumscribed.* I found there was no other retreat for me, in case of an attack, but by either ascending one of the large oaks or pushing off with my boat.

effects: belongings
impediment: obstacle
charged: loaded
reconnoitre: examine
invested: surrounded, so as to prevent escape
circumscribed: limited

It was by this time dusk, and the alligators had nearly ceased their roar, when I was again alarmed by a tumultuous noise that seemed to be in my harbour, and therefore engaged my immediate attention. Returning to my camp I found it undisturbed, and then continued on to the extreme point of the promontory, where I saw a scene, new and surprising, which at first threw my senses into such a tumult that it was some time before I could comprehend what was the matter. However, I soon accounted for the prodigious assemblage* of crocodiles at this place, which exceeded every thing of the kind I had ever heard of.

assemblage: vast gathering

How shall I express myself so as to convey an adequate idea of it to the reader and at the same time avoid raising suspicions of my want of veracity.* Should I say, that the river (in this place) from shore to shore, and perhaps near half a mile above and below me, appeared to be one solid bank of fish, of various kinds, pushing through this narrow pass of St. Juans into the little lake, on their return down the river, and that the alligators were in such incredible numbers, and so close together from shore to shore, that it would have been easy to have walked across on their heads had the animals been harmless. What expressions can sufficiently declare the shocking scene that for some minutes continued, whilst this mighty army of fish were forcing the pass? During this attempt, thousands–I may say hundreds of thousands–of them were caught and swallowed by the devouring alligators. I have seen an alligator take up out of the water several great fish at a time and just squeeze them betwixt his jaws, while the tails of the great trout flapped about his eyes and lips, ere he had swallowed them. The horrid noise of their closing jaws, their plunging amist the broken banks of fish, and rising with their prey some feet upright above the water, the floods of water and blood rushing out of their mouths and the clouds of vapour issuing from their wide nostrils, were truly frightful. This scene continued at intervals during the night as the fish came to the pass. After this sight, shocking and tremendous as it was, I found myself somewhat easier and more reconciled to my situation, being convinced that their extraordinary assemblage here was owing to this annual feast of fish, and that they were so well employed in their own element that I had little occasion to fear their paying me a visit.

veracity: truthfulness

For Thought and Discussion

1. Bartram was a painter as well as a writer. How does the selection from *Travels* demonstrate his eye for artistic detail? Support your answer by citing specific details from the work.

2. Does Bartram in the excerpt you read draw any parallels between his observations of nature and man's spiritual life? Contrast his content with Sewall's in this regard.

3. Does the narrator of *Travels,* who is for the most part scientifically accurate, remain credible throughout the excerpt? If not, at what point in the narrative does his credibility come into question?

4. Would you characterize Bartram's style as plain or ornate? In formulating your answer, consider both sentence style and vocabulary. For what audience is such a style appropriate?

Philip Freneau   1752-1832

Philip Freneau has been called our first truly American poet. Prior to Freneau our notable poets had been immigrants, like Anne Bradstreet and Edward Taylor. In neither theme nor style were they distinctively American. Freneau, however, was American in both.

Freneau's life was largely devoted to the service of political ideals. Born into a wealthy French Huguenot family in New York, Freneau received his education at the College of New Jersey (now Princeton). Here he championed the new political ideas becoming popular in the decade before the Revolutionary War and associated with other students known for their vocal support of American independence. After his graduation in 1771, he tried various occupations, including teaching and a two-year stint in the West Indies as secretary to a wealthy planter. Upon returning to New Jersey in 1778, he enlisted in the New Jersey militia, serving from 1778 to 1780. Then, after shipping aboard an American blockade runner, he was captured by the British and confined in New York Harbor for nearly two months on prison ships so foul that he barely escaped with his life.

After this point Freneau alternated between editorial and seafaring jobs, returning to work in the coastal trade during the intervals when his radically democratic political views cost him an editorial position. He continued writing both poetry and political essays, often combining his poetics and his politics. Irritated by Freneau's outspoken views and scathing personal attacks, George Washington called him ''that rascal Freneau.'' In his last years, experiencing financial disaster and loss of popularity, Freneau made increasingly frequent attempts to drown his unhappiness in liquor. In 1832, when eighty years old, the poet died during a snowstorm while trying to find his way home at night from a tavern.

In content Freneau's poetry reflects the issues of his day. He wrote biting satire against the British and, in poems like ''To the Memory of the Brave Americans,'' patriotic praise of his countrymen who fought in the Revolutionary War. In poems like ''On the Universality and Other Attributes of the God of Nature,'' he espoused the rising Deistic, even Pantheistic, ideas. His poetry also reflected the shift from eighteenth-century neoclassical to nineteenth-century romantic style. By combining neoclassical ideals of regularity and restraint with romantic ideals of innovation and freedom, Freneau's poetry bridged the conflicting poetic attitudes of the two centuries and helped make possible the works of such poets as William Cullen Bryant and Edgar Allan Poe. Interestingly, "The Wild Honey Suckle" expresses attitudes that foreshadow the flowering of English Romanticism by a dozen years.

While Freneau's poetry marks a major poetic shift, it also signals a significant change in religious attitude. A comparison of Freneau's poems to those of the Puritans reveals the extent to which the American mind had changed in one hundred and fifty years. Freneau's view of the world is man-centered, for he replaces the providential, personal relationship of God with mankind with an impersonal and rationalistic divine benevolence.

To the Memory of the Brave Americans Under General Greene, in South Carolina, Who Fell in the Action of September 8, 1781

In the battle of Eutaw Springs, South Carolina, a party of American soldiers pursued a retreating detachment of British troops. Suddenly the British soldiers halted their retreat and made a stand against the colonials. The surprise tactic routed the Americans and turned what seemed glorious victory into stunning defeat. The British, however, lost enough troops in this engagement that the redcoats retreated to the coast, never again posing much of a threat to the Carolinas.

In his **elegy** *on the war dead, Freneau attempts to adapt the conventions of the classical elegy to native American subject matter. The stanzas and meter are regular; the diction is artificially poetic in the eighteenth-century manner. The use of shepherds and spears (ll. 12, 20) to represent the American soldier does seem out of keeping with the realities of the Revolutionary battlefield. Still, the poem shows artistic poise and achieves genuine elevation of feeling.*

At Eutaw Springs the valiant died;
    Their limbs with dust are covered o'er—
Weep on, ye springs, your tearful tide;
    How many heroes are no more!

If in this wreck of ruin they   5
    Can yet be thought to claim a tear,
O smite your gentle breast, and say
    The friends of freedom slumber here!

Thou, who shalt trace this bloody plain,
    If goodness rules thy generous breast,   10
Sigh for the wasted rural reign;
    Sigh for the shepherds, sunk to rest!

Stranger, their humble graves adorn;
    You too may fall, and ask a tear;
'Tis not the beauty of the morn   15
    That proves the evening shall be clear.

They saw their injured country's woe;
    The flaming town, the wasted field;
Then rushed to meet the insulting* foe;   *insulting:* arrogantly
    They took the spear—but left the shield.   20   behaving

Led by thy conquering genius, Greene,
    The Britons they compelled to fly;
None distant viewed the fatal plain,
    None grieved, in such a cause to die—

But, like the Parthian,* famed of old,   25   *Parthian:* in retreat the
    Who, flying, still* their arrows threw,   Parthian cavalry shot
These routed Briton's full as bold,   at their enemies
    Retreated, and retreating slew.   *still:* continually

Now rest in peace, our patriot band;
    Though far from nature's limits thrown,   30
We trust they find a happier land,
    A brighter sunshine of their own.

On the Universality and Other Attributes of the God of Nature

This poem praises the Deists' God. The relationship between God and man is characteristically impersonal. It is instructive to contrast its portrait of God with Edward Taylor's in "The Preface."

All that we see, about, abroad,
What is it all, but nature's God?
In meaner works discover'd here
No less than in the starry sphere.

In seas, on earth, this God is seen;   5
All that exist, upon him lean;
He lives in all, and never stray'd
A moment from the works he made:

His system fix'd on general laws
Bespeaks a wise creating cause;   10
Impartially he rules mankind
And all that on this globe we find.

Unchanged in all that seems to change,
Unbounded space is his great range;

To open vast purpose always true,   15
No time, with him, is old or new.

In all the attributes divine
Unlimited perfectings shine;
In these enwrapt, in these complete,
All virtues in that centre meet.   20

This power who doth all powers transcend,
To all intelligence a friend,
Exists, the greatest and the best
Throughout all worlds, to make them blest.

All that he did he first approved,   25
He all things into *being* loved;
O'er all he made he still presides,
For them in life, or death provides.

On a Honey Bee

Drinking from a Glass of Wine, and Drowned Therein

*The literary technique known as **burlesque** produces humor either by elevating a trivial subject or by deflating an important one. Which method appears in this **apostrophe** to the bee? Notice the **mock-heroic** undercutting by anticlimactic sequence in lines 7-8 and 9-10.*

Thou, born to sip the lake or spring,
Or quaff* the waters of the stream,
Why hither come on vagrant* wing?–
Does Bacchus* tempting seem–
Did he, for you, this glass prepare?–   5
Will I admit you to a share?

Did storms harass or foes perplex,
Did wasps or king-birds bring dismay–
Did wars distress, or labours vex,
Or did you miss your way?–   10
A better seat you could not take
Than on the margin of this lake.

Welcome!–I hail you to my glass:
All welcome, here, you find;
Here, let the cloud of trouble pass,   15
Here, be all care resigned.–
This fluid never fails to please,
And drown the griefs of men or bees.

What forced you here, we cannot know,
And you can scarcely tell–   20
But cheery we would have you go
And bid a fond farewell:
On lighter wings we bid you fly,
Your dart will now all foes defy.

Yet take not, oh! too deep a drink,   25
And in this ocean die;
Here bigger bees than you might sink,
Even bees full six feet high.
Like Pharaoh,* then, you would be said
To perish in a sea of red.   30

Do as you please, your will is mine;
Enjoy it without fear–
And your grave will be this glass of wine,
Your epitaph–a tear–
Go, take your seat in Charon's* boat,   35
We'll tell the hive, you died afloat.

quaff: drink heartily

vagrant: roving

Bacchus: Greek god of wine and revelry

Like Pharaoh: Exodus 14:5-28

Charon's: in Greek mythology, the ferryman who carried the dead across the river of death to Hades

The Wild Honey Suckle

Freneau uses a wildflower to teach the fleeting nature of life. Written in 1786,
this poem foreshadows the romantic use of Nature as a moral teacher.

Fair flower, that dost so comely grow,
Hid in this silent, dull retreat,
Untouched thy honeyed blossoms blow,
Unseen thy little branches greet:
    No roving foot shall crush thee here,   5
    No busy hand provoke a tear.

By Nature's self in white arrayed,
She bade thee shun the vulgar* eye,   *vulgar:* common
And planted here the guardian shade,
And sent soft waters murmuring by;   10
    Thus quietly thy summer goes,
    Thy days declining to repose.

Smit with those charms, that must decay,
I grieve to see your future doom;
They died–nor were those flowers more gay, 15
The flowers that did in Eden bloom;
    Unpitying frost, and Autumn's power
    Shall leave no vestige* of this flower.

vestige: trace

From morning suns and evening dews
At first thy little being came: 20
If nothing once, you nothing lose,
For when you die you are the same;
    The space between, is but an hour,
    The frail duration of a flower.

For Thought and Discussion

1. During their skirmish with Cornwallis's British troops at Eutaw Springs, the colonists under General Nathanael Greene suffered 700 casualties in a single day. What effect does this historical detail have on your understanding and appreciation of Freneau's poem?

2. In your opinion, is Freneau's choice of the pastoral mode for "To the Memory of the Brave Americans" appropriate? Why or why not?

3. In his description of God's orderly creation in "On the Universality and Other Attributes of the God of Nature," what characteristics of the Creator does Freneau present? Does Freneau suggest that this Creator's relationship to man is different from His relationship to the other works of His creation?

4. Analyze Freneau's allusions in "On the Universality and Other Attributes of the God of Nature." Are they primarily Scriptural, literary, or historical? Does he employ more or fewer in this context than in "To the Memory of the Brave Americans"?

5. For what reason do you suppose the form of both "On a Honey Bee" and "The Wild Honey Suckle" is the apostrophe, or direct address? What effect does Freneau gain by employing this form for his nature poetry? What do these two pieces have in common thematically? How do they differ?

Phillis Wheatley
c. 1753-1784

Phillis Wheatley was brought to Boston as a slave from Africa when she was only a child. John Wheatley, a tailor, purchased her as a servant for his wife, who provided an excellent education for the girl, emphasizing history and literature. Phillis began to write poetry as a teen-ager and, encouraged by the Wheatleys, published her first piece in 1770. She then spent several years in England, where she was admired for her learning and wit and where she published her first volume of poetry, *Poems on Various Subjects, Religious and Moral, by Phillis Wheatley, Negro Servant to Mr. John Wheatley of Boston.* After her return to America, Phillis became a free woman in 1778. She married another freed slave, John Peters, with whom she lived in poverty until her death in 1784. Fifty years after Wheatley's death her memoirs were published, and three decades later, in 1864, a volume of her letters appeared.

Wheatley's poetry has received much praise, for she was a genuinely gifted writer. The following selections from her first volume of poetry well illustrate the religious and aesthetic integrity of her poetry.

To the University of Cambridge

While an intrinsic ardor prompts to write,
The muses* promise to assist my pen:
'Twas not long since I left my native shore
The land of errors, and *Egyptian* gloom:
Father of mercy, 'twas thy gracious hand   5
Brought me in safety from those dark abodes.

    Students, to you 'tis giv'n to scan the heights
Above, to traverse the ethereal space,
And mark the systems of revolving worlds.
Still more, ye sons of science ye receive   10
The blissful news by messengers from heav'n,
How *Jesus'* blood for your redemption flows.
See him with hands out-stretcht upon the cross;

Immense compassion in his bosom glows;
He hears revilers, nor resents their scorn: 15
What matchless mercy in the Son of God!
When the whole human race by sin had fall'n,
He deign'd* to die that they might rise again,
And share with him in the sublimest skies,
Life without death, and glory without end.   20

    Improve your privileges while they stay,
Ye pupils, and each hour redeem, that bears
Or* good or bad report of you to heav'n.
Let sin, that baneful* evil to the soul,
By you be shunn'd, nor once remit your guard;   25
Suppress the deadly serpent in its egg.
Ye blooming plants of human race divine,
An *Ethiop** tells you 'tis your greatest foe;
Its transient sweetness turns to endless pain,
And in immense perdition* sinks the soul.   30

muses: goddesses of poetry and learning

deign'd: consented to stoop to

Or: either
baneful: destructive

Ethiop: a black-skinned person

perdition: damnation

On Being Brought from Africa to America

'Twas mercy brought me from my *Pagan* land,
Taught my benighted soul to understand
That there's a God, that there's a *Saviour* too:
Once I redemption neither sought nor knew.
Some view our sable race with scornful eye,   5
"Their colour is a diabolic dye."
Remember, *Christians, Negroes,* black as *Cain,*
May be refin'd, and join th' angelic train.

For Thought and Discussion
1. In "To the University of Cambridge" what is the "native shore" to which Wheatley alludes in lines 4-6? Whom does Wheatley address directly in line 5? In what way has God been gracious to her?
2. Whom does the poet address in the second stanza? At what point does the poem become explicitly Christian in theme? Does this turn in the poem surprise you? Why or why not?
3. What is the predominant poetic meter in the piece? In what line does Wheatley employ allusion?
4. What, according to Wheatley, is the students' "greatest foe"? Although the title of the poem, which actually refers to Harvard College or Cambridge, Massachusetts, localizes it, in what sense is its theme applicable to all students?
5. Discuss Wheatley's use of figurative language in "On Being Brought from Africa to America." In what sense could the phrases "benighted soul," "our sable race," and "black as Cain" refer to the unregenerate condition of all men?

PART TWO

American Romanticism

An Era of Optimism

"In the four corners of the globe, who reads an American book?" scoffed Sydney Smith in Great Britain's prestigious *Edinburgh Review* in 1820. From across the Atlantic came only an embarrassed silence. But the United States did not remain silent for long. Just months before Smith's contemptuous question, an American writer named Washington Irving began publishing a series of essays and tales called *The Sketch Book*. This work, published in book form in 1820, became the first of many American works widely read and respected on both sides of the Atlantic.

Irving's *Sketch Book* popularized in the United States the new literary spirit of romanticism. This spirit dominated American literature from 1820 to 1865, an era known as American Romanticism. The movement crested in 1850-55 with the "American Renaissance," a five-year burst of creative energy producing influential works by all but one of the period's major writers: Ralph Waldo Emerson, Henry David Thoreau, Nathaniel Hawthorne, Herman Melville, and Walt Whitman. (Edgar Allan Poe had died in 1849.) Largely through the efforts of these men, American literature matured and the United States won literary independence from Great Britain.

NATIONAL TENSIONS

Conditions Fueling National Optimism

Underlying the literary romanticism of this period—in fact, helping to fuel it—was a national mood of optimism, a spirit of confidence in the economy, political system, and citizenry of the nation. As the United States surged to the economic forefront among the nations of the world, its population rapidly expanded, fed by waves of European immigrants (five million from 1815 to 1860). As these immigrants spread across the country, they helped to cultivate the soil, to man the growing industrial centers of the North, and to push the frontier farther westward. Technological advances during this era brought the completion of the Erie Canal; the opening of the first railroad; the invention of the reaping machine, the revolver, and the steel plow; the discovery of the process for vulcanizing rubber; the instituting of the first telegraph line; and the drilling of the first oil well. Writers and speakers throughout the country celebrated the splendors of the rapidly expanding nation, especially its twin offers of economic prosperity and political freedom. In short, America's possibilities seemed unlimited.

Issues Undermining National Optimism

Sectionalism Since colonial days there had been marked differences between the nation's regions, particularly the North and South. These economic, political, social, and historical differences provided a rich diversity of American culture. Once the colonies had been bound together into a constitutional union of states, however, this regional diversity began to produce national division. Struggles between the two sections over economic security, slavery expansion, and political leadership increased, requiring the compromises of 1820, 1833, and 1850. These compromises, however, provided only a temporary solution. The issues of slavery and political independence were emotionally charged. Fear increased following the terrorist acts of the radical abolitionist John Brown. Such acts fueled the fiery arguments of extremists in both the North and South and finally tore the union apart by the spring of 1861.

The resulting war, called the Civil War in the North and the War Between the States in the South, exacted a terrible price on the country. The Union victory that followed four years of warfare left huge sections of the South devastated, cost the country five billion dollars, and took the lives of over 600,000 men. Though the war of brothers settled the constitutional question of secession and the moral question of slavery, it also left grim wounds of bitterness and hatred that would take years to heal.

Cultural provincialism Another force during the antebellum period that relates more to American literature than to politics was the issue of provincialism. Was American writing to be universal, comparable to the best European works? Or was it to be narrow and unsophisticated, unworthy of comparison to Europe's best? While other nations accepted the United States as their commercial and military equal, its literature seemed to many–even Americans–culturally inferior, especially to England's. Two factors especially hindered the growth and improvement of American writing. One was the absence of an international copyright law. Because American publishers frequently pirated English works, particularly popular works or those written by well-known authors, American writers received very little critical or financial encouragement to develop their talent. The other factor retarding the development of American literature was the limited perspective and expectation of many American readers. Either they extravagantly praised whatever an American writer produced, whether the work had value or not, or they preferred only English works, not willing to admit the value of any American work.

Out of this cultural uncertainty developed two schools of thought on the issue of a national literature. One school, holding that American writing had to be *strikingly* American, called for a literature as broad as the prairie, as shaggy as the buffalo, as thunderous as Niagara, and as powerful as the Mississippi. The result was oftentimes bizarre. In the post-Revolutionary War period, for example, writers produced long poetic treatments of the country's past or imagined future greatness. Such literature led to what Edgar Allan Poe criticized as the "epic mania."

The opposing school of thought believed that no matter what other elements a writer incorporated into his work, he needed to strive for universality in theme and form. Fortunately for American letters, this second view prevailed, helped by the achievement of the major romantic writers. Nathaniel Hawthorne in *The Scarlet Letter*, worked out his resolution of the universal problem of guilt in terms of American Puritan values. Herman Melville, in *Moby Dick*, tackled the universal problem of evil by using the American whaling industry as his setting and vehicle. Edgar Allan Poe unflinchingly applied universal, not provincial, standards of literary criticism to his own works and those of his contemporaries. As a result, by 1865 American literature stood before a worldwide audience with impressive credentials.

LITERARY ROMANTICISM

Romantic Emphases

Romanticism was a revolt against the literary values of the previous age. This revolt, it is true, was also part of a larger nineteenth-century revolt directed against all traditional values. The romantic revolt has continued to affect American society, particularly its estimation of man's relationship to his fellow men and to God. As a purely literary term, however, *romantic* refers to the cluster of emphases that dominated American writing from 1820 to 1865. Although the term came to mean different things to different people (a study published in 1948 found 11,396 definitions for romanticism), we can distinguish four cornerstones of this second of the four major American literary movements.

Individualism First, romantic individualism regarded man as an individual superior to man in the mass. In the eighteenth century, writers readily accepted the point of view of society or the mass of men over that of the individual because of their faith in universal truth and majority opinion. The frontier tradition in America, which proved the individual man's ability to triumph over circumstances, no doubt helped popularize romantic belief in the individual. Jacksonian democracy, standing on the platform that all men possessed the necessary credentials for public office, brought political power to the common man. The abolitionists' call for the destruction of slavery was, of course, based on the belief in the sanctity of the individual. This emphasis on individualism also influenced religious thought. During the reign of romanticism, cults like Mormonism and Seventh-Day Adventism emerged. In such cults, the teaching of an individual is elevated over the truth of the revealed Word of God.

This doctrine of individualism also contributed to the optimistic but naive notion that man is not a fallen creature, who in sinning has lost the ability to realize his potential. The key Puritan doctrine of total depravity, a somber truth from the Bible, did not appeal to the romantic. He believed, instead, that man could fulfill his potential without supernatural regeneration. The poet Walt Whitman extended this corollary of individualism so far that he made man his god. Because the romantics found man basically good, they were forced to attribute the source of evil to something other than man's heart. Consequently, they imputed the evil they saw around them to the influence of corrupt institutions, like slavery. They believed that the way to improve man is to remove the corrupting influences. Many romantic writers therefore became reformers, attempting to expose and eliminate evil institutions in order to bring man to a state of moral and spiritual health. The Puritan would have recognized that in this rejection of God's truth, the romantics were attacking mere symptoms of the disease (the outward act), not the true cause of that sin (the corrupt, degenerate heart). Thus, in their doctrine of the supremacy of the individual, the romantics were basically in rebellion against God's view of man.

Imagination Second, romantics considered the Imagination to be of primary importance in literary creation. Eighteenth-century writers, believing Reason to be the most important human faculty in the creative process, were loyal to literary tradition and established literary forms. Romantic writers, however, sought to experiment and to follow their own experience and ideas. They often practiced the principle of organicism, or organic form: as a seed determines the eventual shape of the plant, so an idea, romantic writers affirmed, had within it an inherent structure. As a result, literary forms used by older writers seemed obsolete. Under the influence of this doctrine of the Imagination, romantic works differed in both subject matter and form from those of the preceding age.

In the creative process Reason was displaced by Emotion. In fact, feeling was thought superior to rationality as a mode of perceiving and experiencing reality. As the romantic turned away from standards existing outside himself (the seventeenth century had derived them from the Bible; the eighteenth had turned to reason and the opinion of the majority), he came to rely by necessity on his intuition. His standards for truth thus became internal and subjective. Reacting against the Age of Reason, the romantic writer produced a literature that to later critics seemed unrealistic and philosophically shallow because his optimistic view of life seemed only a figment of his imagination.

Nature Third, Nature provided romantics both the means of knowing truth and the actual subject matter of their literature. Although Puritan writers had accepted Nature as a means of revealing God, they had regarded it as much less important than the written Word of God. Eighteenth-century writers had seen Nature as a social model, a picture of the harmonious order that should permeate human society. Romantic writers gave to Nature a much higher position. They claimed that God reveals Himself solely through Nature; therefore, Nature is the moral teacher for men. Moreover, if man communes with the universal spirit through Nature, he can come to understand divine truth and divine ways. Viewed as a remnant of the Edenic paradise, Nature was considered untouched by Adam's fall and thus free from the pollution of society's evil. It therefore offered a place of retreat for men, particularly the artist. Some romantics became virtual pantheists in their worship of Nature as God.

The new role of Nature as romantic subject matter is evident not only in the lavish, picturesque landscapes of Washington Irving and James Fenimore Cooper but also in the less idyllic literary treatment. Nathaniel Hawthorne and Herman Melville, for instance, used Nature to symbolize evil, malignant forces that threaten man's moral and physical destruction.

The distant The fourth cornerstone of the romantic movement was the writer's use of distant settings, both in space and time. Irving's attraction to the mysterious haunts of Europe, Melville's idealization of the South Sea Islands in his early fiction, and Poe's exotic scenes of crime and death brought distant or indefinite settings into prominence. Distancing in time, however, was even more evident. Of all the romantics, Hawthorne showed probably the greatest dependence on the distant, for he set most of his work in the past. In fact, Hawthorne's work was most successful when he turned to the seventeenth and early eighteenth centuries for his material, using the American past to comment on attitudes of his own day. Irving was our first writer to create a legendary past for America. Cooper created the mythological hero Deerslayer (Natty Bumppo) by patterning him after American frontiersmen and explorers and setting him in the untouched wilderness of the eighteenth century.

Even Emerson and Thoreau, who wished to discard the past, were attracted to the distant–the distant future. They envisioned both man and society someday attaining perfection. Their naive vision reflects the nineteenth century's strong attraction to utopias, or perfect worlds. Some writers saw the perfect world in the future, coming as the culmination of man's upward climb to self-realization. Others saw utopia in the past as an age of innocence, free of social complexity and contamination.

Genre Development

Short story As romanticism brought respectability to American letters, American writers made important contributions to two genres: the short story and the novel. Although Washington Irving's major literary form was the sketch, not fiction, his best stories brought to the genre two fictional advancements of special worth: distinctively American settings and characters. Under the hand of Edgar Allan Poe, the short story started taking clearer shape, for Poe contributed the principles of brevity (the work must be short enough to be read in one sitting) and unity (all elements of a story must contribute to a single emotional effect). Nathaniel Hawthorne brought to the short story intense moral and psychological exploration of characters, often by the means of allegory, turning his fiction into a sophisticated evaluation of man and society.

Novel The novel also became a serious art form in the United States during this period. The English novel had originated in the first half of the eighteenth century with the works of Daniel Defoe (1660-1731), Samuel Richardson (1689-1761), and Henry Fielding (1707-54). The first American novels began appearing just after the Revolutionary War, but except for those of Charles Brockden Brown (1771-1810), they tended merely to imitate what was popular in England, and their American elements were little more than incidental. James Fenimore Cooper's Leatherstocking Tales brought a larger-than-life dimension to the American hero. Although often praised more for what he attempted than for what he achieved, Cooper brought the novel to new prominence in American literary history. It remained for Nathaniel Hawthorne and Herman Melville to develop the novel to its full artistic potential.

Literary Groups

Knickerbockers Aided by the country's urban growth, groups of writers gathered in the literary capitals of the East. Most of the major writers were loosely associated with one of three literary circles, two of which today appear relatively minor. The writers centered in New York City were called Knickerbockers after Diedrich Knickerbocker, the fictional historian of Washington Irving's comic *History of New York* and the storyteller of "Rip Van Winkle" and "The Legend of Sleepy Hollow." Included among the so-called Knickerbockers were two other major figures with close ties to New York City: the novelist James Fenimore Cooper and the poet-critic-journalist William Cullen Bryant.

New England School The other relatively minor cluster of writers–although the most influential and popular of the nineteenth century–was the Boston-centered New England School. This group included Henry Wadsworth Longfellow, Oliver

Wendell Holmes, John Greenleaf Whittier, and James Russell Lowell. These poets, also called the "Schoolroom Poets" because their works were extensively taught in schools until well into the twentieth century, popularized for the American public many of the common romantic attitudes and themes.

Transcendental optimists Transcendentalism–defined as "part religion, part philosophy, part revolt against doctrine, part adoration of nature, part Puritan and part Oriental"–spawned some of the most radical ideas of the nineteenth century. The most important writers within American Romanticism–Emerson, Thoreau, Whitman, Poe, Hawthorne, and Melville–were all strongly influenced by transcendentalism. Because not all of this group's six writers responded to the movement in the same way, we can divide them into two factions: three optimists, who supported the movement's beliefs; and three pessimists, who attacked its key tenets. Ralph Waldo Emerson, Henry David Thoreau, and their poetic descendant Walt Whitman were the optimists. The works of these men exemplified the core tenets of transcendentalism and developed ideas still evident in today's literature.

Transcendental pessimists Edgar Allan Poe, Nathaniel Hawthorne, and Herman Melville composed the second group. These writers reacted negatively to many of the beliefs of the optimists. As they evaluated transcendentalism, they discovered that artistically, morally, and philosophically it did not satisfactorily explain the true nature of man and his world. Since the response to transcendental values is the central thrust of American Romanticism, we will examine transcendentalism in detail as we study the works of its chief spokesman, Ralph Waldo Emerson, and of its chief critic, Nathaniel Hawthorne.

RELIGIOUS BACKGROUND

Rebellion Against Orthodoxy

Since transcendentalism originated largely as a religious reaction to the pure rationalism of the Unitarians, we cannot ignore the role of religion in the first half of the nineteenth century. One result of the rebellion against orthodoxy during the eighteenth century had been the creation of a religion founded on reason rather than on faith or revelation. Deism, with numerous religious overtones, was the prevailing eighteenth-century philosophy; Unitarianism was its religious outgrowth and counterpart. Unitarianism's effect upon New England was both rapid and thorough. In 1785 the first New England church became openly Unitarian. By 1815, only three decades later, fourteen of the sixteen Boston Congregational churches founded before the Revolutionary War were also openly Unitarian. These churches astonishingly had been the churches of the Puritans. The extent of the religious decline in America is evident in the five central concepts of Unitarianism. It taught (1) the fatherhood of God, (2) the brotherhood of man, (3) the leadership of Jesus, (4) salvation by character, and (5) the inevitable progress of mankind. Since Unitarians threw out the doctrine of Biblical inspiration and inerrancy, they denied the facts of salvation and damnation, saw sin as a mere matter of morality rather than as an offense against God, and stressed Jesus' role as a great teacher rather than as the divine Son of God.

But even to many of its followers, this movement soon seemed cold and dead. Ralph Waldo Emerson, training for the Unitarian ministry, broke with the movement in 1832 seemingly over the issue of the Lord's Supper. He turned to transcendentalism, but his direction was no less heretical than that in which he had been going before. Whereas Unitarianism emphasized the rational, transcendentalism emphasized the subjective and emotional. The effect of both was to create God in man's image. The transcendental God was the great Soul of the universe pervading all its parts, even the various world religions. Both Unitarianism and transcendentalism deceived many, especially among the influential in education and politics.

Revival Within Orthodoxy

Fortunately these heretical movements did not completely sweep aside the orthodox position. The revival movements of the eighteenth century helped perpetuate belief in salvation through faith in Christ's atonement and in the Word of God as the supreme guide for mankind. In the period from 1800 to 1840, known as the Second Great Awakening, waves of revival surged through various sections of the country and through various denominations. In 1799 the first camp meeting had been held on the banks of the Red River in Kentucky. This form of evangelism, popular for much of the nineteenth century, swept across not only the western areas of Ohio, Pennsylvania, Kentucky, and Tennessee, but also the Southwest. In the large cities of the East, revival came through the preaching of evangelist Charles Grandison Finney (1792-1875). From the early 1840s to 1857, however, religious declension settled over the United States. Then, in response, came the last of our nationwide revivals.

The Great Revival of 1857 grew out of prayer meetings conducted by laymen in the large urban centers of the country, especially New York City. Some revival historians suggest that this movement, which deeply stirred the North and Midwest, was providentially preparing these sections to undergo the rigors of the Civil War.

Although revival did not touch the South at this time, it did come to the Confederacy during the war. Beginning in late 1861 among soldiers stationed near Richmond, Virginia, this revival rapidly spread over all the Confederate forces, bringing the conversion of some 15,000 soldiers.

Advent of Darwinism

Between these last two surges of revival in the late 1850s and early 1860s, an event occurred that brought more attacks against the Word of God than did any other source. That event was the publishing in 1859 of Charles Darwin's *Origin of Species,* the forerunner of evolution's assault on the Bible. That the evolutionary hypothesis profoundly affected American thought appears in the cynicism of numerous later American writers.

"Young Goodman Brown," one of Nathaniel Hawthorne's best short stories, embodies allegorically the changed American attitudes during the nineteenth century. In this tale Brown, the central character, takes a mysterious journey into the dark New England forest. As this recently married young Puritan makes his way at night along the path, he encounters a series of strange experiences. His adventures climax with his vision of a witches' sabbath, where Brown thinks he sees his new bride, named Faith, being taken into the communion of the witches. As he cries out to her to "look up to heaven, and resist the wicked one," the whole scene instantly vanishes, leaving him alone in the darkness. When he returns to his village the next morning, he is a changed man. He no longer trusts the villagers or the Puritan minister, supposing them all to be hypocrites. He shrinks from his wife, believing her to be corrupt. He suspects only the worst of himself and others. Until his dying day, his gloom is unrelieved by any hope or confidence in man or God.

Like Hawthorne's young goodman Brown, nineteenth-century romanticism placed its faith in men. Once its optimistic faith was betrayed, romanticism had lost its foundation. As writers made romanticism their religion, they were shattered by the realization that the goodness of man was a mere phantom. It is no wonder that following the Civil War most American writers reevaluated their beliefs. Tragically, their reevaluation only worsened their confusion. For refusing to recognize God and His claims on them, they turned instead to the evolutionary view of man.

The crucial turning point in our national spirit came thus during American Romanticism. Since then American attitudes have differed radically from those dominant in the earlier centuries of American history. Despite occasional times of revival, the general drift has been further and further from the Biblical principles that provided the foundation for our country. It is no accident therefore that Christians appear more and more out of step with their age. As we turn now to the literature of the romantic writers, we will better understand why.

4 *Knickerbockers*

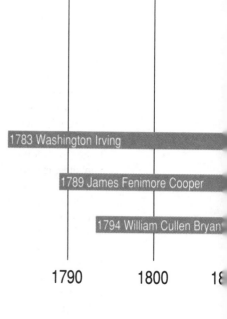

1783 Washington Irving

1789 James Fenimore Cooper

1794 William Cullen Bryan

1790   1800   18

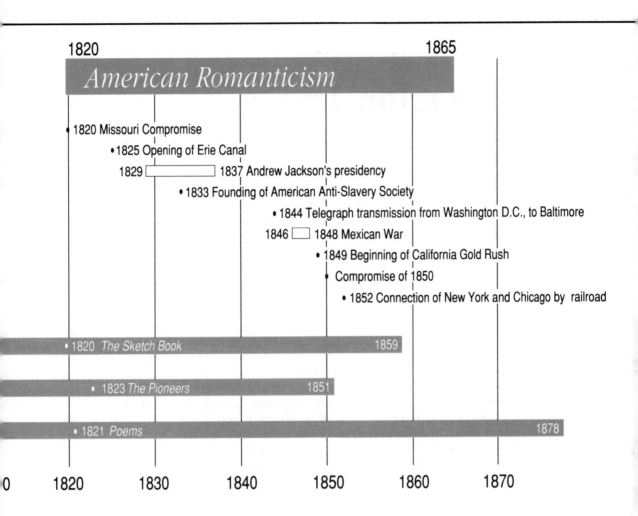

1820   1865

American Romanticism

• 1820 Missouri Compromise

   • 1825 Opening of Erie Canal

  1829 ☐ 1837 Andrew Jackson's presidency

     • 1833 Founding of American Anti-Slavery Society

       • 1844 Telegraph transmission from Washington D.C., to Baltimore

    1846 ☐ 1848 Mexican War

     • 1849 Beginning of California Gold Rush

     • Compromise of 1850

      • 1852 Connection of New York and Chicago by railroad

• 1820 *The Sketch Book*   1859

  • 1823 *The Pioneers*   1851

  • 1821 *Poems*   1878

0   1820   1830   1840   1850   1860   1870

Washington Irving
1783-1859

The work of Washington Irving is our passport into American Romanticism. His collection of essays and tales called *The Sketch Book* made him the first American writer to achieve international fame. A deliberate literary craftsman who sought to entertain his readers, he was also our first professional man of letters.

Although trained as a lawyer and destined to work, reluctantly, in his family's mercantile firm, Irving early revealed literary promise. In the first phase of his career (1783-1815), while cultivating the appearance of a dashing, fashionable young man about town, he wrote a series of newspaper essays (1802-3) and published the *Salmagundi* papers (1807-8). In 1809 he published his first major work, *A History of New York,* supposedly written by an old, eccentric historian named Diedrich Knickerbocker. Comically treating the New York Dutch and their tradition, this mock history pleased many but vexed the stately Dutch families proud of their heritage. Irving's satire undercut the pretensions of these families in particular and of historians in general. It also marked out Irving's future course, for the work, designed solely for entertainment, taught no serious moral lessons. Also in 1809 came the death of his fiancée, Matilda Hoffman. Her death probably accounted for the melancholic cast over much of the rest of his life and work.

In 1815 the scene of Irving's career shifted to Europe. He sailed for England to take charge of the Liverpool branch of the family importing business. When the firm went bankrupt in 1818, he decided to throw himself totally into a literary career. As he traveled throughout England, France, Switzerland, Germany, and Spain, he found stimulation for his imagination. His writing from this period (1815-32) reflects his strong attraction to European materials. He wrote sketchbooks on various European countries as well as a study of Columbus that remained the standard of biography for a hundred years. He also wrote two popular American stories: "Rip Van Winkle" and "The Legend of Sleepy Hollow."

In 1832 Irving returned to the United States, bringing with him a medal from the English Royal Society of Literature, an honorary degree from Oxford, and a reputation well established both here and abroad. In this final phase of his career (1832-59), as dean of American letters, he encouraged other writers and devoted himself to history and biography. He published biographies of Oliver Goldsmith (1840) and of George

Washington (1855-59), for whom he had been named. He traveled west, writing of the picturesque prairie and of Astoria, the fur empire founded by John Jacob Astor. When his fellow New Yorkers attempted to nominate him for the office of the mayor of New York City, Irving declined the honor. After serving in Spain as diplomatic attaché (1842-46), he moved to Sunnyside, his home near Tarrytown, New York. Here he continued to write until his death on November 28, 1859.

Possibly no writer's reputation has hung on so slender a thread as Irving's. His two most famous stories—"Rip Van Winkle" and "The Legend of Sleepy Hollow"—have both established and maintained that reputation. Suffice it to say that *The Sketch Book*, which includes both of his famous stories, is the pivotal work in his career. Irving reveals in its preface, "The Author's Account of Himself," that Europe's storied past and its foreign and exotic settings strongly attracted him. In fact, only four of the selections in *The Sketch Book* are on genuinely American topics: two essays on Indians ("Traits of Indian Character" and "Philip of Pokanoket") and his two memorable works ("Rip Van Winkle" and "The Legend of Sleepy Hollow"). "Rip Van Winkle" exhibits Irving's best traits. Adapting material from German tales, he added the distinctively American settings and characters. His use of the legendary Dutch-American past throws an aura of mystery over the whole work. Rip, the eternal boy-man who never grows up to accept adult responsibilities, is a compelling character type in American fiction.

Often viewed as transitional, Irving's work marked a clear break in American literature. Its goal was no longer moral or religious instruction but entertainment. His style was smooth and urbane, his material pleasurable and innocent. As humorist and folklorist, Irving brought new materials and directions to American literature. Combining the narrative tale and the essay of character, he created the short story, a form that not only brings enjoyment to its readers but also gives them insight into human nature. Generations of American fiction writers as well as readers owe a great debt to Irving.

Rip Van Winkle

"Rip Van Winkle" is not entirely original, for Irving based the story on an old German legend about a goatherd named Peter Klaus. What is original is Irving's Americanization of the tale. Perhaps the American elements he added to the story supply "the charms of storied and poetical association" he believed were missing in America.

Irving uses fictional identities to distance himself from the story. The tale appears in The Sketch Book, *a collection compiled by a certain Geoffrey Crayon. The significance of this pen name is twofold. First, the name Geoffrey links Irving to the English poet Geoffrey Chaucer (1304?-1400) who authored the first great collection of tales in English. Perhaps Irving is implying for himself a position like Chaucer's but at the head of American fiction. He may also be linking his writing with more venerable English literary tradition. Second, the name Crayon suggests Irving's interest in painting, particularly landscape painting—an interest that is reflected in the story's construction.*

In a brief introductory essay not included below, Irving attributes the specific tale, "Rip Van Winkle," to Dutch historian Diedrich Knickerbocker, another of Irving's fictional identities. Supposedly the story had been found among the papers left after Knickerbocker's death. In a note attached to the end of the story, Knickerbocker declares that the account "is beyond the possibility of doubt."

Whoever has made a voyage up the Hudson must remember the Kaatskill* mountains. They are a dismembered* branch of the great Appalachian family, and are seen away to the west of the river, swelling up to a noble height, and lording it over the surrounding country. Every change of season, every change of weather, indeed, every hour of the day, produces some change in the magical hues and shapes of these mountains, and they are regarded by all the good wives, far and near, as perfect barometers. When the weather is fair and settled, they are clothed in blue and purple, and print their bold outlines on the clear evening sky; but, sometimes, when the rest of the landscape is cloudless, they will gather a hood of gray vapors about their summits, which, in the last rays of the setting sun, will glow and light up like a crown of glory.

Kaatskill: Catskill
dismembered: cut off

At the foot of these fairy mountains, the voyager may have descried* the light smoke curling up from a village, whose shingle-roofs gleam among the trees, just where the blue tints of the upland melt away into the fresh green of the nearer landscape. It is a little village of great antiquity, having been founded by some of the Dutch colonists, in the early times of the province, just about the beginning of the government of the good Peter Stuyvesant,* (may he rest in peace!) and there were some of the houses of the original settlers standing within a few years, built of small yellow bricks brought from Holland, having latticed windows and gable fronts, surmounted with weather-cocks.

descried: detected
Peter Stuyvesant: (1592-1672), last governor of the Dutch colony of New Netherlands

In that same village, and in one of these very houses (which, to tell the precise truth, was sadly time-worn and weather-beaten), there lived many years since, while the country was yet a province of Great Britain, a simple good-natured fellow of the name of Rip Van Winkle. He was a descendant of the Van Winkles who figured so gallantly in the chivalrous days of Peter Stuyvesant, and accompanied him to the siege of Fort Christiana.* He inherited, however, but little of the martial* character of his ancestors. I have observed that he was a simple good-natured man; he was, moreover, a kind neighbor, and an obedient henpecked husband. Indeed, to the latter circumstance might be owing that meekness of spirit which gained him such universal popularity; for those men are most apt to be obsequious* and conciliating* abroad, who are under the discipline of shrews at home. Their tempers, doubtless, are rendered pliant and malleable* in the fiery furnace of domestic tribulation; and a curtain lecture* so worth all the sermons in the world for teaching the virtues of patience and longsuffering. A termagant* wife may, therefore, in some respects, be considered a tolerable blessing; and if so, Rip Van Winkle was thrice blessed.

Fort Christiana: In 1655 Stuyvesant's Dutch forces captured this fort from the Swedes.
martial: warlike
obsequious: submissive
conciliating: desirous of friendship
malleable: flexible
curtain lecture: a private lecture given by a wife to her husband
termagant: abusive, quarrelsome

Certain it is, that he was a great favorite among all the good wives of the village, who, as usual, with the amiable sex, took his part in all family squabbles; and never failed, whenever they talked those matters over in their evening gossipings, to lay all the blame on Dame Van Winkle. The children of the village, too, would shout with joy whenever he approached. He assisted at their sports, made their playthings, taught them to fly kites and shoot marbles, and told them long stories of ghosts, witches, and Indians. Whenever he went dodging about the village, he was surrounded by a troop of them, hanging on his shirts,* clambering on his back, and playing a thousand tricks on him with impunity;* and not a dog would bark at him throughout the neighborhood.

---

shirts: clothes
impunity: freedom from punishment

The great error in Rip's composition was an insuperable* aversion to all kinds of profitable labor. It could not be from the want of assiduity* or perseverance; for he would sit on a wet rock, with a rod as long and heavy as a Tartar's lance,* and fish all day without a murmur, even though he should not be encouraged by a single nibble. He would carry a fowling-piece on his shoulder for hours together, trudging through woods and swamps, and up hill and down dale, to shoot a few squirrels or wild pigeons. He would never refuse to assist a neighbor even in the roughest toil, and was a foremost man at all country frolics for husking Indian corn, or building stone-fences; the women of the village, too, used to employ him to run their errands, and to do such little odd jobs as their less obliging husbands would not do for them. In a word Rip was ready to attend to anybody's business but his own; but as to doing family duty, and keeping his farm in order, he found it impossible.

---

insuperable: not able to be overcome
assiduity: diligence
Tartar's lance: a long, spearlike weapon used by the ferocious soldiers of Genghis Khan

---

In fact, he declared it was of no use to work on his farm; it was the most pestilent* little piece of ground in the whole country; everything about it went wrong, and would go wrong, in spite of him. His fences were continually falling to pieces; his cow would either go astray, or get among the cabbages; weeds were sure to grow quicker in his fields than anywhere else; the rain always made a point of setting in just as he had some outdoor work to do; so that though his patrimonial* estate had dwindled away under his management, acre by acre, until there was little more left than a mere patch of Indian corn and potatoes, yet it was the worst conditioned farm in the neighborhood.

---

pestilent: plague-ridden: i.e., deadly
patrimonial: inherited from one's father

His children, too, were as ragged and wild as if they belonged to nobody. His son Rip, an urchin begotten in his own likeness, promised to inherit the habits, with the old clothes of his father. He was generally seen trooping like a colt at his mother's heels, equipped in a pair of his father's cast-off galligaskins,* which he had much ado to hold up with one hand, as a fine lady does her train in bad weather.

---

galligaskins: loose breeches

Rip Van Winkle, however, was one of those happy mortals, of foolish, well-oiled dispositions, who take the world easy, eat white bread or brown, whichever can be got with least thought or trouble, and would rather starve on a penny than work for a pound. If left to himself, he would have whistled life away in perfect contentment; but his wife kept continually dinning* in his ears about his idleness, his carelessness, and the ruin he was bringing on his family. Morning, noon, and night, her tongue was incessantly going, and everything he said or did was sure to produce a torrent of household eloquence. Rip had but one way of replying to all lectures of the kind, and that, by frequent use, had grown into a habit. He shrugged his shoulders, shook his head, cast up his eyes, but said nothing. This, however, always provoked a fresh volley* from his wife; so that he was fain to draw off his forces, and take to the outside of the house—the only side which, in truth, belongs to a hen-pecked husband.

---

dinning: impress through wearying repetition
volley: a bursting forth

Rip's sole domestic adherent was his dog Wolf, who was as much hen-pecked as his master; for Dame Van Winkle regarded them as companions in idleness, and even looked upon Wolf with an evil eye, as the cause of his master's going so far astray. True it is, in all points of spirit befitting an honorable dog, he was as courageous an animal as ever scoured the woods—but what courage can withstand the ever-during and all-besetting terrors of a woman's tongue? The moment Wolf entered the house his crest fell, his tail drooped to the ground, or curled between his legs, he sneaked about with a gallows air,* casting many a sidelong glance at Dame Van Winkle, and at the least flourish of a broomstick or ladle, he would fly to the door with yelping precipitation.*

gallows air: i.e., as though he were about to be executed
precipitation: haste

Times grew worse and worse with Rip Van Winkle as years of matrimony rolled on; a tart temper never mellows with age, and a sharp tongue is the only edged tool that grows keener with constant use. For a long while he used to console himself, when driven from home, by frequenting a kind of perpetual club of the sages, philosophers, and other idle personages of the village; which held its sessions on a bench before a small inn, designated by a rubicund* portrait of His Majesty George the Third.* Here they used to sit in the shade through a long lazy summer's day, talking listlessly over village gossip, or telling endless sleepy stories about nothing. But it would have been worth any statesman's money to have heard the profound discussions that sometimes took place, when by chance an old newspaper fell into their hands from some passing traveler. How solemnly they would listen to the contents, as drawled out by Derrick Van Bummel, the schoolmaster, a dapper,* learned little man, who was not to be daunted by the most gigantic word in the dictionary; and how sagely they would deliberate upon public events some months after they had taken place.

rubicund: red, rosy
George the Third: English king from 1760-1820
dapper: neatly dressed, trim

The opinions of this junto* were completely controlled by Nicholas Vedder, a patriarch of the village, and landlord of the inn, at the door of which he took his seat from morning till night,

just moving sufficiently to avoid the sun and keep in the shade of a large tree; so that the neighbors could tell the hour by his movements as accurately as by a sun-dial. It is true he was rarely heard to speak, but smoked his pipe incessantly. His adherents, however (for every great man has his adherents), perfectly understood him, and knew how to gather his opinions. When anything that was read or related displeased him, he was observed to smoke his pipe vehemently, and to send forth short, frequent and angry puffs; but when pleased, he would inhale the smoke slowly and tranquilly, and emit it in light and placid clouds; and sometimes, taking the pipe from his mouth, and letting the fragrant vapor curl about his nose, would gravely nod his head in token of perfect approbation.*

junto: small, usually secretive, committee or group
approbation: approval

From even this stronghold the unlucky Rip was at length routed by his termagant wife, who would suddenly break in upon the tranquility of the assemblage and call the members all to naught; nor was that august* personage, Nicholas Vedder himself, sacred from the daring tongue of this terrible virago,* who charged him outright with encouraging her husband in habits of idleness.

august: inspiring admiration
virago: a scold, shrew

Poor Rip was at last reduced almost to despair; and his only alternative, to escape from the labor of the farm and clamor of his wife, was to take gun in hand and stroll away into the woods. Here he would sometimes seat himself at the foot of a tree, and share the contents of his wallet* with Wolf, with whom he sympathized as a fellow-sufferer in persecution. "Poor Wolf," he would say, "thy mistress leads thee a dog's life of it; but never mind, my lad, whilst I live thou shalt never want a friend to stand by thee!" Wolf would wag his tail, look wistfully in his master's face, and if dogs can feel pity I verily believe he reciprocated the sentiment with all his heart.

wallet: knapsack

In a long ramble of the kind on a fine autumnal day, Rip had unconsciously scrambled to one of the highest parts of the Kaatskill mountains. He was after his favorite sport of squirrel shooting, and the still solitudes had echoed and re-echoed with the reports of his gun. Panting and fatigued, he threw himself, late in the afternoon, on a green knoll, covered with mountain herbage, that crowned the brow of a precipice. From an opening between the trees he could overlook all the lower country for many a mile of rich woodland. He saw at a distance the lordly Hudson, far, far below him, moving on its silent but majestic course, with the reflection of a purple cloud, or the sail of a lagging bark, here and there sleeping on its glassy bosom, and at last losing itself in the blue highlands.

On the other side he looked down into a deep mountain glen, wild, lonely, and shagged, the bottom filled with fragments from the impending cliffs, and scarcely lighted by the reflected rays of the setting sun. For some time Rip lay musing on this scene; evening was gradually advancing; the mountains began to throw their long blue shadows over the valleys; he saw that it would be dark long before he could reach the village, and he heaved a heavy sigh when he thought of encountering the terrors of Dame Van Winkle.

As he was about to descend, he heard a voice from a distance, hallooing, "Rip Van Winkle! Rip Van Winkle!" He looked round, but could see nothing but a crow winging its solitary flight across the mountain. He thought his fancy must have deceived him, and turned again to descend, when he heard the same cry ring through the still evening air; "Rip Van Winkle! Rip Van Winkle!"—at the same time Wolf bristled up his back, and giving a low growl, skulked* to his master's side, looking fearfully down into the glen. Rip now felt a vague apprehension stealing over him;

he looked anxiously in the same direction, and perceived a strange figure slowly toiling up the rocks, and bending under the weight of something he carried on his back. He was surprised to see any human being in this lonely and unfrequented place, but supposing it to be someone of the neighborhood in need of his assistance, he hastened down to yield it.

skulked: moved stealthily

On nearer approach he was still more surprised at the singularity of the stranger's appearance. He was a short square-built old fellow, with thick bushy hair, and a grizzled beard. His dress was of the antique Dutch fashion—a cloth jerkin strapped round the waist—several pair of breeches, the outer one of ample volume, decorated with rows of buttons down the sides, and bunches at the knees. He bore on his shoulder a stout keg that seemed full of liquor, and made signs for Rip to approach and assist him with the load. Though rather shy and distrustful of this new acquaintance, Rip complied with his usual alacrity;* and mutually relieving one another, they clambered up a narrow gully, apparently the dry bed of a mountain torrent. As they ascended, Rip every now and then heard long rolling peals, like distant thunder, that seemed to issue out of a deep ravine, or rather cleft, between lofty rocks, toward which their rugged path conducted. He paused for an instant, but supposing it to be the muttering of one of those transient thunder-showers which often take place in mountain heights, he proceeded. Passing through the ravine, they came to a hollow, like a small amphitheater, surrounded by perpendicular precipices, over the brinks of which impending trees shot their branches, so that you only caught glimpses of the azure sky and the bright evening cloud. During the whole time Rip and his companion had labored on in silence; for though the former marveled greatly what could be the object of carrying a keg of liquor up this wild mountain, yet there was something strange

and incomprehensible about the unknown, that inspired awe and checked familiarity.

alacrity: cheerful willingness

On entering the amphitheater, new objects of wonder presented themselves. On a level spot in the center was a company of odd-looking personages playing at nine-pins.* They were dressed in a quaint outlandish fashion; some wore short doublets, others jerkins, with long knives in their belts, and most of them had enormous breeches, of similar style with that of the guide's. Their visages, too, were peculiar: one had a large beard, broad face, and small piggish eyes: the face of another seemed to consist entirely of nose, and was surmounted by a white sugar-loaf hat set off with a little red cock's tail. They all had beards, of various shapes and colors. There was one who seemed to be the commander. He was a stout old gentleman, with a weather-beaten countenance; he wore a laced doublet, broad belt and hanger,* high-crowned hat and feather, red stockings, and high-heeled shoes, with roses* in them. The whole group reminded Rip of the figures in an old Flemish painting, in the parlor of Dominie Van Shaick, the village parson, and which had been brought over from Holland at the time of the settlement.

nine-pins: a bowling game played with nine wooden pins
hanger: a short sword
roses: ribbons arranged in the shape of roses

What seemed particularly odd to Rip was, that though these folks were evidently amusing themselves, yet they maintained the gravest faces, the most mysterious silence, and were, withal, the most melancholy party of pleasure he had ever witnessed. Nothing interrupted the stillness of the scene but the noise of the balls, which, whenever they were rolled, echoed along the mountains like rumbling peals of thunder.

As Rip and his companion approached them, they suddenly desisted* from their play, and stared at him with such fixed statue-like gaze, and such strange, uncouth, lack-lustre countenances,

that his heart turned within him, and his knees smote together. His companion now emptied the contents of the keg into large flagons, and made signs to him to wait upon the company. He obeyed with fear and trembling; they quaffed* the liquor in profound silence, and then returned to their game.

desisted: ceased
quaffed: drank heartily

By degrees Rip's awe and apprehension subsided. He even ventured, when no eye was fixed upon him, to taste the beverage, which he found had much of the flavor of excellent Hollands.* He was naturally a thirsty soul, and was soon tempted to repeat the draught. One taste provoked another; and he reiterated his visits to the flagon so often that at length his senses were overpowered, his eyes swam in his head, his head gradually declined, and he fell into a deep sleep.

Hollands: gin made in Holland

On waking, he found himself on the green knoll whence he had first seen the old man of the glen. He rubbed his eyes–it was a bright sunny morning. The birds were hopping and twittering among the bushes, and the eagle was wheeling aloft, and breasting* the pure mountain breeze. "Surely," thought Rip, "I have not slept here all night." He recalled the occurrences before he fell asleep. The strange man with a keg of liquor–the mountain ravine–the wild retreat among the rocks–the woe-begone party at nine-pins–the flagon. "Oh! that flagon! that wicked flagon!" thought Rip–"what excuse shall I make to Dame Van Winkle!"

breasting: advancing against

He looked round for his gun, but in place of the clean well-oiled fowling-piece, he found an old firelock lying by him, the barrel encrusted with rust, the lock falling off, and the stock worm-eaten. He now suspected that the grave roisters* of the mountain had put a trick upon him, and, having dosed him with liquor, had robbed him of his gun. Wolf, too, had disappeared, but he might have strayed away after a squirrel or partridge. He whistled after him and shouted his name, but all in vain; the echoes repeated his whistle and shout, but no dog was to be seen.

---

roisters: revelers

He determined to revisit the scene of the last evening's gambol,* and if he met with any of the party, to demand his dog and gun. As he rose to walk, he found himself stiff in the joints, and wanting in his usual activity. "These mountain beds do not agree with me," thought Rip, "and if this frolic should lay me up with a fit of the rheumatism, I shall have a blessed time with Dame Van Winkle." With some difficulty he got down into the glen: he found the gully up which he and his companion had ascended the preceding evening; but to his astonishment a mountain stream was now foaming down it, leaping from rock to rock, and filling the glen with babbling murmurs. He, however, made shift to scramble up its sides, working his toilsome way through thickets of birch, sassafras, and witch-hazel, and sometimes tripped up or entangled by the wild grapevines that twisted their coils or tendrils from tree to tree, and spread a kind of network in his path.

---

gambol: frolic

At length he reached to where the ravine had opened through the cliffs to the amphitheater; but no traces of such opening remained. The rocks presented a high impenetrable wall over which the torrent came tumbling in a sheet of feathery foam, and fell into a broad deep basin, black from the shadows of the surrounding forest. Here, then, poor Rip was brought to a stand. He again called and whistled after his dog; he was only answered by the cawing of a flock of idle crows, sporting high in air about a dry tree that overhung a sunny precipice; and who, secure in their elevation, seemed to look down and scoff at the poor man's perplexities. What was to be done? the morning was passing away, and Rip felt famished for want of his breakfast. He grieved to give up his dog and gun; he dreaded to meet his wife; but it would not do to starve among the mountains. He shook his head, shouldered the rusty firelock, and, with a heart full of trouble and anxiety, turned his steps homeward.

As he approached the village he met a number of people, but none whom he knew, which somewhat surprised him, for he had thought himself acquainted with everyone in the country round. Their dress, too, was of a different fashion from that to which he was accustomed. They all stared at him with equal marks of surprise, and whenever they cast their eyes upon him, invariably stroked their chins. The constant recurrence of this gesture induced Rip, involuntarily, to do the same, when, to his astonishment, he found his beard had grown a foot long!

He had now entered the skirts of the village. A troop of strange children ran at his heels, hooting after him, and pointing at his gray beard. The dogs, too, not one of which he recognized for an old acquaintance, barked at him as he passed. The very village was altered; it was larger and more populous. There were rows of houses which he had never seen before, and those which had been his familiar haunts had disappeared. Strange names were over the doors—strange faces at the windows—everything was strange. His mind now misgave him; he began to doubt whether both he and the world around him were not bewitched. Surely this was his native village, which he had left but the day before. There stood the Kaatskill mountains—there ran the silver Hudson at a distance—there was every hill and dale precisely as it had always been—Rip was sorely perplexed—"That flagon last night," thought he, "has addled* my poor head sadly!"

---

addled: confused

It was with some difficulty that he found the way to his own house, which he approached with silent awe, expecting every moment to hear the shrill voice of Dame Van Winkle. He found the house gone to decay–the roof fallen in, the windows shattered, and the doors off the hinges. A half-starved dog that looked like Wolf was skulking about it. Rip called him by name, but the cur snarled, showed his teeth, and passed on. This was an unkind cut indeed–"My very dog," sighed poor Rip, "has forgotten me!"

He entered the house, which, to tell the truth, Dame Van Winkle had always kept in neat order. It was empty, forlorn, and apparently abandoned. This desolateness overcame all his connubial* fears–he called loudly for his wife and children–the lonely chambers rang for a moment with his voice, and then all again was silence.

---

connubial: pertaining to marriage

He now hurried forth, and hastened to his old resort, the village inn–but it too was gone. A large rickety wooden building stood in its place, with great gaping windows, some of them broken and mended with old hats and petticoats, and over the door was painted, "the Union Hotel, by Jonathan Doolittle." Instead of the great tree that used to shelter the quiet little Dutch inn of yore, there now was reared a tall naked pole, with something on the top that looked like a red night-cap, and from it was fluttering a flag, on which was a singular assemblage of stars and stripes–all this was strange and incomprehensible. He recognized on the sign, however, the ruby face of King George, under which he had smoked so many a peaceful pipe; but even this was singularly metamorphosed.* The red coat was changed for one of blue and buff,* a sword was held in the hand instead of a scepter, the head was decorated with a cocked hat, and underneath was painted in large characters, GENERAL WASHINGTON.

---

metamorphosed: transformed
buff: color of leather

There was, as usual, a crowd of folk about the door, but none that Rip recollected. The very character of the people seemed changed. There was a busy, bustling, disputatious* tone about it, instead of the accustomed phlegm* and drowsy tranquility. He looked in vain for the sage Nicholas Vedder, with his broad face, double chin, and fair long pipe, uttering clouds of tobacco-smoke instead of idle speeches; or Van Bummel, the schoolmaster, doling forth* the contents of an ancient newspaper. In place of these, a lean, bilious*-looking fellow, with his pockets full of handbills, was haranguing vehemently about rights of citizens–elections–members of congress–liberty–Bunker's Hill–heroes of seventy-six–and other words, which were a perfect Babylonish* jargon to the bewildered Van Winkle.

---

disputatious: argumentative
phlegm: apathy, indifference
doling forth: i.e., reading aloud short passages from
bilious: ill-tempered
Babylonish: foreign, incomprehensible

The appearance of Rip, with his long grizzled beard, his rusty fowling-piece, his uncouth dress, and an army of women and children at his heels, soon attracted the attention of the tavern politicians. They crowded round him, eyeing him from head to foot with great curiosity. The orator bustled up to him, and, drawing him partly aside, inquired "on which side he voted?" Rip stared in vacant stupidity. Another short but busy little fellow pulled him by the arm, and, rising on tiptoe, inquired in his ear, "Whether he was Federal or Democrat?" Rip was equally at a loss to comprehend the question; when a knowing, self-important old gentleman, in a sharp cocked hat, made his way through the crowd, putting them to the right and left with his elbows as he passed, and planting himself before Van Winkle, with one arm akimbo,* the other resting on his cane, his keen eyes and sharp hat penetrating, as it were, into his very soul, demanded in an austere* tone, "what brought him to the election with a gun on his shoulder, and a mob at his heels, and whether he meant to breed a riot in the village?"–"Alas! gentlemen," cried Rip, somewhat dismayed, "I am a poor quiet man, a native of the place, and a loyal subject of the king, God bless him!''

akimbo: hand on hip and elbow bowed outward
austere: severe, stern

Here a general shout burst from the bystanders—"A tory!* a tory! a spy! a refugee! hustle him! away with him!'' It was with great difficulty that the self-important man in the cocked hat restored order; and, having assumed a tenfold austerity of brow, demanded again of the unknown culprit, what he came there for, and whom he was seeking? The poor man humbly assured him that he meant no harm, but merely came there in search of some of his neighbors, who used to keep about the tavern.

tory: one loyal to England during the Revolutionary War

''Well—who are they?—name them.''

Rip bethought himself a moment, and inquired, ''Where's Nicholas Vedder?''

There was a silence for a little while, when an old man replied, in a thin piping voice, ''Nicholas Vedder! why, he is dead and gone these eighteen years! There was a wooden tombstone in the church-yard that used to tell all about him, but that's rotten and gone too.''

''Where's Brom Dutcher?''

''Oh, he went off to the army in the beginning of the war; some say he was killed at the storming of Stony Point—others say he was drowned in a squall at the foot of Anthony's Nose.* I don't know—he never came back again.''

Anthony's Nose: important Revolutionary War fortifications on the Hudson River

''Where's Van Bummel, the schoolmaster?''

''He went off to the wars too, was a great militia general, and is now in congress.''

Rip's heart died away at hearing of these sad changes in his home and friends, and finding himself thus alone in the world. Every answer puzzled him too, by treating of such enormous lapses of time, and of matters which he could not understand: war—congress—Stony Point;—he had no

courage to ask after any more friends, but cried out in despair, ''Does nobody here know Rip Van Winkle?''

''Oh, Rip Van Winkle!'' exclaimed two or three, ''Oh, to be sure! that's Rip Van Winkle yonder, leaning against the tree.''

Rip looked, and beheld a precise counter-part of himself, as he went up the mountain: apparently as lazy, and certainly as ragged. The poor fellow was now completely confounded. He doubted his own identity, and whether he was himself or another man. In the midst of his bewilderment, the man in the cocked hat demanded who he was, and what was his name?

''Who knows,'' exclaimed he, at his wit's end; ''I'm not myself—I'm somebody else—that's me yonder—no—that's somebody else got into my shoes—I was myself last night, but I fell asleep on the mountain, and they've changed my gun, and everything's changed, and I'm changed, and I can't tell what's my name, or who I am!''

The by-standers began now to look at each other, nod, wink significantly, and tap their fingers against their foreheads. There was a whisper, also, about securing the gun, and keeping the old fellow from doing mischief, at the very suggestion of which the self-important man in the cocked hat retired with some precipitation. At this critical moment a fresh comely woman pressed through the throng to get a peep at the gray-bearded man. She had a chubby child in her arms, which, frightened at his looks, began to cry. ''Hush, Rip,'' cried she, ''hush, you little fool; the old man won't hurt you.'' The name of the child, the air of the mother, the tone of her voice, all awakened a train of recollections in his mind. ''What is your name, my good woman?'' asked he.

''Judith Gardenier.''

''And your father's name?''

''Ah, poor man, Rip Van Winkle was his name, but it's twenty years since he went away from home with his gun, and never has been heard of since—his dog came home without him; but whether he shot himself, or was carried away by the Indians, nobody can tell. I was then but a little girl.''

Rip had but one question more to ask; but he put it with a faltering voice:

''Where's your mother?''

''Oh, she too had died but a short time since; she broke a blood-vessel in a fit of passion at a New England peddler.''

There was a drop of comfort, at least, in this intelligence. The honest man could contain himself no longer. He caught his daughter and her child in his arms. ''I am your father!'' cried he–''Young Rip Van Winkle once–old Rip Van Winkle now!– Does anybody know poor Rip Van Winkle?''

All stood amazed, until an old woman, tottering out from among the crowd, put her hand to her brow, and peering under it in his face for a moment, exclaimed, ''Sure enough! it is Rip Van Winkle–it is himself! Welcome home again, old neighbor–Why, where have you been these twenty long years?''

Rip's story was soon told, for the whole twenty years had been to him but as one night. The neighbors stared when they heard it; some were seen to wink at each other, and put their tongues in their cheeks: and the self-important man in the cocked hat, who, when the alarm was over, had returned to the field, screwed down the corners of his mouth, and shook his head–upon which there was a general shaking of the head throughout the assemblage.

It was determined, however, to take the opinion of old Peter Vanderdonk, who was seen slowly advancing up the road. He was a descendant of the historian of that name, who wrote one of the earliest accounts of the province. Peter was the most ancient inhabitant of the village, and well versed in all the wonderful events and traditions of the neighborhood. He recollected Rip at once, and corroborated* his story in the most satisfactory manner. He assured the company that it was a fact, handed down from his ancestor the historian, that the Kaatskill mountains had always been haunted by strange beings. That it was affirmed that the great Hendrick Hudson, the first discoverer of the river and country, kept a kind of vigil there every twenty years, with his crew of the Half-moon; being permitted in this way to revisit the scenes of his enterprise, and keep a guardian eye upon the river, and the great city called by his name. That his father had once seen them in their old Dutch dresses playing at nine-pins in a hollow of the mountain; and that he himself had heard, one summer afternoon, the sound of their balls, like distant peals of thunder.

corroborated: confirmed

To make a long story short, the company broke up, and returned to the more important concerns of the election. Rip's daughter took him home to live with her; she had a snug, well-furnished house, and a stout cheery farmer for a husband, whom Rip recollected for one of the urchins that used to climb upon his back. As to Rip's son and heir, who was the ditto of himself, seen leaning against the tree, he was employed to work on the farm; but evinced an hereditary disposition to attend to any thing else but his business.

Rip now resumed his old walks and habits; he soon found many of his former cronies,* though all rather the worst for the wear and tear of time; and preferred making friends among the rising generation* with whom he soon grew into great favor.

cronies: close companions
rising generation: i.e., children

Having nothing to do at home, and being arrived at the happy age when a man can be idle with impunity, he took his place once more on the bench at the inn door, and was reverenced as one of the patriarchs of the village, and a chronicle of the old times ''before the war.'' It was some time before he could get into the regular track of gossip, or could be made to comprehend the strange events that had taken place during his torpor.* How that there had been a revolutionary war–that the country had thrown off the yoke of old England–and that, instead of being a subject of his Majesty George the Third, he was now a free citizen of the United States. Rip, in fact, was no politician; the changes of states and empires made but little impression on him; but there was one species of despotism* under which he had long groaned, and that was–petticoat government. Happily that was at an end; he had got his neck out of the yoke of matrimony, and could go in and out whenever he pleased, without dreading the tyranny of Dame Van Winkle. Whenever her name was mentioned, however, he shook his head, shrugged his shoulders, and cast up his eyes; which might pass either for an expression of resignation to his fate, or joy at his deliverance.

torpor: inactivity
despotism: absolute power

He used to tell his story to every stranger that arrived at Mr. Doolittle's hotel. He was observed, at first, to vary on some points every time he told it, which was, doubtless, owing to his having so recently awaked. It at last settled down precisely to the tale I have related, and not a man, woman, or child in the neighborhood, but knew it by heart. Some always pretended to doubt the reality of it, and insisted that Rip had been out of his head, and that this was one point on which he always remained flighty. The old Dutch inhabitants, however, almost universally gave it full credit. Even to this day they never hear a thunderstorm of a summer afternoon about the Kaatskill, but they say Hendrick Hudson and his crew are at their game of nine-pins; and it is a common wish of all hen-pecked husbands in the neighborhood, when life hangs heavy on their hands, that they might have a quieting draught out of Rip Van Winkle's flagon.

For Thought and Discussion

1. In what paragraph does Irving specify the time period in which the action of "Rip Van Winkle" is set? How does he link the time setting to the major theme of the story, "petticoat government"?

2. What is the significance of the Catskill Mountains (upstate New York) locale in which Irving sets "Rip Van Winkle"? What is the effect of Irving's reference to the Catskills in both the opening and closing sentences of the story?

3. Paraphrase the final clause of "Rip Van Winkle," stating clearly the meaning on the literal level: "it is a common wish of all hen-pecked husbands . . . that they might have a quieting draught out of Rip Van Winkle's flagon." Next discuss the meaning of this clause in terms of the theme of the story.

4. At what point does Irving introduce the pronoun _I_ to refer to the narrator of the story? What sort of person is the narrator? Is his reaction to the major characters in the story objective or subjective? Notice his occasional insertion of a maxim, or memorable wise saying, in the narrative. (See, for example, the final sentence of paragraph three; the rhetorical question in the middle of paragraph nine; and the first sentence of paragraph ten.) For which character do the narrator's maxims humorously create sympathy?

5. Discuss Irving's achievement in the creation of a memorable, "round" character in Rip Van Winkle. What are Rip's major characteristics? What are his weaknesses? Are these weaknesses realistically portrayed by Irving? Does Rip have any strengths? Do you react positively or negatively to him? Why? Does he grow or change in the course of the story?

James Fenimore Cooper
1789-1851

James Fenimore Cooper, who hated even to write a letter, began writing novels on a dare. One evening in 1819, while reading a current best-selling English novel aloud to his family, Cooper declared in disgust that he could write a better one himself. When his wife playfully dared him to try, he accepted the challenge and six months later published *Precaution* (1820). Although a lackluster effort at best, this moralistic novel set in England was just good enough to launch Cooper's career. For the setting of his second work, *The Spy* (1821), Cooper turned to America during the Revolutionary War. This change to what he knew best was fortunate, for Cooper's treatment of the American past in his subsequent novels made him the first successful American novelist.

Cooper's early life gave no indication of his literary ability. After leaving Yale College during his junior year, he became in 1806 a sailor on a merchant ship and in 1808 a midshipman in the United States Navy. Upon the death in 1809 of his father—for whom Cooperstown, New York, had been named—Cooper inherited a portion of his father's large estate and, in 1811, married into the wealthy Delancey family, shortly thereafter resigning his navy commission. In 1820 the thirty-one-year-old gentleman farmer published his first novel. Two years later, moving from upstate New York to New York City, he became identified with the Knickerbocker writers. From 1826 to 1833 Cooper lived in England and France and traveled extensively in Italy. During this period abroad he staunchly defended his country to Europeans. But when he returned to the States in 1833, he became alarmed at the political and social changes that had occurred during his absence. These changes, spurred by Andrew Jackson's presidency (1829-37), seemed to Cooper to foreshadow the disintegration of leadership and culture in the States. His outspoken criticism of these changes began to diminish his popularity with his countrymen.

In 1837, having moved to Cooperstown on his return from Europe three years earlier, Cooper became involved in a dispute with the local residents over rights to Three Mile Point, a popular picnic area owned by Cooper on Lake Otsego. Suspecting that public access was going to destroy his property rights, he exercised his right of ownership and closed the picnic area to the public. His action received much unfavorable and distorted publicity. The closing of Three Mile Point, coupled with his unflattering social criticism, caused reviewers to attack his work on personal rather than literary grounds. Not a man to take such attacks sitting down, Cooper responded to the libelous matter with lawsuits. The resulting legal battles, many of which he argued and won, further decreased his popularity with the American press. In his last years Cooper became somewhat embittered by the poor reception of his ideas and writings. At his death in 1851, he left more than thirty novels and several volumes of travel literature, naval history, and social commentary.

Cooper's contributions to the American novel are many. He created the first mythological American hero, the larger-than-life portrait of the frontiersman. He introduced social criticism to the American novel in his treatment of the perplexing problem of racial tension, representing racial differences as the ''gifts'' of each race. In Cooper's novels ''gifts'' are the innate or acquired racial and cultural values possessed by an individual or race. Cooper also brought to the American novel his romantic attraction to the forest before its destruction by civilization.

Although later writers, notably Samuel Clemens, attacked Cooper's work as inartistic, his novels have endured. They are not only popular reading material today but are also gaining critical stature as a serious fictional evaluation of our past. Cooper's perspective on the American past is not sentimental and escapist. Although he believed that the country's direction in his day was socially and politically deplorable, he did more than nostalgically re-create the days of the frontier. He addressed issues still crucial today: the relationship of different parts of society, the relationship of the individual to his society, the tension between civil law and natural rights. Of special interest to the Christian is Cooper's source for the moral idealism of Natty Bumppo. Cooper attributes Natty's heroic greatness to the Christian values taught him by Moravian missionaries. This writer, unlike most of his fellow romantics, did not reject the religious past of his country but fashioned his hero so that his actions spring from deeply ingrained, essentially Christian values.

from **The Deerslayer**

The Deerslayer *was the last of Cooper's most famous series of novels, the* Leatherstocking Tales. *Written over a period of nineteen years, these five novels treat the adventures of Natty Bumppo, an American frontiersman patterned after Davy Crockett (1786-1836) and others like him. Although given various names in the novels (i.e., Deerslayer, Hawkeye, and Pathfinder), Natty remains basically the same woodsman throughout the series. Interestingly, however, Cooper's treatment of him changes. The first novels in the series–*The Pioneers *(1823);* The Last of the Mohicans *(1826), his all-time most popular; and* The Prairie *(1827)–portray Natty somewhat realistically, taking him from his mid-thirties to his death in his eighties. After a gap of thirteen years, Cooper wrote the final two:* The Pathfinder *(1840) and* The Deerslayer *(1841). These portray Natty romantically, depicting him in his later thirties (*Pathfinder) *and as a young man (*Deerslayer). *Incidentally, to follow*

Natty's life according to the chronological order, one must read these five novels in alphabetical order of their titles.

The Deerslayer opens with Deerslayer's arrival at Glimmerglass (Lake Otsego) to keep a rendezvous with Chingachgook, a Mohican chieftain, whose fiancée has been kidnapped by the Iroquois. After they warn Thomas Hutter and his two daughters of hostile Indians, the whites and Chingachgook all retreat to the Hutters' Muskrat Castle, a fortified dwelling built on an island in the lake. That night Deerslayer and Hutter return to the mainland to retrieve two canoes. Hutter is captured and Deerslayer, unable to help rescue him, falls asleep in one of the canoes. When he awakes in the morning, he finds that the other canoe has drifted away. In this excerpt from Chapter Seven he now attempts to recover it.

When about a hundred yards from the shore, Deerslayer rose in the canoe, gave three or four vigorous strokes with the paddle, sufficient of themselves to impel* the bark* to land, and then quickly laying aside the instrument of labor, he seized that of war.* He was in the very act of raising the rifle when a sharp report was followed by the buzz of a bullet that passed so near his body as to cause him involuntarily to start. The next instant Deerslayer staggered and fell his whole length in the bottom of the canoe. A yell–it came from a single voice–followed, and an Indian leaped from the bushes upon the open area of the point, bounding toward the canoe. This was the moment the young man desired. He rose on the instant and leveled his own rifle at his uncovered foe, but his finger hesitated about pulling the trigger on one whom he held at such a disadvantage. This little delay, probably, saved the life of the Indian, who bounded back into the cover as swiftly as he had broken out of it. In the meantime Deerslayer had been swiftly approaching the land, and his own canoe reached the point just as his enemy disappeared. As its movements had not been directed, it touched the shore a few yards from the other boat; and though the rifle of his foe had to be loaded, there was not time to secure his prize, and to carry it beyond danger, before he would be exposed to another shot. Under the circumstances, therefore, he did not pause an instant, but dashed into the woods and sought a cover.

impel: push forward
bark: i.e., canoe
laying . . . war: i.e., put aside his paddle for his rifle

On the immediate point there was a small open area, partly in native grass and partly beach, but a dense fringe of bushes lined its upper side. This narrow belt of dwarf vegetation passed, one issued immediately into the high and gloomy vaults of the forest. The land was tolerably level for a few hundred feet, and then it rose precipitously* in a mountainside. The trees were tall, large, and so free from underbrush that they resembled vast columns, irregularly scattered, upholding a dome of leaves. Although they stood tolerably close together, for their ages and size, the eye could penetrate to considerable distances, and bodies of men, even, might have engaged beneath their cover with concert* and intelligence.*

precipitously: steeply
concert: agreement, coordinated effort
intelligence: i.e., groups of men could easily hide themselves and shoot at each other under these trees

Deerslayer knew that his adversary must be employed in reloading, unless he had fled. The former proved to be the case, for the young man had no sooner placed himself behind a tree than he caught a glimpse of the arm of the Indian, his body being concealed by an oak, in the very act of forcing the leathered bullet home. Nothing would have been easier than to spring forward and decide the affair by a close assault on his

unprepared foe, but every feeling of Deerslayer revolted at such a step, although his own life had just been attempted from a cover. He was yet unpracticed in the ruthless expedients* of savage warfare, of which he knew nothing except by tradition and theory, and it struck him as an unfair advantage to assail* an unarmed foe. His color had heightened, his eye frowned, his lips were compressed, and all his energies were collected and ready; but instead of advancing to fire, he dropped his rifle to the usual position of a sportsman in readiness to catch his aim and muttered to himself, unconscious that he was speaking—

expedients: devices, means
assail: attack

"No, no–that may be redskin warfare, but it's not a Christian's gift. Let the miscreant* charge, and then we'll take it out like men, for the canoe he *must* not and *shall* not have. No, no, let him

have time to load, and God will take care of the right!''

miscreant: an unscrupulous wretch, evildoer

All this time the Indian had been so intent on his own movements that he was even ignorant that his enemy was in the wood. His only apprehension was that the canoe would be recovered and carried away before he might be in readiness to prevent it. He had sought the cover from habit, but was within a few feet of the fringe of bushes, and could be at the margin of the forest in readiness to fire in a moment. The distance between him and his enemy was about fifty yards, and the trees were so arranged by nature that the line of sight was not interrupted, except by the particular trees behind which each party stood.

His rifle was no sooner loaded than the savage glanced around him and advanced incautiously as regarded the real,* but stealthily as respected the fancied position of his enemy, until he was fairly exposed. Then Deerslayer stepped from behind his own cover and hailed him.

as . . . real: in respect to Deerslayer's actual position

"Thisaway, redskin; thisaway if you're looking for me," he called out. "I'm young in war but not so young as to stand on an open beach to be shot down like an owl by daylight. It rests on yourself whether it's peace or war atween us, for my gifts are white gifts, and I'm not one of them that thinks it valiant to slay human mortals, singly, in the woods."

The savage was a good deal startled by this sudden discovery of the danger he ran. He had a little knowledge of English, however, and caught the drift of the other's meaning. He was also too well schooled to betray alarm, but, dropping the butt of his rifle to the earth with an air of confidence, he made a gesture of lofty courtesy. All this was done with the ease and self-possession of one accustomed to consider no man his superior. In the midst of the consummate* acting, however, the volcano that raged within caused his eyes to glare and his nostrils to dilate, like those of some wild beast that is suddenly prevented from taking the fatal leap.

consummate: perfect

"Two canoe," he said, in the deep, guttural tones of his race, holding up the number of fingers he mentioned, by way of preventing mistakes; "one for you—one for me."

"No, no, Mingo,* that will never do. You own neither; and neither shall you have, as long as I can prevent it. I know it's war atween your people and mine, but that's no reason why human mortals should slay each other, like savage creatur's that meet in the woods; go your way, then, and leave me to go mine. The world is large enough for us both, and when we meet fairly in battle, why, the Lord will order the fate of each of us."

Mingo: derogatory name for Indian

"Good!" exclaimed the Indian. "My brother missionary—great talk; all about Manitou."*

Manitou: Indian name for the force said to control nature

"Not so—not so, warrior. I'm not good enough for the Moravians* and am too good for most of the other vagabonds that preach about in the woods. No, no, I'm only a hunter, as yet, though afore the peace is made, 'tis like enough there'll be occasion to strike a blow at some of your people. Still, I wish it to be done in fair fight and not in a quarrel about the ownership of a miserable canoe."

Moravians: Protestant group first founded in 1457, active missionaries in America after 1740

"Good! My brother very young—but he very wise. Little warrior—great talker. Chief, sometimes, in council."

"I don't know this, nor do I say it, Injin," returned Deerslayer, coloring a little at the ill-concealed sarcasm of the other's manner. "I look forward to a life in the woods, and I only hope it may be a peaceable one. All young men must go on the warpath, when there's occasion, but war isn't needfully massacre. I've seen enough of the last, this very night, to know that Providence frowns on it; I now invite you to go your own way, while I go mine, and hope that we may part fri'nds."

"Good! My brother has two scalp—gray hair under t'other. Old wisdom—young tongue."

Here the savage advanced with confidence, his hand extended, his face smiling, and his whole bearing denoting amity* and respect. Deerslayer met his offered friendship in a proper spirit, and they shook hands cordially, each endeavoring to assure the other of his sincerity and desire to be at peace.

amity: friendship

"All have his own," said the Indian: "my canoe, mine; your canoe, your'n. Go look: if your'n, you keep, if mine, I keep."

"That's just, redskin, though you must be wrong in thinking the canoe your property. However, seein' is believin', and we'll go down to the shore, where you may look with your own eyes, for it's likely you'll object to trustin' altogether to mine."

The Indian uttered his favorite exclamation of "good!" and then they walked, side by side, toward the shore. There was no apparent distrust in the manner of either, the Indian moving in advance, as if he wished to show his companion that he did not fear turning his back to him. As they reached the open ground, the former pointed toward Deerslayer's boat, and said emphatically—

"No mine—paleface canoe. *This* red man's. No want other man's canoe—want his own."

"You're wrong, redskin, you're altogether wrong. This canoe was left in old Hutter's keeping, and is his'n according to all law, red or white, till its owner comes to claim it. Here's the seats and the stitching of the bark to speak for themselves. No man ever know'd an Injin to turn off such work."

"Good! My brother little ole—big wisdom. Injin no make him. White man's work."

"I'm glad you think so, for holding out to the contrary might have made ill blood atween us, everyone having a right to take possession of his own. I'll just shove the canoe out of reach of dispute at once, as the quickest way of settling difficulties."

While Deerslayer was speaking, he put a foot against the end of the light boat, and giving a vigorous shove, he sent it out into the lake a hundred feet or more, where, taking the true current, it would necessarily float past the point, and be in no further danger of coming ashore. The savage started at this ready and decided expedient, and his companion saw that he cast a hurried and fierce glance at his own canoe, or that which

contained the paddles. The change of manner, however, was but momentary, and then the Iroquois resumed his air of friendliness, and a smile of satisfaction.

"Good!" he repeated, with stronger emphasis then ever. "Young head, old mind. Know how to settle quarrel. Farewell, brother. He go to house in water*—muskrat house—Injin go to camp; tell chiefs no find canoe."

house in water: the Hutters' fortified house

Deerslayer was not sorry to hear this proposal, for he felt anxious to join the females, and he took the offered hand of the Indian very willingly. The parting words were friendly, and while the red man walked calmly towards the wood, with the rifle in the hollow of his arm, without once looking back in uneasiness or distrust, the white man moved toward the remaining canoe, carrying his piece in the same pacific* manner, it is true, but keeping his eyes fastened on the movements of the other. This distrust, however, seemed to be altogether uncalled for, and, as if ashamed to have entertained it, the young man averted his look and stepped carelessly up to his boat. Here he began to push the canoe from the shore and to make his other preparations for departing. He might have been thus employed a minute when, happening to turn his face toward the land, his quick and certain eye told him at a glance the imminent jeopardy in which his life was placed. The black, ferocious eyes of the savage were glancing on him like those of the crouching tiger through a small opening in the bushes, and the muzzle of his rifle seemed already to be opening in a line with his own body.

pacific: peaceful

Then, indeed, the long practice of Deerslayer as a hunter did him good service. Accustomed to fire with the deer on the bound, and often when the precise position of the animal's body had in a manner to be guessed at, he used the same expedients here. To cock and poise his rifle were the acts of a single moment and a single motion; then, aiming almost without sighting, he fired into the bushes where he knew a body ought to be in order to sustain the appalling* countenance* which alone was visible. There was not time to raise the piece any higher, or to take a more deliberate aim. So rapid were his movements that both parties discharged their pieces at the same instant, the concussions mingling in one report. The mountains, indeed, gave back but a single echo. Deerslayer dropped his piece and stood, with head erect, steady as one of the pines in the calm of a June morning, watching the result; while the savage gave the yell that has become historical for its appalling influence, leaped through the bushes, and came bounding across the open ground, flourishing a tomahawk. Still Deerslayer moved not, but stood with his unloaded rifle fallen against his shoulders, while, with a hunter's habits, his hands were mechanically feeling for the powder horn and charger. When about forty feet from his enemy, the savage hurled his keen weapon, but it was with an eye so vacant and a hand so unsteady and feeble that the young man caught it by the handle as it was flying past him. At that instant, the Indian staggered and fell his whole length on the ground.

appalling: filled with dismay
countenance: the expression of the face

"I know'd it—I know'd it!" exclaimed Deerslayer, who was already preparing to force a fresh bullet into his rifle; "I know'd it must come to this as soon as I had got the range from the creatur's eyes. A man sights suddenly and fires quick when his own life's in danger; yes, I know'd it would come to this. I was about the hundredth part of a second too quick for him, or it might have been bad for me! The riptyle's* bullet has just grazed my side—but, say what you will for or ag'in 'em, a redskin is by no means as sartain with powder and ball as a white man. Their gifts don't seem to lie thataway. Even Chingachgook,

great as he is in other matters, isn't downright deadly with the rifle."

riptyle's: reptile's

By this time the piece was reloaded, and Deerslayer, after tossing the tomahawk into the canoe, advanced to his victim and stood over him, leaning on his rifle, in melancholy attention. It was the first instance in which he had seen a man fall in battle—it was the first fellow creature against whom he had ever seriously raised his own hand. The sensations were novel, and regret, with the freshness of our better feelings, mingled with his triumph. The Indian was not dead, though shot directly through the body. He lay on his back, motionless, but his eyes, now full of consciousness, watched each action of his victor—as the fallen bird regards the fowler*—jealous of every movement. The man probably expected the fatal blow which was to precede the loss of his scalp, or perhaps he anticipated that this latter act of cruelty would precede his death. Deerslayer read his thoughts, and he found a melancholy satisfaction in relieving the apprehensions of the helpless savage.

fowler: a hunter of birds

"No, no, redskin," he said, "you've nothing more to fear from me. I am of a Christian stock, and scalping is not of my gifts. I'll just make sartain of your rifle and then come back and do you what sarvice I can. Though here I can't stay much longer, as the crack of three rifles will be apt to bring some of your devils down upon me."

The close of this was said in a sort of a soliloquy, as the young man went in quest of the fallen rifle. The piece was found where its owner had dropped it and was immediately put into the canoe. Laying his own rifle at its side, Deerslayer then returned and stood over the Indian again.

"All inmity* atween you and me's at an ind, redskin," he said, "and you may set your heart at rest on the score of the scalp, or any further injury. My gifts are white, as I've told you, and I hope my conduct will be white also!''

inmity: enmity: i.e., hostility

Could looks have conveyed all they meant, it is probable Deerslayer's innocent vanity on the subject of color would have been rebuked a little, but he comprehended the gratitude that was expressed in the eyes of the dying savage, without in the least detecting the bitter sarcasm that struggled with the better feeling.

''Water!'' exclaimed the thirsty and unfortunate creature, ''give poor Injin water.''

''Aye, water you shall have, if you drink the lake dry. I'll just carry you down to it, that you make take your fill. This is the way, they tell me, with all wounded people—water is their greatest comfort and delight.''

So saying, Deerslayer raised the Indian in his arms and carried him to the lake. Here he first helped him to take an attitude* in which he could appease his burning thirst, after which he seated himself on a stone, and took the head of his wounded adversary in his own lap, and endeavored to soothe his anguish in the best manner he could.

attitude: position

''It would be sinful in me to tell you your time hadn't come, warrior,'' he commenced, ''and therefore I'll not say it. You've passed the middle age already, and considerin' the sort of lives ye lead, your days have been pretty well filled. The principal thing now is to look forward to what comes next. Neither redskin nor paleface, on the whole, calculates much on sleepin' forever, but both expect to live in another world. Each has his gifts, and will be judged by 'em, and I suppose you've thought these matters over enough not to stand in need of sarmons when the trial comes. You'll find your happy hunting grounds, if you've been a just Injin; if an onjust, you'll meet your desarts* in another way. I've my own idees about

these things, but you're too old and exper'enced to need any explanations from one as young as I.''

desarts: deserts: i.e., that which is deserved

''Good!'' exclaimed the Indian, whose voice retained its depth even as life ebbed away; ''young head—ole wisdom!''

''It's sometimes a consolation, when the ind comes, to know that them we've harmed, or *tried* to harm, forgive us. I suppose natur' seeks this relief by way of getting a pardon on 'arth, as we never can know whether He pardons, who is all in all, till judgment itself comes. It's soothing to know that *any* pardon at such times, and that, I conclude, is the secret. Now, as for myself, I overlook altogether your designs ag'in my life; first, because no harm came of 'em; next, because it's your gifts, and natur', and trainin', and I ought not to have trusted you at all; and, finally and chiefly, because I can bear no ill will to a dying man, whether heathen or Christian. So put your heart at ease, so far as I'm consarned; you know best what other matters ought to trouble you, or what ought to give you satisfaction in so trying a moment.''

It is probable that the Indian had some of the fearful glimpses of the unknown state of being which God in mercy seems at times to afford to all the human race, but they were necessarily in conformity with his habits and prejudices. Like most of his people, and like too many of our own, he thought more of dying in a way to gain applause among those he left than to secure a better state of existence hereafter. While Deerslayer was speaking, his mind was a little bewildered, though he felt that the intention was good, and when he had done, a regret passed over his spirit that none of his own tribe were present to witness his stoicism,* under extreme bodily suffering, and the firmness with which he met his end. With the high innate courtesy that so often distinguishes the Indian warrior before he becomes corrupted by too much intercourse with the worst class of the white men, he endeavored to express his thankfulness for the other's good intentions and to let him understand that they were appreciated.

stoicism: indifference to pleasure or pain

"Good!" he repeated, for this was an English word much used by the savages–"good–young head; young *heart,* too. *Old* heart tough; no shed tear. Hear Indian when he die, and no want to lie–what he call him?"

"Deerslayer is the name I bear now, though the Delawares have said that when I get back from this warpath, I shall have a more manly title, provided I can 'arn one."

"That good name for boy–poor name for warrior. He get better quick. No fear *there*"–the savage had strength sufficient, under the strong excitement he felt, to raise a hand and tap the young man on his breast–"eye sartain–finger lightning–aim, death–great warrior soon. No Deerslayer–Hawkeye–Hawkeye–Hawkeye. Shake hand."

For Thought and Discussion

1. Discuss Cooper's description of the natural setting in paragraph two. In what sense is this prose passage poetic in quality? What images does Cooper employ? What kind of mood does Cooper create for the story in this description? Contrast Cooper's conception of nature with Freneau's.

2. Do you consider the dialogue in the story effective? Why or why not? Which dialect does Cooper write more realistically, the Deerslayer's or the Indian's? Why?

3. Find one metaphor and one simile in paragraph eight. To which character does each of these imaginative comparisons refer? Do you consider them appropriate and effective? Why or why not?

4. The excerpt which you read from *The Deerslayer* is often described by critics as Deerslayer's formal rite of initiation into manhood. How does Cooper achieve a ritualistic flavor in this passage? Do you feel that the passage depicts loss of his youthful innocence as well? Why or why not?

5. Why do you suppose Cooper includes a long, philosophical "soliloquy" by Deerslayer in the end of the story? Does it add to or detract from his characterization? What is its function in terms of the passage?

William Cullen Bryant
1794-1878

While still a teen-ager, William Cullen Bryant showed literary promise with the publication of several poems. For more than half a century thereafter, he shaped critical standards of American poetry. As influential editor of a leading New York newspaper, he also shaped national opinion on major social and political issues.

Although his physician-father intended Bryant for a career in medicine, the poet's true interest lay elsewhere. When only fifteen, he entered Williams College as a sophomore. Finding little intellectual challenge there, he left before he had finished his first year and began reading law. After three years of independent study, he entered the legal profession, practicing in Massachusetts for nine years. In 1827, having published "An Essay on American Poetry" and his first volume of verse, Bryant joined the editorial staff of the New York *Evening Post*. Two years later he became part owner and editor-in-chief, a position he held until his death. While continuing to write poetry and essays of literary criticism, Bryant editorially supported abolitionism, free trade, the right to form trade unions, and freedom of speech and of the press. In 1855 he helped organize the Republican party and lent strong support to Lincoln and the Union. When he died in 1878, he left an estate valued at one million dollars and several volumes of poetry, letters, and criticism.

Bryant's romanticism—which frequently invites comparison with that of William Wordsworth (1770-1850), the father of the romantic movement in England—permeates his poetry. Although the form of his verse shows the classical restraint characteristic of the eighteenth century, his themes tend to emphasize nature, death, and the past. Like other romantics Bryant presents Nature as a moral teacher. His poems rarely stop with a natural scene but go on to point out some truth. After 1830 Bryant's verse showed little new in form or content; yet the poet remained active to the end of his life, writing as vigorously in his eighties as he had in his twenties.

Often incorporating religious ideas, Bryant's poetry reflects both the Puritan and the Deistic traditions of the seventeenth and eighteenth centuries. "To a Waterfowl," for instance, states the orthodox Puritan view that a Power (God) providentially guides a man through life. "Thanatopsis," however, sounds a pagan call for resignation to death and denies the fact of an afterlife. Because his religious views lack Biblical consistency, his poetry gives the uncertain sound against which Scripture warns us (see I Cor. 14:8).

Thanatopsis

This poem was first written in 1811, when Bryant was only sixteen. When it was reviewed by the North American Review, *one of the editors exclaimed that no American could have written it. In its original form the poem lacked the first seventeen lines and the last fifteen. Bryant added these two sections when he prepared the poem for inclusion in* Poems *(1821). Not until he added these lines did he identify the message in the poem as coming from Nature.*

Bryant wrote "Thanatopsis" in **blank verse,** *unrhymed iambic pentameter. Each line has five stressed syllables, alternating with five unstressed ones: "She has a voice of gladness, and a smile" (l. 4). These ten syllables divide into five feet of two syllables each. A foot with one unstressed syllable followed by a stressed one is called an* **iamb.** *Since there are five iambs in each line, we call the verse form* **iambic pentameter.** *A line may be divided by a* **caesura** *(pause)—see line 3, for instance: "A various language;/for his gayer hours. . . ."*

The title means "meditation on death." The fact that the poem does not regard man as having a soul or give him any hope of an afterlife shows how far serious poetry had drifted from Puritanism.

To him who in the love of Nature holds
Communion with her visible forms, she speaks
A various language; for his gayer hours
She has a voice of gladness, and a smile
And eloquence of beauty, and she glides   5
Into his darker musings, with a mild
And healing sympathy, that steals away
Their sharpness, ere he is aware. When thoughts
Of the last bitter hour come like a blight
Over thy spirit, and sad images   10
Of the stern agony, and shroud,* and pall,*
And breathless darkness, and the narrow house,*
Make thee to shudder and grow sick at heart;—
Go forth, under the open sky, and list*
To Nature's teachings, while from all around—   15
Earth and her waters, and the depths of air—
Comes a still voice—Yet a few days, and thee
The all-beholding sun shall see no more
In all his course; nor yet in the cold ground,
Where thy pale form was laid, with many tears,   20
Nor in the embrace of ocean, shall exist
Thy image. Earth, that nourished thee, shall claim
Thy growth, to be resolved to earth again,

shroud: garment for the dead/*pall:* a covering, usually black, thrown over a coffin
narrow house: grave
list: listen

And, lost each human trace, surrendering up
Thine individual being, shalt thou go   25
To mix forever with the elements,
To be a brother to the insensible rock
And to the sluggish clod,* which the rude swain*
Turns with his share,* and treads upon. The oak
Shall send his roots abroad, and pierce thy mould.*   30

clod: lump of earth/ rude swain: uneducated farmer
share: plowshare
mould: the decaying corpse

    Yet not to thine eternal resting-place
Shalt thou retire alone, nor couldst thou wish
Couch more magnificent. Thou shalt lie down
With patriarchs of the infant world—with kings,
The powerful of the earth—the wise, the good,   35
Fair forms, and hoary* seers* of ages past,
All in one mighty sepulchre. The hills

hoary: white-(haired), revered/seers: prophets

Rock-ribbed and ancient as the sun,—the vales
Stretching in pensive* quietness between;

pensive: thoughtful

The venerable* woods—rivers that move   40
In majesty, and the complaining* brooks

venerable: aged, worthy of reverence
complaining: murmuring

That make the meadows green; and, poured round all,
Old Ocean's gray and melancholy waste,—
Are but the solemn decorations all
Of the great tomb of man. The golden sun,   45
The planets, all the infinite host of heaven,
Are shining on the sad abodes of death,
Through the still lapse of ages. All that tread
The globe are but a handful to the tribes
That slumber in its bosom.—Take the wings   50
Of morning,* pierce the Barcan wilderness,*
Or lose thyself in the continuous woods
Where rolls the Oregon,* and hears no sound,
Save his own dashings—yet the dead are there:

See Psalms 139:9/ Barcan wilderness: ancient North African desert, thus barren
Oregon: now the Columbia River in the Northwest

And millions in those solitudes, since first   55
The flight of years began, have laid them down
In their last sleep—the dead reign there alone.
So shalt thou rest, and what if thou withdraw
In silence from the living, and no friend
Take note of thy departure? All that breathe   60
Will share thy destiny. The gay will laugh
When thou art gone, the solemn brood of care
Plod on, and each one as before will chase
His favorite phantom; yet all these shall leave
Their mirth and their employments, and shall come   65

And make their bed with thee. As the long train
Of ages glides away, the sons of men,
The youth in life's green spring, and he who goes
In the full strength of years, matron and maid,
The speechless babe, and the gray-headed man—   70
Shall one by one be gathered to thy side,
By those, who in their turn shall follow them.

   So live, that when thy summons comes to join
The innumerable caravan, which moves
To that mysterious realm, where each shall take   75
His chamber in the silent halls of death,
Thou go not, like the quarry-slave at night,
Scourged to his dungeon, but, sustained and soothed
By an unfaltering trust, approach thy grave,
Like one who wraps the drapery of his couch*   80   *couch:* bed
About him, and lies down to pleasant dreams.

To a Waterfowl

This poem grew out of a specific problem Bryant faced when he was twenty-one. One December day, while walking to Plainfield, Massachusetts, to inquire about the opportunites there for practicing law, he felt especially desolate. As he watched a solitary bird fly across the horizon, he sensed a special meaning in the bird's flight. Both he and the bird seemed to be traveling to some definite, though unknown, destination. When he reached the house where he was spending the night, he immediately wrote the poem. Notice that he clarifies the lesson from Nature in stanzas 4 and 8.

   Whither, midst falling dew,
While glow the heavens with the last steps of day,
Far, through their rosy depths, dost thou pursue
   Thy solitary way?

   Vainly the fowler's* eye   5   *fowler's:* hunter's
Might mark thy distant flight to do thee wrong,
As, darkly seen against the crimson sky,
   Thy figure floats along.

   Seek'st thou the plashy* brink   *plashy:* a small pool
Of weedy lake, or marge* of river wide,   10   *marge:* edge: i.e., bank
Or where the rocking billows rise and sink
   On the chafed* ocean-side?   *chafed:* rubbed by
                      waves breaking on
                      the shores

There is a Power whose care
Teaches thy way along that pathless coast—
The desert* and illimitable* air—   15   *desert:* deserted / *illimit-*
    Lone wandering, but not lost.   *able:* boundless

    All day thy wings have fanned,
At that far height, the cold, thin atmosphere,
Yet stoop not, weary, to the welcome land,
    Though the dark night is near.   20

    And soon that toil shall end;
Soon shalt thou find a summer home, and rest,
And scream among thy fellows; reeds shall bend,
    Soon, o'er thy sheltered nest.

    Thou'rt gone, the abyss* of heaven   25   *abyss:* a bottomless
Hath swallowed up thy form; yet, on my heart   void
Deeply hath sunk the lesson thou hast given,
    And shall not soon depart.

    He who, from zone to zone,
Guides through the boundless sky thy certain flight,   30
In the long way that I must tread alone,
    Will lead my steps aright.

For Thought and Discussion

1. To what general audience does Bryant address "Thanatopsis"? Who is the understood *you* of line 14 and the *thee* of line 17? What consolation does Bryant offer to this audience? Is the consolation effective from your point of view?
2. In what ways does the Christian view of death differ from Bryant's? What is the "unfaltering trust" to which Bryant refers in line 79?
3. Summarize Bryant's four major arguments in the long middle stanza of "Thanatopsis" (ll. 31-72).
4. How does Bryant's view of the universe differ in "Thanatopsis" and "To a Waterfowl"? To which view do you react more positively? Why?
5. Why do you suppose Bryant chose to write "Thanatopsis" in blank verse and "To a Waterfowl" in rhymed quatrains? Does the verse form suit the context of each poem?
6. What does the flight of the waterfowl symbolize to the speaker of "To a Waterfowl"? Find and discuss the meaning of at least one other symbol in the poem.

1820

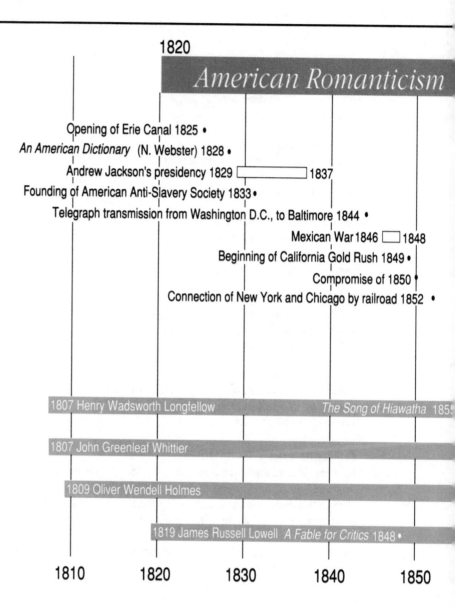

American Romanticism

Opening of Erie Canal 1825 •
An American Dictionary (N. Webster) 1828 •
Andrew Jackson's presidency 1829 ☐ 1837
Founding of American Anti-Slavery Society 1833 •
Telegraph transmission from Washington D.C., to Baltimore 1844 •
Mexican War 1846 ☐ 1848
Beginning of California Gold Rush 1849 •
Compromise of 1850 •
Connection of New York and Chicago by railroad 1852 •

1807 Henry Wadsworth Longfellow   *The Song of Hiawatha* 185

1807 John Greenleaf Whittier

1809 Oliver Wendell Holmes

1819 James Russell Lowell *A Fable for Critics* 1848 •

1810   1820   1830   1840   1850

1865

5 | *New England School*

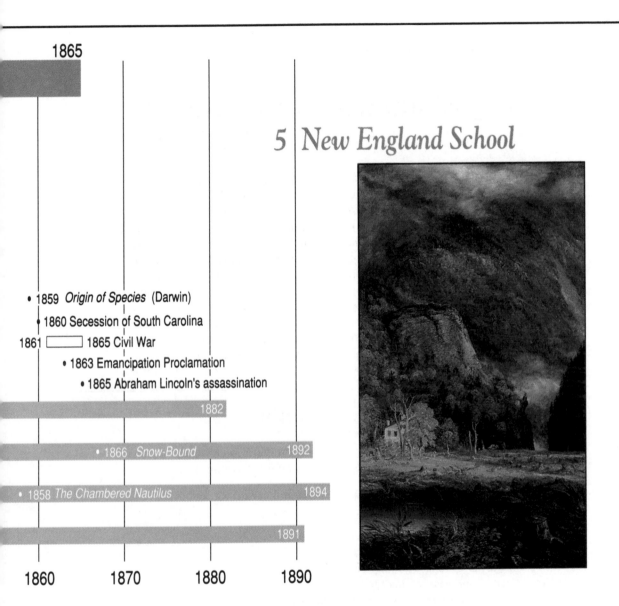

- • 1859 *Origin of Species* (Darwin)
- • 1860 Secession of South Carolina
- 1861 ☐ 1865 Civil War
- • 1863 Emancipation Proclamation
- • 1865 Abraham Lincoln's assassination

1882

• 1866 *Snow-Bound* 1892

• 1858 *The Chambered Nautilus* 1894

1891

| 1860 | 1870 | 1880 | 1890 |

Henry Wadsworth Longfellow
1807-1882

During his lifetime Henry Wadsworth Longfellow achieved remarkable popularity, both in the States and England. He was the first American to have his bust placed in the Poet's Corner of Westminster Abbey. A professor of modern languages at Bowdoin College, Maine, and then at Harvard, Longfellow was our first influential professor-poet. The most versatile of the New England School, he wrote in a variety of genres and verse forms. His epic-length works *Evangeline* (1847), *The Song of Hiawatha* (1855), and *The Courtship of Miles Standish* (1858), all of which drew heavily from America's past, were highly praised in his day. Longfellow's Americanization of European themes and forms has been cited as his greatest achievement. After the death of his second wife in 1861, his work took on a melancholy mood. From this tragedy, however, came some of the poet's best work. Although Longfellow's literary reputation plummeted in the early part of the twentieth century, his poetic craftsmanship, especially in his sonnets, is bringing grudging respect from modern critics.

Mezzo Cammin

This poem, the title of which is Italian meaning "halfway up the road," was never published by Longfellow because of the private nature of its content.

Written at Boppard on the Rhine August 25, 1842, Just Before Leaving for Home

> Half of my life is gone, and I have let
> The years slip from me and have not fulfilled
> The aspiration* of my youth, to build
> Some tower of song with lofty parapet.*
> Not indolence, nor pleasure, nor the fret   5
> Of restless passions that would not be stilled,
> But sorrow, and a care that almost killed,*
> Kept me from what I may accomplish yet;
> Though, half-way up the hill, I see the Past
> Lying beneath me with its sounds and sights,–   10
> A city in the twilight dim and vast,
> With smoking roofs, soft bells, and gleaming lights,–
> And hear above me on the autumnal blast
> The cataract* of Death far thundering from the heights.

aspiration: high ambition
parapet: low bordering wall on the top of a tower

But . . . killed: Longfellow's first wife, Mary, had died in 1835 in Rotterdam, during his previous trip abroad.

cataract: waterfall

from Divina Commedia

To relieve his grief after his second wife's tragic death, Longfellow turned to the task of translating the Divine Comedy, *the greatest work by the fourteenth-century Italian poet Dante Alighieri. While translating this work into English, Longfellow wrote two* **sonnets** *to precede each of the three parts of Dante's work.*

Oft have I seen at some cathedral door
  A laborer, pausing in the dust and heat,
  Lay down his burden, and with reverent feet
  Enter, and cross himself, and on the floor
Kneel to repeat his paternoster* o'er;   5
  Far off the noises of the world retreat;
  The loud vociferations* of the street
  Become an undistinguishable roar.
So, as I enter here from day to day,
  And leave my burden at this minster* gate,   10
  Kneeling in prayer, and not ashamed to pray,
The tumult of the time disconsolate*
  To inarticulate* murmurs dies away,
  While the eternal ages watch and wait.

paternoster: the Lord's Prayer (in Latin the opening words are "Pater Noster")

vociferations: shouts

minster: cathedral

disconsolate: inconsolable

inarticulate: uttered without distinct sounds

For Thought and Discussion

1. Determine the rhyme scheme and outline the structure of "Mezzo Cammin."
2. Many critics have described the tone of "Mezzo Cammin" as one of self-pity. Do you agree with their assessment? Why or why not? What, if any, portion of the poem is hopeful?
3. Discuss the role of nature in "Mezzo Cammin." Contrast Longfellow's view of nature in this context with Bryant's view.
4. Determine the rhyme scheme and outline the structure of the introductory sonnet to *Divina Commedia.* How is this sonnet similar in form to "Mezzo Cammin"?
5. The sonnet from *Divina Commedia* is built around the central comparison of a laborer's entering a cathedral for a brief respite from the cares of life to Longfellow's own daily preparation to enter upon the large task of making an English poetic translation of Dante's *Divine Comedy.* What details in the poem contribute to Longfellow's development of this central metaphor? In what sense is Dante's work a cathedral? What happens to the persona as he "enter[s] here from day to day" (l. 9)? If this sonnet, like "Mezzo Cammin," is autobiographical, which phrases of the work might you appreciate better if you had knowledge of specific events which prompted Longfellow's expression?

John Greenleaf Whittier
1807-1892

John Greenleaf Whittier, the foremost voice in the literary war against slavery, was a self-made poet strongly influenced by the Scottish poet Robert Burns. The least typical of the New England school, Whittier was a leading writer with almost no formal schooling, a devout Quaker, and an outspoken abolitionist nearly killed twice by mob reaction to his activities. A prolific writer, he published more than thirty volumes during his lifetime. His most popular was *Snow-Bound* (1866), which recounted the experiences of a household during a New England snowstorm. Whittier used this narrative not only to give a detailed picture of rural life but also to express his philosophical views on slavery, social reform, human guilt, and death. By the time he died in 1892, his popularity was second only to Longfellow's.

Ichabod

Whittier wrote this **dirge** *(a poem expressing lament or mourning) in disillusionment over Daniel Webster's speech in support of the Compromise of 1850, which allowed slavery in the new territory gained from the Mexican War.*

So fallen! so lost! the light withdrawn
    Which once he wore!
The glory from his gray hairs gone
    Forevermore!

Revile him not, the Tempter hath   5
    A snare for all;
And pitying tears, not scorn and wrath,
    Befit his fall!

Oh, dumb be passion's stormy rage,
    When he who might   10
Have lighted up and led his age,
    Falls back in night.

Scorn! would the angels laugh, to mark
    A bright soul driven,
Fiend-goaded, down the endless dark,   15
    From hope and heaven!

Let not the land once proud of him
    Insult him now,
Nor brand with deeper shame his dim,
    Dishonored brow.   20

But let its humbled sons, instead,
    From sea to lake,
A long lament, as for the dead,
    In sadness make.

Of all we loved and honored, naught   25
    Save power remains;
A fallen angel's pride of thought,
    Still strong in chains.

All else is gone; from those great eyes
    The soul has fled: 30
When faith is lost, when honor dies,
    The man is dead!

Then pay the reverence of old days
    To his dead fame;
Walk backwards, with averted gaze,   35
    And hide the shame!

First-Day Thoughts

Whittier's Quaker background pervades this poem. "First-day" is the term Quakers substituted for "Sunday" in order to avoid reference to pagan gods for whom the days of the week had been named. The Quaker doctrine of the "Inner Light"–the notion that all men possess within them the presence of God to guide them–brought Quakers (known officially as the Society of Friends) to de-emphasize the Bible and to emphasize men's intuitive goodness and desire to serve truth. This doctrine, combined with other religious and political positions, had caused the Puritans in the seventeenth century to condemn Quakers as heretics. In fact, even though certain sentiments in the poem attract the Christian (the spirit of worship, ll. 1-14, and the poet's desire to serve God, ll. 15-22), this poem is marred for the Christian reader by what it assumes to be true about the nature of man.

In calm and cool and silence, once again
 I find my old accustomed place among
 My brethren, where, perchance, no human tongue
 Shall utter words; where never hymn is sung,
 Nor deep-toned organ blown, nor censer* swung,   5
Nor dim light falling through the pictured pane!*
There, syllabled by silence, let me hear
The still small voice which reached the prophet's* ear;
Read in my heart a still diviner law
Than Israel's leader* on his tables saw!   10
There let me strive with each besetting sin,
 Recall my wandering fancies, and restrain
 The sore disquiet of a restless brain;
 And, as the path of duty is made plain,
May grace be given that I may walk therein,   15
 Not like the hireling,* for his selfish gain,
With backward glances and reluctant tread,
Making a merit of his coward dread,
 But, cheerful, in the light around me thrown,
 Walking as one to pleasant service led;   20
 Doing God's will as if it were my own,
Yet trusting not in mine, but in his strength alone!

censer: vessel for incense
pictured pane: i.e., a stained-glass window

prophet's: Elijah's (cf. I Kings 19:12)
Israel's leader: Moses' (cf. Exod. 20:1-17; Prov. 3:3; Jer. 17:1)

hireling: hired man: see John 10:12

For Thought and Discussion

1. Discuss the significance of the title "Ichabod," which Whittier derives from I Samuel 4:19-22. Are there any parallels between the Biblical account and Whittier's lament over Webster's support of slavery other than the etymological meaning of the title? Does the title strengthen Whittier's theme in "Ichabod," or does it detract from it? Why?

2. Find as many Biblical allusions as possible in "Ichabod," and discuss the appropriateness of each in terms of Whittier's theme.

3. In the first full sentence of "First-Day Thoughts," Whittier includes a negative catalogue, or, in this case, a list of what the speaker does not expect to find as he takes his place with his brethren. List the five elements of this negative catalogue. In what way would the effect of Whittier's poem be different had he not included this catalogue?

4. Determine the poetic meter of "First-Day Thoughts." Only one line is irregular. Which line is it? Why do you suppose Whittier chose to make this particular line irregular?

5. In which poem do you believe Whittier's Biblical allusions to be more effective, "Ichabod" or "First-Day Thoughts"? Why?

James Russell Lowell
1819-1891

James Russell Lowell, like Whittier, was an avid poetic spokesman for various reforms in the nineteenth century. Unlike the rest of the New England School, Lowell was highly influential also through his prose. His 1865 essay on the transcendentalist Henry David Thoreau, in fact, destroyed Thoreau's reputation for the rest of the century. Lowell was an astute critic: *A Fable for Critics* (1848), a verse-satire on contemporary writers, accurately assessed their strengths and weaknesses. *The Biglow Papers* (1848, 1867), two series of dialect works by Hosea Biglow, a homespun village bard, caught the New England dialect beautifully. During his lifetime Lowell held numerous positions of honor, serving as Smith Professor of Modern Languages at Harvard (1855-76); first editor of the *Atlantic Monthly* (1857-61); coeditor of the *North American Review* (1863-72); and, like Washington Irving, minister to Spain (1866-80) and to England (1880-85). Due to his influence and output, Lowell deserves recognition as an important American writer.

from A Fable for Critics

[Ralph Waldo Emerson]

"There comes Emerson first, whose rich words, every one,
Are like gold nails* in temples to hang trophies on,
Whose prose is grand verse, while his verse, heaven knows,
Is some of it pr–No, 'tis not even prose;
I'm speaking of metres; some poems have welled   5
From those rare depths of soul that have ne'er been excelled;
They're not epics, but that doesn't matter a pin,
In creating, the only hard thing's to begin;
A grass-blade's no easier to make than an oak;
If you've once found the way, you've achieved the grand stroke;   10
In the worst of his poems are mines of rich matter,
But thrown in a heap with a crash and a clatter;
Now it is not one thing nor another alone
Makes a poem, but rather the general tone,
The something pervading, uniting the whole,   15
The before unconceived, unconceivable soul,
So that just in removing this trifle or that, you
Take away, as it were, a chief limb of the statue;
Roots, wood, bark, and leaves singly perfect may be,
But, clapt hodge-podge together, they don't make a tree.   20

nails: see Ecclesiastes 12:11

[William Cullen Bryant]

"There is Bryant, as quiet, as cool, and as dignified,
As a smooth, silent iceberg, that never is ignified,*
Save when by reflection 'tis kindled o' nights
With a semblance of flame by the chill Northern Lights.
He may rank (Griswold* says so) first bard of your nation   25
(There's no doubt that he stands in supreme iceolation),
Your topmost Parnassus* he may set his heel on,
But no warm applauses come, peal following peal on,–
He's too smooth and too polished to hang any zeal on:
Unqualified merits, I'll grant, if you choose, he has 'em,   30
But he lacks the one merit of kindling enthusiasm;
If he stir you at all, it is just, on my soul,
Like being stirred up with the very North Pole.

ignified: set on fire

Griswold: Rufus Wilmot Griswold (1815-57), popular editor at the middle of the nineteenth century

Parnassus: the Greek mountain regarded as sacred to Apollo (the god of poetry) and his Muses (the goddesses of the various arts)

[Edgar Allan Poe]

"There comes Poe, with his raven, like Barnaby Rudge,*
Three-fifths of him genius and two-fifths sheer fudge . . .   35
Who has written some things quite the best of their kind,
But the heart somehow seems all squeezed out by the mind,
Who–But hey-day! What's this? Messieurs Mathews* and Poe,
You mustn't fling mud-balls at Longfellow so,*
Does it make a man worse that his character's such   40
As to make his friends love him (as you think) too much?
Why, there is not a bard at this moment alive
More willing than he that his fellows should thrive;
While you are abusing him thus, even now
He would help either one of you out of a slough;*   45
You may say that he's smooth and all that till you're hoarse,
But remember that elegance also is force.

Barnaby Rudge: central character, who owned a raven, in Charles Dickens's *Barnaby Rudge* (1841)
Mathews: a writer critical of Longfellow's poetic form and subject matter
You . . . so: Poe bitterly attacked Longfellow, even accusing him of plagiarism
slough: a stagnant swamp

[James Russell Lowell]

"There is Lowell,* who's striving Parnassus to climb
With a whole bale of *isms* tied together with rhyme,
He might get on alone, spite of brambles and boulders,
But he can't with that bundle* he has on his shoulders   50
The top of the hill he will ne'er come nigh reaching
Till he learns the distinction 'twix singing and preaching;
His lyre has some chords that would ring pretty well,
But he'd rather by half make a drum of the shell,   55
And rattle away till he's old as Methusalem,*
At the head of a march to the last new Jerusalem."*

Lowell: the poet himself

bundle: his "bale of *isms*"

Methusalem: Genesis 5:27
new Jerusalem: the millennial kingdom

The Courtin'

The poem typifies the New England dialect Lowell used throughout his two series of Biglow Papers. *One of the few nonsatiric works in these papers, this poem was originally written to satisfy a printer's request for something to fill up a blank page in the first series. For the second series Lowell expanded his description of the characters and situation, creating the version reprinted here.*

God makes sech nights, all white an' still
 Fur'z you can look or listen,
Moonshine an' snow on field an' hill,
 All silence an' all glisten.

Zekle crep' up quite unbeknown
 An' peeked in thru' the winder,
An' there sot Huldy all alone,
 'ith no one nigh to hender.

A fireplace filled the room's one side
    With half a cord o' wood in–   10
There warn't no stoves (tell comfort died)
    To bake ye to a puddin'.

The wa'nut logs shot sparkles out
    Towards the pootiest, bless her,
An' leetle flames danced all about   15
    The chiny on the dresser.

Agin the chimbley crook-necks hung,
    An' in amongst 'em rusted
The ole queen's-arm thet gran'ther Young
    Fetched back f'om Concord busted.   20

The very room, coz she was in,
    Seemed warm f'om floor to ceilin',
An' she looked full ez rosy agin
    Ez the apples she was peelin'.

'Twas kin' 'o kingdom-come to look   25
    On sech a blessed cretur,
A dogrose blushin' to a brook
    Ain't modester nor sweeter.

He was six foot o' man, A 1,
    Clear grit an' human natur'.   30
None couldn't quicker pitch a ton
    Nor dror a furrer straighter.

He'd sparked it with full twenty gals,
    He'd squired 'em, danced 'em, druv 'em,
Fust this one, an' then thet, by spells–   35
    All is, he couldn't love 'em.

But long o' her his veins 'ould run
    All crinkly like curled maple,
The side she breshed felt full o' sun
    Ez a south slope in Ap'il.   40

She thought no v'ice hed sech a swing
    Ez hisn in the choir;
My! when he made Ole Hunderd ring,
    She *knowed* the Lord was nigher.

An' she blush scarlit, right in prayer,   45
    When her new meetin'-bunnet
Felt somehow thru' its crown a pair
    O' blue eyes sot upun it.

Thet night, I tell ye, she looked *some!*
    She seemed to 've gut a new soul,   50
For she felt sartin-sure he'd come,
    Down to her very shoe-sole.

She heered a foot, an' knowed it tu,
   A-raspin' on the scraper,–
All ways to once her feelin's flew   55
   Like sparks in burnt-up paper.

He kin' o' l'tered on the mat,
   Some doubtfle o' the sekle,
His heart kep' goin' pity-pat,
   But hern went pity Zekle.   60

An' yit she gin her cheer a jerk
   Ez though she wished him furder,
An' on her apples kep' to work,
   Parin' away like murder.

"You want to see my Pa, I s'pose?"   65
   "Wal . . . no . . . I come dasignin' "–
"To see my Ma? She's sprinklin' clo'es
   Agin to-morrer's i'nin'."

To say why gals acts so or so,
   Or don't, 'ould be persumin';   70
Mebby to mean *yes* an' say *no*
   Comes nateral to women.

He stood a spell on one foot fust,
   Then stood a spell on t'other,
An' on which one he felt the wust   75
   He couldn't ha' told ye nuther.

Says he, "I'd better call agin!"
   Says she, "Think likely, Mister:"
Thet last word pricked him like a pin,
   An' . . . Wal, he up an' kist her.   80

When Ma bimeby upon 'em slips,
   Huldy sot pale ez ashes,
All kin' o' smily roun' the lips
   An' teary roun' the lashes.

For she was jes' the quiet kind   85
   Whose naturs never vary,
Like streams that keep a summer mind
   Snowhid in Jenooary.

The blood clost roun' her heart felt glued
   Too tight for all expressin',   90
Tell mother see how metters stood,
   An' gin 'em both her blessin'.

Then her red come back like the tide
   Down to the Bay o' Fundy,
An' all I know is they was cried   95
   In meetin' come nex' Sunday.

The Lesson

In this poem Lowell uses nature to teach a lesson about man's pride. The comparison of man's reasoning to the firefly's reveals the foolishness of man's attempts to define God in terms of himself. In the manner of a sermon, the last few lines draw the "lesson" from the illustration. Benjamin Franklin's "The Ephemera" is an eighteenth-century prose parallel to Lowell's poem.

I sat and watched the walls of night
With cracks of sudden lightning glow,
And listened while with clumsy might
The thunder wallowed to and fro.
The rain fell softly now; the squall,   5

That to a torrent drove the trees,
Had whirled beyond us to let fall
Its tumult on the whitening seas.
But still the lightning crinkled keen,
Or fluttered fitful from behind   10
The leaden drifts, then only seen,
That rumbled eastward on the wind.
Still as gloom followed after glare,
While bated breath the pine-trees drew,
Tiny Salmoneus* of the air,   15
His mimic bolts the firefly threw.
He thought, no doubt, "Those flashes grand,
That light for leagues the shuddering sky,
Are made, a fool could understand,
By some superior kind of fly.   20
He's of our race's elder branch
His family-arms the same as ours,
Both born the twy-forked* flame to launch,
Of kindred, if unequal, powers."
And is man wiser? Man who takes
His consciousness the law to be   25
Of all beyond his ken,* and makes
God but a bigger kind of Me?

Salmoneus: legendary king who pretended to be Zeus by flinging torches into the air to mimic lightning and making noise like thunder with his chariot. Zeus retaliated by striking Salmoneus with a real bolt of lightning.

twy-forked: divided in two, like a fork

ken: understanding

For Thought and Discussion

1. What two lines in Lowell's stanza on Emerson from *A Fable for Critics* are characterized by feminine rhyme? Check the glossary of this text if you do not know what feminine rhyme is.

2. Which line in Lowell's stanza on Bryant ends with a pun? Explain the significance of the pun in Lowell's context.

3. Summarize the narrative (story) of "The Courtin'." From what point of view is the poem narrated? What kind of person is the narrator?

4. Discuss the significance of the title of "The Lesson." Would the poem make a different impression if the title were changed?

5. Lines 14-16 are the most difficult of "The Lesson." Paraphrase lines 14-16, answering these questions: What is the verb in the sentence? What is the direct object? What is the grammatical function of the phrase "the firefly"? Next determine the antecedent of the pronoun *He* in line 17. Does Lowell's allusion to classical mythology in this passage enhance or detract from the meaning of the poem? Why?

Oliver Wendell Holmes
1809-1894

Oliver Wendell Holmes excelled in humorous prose and verse as well as serious poetry. Trained in medicine at Boston (1830-33) and Paris (1833-35), Holmes served as medical professor at Dartmouth (1838-40) and Harvard (1847-82). Yet he found time to lecture widely on literary topics and to produce four witty conversation books (for example, *The Autocrat of the Breakfast Table),* two biographies (one of Ralph Waldo Emerson, with whom Holmes had little spiritual kinship), three medical novels, and a nearly endless flow of poems, much of which was **occasional verse** (written for a specific occasion). A leading contributor to the *Atlantic Monthly* (Holmes had named it), he enjoyed a wide reading audience on both sides of the Atlantic. A scientific rationalist and outspoken Unitarian, Holmes sought to destroy the conservative religion of his fathers. His most famous attack appears in ''The Deacon's Masterpiece or, The Wonderful 'One-Hoss Shay': A Logical Story'' (1858), an allegorical **satire** on Jonathan Edwards and New England Calvinism. Although significant in the development of medical practice, Holmes is remembered today primarily for his avocation, literature, and especially for his light verse. His son, named after him, became equally well known as associate justice of the Supreme Court from 1902 to 1932.

Old Ironsides

Holmes wrote this patriotic poem to protest the naval order to dismantle the frigate Constitution. *The venerable ship (first launched in 1797) had served both in the War of 1812 and in the war at Tripoli (1801-5) over the tribute demanded by the Barbary pirates preying on American shipping in the Mediterranean. Holmes's poem aroused so much public interest that the vessel was saved, rebuilt, and restored to service in 1833. The poem also launched Holmes's literary career.*

Ay, tear her tattered ensign* down!
    Long has it waved on high,
And many an eye has danced to see
    That banner in the sky;
Beneath it rung the battle shout,   5
    And burst the cannon's roar;–
The meteor of the ocean air
    Shall sweep the clouds no more.

Her deck, once red with heroes' blood,
    Where knelt the vanquished foe,   10
When winds were hurrying o'er the flood,
    And waves were white below,
No more shall feel the victor's tread,
    Or know the conquered knee;–
The harpies* of the shore shall pluck   15
    The eagle of the sea!

Oh, better that her shattered hulk
    Should sink beneath the wave;
Her thunders shook the mighty deep,
    And there should be her grave;   20
Nail to the mast her holy flag,
    Set every threadbare sail,
And give her to the god of storms,
    The lightning and the gale!

ensign: flag

harpies: looters: myth-
ological creatures,
half bird and half
woman, who ate the
souls of the dead

The Chambered Nautilus

This poem, Holmes's personal favorite and also his most famous, is atypically serious. The nautilus, which is a shellfish resembling a large snail, builds a new chamber for itself each year. Like Bryant (see "To a Waterfowl"), Holmes uses an object from nature to teach a moral lesson (see the last two stanzas). Is Holmes's lesson Biblical?

This is the ship of pearl, which, poets feign,*
    Sails the unshadowed main,–
    The venturous bark that flings
On the sweet summer wind its purpled wings
In gulfs enchanted, where the Siren* sings,   5
    And coral reefs lie bare,
Where the cold sea-maids* rise to sun their streaming hair.

Its webs of living gauze no more unfurl;
    Wrecked is the ship of pearl!
    And every chambered cell,   10
Where its dim dreaming life was wont to dwell,
As the frail tenant shaped his growing shell,
    Before thee lies revealed,–
Its irised* ceiling rent, its sunless crypt unsealed!

Year after year beheld the silent toil   15
    That spread his lustrous coil;
    Still, as the spiral grew,
He left the past year's dwelling for the new,
Stole with soft step its shining archway through,
    Built up its idle door,   20
Stretched in his last-found home, and knew the old no more.

feign: portray

Siren: in Greek mythology a nymph whose singing lures sailors onto the rocks
sea-maids: mermaids

irised: colored like the rainbow

Thanks for the heavenly message brought by thee,
    Child of the wandering sea,
    Cast from her lap, forlorn!
From thy dead lips a clearer note is born   25
Than ever Triton* blew from wreathèd horn!
    While on mine ear it rings,
Through the deep caves of thought I hear a voice that sings:–

Triton: Greek sea god who called up or calmed storms by blowing through a shell

Build thee more stately mansions, O my soul,
    As the swift seasons roll!   30
    Leave thy low-vaulted past!
Let each new temple, nobler than the last,
Shut thee from heaven with a dome more vast,
    Till thou at length art free,
Leaving thine outgrown shell by life's unresting sea!   35

For Thought and Discussion

1. Explain the irony of the first line and the final stanza of "Old Ironsides." What is the purpose of Holmes's irony in this poem? Is it effective? Why or why not?

2. What is the purpose of lines 2-14 of "Old Ironsides"? After determining their function, make an outline of the structure of the entire poem. Notice Holmes's juxtaposition of imperative sentences with declarative sentences in past tense. What relationship does sentence mode have to structure and irony in "Old Ironsides"?

3. Consult an encyclopedia to determine whether Holmes's description of the nautilus is scientifically sound, paying attention to these points: a) What are the "purpled wings" (l. 4) and "webs of living gauze" (l. 8) referred to by Holmes? b) Does the nautilus toil to build successively larger chambers for itself? c) In which chamber does it live?

4. To whom or what is stanza 4 of "The Chambered Nautilus" addressed? In your opinion is "thy dead lips" (l. 25) an effective image? To whom or what is stanza 5 addressed? Make a simple outline of the content of the poem.

5. In the often quoted final stanza of "The Chambered Nautilus," Holmes argues that the example of the nautilus should inspire man to spiritual progress. Discuss Holmes's concept of spiritual progress, considering the following points: What does spiritual progress mean to the poet? By what means does he suggest one may realize such progress? What is the ultimate end of spiritual progress? Why is the phrase "Shut thee from heaven" (l. 33) problematic? What does it mean in the literal sense? What does it mean in terms of Holmes's theme? After reading the poem, do you have a clear understanding of Holmes's concept of spiritual progress? Does Holmes state his philosophy clearly enough for you to evaluate its soundness from a Biblical perspective?

6 *Transcendental Optimists*

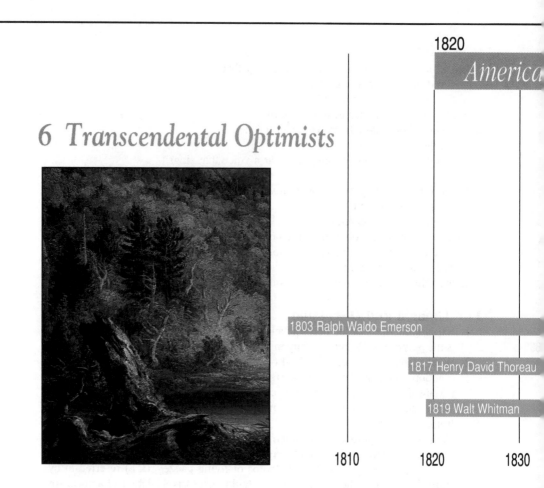

1820

America

1803 Ralph Waldo Emerson

1817 Henry David Thoreau

1819 Walt Whitman

1810   1820   1830

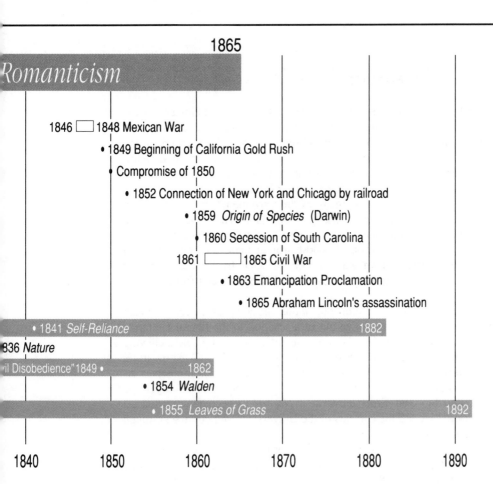

1865

Romanticism

1846 ☐ 1848 Mexican War

• 1849 Beginning of California Gold Rush

• Compromise of 1850

• 1852 Connection of New York and Chicago by railroad

• 1859 *Origin of Species* (Darwin)

• 1860 Secession of South Carolina

1861 ☐ 1865 Civil War

• 1863 Emancipation Proclamation

• 1865 Abraham Lincoln's assassination

• 1841 *Self-Reliance*   1882

836 *Nature*

il Disobedience" 1849 •   1862

• 1854 *Walden*

• 1855 *Leaves of Grass*   1892

1840   1850   1860   1870   1880   1890

Transcendentalism

Transcendentalism was not an organized system of thought but a cluster of ideas that influenced New England writers during the middle third of the nineteenth century. Its beliefs affected in varying degrees virtually all American writers during the romantic period. Ralph Waldo Emerson, Henry David Thoreau, and Walt Whitman were important spokesmen for the movement; Edgar Allan Poe, Nathaniel Hawthorne, and Herman Melville were sharp critics of it.

The term *transcendental,* as well as many of the movement's ideas, originated with the German philosopher Immanuel Kant (1724-1804), who used the term to refer to knowledge not known through the five senses. According to Kant, men can know something other than the physical world around them. An outgrowth of German idealism, transcendentalism was strongly affected by both Eastern and Western mysticism: by Hinduism from the Orient and Neoplatonism from Western Europe.

A rather awkward composite of philosophical bits and scraps, transcendentalism masqueraded as a religion, having grown out of a reaction to the liberal Unitarian Church. Fundamentally anti-Christian, the movement discarded the Bible, believing its truths relevant only to the original writers, not to present readers. To know truth, transcendentalists turned instead to Nature, which they believed communicates divine ideas directly to persons willing to listen. In this communication such persons become virtually united to God. Emerson wrote in *Nature,* "I become a transparent eyeball; I am nothing; I see all; the currents of the Universal Being circulate through me; I am part or parcel of God."

This "Universal Being" Emerson spoke of is not the God of the Bible. Transcendentalists taught that the Biblical God is only the Jewish version of the true God and thus no different from the gods claimed by other religions in the world. The true God, they declared, is the Over-Soul, a spiritual presence residing in every part of the universe. The tendency of some transcendentalists to regard Nature and God as synonymous led them to pantheism, the worship of the universe as God.

Transcendentalists also held that since the Over-Soul permeates everything, all things belong to one gigantic whole with each part as important as any other. This teaching not only departed from the Biblical conception of man as the pinnacle of God's earthly creation but also erased the Puritan distinction between renate (reborn) and reprobate (unsaved) man. A corollary of this position was the belief in man's natural goodness. Transcendentalists taught the "green apple theory," that men progressively ripen toward the ideal. This notion of natural goodness elevated the self. The most important object became the individual, not society. Thoreau and Whitman, in fact, raised the "I" to incredible heights of egotism. Transcendentalism thus provided a religio-philosophical basis for the romantic view of man.

The tenets of this movement spread primarily through the lecture circuit, the lyceum. Its chief literary spokesman was Emerson, whose *Nature* along with Thoreau's *Walden* gave the movement its most enduring literary expression. *The Dial* was the short-lived, official publication of transcendentalism. Brook Farm, an experimental commune, sought to translate transcendental teachings into both art and life. Although the post-Civil War re-evaluation of American ideals signalled the death of transcendentalism, its values and assumptions have lived on into our day.

Ralph Waldo Emerson
1803-1882

As the philosophical leader of transcendentalism, Ralph Waldo Emerson exerted great influence on American literature. Through both the resounding rhetoric of his popular lectures and the example of his life, he brought transcendentalist beliefs with great force to the American public of his day. Since these beliefs are a substitute religion that deviates from the truth of God's Word and since their influence was so widespread, Emerson, their most powerful literary spokesman, may be justly described as the nineteenth century's arch-heretic.

In 1803, exactly one hundred years after Jonathan Edwards's birth, Emerson was born into a long line of New England ministers. After graduation from Harvard and brief attendance at Harvard Divinity School, Emerson entered the Unitarian ministry. In 1829 he was ordained as assistant minister of Boston's Second Church–a prestigious Unitarian church that had been, in the seventeenth century, a center of Puritan orthodoxy under the ministries of both Increase and Cotton Mather. As his doubts about the creed and rites of the church increased, Emerson found himself moving toward rejection of even the Unitarian ministry. In 1832, a year after his wife's death, he resigned from the church, apparently over administering the Lord's Supper. For the next three years he traveled in Europe, meeting famous men like William Wordsworth and Samuel Taylor Coleridge and finding especially in the English essayist and thinker Thomas Carlyle a kindred spirit. After returning to the States in 1834, he remarried and plunged into lecturing, his real vocation.

The next decade, 1835-45, was the most important of Emerson's life, for in these years he published the works that defined the transcendental spirit. His lengthy essay *Nature* (1836) launched the movement into the mainstream of American philosophy. In two significant addresses delivered at Harvard, he further developed his concepts. "The American Scholar" (1837), delivered to the Harvard chapter of Phi Beta Kappa, was described by Oliver Wendell Holmes as America's "intellectual declaration of independence" because it called for a new scheme of education to break the country's cultural ties to Europe, especially to England. "The Divinity

School Address'' (1838), which shocked the staid Unitarians of Harvard and severed all ties between Emerson and the college for the next quarter century, asserted the divinity of man and renounced historic Christianity.

As Emerson's popularity grew, his lecture engagements took him throughout the Midwest and even into the frontier areas of the thinly settled West. The publishing of *Essays: First Series* (1841) and *Essays: Second Series* (1844) carried transcendental ideas further into the American mind. With Thoreau as his assistant, Emerson edited the official publication of transcendentalism, *The Dial,* for the last two years of its four-year existence. In 1847 he published his first book of poetry; twenty years later, his second. Defining poetry as ''meter-making argument,'' Emerson used his verse to repreach the ideas of his earlier days. As he and Thoreau drifted apart, the younger man not at all content to be merely Emerson's echo, a brash New York poet named Walt Whitman started to write poetry he claimed owed its genesis to Emerson's influence.

In his last years Emerson found respectability, enjoying the favors of the wealthy and the prestige of speaking engagements at Harvard. When rumors circulated that he had retracted his heresy and returned to orthodoxy, Emerson issued a denial, content to die with his transcendental views still intact. He was buried in 1882 in Sleepy Hollow Cemetery in Concord, Massachusetts, near where he had seen both Thoreau and Hawthorne laid to rest.

Emerson's essays and poems are not easy to read, for his style differs markedly from the traditional. The pithy, memorable sentences that pervade his prose, like the thoughts themselves, often are taken from his journals. These journals he mined for materials for his lectures, which, having delivered, he revised for publication as essays. This process of composition caused the sentence unit to dominate the paragraph. Few paragraphs have topic sentences followed by supporting details. Instead, Emerson's paragraphs typically function as collecting units for his sentences. Their development simply follows the windings of his thought. Even the poems suffer from weak integration of meaning with form, all too often leaving the impression of a succession of separate sentences.

As a thinker, if not as a stylist, Emerson remains the pivotal figure in American literature, for later writers tend either to support and extend his views or to argue against them. His influence now lives mainly through the work of two disciples, both more popular today than he: Henry David Thoreau, the zealous practitioner of Emersonian concepts; and Walt Whitman, the poet-prophet, who extended them to their logical but, to Emerson, not altogether welcome conclusions. From a Christian perspective this influence has been unwholesome. Emerson's doctrines of the divinity of man, the perfectibility of society, and the irrelevance of the Bible all attack the very basis of orthodox Christianity. It is no wonder, then, that Christians must repudiate the teachings both of Emerson and of his philosophical descendants.

from Nature

In this first published essay Emerson strikes an optimistic note about Nature's benefits to mankind. The essay opens with Emerson's charge that men err by depending on the past. By this he means that men should not depend on the Bible for truth because only for the original writers themselves did the revelation have any relevancy. Emerson then defines Nature in two senses: as the philosophical "Not-Me" and as the common-sense "essences unchanged by man." The essay unfolds through Emerson's description of the various benefits Nature brings to man: commodity (usefulness), beauty, language, discipline (conduct), idealism, and spirit. In his last section, "Prospects," from which this excerpt is taken, Emerson eloquently attributes to the poet (Emerson himself) a vision of the future when all men shall subscribe to transcendentalism. Notice that everything disagreeable–including even evil–disappears in the utopian future Emerson imagines.

So shall we come to look at the world with new eyes. It shall answer the endless inquiry of the intellect,–What is truth? and of the affections,* What is good? by yielding itself passive to the educated Will. Then shall come to pass what my poet said; "Nature is not fixed but fluid. Spirit alters, moulds, makes it. The immobility or bruteness of nature, is the absence of spirit; to pure spirit, it is fluid, it is volatile,* it is obedient. Every spirit builds itself a house; and beyond its house a world; and beyond its world, a heaven. Know then, that the world exists for you. For you is the phenomenon perfect. What we are, that only can we see. All that Adam had, all that Caesar could, you have and can do. Adam called his house, heaven and earth; Caesar called his house, Rome; you perhaps call yours, a cobler's trade; a hundred acres of ploughed land; or a scholar's garret.* Yet line for line and point for point, your dominion is as great as theirs, though without fine names. Build, therefore, your own world. As fast as you conform your life to the pure idea in your mind, that will unfold its great proportions. A correspondent revolution in things will attend the influx* of the spirit. So fast will disagreeable appearances, swine, spiders, snakes, pests, madhouses, prisons, enemies, vanish; they are temporary and shall be no more seen. The sordor* and filths of nature, the sun shall dry up, and the wind exhale. As when the summer comes from the south the snowbanks melt, and the face of the earth becomes green before it, so shall the advancing spirit create its ornaments along its path, and carry with it the beauty it visits and the song which enchants it; it shall draw beautiful faces, warm hearts, wise discourse, and heroic acts, around its way, until evil is no more seen. The kingdom of man over nature, which cometh not with observation,*–a dominion such as now is beyond his dream of God,–he shall enter without more wonder than the blind man feels who is gradually restored to perfect sight."

affections: emotions
volatile: changeable
garret: attic room
influx: a flowing in
sordor: sordidness
The . . . observation: Luke 17:20

from Self-Reliance

Emerson's title for this essay means something different from what it seems to suggest. The reliance is not upon one's self but upon the Over-Soul within all men. Emerson's emphasis on romantic individualism made this essay one of the most popular works of the nineteenth century.

Emerson's training for the Unitarian ministry doubtlessly affected his organization; for the essay follows the three-part sermonic form: doctrine, grounds, and application. In the first section he defines the doctrine by setting self-reliance against its two negatives: conformity and consistency. In the second section he gives the grounds for his doctrine of individualism: namely that the intuition receives truth from the Over-Soul, and reason convinces man that these intuitions are truth. Emerson's transitional statement to the essay's final section, which is not included here, shows the magnitude of the intellectual revolution he is advocating: "It is easy to see that a greater self-reliance must work a revolution in all the offices and relations of men; in their religion; in their education; in their pursuits; their modes of living; their associations; in their property; in their speculative views."

There is a time in every man's education when he arrives at the conviction that envy is ignorance; that imitation is suicide; that he must take himself for better for worse as his portion; that though the wide universe is full of good, no kernel of nourishing corn can come to him but through his toil bestowed on that plot of ground which is given to him to till. The power which resides in him is new in nature, and none but he knows what that is which he can do, nor does he know until he has tried. . . .

Trust thyself: every heart vibrates to that iron string. Accept the place the divine providence has found for you, the society of your contemporaries, the connection of events. Great men have always done so, and confided themselves childlike to the genius of their age, betraying their perception that the absolutely trustworthy was seated at their heart, working through their hands, predominating in all their being. And we are now men, and must accept in the highest mind the same transcendent destiny; and not minors and invalids in a protected corner, not cowards fleeing before a revolution, but guides, redeemers, and benefactors, obeying the Almighty effort and advancing on Chaos and the Dark.

What pretty oracles* nature yields us on this text in the face and behavior of children, babes, and even brutes! That divided and rebel mind, that distrust of a sentiment because our arithmetic has computed the strength and means opposed to our purpose, these have not. Their mind being whole, their eye is as yet unconquered, and when we look in their faces we are disconcerted. Infancy conforms to nobody; all conform to it; so that one babe commonly makes four or five out of the adults who prattle and play to it. So God has armed youth and puberty and manhood no less with its own piquancy* and charm, and made it enviable and gracious and its claims not to be put by, if it will stand by itself. Do not think the youth has no force, because he cannot speak to you and me. Hark! in the next room his voice is sufficiently clear and emphatic. It seems he knows how to speak to his contemporaries. Bashful or bold then, he will know how to make us seniors very unnecessary.

oracles: prophecies
piquancy: liveliness

These are the voices which we hear in solitude, but they grow faint and inaudible as we enter into the world. Society everywhere is in conspiracy against the manhood of every one of its members. Society is a joint-stock company, in which the members agree, for the better securing of his bread to each shareholder, to surrender the liberty and culture of the eater. The virtue in most request* is conformity. Self-reliance is its aversion. It loves not realites and creators, but names and customs.

in . . . request: in great demand

Whoso would be a man, must be a nonconformist. He who would gather immortal palms must not be hindered by the name of goodness, but must explore if it be goodness. Nothing is at last sacred but the integrity of your own mind. Absolve* you to yourself, and you shall have the suffrage* of the world. I remember an answer which when quite young I was prompted to make to a valued adviser who was wont to importune* me with the dear old doctrines of the church. On my saying, ''What have I to do with the sacredness of traditions, if I live wholly from within?'' my friend suggested, ''But these impulses may be from below, not from above.'' I replied, ''They do not seem to me to be such; but if I am the Devil's child, I will live then from the Devil.'' No law can be sacred to me but that of my nature. Good and bad are but names very readily transferable to that or this; the only right is what is after my constitution; the only wrong what is against it. . . .

Absolve: acquit
suffrage: assent
importune: harass

The other terror that scares us from self-trust is our consistency; a reverence for our past act or word because the eyes of others have no other data for computing our orbit than our past acts, and we are loth to disappoint them.

A foolish consistency is the hobgoblin* of little minds, adored by little statesmen and philosophers and divines. With consistency a great soul has simply nothing to do. He may as well concern himself with his shadow on the wall. Speak what you think now in hard words and tomorrow speak what tomorrow thinks in hard words again, though it contradict every thing you said today.–''Ah, so you shall be sure to be misunderstood.''–Is it so bad then to be misunderstood? Pythagoras was misunderstood, and Socrates, and Jesus, and Luther, and Copernicus, and Galileo, and Newton, and every pure and wise spirit that ever took flesh. To be great is to be misunderstood. . . .

hobgoblin: an imaginary cause of terror or dread

[The Grounds for Self-Reliance]

The magnetism which all original action exerts is explained when we inquire the reason of self-trust. Who is the Trustee? What is the aboriginal* Self, on which a universal reliance may be grounded? What is the nature and power of that science-baffling star, without parallax,* without calculable elements, which shoots a ray of beauty even into trivial and impure actions, if the least mark of independence appear? The inquiry leads us to that source, at once the essence of genius, of virtue, and of life, which we call Spontaneity or Instinct. We denote this primary wisdom as Intuition, whilst all later teachings are tuitions. In that deep force, the last fact behind which analysis cannot go, all things find their common origin. For the sense of being which in calm hours rises, we know not how, in the soul, is not diverse from things, from space, from light, from time, from man, but one with them and proceeds obviously from the same source whence their life and being also proceed. We first share the life by which things exist and afterwards see them as appearances in nature and forget that we have shared their cause. Here is the fountain of action and of thought. Here are the lungs of that inspiration which giveth man wisdom and which cannot be denied without impiety and atheism. We lie in the lap of immense intelligence, which makes us receivers of its truth and organs of its activity. When we discern justice, when we discern truth, we do nothing of ourselves, but allow a passage to its beams. If we ask whence this comes, if we seek to pry into the soul that causes, all philosophy is at fault. Its presence or its absence is all we can affirm. Every man discriminates between the voluntary acts of his mind and his involuntary perceptions, and knows that to his involuntary perceptions a perfect faith is due. He may err in the expression of them, but he knows that these things are so, like day and night, not to be disputed. My wilful actions and acquisitions are but roving; the idlest reverie, the faintest native emotion, command my curiosity and respect. Thoughtless people contradict as readily the statement of perceptions as of opinions, or rather much more readily; for they do not distinguish between perception and notion. They fancy that I choose to see this or that thing. But perception is not whimsical, but fatal. If I see a trait, my children will see it after me, and in course of time all mankind,—although it may chance that no one has seen it before me. For my perception of it is as much a fact as the sun.

---

aboriginal: first, original
parallax: apparent change in the direction of an object, caused by a change in observational position that provides a new line of sight

The relations of the soul to the divine spirit are so pure that it is profane* to seek to interpose* helps. It must be that when God speaketh he should communicate, not one thing, but all things; should fill the world with his voice; should scatter forth light, nature, time, souls, from the center of the present thought; and new date and new create the whole. Whenever a mind is simple and receives a divine wisdom, old things pass away—means, teachers, texts, temples fall; it lives now, and absorbs past and future into the present hour. All things are made sacred by relation to it—one as much as another. All things are dissolved to their center by their cause, and in the universal miracle petty and particular miracles disappear. If therefore a man claims to know and speak of God and carries you backward to the phraseology of some old moldered nation in another country, in another world, believe him not. Is the acorn better than the oak which is its fulness and completion? Is the parent better than the child into whom he has cast his ripened being? Whence then this worship of the past? The centuries are conspirators against the sanity and authority of the soul. Time and space are but physiological colors which the eye makes, but the soul is light: where it is, is day; where it was, is night; and history is an impertinence* and an injury if it be any thing more than a cheerful apologue* or parable of my being and becoming.

---

profane: irreverent
interpose: to put between
impertinence: deliberate disrespectfulness, irrelevancy
apologue: a fable or tale having a moral

Man is timid and apologetic; he is no longer upright; he dares not say "I think," "I am," but quotes some saint or sage. He is ashamed before the blade of grass or the blowing rose.

Concord Hymn

This poem commemorates the Battle of Concord, fought on land owned by Emerson's stepgrandfather. Its famous line, "And fired the shot heard round the world," refers to the minutemen's repulsion of the redcoats on April 19, 1775. The last stanza of this poem is a prayer. How does it compare with the concluding prayer of an Edward Taylor poem?

Sung* at the Completion of the Battle Monument, July 4, 1837

By the rude bridge that arched the flood,*
    Their flag to April's breeze unfurled,
Here once the embattled farmers stood
    And fired the shot heard round the world.

The foe long since in silence slept;   5
    Alike the conqueror silent sleeps;
And Time the ruined bridge has swept
    Down the dark stream which seaward creeps.

On this green bank, by this soft stream,
    We set today a votive* stone;   10
That memory may their deed redeem,
    When, like our sires,* our sons are gone.

Sung: to the tune of "Old Hundred"

flood: poetic term for river

votive: offered as an expression of gratitude

sires: fathers

Spirit, that made those heroes dare
    To die, and leave their children free,
Bid Time and Nature gently spare   15
    The shaft* we raise to them and thee.

shaft: the monument

Brahma

This poem puzzled many of Emerson's contemporary readers. "If you tell them to say Jehovah instead of Brahma," Emerson told his daughter, "they will not feel any perplexity." The persistent oriental strain in Emerson's work is very much evident in this poem. To the Hindu, Brahma is the supreme soul of the universe, from which all things originate, to which all things return, and in which all things are reconciled. What does Emerson imply in the last stanza concerning the relationship between Jehovah and Brahma?

If the red slayer* think he slays,
    Or if the slain think he is slain,
They know not well the subtle ways
    I keep, and pass, and turn again.

slayer: personification
of death

Far or forgot to me is near;   5
    Shadow and sunlight are the same;
The vanished gods to me appear;
    And one to me are shame and fame.

They reckon ill who leave me out;
    When me they fly, I am the wings;   10
I am the doubter and the doubt,
    And I the hymn the Brahmin* sings.

Brahmin: a member of
the highest caste in
the Hindu religion

The strong gods pine for my abode,
    And pine in vain the sacred Seven,*
But thou, meek lover of the good!   15
    Find me, and turn thy back on heaven.

sacred Seven: the sev-
en most revered
saints in Hinduism

Hamatreya

This poem is Emerson's New England version of a section of the Vishnu Purana, *a Hindu sacred book. The title of the poem probably derives from "Maitreya," a Hindu god named in Emerson's source, or from a Greek term translated "Earth-Mother." Instead of speaking of great kings who have disappeared with their kingdoms, Emerson speaks here of New England farmers who foolishly believe that they possess the land they farm. This poem compares favorably with Thoreau's treatment of land ownership at the beginning of Chapter 2 of* Walden: *"Where I Lived, and What I Lived For." Notice that lines 1 and 3 of this poem (1847) anticipate the cataloging technique of Walt Whitman's* Leaves of Grass *(1855). Notice also that there are at least two voices in Emerson's poem. Whose are they?*

Bulkeley, Hunt, Willard, Hosmer, Meriam, Flint,*
Possessed the land which rendered to their toil
Hay, corn, roots, hemp, flax,* apples, wool and wood.
Each of these landlords walked amidst his farm,
Saying, " 'Tis mine, my children's and my name's.   5
How sweet the west wind sounds in my own trees!
How graceful climb those shadows on my hill!
I fancy these pure waters and the flags*
Know me, as does my dog: we sympathize;
And, I affirm, my actions smack of the soil."   10

Where are these men? Asleep beneath their grounds:
And strangers, fond* as they, their furrows plough.
Earth laughs in flowers, to see her boastful boys
Earth-proud, proud of the earth which is not theirs;
Who steer the plough, but cannot steer their feet   15
Clear of the grave.
They added ridge to valley, brook to pond,
And sighed for all that bounded their domain;
"This suits me for a pasture; that's my park;
We must have clay, lime, gravel, granite-ledge,   20
And misty lowland, where to go for peat.
The land is well,—lies fairly to the south.
'Tis good, when you have crossed the sea and back,
To find the sitfast acres where you left them."
Ah! the hot owner sees not Death, who adds   25
Him to his land, a lump of mould the more.
Hear what the Earth says:

Bulkeley . . . Flint: the first settlers in the Concord area

flax: a plant that yields the fiber for making linen

flags: a variety of iris, growing in moist places

fond: foolish

Earth-Song

"Mine and yours;
Mine, not yours.
Earth endures;   30
Stars abide–
Shine down in the old sea;
Old are the shores;
But where are old men?
I who have seen much,   35
Such have I never seen.

"The lawyer's deed
Ran sure,
In tail,*   *tail:* entail: a restricted
To them, and to their heirs   40   line of inheritance
Who shall succeed,
Without fail,
Forevermore.

"Here is the land,
Shaggy with wood,   45
With its old valley,
Mound and flood.
But the heritors?–
Fled like the flood's foam.
The lawyer, and the laws,   50
And the kingdom,
Clean swept herefrom.

"They called me theirs,
Who so controlled me;
Yet every one   55
Wished to stay, and is gone,
How am I theirs,
If they cannot hold me,
But I hold them?"

When I heard the Earth-song   60
I was no longer brave;
My avarice* cooled   *avarice:* greed
Like lust in the chill of the grave.

For Thought and Discussion

1. What is the antecedent of the pronoun *It* in line 2 of the selection from *Nature?* What, according to Emerson, will "yield itself passive to the educated Will"?

2. Might "Build, therefore, your own world" be considered the theme of the selection from *Nature?* Does Emerson suggest how one should go about such building? What will be the result of such building? Compare Emerson's philosophy of building to Holmes's in "The Chambered Nautilus." Next evaluate both in light of Christ's teachings in Matthew 7:24-27 and Luke 6:46-49.

3. Evaluate each of the following pithy, quotable sayings from *Self-Reliance,* using conformity to Biblical teaching to test the soundness of each saying.
   a. "Trust Thyself."
   b. "Accept the place the divine providence has found for you."
   c. "Nothing is at last sacred but the integrity of your own mind."
   d. "No law can be sacred to me but that of my nature."
   e. "We lie in the lap of immense intelligence, which makes us receivers of its truth and organs of its activities."

4. Select three sentences from *Self-Reliance* that contain metaphors, and discuss the appropriateness of each to Emerson's purpose in the essay.

5. The final stanza of "Concord Hymn" is a prayer. To whom is it addressed? What requests does the speaker make in this prayer? Why are "Time" and "Nature" capitalized in this stanza? To whom has the monument at Concord been raised?

6. Who is the speaker of "Brahma"? To whom is the poem addressed? What final injunction does the speaker deliver to the hearer of the poem?

7. In what lines of "Hamatreya" does Emerson express the theme of the poem? In whose voice are these lines spoken? What do these lines reveal about Emerson's philosophy?

Henry David Thoreau
1817-1862

"Whoso would be a man," Emerson wrote in "Self-Reliance," "must be a nonconformist." By that standard Henry David Thoreau must have been quite a man. Refusing to conform to the expectations of his Concord neighbors, he did not marry, pay his poll tax regularly, buy property, or work at a regular job. Perpetuating this lifestyle through his writings, Thoreau has influenced devoted followers to adapt his ideas to conditions in the United States and in other countries such as Britain and India. In fact, two modern movements—the idealization of primitive life and civil disobedience through passive resistance—are outgrowths of Thoreau's works. Naturalist, philosopher, and artist, Thoreau is an avid proponent of transcendental ideas.

The central event in Thoreau's life was his residence at Walden Pond from 1845 to 1847. Prior to this period, his life had been relatively uneventful. The son of a pencil manufacturer of French heritage, Thoreau spent most of his life in Concord, Massachusetts. After graduating from Harvard in 1837, he tried teaching in the town school but resigned after two weeks rather than administer corporal punishment to students. Later he formed his own private, experimental school that prospered until his partner, his brother John, fell ill in 1841. Deciding then to abandon teaching, he accepted Emerson's invitation to live with the Emersons, working manually for his room and board. Twice in the 1840s he lived in the Emerson household, this first time from 1841 to 1843. Equally attracted to transcendentalism, Emerson and Thoreau served for two years as editor and editorial assistant, respectively, of *The Dial,* the official publication of transcendentalists. In 1844 Emerson bought a parcel of wooded land on Walden Pond about two miles from his home. Thoreau, wishing a secluded place to concentrate on his writing, got Emerson's permission to live on this land.

The pivotal Walden experience—which lasted from July 4, 1845, to September 6, 1847—was Thoreau's experimental step of self-reliance. He built his cabin for $28.12 $\frac{1}{2}$ and fed himself on an average of twenty-seven cents per week. Freed from economic demands (approximately six weeks' labor supported him for twelve months), Thoreau wrote his first book, *A Week on the Concord and Merrimack Rivers* (1849), and a substantial portion of *Walden or Life in the Woods* (1854). The experiment ended when Thoreau decided that he had other lives to live. One month later he moved for the second time back into Emerson's house, this time for nine months while Emerson lectured in England. Following Emerson's return in 1848, Thoreau rejoined his parents, with whom he lived until his death.

After the Walden period, in the final fifteen years of his life, Thoreau became more openly political. He had been arrested in 1846 and placed in jail for not paying his poll tax (a small tax levied on all citizens of a community whether or not they owned property). He determined to stay in jail in order to register his opposition to the Mexican War, which he believed was designed to enlarge the number of slave states. He was, however, released from jail after one night's stay when an aunt paid his tax for him. Out of this experience grew his essay ''Civil Disobedience'' (1849), which forcefully expresses the notion, espoused by modern radicals, that conscience is above the law and that each individual has the right—in fact, the duty—to violate any law he regards as unjust. Thoreau resisted the government also by participating in the illegal Underground Railroad that secretively brought escaped slaves into Canada. In his lectures he justified John Brown's maniacal raid in 1859 on the federal arsenal at Harpers Ferry in western Virginia to secure arms for a slave revolt in the South. As the Civil War erupted, his activism came to an end, for he fell seriously ill with tuberculosis. In spite of a trip to Minnesota for a change of climate, his condition steadily worsened. He died in the spring of 1862 at the age of forty-four.

Thoreau left two major works: ''Civil Disobedience'' and *Walden*. In the first of these, originally a lecture entitled ''The Relation of the Individual to the State,'' Thoreau argues that the best type of government governs not at all. Called a philosophical anarchist, he bases his argument on the assumption that because men are naturally good, they will do the right thing when faced with a choice. Optimistically, even naively, ignoring contrary historical evidence that men choose to follow their depraved nature, he envisions a perfect state where governments will be obsolete.

Thoreau's most influential work is *Walden,* a work he revised at least seven times over a period of at least six years. The purpose of *Walden* can be stated best by the motto Thoreau attached to the first edition: ''I do not propose to write an ode to dejection but to brag as lustily as chanticleer in the morning, standing on his roost, if only to wake my neighbors up.'' That this work is complex and multifaceted is evident in the various ways it may be read. It is, first, a book on nature recording Thoreau's observation of the world around him and his interpretation of the spiritual significance of that world. It is, second, an autobiography recording the inner life of its author. It is, third, inspirational literature calling its readers to a better life, one stripped of all nonessentials. It is, fourth, an expression of transcendental assumptions deriving basically from Emerson. It is, fifth, a work of social criticism recommending a certain ideal of life and pointing out the deficiencies of contemporary living. It is, finally, an artistic creation carefully shaped so as to fuse all its parts into one coherent, unified whole.

Although the form of Thoreau's writing might be considered attractive, his assumptions and values demand the kind of careful scrutiny that only a Biblically grounded Christian can bring to an evaluation of its content. Thoreau conceives a world that begins and ends with self, denies the fact of man's corrupt nature, believes in salvation through self-achievement, and worships God only in nature. A hero to modern radicals, the father of twentieth-century primitivism, an anarchist seeking to pull down divinely instituted government, Thoreau is no model for the Christian.

from Civil Disobedience

Civil disobedience, which owes its origin to Henry David Thoreau, has been one of the most influential weapons in the arsenal of the modern revolutionary. In his essay Thoreau applies transcendental principles to politics. His argument rests on the assumption that the individual is above the state, that conscience is superior to law. According to Thoreau, a person may justifiably break any law he considers bad; for if enough people break a law, the state will be forced to change it. Although his own technique for breaking the law was passive, nonviolent resistance, his reference to the blood of conscience (p. 213) has caused some readers to misinterpret his comment as a call for bloody revolution.

Thoreau classifies the citizens (and government) of his day into three categories. At the bottom are the mass of men who serve the state with only their bodies (characteristic of an absolute, or unlimited, monarchy). At the next level are those who serve the state with their heads (characteristic of a limited monarchy). At the third level are those who serve the state with their conscience (characteristic of a democracy). Above these three levels is a nonexistent, visionary state, where those similar to Thoreau can live as neighbors to the state rather than as subjects to it.

Thoreau's ideas have a certain attractiveness to the modern Christian, who more often than not may find himself in disagreement with governmental policies and actions. But such ideas must be carefully weighed. Is there support in the Bible for obeying only those laws that one considers wise? Can one Scripturally exempt himself from political authority? Both Paul (Rom. 13:1-7) and Peter (I Pet. 2:13-14) insisted on the believer's submission to the law and the ministers of the law, in a time when neither the government nor its local magistrates were sympathetic toward Christianity. Jesus set His disciples an example of paying an oppressive tax (Matt. 17:24-27). Only when His followers were prevented by governmental edict from obeying a specific command of God did they refuse to obey the political authorities (Acts 4:19-20). And then they did not, in the manner of today's social activists, question the right of the government to punish them or try to disrupt governmental functions. By their actions, they turned physical defeat into moral and spiritual victory.

This is not to say that Christian citizens should neglect what legal means of redress are available to them. Paul, in fact, escaped the jurisdiction of Festus by appealing to Caesar (Acts 25). Thoreau would have scorned such means. This is also not to say that Christian citizens should keep silent and remain passive in the presence of abuses when they can make their influence count. In a society ruled by a representative government that guarantees the freedoms of speech, press, and assembly, Christians have not only the right but the responsibility to speak out for *moral and spiritual righteousness. When to obey the government is to disobey specific Biblical commands and when legal appeal and personal influence have failed, Christians are bound to withhold obedience and submit to whatever punishment their disobedience entails.*

It is to Thoreau's credit that he willingly went to prison, accepting the punishment required by law for his disobedience. But his submission to imprisonment was part of a deliberate strategy to persuade the public. It was not an act motivated by any conviction that the government had political authority over him. To "despise government," as Thoreau did, is an expression of the unregenerate rather than of the regenerate mind (II Pet. 2:10). Christian protest must look to the Scriptures, not to Thoreau, for a pattern of behavior in times of conflict with society.

I heartily accept the motto,* "That government is best which governs least"; and I should like to see it acted up to more rapidly and systematically. Carried out, it finally amounts to this, which also I believe–"That government is best which governs not at all"; and when men are prepared for it, that will be the kind of government which they will have. Government is at best but an expedient;* but most governments are usually, and all governments are sometimes, inexpedient. The objections which have been brought against a standing army,* and they are many and weighty, and deserve to prevail, may also at last be brought against a standing government. The standing army is only an arm of the standing government. The government itself, which is only the mode which the people have chosen to execute their will, is equally liable to be abused and perverted before the people can act through it. Witness the present Mexican war,* the work of comparatively a few individuals using the standing government as their tool; for, in the outset, the people would not have consented to this measure. . . .

---

motto: printed on the masthead of a journal to which Thoreau occasionally contributed

expedient: device, a means to an end

standing army: an army prepared at all times for action, especially during peacetime

Mexican War: Thoreau opposed the Mexican War (1846-48) because he thought its purpose was the extension of slave territory.

But, to speak practically and as a citizen, unlike those who call themselves no-government men, I ask for, not at once no government, but *at once* a better government. Let every man make known what kind of government would command his respect, and that will be one step toward obtaining it.

After all, the practical reason why, when the power is once in the hands of the people, a majority are permitted, and for a long period continue, to rule is not because they are most likely to be in the right, nor because this seems fairest to the minority, but because they are physically the strongest. But a government in which the majority rule in all cases cannot be based on justice, even as far as men understand it. Can there not be a government in which majorities do not virtually decide right and wrong, but conscience?–in which majorities decide only those questions to which the rule of expediency is applicable? Must the citizen ever for a moment, or in the least degree, resign his conscience to the legislator? Why has every man a conscience, then? I think that we should be men first, and subjects afterward. It is not desirable to cultivate a respect for the law, so much as for the right. The only obligation which I have a right to assume is to do at any time what I think right. . . .

Unjust laws exist: shall we be content to obey them, or shall we endeavor to amend them, and obey them until we have succeeded, or shall we transgress them at once? Men generally, under such a government as this, think that they ought to wait until they have persuaded the majority to alter them. They think that, if they should resist, the remedy would be worse than the evil. But it is the fault of the government itself that the remedy *is* worse than the evil. *It* makes it worse. Why is it not more apt to anticipate and provide for reform? Why does it not cherish its wise minority? Why does it cry and resist before it is hurt? Why does it not encourage its citizens to be on the alert to point out its faults, and *do* better than it would have them? Why does it always crucify Christ, and excommunicate Copernicus* and Luther,* and pronounce Washington and Franklin rebels?

Copernicus: (1473-1543) a Polish astronomer threatened with excommunication from the Roman Catholic church for asserting that the earth is not the center of the universe
Martin Luther: (1483-1546) the father of the Reformation, was excommunicated in 1521

One would think, that a deliberate and practical denial of its authority was the only offence never contemplated by government; else, why has it not assigned its definite, its suitable and proportionate, penalty? If a man who has no property refuses but once to earn nine shillings for the State,* he is put in prison for a period unlimited by any law that I know, and determined only by the discretion of those who placed him there; but if he should steal ninety times nine shillings from the State, he is soon permitted to go at large again.

State: reference to the poll tax

If the injustice is part of the necessary friction of the machine of government, let it go, let it go: perchance it will wear smooth—certainly the machine will wear out. If the injustice has a spring, or a pulley, or a rope, or a crank, exclusively for itself, then perhaps you may consider whether the remedy will not be worse than the evil; but if it is of such a nature that it requires you to be the agent of injustice to another, then, I say, break the law. Let your life be a counter-friction to stop the machine. What I have to do is to see, at any rate, that I do not lend myself to the wrong which I condemn.

As for adopting the ways which the State has provided for remedying the evil, I know not of such ways. They take too much time, and a man's life will be gone. I have other affairs to attend to. I came into this world, not chiefly to make this a good place to live in, but to live in it, be it good or bad. A man has not everything to do, but something; and because he cannot do *everything,* it is not necessary that he should do *something* wrong. It is not my business to be petitioning the Governor or the Legislature any more than it is theirs to petition me; and if they should not hear my petition, what should I do then? But in this case the State has provided no way: its very Constitution is the evil. This may seem to be harsh and stubborn and unconciliatory;* but it is to treat with the utmost kindness and consideration the only spirit that can appreciate or deserves it. So is all change for the better, like birth and death, which convulse the body.*

---

unconciliatory: not promoting reconciliation
So . . . body: Note Thoreau's belief in progress; here he states a position that justifies all revolution.

Under a government which imprisons any unjustly, the true place for a just man is also a prison.

The proper place today, the only place which Massachusetts has provided for her freer and less desponding* spirits, is in her prisons, to be put out and locked out of the State by her own act, as they have already put themselves out by their principles. It is there that the fugitive slave, and the Mexican prisoner on parole, and the Indian come to plead the wrongs of his race should find them; on that separate, but more free and honorable, ground, where the State places those who are not *with* her, but *against* her,*–the only house in a slave State in which a free man can abide with honor. If any think that their influence would be lost there, and their voices no longer afflict the ear of the State, that they would not be as an enemy within its walls, they do not know by how much truth is stronger than error, nor how much more eloquently and effectively he can combat injustice who has experienced a little in his own person. Cast your whole vote, not a strip of paper merely, but your whole influence. A minority is powerless while it conforms to the majority; it is not even a minority then; but it is irresistible when it clogs by its whole weight. If the alternative is to keep all just men in prison, or give up war and slavery, the State will not hesitate which to choose. If a thousand men were not to pay their tax-bills this year, that would not be a violent and bloody measure, as it would be to pay them, and enable the State to commit violence and shed innocent blood. This is, in fact, the definition of a peaceable revolution, if any such is possible. If the tax-gatherer, or any other public officer, asks me, as one has done, "But what shall I do?" my answer is, "If you really wish to do anything, resign your office." When the subject has refused allegiance, and the officer has resigned his office, then the revolution is accomplished. But even suppose blood should flow. Is there not a sort of blood shed when the conscience is wounded? Through this wound a man's real manhood and immortality flow out, and he bleeds to an everlasting death. I see this blood flowing now. . . .

desponding: disheartened
those . . . her: cf. Luke 9:50

Walden

Walden's style has been frequently praised. Like Emerson, Thoreau seemed to prefer the sentence unit rather than the paragraph. As a result, numerous sentences leap from the work into the reader's mind, becoming memorable not only because of concrete details but also because of metaphor, simile, hyperbole, and surprise. These examples are typical: **metaphor**(*"Time is but the stream I go a-fishing in"*); **simile** (*". . . you will see the sun glimmer on both its surfaces, as if it were a cimeter"*); **hyperbole,** *or exaggeration* (*"Men say that a stitch in time saves nine, and so they take a thousand stitches today to save nine tomorrow"*); **surprise,** *or the violation of the reader's expectations (notice that the rest of this sentence does not fulfill the expectation raised by* misfortune; *"I see young men, my townsmen, whose misfortune it is to have inherited farms, houses, barns, cattle, and farming tools; for these are more easily acquired than got rid of"*).

The content of Walden *raises key questions, especially for Christians. Can one live a life like Thoreau's today? Are Thoreau's goals Christian or non-Christian? Should the Christian follow Thoreau's example?*

To answer these questions, we must accurately interpret Thoreau's experiment before we can evaluate it. We must grant to Thoreau his own view of the months at Walden Pond. He saw the experience as a time of testing his self-resources and of seeking spiritual freedom through separation from the normal physical comforts of society. The experience thus combined two elements of the transcendental mind: romantic individualism and mystical asceticism (the denial of material benefits in order to experience the divine as real and near).

We must also take seriously Thoreau's intention of correcting society. His cabin on the pond was not a refuge from society. It provided him instead with a vantage point outside society, a position from which he could analyze contemporary life and measure it against his own values. His cabin was also a stage on which to live out in the public view the principles he had learned from Emerson. Although carefully situated so as to be close to Nature, it was within two miles of Concord. Thus Thoreau was not so far removed from other men as to keep him from their notice.

Thoreau's setting, which permitted the fullest exposure to Nature, exemplified romantic primitivism. Although Thoreau was not necessarily advocating a life close to Nature at all times for all men, the **tone** *of* Walden *seems to represent civilized existence as pale and sterile by comparison. Man is less fortunate because he has distanced himself from his natural surroundings. The primitive life, for Thoreau, is therapeutic. It is a means of recovering a former happier consciousness not dulled by civilization.*

Thoreau's Walden experiment, like his position on civil disobedience, must be carefully examined in the light of the Scriptures. First, the ideal of self-reliance is not derived from the Bible but from human egotism. By Christ ''all things consist'' (Col. 1:17); in Christ ''we live, and move, and have our being'' (Acts 17:28). Even in merely human terms Thoreau's self-sufficiency is questionable. As James Russell Lowell has pointed out, Thoreau lived on another man's land, borrowed tools from his neighbors, and made frequent trips to Concord for supplies.

Second, as an ascetic withdrawal from society, the Walden experience is also questionable. It is true that there is some value in detaching oneself on occasion from daily routine and common comforts in order to view life more objectively. In the hurly-burly of life, Christians, like others, can lose sight of their goals and miss life's opportunities. Physical deprivation can remind us that the most important values are spiritual rather than material. But practicing asceticism, or physical self-denial for spiritual advancement, is a pagan practice rather than a Christian one (Col. 2:20-23; I Tim. 4:1-3). A better example than Thoreau for Christians is the Puritans. They acknowledged the superiority of the spiritual to the physical and practiced a strict frugality. Yet they were quite ready to accept their physical blessings with thanks. Moreover, they used their material advantages as resources in their service of God, for they understood that Christian duty carries the believer into the world of men rather than away from it.

Third, Thoreau's aim of correcting society would be admirable were it not for the inadequacy of his principles and his obvious deficiencies of character. His call for a simpler life more in touch with the motions of Nature has nothing to do with the traditional virtues of humble country living. His call for an awakening of man's faculties to the symphony of Nature yields no praise to the Creator revealed in Scripture. His celebration of Nature is instead an expression of romantic primitivism, which assumes that man, like the other animals, is happiest in a natural habitat and least happy when subjected to the institutions of society. It denies any real distinction between man and the lower creation and gives priority to those faculties man shares with the lower animals (notice Thoreau's emphasis on the cultivation of the senses). Romantic primitivism—like its descendant, modern behaviorism—does not allow man a soul. It therefore recognizes on the part of man no greater responsibility to the Creator than that of any other animal. As Thoreau lay dying of tuberculosis, he was asked by his aunt Maria whether he had made his peace with God. Said Thoreau, "I did not know that we had quarreled."

One cannot read far in Walden *without becoming aware of the egotism behind the author's principles and actions. Trivialities become momentous because he is observing them. Momentous world events are trivial because he has not observed them. The newspaper, for this reason, is a waste of his time. Thoreau has a way of rationalizing his failure in certain endeavors by denying the value of success in them. If a lecture failed to interest an audience, then so much the better for the lecture. It would be no credit to his ideas to have them appreciated by mediocre minds. If the citizens of Concord looked down their noses at him, he would look down his nose at them. Obviously these responses are not the answer to the needs of the world.* Walden *legitimately calls attention to some of man's problems, but it cannot provide their solution.*

from Economy*

When I wrote the following pages, or rather the bulk of them, I lived alone, in the woods, a mile from any neighbor, in a house which I had built myself, on the shore of Walden Pond, in Concord, Massachusetts, and earned my living by the labor of my hands only. I lived there two years and two months. At present I am a sojourner* in civilized life again.

Economy: In "Economy," his first chapter, Thoreau, speaks of both financial and spiritual economy.
sojourner: temporary resident

I have traveled a good deal in Concord; and everywhere, in shops, and offices, and fields, the inhabitants have appeared to me to be doing penance in a thousand remarkable ways. What I have heard of Bramins* sitting exposed to four fires and looking in the face of the sun; or hanging suspended, with their heads downward, over flames; or looking at the heavens over their shoulders "until it becomes impossible for them to resume their natural position, while from the twist of the neck nothing but liquids can pass into the stomach"; or dwelling, chained for life, at the foot of a tree; or measuring with their bodies, like caterpillars, the breadth of vast empires, or standing on one leg on the tops of pillars—even these forms of conscious penance are hardly more incredible and astonishing than the scenes which I daily witness. The twelve labors of Hercules* were trifling in comparison with those which my neighbors have undertaken; for they were only twelve, and had an end; but I could never see that these men slew or captured any monster or finished any labor. They have no friend Iolas* to burn with a hot iron the root of the hydra's head, but as soon as one head is crushed, two spring up.

Bramins: members of the highest Hindu caste of India
Hercules: the son of the Greek god Zeus and a human mother; required to perform twelve superhuman feats to win his freedom from slavery
Iolas: Hercules' servant, who aided him in killing the nine-headed monster, Hydra.

I see young men, my townsmen, whose misfortune it is to have inherited farms, houses, barns, cattle, and farming tools; for these are more easily acquired than got rid of. Better if they had been born in the open pasture and suckled* by a wolf, that they might have seen with clearer eyes what field they were called to labor in. Who made them serfs* of the soil? Why should they eat their sixty acres, when man is condemned to eat only his peck of dirt? Why should they begin digging their graves as soon as they are born? They have got to live a man's life, pushing all these things before them, and get on as well as they can. How many a poor immortal soul have I met well nigh crushed and smothered under its load, creeping down the road of life, pushing before it a barn seventy-five feet by forty, its Augean stables* never cleansed, and one hundred acres of land, tillage, mowing, pasture, and wood-lot! The portionless, who struggle with no such unnecessary inherited encumbrances, find it labor enough to subdue and cultivate a few cubic feet of flesh.

suckled: nursed
serfs: slaves
Augean stables: the fifth of Hercules' labors: to cleanse the stables where King Augeas had kept three thousand oxen for thirty years

But men labor under a mistake. The better part of the man is soon ploughed into the soil for compost. By a seeming fate, commonly called necessity, they are employed, as it says in an old book, laying up treasures which moth and rust will corrupt and thieves break through and steal.*

It is a fool's life, as they will find when they get to the end of it, if not before. . . .

thieves . . . steal: Matthew 6:19

from Where I Lived, and What I Lived For

At a certain season of our life we are accustomed to consider every spot as the possible site of a house. I have thus surveyed* the country on every side within a dozen miles of where I live. In imagination I have bought all the farms in succession, for all were to be bought, and I knew their price. I walked over each farmer's premises, tasted his wild apples, discoursed on husbandry* with him, took his farm at his price, at any price, mortgaging it to him in my mind; even put a higher price on it–took everything but a deed of it–took his word for his deed, for I dearly loved to talk–cultivated it, and him too to some extent, I trust, and withdrew when I had enjoyed it long enough, leaving him to carry it on. This experience entitled me to be regarded as a sort of real-estate broker by my friends. Wherever I sat, there I might live, and the landscape radiated from me accordingly. What is a house but a *sedes,** a seat?–better if a country seat. I discovered many a site for a house not likely to be soon improved, which some might have thought too far from the village, but to my eyes the village was too far from it. Well, there I might live, I said; and there I did live, for an hour, a summer and a winter life; saw how I could let the years run off, buffet the winter through, and see the spring come in. The future inhabitants of this region, wherever they may place their houses, may be sure that they have been anticipated. An afternoon sufficed to lay out the land into orchard, woodlot, and pasture, and to decide what fine oaks or pines should be left to stand before the door, and whence each blasted* tree could be seen to the best advantage; and then I let it lie fallow* perchance,* for a man is rich in proportion to the number of things which he can afford to let alone.

I . . . surveyed: Thoreau's occupation was that of a surveyor; here the term means to inspect carefully.
husbandry: farming
sedes: Lat., seat, residence
blasted: budding
fallow: uncultivated, unused
perchance: possibly, perhaps

"I am monarch of all I *survey,*
My right there is none to dispute."*

I . . . dispute: from William Cowper's "Verses Supposed to be Written by Alexander Selkirk" (Thoreau italicizes *survey* to pun on his own profession as a surveyor.)

The present was my next* experiment of this kind, which I purpose to describe more at length, for convenience, putting the experience of two years into one. As I have said, I do not propose to write an ode to dejection, but to brag as lustily as chanticleer* in the morning, standing on his roost, if only to wake my neighbors up.*

my next: His first experiment, evidently, was the near purchase of the Hollowell farm.
chanticleer: the rooster
I . . . up: This statement is the epigraph for the first edition of *Walden*

When first I took up my abode in the woods, that is, began to spend my nights as well as days there, which, by accident, was on Independence Day, or the Fourth of July, 1845, my house was not finished for winter, but was merely a defense against the rain, without plastering or chimney, the walls being of rough weather-stained boards, with wide chinks, which made it cool at night. . . .

I went to the woods because I wished to live deliberately, to front* only the essential facts of life, and see if I could not learn what it had to teach, and not, when I came to die, discover that I had not lived. I did not wish to live what was not life, living is so dear; nor did I wish to practice resignation, unless it was quite necessary. I wanted to live deep and suck out all the marrow of life, to live so sturdily and Spartan-like* as to put to rout* all that was not life, cut a broad swath* and shave close, to drive life into a corner, and reduce it to its lowest terms, and, if it proved to be mean,* why then to get the whole and genuine meanness of it, and publish its meanness to the world; or if it were sublime, to know it by experience, and be able to give a true account of it in my next excursion. For most men, it appears to me, are in a strange uncertainty about it, whether it is of the devil or of God, and have *somewhat hastily* concluded that it is the chief end of man here to "glorify God and enjoy him forever."*

front: face
Spartan-like: ascetic: i.e., a life of self-denial
rout: flight
swath: the width of a scythe or mowing-machine blade
mean: petty, ignoble
glorify . . . forever: The opening lines of the "Shorter Catechism" in *New England Primer* are "Man's chief end is to glorify God, and to enjoy Him forever."

Still we live meanly, like ants; though the fable tells us that we were long ago changed into men;* like pygmies we fight with cranes;* it is error upon error, and clout upon clout, and our best virtue has for its occasion a superfluous* and evitable* wretchedness. Our life is frittered away by detail. An honest man has hardly need to count more than his ten fingers, or in extreme cases he may add his ten toes, and lump the rest. Simplicity, simplicity, simplicity! I say, let your affairs be as two or three, and not a hundred or a thousand; instead of a million count half a dozen, and keep your accounts on your thumb nail. In the midst of this chopping sea of civilized life, such are the clouds and storms and quicksands and thousand-and-one items to be allowed for, that a man has to live, if he would not founder* and go to the bottom and not make his port at all, by dead reckoning,* and he must be a great calculator indeed who succeeds. Simplify, simplify. Instead of three meals a day, if it be necessary eat but one; instead of a hundred dishes, five; and reduce other things in proportion. . . .

changed . . . men: According to Greek mythology, Zeus repeopled a kingdom by turning the ants into men.
fight . . . cranes: In the *Iliad* the Trojans are compared to cranes fighting with pygmies.
superfluous: unnecessary
evitable: avoidable
founder: sink
dead reckoning: the computation of a vessel's position at sea by not using the aid of the stars

Why should we live with such hurry and waste of life? We are determined to be starved before we are hungry. Men say that a stitch in time saves nine, and so they take a thousand stitches today to save nine tomorrow. . . .

Let us spend one day as deliberately as Nature, and not be thrown off the track by every nutshell and mosquito's wing that falls on the rails. Let us rise early and fast, or break fast, gently and without perturbation;* let company come and let company go, let the bells ring and the children cry–determined to make a day of it. Why should we knock under and go with the stream? Let us not be upset and overwhelmed in that terrible rapid and whirlpool called a dinner, situated in the meridian* shallows. Weather this danger and you are safe, for the rest of the way is down hill. With unrelaxed nerves, with morning vigor, sail by it, looking another way, tied to the mast like Ulysses.* If the engine whistles, let it whistle till it is hoarse for its pains. If the bell rings, why should we run? We will consider what kind of music they are like. Let us settle ourselves, and work and wedge our feet downward through the mud and slush of opinion, and prejudice, and tradition, and delusion, and appearance, that alluvion* which covers the globe, through Paris and London, through New York and Boston and Concord, through church and state, through poetry and philosophy and religion, till we come to a hard bottom and rocks in place, which we can call *reality,* and say, This is, and no mistake; and then begin, having a *point d' appui,* * below freshet and frost and fire, a place where you might found a wall or a state, or set a lamp-post safely, or perhaps a gauge, not a Nilometer,* but a Realometer, that future ages might know how deep a freshet of shams and appearances had gathered from time to time. If you stand right fronting and face to face to a fact, you will see the sun glimmer on both its surfaces, as if it were a cimeter,* and feel its sweet edge dividing you through the heart and marrow, and so you will happily conclude your mortal career. Be it life or death, we crave only reality. If we are really dying, let us hear the rattle in our throats and feel cold in the extremities; if we are alive, let us go about our business.

perturbation: agitation, disquiet
meridian: midday
Ulysses: Ulysses commanded his sailors to tie him to the mast so that he could hear the song of the Sirens but yet not yield to their fatal entreaties.
alluvion: a deposit, as of mud or sand, brought and laid down by running water
point d'appui: Fr., point of support, base
Nilometer: a gauge used by the ancient Egyptians to measure the flood states of the Nile River.
cimeter: obsolete for "scimitar," an oriental saber with a curved blade

Time is but the stream I go a-fishing in. I drink at it; but while I drink I see the sandy bottom and detect how shallow it is. Its thin current slides away, but eternity remains. I would drink deeper; fish in the sky, whose bottom is pebbly with stars. I cannot count one. I know not the first letter of the alphabet. I have always been regretting that I was not as wise as the day I was born. The intellect is a cleaver; it discerns and rifts its way into the secret of things. I do not wish to be any more busy with my hands than is necessary. My head is hands and feet. I feel all my best faculties concentrated in it. My instinct tells me that my head is an organ for burrowing, as some creatures use their snout and forepaws, and with it I would mine and burrow my way through these hills. I think that the richest vein is somewhere hereabouts; so by the divining rod* and thin rising vapors I judge; and here I will begin to mine.

divining rod: a forked stick that is supposed to indicate the presence of water or metal underground

from Conclusion

I left the woods for as good a reason as I went there. Perhaps it seemed to me that I had several more lives to live, and could not spare any more time for that one. It is remarkable how easily and insensibly we fall into a particular route, and make a beaten track for ourselves. I had not lived there a week before my feet wore a path from my

door to the pond-side; and though it is five or six years since I trod it, it is still quite distinct. It is true, I fear that others may have fallen into it, and so helped to keep it open. The surface of the earth is soft and impressible by the feet of men; and so with the paths which the mind travels. How worn and dusty, then, must be the highways of the world, how deep the ruts of tradition and conformity! I did not wish to take a cabin passage, but rather to go before the mast and on the deck of the world, for there I could best see the moonlight amid the mountains. I do not wish to go below now.

I learned this, at least, by my experiment; that if one advances confidently in the direction of his dreams, and endeavors to live the life which he has imagined, he will meet with a success unexpected in common hours. He will put some things behind, will pass an invisible boundary; new, universal, and more liberal laws will begin to establish themselves around and within him; or the old laws be expanded, and interpreted in his favor in a more liberal sense, and he will live with the license of a higher order of beings. In proportion as he simplifies his life, the laws of the universe will appear less complex, and solitude will not be solitude, nor poverty poverty, nor weakness weakness. If you have built castles in the air, your work need not be lost; that is where they should be. Now put the foundations under them. . . .

The life in us is like the water in the river. It may rise this year higher than man has ever known it, and flood the parched uplands; even this may be the eventful year, which will drown out all our muskrats. It was not always dry land where we dwell. I see far inland the banks which the stream anciently washed, before science began to record its freshets. Every one has heard the story* which has gone the rounds of New England, of a strong and beautiful bug which came out of the dry leaf of an old table of apple-tree wood, which had stood in a farmer's kitchen for sixty years, first in Connecticut, and afterward in Massachusetts,—from an egg deposited in the living tree many years earlier still, as appeared by counting the annual layers beyond it; which was heard gnawing out for several weeks, hatched perchance by the heat of an urn. Who does not feel his faith in a resurrection and immortality strengthened by hearing of this? Who knows what beautiful and winged life, whose egg has been buried for ages under many concentric layers of woodenness in the dead dry life of society, deposited at first in the alburnum* of the green and living tree, which has been gradually converted into the semblance of its well-seasoned tomb,—heard perchance gnawing out now for years by the astonished family of man, as they sat around the festive board,—may unexpectedly come forth from amidst society's most trivial and handselled* furniture, to enjoy its perfect summer life at last!

story: Melville used this well-known story as the basis for his "The Apple-Tree Table."
alburnum: sapwood
handselled: given as a token

from Journals

Like Emerson, who suggested in 1837 that Thoreau keep a journal, Thoreau mined his notebook jottings for ideas to incorporate into his essays and books. All together, the nearly daily entries from 1837 to 1861 total more than two million words and fill fourteen printed volumes. The brief excerpts below represent Thoreau's extensive journal comments on the art of writing.

February 3, 1859

The writer must to some extent inspire himself. Most of his sentences may at first lie dead in his essay, but when all are arranged, some life and color will be reflected on them from the mature and successful lines; they will appear to pulsate with fresh life, and he will be enabled to eke out* their slumbering sense, and make them worthy of their neighborhood. In his first essay on a given theme, he produces scarcely more than a frame and groundwork for his sentiment and poetry. Each clear thought that he attains to draws in its train many divided thoughts or perceptions. The writer has much to do even to create a theme for himself. Most that is first written on any subject is a mere groping after it, mere rubble-stone and foundation. It is only when many observations of different periods have been brought together that he begins to grasp his subject and can make one pertinent and just observation.

eke out: supplement: i.e., clarify

February 20, 1859

In the composition it is the greatest art to find out as quickly as possible which are the best passages you have written, and tear the rest away to come at them. Even the poorest parts will be most effective when they serve these, as pediments* to the column. . . .

pediments: the broad triangular parts above doors or columns

March 11, 1859

Find out as soon as possible what are the best things in your composition, and then shape the rest to fit them.

For Thought and Discussion

1. Listed below are several points paraphrased from the excerpt of "Civil Disobedience." Choose one of these points and defend or refute the idea embodied therein:
   a. Our country should have no standing army.
   b. The citizen should not delegate the task of lawmaking to elected legislators.
   c. With regard to the justice of existing laws, the majority should not rule.
   d. The law makes well-intentioned men the agents of injustice.
   e. It is better to break the law than to petition the governor or legislature.
   f. All change is for the better.

2. Thoreau's "Civil Disobedience" is usually regarded as an effective piece of persuasion. Cite and discuss at least two examples which illustrate Thoreau's employment of the following persuasive techniques: rhetorical questions, metaphorical language, analogy, definition.

3. Choose one paragraph from "Where I Lived, and What I Lived For" in which Thoreau uses both figurative language and allusion. Evaluate the effectiveness of the passage in terms of Thoreau's purpose in *Walden,* mentioning specific phrases or sentences and labeling specific devices or allusions employed.

4. After reading the selections from Thoreau's *Journals,* list five guidelines for the process of writing. What evidence do you find in Thoreau's writing that he follows his own guidelines?

Walt Whitman   1819-1892

"I look in vain for the poet whom I describe," wrote Emerson in 1844. Eleven years later, almost as if in answer to Emerson's call, Walt Whitman published a collection of poems entitled *Leaves of Grass.* In these poems Whitman in effect, proclaimed himself as "National Poet of the United States." Reworking this collection for the rest of his life, Whitman created a style of poetry that radically departed from the traditional conception of verse. His work has left a strong imprint on later American poets, especially those of the twentieth century. His most harmful long-range effect has been to encourage total freedom both in subject matter and in poetic form.

Whitman's biography cannot be known apart from *Leaves of Grass.* Before the first edition appeared in 1855, Whitman's life seemed unpromising. He had drifted from job to job, taking turns at carpentry, journalism, printing, editing, and schoolteaching. Yet he had also gained familiarity with the country and people he was to celebrate in his poetry. During his boyhood he had lived in rural Long Island and in urban Brooklyn. During his adult life he had traveled to New Orleans and throughout the Midwest. He had read widely in the works of Shakespeare, Homer, Dante, and the Hindu poets and in the Bible, although its truths evidently made no impact on him. He had also absorbed the works of one American writer with whom he felt a special kinship–Emerson. Whitman later declared, "I was simmering, simmering, simmering; Emerson brought me to a boil."

What boiled forth from Whitman in 1855 was *Leaves of Grass,* a thin volume of twelve poems set in print by the poet himself. For the next thirty-seven years he worked on this collection, adding new poems, dropping old ones, and constantly rearranging the others.

As the Civil War engulfed the nation, Whitman too was drawn into the conflict. Although too old to enlist, he voluntarily served in Washington, D.C., as a male nurse among the wounded. From this experience came *Drum-Taps,* a collection of poems on the war and the assassination of President Lincoln. After the war ended, he worked at a government job until 1873, when a stroke partially paralyzed him and forced him into retirement. As he continued issuing revisions of *Leaves of Grass,* public resistance gradually gave way to tentative acceptance. Although his countrymen's praise remained muted, in his last years Whitman achieved international recognition. Praised, surprisingly, as the "good gray poet," Whitman prepared the last edition of his magnum opus, the "death-bed edition," in 1891-92 and died in March 1892.

Whitman's writing unleashed new forces in American verse. No longer, stated Whitman in "Song of Myself," were any subjects forbidden to the poet: "Through me forbidden voices,/Voices of sexes and lust, voices veil'd and I remove the veil,/Voices indecent by me clarified and transfigur'd.'' Even Thoreau and Emerson, who liked Whitman's religious philosophy, were bothered by the volume's sexual frankness and depiction of immorality. Whittier read only a few lines of the copy Whitman sent him before burning it.

Other astute critics attacked Whitman's work as obnoxious in its praise of self and deification of man. This disciple of Emerson proclaimed a new religious creed: ''I believe in the flesh and the appetites,/Seeing, hearing, feeling, are miracles, and each part and tag of me is a miracle./Divine am I inside and out, and I make holy whatever I touch or am touch'd from.'' With his own mind as his church, Whitman founded a new cult of self-worship, its tenets drawn from transcendentalism.

Whitman's writing also affected poetic form. He abandoned rhyme and meter to write in **free verse,** a form that uses lines irregular in length without fixed metrical patterns and usually without rhyme. Other characteristics of his verse include the **catalogs** and experimental diction: for example, neologisms (coined words like *presidentiad, partialisms*), slang *(Kanuck, Cuff)*, archaisms *(nay, anon)*, and foreign words *(ma femme, habitan)*. After Whitman, American poetry was never again the same.

Whitman's verse thus reveals the poet to be the true heir of Emerson's optimistic view on man's perfectability, goodness, and unity with Nature. Probably the single most powerful influence on modern American poets, Whitman tangibly represents this country's mid-nineteenth-century drift away from the spiritual values and ideals of our forefathers. In extending Emerson's ideas to their logical outcome, Whitman illustrates the destructive effects of transcendentalism on the American mind. Understanding his contribution is necessary in our tracing a major current of degeneration in American literature and life.

I Hear America Singing

This poem is one of a cluster of poems called ''Inscriptions'' and attached to the beginning of Leaves of Grass. *Like almost all of Whitman's verse, it reflects Emerson's statement in ''The Poet'' that ''America is a poem in our eyes.'' Here Whitman sings of common Americans busy at their jobs. Notice especially the cataloging technique in lines 2-9.*

I hear America singing, the varied carols I hear,
Those of mechanics, each one singing his as it should be blithe* and strong,   *blithe:* joyous
The carpenter singing his as he measures his plank or beam,
The mason singing his as he makes ready for work, or leaves off work,
The boatman singing what belongs to him in his boat, the deckhand singing on the
   steamboat deck,   5

The shoemaker singing as he sits on his bench, the hatter singing as he stands,
The wood-cutter's song, the ploughboy's on his way in the morning, or at noon
　　intermission or at sundown,
The delicious singing of the mother, or of the young wife at work, or of the girl sewing
　　or washing,
Each singing what belongs to him or her and to none else,
The day what belongs to the day—at night the party of young fellows, robust, friendly,
Singing with open mouths their strong melodious songs.　　　　　　　　　　11

from Song of Myself

*The longest of Whitman's poems, ''Song of Myself'' is the foundation of all nine
editions of* Leaves of Grass. *Constructed of fifty-two sections, the poem develops
Whitman's concept of Self. What causes confusion is the fact that ''self'' refers both
to the individual poet (as in line 8) and to the mystical ''self'' unifying all men.*

*The three sections reprinted here are all significant parts. In section 1 Whitman
expresses his poetic theory; in section 6 he explores six meanings of the central*
image *in his entire work–grass; and in section 52 he defines his poetry and illustrates his belief in the underlying unity of mankind and nature.*

1

I celebrate myself, and sing myself,
And what I assume you shall assume,
For every atom belonging to me as good belongs to you.

I loafe and invite my soul,
I lean and loafe at my ease observing a spear of summer grass.　　　　5

My tongue, every atom of my blood, form'd from this soil, this air,
Born here of parents born here from parents the same, and parents the same,
I, now thirty-seven years old in perfect health begin,
Hoping to cease not till death.

Creeds, and schools in abeyance,* 10
Retiring back a while sufficed at what they are, but never forgotten,
I harbor for good or bad, I permit to speak at every hazard,
Nature without check with original energy.*

abeyance: suspension, temporary inactivity

Nature . . . energy: This line summarizes Whitman's subject matter, limitations, and mode of poetic utterance in "Song of Myself."

6

A child said *What is the grass?* fetching it to me with full hands,
How could I answer the child? I do not know what it is any more than he.

I guess it must be the flag of my disposition,* out of hopeful green stuff woven.

disposition: frame of mind

Or I guess it is the handkerchief of the Lord,
A scented gift and remembrancer designedly dropt,
Bearing the owner's name someway in the corners, that we may see and remark, and
    say *Whose?*
Or I guess the grass is itself a child, the produced babe of the vegetation.

Or I guess it is a uniform hieroglyphic,*
And it means, Sprouting alike in broad zones and narrow zones,
Growing among black folks as among white,
Kanuck, Tuckahoe, Congressman, Cuff,* I give them the same, I receive them the same.

hieroglyphic: picture writing

Kanuck . . . Cuff: Three are slang terms; *Kanuck* is a French-Canadian; *Tuckahoe* is a Tide- water Virginian; *Cuff* is a Negro. Why is *Congressman* includ- ed in this list?

And now it seems to me the beautiful uncut hair of graves. 25

Tenderly will I use you curling grass,
It may be you transpire from the breasts of young men,
It may be if I had known them I would have loved them,
It may be you are from old people, or from offspring taken soon out of their mothers'
    laps,
And here you are the mothers' laps. 30

This grass is very dark to be from the white heads of old mothers,
Darker than the colorless beards of old men,
Dark to come from under the faint red roofs of mouths.

O I perceive after all so many uttering tongues,
And I perceive they do not come from the roofs of mouths for nothing.   35

I wish I could translate the hints about the dead young men and women,
And the hints about old men and mothers, and the offspring taken soon out of their laps.

What do you think has become of the young and old men?
And what do you think has become of the women and children?

They are alive and well somewhere,   40
The smallest sprout shows there is really no death,
And if ever there was it led forward life, and does not wait at the end to arrest it,
And ceas'd the moment life appear'd.

All goes onward and outward, nothing collapses,
And to die is different from what any one supposed, and luckier.   45

52

The spotted hawk swoops by and accuses me, he complains of my gab and my loitering.

I too am not a bit tamed, I too am untranslatable,
I sound my barbaric yawp* over the roofs of the world.

yawp: loud cry or yell

The last scud* of day holds back for me.
It flings my likeness after the rest and true as any on the shadow'd wilds,   50
It coaxes me to the vapor and the dusk.

scud: light wind-driven clouds

I depart as air, I shake my white locks at the runaway sun,
I effuse* my flesh in eddies, and drift it in lacy jags.*

effuse: pour out, flow/ *lacy jags:* rags, tatters

I bequeath myself to the dirt to grow from the grass I love,
If you want me again look for me under your boot-soles.   55

You will hardly know who I am or what I mean,
But I shall be good health to you nevertheless,
And filter and fibre your blood.

Failing to fetch me at first keep encouraged,
Missing me one place search another,   60
I stop somewhere waiting for you.

O Captain! My Captain!

One of Whitman's most traditional poems, "O Captain! My Captain!" represents the nation as a ship with its president as the captain. The voice heard in the lament is a public voice mourning the death of Abraham Lincoln.

O Captain! my Captain! our fearful trip is done,
The ship has weather'd every rack, the prize we sought is won,
The port is near, the bells I hear, the people all exulting,*
While follow eyes the steady keel,* the vessel grim and daring;
    But O heart! heart! heart!   5
      O the bleeding drops of red,
         Where on the deck my Captain lies,
            Fallen cold and dead.

exulting: rejoicing greatly

keel: the main structural member of a vessel, the backbone of a ship

O Captain! my Captain! rise up and hear the bells;
Rise up–for you the flag is flung–for you the bugle trills,   10
For you bouquets and ribbon'd wreaths–for you the shores a-crowding,
For you they call, the swaying mass, their eager faces turning;
    Here Captain! dear father!
      This arm beneath your head!
         It is some dream that on the deck,   15
            You've fallen cold and dead.

My Captain does not answer, his lips are pale and still,
My father does not feel my arm, he has no pulse nor will,
The ship is anchor'd safe and sound, its voyage closed and done,
From fearful trip the victor ship comes in with object won;   20
    Exult O shores, and ring O bells!
      But I with mournful tread,
         Walk the deck my Captain lies,
            Fallen cold and dead.

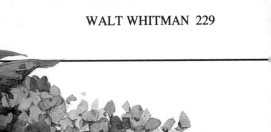

When Lilacs Last in the Dooryard Bloom'd

*In this poem we hear Whitman's personal voice. This **elegy** has been called "a masterpiece expressing personal grief and reconciliation."*

*Whitman develops the poem by three symbols: the lilac, the star, and the hermit thrush. He takes up each separately in section 1, intertwines them, and finally brings all three together in the next to the last line. In his treatment of the lilac itself, the **image** expands from a single bough (l. 17) to armfuls of lilacs (ll. 52-53).*

*Whitman develops two **themes** in this poem: his country and death. Woven throughout the poem is his praise of the beauty of the United States (see section 11 especially). The theme of death is embodied in the bird's song (section 14) and the poet's vision (section 15).*

Although Whitman never met President Lincoln personally, he often saw him and greatly admired him. Lincoln's death on April 15, 1865, came when the lilacs were in bloom in Brooklyn. Whitman later observed, "By one of those caprices that enter and give tinge to events without being at all a part of them, I find myself always reminded of the great tragedy of that day by the sight and odor of these blossoms. It never fails." Thus in the manner characteristic of romantic poetry and of poetry ever since, a major symbol is based on very private associations.

Notice that this poem follows the traditional form of the elegy by moving from an expression of uncontrollable grief toward acceptance of death. In section 2, for instance, the poet's grief seems inconsolable. In the section that follows, he seems deliberately to turn from his grief to distract himself with the lilacs (section 3), the hermit thrush (section 4), and the progress of Lincoln's coffin from Washington to Springfield, Illinois (sections 5 and 6). In section 7 the poet confronts the fact of death by universalizing, or broadening, the one death (Lincoln's) to include all deaths. In section 14 Nature educates the poet through the thrush's song of death, which awakens a response in the poet's soul. He then sees death as different from what he had formerly imagined (section 15). Finally, in section 16, as the visions retreat with the coming of day, the poet becomes reconciled to the death that had earlier seemed so devastating.

1

When lilacs last in the dooryard bloom'd,
And the great star early droop'd in the western sky in the night,
I mourn'd, and yet shall mourn with ever-returning spring.

Ever-returning spring, trinity* sure to me you bring,
Lilac blooming perennial and drooping star in the west,   5
And thought of him I love.

trinity: lilac, star, and
thrush

2

O powerful western fallen star!
O shades of night–O moody, tearful night!
O great star disappear'd–O the black murk that hides the star!
O cruel hands that hold me powerless–O helpless soul of me!   10
O harsh surrounding cloud that will not free my soul.

3

In the dooryard fronting an old farm-house near the white-wash'd palings,
Stands the lilac-bush tall-growing with heart-shaped leaves of rich green,
With many a pointed blossom rising delicate, with the perfume strong I love,
With every leaf a miracle–and from this bush in the dooryard,   15
With delicate-color'd blossoms and heart-shaped leaves of rich green,
A sprig with its flower I break.

4

In the swamp in secluded recesses,
A shy and hidden bird is warbling a song.

Solitary the thrush,   20
The hermit withdrawn to himself, avoiding the settlements,
Sings by himself a song.

Song of the bleeding throat,
Death's outlet song of life, (for well dear brother I know,
If thou wast not granted to sing thou would'st surely die).

5

Over the breast of the spring, the land, amid cities,
Amid lanes and through old woods, where lately the violets peep'd from the ground,
    spotting the gray debris,
Amid the grass in the fields each side of the lanes, passing the endless grass,
Passing the yellow-spear'd wheat, every grain from its shroud in the dark-brown fields
    uprisen,
Passing the apple-tree blows of white and pink in the orchards,   30
Carrying a corpse to where it shall rest in the grave,
Night and day journeys a coffin,

6

Coffin that passes through lanes and streets,
Through day and night with the great cloud darkening the land,
With the pomp of the inloop'd* flags with the cities draped in black,   35
With the show of the States themselves as of crape-veil'd* women standing,
With processions long and winding and the flambeaus* of the night,
With the countless torches lit, with the silent sea of faces and the unbared heads,
With the waiting depot, the arriving coffin, and the sombre faces,
With dirges* through the night, with the thousand voices rising strong and solemn,
With all the mournful voices of the dirges pour'd around the coffin,
The dim-lit churches and the shuddering organs—where amid these you journey,
With the tolling tolling bells' perpetual clang,
Here, coffin that slowly passes,
I give you my sprig of lilac.   45

inloop'd: suggesting the shape of a loop
crape-veil'd: veiled with black crepe as a sign of mourning
flambeaus: burning torches
dirges: songs of mourning

7

(Nor for you, for one alone,
Blossoms and branches green to coffins all I bring,
For fresh as the morning, thus would I chant a song for you O sane and sacred death.

All over bouquets of roses,
O death, I cover you over with roses and early lilies,   50
But mostly and now the lilac that blooms the first,
Copious I break, I break the sprigs from the bushes,
With loaded arms I come, pouring for you,
For you and the coffins all of you O death.)

8

O western orb* sailing the heaven,   55
Now I know what you must have meant as a month since I walk'd,
As I walk'd in silence the transparent shadowy night,
As I saw you had something to tell as you bent to me night after night,
As you droop'd from the sky low down as if to my side, (while the other stars all
    look'd on,)
As we wander'd together the solemn night, (for something I know not what kept me
    from sleep,)   60
As the night advanced, and I saw on the rim of the west how full you were of woe,
As I stood on the rising ground in the breeze in the cool transparent night,
As I watch'd where you pass'd and was lost in the netherward black of the night,
As my soul in its trouble dissatisfied sank, as where you sad orb,
Concluded, dropt in the night, and was gone.   65

orb: a rounded mass: i.e., the star

9

Sing on there in the swamp,
O singer bashful and tender, I hear your notes, I hear your call,
I hear, I come presently,* I understand you,
But a moment I linger, for the lustrous star has detain'd me,
The star my departing comrade holds and detains me.   70

presently: after a little while

10

O how shall I warble myself for the dead one there I loved?
And how shall I deck my song for the large sweet soul that has gone?
And what shall my perfume be for the grave of him I love?

Sea-winds blown from east and west,
Blown from the Eastern sea and blown from the Western sea, till there on the prairies
    meeting,   75
These and with these and the breath of my chant,
I'll perfume the grave of him I love.

11

O what shall I hang on the chamber walls?
And what shall the pictures be that I hang on the walls,
To adorn the burial-house of him I love?   80

Pictures of growing spring and farms and homes,
With the Fourth-month eve at sundown, and the gray smoke lucid* and bright,   *lucid:* lit., shining
With floods of the yellow gold of the gorgeous, indolent,* sinking sun, burning,   *indolent:* idle
    expanding the air,
With the fresh sweet herbage* under foot, and the pale green leaves of the trees prolific,* *herbage:* grass/*prolif-*
In the distance the flowing glaze, the breast of the river, with a wind-dapple here and   *ic:* in great
    there,   85 abundance
With ranging hills on the banks, with many a line against the sky, and shadows,
And the city at hand with dwellings so dense, and stacks of chimneys,
And all the scenes of life and the workshops, and the workmen homeward returning.

12

Lo, body and soul–this land,
My own Manhattan with spires, and the sparkling and hurrying tides, and the ships,
The varied and ample land, the South and the North in the light, Ohio's shores and
    flashing Missouri,
And ever the far-spreading prairies cover'd with grass and corn.

Lo, the most excellent sun so calm and haughty,
The violet and purple morn with just-felt breezes,
The gentle soft-born measureless light,   95
The miracle spreading bathing all, the fulfill'd noon,
The coming eve delicious, the welcome night and the stars,
Over my cities shining all, enveloping man and land.

13

Sing on, sing on you gray-brown bird,
Sing from the swamps, the recesses,* pour your chant from the bushes,   100 *recesses:* quiet, se-
Limitless out of the dusk, out of the cedars and pines.   cluded spots

Sing on dearest brother, warble your reedy song,
Loud human song, with voice of uttermost woe.

O liquid and free and tender!
O wild and loose to my soul–O wondrous singer,   105
You only I hear–yet the star holds me, (but will soon depart,)
Yet the lilac with mastering odor holds me.

14

Now while I sat in the day and look'd forth,
In the close of the day with its light and the fields of spring, and the farmers preparing
      their crops,
In the large unconscious scenery of my land with its lakes and forests,   110
In the heavenly aerial beauty, (after the perturb'd winds and the storms,)
Under the arching heavens of the afternoon swift passing, and the voices of children and
      women,
The many-moving sea-tides, and I saw ships how they sail'd,
And the summer approaching with richness, and the fields all busy with labor,
And the infinite separate houses, how they all went on, each with its meals and minutia*   *minutia*: small unim-
      of daily usages,   portant detail
                                                                                        115
And the streets how their throbbings throbb'd, and the cities pent—lo, then and there,
Falling upon them all and among them all, enveloping me with the rest,
Appear'd the cloud, appear'd the long black trail,
And I knew death, its thought, and the sacred knowledge of death.

Then with the knowledge of death as walking one side of me,   120
And the thought of death close-walking the other side of me,
And I in the middle as with companions, and as holding the hands of companions,
I fled forth to the hiding receiving night that talks not,
Down to the shores of the water, the path by the swamp in the dimness,
To the solemn shadowy cedars and ghostly pines so still.   125

And the singer so shy to the rest receiv'd me,
The gray-brown bird I know receiv'd us comrades three,
And he sang the carol of death, and a verse for him I love.

From deep secluded recesses,
From the fragrant cedars and the ghostly pines so still,   130
Came the carol of the bird.

And the charm of the carol rapt me,
As I held as if by their hands my comrades in the night,
And the voice of my spirit tallied the song of the bird.*   The italicized passage
                                                                 beginning with line
                                                                 135 represents Whit-
Come lovely and soothing death,   135   man's translation of
Undulate round the world, serenely arriving, arriving,   the bird's song.
In the day, in the night, to all, to each,
Sooner or later delicate death.

Prais'd be the fathomless universe,
For life and joy, and for objects and knowledge curious,   140
And for love, sweet love—but praise! praise! praise!
For the sure-enwinding arms of cool-enfolding death.

Dark mother always gliding near with soft feet,
Have none chanted for thee a chant of fullest welcome?
Then I chant it for thee, I glorify thee above all,   145
I bring thee a song that when thou must indeed come, come unfalteringly.

Approach strong deliveress,
When it is so, when thou hast taken them I joyously sing the dead,
Lost in the loving floating ocean of thee,
Laved* in the flood of thy bliss O death.   150   *Laved*: bathed

From me to thee glad serenades,
Dances for thee I propose saluting thee, adornments and feastings for thee,
And the sights of the open landscape and the high-spread sky are fitting,
And life and the fields, and the huge and thoughtful night.

The night in silence under many a star,   155
The ocean shore and the husky whispering wave whose voice I know,
And the soul turning to thee O vast and well-veil'd death,
And the body gratefully nestling close to thee.

Over the tree-tops I float thee a song,
Over the rising and sinking waves, over the myriad fields and the prairies wide,
Over the dense-pack'd cities all and the teeming wharves and ways,
I float this carol with joy, with joy to thee O death.

15

To the tally of my soul,
Loud and strong kept up the gray-brown bird,
With pure deliberate notes spreading filling the night.   165

Loud in the pines and cedars dim,
Clear in the freshness moist and the swamp-perfume,
And I with my comrades there in the night.

While my sight that was bound in my eyes unclosed,
As to long panoramas* of visions.   170

And I saw askant* the armies,
I saw as in noiseless dreams hundreds of battle-flags,
Borne through the smoke of the battles and pierc'd with missiles I saw them,
And carried hither and yon through the smoke, and torn and bloody,
And at last but a few shreds left on the staffs, (and all in silence,) 175
And the staffs all splinter'd and broken.

I saw battle-corpses, myriads of them,
And the white skeletons of young men, I saw them,
I saw the debris and debris of all the slain soldiers of the war,
But I saw they were not as was thought,   180
They themselves were fully at rest, they suffer'd not,
The living remain'd and suffer'd, the mother suffer'd,
And the wife and the child and the musing comrade suffer'd
And the armies that remain'd suffer'd.

16

Passing the visions, passing the night,   185
Passing, unloosing the hold of my comrade's hands,
Passing the song of the hermit bird and the tallying song of my soul,
Victorious song, death's outlet song, yet varying ever-altering song,
As low, and wailing, yet clear the notes, rising and falling, flooding the night,
Sadly sinking and fainting, as warning and warning, and yet again bursting with joy,
Covering the earth and filling the spread of the heaven,   191
As that powerful psalm in the night I heard from recesses,
Passing, I leave thee lilac with heart-shaped leaves,
I leave thee there in the door-yard, blooming, returning with spring.

I cease from my song for thee,   195
From my gaze on thee in the west, fronting the west, communing with thee,
O comrade lustrous with silver face in the night.

Yet each to keep and all, retrievements* out of the night,
The song, the wondrous chant of the gray-brown bird,

panoramas: a series of pictures arranged to unroll and pass before a spectator
askant: distrustfully

retrievements: remembrances

And the tallying chant, the echo arous'd in my soul,   200
With the lustrous and drooping star with the countenance full of woe,
With the holders holding my hand hearing the call of the bird.
Comrades mine and I in the midst, and their memory ever to keep, for the dead I loved
    so well,
For the sweetest, wisest soul of all my days and lands—and this for his dear sake,
Lilac and star and bird twined with the chant of my soul,   205
There in the fragrant pines and the cedars dusk and dim.

For Thought and Discussion

1. How many times does Whitman use forms of the verb *sing* and the noun *song* in "I Hear America Singing"? Is there any line in which he does not use one of these forms? Which line of the poem begins and ends with the same clause? How is this clause related to Whitman's repetition of *sing* and its variants? Which line begins and ends with a variant of *sing?* What is the effect of Whitman's repetition of this key word throughout the poem? Does this repetition intensify or detract from the meaning of the poem? Why? As a reader, do you react positively or negatively to re-encountering this word and its variants as you move from line to line of the poem? After considering all these questions, write a paragraph on Whitman's use of repetition to convey theme in "I Hear America Singing."

2. In "Song of Myself" Whitman again uses repetition but it is a different type of repetition than that used in the first poem. In which lines of "Song of Myself" does he repeat a word, a phrase, or a grammatical pattern within a single line of poetry? What is the effect of this variety in repetition?

3. How does Whitman use the symbol of grass to convey his beliefs in immortality and pantheism in sections 6 and 52 of "Song of Myself"? In what major way does Whitman's grass symbolism differ from the associations made with grass in the following Scriptural passages: Psalm 102:4, 11; Psalm 103:15-16; Isaiah 40:6-8; 1 Peter 1:24-25?

4. According to some critics, Whitman's primary source for the form, style, and major imagery of *Leaves of Grass* was the King James Version of the Bible. Why do you suppose Whitman chose the Bible as his model? Which works by Whitman are stylistically akin to Hebrew poetry in their use of repetition and parallelism? Can you find any Biblical allusions in Whitman's works?

5. In contrast to "When Lilacs Last in the Dooryard Bloom'd," Whitman's "O Captain! My Captain!" is a conventional poem. How do the two pieces differ in rhythm and in stanza form? In which poem does Whitman employ rhyme? Why do you suppose Whitman chose a traditional poetic style for one and free verse for the other? How does the poetic style for each contribute to or reinforce the content of each poem?

7 *Transcendental Pessimists*

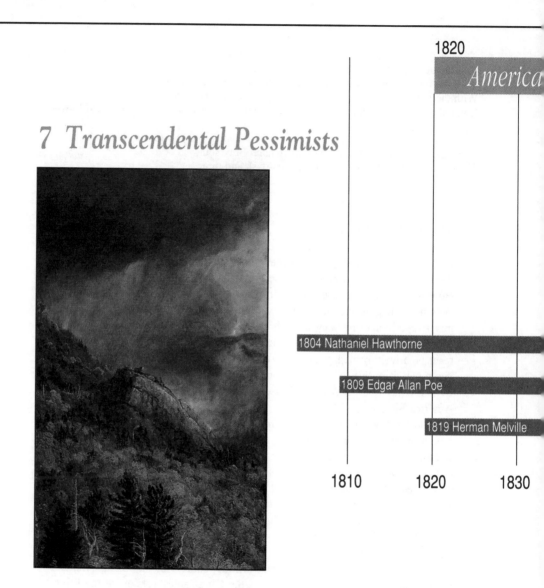

1820

America

1804 Nathaniel Hawthorne

1809 Edgar Allan Poe

1819 Herman Melville

1810   1820   1830

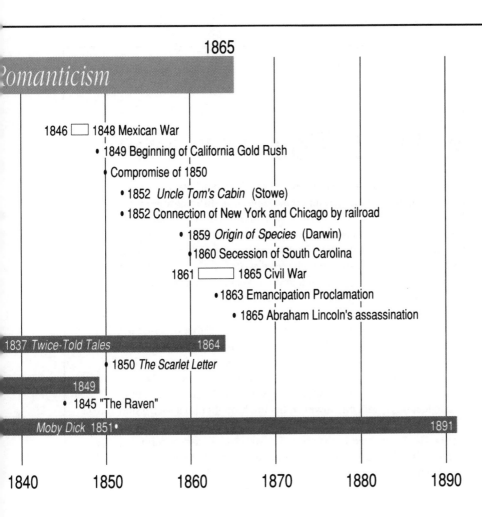

1865

Romanticism

1846 ☐ 1848 Mexican War
• 1849 Beginning of California Gold Rush
• Compromise of 1850
• 1852 *Uncle Tom's Cabin* (Stowe)
• 1852 Connection of New York and Chicago by railroad
• 1859 *Origin of Species* (Darwin)
• 1860 Secession of South Carolina
1861 ☐ 1865 Civil War
• 1863 Emancipation Proclamation
• 1865 Abraham Lincoln's assassination

1837 *Twice-Told Tales*   1864
• 1850 *The Scarlet Letter*

1849
• 1845 "The Raven"

Moby Dick 1851•   1891

1840   1850   1860   1870   1880   1890

Edgar Allan Poe 1809-1849

Edgar Allan Poe's life and writings have intrigued many readers. Because much of the biographical information is distorted and unreliable, it is difficult to separate legend from fact. In fact, several "Poes" exist. One is the tragic American writer romantically doomed to failure by internal and external forces too strong for him to control. Another is the literary "lightweight" whose works reveal technical skill but yield no significant content. A third is the obsessed writer whose works mirror his own mental torment and psychological disintegration. While none of these views is totally accurate, all suggest important features of one of today's most widely read nineteenth-century authors.

Poe's life unquestionably had elements of tragedy. His actor-father deserted the family when the boy was only a year old. His actress-mother died from tuberculosis when he was two. He was then informally adopted by the Allans—a wealthy, childless couple from Richmond, Virginia, who gave Poe his middle name. Educated both in England (1815-20) and in Virginia, Poe developed into a young man of academic promise. From his late teen-age years on, however, his life brought him a succession of disappointments. He left the University of Virginia after one term because of heavy gambling debts. He then served in the army for two years before securing an appointment to West Point, where for eight months he chafed under regulations until his deliberate defiance of the rules brought his dismissal. However, by this time he was a published poet: his first volume, *Tamerlane and Other Poems,* appeared anonymously in 1827 when he was eighteen; other volumes followed in 1829 and 1831.

In 1832, having received little recognition from his verse, Poe turned to fiction. In 1833 he won first prize in a Baltimore newspaper contest for his short story "Ms. Found in a Bottle." Over the next dozen years his carefully thought out and executed short stories helped raise the **genre** to artistic stature. Unable to support himself solely by his writing, Poe worked as an editor. While invariably improving the literary quality of the publications he edited, he almost always lost these jobs because of quarrels with the owners. In his scathing reviews of writers he disliked, he belittled works more for personal or professional reasons than for truly aesthetic ones. His unsubstantiated charges of plagiarism against Longfellow made Poe unpopular with many American readers.

In 1835 Poe married his thirteen-year-old cousin, Virginia Clemm. This marriage, made public in 1836, brought Poe a more stable home environment than he had ever known. From 1836 to 1844 he enjoyed a period of significant literary accomplishment although he remained in poverty and was hampered by bouts of drinking and depression. When Virigina died in 1847 after five years of progressively worsening illness, Poe threw himself recklessly into his work. In 1849, two years after the death of his wife, Poe heard that Mrs. Shelton, a childhood sweetheart, had been recently widowed. Traveling to Richmond to renew their acquaintance, Poe secured her promise to marry him. On his way back to Philadelphia after this engagement, he stopped off in Baltimore. Here he was discovered lying in a gutter in a coma. Taken to a hospital, Poe remained delirious until his death four days later on October 7.

Poe stands today as the first American writer to influence his successors in poetry, fiction, *and* criticism. What significantly shaped his stories and poems was a set of aesthetic principles stated in his criticism. These principles were the result of Poe's conception of the human mind as divided into three faculties, or compartments: Intellect, Soul, and Conscience. Truth appeals to the first, Beauty to the second, and Duty to the third. Since these compartments, Poe believed, are separate, neither truth nor morality appeals to the Soul. In his practical criticism Poe attacked strongly a contemporary tendency he called the "heresy of the Didactic." The didacticism in the works of contemporary poets like Longfellow seemed inartistic to Poe. The inability to appreciate the didactic was, however, a blindness. The notion that beauty and truth are mutually exclusive is certainly false, as examples of the Bible and of great writers like Spenser, Shakespeare, Milton, and Bunyan make clear.

Also, Poe's principle of proper length also governed his literary style. According to Poe, both poetry and fiction had to be short enough to be read in one sitting. The limit for a poem, he felt, is about one hundred lines. Poe's insistence that a work must satisfy high literary standards, not just develop American content, made his contribution instrumental in the development of a national literature comparable to England's.

Moreover, Poe's short stories and poems illustrate his principle that a single emotion or **mood** ought to dominate a literary work. In poetry the mood Poe generally sought was melancholy, produced by reflections on the death of a beautiful woman. In fiction his desired mood was horror or terror, with each detail of the story contributing to the single emotional effect.

Although romantic in principle and practice, Poe was not a transcendentalist. In fact, he uttered a distinct "No" on aesthetic grounds to transcendental optimism. Poe's works undercut the concept of mankind's upward progression to perfection by picturing characters caught in a downward process of psychological and moral disintegration. Poe's world is no benevolent creation revealing truth to men, but a twisted, nightmarish landscape of failure, malevolence, and death. Poe also strikes a persistent note of pessimism about man's achievements and capabilities. Although Poe's perspective is not Biblically or even morally sound, his delineations of depraved men, twisted and tortured by their innermost natures, are in keeping with what we know of the effects of sin and, in fact, parallel the portraits given by Hawthorne and Melville, the other two romantic pessimists.

Poe's work significantly raised the consciousness of the American public concerning literary aesthetics. In terms of ethical significance, however, it is deficient, especially for the Christian reader. Although we may find Poe's stories entertaining, we cannot overlook his preoccupation with the morbid side of man's nature. Thus his work is finally a weak refutation of transcendental optimism.

To Helen

Critics believe that Poe received inspiration from a schoolmate's mother, Mrs. Jane Stith Stanard, whose beauty and whose tragic death in 1824 touched the fifteen-year-old poet deeply. The Helen of the title is the legendary Helen of Troy, the classical epitome of beauty. Helen's beauty caused her abduction from Macedonia by Paris of Troy and thus touched off the Trojan War, which serves as backdrop for the Iliad. *Notice that this poem, like the ''Sonnet–To Science,'' is an* **apostrophe.**

Helen, thy beauty is to me
    Like those Nicéan barks* of yore,
That gently, o'er a perfumed sea,
    The weary, way-worn wanderer* bore
    To his own native shore.   5

On desperate seas long wont to roam,
    Thy hyacinth* hair, thy classic face,
Thy Naiad airs have brought me home
    To the glory that was Greece
And the grandeur that was Rome.   10

Lo! in yon brilliant window-niche
    How statue-like I see thee stand!
    The agate* lamp within thy hand,
Ah, Psyche,* from the regions which
    Are Holy-Land!   15

Nicéan barks: poetic term for ships

The . . . wanderer: i.e., Ulysses, who wandered for ten years before returning home after the Trojan War (Notice the alliteration of *w*'s in this line.)
hyacinth: curly

agate: stone

Psyche: Gr., soul: Greek goddess of enviable beauty (Poe regards the world of imagination as his Holy Land.)

The Raven

*"The Raven" is the most famous of Poe's poems. Published in 1845, it brought the poet his first taste of fame. In "The Philosophy of Composition" Poe explains how he wrote the poem and why he chose its technical features. He notes that the structure of the poem develops from the arrangement of the speaker's questions from playful to climactic (see especially ll. 85-90). Poe also notes that the raven becomes an emblem, or **symbol,** in the last two stanzas. Notice that the **theme** of the poem is the one Poe regarded as the most poetic—the death of a beautiful woman.*

Once upon a midnight dreary, while I pondered, weak and weary,
Over many a quaint and curious volume of forgotten lore,*
While I nodded, nearly napping, suddenly there came a tapping,
As of some one gently rapping, rapping at my chamber door.
" 'Tis some visitor," I muttered, "tapping at my chamber door—   5
    Only this, and nothing more."

lore: accumulated fact, tradition, or belief about a particular subject

Ah, distinctly I remember it was in the bleak December,
And each separate dying ember wrought its ghost upon the floor.
Eagerly I wished the morrow;–vainly I had sought to borrow
From my books surcease* of sorrow–sorrow for the lost Lenore*   10
For the rare and radiant maiden whom the angels name Lenore—
    Nameless here* for evermore.

surcease: an end/*Lenore:* suggestive of Poe's wife Virginia or his youthful sweetheart
here: i.e., in this world

And the silken sad uncertain rustling of each purple curtain
Thrilled me–filled me with fantastic terrors never felt before;
So that now, to still the beating of my heart, I stood repeating   15
" 'Tis some visitor entreating entrance at my chamber door—
Some late visitor entreating entrance at my chamber door;–
    This it is, and nothing more."

Presently my soul grew stronger; hesitating then no longer,
"Sir," said I, "or Madam, truly your forgiveness I implore;   20
But the fact is I was napping, and so gently you came rapping,
And so faintly you came tapping, tapping at my chamber door,
That I scarce was sure I heard you"–here I opened wide the door;–
    Darkness there, and nothing more.

Deep into that darkness peering, long I stood there wondering, fearing,
Doubting, dreaming dreams no mortal ever dared to dream before;
But the silence was unbroken, and the darkness gave no token,
And the only word there spoken was the whispered word, "Lenore!"
This I whispered, and an echo murmured back the word, "Lenore!"
      Merely this, and nothing more.   30

Back into the chamber turning, all my soul within me burning,
Soon I heard again a tapping somewhat louder than before.
"Surely," said I, "surely that is something at my window lattice;
Let me see, then, what thereat is,* and this mystery explore–   *thereat is:* comic
Let my heart be still a moment and this mystery explore;–   35   rhyme: cf. *lattice*
      'Tis the wind and nothing more!"

Open here I flung the shutter, when, with many a flirt and flutter,
In there stepped a stately raven of the saintly days of yore;*   *yore:* time long past
Not the least obeisance* made he; not an instant stopped or stayed he;   *obeisance:* gesture,
But, with mien* of lord or lady, perched above my chamber door–   40   such as a bow, ex-
Perched upon a bust of Pallas* just above my chamber door–   pressing respect
      Perched, and, sat, and nothing more.   *mien:* expression or
                                     bearing

Then this ebony bird beguiling* my sad fancy into smiling,   *Pallas:* Athena, the
By the grave and stern decorum* of the countenance it wore,   goddess of wis-
"Though thy crest be shorn and shaven, thou," I said, "art sure no craven,* dom, the patron
Ghastly grim and ancient raven wandering from the Nightly shore–   goddess of Athens
Tell me what thy lordly name is on the Night's Plutonian* shore!"   *beguiling:* diverting
      Quoth the raven, "Nevermore."   *decorum:* propriety

                                       craven: coward

Much I marvelled this ungainly* fowl to hear discourse so plainly,   *Night's Plutonian:* In
Though its answer little meaning–little relevancy bore;   50   Roman myth Pluto
For we cannot help agreeing that no living human being   ruled Hades, the
Ever yet was blessed with seeing bird above his chamber door–   home of the dead.
Bird or beast upon the sculptured bust above his chamber door,   *ungainly:* without
      With such name as "Nevermore."   grace, clumsy

But the raven, sitting lonely on the placid* bust, spoke only   55   *placid:* undisturbed,
That one word, as if his soul in that one word he did outpour.   calm
Nothing farther then he uttered–not a feather then he fluttered–
Till I scarcely more than muttered "Other friends have flown before–
On the morrow *he* will leave me, as my hopes have flown before."
      Then the bird said "Nevermore."   60

Startled at the stillness broken by reply so aptly spoken,
"Doubtless," said I, "what it utters is its only stock and store
Caught from some unhappy master whom unmerciful Disaster
Followed fast and followed faster till his songs one burden bore–
Till the dirges* of his Hope that melancholy burden bore   65   *dirges:* funeral
      Of 'Never–nevermore.' "   hymns

But the raven still beguiling all my fancy into smiling,
Straight I wheeled a cushioned seat in front of bird and bust and door;
Then, upon the velvet sinking, I betook myself to linking
Fancy unto fancy, thinking what this ominous bird of yore–   70
What this grim, ungainly, ghastly, gaunt, and ominous bird of yore
      Meant in croaking "Nevermore."

This I sat engaged in guessing, but no syllable expressing
To the fowl whose fiery eyes now burned into my bosom's core;
This and more I sat divining,* with my head at ease reclining   75   *divining:* inferring,
On the cushion's velvet lining that the lamplight gloated,* o'er   concluding
But whose velvet violet lining with the lamplight gloating o'er,
      She shall press, ah, nevermore!   *gloated:* double
                                                                          meaning: to look
                                                                          down on with evil
                                                                          satisfaction and to
                                                                          refract or reflect
Then, methought, the air grew denser, perfumed from an unseen censer   light
Swung by angels whose faint foot-falls tinkled on the tufted floor. 80
"Wretch," I cried, "thy God hath lent thee–by these angels he hath sent thee
Respite*–respite and nepenthe* from thy memories of Lenore!   *Respite:* rest/*nepen-
Quaff* oh quaff this kind nepenthe and forget this lost Lenore!"   *the:* in classical
      Quoth the raven, "Nevermore."   myth a drink ban-
                                                                          ishing sorrow
                                                                          Quaff: drink heartily

"Prophet!" said I, "thing of evil!–prophet still, if bird or devil!– 85
Whether Tempter sent, or whether tempest tossed thee here ashore,
Desolate, yet all undaunted, on this desert land enchanted–
On this home by Horror haunted–tell me truly, I implore–
Is there—*is* there balm in Gilead?*–tell me–tell me, I implore!"   *balm in Gilead:* see
      Quoth the raven, "Nevermore."   90   Jeremiah 8:22; ref-
                                                                          erence to medici-
                                                                          nal herb

"Prophet!" said I, "thing of evil–prophet still, if bird or devil!
By that Heaven that bends above us–by that God we both adore–
Tell this soul with sorrow laden if, within the distant Aidenn,*   *Aidenn:* Eden or
It shall clasp a sainted maiden whom the angels name Lenore–   heaven
Clasp a rare and radiant maiden whom the angels name Lenore."   95
      Quoth the raven, "Nevermore."

"Be that word our sign of parting, bird or fiend!" I shrieked, upstarting–
"Get thee back into the tempest and the Night's Plutonian shore!
Leave no black plume as a token of that lie thy soul hath spoken!
Leave my loneliness unbroken!–quit the bust above my door!   100
Take thy beak from out my heart, and take thy form from off my door!"
     Quoth the raven, "Nevermore."

And the raven, never flitting, still is sitting, still is sitting
On the pallid bust of Pallas just above my chamber door;
And his eyes have all the seeming of a demon's that is dreaming,   105
And the lamp-light o'er him streaming throws his shadow on the floor;
And my soul from out that shadow that lies floating on the floor
     Shall be lifted–nevermore!

Sonnet–To Science

*This **sonnet** contrasts the real world of scientific investigation with the imaginary world of the poet. The first eight lines express the romantic poet's dislike of the scientific attitude while the last six lines show science's destructive effect on the world of the imagination.*

Science! true daughter of Old Time thou art!
    Who alterest all things with thy peering eyes.
Why preyest thou thus upon the poet's heart,
    Vulture, whose wings are dull realities?
How should he love thee? or how deem* thee wise?   5   *deem:* think, consider
    Who wouldst not leave him in his wandering
To seek for treasure in the jewelled skies,
    Albeit he soared with an undaunted* wing?   *undaunted:* fearless
Hast thou not dragged Diana* from her car?   *Diana:* the Roman goddess whose "car" (chariot) was the moon
    And driven the Hamadryad* from the wood   10
To seek a shelter in some happier star?   *Hamadryad:* a female spirit of the trees in Greek mythology
    Hast thou not torn the Naiad* from her flood,   *Naiad:* a female spirit of rivers and lakes
The Elfin* from the green grass, and from me   *Elfin:* elves
The summer dream beneath the tamarind* tree?   *tamarind:* a tree idealized in oriental poetry

To My Mother

This poem is addressed not to Poe's real mother, who had died when he was two, but to his aunt and mother-in-law, Maria Poe Clemm. Written after his wife's death in 1847, this **sonnet** *seems unrepresentative of Poe's verse by virtue of its strong personal feeling.*

Because I feel that, in the Heavens above,
　　The angels, whispering to one another,
Can find, among their burning terms of love,
　　None so devotional as that of "Mother,"
Therefore by that dear name I long have called you—　　　　5
　　You who are more than mother unto me,
And fill my heart of hearts, where Death installed you
　　In setting my Virginia's spirit free.
My mother—my own mother, who died early,
　　Was but the mother of myself; but you　　　　　　　　10
Are mother to the one I loved so dearly,
　　And thus are dearer than the mother I knew
By that infinity with which my wife
　　Was dearer to my soul than its soul-life.

Annabel Lee

This poem, like "The Raven," establishes an atmosphere, incorporates a narrative, and culminates in the first-person narrator's defiant resolve in the face of loneliness and loss.

It was many and many a year ago,
　　In a kingdom by the sea,
That a maiden there lived whom you may know
　　By the name of Annabel Lee;—
And this maiden she lived with no other thought　　　　5
　　Than to love and be loved by me.

She was a child and *I* was a child,*
    In this kingdom by the sea,
But we loved with a love that was more than love–
    I and my Annabel Lee–   10
With a love that the wingèd seraphs* of Heaven
    Coveted her and me.

And this was the reason that, long ago,
    In this kingdom by the sea,
A wind blew out of a cloud by night   15
    Chilling my Annabel Lee;
So that her high-born kinsman came
    And bore her away from me,
To shut her up in a sepulchre
    In this kingdom by the sea.   20

The angels, not half so happy in Heaven,
    Went envying her and me;
Yes! that was the reason (as all men know,
    In this kingdom by the sea)
That the wind came out of the cloud, chilling   25
    And killing my Annabel Lee.

But our love it was stronger by far than the love
    Of those who were older than we–
    Of many far wiser than we–
And neither the angels in Heaven above   30
    Nor the demons down under the sea
Can ever dissever* my soul from the soul
    Of the beautiful Annabel Lee:–
For the moon never beams without bringing me dreams
    Of the beautiful Annabel Lee;   35

And the stars never rise but I see the bright eyes
    Of the beautiful Annabel Lee;
And so, all the night-tide, I lie down by the side
Of my darling, my darling, my life and my bride
    In her sepulchre there by the sea–   40
    In her tomb by the side of the sea.

She . . . child: Some versions transpose the two halves of this line.

seraphs: one of the highest orders of angels: see Isaiah 6:2 (Poe, however, does not accept the Biblical concept of angels.)

dissever: to separate

The Purloined Letter

"The Purloined Letter" well illustrates one of Poe's artistic principles in that it is a tale intended simply to entertain, not to teach. The story's mood, however, is somewhat atypical. There are none of the ghoulish details evident in many of Poe's other stories. But this absence of "horror and terror" does not diminish the story's interest. The bantering tone as well as the game of wits between the hero Dupin and the Minister provide ample enjoyment.

Dupin, the central character in "The Purloined Letter," is also the protagonist in two other Poe mysteries. Poe's three Dupin stories laid the groundwork for much of our modern detective fiction. Such famous sleuths as Sherlock Holmes, Hercule Poirot, and Miss Marple can all be traced to the analytical Dupin whose greatest weapon in the fight against crime was not a superior arsenal but a superior mind.

Nil sapientiae odiosius acumine nimio.*

—Seneca.

At Paris, just after dark one gusty evening in the autumn of 18–, I was enjoying the twofold luxury of meditation and a meerschaum,* in company with my friend C. Auguste Dupin, in his little back library, or book-closet, *au troisieme,** No. 33, Rue Dunot, Faubourg St. Germain. For one hour at least we had maintained a profound silence; while each, to any casual observer, might have seemed intently and exclusively occupied with the curling eddies of smoke that oppressed the atmosphere of the chamber. For myself, however, I was mentally discussing certain topics which had formed matter for conversation between us at an earlier period of the evening; I mean the affair of the Rue Morgue, and the mystery attending the murder of Marie Rogêt. I looked upon it, therefore, as something of a co-

incidence, when the door of our apartment was thrown open and admitted our old acquaintance, Monsieur G—, the Prefect of the Parisian police.

Nil . . . nimio: "Nothing is more troublesome to wisdom than too much cunning."
meerschaum: a tobacco pipe
au troisieme: on the fourth floor

We gave him a hearty welcome; for there was nearly half as much of the entertaining as of the contemptible about the man, and we had not seen him for several years. We had been sitting in the dark, and Dupin now arose for the purpose of lighting a lamp, but sat down again, without doing so, upon G.'s saying that he had called to consult us, or rather to ask the opinion of my friend, about some official business which had occasioned a great deal of trouble.

"If it is any point requiring reflection," observed Dupin, as he forbore to enkindle the wick, "we shall examine it to better purpose in the dark."

"That is another of your odd notions," said the Prefect, who had a fashion of calling every thing "odd" that was beyond his comprehension, and thus lived amid an absolute legion of "oddities."

"Very true," said Dupin, as he supplied his visitor with a pipe, and rolled towards him a comfortable chair.

"And what is the difficulty now?" I asked. "Nothing more in the assassination way, I hope?"

"Oh no; nothing of that nature. The fact is, the business is *very* simple indeed, and I make no doubt that we can manage it sufficiently well ourselves; but then I thought Dupin would like to hear the details of it, because it is so excessively *odd*."

"Simple and odd," said Dupin.

"Why, yes; and not exactly that, either. The fact is, we have all been a good deal puzzled because the affair *is* so simple, and yet baffles us altogether."

"Perhaps it is the very simplicity of the thing which puts you at fault," said my friend.

"What nonsense you *do* talk!" replied the Prefect, laughing heartily.

"Perhaps the mystery is a little *too* plain," said Dupin.

"Oh, good heavens! who ever heard of such an idea?"

"A little *too* self-evident."

"Ha! ha! ha!–ha! ha! ha!–ho! ho! ho!"– roared our visitor, profoundly amused, "oh, Dupin, you will be the death of me yet!"

"And what, after all, *is* the matter on hand?" I asked.

"Why, I will tell you," replied the Prefect, as he gave a long, steady, and contemplative puff, and settled himself in his chair. "I will tell you in a few words; but, before I begin, let me caution you that this is an affair demanding the greatest secrecy, and that I should most probably lose the position I now hold, were it known that I confided it to any one."

"Proceed," said I.

"Or not," said Dupin.

"Well, then; I have received personal information, from a very high quarter, that a certain document of the last importance, has been purloined from the royal apartments. The individual who purloined it is known; this beyond a doubt; he was seen to take it. It is known, also, that it still remains in his possession."

"How is this known?" asked Dupin.

"It is clearly inferred," replied the Prefect, "from the nature of the document, and from the non-appearance of certain results which would at once arise from its passing *out* of the robber's possession;–that is to say, from his employing it as he must design in the end to employ it."

"Be a little more explicit," I said.

"Well, I may venture so far as to say that the paper gives its holder a certain power in a certain quarter where such power is immensely valuable." The Prefect was fond of the cant* of diplomacy.

---

cant: special vocabulary understood only by members of a certain group

---

"Still I do not quite understand," said Dupin.

"No? Well; the disclosure of the document to a third person, who shall be nameless, would bring in question the honor of a personage of most exalted station; and this fact gives the holder of the document an ascendancy over the illustrious personage whose honor and peace are so jeopardized."

"But this ascendancy," I interposed, "would depend upon the robber's knowledge of the loser's knowledge of the robber. Who would dare–"

"The thief," said G., "is the Minister D—, who dares all things, those unbecoming as well as those becoming a man. The method of the theft was not less ingenious than bold. The document in question–a letter, to be frank–had been received by the personage robbed while alone in the royal *boudoir*. During its perusal she was suddenly interrupted by the entrance of the other exalted personage from whom especially it was her wish to conceal it. After a hurried and vain endeavor to thrust it in a drawer, she was forced to place it, open as it was, upon a table. The address, however, was uppermost, and, the contents thus unexposed, the letter escaped notice. At this juncture enters the Minister D—. His lynx eye immediately perceives the paper, recognises the handwriting of the address, observes the confusion of the personage addressed, and fathoms her secret. After some business transactions, hurried through in his ordinary manner, he produces a letter somewhat similar to the one in question, opens it, pretends to read it, and then places it in close juxtaposition to the other. Again he converses, for some fifteen minutes, upon the public affairs. At length, in taking leave, he takes also from the table the letter to which he had no claim. Its rightful owner saw, but, of course, dared not call attention to the act, in the presence of the third personage who stood at her elbow. The minister decamped; leaving his own letter–one of no importance–upon the table.''

"Here, then," said Dupin to me, "you have precisely what you demand to make the ascendancy complete–the robber's knowledge of the loser's knowledge of the robber."

"Yes," replied the Prefect; "and the power thus attained has, for some months past, been wielded, for political purposes, to a very dangerous extent. The personage robbed is more thoroughly convinced, every day, of the necessity of reclaiming her letter. But this, of course, cannot be done openly. In fine, driven to despair, she has committed the matter to me."

"Than whom," said Dupin, amid a perfect whirlwind of smoke, "no more sagacious* agent could, I suppose, be desired, or even imagined."

sagacious: wise

"You flatter me," replied the Prefect; "but it is possible that some such opinion may have been entertained."

"It is clear," said I, "as you observe, that the letter is still in possession of the minister; since it is this possession, and not any employment of the letter, which bestows the power. With the employment the power departs."

"True," said G.; "and upon this conviction I proceeded. My first care was to make thorough search of the minister's hotel; and here my chief embarrassment lay in the necessity of searching without his knowledge. Beyond all things, I have been warned of the danger which would result from giving him reason to suspect our design."

"But," said I, "you are quite *au fait** in these investigations. The Parisian police have done this thing often before."

au fait: proficient; expert

"O yes; and for this reason I did not despair. The habits of the minister gave me, too, a great advantage. He is frequently absent from home all night. His servants are by no means numerous. They sleep at a distance from their master's apartment, and, being chiefly Neapolitans,* are readily made drunk. I have keys, as you know, with which I can open any chamber or cabinet in Paris. For three months a night has not passed, during the greater part of which I have not been engaged, personally, in ransacking the D— Hôtel. My honor is interested, and, to mention a great secret, the reward is enormous. So I did not abandon the search until I had become fully satisfied that the thief is a more astute man than myself. I fancy that I have investigated every nook and corner of the premises in which it is possible that the paper can be concealed."

Neapolitans: natives of Naples, Italy

"But is it not possible," I suggested, "that although the letter may be in possession of the minister, as it unquestionably is, he may have concealed it elsewhere than upon his own premises?''

''This is barely possible,'' said Dupin. ''The present peculiar condition of affairs at court, and especially of those intrigues in which D— is known to be involved, would render the instant availability of the document–its susceptibility of being produced at a moment's notice–a point of nearly equal importance with its possession.''

''Its susceptibility of being produced?'' said I.

''That is to say, of being *destroyed*,'' said Dupin.

''True,'' I observed; ''the paper is clearly then upon the premises. As for its being upon the person of the minister, we may consider that as out of the question.''

''Entirely,'' said the Prefect. ''He has been twice waylaid, as if by footpads,* and his person rigorously searched under my own inspection.''

---

footpads: highwaymen or street robbers

''You might have spared yourself this trouble,'' said Dupin. ''D—, I presume, is not altogether a fool, and, if not, must have anticipated these waylayings, as a matter of course.''

''Not *altogether* a fool,'' said G., ''but then he's a poet, which I take to be only one remove from a fool.''

''True,'' said Dupin, after a long and thoughtful whiff from his meerschaum, ''although I have been guilty of certain doggerel* myself.''

---

doggerel: trivial verse

''Suppose you detail,'' said I, ''the particulars of your search.''

''Why the fact is, we took our time, and we searched *every where*. I have had long experience in these affairs. I took the entire building, room by room; devoting the nights of a whole week to each. We examined, first, the furniture of each apartment. We opened every possible drawer; and I presume you know that, to a properly trained police agent, such a thing as a *secret* drawer is impossible. Any man is a dolt who permits a 'secret'

drawer to escape him in a search of this kind. The thing is *so* plain. There is a certain amount of bulk–of space–to be accounted for in every cabinet. Then we have accurate rules. The fiftieth part of a line could not escape us. After the cabinets we took the chairs. The cushions we probed with the fine long needles you have seen me employ. From the tables we removed the tops.''

''Why so?''

''Sometimes the top of a table, or other similarly arranged piece of furniture, is removed by the person wishing to conceal an article; then the leg is excavated, the article deposited within the cavity, and the top replaced. The bottoms and tops of bed-posts are employed in the same way.''

''But could not the cavity be detected by sounding?'' I asked.

''By no means, if, when the article is deposited, a sufficient wadding of cotton be placed around it. Besides, in our case, we were obliged to proceed without noise.''

''But you could not have removed–you could not have taken to pieces *all* articles of furniture in which it would have been possible to make a deposit in the manner you mention. A letter may be compressed into a thin spiral roll, not differing much in shape or bulk from a large knitting-needle, and in this form it might be inserted into the rung of a chair, for example. You did not take to pieces all the chairs?''

''Certainly not; but we did better–we examined the rungs of every chair in the hotel, and, indeed, the jointings of every description of furniture, by the aid of a most powerful microscope. Had there been any traces of recent disturbance we should not have failed to detect it instantly. A single grain of gimlet*-dust, for example, would have been as obvious as an apple. Any disorder in the glueing–any unusual gaping in the joints–would have sufficed to insure detection.''

---

gimlet: a small hand tool for boring holes

''I presume you looked to the mirrors, between the boards and the plates, and you probed the beds and the bed-clothes, as well as the curtains and carpets.''

''That of course; and when we had absolutely completed every particle of the furniture in this way, then we examined the house itself. We divided its entire surface into compartments, which we numbered, so that none might be missed; then we scrutinized each individual square inch throughout the premises, including the two houses immediately adjoining, with the microscope, as before.''

''The two houses adjoining!'' I exclaimed; ''you must have had a great deal of trouble.''

''We had; but the reward offered is prodigious.''*

---

prodigious: enormous

''You include the *grounds* about the houses?''

''All the grounds are paved with brick. They gave us comparatively little trouble. We examined the moss between the bricks, and found it undisturbed.''

''You looked among D—'s papers, of course, and into the books of the library?''

''Certainly; we opened every package and parcel; we not only opened every book, but we turned over every leaf in each volume, not contenting ourselves with a mere shake, according to the fashion of some of our police officers. We also measured the thickness of every book-*cover,* with the most accurate admeasurement, and applied to each the most jealous scrutiny of the microscope. Had any of the bindings been recently meddled with, it would have been utterly impossible that the fact should have escaped observation. Some five or six volumes, just from the hands of the binder, we carefully probed, longitudinally, with the needles.''

''You explored the floors beneath the carpets?''

''Beyond doubt. We removed every carpet, and examined the boards with the microscope.''

''And the paper on the walls?''

''Yes.''

''You looked into the cellars?''

''We did.''

''Then,'' I said, ''you have been making a miscalculation, and the letter is *not* upon the premises, as you suppose.''

''I fear you are right there,'' said the Prefect. ''And now, Dupin, what would you advise me to do?''

''To make a thorough re-search of the premises.''

''That is absolutely needless,'' replied G—. ''I am not more sure that I breathe than I am that the letter is not at the Hôtel.''

''I have no better advice to give you,'' said Dupin. ''You have, of course, an accurate description of the letter?''

''Oh yes!''–And here the Prefect, producing a memorandum-book, proceeded to read aloud a minute account of the internal, and especially of the external appearance of the missing document. Soon after finishing the perusal of this description, he took his departure, more entirely depressed in spirits than I had ever known the good gentleman before.

In about a month afterwards he paid us another visit, and found us occupied very nearly as before. He took a pipe and a chair and entered into some ordinary conversation. At length I said,–

''Well, but G—, what of the purloined letter? I presume you have at last made up your mind that there is no such thing as overreaching the Minister?''

''Confound him, say I–yes; I made the re-examination, however, as Dupin suggested–but it was all labor lost, as I knew it would be.''

''How much was the reward offered, did you say?'' asked Dupin.

''Why, a very great deal–a *very* liberal reward–I don't like to say how much, precisely; but one thing I *will* say, that I would n't mind giving my individual check for fifty thousand francs to any one who could obtain me that letter. The fact is, it is becoming of more and more importance every day; and the reward has been lately doubled. If it were trebled, however, I could do no more than I have done.''

"Why, yes," said Dupin, drawlingly, between the whiffs of his meerschaum, "I really–think, G—, you have not exerted yourself–to the utmost in this matter. You might–do a little more, I think, eh?"

"How?–in what way?"

"Why–puff, puff–you might–puff, puff–employ counsel in the matter, eh?–puff, puff, puff. Do you remember the story they tell of Abernethy?"

"No; hang Abernethy!"

"To be sure! hang him and welcome. But, once upon a time, a certain rich miser conceived the design of spunging upon this Abernethy for a medical opinion. Getting up, for this purpose, an ordinary conversation in a private company, he insinuated his case to the physician, as that of an imaginary individual.

" 'We will suppose,' said the miser, 'that his symptoms are such and such; now, doctor, what would *you* have directed him to take?'

" 'Take!' said Abernethy, 'why, take *advice, to be sure.* ' "

"But," said the Prefect, a little discomposed, "I am *perfectly* willing to take advice, and to pay for it. I would *really* give fifty thousand francs to any one who would aid me in the matter."

"In that case," replied Dupin, opening a drawer, and producing a checkbook, "you may as well fill me up a check for the amount mentioned. When you have signed it, I will hand you the letter."

I was astounded. The Prefect appeared absolutely thunderstricken. For some minutes he remained speechless and motionless, looking incredulously at my friend with open mouth, and eyes that seemed starting from their sockets; then, apparently recovering himself in some measure, he seized a pen, and after several pauses and vacant stares, finally filled up and signed a check for fifty thousand francs, and handed it across the table to Dupin. The latter examined it carefully and deposited it in his pocket-book; then, unlocking an *escritoire,** took thence a letter and gave it to the Prefect. This functionary* grasped it in a perfect agony of joy, opened it with a trembling hand, cast a rapid glance at its contents, and then, scrambling and struggling to the door, rushed at length unceremoniously from the room and from the house, without having uttered a syllable since Dupin had requested him to fill up the check.

---

escritoire: a writing table
functionary: official

When he had gone, my friend entered into some explanations.

"The Parisian police," he said, "are exceedingly able in their way. They are persevering, ingenious, cunning, and thoroughly versed in the knowledge which their duties seem chiefly to demand. Thus, when G— detailed to us his mode of searching the premises at the Hôtel D—, I felt entire confidence in his having made a satisfactory investigation–so far as his labors extended.''

"So far as his labors extended?" said I.

"Yes," said Dupin. "The measures adopted were not only the best of their kind, but carried out to absolute perfection. Had the letter been deposited within the range of their search, these fellows would, beyond a question, have found it."

I merely laughed–but he seemed quite serious in all that he said.

"The measures, then," he continued, "were good in their kind, and well executed; their defect lay in their being inapplicable to the case, and to the man. A certain set of highly ingenious resources are, with the Prefect, a sort of Procrustean* bed, to which he forcibly adapts his designs. But he perpetually errs by being too deep or too shallow, for the matter in hand; and many a schoolboy is a better reasoner than he. I knew one about eight years of age, whose success at guessing in the game of 'even and odd' attracted universal admiration. This game is simple, and is played with marbles. One player holds in his hand a number of these toys, and demands of another whether that number is even or odd. If the guess is right, the guesser wins one; if wrong, he loses one. The boy to whom I allude won all the marbles of the school. Of course he had some principle of guessing; and this lay in mere observation and admeasurement of the astuteness of his opponents. For example, an arrant simpleton* is his opponent, and, holding up his closed hand, asks, 'are they even or odd?' Our schoolboy replies, 'odd,' and loses; but upon the second trial he wins, for he then says to himself, 'the simpleton had them even upon the first trial, and his amount of cunning is just sufficient to make him have them odd upon the second; I will therefore guess odd;'–and he guesses odd, and wins. Now, with a simpleton a degree above the first, he would have reasoned thus: 'This fellow finds that in the first instance I guessed odd, and, in the second, he will propose to himself upon the first impulse, a simple variation from even to odd, as did the first simpleton; but then a second thought will suggest that this is too simple a variation, and finally he will decide upon putting it even as before. I will therefore guess even;'–he guesses even, and wins. Now this mode of reasoning in the schoolboy, whom his fellows termed 'lucky,'–what, in its last analysis, is it?''

Procrustean: refers to the mythical Procrustes whose view of hospitality was to provide an iron bed for travelers. If a stranger was too short, he was stretched to fit the bed; if too long, he was cut "down to size."
arrant simpleton: i.e., a complete simpleton

"It is merely," I said, "an identification of the reasoner's intellect with that of his opponent."

"It is," said Dupin; "and, upon inquiring of the boy by what means he effected the *thorough* identification in which his success consisted, I received answer as follows: 'When I wish to find out how wise, or how stupid, or how good, or how wicked is any one, or what are his thoughts at the moment, I fashion the expression of my face, as accurately as possible, in accordance with the expression of his, and then wait to see what thoughts or sentiments arise in my mind or heart, as if to match or correspond with the expression.' This response of the schoolboy lies at the bottom of all the spurious profundity* which has been attributed to Rochefoucauld, to La Bougive, to Machiavelli, and to Campanella.''

spurious profundity: false depth of intellect

"And the identification," I said, "of the reasoner's intellect with that of his opponent, depends, if I understand you aright, upon the accuracy with which the opponent's intellect is admeasured."

"For its practical value it depends upon this," replied Dupin; "and the Prefect and his cohort fail so frequently, first, by default of this identification, and, secondly, by ill-admeasurement, or rather through non-admeasurement, of the intellect with which they are engaged. They consider only their *own* ideas of ingenuity; and, in searching for anything hidden, advert only to the modes in which *they* would have hidden it. They are right in this much–that their own ingenuity is a faithful representative of that of *the mass;* but when the cunning of the individual felon is diverse in character from their own, the felon foils them, of course. This always happens when it is above their own, and very usually when it is below. They have no variation of principle in their investigations; at best, when urged by some unusual emergency–by some extraordinary reward–they extend or exaggerate their old modes of *practice,* without touching their principles. What, for example, in this case of D—, has been done to vary the principle of action? What is all this boring, and probing, and sounding, and scrutinizing with the microscope, and dividing the surface of the building into registered square inches–what is it all but an exaggeration *of the application* of the one principle or set of principles of search, which are based upon the one set of notions regarding human ingenuity, to which the Prefect, in the long routine of his duty, has been accustomed? Do you not see he has taken it for granted that *all* men proceed to conceal a letter,–not exactly in a gimlet-hole bored in a chair-leg–but, at least, in *some* out-of-the-way hole or corner suggested by the same tenor of thought which would urge a man to secrete a letter in a gimlet-hole bored in a chair-leg? And do you not see also, that such *recherchés** nooks for concealment are adapted only for ordinary occasions, and would be adopted only by ordinary intellects; for, in all cases of concealment, a disposal of the article concealed–a disposal of it in this *recherché* manner,–is, in the very first instance, presumable and presumed; and thus its discovery depends, not at all upon the acumen,* but altogether upon the mere care, patience, and determination of the seekers; and where the case is of importance–or, what amounts to the same thing in the *policial* eyes, when the reward is of magnitude,–the qualities in question have *never* been known to fail. You will now understand what I meant in suggesting that, had the purloined letter been hidden any where within the limits of the Prefect's examination–in other words, had the principle of its concealment been comprehended within the principles of the Prefect–its discovery would have been a matter altogether beyond question. This functionary, however, has been thoroughly mystified; and the remote source of his defeat lies in the supposition that the Minister is a fool, because he has acquired renown as a poet. All fools are poets; this the Prefect *feels;* and he is merely guilty of a *non distributio medii** in thence inferring that all poets are fools."

recherchés: out of the way
acumen: accuracy of judgment
non . . . medii: Latin phrase referring to faulty logic

"But is this really the poet?" I asked. "There are two brothers, I know; and both have attained reputation in letters. The Minister I believe has written learnedly on the Differential Calculus. He is a mathematician, and no poet."

"You are mistaken; I know him well; he is both. As poet *and* mathematician, he would rea-

son well; as mere mathematician, he could not have reasoned at all, and thus would have been at the mercy of the Prefect."

"You surprise me," I said, "by these opinions, which have been contradicted by the voice of the world. You do not mean to set at naught the well-digested idea of centuries. The mathematical reason has long been regarded as the reason *par excellence.*"

" *'Il y a à parier,'* " replied Dupin, quoting from Chamfort, " *'que toute idée publique, toute convention reçue, est une sottise, car elle a convenu au plus grand nombre.'** The mathematicians, I grant you, have done their best to promulgate* the popular error to which you allude, and which is none the less an error for its promulgation as truth. With an art worthy a better cause, for example, they have insinuated the term 'analysis' into application to algebra. The French are the originators of this particular deception; but if a term is of any importance–if words derive any value from applicability–then 'analysis' conveys 'algebra' about as much as, in Latin, *'ambitus'* implies 'ambition,' *'religio'* 'religion,' or *'homines honesti,'* a set of *honorable* men."*

Il . . . nombre: from the French writer Chamfort, "Probably every widely accepted idea and custom shows a lack of intelligence common to the masses."
promulgate: to make known by public declaration
then . . . men: Dupin is saying that derived words often have a different meaning from the words from which they came.

"You have a quarrel on hand, I see," said I, "with some of the algebraists of Paris; but proceed."

"I dispute the availability, and thus the value, of that reason which is cultivated in any especial form other than the abstractly logical. I dispute, in particular, the reason educed* by mathematical study. The mathematics are the science of form and quantity; mathematical reasoning is merely logic applied to observation upon form and quantity. The great error lies in supposing that even the truths of what is called *pure* algebra, are abstract or general truths. And this error is so egregious* that I am confounded at the universality with which it has been received. Mathematical axioms are *not* axioms of general truth. What is true of *relation*–of form and quantity–is often grossly false in regard to morals, for example. In this latter science it is very usually *un*true that the aggregated parts are equal to the whole. In chemistry also the axiom fails. In the consideration of motive it fails; for two motives, each of a given value, have not, necessarily, a value when united, equal to the sum of their values apart. There are numerous other mathematical truths which are only truths within the limits of *relation*. But the mathematician argues, from his *finite truths*, through habit, as if they were of an absolutely general applicability–as the world indeed imagines them to be. Bryant, in his very learned 'Mythology,' mentions an analogous source of error, when he says that 'although the Pagan fables are not believed, yet we forget ourselves continually, and make inferences from them as existing realities.' With the algebraists, however, who are Pagans themselves, the 'Pagan fables' *are* believed, and the inferences are made, not so much through lapse of memory, as through an unaccountable addling of the brains. In short, I never yet encountered the mere mathematician who could be trusted out of equal roots, or one who did not clandestinely* hold it as a point of his faith that $x^2 + px$ was absolutely and unconditionally equal to q. Say to one of these gentlemen, by way of experiment, if you please, that you believe occasions may occur where $x^2 + px$ is *not* altogether equal to q, and, having made him understand what you mean, get out of his reach as speedily as convenient, for, beyond doubt, he will endeavor to knock you down.

educed: brought out; elicited
egregious: extremely bad; flagrant
clandestinely: secretly

"I mean to say," continued Dupin, while I merely laughed at his last observations, "that if the Minister had been no more than a mathemati-

cian, the Prefect would have been under no necessity of giving me this check. I knew him, however, as both mathematician and poet, and my measures were adapted to his capacity, with reference to the circumstances by which he was surrounded. I knew him as a courtier,* too, and as a bold *intriguant.** Such a man, I considered, could not fail to be aware of the ordinary *policial* modes of action. He could not have failed to anticipate–and events have proved that he did not fail to anticipate–the waylayings to which he was subjected. He must have forseen, I reflected, the secret investigations of his premises. His frequent absences from home at night, which were hailed by the Prefect as certain aids to his success, I regarded only as *ruses,** to afford opportunity for thorough search to the police, and thus the sooner to impress them with the conviction to which G—, in fact, did finally arrive–the conviction that the letter was not upon the premises. I felt, also, that the whole train of thought, which I was at some pains in detailing to you just now, concerning the invariable principle of *policial* action in searches for articles concealed–I felt that this whole train of thought would necessarily pass through the mind of the Minister. It would imperatively lead him to despise all the ordinary *nooks* of concealment. *He* could not, I reflected, be so weak as not to see that the most intricate and remote recess of his hotel would be as open as his commonest closets to the eyes, to the probes, to the gimlets, and to the microscopes of the Prefect. I saw, in fine, that he would be driven, as a matter of course, to *simplicity,* if not deliberately induced to it as a matter of choice. You will remember, perhaps, how desperately the Prefect laughed when I suggested, upon our first interview, that it was just possible this mystery troubled him so much on account of its being so *very* self-evident."

courtier: one who seeks favor by flattery
intriguant: one who schemes
ruses: actions meant to mislead

"Yes," said I, "I remember his merriment well. I really thought he would have fallen into convulsions."

"The material world," continued Dupin, "abounds with very strict analogies to the immaterial; and thus some color of truth has been given to the rhetorical dogma, that metaphor, or simile, may be made to strengthen an argument, as well as to embellish a description. The principle of the *vis inertiae*,* for example, seems to be identical in physics and metaphysics. It is not more true in the former, that a large body is with more difficulty set in motion than a smaller one, and that its subsequent *momentum* is commensurate with this difficulty, than it is, in the latter, that intellects of the vaster capacity, while more constant, and more eventful in their movements than those of inferior grade, are yet the less readily moved, and more embarrassed and full of hesitation in the first few steps of their progress. Again: have you ever noticed which of the street signs, over the shop doors, are the most attractive of attention?"

vis inertiae: the power of inertia; passive resistance to force applied

"I have never given the matter a thought," I said.

"There is a game of puzzles," he resumed, "which is played upon a map. One party playing requires another to find a given word—the name of town, river, state or empire—any word, in short, upon the motley and perplexed surface of the chart. A novice in the game generally seeks to embarrass his opponents by giving them the most minutely lettered names; but the adept selects such words as stretch, in large characters, from one end of the chart to the other. These, like the over-largely lettered signs and placards of the street, escape observation by dint of being excessively obvious; and here the physical oversight is precisely analogous with the moral inapprehension by which the intellect suffers to pass unnoticed those considerations which are too obtrusively and too palpably* self-evident. But this is

a point, it appears, somewhat above or beneath the understanding of the Prefect. He never once thought it probable, or possible, that the Minister had deposited the letter immediately beneath the nose of the whole world, by way of best preventing any portion of that world from perceiving it.

palpably: obviously

"But the more I reflected upon the daring, dashing, and discriminating ingenuity of D—; upon the fact that the document must always have been *at hand,* if he intended to use it to good purpose; and upon the decisive evidence, obtained by the Prefect, that it was not hidden within the limits of that dignitary's ordinary search—the more satisfied I became that, to conceal this letter, the Minister had resorted to the comprehensive and sagacious expedient of not attempting to conceal it at all.

"Full of these ideas, I prepared myself with a pair of green spectacles, and called one fine morning, quite by accident, at the Ministerial hotel. I found D— at home, yawning, lounging, and dawdling, as usual, and pretending to be in the last extremity of *ennui.** He is, perhaps, the most really energetic human being now alive—but that is only when nobody sees him.

ennui: boredom

"To be even with him, I complained of my weak eyes, and lamented the necessity of the spectacles, under cover of which I cautiously and thoroughly surveyed the apartment, while seemingly intent only upon the conversation of my host.

"I paid special attention to a large writing-table, near which he sat, and upon which lay confusedly, some miscellaneous letters and other papers, with one or two musical instruments and a few books. Here, however, after a long and very deliberate scrutiny, I saw nothing to excite particular suspicion.

"At length my eyes, in going the circuit of the room, fell upon a trumpery fillagree card-rack of paste-board, that hung dangling by a dirty blue ribbon, from a little brass knob just beneath the middle of the mantelpiece. In this rack, which had three or four compartments, were five or six visiting cards and a solitary letter. This last was much soiled and crumpled. It was torn nearly in two, across the middle–as if a design, in the first instance, to tear it entirely up as worthless, had been altered, or stayed, in the second. It had a large black seal, bearing the D— cipher *very* conspicuously, and was addressed, in a diminutive female hand, to D—, the minister, himself. It was thrust carelessly, and even, as it seemed, contemptuously, into one of the upper divisions of the rack.

"No sooner had I glanced at this letter, than I concluded it to be that of which I was in search. To be sure, it was, to all appearance, radically different from the one of which the Prefect had read us so minute a description. Here the seal was large and black, with the D— cipher; there it was small and red, with the ducal arms of the S— family. Here, the address, to the Minister, was diminutive and feminine; there the superscription, to a certain royal personage, was markedly bold and decided; the size alone formed a point of correspondence. But, then, the *radicalness* of these differences, which was excessive; the dirt; the soiled and torn condition of the paper so inconsistent with the *true* methodical habits of D—, and so suggestive of a design to delude the beholder into an idea of the worthlessness of the document; these things, together with the hyperobtrusive situation of this document, full in the view of every visitor, and thus exactly in accordance with the conclusions to which I had previously arrived; these things, I say, were strongly corroborative* of suspicion, in one who came with the intention to suspect.

---

corroborative: supportive

"I protracted my visit as long as possible, and, while I maintained a most animated discussion with the Minister, on a topic which I knew well had never failed to interest and excite him, I kept my attention really riveted upon the letter. In this

examination, I committed to memory its external appearance and arrangement in the rack; and also fell, at length, upon a discovery which set at rest whatever trivial doubt I might have entertained. In scrutinizing the edges of the paper, I observed them to be more *chafed* than seemed necessary. They presented the *broken* appearance which is manifested when a stiff paper, having been once folded and pressed with a folder, is refolded in a reversed direction, in the same creases or edges which had formed the original fold. This discovery was sufficient. It was clear to me that the letter had been turned, as a glove, inside out, re-directed, and re-sealed. I bade the minister good morning, and took my departure at once, leaving a gold snuff-box upon the table.

"The next morning I called for the snuff-box, when we resumed, quite eagerly, the conversation of the preceding day. While thus engaged, however, a loud report, as if of a pistol, was heard immediately beneath the windows of the hotel, and was succeeded by a series of fearful screams, and the shoutings of a mob. D— rushed to a casement, threw it open, and looked out. In the meantime, I stepped to the card-rack, took the letter, put it in my pocket, and replaced it by a *fac-simile,* (so far as regards externals,) which I had carefully prepared at my lodgings; imitating the D— cipher, very readily, by means of a seal formed of bread.

"The disturbance in the street had been occasioned by the frantic behavior of a man with a musket. He had fired it among a crowd of women and children. It proved, however, to have been without ball, and the fellow was suffered to go his way as a lunatic or a drunkard. When he had gone, D— came from the window, whither I had followed him immediately upon securing the object in view. Soon afterwards I bade him farewell. The pretended lunatic was a man in my own pay."

"But what purpose had you," I asked, "in replacing the letter by a *fac-simile?* Would it not have been better, at the first visit, to have seized it openly, and departed?"

"D—," replied Dupin, "is a desperate man, and a man of nerve. His hotel, too, is not without attendants devoted to his interests. Had I made the wild attempt you suggest, I might never have left the Ministerial presence alive. The good people of Paris might have heard of me no more. But I had an object apart from these considerations. You know my political prepossessions. In this matter, I act as a partisan of the lady concerned. For eighteen months the Minister has had her in his power. She has now him in hers; since, being unaware that the letter is not in his possession, he will proceed with his exactions as if it was. Thus will he inevitably commit himself, at once, to his political destruction. His downfall, too, will not be more precipitate* than awkward. It is all very well to talk about the *facilis descensus Averni;** but in all kinds of climbing, as Catalani said of singing, it is far more easy to get up than to come down. In the present instance I have no sympathy—at least no pity—for him who descends. He is that *monstrum horrendum,* an unprincipled man of genius. I confess, however, that I should like very well to know the precise character of his thoughts, when, being defied by her whom the Prefect terms 'a certain personage,' he is reduced to opening the letter which I left for him in the card rack."

precipitate: rash; overhasty
facilis . . . Averni: "easy descent [to] the lower world"

"How? did you put any thing particular in it?"

"Why—it did not seem altogether right to leave the interior blank—that would have been insulting. D—, at Vienna once, did me an evil turn, which I told him, quite good-humoredly, that I should remember. So, as I knew he would feel some curiosity in regard to the identity of the person who had outwitted him, I thought it a pity not to give him a clue. He is well acquainted with my MS.,* and I just copied into the middle of the blank sheet the words—

　　　—Un dessein si funeste,
S'il n'est digne d'Atrée, est digne de Thyeste.*

MS.: handwriting
S'il . . . Thyeste: "A plan so deadly, even if it is not worthy of Atreus, it is worthy of Thyestes." The narrator is implying that the minister had a good plan but did not carry it out successfully.

They are to be found in Crébillon's 'Atrée.' "

For Thought and Discussion

1. Make a list of the adjectives that Poe employs in the first two stanzas of "The Raven." What kind of mood do they establish for the poem?

2. Examine carefully the climax of "The Raven" and its aftermath, treating the poem as a story that has a carefully planned plot line. After having asked the raven a number of questions and receiving the same answer each time, the speaker poses a final question, the question that to him is most crucial. First he states the question in broad terms, employing a phrase from the prophet Jeremiah. In which stanza does this question occur? Then the speaker restates his question in specific, personal terms, and in so doing, he reveals his own concept of the "balm of Gilead." What ultimate, eternal source of soothing and healing does the speaker desire? According to the raven, will the speaker ever realize this final comfort? How does the speaker react to the raven's answer? What is your evaluation of the philosophy implied in this portion of Poe's narrative?

3. Contrast Poe's tone in "Sonnet–To Science" and "To My Mother." How does Poe's attitude toward his subject differ in these two sonnets? In which poem does Poe incorporate a greater contrast in feeling between the octave (first eight lines) and the sestet (last six lines)? Notice that in "Sonnet–To Science" Poe establishes his tone in the sestet chiefly by his choice of verbs, but in "To My Mother" his repetition of the word *mother* and the pronoun *my* is instrumental to his tone. What is the antecedent of the pronoun *its* in the last line of "To My

Mother''? Does Poe's repetition of *soul* in this line intensify the meaning of the poem, or is it an impediment to your understanding of his point?

4. Compare the psychological state of mind of the persona at the end of ''Annabel Lee'' to that of the persona at the end of ''The Raven.'' In what ways is Poe's depiction of love similar in these two poems?

5. In ''The Purloined Letter,'' one of Poe's most famous analytical tales, the master detective Dupin successfully solves the mystery by using logical deductive reasoning. What is the actual crime he solves, and who are the characters involved? What is the general premise with which Dupin begins his attempt at solving the crime? How is Dupin's allusion to the schoolboy who won all the marbles in his school appropriate? How does the Prefect display faulty logic in his attempt to solve the crime? What specific part of either Dupin's or the Prefect's attempts at the solution do you find most intriguing? What examples of foreshadowing can you find early in the story that prepare you for the obvious solution to the crime?

6. The purpose of Poe's story is clearly to entertain the reader. How does the tone of the story reflect the author's purpose? Give examples from the story which illustrate the tone he sets. Notice especially the opening and closing quotations and the classical allusions he uses throughout the story. Do these allusions strengthen or weaken the unified effect Poe sought to achieve?

7. What advantages does Poe gain by selecting Dupin's friend and confidant as the first-person narrator rather than having Dupin himself relate the events of the story? In what way does the reader identify with the narrator? At what point in the story does it become most apparent that Dupin's deductive skills are superior to those of the narrator? Why do you think Poe chooses to have the Prefect leave before Dupin begins his explanation to the narrator concerning his solving of the crime?

Nathaniel Hawthorne
1804-1864

No other nineteenth-century American author was more strongly attracted to his country's history than was Nathaniel Hawthorne. One force encouraging him to turn to the past and use native American materials was the literary nationalism prevalent within American Romanticism. Another force was the impact on Hawthorne of the actions of two seventeenth-century ancestors. The first American member of the family, Major William Hathorne (Nathaniel added the *w* to the family name after his graduation from college), had played an active role in the persecution of Quakers. His son, Judge John Hathorne, had served as one of the magistrates ordering the execution of twenty persons during the 1692 Salem witchcraft trials. A third force was Hawthorne's sympathy with many Puritan values and viewpoints even though he evidently rejected the Puritan's faith in Christ and trust in the Bible. Whenever Hawthorne portrayed a fictional conflict between the moral realism of Puritanism and the optimistic naiveté of transcendentalism, he invariably sided with the Puritan view of man's nature. In fact, of all the American romantics, only Hawthorne expressed a viewpoint based on values sympathetic to those of Christianity.

Hawthorne's literary career developed in three stages. After graduation from Bowdoin College in 1825, Hawthorne entered a period of literary preparation (1825-37). For twelve years the fledgling writer isolated himself in order to read widely and practice writing. Although some critics have interpreted this period as Hawthorne's neurotic withdrawal from the world, it is more accurately viewed as his writing apprenticeship. Hawthorne evidently regarded it so, for it appears that he destroyed much of what he wrote during this time. The preparatory period ended in 1837 when he published eighteen tales in a volume entitled *Twice-Told Tales*.

This collection ushered in the short-story phase of Hawthorne's career (1837-50). Like Poe, Hawthorne took his craft seriously and consequently helped elevate the short story to the status of an important artistic form. He infused his American settings with the universal themes of isolation, guilt, and pride. During this middle portion of his career, Hawthorne worked from 1839 to 1841 in Boston at the port's Custom House (the government building in which taxes on imported goods were collected and ships were cleared for entering or leaving the country). He then lived for several months in 1841 at the experimental transcendental community Brook Farm. In 1842, at the age of thirty-eight, Hawthorne married Sophia Peabody, who he believed helped him overcome a morbid tendency to observe life rather than actually to participate in it. In 1846, the same year in which he published his second major short-story collection–*Mosses from an Old Manse*–he began working in the Salem Custom House. But the election of 1849 replaced the Democrats with the Whigs, and the staunch Democrat lost his job to the spoils system (granting of government offices to members of the political party in power). Forced to turn to some other means of earning a living and yet freed from the demands of a regular job, he began writing a story that had been steadily growing in his imagination. After having worked nine hours a day for six months, he produced one of America's greatest novels, *The Scarlet Letter*.

This work introduced the novel phase of Hawthorne's career (1850-64). It also brought him friendship with Herman Melville, who, recognizing a kindred spirit in Hawthorne, dedicated *Moby Dick* (1851) to him. From 1851 to 1853 Hawthorne published two more novels (*The House of the Seven Gables,* 1851; and *The Blithedale Romance,* 1852), another collection of short stories, two books for children, and the official campaign biography for his college friend

Franklin Pierce, who ran on the Democratic ticket for president. After Pierce's election in 1853, Hawthorne was rewarded with an appointment as United States consul at Liverpool, England. For the next four years Hawthorne did very little writing. When his term as consul ended, he vacationed in Europe, absorbing the continental background for his last published novel, *The Marble Faun* (1860), a story set in Italy rather than in New England. After Hawthorne's return to the United States in 1860, he wrote steadily but could not recapture the artistic control he had possessed during the early 1850s. He started four different novels but finished none. On May 19, 1864, while on vacation in New Hampshire, Hawthorne died quietly in his sleep.

Hawthorne's tales and novels reveal his interest in the past and present. While generally using **settings** from the past, his fiction employs universal **themes.** Content neither to re-create nostalgically the past nor simply to present without comment the present, he evaluated both past and present, especially the beliefs of his contemporaries. As Melville pointed out in a review of Hawthorne's *Twice-Told Tales,* Hawthorne derived his view of mankind's nature and potential directly from Puritanism. Melville attributed Hawthorne's artistic power to "a touch of Puritanic gloom," which develops from a "sense of Innate Depravity and Original Sin, from whose visitations, in some shape or other, no deeply thinking mind is always and wholly free." Because Hawthorne accepted man's sinfulness as reality, he distrusted—and refuted in his fiction—the naive optimism of contemporaries who believed that man's nature is innately good, change brings inevitable improvement, and earthly perfection lies within man's grasp.

Hawthorne expressed this romantic pessimism in a style characterized by allegory, ambiguity, and ambivalence. **Allegory** (a story with a literal and an implied level of meaning) helps his fiction transcend its realistic settings and characters and achieve universality. Subtitles (e.g., "A Parable," subtitle for "The Minister's Black Veil") or explicit comments within a tale (e.g., "Jollity and gloom were contending for an empire," part of the introduction in the "The Maypole of Merry Mount") often imply the existence of an allegorical level. The local, historical clash in the 1620s between the Merry Mount and the Plymouth settlers, for instance, mirrors the conflict between two opposing philosophies of life: self-gratification (Merry Mount) and self-denial (Plymouth). The prominence in his fiction of symbolic details like a railroad also suggests Hawthorne's partiality for allegory.

The other two prevalent characteristics of Hawthorne's style are intertwined. **Ambiguity** (doubleness or inconclusiveness of meaning) complicates the interpretation of his fiction. He frequently presents readers with several ways of viewing details in a story: for instance, in *The Scarlet Letter* there is basis for four views of the *A* on Dimmesdale's breast, including the possibility of the letter's not existing at all. This ambiguity of Hawthorne's style has attracted many modern readers, especially those who believe life to be ultimately unknowable and full of unresolved puzzles.

A special form of Hawthorne's ambiguity is his **ambivalence** (the coexistence of conflicting feelings or attitudes of an author or a reader). His ambivalence towards Puritanism, for example, reflects a kind of love-hate relationship between Hawthorne and the Puritan past: he both sympathized with and condemned Puritan values. In addition, his style is typical of the nineteenth century: difficult vocabulary, long sentences, and often stilted dialogue. But while his style may create difficulty for modern readers, his insight into human nature more than compensates for the difficulty.

Hawthorne's work powerfully voices the reaction within American Romanticism to transcendental optimism. Although a religious skeptic, Hawthorne held the Biblical view of man as a flawed creature, unable to secure his own salvation or perfection. Hawthorne's fiction illustrates the truth that mankind's attempts to deny this moral reality produce only foolish pride and consequent failure.

The Maypole of Merry Mount

This story illustrates Hawthorne's characteristic handling of "the Actual" and "the Imaginary." Although the story has historical basis, Hawthorne makes the original incident very much his own by adding a **plot** *with fictional* **setting, characters,** *and events so as to communicate a* **theme** *of universal importance.*

Hawthorne's references to the literary and the classical past emphasize the timelessness of this tale's conflict between self-gratification and self-denial. Like Edmund Spenser in The Faerie Queene, *Hawthorne uses the forest as a symbolic setting for man's lawlessness and moral confusion. Like John Milton in* Comus, *Hawthorne recognizes that man often allows his animal nature to dominate his spiritual nature. Like the Puritans, who believed that Satan ruled the wilderness and God (in the person of His ministers) ruled the clearing (i.e., the civilized portions), Hawthorne has no romantic illusions about what men become when left to follow their natural desires.*

Hawthorne also wove a number of classical and folklore elements into this story. Historically, the maypole was the center of English rites celebrated on May 1 to welcome the return of spring. The "fauns" (woodland deities having the ears, horns, tail, and legs of a goat) and "nymphs" (goddesses pictured as beautiful maidens) also link the Merry Mounters to classical pagan times. Set against these symbols and allusions is the central, sobering **symbol** *of the Puritan community: the whipping post.*

Hawthorne's **tone** *at first seems confusing because the story appears to attack both the Puritans and the Merry Mounters. In reality, Hawthorne blends perspectives that allow him to view the Merry Mounters through the Puritans' eyes, the Puritans through the Merry Mounters' eyes, and both sides through Edith's and Edgar's eyes. To interpret the story, the reader must carefully consider the role played by the two young lovers, chosen queen and king of May.*

Bright were the days at Merry Mount, when the Maypole was the banner staff of that gay colony! They who reared it, should their banner be triumphant, were to pour sunshine over New England's rugged hills, and scatter flower seeds throughout the soil. Jollity and gloom were contending for an empire. Midsummer eve had come, bringing deep verdure* to the forest, and roses in her lap, of a more vivid hue than the tender buds of Spring. But May, or her mirthful spirit, dwelt all the year round at Merry Mount, sporting with the Summer months, and revelling with Autumn, and basking in the glow of Winter's fireside. Through a world of toil and care she flitted with a dreamlike smile, and came hither to find a home among the lightsome* hearts of Merry Mount.

verdure: fresh greenness of vegetation
lightsome: untroubled, cheerful

Never had the Maypole been so gayly decked as at sunset on midsummer eve. This venerated emblem was a pine-tree, which had preserved the slender grace of youth, while it equalled the loftiest height of the old wood monarchs. From its top streamed a silken banner, colored like the rainbow. Down nearly to the ground the pole was dressed with birchen boughs, and others of the liveliest green, and some with silvery leaves, fastened by ribbons that fluttered in fantastic* knots of twenty different colors, but no sad ones. Garden flowers, and blossoms of the wilderness, laughed gladly forth amid the verdure, so fresh and dewy that they must have grown by magic on that happy pine-tree. Where this green and flowery splendor terminated, the shaft of the Maypole was stained with the seven brilliant hues of the banner at its top. On the lowest green bough hung an abundant wreath of roses, some that had been gathered in the sunniest spots of the forest, and others, of still richer blush, which the colonists had reared from English seed. O, people of the Golden Age, the chief of your husbandry was to raise flowers!

fantastic: oddly shaped

But what was the wild throng that stood hand in hand about the Maypole? It could not be that the fauns and nymphs, when driven from their classic groves and homes of ancient fable, had sought refuge, as all the persecuted did, in the fresh woods of the West. These were Gothic* monsters, though perhaps of Grecian ancestry. On the shoulders of a comely* youth uprose the head and branching antlers of a stag; a second, human in all other points, had the grim visage of a wolf; a third, still with the trunk and limbs of a mortal man, showed the beard and horns of a venerable* he-goat. There was the likeness of a bear erect, brute in all but his hind legs, which were adorned with pink silk stockings. And here again, almost as wondrous, stood a real bear of the dark forest, lending each of his fore paws to the grasp of a human hand, and as ready for the dance as any in that circle. His inferior nature rose half way, to meet his companions as they stooped. Other faces wore the similitude* of man or woman, but distorted or extravagant, with red noses pendulous* before their mouths, which seemed of awful depth, and stretched from ear to ear in an eternal fit of laughter. Here might be seen the Salvage Man,* well known in heraldry, hairy as a baboon, and girdled with green leaves. By his side, a noble figure, but still a counterfeit, appeared an Indian hunter, with feathery crest and wampum belt. Many of this strange company wore foolscaps, and had little bells appended* to their garments, tinkling with a silvery sound, responsive to the inaudible music of their gleesome spirits. Some youths and maidens were of soberer garb, yet well maintained their places in the irregular throng by the expression of wild revelry upon their features. Such were the colonists of Merry Mount, as they stood in the broad smile of sunset round their venerated Maypole.

Gothic: grotesque, barbaric
comely: handsome
venerable: aged
similitude: similarity
pendulous: hanging, especially so as to swing
Salvage Man: i.e., savage man
appended: attached

Had a wanderer, bewildered in the melancholy forest, heard their mirth, and stolen a half-affrighted glance, he might have fancied them the crew of Comus,* some already transformed to brutes, some midway between man and beast, and the others rioting in the flow of tipsy jollity that foreran the change. But a band of Puritans, who watched the scene, invisible themselves, compared the masques* to those devils and ruined souls with whom their superstition peopled the black wilderness.

Comus: an enchanter
masques: masquerades

Within the ring of monsters appeared the two airiest forms that had ever trodden on any more solid footing than a purple and golden cloud. One was a youth in glistening apparel, with a scarf of the rainbow pattern crosswise on his breast. His right hand held a gilded staff, the ensign of high dignity among the revellers, and his left grasped the slender fingers of a fair maiden, not less gayly decorated than himself. Bright roses glowed in contrast with the dark and glossy curls of each, and were scattered round their feet, or had sprung up spontaneously there. Behind this lightsome couple, so close to the Maypole that its boughs shaded his jovial face, stood the figure of an English priest, canonically dressed,* yet decked with flowers, in heathen fashion, and wearing a chaplet of the native vine leaves. By the riot of his rolling eye, and the pagan decorations of his holy garb, he seemed the wildest monster there, and the very Comus of the crew.

canonically dressed: dressed like a priest

"Votaries* of the Maypole," cried the flower-decked priest, "merrily, all day long, have the woods echoed to your mirth. But be this your merriest hour, my hearts! Lo, here stands the Lord and Lady of the May, whom I, a clerk* of Oxford, and high priest of Merry Mount, am presently to join in holy matrimony. Up with your nimble spirits, ye morris-dancers, green men, and glee maidens, bears and wolves, and horned gentlemen! Come; a chorus now, rich with the old mirth of Merry England, and the wilder glee of this fresh forest; and then a dance, to show the youthful pair what life is made of, and how airily they should go through it! All ye that love the Maypole, lend your voices to the nuptial* song of the Lord and Lady of the May!"

Votaries: those bound by a vow or promise
clerk: member of the clergy
nuptial: pertaining to marriage

This wedlock was more serious than most affairs of Merry Mount, where jest and delusion, trick and fantasy, kept up a continual carnival. The Lord and Lady of the May, though their titles must be laid down at sunset, were really and truly to be partners for the dance of life, beginning the measure that same bright eve. The wreath of roses, that hung from the lowest green bough of the Maypole, had been twined for them, and would be thrown over both their heads, in symbol of their flowery union. When the priest had spoken, therefore, a riotous uproar burst from the rout of monstrous figures.

"Begin you the stave,* reverend Sir," cried they all; "and never did the woods ring to such a merry peal as we of the Maypole shall send up!"

stave: a verse of music

Immediately a prelude of pipe, cithern,* and viol,* touched with practiced minstrelsy,* began to play from a neighboring thicket, in such a mirthful cadence that the boughs of the Maypole quivered to the sound. But the May Lord, he of the gilded staff, chancing to look into his Lady's eyes, was wonder struck at the almost pensive* glance that met his own.

cithern: guitarlike instrument
viol: ancestor of the violin
minstrelsy: musical artistry
pensive: sadly thoughtful

"Edith, sweet Lady of the May," whispered he reproachfully, "is yon wreath of roses a garland to hang above our graves, that you look so sad? O, Edith, this is our golden time! Tarnish it not by any pensive shadow of the mind; for it may be that nothing of futurity will be brighter than the mere remembrance of what is now passing."

"That was the very thought that saddened me! How came it in your mind too?" said Edith, in a still lower tone than he, for it was high treason to be sad at Merry Mount. "Therefore do I sigh amid the festive music. And besides, dear Edgar, I struggle as with a dream, and fancy that these shapes of our jovial friends are visionary, and their mirth unreal, and that we are no true Lord and Lady of the May. What is the mystery in my heart?"

Just then, as if a spell had loosened them, down came a little shower of withering rose leaves from the Maypole. Alas, for the young lovers! No sooner had their hearts glowed with real passion than they were sensible of something vague and unsubstantial in their former pleasures, and felt a dreary presentiment* of inevitable change. From the moment that they truly loved, they had subjected themselves to earth's doom of care and sorrow, and troubled joy, and had no more a home at Merry Mount. That was Edith's mystery. Now leave we the priest to marry them, and the masquers to sport round the Maypole, till the last sunbeam be withdrawn from its summit, and the shadows of the forest mingle gloomily in the dance. Meanwhile, we may discover who these gay people were.

presentiment: a foreboding

Two hundred years ago, and more, the old world and its inhabitants became mutually weary of each other. Men voyaged by thousands to the West: some to barter glass beads, and such like jewels, for the furs of the Indian hunter; some to conquer virgin empires; and one stern band to pray. But none of these motives had much weight with the colonists of Merry Mount. Their leaders were men who had sported so long with life, that when Thought and Wisdom came, even these unwelcome guests were led astray by the crowd of vanities which they should have put to flight. Erring Thought and perverted Wisdom were made to put on masques, and play the fool. The men of whom we speak, after losing the heart's fresh gayety, imagined a wild philosophy of pleasure, and came hither to act out their latest day-dream. They gathered followers from all that giddy tribe whose whole life is like the festal days of soberer men. In their train were minstrels, not unknown in London streets; wandering players, whose theatres had been the halls of noblemen; mummers,* rope-dancers, and mountebanks,* who would long be missed at wakes,* church ales, and fairs; in a word, mirth makers of every sort, such as abounded in that age, but now began to be discountenanced* by the rapid growth of Puritanism. Light had their footsteps been on land, and as lightly they came across the sea. Many had been maddened by their previous troubles into a gay despair; others were as madly gay in the flush of youth, like the May Lord and his Lady; but whatever might be the quality of their mirth, old and young were gay at Merry Mount. The young deemed themselves happy. The elder spirits, if they knew that mirth was but the counterfeit of happiness, yet followed the false shadow wilfully, because at least her garments glittered brightest. Sworn triflers of a lifetime, they would not venture among the sober truths of life not even to be truly blest.

mummers: masked or disguised players
mountebanks: those who draw crowds with tricks, jokes, etc.
wakes: watches over a body of a dead person, often accompanied by festivity
discountenanced: looked at with disfavor

All the hereditary pastimes of Old England were transplanted hither. The King of Christmas was duly crowned, and the Lord of Misrule bore potent* sway. On the Eve of St. John, they felled whole acres of the forest to make bonfires, and danced by the blaze all night, crowned with garlands, and throwing flowers into the flame. At harvest time, though their crop was of the smallest, they made an image with the sheaves of Indian corn, and wreathed it with autumnal garlands, and bore it home triumphantly. But what chiefly characterized the colonists of Merry Mount was their veneration for the Maypole. It has made their true history a poet's tale. Spring decked the hallowed emblem with young blossoms and fresh green boughs; Summer brought roses of the deepest blush, and the perfected foliage of the forest; Autumn enriched it with that red and yellow gorgeousness which converts each wildwood leaf into a painted flower; and Winter silvered it with sleet, and hung it round with icicles, till it flashed in the cold sunshine, itself a frozen sunbeam. Thus each alternate season did homage to the Maypole, and paid it a tribute of its own richest splendor. Its votaries danced round it, once, at least, in every month; sometimes they called it their religion, or their altar; but always, it was the banner staff of Merry Mount.

potent: holding great authority

Unfortunately, there were men in the new world of a sterner faith than those Maypole worshippers. Not far from Merry Mount was a settlement of Puritans, most dismal wretches, who said their prayers before daylight, and then wrought* in the forest or the cornfield till evening made it prayer time again. Their weapons were always at hand to shoot down the straggling savage. When they met in conclave,* it was never to keep up the old English mirth, but to hear sermons three hours long, or to proclaim bounties on the heads of wolves and the scalps of Indians. Their festivals were fast days, and their chief pastime the singing of psalms. Woe to the youth or maiden who did but dream of a dance! The selectman nodded to the constable; and there sat the light-

heeled reprobate in the stocks; or if he danced, it was round the whipping-post, which might be termed the Puritan Maypole.

wrought: worked
conclave: secret meeting

A party of these grim Puritans, toiling through the difficult woods, each with a horse-load of iron armor to burden his footsteps, would sometimes draw near the sunny precincts of Merry Mount. There were the silken colonists, sporting round their Maypole; perhaps teaching a bear to dance, or striving to communicate their mirth to the grave Indian; or masquerading in the skins of deer and wolves, which they had hunted for that especial purpose. Often, the whole colony were playing at blindman's buff, magistrates and all, with their eyes bandaged, except a single scapegoat, whom the blinded sinners pursued by the tinkling of the bells at his garments. Once, it is said, they were seen following a flower-decked corpse, with merriment and festive music, to his grave. But did the dead man laugh? In their quietest times, they sang ballads and told tales, for the edification of their pious visitors; or perplexed them with juggling tricks; or grinned at them through horse collars; and when sport itself grew wearisome, they made game of their own stupidity, and began a yawning match. At the very least of these enormities, the men of iron shook their heads and frowned so darkly that the revellers looked up imagining that a momentary cloud had overcast the sunshine, which was to be perpetual there. On the other hand, the Puritans affirmed that, when a psalm was pealing from their place of worship, the echo which the forest sent them back seemed often like the chorus of a jolly catch,* closing with a roar of laughter. Who but the fiend, and his bond slaves, the crew of Merry Mount, had thus disturbed them? In due time, a feud arose, stern and bitter on one side, and as serious on the other as anything could be among such light spirits as had sworn allegiance to the Maypole. The future complexion* of New England was involved in this important quarrel. Should the grizzly saints establish their jurisdiction over the gay sinners, then would their spirits darken all the clime, and make it a land of clouded visages, of hard toil, of sermon and psalm forever. But should the banner staff of Merry Mount be fortunate, sunshine would break upon the hills, and flowers would beautify the forests, and late posterity do homage to the Maypole.

---

jolly catch: round sung by three or more voices
complexion: general character

After these authentic passages from history, we return to the nuptials of the Lord and Lady of the May. Alas! we have delayed too long, and must darken our tale too suddenly. As we glance again at the Maypole, a solitary sunbeam is fading from the summit, and leaves only a faint, golden tinge blended with the hues of the rainbow banner. Even that dim light is now withdrawn, relinquishing the whole domain of Merry Mount to the evening gloom, which has rushed so instantaneously from the black surrounding woods. But some of these black shadows have rushed forth in human shape.

Yes, with the setting sun, the last day of mirth had passed from Merry Mount. The ring of gay masquers was disordered and broken; the stag lowered his antlers in dismay; the wolf grew weaker than a lamb; the bells of the morris-dancers tinkled with a tremulous affright. The Puritans had played a characteristic part in the Maypole mummeries. Their darksome figures were intermixed with the wild shapes of their foes, and made the scene a picture of the moment, when waking thoughts start up amid the scattered fantasies of a dream. The leader of the hostile party stood in the centre of the circle, while the route of monsters cowered around him, like evil spirits in the presence of a dread magician. No fantastic foolery could look him in the face. So stern was the energy of his aspect, that the whole man, visage, frame, and soul, seemed wrought of iron, gifted with life and thought, yet all of one sub-

stance with his headpiece and breastplate. It was the Puritan of Puritans; it was Endicott himself!

"Stand off, priest of Baal!" said he, with a grim frown, and laying no reverent hand upon the surplice.* "I know thee, Blackstone! Thou art the man who couldst not abide the rule even of thine own corrupted church, and hast come hither to preach iniquity, and to give example of it in thy life. But now shall it be seen that the Lord hath sanctified this wilderness for his peculiar people. Woe unto them that would defile it! And first, for this flower-decked abomination, the altar of thy worship!"

---

surplice: a loose, white gown worn by a priest

And with his keen sword Endicott assaulted the hallowed Maypole. Nor long did it resist his arm. It groaned with a dismal sound; it showered leaves and rosebuds upon the remorseless enthusiast;* and finally, with all its green boughs and ribbons and flowers, symbolic of departed pleasures, down fell the banner staff of Merry Mount. As it sank, tradition says, the evening sky grew darker, and the woods threw forth a more sombre shadow.

---

enthusiast: religious fanatic

"There," cried Endicott, looking triumphantly on his work, "there lies the only Maypole in New England! The thought is strong within me that, by its fall, is shadowed forth the fate of light and idle mirth makers, amongst us and our posterity. Amen, saith John Endicott."

"Amen!" echoed his followers.

But the votaries of the Maypole gave one groan for their idol. At the sound, the Puritan leader glanced at the crew of Comus, each a figure of broad mirth, yet, at this moment, strangely expressive of sorrow and dismay.

"Valiant captain," quoth Peter Palfrey, the ancient of the band, "what order shall be taken with the prisoners?"

"I thought not to repent me of cutting down a Maypole," replied Endicott, "yet now I could find in my heart to plant it again, and give each of these bestial pagans one other dance around their idol. It would have served rarely for a whipping-post!''

''But there are pine-trees enow,''* suggested the lieutenant.

enow: enough

''True, good Ancient,'' said the leader. ''Wherefore, bind the heathen crew, and bestow on them a small matter of stripes apiece, as earnest of our future justice. Set some of the rogues in the stocks to rest themselves, so soon as Providence shall bring us to one of our own well-ordered settlements where such accommodations may be found. Further penalties, such as branding and cropping of ears, shall be thought of hereafter.''

''How many stripes for the priest?'' inquired Ancient Palfrey.

''None as yet,'' answered Endicott, bending his iron frown upon the culprit. ''It must be for the Great and General Court to determine, whether stripes and long imprisonment, and other grievous penalty, may atone for his transgressions. Let him look to himself! For such as violate our civil order, it may be permitted us to show mercy. But woe to the wretch that troubleth our religion.''

''And this dancing bear,'' resumed the officer. ''Must he share the stripes of his fellows?''

''Shoot him through the head!'' said the energetic Puritan. ''I suspect witchcraft in the beast.''

''Here be a couple of shining ones,'' continued Peter Palfrey, pointing his weapon at the Lord and Lady of the May. ''They seem to be of high station among these misdoers. Methinks their dignity will not be fitted with less than a double share of stripes.''

Endicott rested on his sword, and closely surveyed the dress and aspect of the hapless pair. There they stood, pale, downcast, and apprehensive. Yet there was an air of mutual support and of pure affection, seeking aid and giving it, that showed them to be man and wife, with the sanction of a priest upon their love. The youth, in the peril of the moment, had dropped his gilded staff, and thrown his arm about the Lady of the May, who leaned against his breast, too lightly to burden him, but with weight enough to express that their destinies were linked together, for good or evil. They looked first at each other, and then into the grim captain's face. There they stood, in the first hour of wedlock, while the idle pleasures, of which their companions were the emblems, had given place to the sternest cares of life, personified by the dark Puritans. But never had their youthful beauty seemed so pure and high as when its glow was chastened by adversity.

''Youth,'' said Endicott, ''ye stand in an evil case, thou and thy maiden wife. Make ready presently, for I am minded that ye shall both have a token to remember your wedding day!''

''Stern man,'' cried the May Lord, ''how can I move thee? Were the means at hand, I would resist to the death. Being powerless, I entreat! Do with me as thou wilt, but let Edith go untouched!''

''Not so,'' replied the immitigable* zealot. ''We are not wont to show an idle courtesy to that sex, which requireth the stricter discipline. What sayest thou, maid? Shall thy silken bridegroom suffer thy share of the penalty, besides his own?''

immitigable: unsoftened

''Be it death,'' said Edith, ''and lay it all on me!''

Truly, as Endicott had said, the poor lovers stood in a woful case. Their foes were triumphant, their friends captive and abased, their home desolate, the benighted* wilderness around them, and a rigorous destiny, in the shape of the Puritan leader, their only guide. Yet the deepening twilight could not altogether conceal that the iron man was softened; he smiled at the fair spectacle of early love; he almost sighed for the inevitable blight of early hopes.

benighted: dark, both literally and figuratively

"The troubles of life have come hastily on this young couple," observed Endicott. "We will see how they comport* themselves under their present trials ere we burden them with greater. If, among the spoil, there be any garments of a more decent fashion, let them be put upon this May Lord and his Lady, instead of their glistening vanities. Look to it, some of you."

comport: behave

"And shall not the youth's hair be cut?" asked Peter Palfrey, looking with abhorrence at the love-lock and long glossy curls of the young man.

"Crop it forthwith, and that in the true pumpkin-shell fashion," answered the captain. "Then bring them along with us, but more gently than their fellows. There be qualities in the youth, which may make him valiant to fight, and sober to toil, and pious to pray; and in the maiden, that may fit her to become a mother in our Israel, bringing up babes in better nurture than her own

hath been. Nor think ye, young ones, that they are the happiest, even in our lifetime of a moment, who misspend it in dancing round a Maypole!"

And Endicott, the severest Puritan of all who laid the rock foundation of New England, lifted the wreath of roses from the ruin of the Maypole, and threw it, with his own gauntleted* hand, over the heads of the Lord and Lady of the May. It was a deed of prophecy. As the moral gloom of the world overpowers all systematic gayety, even so was their home of wild mirth made desolate amid the sad forest. They returned to it no more. But as their flowery garland was wreathed of the brightest roses that had grown there, so, in the tie that united them, were intertwined all the purest and best of their early joys. They went heavenward, supporting each other along the difficult path which it was their lot to tread, and never wasted one regretful thought on the vanities of Merry Mount.

gauntleted: gloved hand (A gauntlet was a glove covered with metal plates to protect the hand.)

The Celestial Railroad

"The Celestial Railroad" is Hawthorne's **satire** *on his contemporaries' modernized religion, especially transcendentalism and Unitarianism. Inspired by John Bunyan's* The Pilgrim's Progress *(1679), Hawthorne's story attacks the liberal notions of the way to heaven. The story is infused with* **irony.**

Despite its many parallels with Bunyan's work, this story has genuine originality, especially in the relationship between the pilgrim and Mr. Smooth-it-away and in the satire on the attempts of Hawthorne's contemporaries to find an easy pathway to heaven. Since satire is basically didactic in its correction of human weakness by ridicule, Hawthorne reveals clearly that his sympathy lies not with the liberal theology of his day but with the Puritan view of this life and the next.

In this **allegory** *the characters seem to personify categories of human values (i.e., Mr. Smooth-it-away, Mr. Live-for-the-world, Mr. Take-it-easy, Mr. Flimsy-faith). As characters, they are underdeveloped, clearly two-dimensional, flat. Their abstractness, however, is essential; type characters are required for allegory, which attempts to say something universal about man and his experiences.*

Notice that this story is told from a first-person **point of view.** *Do not confuse the "I" telling the story with the author. The "I" is fictional like the other characters.*

Not a great while ago, passing through the gate of dreams, I visited that region of the earth in which lies the famous City of Destruction. It interested me much to learn that by the public spirit of some of the inhabitants a railroad has recently been established between this populous and flourishing town and the Celestial City. Having a little time upon my hands, I resolved to gratify a liberal curiosity by making a trip thither. Accordingly, one fine morning after paying my bill at the hotel, and directing the porter to stow my luggage behind a coach, I took my seat in the vehicle and set out for the station-house. It was my good fortune to enjoy the company of a gentleman—one Mr. Smooth-it-away—who, though he had never actually visited the Celestial City, yet seemed as well acquainted with its laws, customs, policy, and statistics, as with those of the City of Destruction, of which he was a native townsman. Being, moreover, a director of the railroad corporation and one of its largest stockholders, he had it in his power to give me all desirable information respecting that praiseworthy enterprise.

Our coach rattled out of the city, and at a short distance from its outskirts passed over a bridge of elegant construction, but somewhat too slight, as I imagined, to sustain any considerable weight. On both sides lay an extensive quagmire,* which could not have been more disagreeable, either to sight or smell, had all the kennels* of the earth emptied their pollution there.

quagmire: swamp
kennels: gutters

"This," remarked Mr. Smooth-it-away, "is the famous Slough of Despond*—a disgrace to all the neighborhood; and the greater that it might so easily be converted into firm ground."

Slough of Despond: cf. Bunyan's *Pilgrim's Progress*

"I have understood," said I, "that efforts have been made for that purpose from time immemorial. Bunyan mentions that above twenty thousand cartloads of wholesome instructions had been thrown in here without effect."

"Very probably! And what effect could be anticipated from such unsubstantial stuff?" cried Mr. Smooth-it-away. "You observe this convenient bridge. We obtained a sufficient foundation for it by throwing into the slough* some editions of books of morality; volumes of French philosophy and German rationalism; tracts, sermons, and essays of modern clergymen; extracts from Plato, Confucius, and various Hindoo sages, together with a few ingenious commentaries upon texts of Scripture,—all of which by some scientific process, have been converted into a mass like granite. The whole bog might be filled up with similar matter."

slough: a depression or hollow usually filled with deep mud or mire

It really seemed to me, however, that the bridge vibrated and heaved up and down in a very formidable manner; and, in spite of Mr. Smooth-it-away's testimony to the solidity of its foundation, I should be loath to cross it in a crowded omnibus,* especially if each passenger were encumbered with as heavy luggage as that gentleman and myself. Nevertheless we got over without accident, and soon found ourselves at the station-house. This very neat and spacious edifice is erected on the site of the little wicket gate, which formerly, as all old pilgrims will recollect, stood directly across the highway, and, by its inconvenient narrowness, was a great obstruction to the traveller of liberal mind and expansive stomach. The reader of John Bunyan will be glad to know that Christian's old friend Evangelist, who was accustomed to supply each pilgrim with a mystic* roll, now presides at the ticket office. Some malicious persons it is true deny the identity of this reputable character with the Evangelist of old times, and even pretend to bring competent evidence of an imposture. Without involving myself in a dispute I shall merely observe that, so far as my experience goes, the square pieces of pasteboard now delivered to passengers are much more convenient and useful along the road than the antique roll of parchment. Whether they will be as readily received at the gate of the Celestial City I decline giving an opinion.

omnibus: bus
mystic: mysteriously symbolic

A large number of passengers were already at the station-house awaiting the departure of the cars. By the aspect and demeanor of these persons it was easy to judge that the feelings of the community had undergone a very favorable change in reference to the celestial pilgrimage. It would have done Bunyan's heart good to see it. Instead of a lonely and ragged man with a huge burden on his back, plodding along sorrowfully on foot while the whole city hooted after him, here were parties of the first gentry and most respectable people in the neighborhood setting forth towards the Celestial City as cheerfully as if the pilgrimage were merely a summer tour. Among the gentlemen were characters of deserved eminence–magistrates, politicians, and men of wealth, by whose example religion could not but be greatly recommended to their meaner* brethren. In the ladies' apartment, too, I rejoiced to distinguish some of those flowers of fashionable society who are so well fitted to adorn the most elevated circles of the Celestial City. There was much pleasant conversation about the news of the day, topics of business and politics, or the lighter matters of amusement; while religion, though indubitably* the main thing at heart, was thrown tastefully into the background. Even an infidel* would have heard little or nothing to shock his sensibility.

meaner: inferior
indubitably: unquestionably
infidel: one with no religious beliefs

One great convenience of the new method of going on pilgrimage I must not forget to mention. Our enormous burdens, instead of being carried on our shoulders as had been the custom of old, were all snugly deposited in the baggage car, and, as I was assured, would be delivered to their respective owners at the journey's end. Another thing, likewise, the benevolent reader will be delighted to understand. It may be remembered that there was an ancient feud between Prince Beelzebub* and the keeper of the wicket gate, and that the adherents* of the former distinguished personage were accustomed to shoot deadly arrows at honest pilgrims while knocking at the door. This dispute, much to the credit as well of the illustrious potentate above mentioned as of the worthy and enlightened directors of the railroad, has been pacifically* arranged on the principle of mutual compromise. The prince's subjects are now pretty numerously employed about the station-house, some in taking care of the baggage, others in collecting fuel, feeding the engines, and

such congenial occupations; and I can conscientiously affirm that persons more attentive to their business, more willing to accommodate, or more generally agreeable to the passengers, are not to be found on any railroad. Every good heart must surely exult at so satisfactory an arrangement of an immemorial difficulty.

ancient . . . Beelzebub: see Matthew 12:24
adherents: supporters
pacifically: peacefully

"Where is Mr. Greatheart?" inquired I. "Beyond a doubt the directors have engaged that famous old champion to be chief conductor on the railroad?"

"Why, no," said Mr. Smooth-it-away, with a dry cough. "He was offered the situation of brakeman; but, to tell you the truth, our friend Greatheart has grown preposterously stiff and narrow in his old age. He has so often guided pilgrims over the road on foot that he considers it a sin to travel in any other fashion. Besides, the old fellow had entered so heartily into the ancient feud with Prince Beelzebub that he would have been perpetually at blows or ill language with some of the prince's subjects, and thus have embroiled* us anew. So, on the whole, we were not sorry when honest Greatheart went off to the Celestial City in a huff and left us at liberty to choose a more suitable and accommodating man. Yonder comes the engineer of the train. You will probably recognize him at once."

embroiled: entangled

The engine at this moment took its station in advance of the cars, looking, I must confess, much more like a sort of mechanical demon that would hurry us to the infernal regions than a laudable* contrivance* for smoothing our way to the Celestial City. On its top sat a personage almost enveloped in smoke and flame, which, not to startle the reader, appeared to gush from his own mouth and stomach as well as from the engine's brazen* abdomen.

laudable: praiseworthy
contrivance: means
brazen: brass

"Do my eyes deceive me?" cried I. "What on earth is this! A living creature? If so, he is own brother to the engine he rides upon!"

"Poh, poh, you are obtuse!"* said Mr. Smooth-it-away, with a hearty laugh. "Don't you know Apollyon, Christian's old enemy, with whom he fought so fierce a battle in the Valley of Humiliation? He was the very fellow to manage the engine; and so we have reconciled him to the custom of going on pilgrimage, and engaged him as chief engineer."

obtuse: dull or stupid

"Bravo, bravo!" exclaimed I, with irrepressible enthusiasm; "this shows the liberality of the age; this proves, if anything can, that all musty prejudices are in a fair way to be obliterated. And how will Christian rejoice to hear of this happy transformation of his old antagonist! I promise myself great pleasure in informing him of it when we reach the Celestial City."

The passengers being all comfortably seated, we now rattled away merrily, accomplishing a greater distance in ten minutes than Christian probably trudged over in a day. It was laughable, while we glanced along, as it were, at the tail of a thunderbolt, to observe two dusty foot travellers in the old pilgrim guise, with cockle shell and staff, their mystic rolls of parchment in their hands and their intolerable burdens on their backs. The preposterous obstinacy of these honest people in persisting to groan and stumble along the difficult pathway rather than take advantage of modern improvements, excited great mirth among our wiser brotherhood. We greeted the two pilgrims with many pleasant gibes* and a roar of laughter; whereupon they gazed at us with such woful and absurdly compassionate visages that our merriment grew tenfold more obstreperous.* Apollyon also entered heartily into the fun, and contrived to flirt the smoke and flame of the engine, or of his own breath, into their faces, and envelop them in an atmosphere of scalding steam. These little practical jokes amused us mightily, and doubtless afforded the pilgrims the gratification of considering themselves martyrs.

gibes: heckling or mocking remarks
obstreperous: noisily defiant

At some distance from the railroad Mr. Smooth-it-away pointed to a large, antique edifice, which, he observed, was a tavern of long standing, and had formerly been a noted stopping-place for pilgrims. In Bunyan's road-book it is mentioned as the Interpreter's House.

"I have long had a curiosity to visit that old mansion," remarked I.

"It is not one of our stations, as you perceive," said my companion. "The keeper was violently opposed to the railroad; and well he might be, as the track left his house of entertainment on one side, and thus was pretty certain to deprive him of all his reputable customers. But the footpath still passes his door, and the old gentleman now and then receives a call from some simple traveller, and entertains him with fare* as old-fashioned as himself."

fare: food and drink

Before our talk on this subject came to a conclusion we were rushing by the place where Christian's burden fell from his shoulders at the sight of the Cross. This served as a theme for Mr. Smooth-it-away, Mr. Live-for-the-world, Mr. Hide-sin-in-the-heart, Mr. Scaly-conscience, and a knot of gentlemen from the town of Shun-repentance, to descant* upon the inestimable advantages resulting from the safety of our baggage. Myself, and all the passengers indeed, joined with great unanimity* in this view of the matter; for our burdens were rich in many things esteemed precious throughout the world; and, especially, we each of us possessed a great variety of favorite Habits, which we trusted would not be out of fashion even in the polite circles of the Celestial City. It would

down, it will remain an eternal monument of the builder's skill and enterprise. It is a great though incidental advantage that the materials from the heart of the Hill Difficulty have been employed in filling up the Valley of Humiliation, thus obviating* the necessity of descending into that disagreeable and unwholesome hollow.

descant: discourse
unanimity: complete agreement
obviating: preventing

"This is a wonderful improvement, indeed," said I. "Yet I should have been glad of an opportunity to visit the Palace Beautiful and be introduced to the charming young ladies–Miss Prudence, Miss Piety, Miss Charity, and the rest–who have the kindness to entertain pilgrims there."

"Young ladies!" cried Mr. Smooth-it-away, as soon as he could speak for laughing. "And charming young ladies! Why, my dear fellow, they are old maids, every soul of them–prim, starched, dry, and angular; and not one of them, I will venture to say, has altered so much as the fashion of her gown since the days of Christian's pilgrimage."

"Ah, well," said I, much comforted, "then I can very readily dispense with their acquaintance."

The respectable Apollyon was now putting on the steam at a prodigious* rate, anxious, perhaps, to get rid of the unpleasant reminiscences connected with the spot where he had so disastrously encountered Christian. Consulting Mr. Bunyan's road-book, I perceived that we must now be within a few miles of the Valley of the Shadow of Death, into which doleful region, at our present speed, we should plunge much sooner than seemed at all desirable. In truth, I expected nothing better than to find myself in the ditch on one side or the quag on the other; but on communicating my apprehensions to Mr. Smooth-it-away, he assured me that the difficulties of this passage, even in its worst condition, had been vastly exaggerated, and that, in its present state of im-

have been a sad spectacle to see such an assortment of valuable articles tumbling into the sepulchre. Thus pleasantly conversing on the favorable circumstances of our position as compared with those of past pilgrims and of narrow-minded ones at the present day, we soon found ourselves at the foot of the Hill Difficulty. Through the very heart of this rocky mountain a tunnel has been constructed of most admirable architecture, with a lofty arch and a spacious double track; so that, unless the earth and rocks should chance to crumble provement, I might consider myself as safe as on any railroad in Christendom.

prodigious: extraordinary

Even while we were speaking the train shot into the entrance of this dreaded Valley. Though I plead guilty to some foolish palpitations of the heart during our headlong rush over the causeway* here constructed, yet it were unjust to withhold the highest encomiums* on the boldness of its original conception and the ingenuity of those who executed it. It was gratifying, likewise, to observe how much care had been taken to dispel the everlasting gloom and supply the defect of cheerful sunshine, not a ray of which has ever penetrated among these awful shadows. For this purpose, the inflammable gas which exudes plentifully from the soil is collected by means of pipes, and thence communicated to a quadruple row of lamps along the whole extent of the passage. Thus a radiance has been created even out of the fiery and sulphurous curse that rests forever upon the valley—a radiance hurtful, however, to the eyes, and somewhat bewildering, as I discovered by the changes which it wrought in the visages of my companions. In this respect, as compared with natural daylight, there is the same difference as between truth and falsehood; but if the reader have ever travelled through the dark Valley, he will have learned to be thankful for any light that he could get—if not from the sky above, then from the blasted* soil beneath. Such was the red brilliancy of these lamps that they appeared to build walls of fire on both sides of the track, between which we held our course at lightning speed, while a reverberating thunder filled the Valley with its echoes. Had the engine run off the track,—a catastrophe, it is whispered, by no means unprecedented,—the bottomless pit, if there be any such place, would undoubtedly have received us. Just as some dismal fooleries of this nature had made my heart quake there came a tremendous shriek, careering* along the valley as if a thousand devils had burst their lungs to utter it, but

which proved to be merely the whistle of the engine on arriving at a stopping-place.

causeway: raised roadway, as across a marshland
encomiums: tributes
blasted: blighted, perhaps condemned
careering: rushing headlong

The spot where we had now paused is the same that our friend Bunyan—a truthful man, but infected with many fantastic notions—has designated, in terms plainer than I like to repeat, as the mouth of the infernal region. This, however, must be a mistake, inasmuch as Mr. Smooth-it-away, while we remained in the smoky and lurid* cavern, took occasion to prove that Tophet* has not even a metaphorical existence. The place, he assured us, is no other than the crater of a half-extinct volcano, in which the directors had caused forges to be set up for the manufacture of railroad iron. Hence, also, is obtained a plentiful supply of fuel for the use of the engines. Whoever had gazed into the dismal obscurity of the broad cavern mouth, whence ever and anon* darted huge tongues of dusky flame, and had seen the strange, half-shaped monsters, and visions of faces horribly grotesque, into which the smoke seemed to wreathe itself, and had heard the awful murmurs, and shrieks, and deep shuddering whispers of the blast, sometimes forming themselves into words almost articulate, would have seized upon Mr. Smooth-it-away's comfortable explanation as greedily as we did. The inhabitants of the cavern, moreover, were unlovely personages, dark, smoke-begrimed, generally deformed, with misshapen feet, and a glow of dusky redness in their eyes as if their hearts had caught fire and were blazing out of the upper windows. It struck me as a peculiarity that the laborers at the forge and those who brought fuel to the engine, when they began to draw short breath, positively emitted smoke from their mouth and nostrils.

lurid: glowing
Tophet: lit., "place of fire": symbolic reference to the "lake of fire"
anon: again

Among the idlers about the train, most of whom were puffing cigars which they had lighted at the flame of the crater, I was perplexed to notice several who, to my certain knowledge, had heretofore set forth by railroad for the Celestial City. They looked dark, wild, and smoky, with a singular resemblance, indeed, to the native inhabitants, like whom, also, they had a disagreeable propensity to ill-natured gibes and sneers, the habit of which had wrought a settled contortion of their visages. Having been on speaking terms with one of these persons,–an indolent,* good-for-nothing fellow, who went by the name of Take-it-easy,–I called him, and inquired what was his business there.

indolent: lazy

"Did you not start," said I, "for the Celestial City?"

"That's a fact," said Mr. Take-it-easy, carelessly puffing some smoke into my eyes. "But I heard such bad accounts that I never took pains to climb the hill on which the city stands. No business doing, no fun going on, nothing to drink, and no smoking allowed, and a thrumming of church music from morning till night. I would not stay in such a place if they offered me house room and living free."

"But my good Mr. Take-it-easy," cried I, "why take up your residence here, of all places in the world?"

"Oh," said the loafer, with a grin, "it is very warm hereabouts, and I meet with plenty of old acquaintances, and altogether the place suits me. I hope to see you back again some day soon. A pleasant journey to you."

While he was speaking the bell of the engine rang, and we dashed away after dropping a few passengers, but receiving no new ones. Rattling onward through the Valley, we were dazzled with the fiercely gleaming gas lamps, as before. But sometimes, in the dark of intense brightness, grim faces, that bore the aspect and expression of individual sins, or evil passions, seemed to thrust themselves through the veil of light, glaring upon us, and stretching forth a great, dusky hand, as if to impede our progress. I almost thought that they were my own sins that appalled me there. These were freaks of imagination–nothing more, certainly–mere delusions, which I ought to be heartily ashamed of; but all through the Dark Valley I was tormented, and pestered, and dolefully bewildered with the same kind of waking dreams. The mephitic* gases of that region intoxicate the brain. As the light of natural day, however, began to struggle with the glow of the lanterns, these vain imaginations lost their vividness, and finally vanished with the first ray of sunshine that greeted our escape from the Valley of the Shadow of

Death. Ere we had gone a mile beyond it I could well-nigh have taken my oath that this whole gloomy passage was a dream.

mephitic: smelly

At the end of the valley, as John Bunyan mentions, is a cavern, where, in his days, dwelt two cruel giants, Pope and Pagan, who had strown the ground about their residence with the bones of slaughtered pilgrims. These vile old troglodytes* are no longer there; but into their deserted cave another terrible giant has thrust himself, and makes it his business to seize upon honest travellers and fatten them for his table with plentiful meals of smoke, mist, moonshine, raw potatoes, and sawdust. He is a German by birth, and is called Giant Transcendentalist; but as to his form, his features, his substance, and his nature generally, it is the chief peculiarity of this huge miscreant* that neither he for himself, nor anybody for him, has ever been able to describe them. As we rushed by the cavern's mouth we caught a hasty glimpse of him, looking somewhat like an ill-proportioned figure, but considerably more like a heap of fog and duskiness. He shouted after us, but in so strange a phraseology that we knew not what he meant, nor whether to be encouraged or affrighted.

troglodytes: those resembling cavemen
miscreant: heretic or infidel

It was late in the day when the train thundered into the ancient city of Vanity, where Vanity Fair is still at the height of prosperity, and exhibits an epitome* of whatever is brilliant, gay, and fascinating beneath the sun. As I purposed to make a considerable stay here, it gratified me to learn that there is no longer the want of harmony between the town's-people and pilgrims, which impelled the former to such lamentably mistaken measures as the persecution of Christian and the fiery martyrdom of Faithful. On the contrary, as the new railroad brings with it great trade and a constant influx of strangers, the lord of Vanity Fair is its chief patron, and the capitalists of the city are among the largest stockholders. Many passengers stop to take their pleasure or make their profit in the Fair, instead of going onward to the Celestial City. Indeed, such are the charms of the place that people often affirm it to be the true and only heaven, stoutly contending that there is no other, that those who seek further are mere dreamers, and that, if the fabled brightness of the Celestial City lay but a bare mile beyond the gates of Vanity, they would not be fools enough to go thither. Without subscribing to these perhaps exaggerated encomiums, I can truly say that my abode in the city was mainly agreeable, and my intercourse with the inhabitants productive of much amusement and instruction.

epitome: embodiment

Being naturally of a serious turn, my attention was directed to the solid advantages derivable from a residence here, rather than to the effervescent* pleasures which are the grand object with too many visitants. The Christian reader, if he have had no accounts of the city later than Bunyan's time, will be surprised to hear that almost every street has its church, and that the reverend clergy are nowhere held in higher respect than at Vanity Fair. And well do they deserve such honorable estimation; for the maxims of wisdom and virtue which fall from their lips come from as deep a spiritual source, and tend to as lofty a religious aim, as those of the sagest philosophers of old. In justification of this high praise I need only mention the names of the Rev. Mr. Shallowdeep, the Rev. Mr. Stumble-at-truth, that fine old clerical character the Rev. Mr. This-to-day, who expects shortly to resign his pulpit to the Rev. Mr. That-to-morrow; together with the Rev. Mr. Bewilderment, Rev. Mr. Clog-the-spirit, and, last and greatest, the Rev. Dr. Wind-of-doctrine. The labors of these eminent divines are aided by those of innumerable lecturers, who diffuse such a various profundity, in all subjects of human or celestial science, that any man may acquire an omnigenous* erudition* without the trouble of even learning to read. Thus literature is etherealized* by assuming for its medium the human voice; and knowledge, depositing all its heavier particles, except, doubtless, its gold, becomes exhaled into a sound, which forthwith steals into the ever-open ear of the community. These ingenious methods constitute a sort of machinery, by which thought and study are done to every person's hand without his putting himself to the slightest inconvenience in the matter. There is another species of machine for the wholesale manufacture of individual morality. This excellent result is effected by societies for all manner of virtuous purposes, with which a man has merely to connect himself, throwing, as it were, his quota of virtue into the common stock, and the president and directors will take care that the aggregate* amount be well applied. All these, and other wonderful improvements in ethics, religion, and literature, being made plain to my comprehension by the ingenious Mr. Smooth-it-away, inspired me with a vast admiration of Vanity Fair.

effervescent: bubbling: i.e., short-lived
omnigenous: of all kinds
erudition: learning
etherealized: spiritualized
aggregate: total

It would fill a volume, in an age of pamphlets, were I to record all of my observations in this great capital of human business and pleasure. There was an unlimited range of society–the powerful, the wise, the witty, and the famous in every walk of life; princes, presidents, poets, generals, artists, actors, and philanthropists,–all making their own market at the fair, and deeming no price too exorbitant for such commodities as hit their fancy. It was well worth one's while, even if he had no idea of buying or selling, to loiter through the bazaars and observe the various sorts of traffic that were going forward.

Some of the purchasers, I thought, made very foolish bargains. For instance, a young man having inherited a splendid fortune, laid out a considerable portion of it in the purchase of diseases, and finally spent all the rest for a heavy lot of repentance and a suit of rags. A very pretty girl bartered a heart as clear as crystal, and which seemed her most valuable possession, for another jewel of the same kind, but so worn and defaced as to be utterly worthless. In one shop there were a great many crowns of laurel and myrtle,* which soldiers, authors, statesmen, and various other people pressed eagerly to buy; some purchased these paltry wreaths with their lives, others by a toilsome servitude of years, and many sacrificed whatever was most valuable, yet finally slunk away without the crown. There was a sort of stock or scrip,* called Conscience, which seemed to be in great demand, and would purchase almost anything. Indeed, few rich commodities were to be obtained without paying a heavy sum in this particular stock, and a man's business was seldom very lucrative unless he knew precisely when and how to throw his hoard of conscience into the market. Yet as this stock was the only thing of permanent value, whoever parted with it was sure to find himself a loser in the long run. Several of the speculations were of a questionable character. Occasionally a member of Congress recruited his pocket by the sale of his constituents; and I was assured that public officers have often sold their country at very moderate prices. Thousands sold their happiness for a whim. Gilded chains were in great demand, and purchased with almost any sacrifice. In truth, those who desired, according to the old adage, to sell anything valuable for a song, might find customers all over the Fair; and there were innumerable messes of pottage, piping hot, for such as chose to buy them with their birthrights. A few articles, however, could not be found genuine at Vanity Fair. If a customer wished to renew his stock of youth the dealers offered him a set of false teeth and an auburn wig; if he demanded peace of mind, they recommended opium or a brandy bottle.

laurel and myrtle: laurel wreaths, awards of honor in ancient times
scrip: provisional certificate entitling one to a fractional share of stock

Tracts of land and golden mansions, situate in the Celestial City, were often exchanged, at very disadvantageous rates, for a few years' lease of small, dismal, inconvenient tenements in Vanity Fair. Prince Beelzebub himself took great interest in this sort of traffic, and sometimes condescended to meddle with smaller matters. I once had the pleasure to see him bargaining with a miser for his soul, which, after much ingenious skirmishing on both sides, his highness succeeded in obtaining at about the value of sixpence. The prince remarked with a smile, that he was a loser by the transaction.

Day after day, as I walked the streets of Vanity, my manners and deportment became more and more like those of the inhabitants. The place began to seem like home; the idea of pursuing my travels to the Celestial City was almost obliterated from my mind. I was reminded of it, however, by the sight of the same pair of simple pilgrims at whom we had laughed so heartily when Apollyon puffed smoke and steam into their faces at the commencement of our journey. There they stood amidst the densest bustle of Vanity; the dealers offering them their purple and fine linen and jewels, the men of wit and humor gibing at them, a pair of buxom* ladies ogling* them askance,* while the benevolent Mr. Smooth-it-away whispered some of his wisdom at their elbows, and pointed to a newly-erected temple; but there were these worthy simpletons, making the scene look wild and monstrous, merely by their sturdy repudiation* of all part in its business or pleasures.

buxom: gay, lively
ogling: staring at flirtatiously
askance: with a side glance
repudiation: rejection

One of them—his name was Stick-to-the-right—perceived in my face, I suppose, a species of sympathy and almost admiration, which, to my own great surprise, I could not help feeling for this pragmatic* couple. It prompted him to address me.

pragmatic: practical, active

"Sir," inquired he, with a sad, yet mild and kindly voice, "do you call yourself a pilgrim?"

"Yes," I replied, "my right to that appellation* is indubitable. I am merely a sojourner here in Vanity Fair, being bound to the Celestial City by the new railroad."

appellation: name or title

"Alas, friend," rejoined Mr. Stick-to-the-right, "I do assure you, and beseech you to receive the truth of my words, that that whole concern is a bubble. You may travel on it all your lifetime, were you to live thousands of years, and

yet never get beyond the limits of Vanity Fair. Yea, though you should deem yourself entering the gates of the blessed city, it will be nothing but a miserable delusion.''

''The Lord of the Celestial City,'' began the other pilgrim, whose name was Mr. Foot-it-to-heaven, ''has refused, and will refuse, to grant an act of incorporation for this railroad; and unless that be obtained, no passenger can ever hope to enter his dominions. Wherefore every man who buys a ticket must lay his account with losing the purchase money, which is the value of his own soul.''

''Poh, nonsense!'' said Mr. Smooth-it-away, taking my arm and leading me off, ''these fellows ought to be indicted for a libel. If the law stood as it once did in Vanity Fair we should see them grinning through the iron bars of the prison window.''

This incident made a considerable impression on my mind, and contributed with other circumstances to indispose me to a permanent residence in the city of Vanity; although, of course, I was not simple enough to give up my original plan of gliding along easily and commodiously* by railroad. Still, I grew anxious to be gone. There was one strange thing that troubled me. Amid the occupations or amusements of the Fair, nothing was more common than for a person–whether at feast, theatre, or church, or trafficking for wealth and honors, or whatever he might be doing, and however unseasonable the interruption–suddenly to vanish like a soap bubble, and be never more seen of his fellows; and so accustomed were the latter to such little accidents that they went on with their business as quietly as if nothing had happened. But it was otherwise with me.

---

commodiously: conveniently

Finally, after a pretty long residence at the Fair, I resumed my journey towards the Celestial City, still with Mr. Smooth-it-away at my side. At a short distance beyond the suburbs of Vanity we passed the ancient silver mine, of which Demas was the first discoverer, and which is now wrought to great advantage, supplying nearly all the coined currency of the world. A little further onward was the spot where Lot's wife had stood forever under the semblance of a pillar of salt. Curious travellers have long since carried it away piecemeal. Had all regrets been punished as rigorously as this poor dame's were, my yearning for the relinquished delights of Vanity Fair might have produced a similar change in my own corporeal* substance, and left me a warning to future pilgrims.

---

corporeal: pertaining to the body

The next remarkable object was a large edifice, constructed of mossgrown stone, but in a modern and airy style of architecture. The engine came to a pause in its vicinity, with the usual tremendous shriek.

''This was formerly the castle of the redoubted* giant Despair,'' observed Mr. Smooth-it-away; ''but since his death Mr. Flimsy-faith has repaired it, and keeps an excellent house of entertainment here. It is one of our stopping-places.''

---

redoubted: dreaded

''It seems but slightly put together,'' remarked I, looking at the frail yet ponderous walls. ''I do not envy Mr. Flimsy-faith his habitation. Some day it will thunder down upon the heads of the occupants.''

''We shall escape at all events,'' said Mr. Smooth-it-away, ''for Apollyon is putting on the steam again.''

The road now plunged into a gorge of the Delectable Mountains, and traversed the field where in former ages the blind men wandered and stumbled among the tombs. One of these ancient tombstones had been thrust across the track by some malicious person, and gave the train of cars a terrible jolt. Far up the rugged side of a mountain I perceived a rusty iron door, half overgrown with bushes and creeping plants, but with smoke issuing from its crevices.

''Is that,'' inquired I, ''the very door in the hill-side which the shepherds assured Christian was a by-way to hell?''

"That was a joke on the part of the shepherds," said Mr. Smooth-it-away, with a smile. "It is neither more nor less than the door of a cavern which they use as a smoke-house for the preparation of mutton hams."

My recollections of the journey are now, for a little space, dim and confused, inasmuch as a singular drowsiness here overcame me, owing to the fact that we were passing over the enchanted ground, the air of which encourages a disposition to sleep. I awoke, however, as soon as we crossed the borders of the pleasant land of Beulah. All the passengers were rubbing their eyes, comparing watches, and congratulating one another on the prospect of arriving so seasonably at the journey's end. The sweet breezes of this happy clime came refreshingly to our nostrils; we beheld the glimmering gush of silver fountains, overhung by trees of beautiful foliage and delicious fruit, which were propagated by grafts from the celestial gardens. Once, as we dashed onward like a hurricane, there was a flutter of wings and the bright appearance of an angel in the air, speeding forth on some heavenly mission. The engine now announced the close vicinity of the final station-house by one last and horrible scream, in which there seemed to be distinguishable every kind of wailing and woe, and bitter fierceness of wrath, all mixed up with the wild laughter of a devil or a madman. Throughout our journey, at every stopping-place, Apollyon had exercised his ingenuity in screwing the most abominable sounds out of the whistle of the steam-engine; but in this closing effort he outdid himself and created an infernal uproar, which, besides disturbing the peaceful inhabitants of Beulah, must have sent its discord even through the celestial gates.

While the horrid clamor was still ringing in our ears we heard an exulting strain, as if a thousand instruments of music, with height and depth and sweetness in their tones, at once tender and triumphant, were struck in unison, to greet the approach of some illustrious hero, who had fought the good fight and won a glorious victory, and was come to lay aside his battered arms forever. Looking to ascertain what might be the occasion of this glad harmony, I perceived, on alighting from the cars, that a multitude of shining ones had assembled on the other side of the river, to welcome two poor pilgrims, who were just emerging from its depths. They were the same whom Apollyon and ourselves had persecuted with taunts, and gibes, and scalding steam, at the commencement of our journey–the same whose unworldly aspect and impressive words had stirred my conscience amid the wild revellers of Vanity Fair.

"How amazingly well those men have got on," cried I to Mr. Smooth-it-away. "I wish we were secure of as good a reception."

"Never fear, never fear!" answered my friend. "Come, make haste; the ferry boat will be off directly, and in three minutes you will be on the other side of the river. No doubt you will find coaches to carry you up to the city gates."

A steam ferry boat, the last improvement on this important route, lay at the river side, puffing, snorting, and emitting all those other disagreeable utterances which betoken the departure to be immediate. I hurried on board with the rest of the passengers, most of whom were in great perturbation:* some bawling out for their baggage; some tearing their hair and exclaiming that the boat would explode or sink; some already pale with the heaving of the stream; some gazing affrighted at the ugly aspect of the steersman; and some still dizzy with the slumberous influences of the Enchanted Ground. Looking back to the shore, I was amazed to discern Mr. Smooth-it-away waving his hand in token of farewell.

---

perturbation: agitation

"Don't you go over to the Celestial City?" exclaimed I.

"Oh, no!" answered he with a queer smile, and that same disagreeable contortion of visage which I had remarked in the inhabitants of the Dark Valley. "Oh, no! I have come thus far only for the sake of your pleasant company. Good-by! We shall meet again.''

And then did my excellent friend Mr. Smooth-it-away laugh out-right, in the midst of which cachinnation* a smoke-wreath issued from his mouth and nostrils, while a twinkle of lurid flame darted out of either eye, proving indubitably that his heart was all of a red blaze. The impudent fiend! To deny the existence of Tophet, when he felt its fiery tortures raging within his breast. I rushed to the side of the boat, intending to fling myself on shore; but the wheels, as they began their revolutions, threw a dash of spray over me so cold–so deadly cold, with the chill that will never leave those waters until Death be drowned in his own river–that with a shiver and a heart-quake I awoke. Thank Heaven it was a Dream!

cachinnation: loud, hard laughter

The Minister's Black Veil

A Parable

The subtitle of this story, "A Parable," indicates that Hawthorne wished his readers to see a universal, symbolic level of meaning in the tale. It, therefore, is not just about a minister who wears a black veil but about us all. As a **symbol** *the veil implies the story's* **theme:** *to prevent himself from becoming hypocritical or proud, man should not hide the worst side of his nature from others–or from himself.*

The sexton* stood in the porch of Milford meeting-house, pulling busily at the bell-rope. The old people of the village came stooping along the street. Children, with bright faces, tripped merrily beside their parents, or mimicked a graver gait, in the conscious dignity of their Sunday clothes. Spruce bachelors looked sidelong at the pretty maidens, and fancied that the Sabbath sunshine made them prettier than on week days. When the throng had mostly streamed into the porch, the sexton began to toll the bell, keeping his eye on the Reverend Mr. Hooper's door. The first glimpse of the clergyman's figure was the signal for the bell to cease its summons.

sexton: a church caretaker, often responsible for bell-ringing

"But what has good Parson Hooper got upon his face?" cried the sexton in astonishment.

All within hearing immediately turned about, and beheld the semblance* of Mr. Hooper, pacing slowly his meditative way towards the meeting-house. With one accord they started, expressing more wonder than if some strange minister were coming to dust the cushions of Mr. Hooper's pulpit.

semblance: appearance

"Are you sure it is our parson?" inquired Goodman Gray of the sexton.

"Of a certainty it is good Mr. Hooper," replied the sexton. "He was to have exchanged pulpits with Parson Shute, of Westbury; but Parson Shute sent to excuse himself yesterday, being to preach a funeral sermon."

The cause of so much amazement may appear sufficiently slight. Mr. Hooper, a gentlemanly person, of about thirty, though still a bachelor, was dressed with due clerical neatness, as if a careful wife had starched his band, and brushed the weekly dust from his Sunday's garb. There was but one thing remarkable in his appearance. Swathed about his forehead, and hanging down over his face, so low as to be shaken by his breath, Mr. Hooper had on a black veil. On a nearer view it seemed to consist of two folds of crape,* which entirely concealed his features, except the mouth and chin, but probably did not intercept his sight, further than to give a darkened aspect to all living and inanimate things. With this gloomy shade before him, good Mr. Hooper walked onward, at a slow and quiet pace, stooping somewhat, and looking on the ground, as is customary with abstracted* men, yet nodding kindly to those of his parishioners who still waited on the meeting-house steps. But so wonder-struck were they that his greeting hardly met with a return.

---

crape: also crepe, a light, soft, thin fabric
abstracted: preoccupied, lost in thought

"I can't really feel as if good Mr. Hooper's face was behind that piece of crape," said the sexton.

"I don't like it," muttered an old woman, as she hobbled into the meeting-house. "He has changed himself into something awful, only by hiding his face."

"Our parson has gone mad!" cried Goodman Gray, following him across the threshold.

A rumor of some unaccountable phenomenon had preceded Mr. Hooper into the meeting-house, and set all the congregation astir. Few could refrain from twisting their heads towards the door; many stood upright, and turned directly about; while several little boys clambered upon the seats, and came down again with a terrible racket. There was a general bustle, a rustling of the women's gowns and shuffling of the men's feet, greatly at variance with that hushed repose which should attend the entrance of the minister. But Mr. Hooper appeared not to notice the perturbation of his people. He entered with an almost noiseless step, bent his head mildly to the pews on each side, and bowed as he passed his oldest parishioner, a white-haired great-grandsire, who occupied an arm-chair in the centre of the aisle. It was strange to observe how slowly this venerable man became conscious of something singular in the appearance of his pastor. He seemed not fully to partake of the prevailing wonder, till Mr. Hooper had ascended the stairs, and showed himself in the pulpit, face to face with his congregation, except for the black veil. That mysterious emblem was never once withdrawn. It shook with his measured breath, as he gave out the psalm; it threw its obscurity between him and the holy page, as he read the Scriptures; and while he prayed, the veil lay heavily on his uplifted countenance. Did he seek to hide it from the dread Being whom he was addressing?

Such was the effect of this simple piece of crape, that more than one woman of delicate nerves was forced to leave the meeting-house. Yet perhaps the pale-faced congregation was almost as fearful a sight to the minister, as his black veil to them.

Mr. Hooper had the reputation of a good preacher, but not an energetic one: he strove to win his people heavenward by mild, persuasive influences, rather than to drive them thither by the thunders of the Word. The sermon which he now delivered was marked by the same characteristics of style and manner as the general series of his pulpit oratory. But there was something, either in the sentiment* of the discourse itself, or in the imagination of the auditors, which made it greatly the most powerful effort that they had ever heard from their pastor's lips. It was tinged, rather more darkly than usual, with the gentle gloom of Mr. Hooper's temperament. The subject had reference to secret sin, and those sad mysteries which we hide from our nearest and dearest, and would fain* conceal from our own consciousness, even forgetting that the Omniscient can detect them. A subtle power was breathed into his words. Each member of the congregation, the most innocent girl, and the man of hardened breast, felt as if the preacher had crept upon them, behind his awful veil, and discovered their hoarded iniquity of deed or thought. Many spread their clasped hands on their bosoms. There was nothing terrible in what Mr. Hooper said, at least, no violence; and yet, with every tremor of his melancholy voice, the hearers quaked. An unsought pathos* came hand in hand with awe. So sensible were the audience of some unwonted* attribute in their minister, that they longed for a breath of wind to blow aside the veil, almost believing that a stranger's visage would be discovered, though the form, gesture, and voice were those of Mr. Hooper.

---

sentiment: i.e., emotional import of the passage
fain: gladly
pathos: strong feeling of sympathy or pity
unwonted: unusual

At the close of the services, the people hurried out with indecorous* confusion, eager to communicate their pent-up amazement, and conscious of lighter spirits the moment they lost sight of the black veil. Some gathered in little circles, huddled closely together, with their mouths all whispering in the centre; some went homeward alone, wrapt in silent meditation; some talked loudly, and profaned the Sabbath day with ostentatious* laughter. A few shook their sagacious* heads, intimating* that they could penetrate the mystery; while one or two affirmed that there was no mystery at all, but only that Mr. Hooper's eyes were so weakened by the midnight lamp, as to require a shade. After a brief interval, forth came good Mr. Hooper also, in the rear of his flock. Turning his veiled face from one group to another, he paid due reverence to the hoary* heads, saluted the middled aged with kind dignity as their friend and spiritual guide, greeted the young with mingled authority and love, and laid his hands on the little children's heads to bless them. Such was always his custom on the Sabbath day. Strange and bewildered looks repaid him for his courtesy. None, as on former occasions, aspired to the honor of walking by their pastor's side. Old Squire Saunders, doubtless by an accidental lapse of memory, neglected to invite Mr. Hooper to his table, where the good clergyman had been wont to bless the food, almost every Sunday since his settlement. He returned, therefore, to the parsonage, and, at the moment of closing the door, was observed to look back upon the people, all of whom had their eyes fixed upon the minister. A sad smile gleamed faintly from beneath the black veil, and flickered about his mouth, glimmering as he disappeared.

---

indecorous: lacking good taste or propriety
ostentatious: showy
sagacious: wise
intimating: implying
hoary: gray or white

"How strange," said a lady, "that a simple black veil, such as any woman might wear on her bonnet, should become such a terrible thing on Mr. Hooper's face!"

"Something must surely be amiss with Mr. Hooper's intellects," observed her husband, the physician of the village. "But the strangest part of the affair is the effect of this vagary,* even on a sober-minded man like myself. The black veil, though it covers only our pastor's face, throws its influence over his whole person, and makes him ghostlike from head to foot. Do you not feel it so?"

---

vagary: flight of imagination

"Truly I do," replied the lady; "and I would not be alone with him for the world. I wonder he is not afraid to be alone with himself!"

"Men sometimes are so," said her husband.

The afternoon service was attended with similar circumstances. At its conclusion, the bell tolled for the funeral of a young lady. The relatives and friends were assembled in the house, and the more distant acquaintances stood about the door, speaking of the good qualities of the deceased, when their talk was interrupted by the appearance of Mr. Hooper, still covered with his black veil. It was now an appropriate emblem. The clergyman stepped into the room where the corpse was laid, and bent over the coffin, to take a last farewell of his deceased parishioner. As he stooped, the veil hung straight down from his forehead, so that, if her eyelids had not been closed forever, the dead maiden might have seen his face. Could Mr. Hooper be fearful of her glance, that he so hastily caught back the black veil? A person who watched the interview between the dead and the living, scrupled* not to affirm, that, at the instant when the clergyman's features were disclosed, the corpse had slightly shuddered, rustling the shroud and muslin cap, though the countenance retained the composure of death. A superstitious old woman was the only witness of the prodigy.* From the coffin Mr. Hooper passed into the chamber of the mourners, and thence to the head of the staircase, to make the funeral prayer. It was a tender and heart-dissolving prayer, full of sorrow, yet so imbued* with celestial hopes, that the music of a heavenly harp, swept by the fingers of the dead, seemed faintly to be heard among the saddest accents of the minister. The people trembled, though they but darkly understood him when he prayed that they, and himself, and all of mortal race, might be ready, as he trusted this young maiden had been, for the dreadful hour that should snatch the veil from their faces. The bearers went heavily forth, and the mourners followed, saddening all the street, with the dead before them, and Mr. Hooper in his black veil behind.

scrupled: hesitated
prodigy: marvel, omen
imbued: saturated

"Why do you look back?" said one in the procession to his partner.

"I had a fancy," replied she, "that the minister and the maiden's spirit were walking hand in hand."

"And so had I, at the same moment," said the other.

That night, the handsomest couple in Milford village were to be joined in wedlock. Though reckoned a melancholy man, Mr. Hooper had a placid cheerfulness for such occasions, which often excited a sympathetic smile where livelier merriment would have been thrown away. There was no quality of his disposition which made him more beloved than this. The company at the wed-

ding awaited his arrival with impatience, trusting that the strange awe, which had gathered over him throughout the day, would now be dispelled. But such was not the result. When Mr. Hooper came, the first thing that their eyes rested on was the same horrible black veil, which had added deeper gloom to the funeral, and could portend* nothing but evil to the wedding. Such was its immediate effect on the guests that a cloud seemed to have rolled duskily from beneath the black crape, and dimmed the light of the candles. The bridal pair stood up before the minister. But the bride's cold fingers quivered in the tremulous* hand of the bridegroom, and her deathlike paleness caused a whisper that the maiden who had been buried a few hours before was come from her grave to be married. If ever another wedding were so dismal, it was that famous one where they tolled the wedding knell.* After performing the ceremony, Mr. Hooper raised a glass of wine to his lips, wishing happiness to the new-married couple in a strain of mild pleasantry that ought to have brightened the features of the guests, like a cheerful gleam from the hearth. At that instant, catching a glimpse of his figure in the looking-glass, the black veil involved his own spirit in the horror with which it overwhelmed all others. His frame shuddered, his lips grew white, he spilt the untasted wine upon the carpet, and rushed forth into the darkness. For the Earth, too, had on her Black Veil.

portend: foretell
tremulous: trembling
knell: slow, solemn sounding of a bell

The next day, the whole village of Milford talked of little else than Parson Hooper's black veil. That, and the mystery concealed behind it, supplied a topic for discussion between acquaintances meeting in the street, and good women gossiping at their open windows. It was the first item of news that the tavern-keeper told to his guests. The children babbled of it on their way to school. One imitative little imp covered his face with an old black handkerchief, thereby so af-

frighting his playmates that the panic seized himself, and he well-nigh lost his wits by his own waggery.*

waggery: playful behavior

It was remarkable that of all the busybodies and impertinent* people in the parish, not one ventured to put the plain question to Mr. Hooper, wherefore he did this thing. Hitherto, whenever there appeared the slightest call for such interference, he had never lacked advisers, nor shown himself averse* to be guided by their judgment. If he erred at all, it was by so painful a degree of self-distrust, that even the mildest censure* would lead him to consider an indifferent action as a crime. Yet, though so well acquainted with this amiable weakness, no individual among his parishioners chose to make the black veil a subject of friendly remonstrance.* There was a feeling of dread, neither plainly confessed nor carefully concealed, which caused each to shift the responsibility upon another, till at length it was found expedient* to send a deputation of the church, in order to deal with Mr. Hooper about the mystery, before it should grow into a scandal. Never did an embassy so ill discharge its duties. The minister received them with friendly courtesy, but became silent, after they were seated, leaving to his visitors the whole burden of introducing their important business. The topic, it might be supposed, was obvious enough. There was the black veil swathed round Mr. Hooper's forehead, and concealing every feature above his placid mouth, on which, at times, they could perceive the glimmering of a melancholy smile. But that piece of crape, to their imagination, seemed to hang down before his heart, the symbol of a fearful secret between him and them. Were the veil but cast aside, they might speak freely of it, but not till then. Thus they sat a considerable time, speechless, confused, and shrinking uneasily from Mr. Hooper's eye, which they felt to be fixed upon them with an invisible glance. Finally, the deputies returned abashed* to their constituents,* pronouncing the matter too weighty to be handled, except by a council of the churches, if, indeed, it might not require a general synod.

---

impertinent: rude
averse: reluctant
censure: disapproval
remonstrance: reproof
expedient: appropriate
abashed: ashamed
constituents: those represented by another

But there was one person in the village unappalled by the awe with which the black veil had impressed all beside herself. When the deputies returned without an explanation, or even venturing to demand one, she, with the calm energy of her character, determined to chase away the strange cloud that appeared to be settling around Mr. Hooper, every moment more darkly than before. As his plighted wife, it should be her privilege to know what the black veil concealed. At the minister's first visit, therefore, she entered upon the subject with a direct simplicity, which made the task easier both for him and her. After he had seated himself, she fixed her eyes steadfastly upon the veil, but could discern nothing of the dreadful gloom that had so overawed the multitude: it was but a double fold of crape, hanging down from his forehead to his mouth, and slightly stirring with his breath.

"No," said she aloud, and smiling, "there is nothing terrible in this piece of crape, except that it hides a face which I am always glad to look upon. Come, good sir, let the sun shine from behind the cloud. First lay aside your black veil: then tell me why you put it on."

Mr. Hooper's smile glimmered faintly.

"There is an hour to come," said he, "when all of us shall cast aside our veils. Take it not amiss, beloved friend, if I wear this piece of crape till then."

"Your words are a mystery, too," returned the young lady. "Take away the veil from them, at least."

"Elizabeth, I will," said he, "so far as my vow may suffer me. Know, then, this veil is a type and a symbol, and I am bound to wear it ever, both in light and darkness, in solitude and before the gaze of multitudes, and as with strangers, so with my familiar friends. No mortal eye will see it withdrawn. This dismal shade must separate me from the world: even you, Elizabeth, can never come behind it!"

"What grievous affliction hath befallen you," she earnestly inquired, "that you should thus darken your eyes forever?"

"If it be a sign of mourning," replied Mr. Hooper, "I, perhaps, like most other mortals, have sorrows dark enough to be typified by a black veil."

"But what if the world will not believe that it is the type of an innocent sorrow?" urged Elizabeth. "Beloved and respected as you are, there may be whispers that you hide your face under the consciousness of secret sin. For the sake of your holy office, do away this scandal!"

The color rose into her cheeks as she intimated the nature of the rumors that were already abroad in the village. But Mr. Hooper's mildness did not forsake him. He even smiled again–that same sad smile, which always appeared like a faint glimmering of light, proceeding from the obscurity beneath the veil.

"If I hide my face for sorrow, there is cause enough," he merely replied; "and if I cover it for secret sin, what mortal might not do the same?"

And with this gentle, but unconquerable obstinacy did he resist all her entreaties. At length Elizabeth sat silent. For a few moments she appeared lost in thought, considering, probably, what new methods might be tried to withdraw her lover from so dark a fantasy, which, if it had no other meaning, was perhaps a symptom of mental disease. Though of a firmer character than his own, the tears rolled down her cheeks. But, in an instant, as it were, a new feeling took the place of sorrow: her eyes were fixed insensibly on the black veil, when, like a sudden twilight in the air, its terrors fell around her. She arose, and stood trembling before him.

"And do you feel it then, at last?" said he mournfully.

She made no reply, but covered her eyes with her hand, and turned to leave the room. He rushed forward and caught her arm.

"Have patience with me, Elizabeth!" cried he, passionately. "Do not desert me, though this veil must be between us here on earth. Be mine, and hereafter there shall be no veil over my face, no darkness between our souls! It is but a mortal veil–it is not for eternity! O! you know not how lonely I am, and how frightened, to be alone behind my black veil. Do not leave me in this miserable obscurity forever!"

"Lift the veil but once, and look me in the face," said she.

"Never! It cannot be!" replied Mr. Hooper.

"Then farewell!" said Elizabeth.

She withdrew her arm from his grasp, and slowly departed, pausing at the door, to give one long shuddering gaze, that seemed almost to penetrate the mystery of the black veil. But, even amid his grief, Mr. Hooper smiled to think that only a material emblem had separated him from happiness, though the horrors, which it shadowed forth, must be drawn darkly between the fondest of lovers.

From that time no attempts were made to remove Mr. Hooper's black veil, or, by a direct appeal, to discover the secret which it was supposed to hide. By persons who claimed a superiority to popular prejudice, it was reckoned merely an eccentric whim, such as often mingles with the sober actions of men otherwise rational, and tinges them all with its own semblance of insanity.

But with the multitude, good Mr. Hooper was irreparably* a bugbear.* He could not walk the street with any peace of mind, so conscious was he that the gentle and timid would turn aside to avoid him, and that others would make it a point of hardihood to throw themselves in his way. The impertinence of the latter class compelled him to give up his customary walk at sunset to the burial ground; for when he leaned pensively* over the gate, there would always be faces behind the gravestones, peeping at his black veil. A fable went the rounds that the stare of the dead people drove him thence. It grieved him, to the very depth of his kind heart, to observe how the children fled from his approach, breaking up their merriest sports, while his melancholy figure was yet afar off. Their instinctive dread caused him to feel more strongly than aught else, that a preternatural* horror was interwoven with the threads of the black crape. In truth, his own antipathy* to the veil was known to be so great, that he never willingly passed before a mirror, nor stooped to drink at a still fountain, lest, in its peaceful bosom, he should be affrighted by himself. This was what gave plausibility* to the whispers, that Mr. Hooper's conscience tortured him for some great crime too horrible to be entirely concealed, or otherwise than so obscurely intimated. Thus, from beneath the black veil, there rolled a cloud into the sunshine, an ambiguity of sin or sorrow, which enveloped the poor minister, so that love or sympathy could never reach him. It was said that ghost and fiend consorted with him there. With self-shudderings and outward terrors, he walked continually in its shadow, groping darkly within his own soul, or gazing through a medium that saddened the whole world. Even the lawless wind, it was believed, respected his dreadful secret, and never blew aside the veil. But still good Mr. Hooper sadly smiled at the pale visages of the worldly throng as he passed by.

irreparably: beyond repair
bugbear: object of excessive dread
pensively: thoughfully
preternatural: abnormal
antipathy: opposition
plausibility: likelihood

Among all its bad influences, the black veil had the one desirable effect, of making its wearer a very efficient clergyman. By the aid of his mysterious emblem–for there was no other apparent cause–he became a man of awful power over souls that were in agony for sin. His converts always regarded him with a dread peculiar to themselves, affirming, though but figuratively, that, before he brought them to celestial light, they had been with him behind the black veil. Its gloom, indeed, enabled him to sympathize with all dark affections. Dying sinners cried aloud for Mr. Hooper, and would not yield their breath till he appeared; though ever, as he stooped to whisper consolation, they shuddered at the veiled face so near their own. Such were the terrors of the black veil, even when Death had bared his visage! Strangers came long distances to attend service at his church, with the mere idle purpose of gazing at his figure, because it was forbidden them to behold his face. But many were made to quake ere they departed! Once, during Governor Belcher's administration, Mr. Hooper was appointed to preach the election sermon.* Covered with his black veil, he stood before the chief magistrate, the council, and the representatives, and wrought so deep an impression, that the legislative measures of that year were characterized by all the gloom and piety of our earliest ancestral sway.

election sermon: delivered at the time of elections in New England

In this manner Mr. Hooper spent a long life, irreproachable in outward act, yet shrouded in dismal suspicions; kind and loving, though unloved, and dimly feared; a man apart from men, shunned in their health and joy, but ever summoned to their aid in mortal anguish. As years wore on, shedding their snows above his sable

veil, he acquired a name throughout the New England churches, and they called him Father Hooper. Nearly all his parishioners, who were of mature age when he was settled, had been borne away by many a funeral: he had one congregation in the church, and a more crowded one in the churchyard; and having wrought so late into the evening, and done his work so well, it was now good Father Hooper's turn to rest.

Several persons were visible by the shaded candle-light, in the death chamber of the old clergyman. Natural connections he had none. But there was the decorously* grave, though unmoved physician, seeking only to mitigate* the last pangs of the patient whom he could not save. There were the deacons, and other eminently pious members of his church. There, also, was the Reverend Mr. Clark, of Westbury, a young and zealous divine, who had ridden in haste to pray by the bedside of the expiring minister. There was the nurse, no hired handmaiden of death, but one whose calm affection had endured thus long in secrecy, in solitude, amid the chill of age, and would not perish, even at the dying hour. Who, but Elizabeth! And there lay the hoary head of good Father Hooper upon the death pillow, with the black veil still swathed about his brow, and reaching down his face, so that each more difficult gasp of his faint breath caused it to stir. All through life that piece of crape had hung between him and the world: it had separated him from cheerful brotherhood and woman's love, and kept him in that saddest of all prisons, his own heart; and still it lay upon his face, as if to deepen the gloom of his darksome chamber, and shade him from the sunshine of eternity.

decorously: properly
mitigate: moderate

For some time previous, his mind had been confused, wavering doubtfully between the past and the present, and hovering foreward, as it were, at intervals, into the indistinctness of the world to come. There had been feverish turns,

which tossed him from side to side, and wore away what little strength he had. But in his most convulsive struggles, and in the wildest vagaries of his intellect, when no other thought retained its sober influence, he still showed an awful solicitude lest the black veil should slip aside. Even if his bewildered soul could have forgotten, there was a faithful woman at his pillow, who, with averted eyes, would have covered that aged face,* which she had last beheld in the comeliness of manhood. At length the death-stricken old man lay quietly in the torpor* of mental and bodily exhaustion, with an imperceptible* pulse, and breath that grew fainter and fainter, except when a long, deep, and irregular inspiration* seemed to prelude* the flight of his spirit.

covered . . . face: cf. Genesis 9:23
torpor: inactivity
imperceptible: not perceived, not felt
inspiration: the act of breathing in
prelude: introduce

The minister of Westbury approached the bedside.

"Venerable Father Hooper," said he, "the moment of your release is at hand. Are you ready for the lifting of the veil that shuts in time from eternity?"

Father Hooper at first replied merely by a feeble motion of his head; then, apprehensive, perhaps, that his meaning might be doubtful, he exerted himself to speak.

"Yea," said he, in faint accents, "my soul hath a patient weariness until that veil be lifted."

"And is it fitting," resumed Reverend Mr. Clark, "that a man so given to prayer, of such a blameless example, holy in deed and thought, so far as mortal judgment may pronounce; is it fitting that a father in the church should leave a shadow on his memory, that may seem to blacken a life so pure? I pray you, my venerable brother, let not this thing be! Suffer us to be gladdened by your triumphant aspect* as you go to your reward. Before the veil of eternity be lifted, let me cast aside this black veil from your face!"

aspect: a particular facial expression

And thus speaking, the Reverend Mr. Clark bent forward to reveal the mystery of so many years. But, exerting a sudden energy, that made all the beholders stand aghast, Father Hooper snatched both his hands from beneath the bedclothes, and pressed them strongly on the black veil, resolute to struggle, if the minister of Westbury would contend with a dying man.

"Never!" cried the veiled clergyman. "On earth, never!"

"Dark old man!" exclaimed the affrighted minister, "with what horrible crime upon your soul are you now passing to the judgment?"

Father Hooper's breath heaved; it rattled in his throat; but, with a mighty effort, grasping forward with his hands, he caught hold of life, and held it back till he should speak. He even raised himself in bed; and there he sat, shivering with the arms of death around him, while the black veil hung down, awful, at that last moment, in the gathered terrors of a lifetime. And yet the faint, sad smile, so often there, now seemed to glimmer from its obscurity, and linger on Father Hooper's lips.

"Why do you tremble at me alone?" cried he, turning his veiled face round the circle of pale spectators. "Tremble also at each other! Have men avoided me, and women shown no pity, and children screamed and fled, only for my black veil? What, but the mystery which it obscurely typifies, has made this piece of crape so awful? When the friend shows his inmost heart to his friend; the lover to his best beloved; when man does not vainly shrink from the eye of the Creator, loathsomely treasuring up the secret of his sin; then deem me a monster, for the symbol beneath which I have lived, and die! I look around me, and lo! on every visage a Black Veil!"

While his auditors shrank from one another, in mutual affright, Father Hooper fell back upon his pillow, a veiled corpse, with a faint smile lingering on the lips. Still veiled, they laid him in his coffin, and a veiled corpse they bore him to the grave. The grass of many years has sprung up and withered on that grave, the burial stone is moss-grown, and good Mr. Hooper's face is dust; but awful is still the thought that it mouldered beneath the Black Veil!

The Birthmark

"The Birthmark," first published in 1843, is an early example of the mad scientist story. Hawthorne characteristically made the tale center more on moral issues than on bizarre events. This tale strongly condemns the egotism of science as well as the romantic dreams of creating perfection on earth (see Emerson and Thoreau). Notice Hawthorne's strategy of characterization in this story. Georgiana is the most fully realized of the three characters. She can be called a **round character** *because of her lifelikeness. Aylmer and his laboratory assistant, Aminadab, both are two-dimensional,* **flat characters.** *Hawthorne seems to make these two figures complementary: Aylmer represents the mental part of mankind; Aminadab, the fleshy part.*

In the latter part of the last century there lived a man of science, an eminent* proficient in every branch of natural philosophy, who not long before our story opens had made experience of a spiritual affinity* more attractive than any chemical one. He had left his laboratory to the care of an assistant, cleared his fine countenance from the furnace smoke, washed the stain of acids from his fingers, and persuaded a beautiful woman to become his wife. In those days when the comparatively recent discovery of electricity and other kindred mysteries of Nature seemed to open paths into the region of miracle, it was not unusual for the love of science to rival the love of woman in its depth and absorbing energy. The higher intellect, the imagination, the spirit, and even the heart might all find their congenial* aliment* in pursuits which, as some of their ardent votaries believed, would ascend from one step of powerful intelligence to another, until the philosopher should lay his hand on the secret of creative force and perhaps make new worlds for himself. We know not whether Aylmer possessed this degree of faith in man's ultimate control over Nature. He had devoted himself, however, too unreservedly to scientific studies ever to be weaned from them by any second passion. His love for his young wife might prove the stronger of the two; but it could only be by intertwining itself with his love of science, and uniting the strength of the latter to his own.

---

eminent: i.e., an outstanding person
affinity: relationship
congenial: sympathetic
aliment: support

Such a union accordingly took place, and was attended with truly remarkable consequences and a deeply impressive moral. One day, very soon after their marriage, Aylmer sat gazing at his wife with a trouble in his countenance that grew stronger until he spoke.

"Georgiana," said he, "has it never occurred to you that the mark upon your cheek might be removed?"

"No, indeed," said she, smiling; but perceiving the seriousness of his manner, she blushed deeply. "To tell you the truth it has been so often called a charm that I was simple enough to imagine it might be so."

"Ah, upon another face perhaps it might," replied her husband; "but never on yours. No,

dearest Georgiana, you came so nearly perfect from the hand of Nature that this slightest possible defect, which we hesitate whether to term a defect or a beauty, shocks me, as being the visible mark of earthly imperfection."

"Shocks you, my husband!" cried Georgiana, deeply hurt; at first reddening with momentary anger, but then bursting into tears. "Then why did you take me from my mother's side? You cannot love what shocks you!"

To explain this conversation it must be mentioned that in the centre of Georgiana's left cheek there was a singular mark, deeply interwoven, as it were, with the texture and substance of her face. In the usual state of her complexion–a healthy though delicate bloom–the mark wore a tint of deeper crimson, which imperfectly defined its shape amid the surrounding rosiness. When she

blushed it gradually became more indistinct, and finally vanished amid the triumphant rush of blood that bathed the whole cheek with its brilliant glow. But if any shifting motion caused her to turn pale there was the mark again, a crimson stain upon the snow, in what Aylmer sometimes deemed an almost fearful distinctness. Its shape bore not a little similarity to the human hand, though of the smallest pygmy size. Georgiana's lovers were wont to say that some fairy at her birth hour had laid her tiny hand upon the infant's cheek, and left this impress there in token of the magic endowments* that were to give her such sway over all hearts. Many a desperate swain* would have risked life for the privilege of pressing his lips to the mysterious hand. It must not be concealed, however, that the impression wrought by this fairy sign manual* varied exceedingly, according to the difference of temperament in the beholders. Some fastidious persons–but they were exclusively of her own sex–affirmed that the bloody hand, as they chose to call it, quite destroyed the effect of Georgiana's beauty, and rendered her countenance even hideous. But it would be as reasonable to say that one of those small blue stains which sometimes occur in the purest statuary marble would convert the Eve of Powers* to a monster. Masculine observers, if the birthmark did not heighten their admiration, contented themselves with wishing it away, that the world might possess one living specimen of ideal loveliness without the semblance* of a flaw. After his marriage,—for he thought little or nothing about the matter before,—Aylmer discovered that this was the case with himself.

endowments: natural qualities or attributes
swain: lover
manual: pertaining to the hands
Eve of Powers: nineteenth-century statue titled *Eve Before the Fall*
semblance. barest trace

Had she been less beautiful,–if Envy's self could have found aught else to sneer at,–he might have felt his affection heightened by the prettiness of this mimic hand, now vaguely portrayed, now lost, now stealing forth again and glimmering to and fro with every pulse of emotion that throbbed within her heart; but seeing her otherwise so perfect, he found this one defect grow more and more intolerable with every moment of their united lives. It was the fatal flaw of humanity which Nature, in one shape or another, stamps ineffaceably* on all her productions, either to imply that they are temporary and finite, or that their perfection must be wrought by toil and pain. The crimson hand expressed the ineludible* gripe* in which mortality clutches the highest and purest of earthly mold, degrading them into kindred with the lowest, and even with the very brutes, like whom their visible frames return to dust. In this manner, selecting it as the symbol of his wife's liability* to sin, sorrow, decay, and death, Aylmer's sombre imagination was not long in rendering the birthmark a frightful object, causing him more trouble and horror than ever Georgiana's beauty, whether of soul or sense, had given him delight.

---

ineffaceably: indelibly
ineludible: inescapable
gripe: grip, grasp
liability: likelihood

At all the seasons which should have been their happiest, he invariably and without intending it, nay, in spite of a purpose to the contrary, reverted to this one disastrous topic. Trifling as it at first appeared, it so connected itself with innumerable trains of thought and modes of feeling that it became the central point of all. With the morning twilight Aylmer opened his eyes upon his wife's face and recognized the symbol of imperfection; and when they sat together at the evening hearth his eyes wandered stealthily to her cheek, and beheld, flickering with the blaze of the wood fire, the spectral* hand that wrote mortality where he would fain* have worshipped. Georgiana soon learned to shudder at his gaze. It needed but a glance with the peculiar expression that his face often wore to change the roses of her cheek into a deathlike paleness, amid which the crimson hand was brought strongly out, like a bas-relief* of ruby on the whitest marble.

---

spectral: ghostlike
fain: gladly
bas-relief: low relief: i.e., slight projection of a sculptured figure from a flat background

---

Late one night when the lights were growing dim, so as hardly to betray the stain on the poor wife's cheek, she herself, for the first time, voluntarily took up the subject.

"Do your remember, my dear Aylmer," said she, with a feeble attempt at a smile, "have you any recollection of a dream last night about this odious* hand?"

---

odious: offensive

"None! none whatever!" replied Aylmer, starting; but then he added, in a dry, cold tone, affected for the sake of concealing the real depth of his emotion, "I might well dream of it; for before I fell asleep it had taken a pretty firm hold on my fancy."

"And you did dream of it?" continued Georgiana, hastily; for she dreaded lest a gush of tears should interrupt what she had to say. "A terrible dream! I wonder that you can forget it. Is it possible to forget this one expression?–'It is in her heart now; we must have it out!' Reflect, my husband; for by all means I would have you recall that dream."

The mind is in a sad state when Sleep, the all-involving, cannot confine her spectres within the dim region of her sway, but suffers them to break forth, affrighting this actual life with secrets that perchance* belong to a deeper one. Aylmer now remembered his dream. He had fancied himself with his servant Aminadab, attempting an operation for the removal of the birthmark; but the deeper went the knife, the deeper sank the hand, until at length its tiny grasp appeared to have caught hold of Georgiana's heart; whence, however, her husband was inexorably resolved* to cut or wrench it away.

perchance: perhaps
inexorably resolved: unyielding in his resolve

When the dream had shaped itself perfectly in his memory, Aylmer sat in his wife's presence with a guilty feeling. Truth often finds its way to the mind close muffled in robes of sleep, and then speaks with uncompromising directness of matters in regard to which we practice an unconscious self-deception during our waking moments. Until now he had not been aware of the tyrannizing influence acquired by one idea over his mind, and of the lengths which he might find in his heart to go for the sake of giving himself peace.

"Aylmer," resumed Georgiana, solemnly, "I know not what may be the cost to both of us to rid me of this fatal birthmark. Perhaps its removal may cause cureless deformity; or it may be the stain goes as deep as life itself. Again: do we know that there is a possibility, on any terms, of unclasping the firm gripe of this little hand which was laid upon me before I came into the world?"

"Dearest Georgiana, I have spent much thought upon the subject," hastily interrupted Aylmer. "I am convinced of the perfect practicability of its removal."

"If there be the remotest possibility of it," continued Georgiana, "let the attempt be made at whatever risk. Danger is nothing to me; for life, while this hateful mark makes me the object of your horror and disgust,–life is a burden which I would fling down with joy. Either remove this dreadful hand, or take my wretched life! You have deep science. All the world bears witness of it. You have achieved great wonders. Cannot you remove this little, little mark, which I cover with the tips of two small fingers? Is this beyond your power, for the sake of your own peace, and to save your poor wife from madness?"

"Noblest, dearest, tenderest wife," cried Aylmer, rapturously, "doubt not my power. I have already given this matter the deepest thought–thought which might almost have enlightened me to create a being less perfect than

yourself. Georgiana, you have led me deeper than ever into the heart of science. I feel myself fully competent to render this dear cheek as faultless as its fellow; and then, most beloved, what will be my triumph when I shall have corrected what Nature left imperfect in her fairest work! Even Pygmalion, when his sculptured woman assumed life, felt not greater ecstasy than mine will be."

Pygmalion: mythological king who fell in love with a statue

"It is resolved, then," said Georgiana, faintly smiling. "And, Aylmer, spare me not, though you should find the birthmark take refuge in my heart at last."

Her husband tenderly kissed her cheek–her right cheek–not that which bore the impress of the crimson hand.

The next day Aylmer apprised* his wife of a plan that he had formed whereby he might have opportunity for the intense thought and constant watchfulness which the proposed operation would require; while Georgiana, likewise, would enjoy the perfect repose* essential to its success. They were to seclude themselves in the extensive apartments occupied by Aylmer as a laboratory, and where, during his toilsome youth, he had made discoveries in the elemental powers of Nature that had roused the admiration of all the learned societies in Europe. Seated calmly in this laboratory, the pale philosopher had investigated the secrets of the highest cloud region and of the profoundest mines; he had satisfied himself of the causes that kindled and kept alive the fires of the volcano; and had explained the mystery of fountains, and how it is that they gush forth, some so bright and pure, and others with such rich medicinal virtues, from the dark bosom of the earth. Here, too, at an earlier period, he had studied the wonders of the human frame, and attempted to fathom the very process by which Nature assimilates* all her precious influences from earth and air, and from the spiritual world, to create and foster man, her masterpiece. The latter pursuit, however, Aylmer had long laid aside in unwilling recognition of the truth–against which all seekers sooner or later stumble—that our great creative Mother, while she amuses us with apparently working in the broadest sunshine, is yet severely careful to keep her own secrets, and, in spite of her pretended openness, shows us nothing but results. She permits us, indeed, to mar, but seldom to mend, and, like a jealous patentee,* on no account to make. Now, however, Aylmer resumed these half-forgotten investigations; not, of course, with such hopes or wishes as first suggested them; but because they involved much physiological* truth and lay in the path of his proposed scheme for the treatment of Georgiana.

apprised: informed
repose: rest
assimilates: transforms
patentee: one given an exclusive right
physiological: pertaining to the normal function of a living organism

As he led her over the threshold of the laboratory, Georgiana was cold and tremulous. Aylmer looked cheerfully into her face, with intent to reassure her, but was so startled with the intense glow of the birthmark upon the whiteness of her cheek that he could not restrain a strong convulsive shudder. His wife fainted.

"Aminadab! Aminadab!" shouted Aylmer, stamping violently on the floor.

Forthwith there issued from an inner apartment a man of low stature, but bulky frame, with shaggy hair hanging about his visage, which was grimed with the vapors of the furnace. This personage had been Aylmer's underworker during his whole scientific career, and was admirably fitted for that office by his great mechanical readiness, and the skill with which, while incapable of comprehending a single principle, he executed all the details of his master's experiments. With his vast strength, his shaggy hair, his smoky aspect, and the indescribable earthiness that incrusted him, he seemed to represent man's physical nature; while Aylmer's slender figure, and pale, intellectual face, were no less apt a type of the spiritual element.

"Throw open the door of the boudoir, Aminadab," said Aylmer, "and burn a pastil."*

pastil: a tablet burned to deodorize the air

"Yes, master," answered Aminadab, looking intently at the lifeless form of Georgiana; and then he muttered to himself, "If she were my wife, I'd never part with that birthmark."

When Georgiana recovered consciousness she found herself breathing an atmosphere of penetrating fragrance, the gentle potency of which had recalled her from her deathlike faintness. The scene around her looked like enchantment. Aylmer had converted those smoky, dingy, sombre rooms, where he had spent his brightest years in recondite* pursuits, into a series of beautiful apartments not unfit to be the secluded abode of a lovely woman. The walls were hung with gorgeous curtains, which imparted the combination of grandeur and grace that no other species of adornment can achieve; and as they fell from the ceiling to the floor, their rich and ponderous* folds, concealing all angles and straight lines, appeared to shut in the scene from infinite space. For aught Georgiana knew, it might be a pavilion* among the clouds. And Aylmer, excluding the sunshine, which would have interfered with his chemical processes, had supplied its place with perfumed lamps, emitting flames of various hue, but all uniting in a soft, impurpled radiance. He now knelt by his wife's side, watching her earnestly, but without alarm; for he was confident in his science, and felt that he could draw a magic circle round her within which no evil might intrude.

recondite: delving into matters difficult to understand
ponderous: massive
pavilion: an ornate tent

"Where am I? Ah, I remember," said Georgiana, faintly; and she placed her hand over her cheek to hide the terrible mark from her husband's eyes.

"Fear not, dearest!" exclaimed he. "Do not shrink from me! Believe me, Georgiana, I even rejoice in this single imperfection, since it will be such a rapture to remove it."

"Oh, spare me!" sadly replied his wife. "Pray do not look at it again. I never can forget that convulsive shudder."

In order to soothe Georgiana, and, as it were, to release her mind from the burden of actual things, Aylmer now put in practice some of the light and playful secrets which science had taught him among its profounder lore. Airy figures, absolutely bodiless ideas, and forms of unsubstantial beauty came and danced before her, imprinting their momentary footsteps on beams of light. Though she had some indistinct idea of the method of these optical phenomena, still the illusion was almost perfect enough to warrant the belief that her husband possessed sway over the spiritual world. Then again, when she felt a wish to look forth from her seclusion, immediately, as if her thoughts were answered, the procession of external existence flitted across a screen. The scenery and the figures of actual life were perfectly represented, but with that bewitching, yet indescribable difference which always makes a picture, an image, or a shadow so much more attractive than the original. When wearied of this, Aylmer bade her cast her eyes upon a vessel containing a quantity of earth. She did so, with little interest at first; but was soon startled to perceive the germ of a plant shooting upward from the soil. Then came the slender stalk; the leaves gradually unfolded themselves; and amid them was a perfect and lovely flower.

"It is magical!" cried Georgiana. "I dare not touch it."

"Nay, pluck it," answered Aylmer,—"pluck it, and inhale its brief perfume while you may. The flower will wither in a few moments and leave nothing save its brown seed vessels; but thence may be perpetuated a race as ephemeral* as itself."

ephemeral: short-lived

But Georgiana had no sooner touched the flower than the whole plant suffered a blight,* its leaves turning coalblack as if by the agency of fire.

blight: an environmental condition that injures or kills

"There was too powerful a stimulus," said Aylmer, thoughtfully.

To make up for this abortive* experiment, he proposed to take her portrait by a scientific process of his own invention. It was to be effected by rays of light striking upon a polished plate of metal. Georgiana assented; but, on looking at the result, was affrighted to find the features of the portrait blurred and indefinable; while the minute figure of a hand appeared where the cheek should have been. Aylmer snatched the metallic plate and threw it into a jar of corrosive acid.

abortive: fruitless

Soon, however, he forgot these mortifying failures. In the intervals of study and chemical experiment he came to her flushed and exhausted, but seemed invigorated by her presence, and spoke in glowing language of the resources of his art. He gave a history of the long dynasty of the alchemists,* who spent so many ages in quest of the universal solvent by which the golden principle might be elicited* from all things vile and base. Aylmer appeared to believe that, by the plainest scientific logic, it was altogether within the limits of possibility to discover this long-sought medium; "but," he added, "a philosopher who should go deep enough to acquire the power would attain too lofty a wisdom to stoop to the exercise of it." Not less singular were his opinions in regard to the elixir vitae.* He more than intimated that it was at his option to concoct a liquid that should prolong life for years, perhaps interminably; but that it would produce a discord in Nature which all the world, and chiefly the quaffer* of the immortal nostrum,* would find cause to curse.

alchemists: psuedoscientists who tried to make gold
elicited: brought out
elixir vitae: lit. elixir of life (Elixir is a medicinal potion believed to possess unusual powers.)
quaffer: i.e., the one who drinks
nostrum: quack potion

"Aylmer, are you in earnest?" asked Georgiana, looking at him with amazement and fear. "It is terrible to possess such power, or even dream of possessing it."

"Oh, do not tremble, my love," said her husband. "I would not wrong either you or myself by working such inharmonious effects upon our lives; but I would have you consider how trifling, in comparison, is the skill requisite* to remove this little hand."

requisite: necessary

At the mention of the birthmark, Georgiana, as usual, shrank as if a redhot iron had touched her cheek.

Again Aylmer applied himself to his labors. She could hear his voice in the distant furnace room giving directions to Aminadab, whose harsh, uncouth, misshapen tones were audible in response, more like the grunt or growl of a brute than human speech. After hours of absence, Aylmer reappeared and proposed that she should now examine his cabinet of chemical products and natural treasures of the earth. Among the former he showed her a small vial, in which, he remarked, was contained a gentle yet most powerful fragrance, capable of impregnating* all the breezes that blow across the kingdom. They were of inestimable value, the contents of that little vial; and, as he said so, he threw some of the perfume into the air and filled the room with piercing and invigorating delight.

impregnating: saturating

"And what is this?" asked Georgiana, pointing to a small crystal globe containing a gold-colored liquid. "It is so beautiful to the eye that I could imagine it the elixir of life."

"In one sense it is," replied Aylmer; "or, rather, the elixir of immortality. It is the most precious poison that ever was concocted in this world. By its aid I could apportion* the lifetime of any mortal at whom you might point your finger. The strength of the dose would determine whether he were to linger out years, or drop dead in the midst of a breath. No king on his guarded throne could keep his life if I, in my private station, should deem that the welfare of millions justified me in depriving him of it."

apportion: allot

"Why do you keep such a terrific drug?" inquired Georgiana in horror.

"Do not mistrust me, dearest," said her husband, smiling; "its virtuous potency is yet greater than its harmful one. But see! here is a powerful cosmetic. With a few drops of this in a vase of water, freckles may be washed away as easily as the hands are cleansed. A stronger infusion would take the blood out of the cheek, and leave the rosiest beauty a pale ghost.''

''Is it with this lotion that you intend to bathe my cheek?'' asked Georgiana, anxiously.

''Oh, no,'' hastily replied her husband; ''this is merely superficial. Your case demands a remedy that shall go deeper.''

In his interviews with Georgiana, Aylmer generally made minute inquiries as to her sensations and whether the confinement of the rooms and the temperature of the atmosphere agreed with her. These questions had such a particular drift that Georgiana began to conjecture that she was already subjected to certain physical influences, either breathed in with the fragrant air or taken with her food. She fancied likewise, but it might be altogether fancy, that there was a stirring up of her system—a strange, indefinite sensation creeping through her veins, and tingling, half painfully, half pleasurably, at her heart. Still, whenever she dared to look into the mirror, there she beheld herself pale as a white rose and with the crimson birthmark stamped upon her cheek. Not even Aylmer now hated it so much as she.

To dispel the tedium of the hours which her husband found it necessary to devote to the processes of combination and analysis, Georgiana turned over the volumes of his scientific library. In many dark old tomes* she met with chapters full of romance and poetry. There were the works of the philosophers of the middle ages, such as Albertus Magnus, Cornelius Agrippa, Paracelsus, and the famous friar who created the prophetic Brazen Head. All these antique naturalists stood in advance of their centuries, yet were imbued with some of their credulity,* and therefore were believed, and perhaps imagined themselves to have acquired from the investigation of Nature a power above Nature, and from physics a sway over the spiritual world. Hardly less curious and imaginative were the early volumes of the Transactions of the Royal Society, in which the members, knowing little of the limits of natural possibility, were

continually recording wonders or proposing methods whereby wonders might be wrought.

tomes: large scholarly books
credulity: gullibility

But to Georgiana the most engrossing volume was a large folio* from her husband's own hand, in which he had recorded every experiment of his scientific career, its original aim, the methods adopted for its development, and its final success or failure, with the circumstances to which either event was attributable. The book, in truth, was both the history and emblem of his ardent, ambitious, imaginative, yet practical and laborious life. He handled physical details as if there were nothing beyond them; yet spiritualized them all, and redeemed himself from materialism by his strong and eager aspiration towards the infinite. In his grasp the veriest* clod of earth assumed a soul. Georgiana, as she read, reverenced Aylmer and loved him more profoundly than ever, but with a less entire dependence on his judgment than heretofore. Much as he had accomplished, she could not but observe that most splendid successes were almost invariably failures, if compared with the ideal at which he aimed. His brightest diamonds were the merest pebbles, and felt to be so by himself, in comparison with the inestimable gems which lay hidden beyond his reach. The volume, rich with achievements that had won renown for its author, was yet as melancholy a record as ever mortal hand had penned. It was the sad confession and continual exemplification* of the shortcomings of the composite* man, the spirit burdened with clay and working in matter, and of the despair that assails* the higher nature at finding itself so miserably thwarted by the earthly part. Perhaps every man of genius in whatever sphere might recognize the image of his own experience in Aylmer's journal.

folio: large-sized manuscript
veriest: truest
exemplification: example
composite: compound
assails: attacks

So deeply did these reflections affect Georgiana that she laid her face upon the open volume and burst into tears. In this situation she was found by her husband.

"It is dangerous to read in a sorcerer's books," said he with a smile, though his countenance was uneasy and displeased. "Georgiana, there are pages in that volume which I can scarcely glance over and keep my senses. Take heed lest it prove as detrimental to you."

"It has made me worship you more than ever," said she.

"Ah, wait for this one success," rejoined he, "then worship if you will. I shall deem myself hardly unworthy of it. But come, I have sought you for the luxury of your voice. Sing to me, dearest."

So she poured out the liquid music of her voice to quench the thirst of his spirit. He then took his leave with a boyish exuberance of gaiety, assuring her that her seclusion would endure but a little longer, and that the result was already certain. Scarcely had he departed when Georgiana felt irresistibly impelled to follow him. She had forgotten to inform Aylmer of a symptom which for two or three hours past had begun to excite her attention. It was a sensation in the fatal birthmark, not painful, but which induced a restlessness throughout her system. Hastening after her husband, she intruded for the first time into the laboratory.

The first thing that struck her eye was the furnace, that hot and feverish worker, with the intense glow of its fire, which by the quantities of soot clustered above it seemed to have been burning for ages. There was a distilling apparatus in full operation. Around the room were retorts, tubes, cylinders, crucibles, and other apparatus of chemical research. An electrical machine stood ready for immediate use. The atmosphere felt oppressively close; and was tainted with gaseous odors which had been tormented forth by the processes of science. The severe and homely simplicity of the apartment with its naked walls and brick pavement, looked strange, accustomed as Georgiana had become to the fantastic elegance of her boudoir.* But what chiefly, indeed almost solely, drew her attention, was the aspect of Aylmer himself.

boudoir: woman's private sitting room

He was pale as death, anxious and absorbed, and hung over the furnace as if it depended upon his utmost watchfulness whether the liquid which it was distilling should be the draught* of immortal happiness or misery. How different from the sanguine* and joyous mien* that he had assumed for Georgiana's encouragement!

draught: drink
sanguine: cheerful
mien: expression

"Carefully now, Aminadab; carefully, thou human machine; carefully, thou man of clay!" muttered Aylmer, more to himself than his assistant. "Now, if there be a thought too much or too little, it is all over."

"Ho! ho!" mumbled Aminadab. "Look, master! look!"

Aylmer raised his eyes hastily, and at first reddened, then grew paler than ever, on beholding Georgiana. He rushed towards her and seized her arm with a gripe that left the print of his fingers upon it.

"Why do you come hither? Have you no trust in your husband?" cried he, impetuously. "Would you throw the blight of that fatal birthmark over my labors? It is not well done. Go, prying woman, go!"

"Nay, Aylmer," said Georgiana with the firmness of which she possessed no stinted* endowment, "it is not you that have a right to complain. You mistrust your wife; you have concealed the anxiety with which you watch the development of this experiment. Think not so unworthily of me, my husband. Tell me all the risk we run, and fear not that I shall shrink; for my share in it is far less than your own."

stinted: limited

"No, no, Georgiana!" said Aylmer, impatiently; "it must not be."

"I submit," replied she calmly. "And, Aylmer, I shall quaff whatever draught you bring me; but it will be on the same principle that would induce me to take a dose of poison if offered by your hand."

"My noble wife," said Aylmer, deeply moved; "I knew not the height and depth of your nature until now. Nothing shall be concealed. Know, then, that this crimson hand, superficial as it seems, has clutched its grasp into your being with a strength of which I had no previous conception. I have already administered agents powerful enough to do aught except to change your entire physical system. Only one thing remains to be tried. If that fails us we are ruined."

"Why did you hesitate to tell me this?" asked she.

"Because, Georgiana," said Aylmer, in a low voice, "there is danger."

"Danger? There is but one danger—that this horrible stigma shall be left upon my cheek!" cried Georgiana. "Remove it, remove it, whatever be the cost, or we shall both go mad!"

"Heaven knows your words are too true," said Aylmer, sadly. "And now, dearest, return to your boudoir. In a little while all will be tested."

He conducted her back and took leave of her with a solemn tenderness which spoke far more than his words how much was now at stake. After his departure Georgiana became rapt in musings. She considered the character of Aylmer, and did it completer justice than at any previous moment. Her heart exulted, while it trembled, at his honorable love—so pure and lofty that it would accept nothing less than perfection nor miserably make itself contented with an earthlier nature than he had dreamed of. She felt how much more precious was such a sentiment than that meaner kind which would have borne with the imperfection for her sake, and have been guilty of treason to holy love

by degrading its perfect idea to the level of the actual; and with her whole spirit she prayed that, for a single moment, she might satisfy his highest and deepest conception. Longer than one moment she well knew it could not be; for his spirit was ever on the march, ever ascending, and each instant required something that was beyond the scope of the instant before.

The sound of her husband's footsteps aroused her. He bore a crystal goblet containing a liquor colorless as water, but bright enough to be the draught of immortality. Aylmer was pale; but it seemed rather the consequence of a highly-wrought state of mind and tension of spirit than of fear or doubt.

"The concoction of the draught has been perfect," said he, in answer to Georgiana's look. "Unless my science have deceived me, it cannot fail."

"Save on your account, my dearest Aylmer," observed his wife, "I might wish to put off this birthmark of mortality by relinquishing mortality itself in preference to any other mode. Life is but a sad possession to those who have attained precisely the degree of moral advancement at which I stand. Were I weaker and blinder it might be happiness. Were I stronger, it might be endured hopefully. But, being what I find myself, me thinks I am of all mortals the most fit to die."

"You are fit for heaven without tasting death!" replied her husband. "But why do we speak of dying? The draught cannot fail. Behold its effect upon this plant."

On the window seat there stood a geranium diseased with yellow blotches, which had overspread all its leaves. Aylmer poured a small quantity of the liquid upon the soil in which it grew. In a little time, when the roots of the plant had taken up the moisture, the unsightly blotches began to be extinguished in a living verdure.

"There needed no proof," said Georgiana, quietly. "Give me the goblet. I joyfully stake all upon your word."

"Drink, then, thou lofty creature!" exclaimed Aylmer, with fervid* admiration. "There is no taint of imperfection on thy spirit. Thy sensible frame, too, shall soon be all perfect."

fervid: impassioned

She quaffed the liquid and returned the goblet to his hand.

"It is grateful," said she with a placid smile. "Methinks it is like water from a heavenly fountain; for it contains I know not what of unobtrusive fragrance and deliciousness. It allays a feverish thirst that had parched me for many days. Now, dearest, let me sleep. My earthly senses are closing over my spirit like the leaves around the heart of a rose at sunset."

She spoke the last words with a gentle reluctance, as if it required almost more energy than she could command to pronounce the faint and lingering syllables. Scarcely had they loitered through her lips ere she was lost in slumber. Aylmer sat by her side, watching her aspect with the emotions proper to a man the whole value of whose existence was involved in the process now to be tested. Mingled with this mood, however, was the philosophic investigation characteristic of the man of science. Not the minutest symptom escaped him. A heightened flush of the cheek, a slight irregularity of breath, a quiver of the eyelid, a hardly perceptible tremor through the frame,—such were the details which, as the moments passed, he wrote down in his folio volume. Intense thought had set its stamp upon every previous page of that volume, but the thoughts of years were all concentrated upon the last.

While thus employed, he failed not to gaze often at the fatal hand, and not without a shudder. Yet once, by a strange and unaccountable impulse, he pressed it with his lips. His spirit recoiled, however, in the very act; and Georgiana, out of the midst of her deep sleep, moved uneasily and murmured as if in remonstrance.* Again Aylmer resumed his watch. Nor was it without avail. The crimson hand, which at first had been strong-

ly visible upon the marble paleness of Georgiana's cheek, now grew more faintly outlined. She remained not less pale than ever; but the birthmark, with every breath that came and went, lost somewhat of its former distinctness. Its presence had been awful; its departure was more awful still. Watch the stain of the rainbow fading out of the sky, and you will know how that mysterious symbol passed away.

remonstrance: reproof

"By Heaven! it is well-nigh gone!" said Aylmer to himself, in almost irrepressible ecstasy. "I can scarcely trace it now. Success! success! And now it is like the faintest rose color. The lightest flush of blood across her cheek would overcome it. But she is so pale!"

He drew aside the window curtain and suffered the light of natural day to fall into the room and rest upon her cheek. At the same time he heard a gross, hoarse chuckle, which he had long known as his servant Aminadab's expression of delight.

"Ah, clod! ah, earthly mass!" cried Aylmer, laughing a sort of frenzy, "you have served me well! Matter and spirit—earth and heaven—have both done their part in this! Laugh, thing of the senses! You have earned the right to laugh."

These exclamations broke Georgiana's sleep. She slowly unclosed her eyes and gazed into the mirror which her husband had arranged for that purpose. A faint smile flitted over her lips when she recognized how barely perceptible was now that crimson hand which had once blazed forth with such disastrous brilliancy as to scare away all their happiness. But then her eyes sought Aylmer's face with a trouble and anxiety that he could by no means account for.

"My poor Aylmer!" murmured she.

"Poor? Nay, richest, happiest, most favored!" exclaimed he. "My peerless bride, it is successful! You are perfect!"

"My poor Aylmer," she repeated, with a more than human tenderness, "you have aimed loftily; you have done nobly. Do not repent that with so high and pure a feeling, you have rejected the best the earth could offer. Aylmer, dearest Aylmer, I am dying!''

Alas! it was too true! The fatal hand had grappled with the mystery of life, and was the bond by which an angelic spirit kept itself in union with a mortal frame. As the last crimson tint of the birthmark–that sole token of human imperfection–faded from her cheek, the parting breath of the now perfect woman passed into the atmosphere, and her soul, lingering a moment near her husband, took its heavenward flight. Then a hoarse, chuckling laugh was heard again! Thus ever does the gross fatality of earth exult in its invariable triumph over the immortal essence which, in this dim sphere of half development, demands the completeness of a higher state. Yet, had Aylmer reached a profounder wisdom, he need not thus have flung away the happiness which would have woven his mortal life of the selfsame texture with the celestial. The momentary circumstance was too strong for him; he failed to look beyond the shadowy scope of time, and living once for all in eternity, to find the perfect future in the present.

For Thought and Discussion

1. In the first paragraph of ''The Maypole of Merry Mount,'' Hawthorne defines the conflict of the story in one simple, direct sentence. What is the sentence? What parties of characters in the story represent the two conflicting forces? Which of these two parties does Hawthorne associate with English folk customs, Anglicanism, and even paganism? (Find at least one passage in which Hawthorne makes each of these associations.) Which of the conflicting parties do we usually associate with New England and the founding of America? In which sentence in the final paragraph does Hawthorne relate the theme and reveal the outcome of the conflict?

2. Hawthorne associates Puritans with iron. Find several sentences in ''The Maypole of Merry Mount'' in which the word *iron* or a variant form of it appears. What qualities of iron does Hawthorne associate with the Puritans? (Include both the positive and negative qualities that he uses.) The Merry Mounters, on the other hand, are described as ''silken colonists.'' Why is this image appropriate? Do you think it was necessary to the survival of our nation that our ancestors be men of ''iron?'' Why?

3. Discuss the modes of transportation used by the pilgrims in ''The Celestial Railroad.'' In what sense is this narrative detail appropriate to the mode of satirical allegory Hawthorne uses for this work? What modes of transportation does Christian employ in Bunyan's *The Pilgrim's Progress?* Can you determine anything about Hawthorne's attitude toward modern modes of transportation by reading ''The Celestial Railroad''?

4. Father Hooper of ''The Minister's Black Veil'' isolates himself from his fellow man in order to demonstrate the effect of man's sin, which separates him both from God and man. How does Hooper's congregation react to the veil? How does Elizabeth react? How do other members of the community react? What does Hooper forfeit in terms of human relationships because he refuses to cast off the veil? Do any of the characters in the story change their attitudes toward the veil after a time? In your opinion, does Hooper's self-imposed isolation represent self-denial for the edification of others, or is it symbolic of misdirected religious zeal? Discuss Hawthorne's theme in light of I John 1:8-10.

5. To what object is Georgiana's birthmark similar in shape? Find other references to this object in the story. In light of these references, what does it symbolize?

Herman Melville 1819-1891

Like Edgar Allan Poe and Nathaniel Hawthorne, Herman Melville attacked the optimism of the American transcendentalists. His "No" to their values came not for essentially artistic or moral reasons (as Poe's and Hawthorne's, respectively, had come) but for primarily philosophical reasons. At first a popular author, Melville soon became preoccupied with philosophical issues in his writing. As a result, American readers lost interest in his works. Long before his death, his literary reputation had sunk into oblivion, not to be rescued until the 1920s, some thirty years after his death. Today, however, Melville is regarded as one of America's most important literary voices.

Melville was born into a prosperous, socially prominent New York family, the third of eight children. Because of his father's bankruptcy in 1830 and death two years later, Melville spent the second decade of his life in genteel poverty. Handicapped by an irregular education and unable to settle on an occupation (he tried clerking, banking, and teaching), in 1839, when almost twenty years old, he sailed as a cabin boy–while actually performing the duties of an apprentice seaman–to Liverpool, England. On returning to the States, he taught school again for a short time, then traveled to the Midwest. Soon back in the East, Melville tried unsuccessfully to find a job in New York City. In January 1841, he once more shipped to sea. For the next three and a half years, on various ships sailing in various parts of the ocean, Melville stored up the experiences that were to permeate his best fiction.

In 1846 Melville launched his writing career by publishing *Typee*. This first novel, which romanticized his actual experiences among cannibals in the South Sea Islands, whetted the American public's appetite for more. In rapid order Melville, drawing again and again upon his sailing experiences, published four more novels: *Omoo* (1847), *Mardi* (1849), *Redburn* (1849), and *White Jacket* (1850). In 1851 appeared his greatest work, *Moby Dick*. This novel reflected both Melville's eighteen months aboard the whaling ship *Acushnet,* which he called "my Yale College and my Harvard," and his recent acquaintance with Nathaniel Hawthorne, to whom he dedicated the novel. This work also clearly revealed what his earlier novels had been hinting at–that his fiction was increasingly moving toward **symbol** and **ambiguity.** After 1851 Melville's popularity rapidly fell as he ceased mining his own experiences and began grappling with complex philosophical issues. As subsequent works further widened the breach between author's interest and public expectation, a disastrous fire in 1853 at Harpers, his publishers, destroyed the printing plates and most of the unsold copies of his early novels.

Melville turned at this point in his career to writing short stories for American literary periodicals. Although spurred by financial difficulties, he wrote tales so much like his novels that they did little to slow the descent of his popularity. Melville's short-story phase (1853-56) ended with the publication of *The Piazza Tales* (1856), a collection of works including "Bartleby the Scrivener," "Benito Cereno," and the *Encantadas* sketches.

From 1858 to 1866 Melville published nothing. For a time (1857-60) he traveled the lecture circuit in an almost futile attempt to ease his financial woes. Then in 1866 he issued his first collection of poems, *Battle-Pieces and Aspects of the War*. After this work appeared, he directed his creative energy toward writing poetry. (The only exception is the short novel *Billy Budd*, written in Melville's last years but not published until 1924 during the revival of interest in his works.) All together he published four volumes of poetry, most as privately printed, limited editions. During his last two decades, Melville supported his family by working as a customs inspector at the port of New York. His death in 1891 passed virtually unnoticed by most Americans.

In his fiction Melville adopted a realistic style, attempting to represent the world exactly as he saw it. Like Hawthorne, he often chose to write about the dark side of man's nature. Melville depicted evil as a powerful force by which men are dominated far more often than by the goodness supposed by transcendentalism to exist within them. A major **theme** of his writings is patience, which appears in his characters' stoical resistance to the evil forces in the world.

Because Melville raises questions about God's goodness and the prevalence of goodness in the world, he has attracted much sympathetic attention from twentieth-century critics who find his outlook modern. The dominant spirit of his writing is rebellion against God; his best-known character, Captain Ahab of *Moby Dick*, hurls defiance at God. Melville quarrels with God for having provided no meaning in the universe and virtually no hope of ultimate victory over the forces that oppose men. While his refutation of transcendentalism is valuable to the Christian, his refusal to accept the Biblical view of God and man mars his work. His writing is that of a searcher who, having turned away from the truth of God's Word, offers only questions, not answers.

Bartleby the Scrivener

Although critics quarrel about the theme of "Bartleby," it is an intriguing piece of fiction with a well-structured plot and a well-defined conflict. Melville's two major characters, Bartleby and the narrator, are among the most fascinating in American literature. The three minor characters are also vividly portrayed, adding even more interest for the reader. Finally, the effective use of humor and irony as well as the questions the story provokes concerning man's responsibility toward his fellow man make Melville's accomplishment in the work impressive.

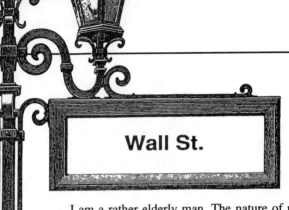

Wall St.

I am a rather elderly man. The nature of my avocations, for the last thirty years, has brought me into more than ordinary contact with what would seem an interesting and somewhat singular set of men, of whom, as yet, nothing, that I know of, has ever been written—I mean, the law-copyists, or scriveners.* I have known very many of them, professionally and privately, and, if I pleased, could relate divers histories, at which good-natured gentlemen might smile, and sentimental souls might weep. But I waive the biographies of all other scriveners, for a few passages in the life of Bartleby, who was a scrivener, the strangest I ever saw, or heard of. While, of other law-copyists, I might write the complete life, of Bartleby nothing of that sort can be done. I believe that no materials exist, for a full and satisfactory biography of this man. It is an irreparable loss to literature. Bartleby was one of those beings of whom nothing is ascertainable, except from the original sources, and, in his case, those are very small. What my own astonished eyes saw of Bartleby, *that* is all I know of him, except, indeed, one vague report, which will appear in the sequel.

scriveners: those who had to copy by hand legal documents before the invention of the typewriter

Ere introducing the scrivener, as he first appeared to me, it is fit I make some mention of myself, my *employés,* my business, my chambers, and general surroundings; because some such description is indispensable to an adequate understanding of the chief character about to be presented. Imprimis:* I am a man who, from his youth upwards, has been filled with a profound conviction that the easiest way of life is the best. Hence, though I belong to a profession prover-

bially energetic and nervous, even to turbulence, at times, yet nothing of that sort have I ever suffered to invade my peace. I am one of those unambitious lawyers who never addresses a jury, or in any way draws down public applause; but, in the cool tranquillity of a snug retreat, do a snug business among rich men's bonds, and mortgages, and title-deeds. All who know me, consider me an eminently *safe* man. The late John Jacob Astor,* a personage little given to poetic enthusiasm, had no hesitation in pronouncing my first grand point to be prudence; my next, method. I do not speak it in vanity, but simply record the fact, that I was not unemployed in my profession by the late John Jacob Astor; a name which, I admit, I love to repeat; for it hath a rounded and orbicular sound to it, and rings like unto bullion. I will freely add, that I was not insensible to the late John Jacob Astor's good opinion.

Imprimis: i.e., in the first place
John Jacob Astor: a wealthy, influential businessman in the late eighteenth and early nineteenth centuries

Some time prior to the period at which this little history begins, my avocations had been largely increased. The good old office, now extinct in the State of New York, of a Master in Chancery,* had been conferred upon me. It was not a very arduous* office, but very pleasantly remunerative. I seldom lose my temper; much more seldom indulge in dangerous indignation at wrongs and outrages; but, I must be permitted to be rash here, and declare, that I consider the sudden and violent abrogation* of the office of Master in Chancery, by the new Constitution,* as a—premature act; inasmuch as I had counted upon a life-lease of the profits, whereas I only received those of a few short years. But this is by the way.

Master in Chancery: a judge in an equity court, a court which handles cases not handled in law courts, cases such as those involving the rewriting of contracts or the suing of businesses
arduous: difficult
abrogation: abolishment
Constitution: i.e., the constitution of the state of New York

My chambers were up stairs, at No. – Wall Street. At one end, they looked upon the white wall of the interior of a spacious sky-light shaft, penetrating the building from top to bottom.

This view might have been considered rather tame than otherwise, deficient in what landscape painters call "life." But, if so, the view from the other end of my chambers offered, at least, a contrast, if nothing more. In that direction, my windows commanded an unobstructed view of a lofty brick wall, black by age and everlasting shade; which wall required no spy-glass to bring out its lurking beauties, but, for the benefit of all near-sighted spectators, was pushed up to within ten feet of my window panes. Owing to the great height of the surrounding buildings, and my chambers being on the second floor, the interval between this wall and mine not a little resembled a huge square cistern.

At the period just preceding the advent of Bartleby, I had two persons as copyists in my employment, and a promising lad as an office-boy. First, Turkey; second, Nippers; third, Ginger Nut. These may seem names, the like of which are not usually found in the Directory. In truth, they were nicknames, mutually conferred upon each other by my three clerks, and were deemed expressive of their respective persons or characters. Turkey was a short, pursy Englishman, of about my own age—that is, somewhere not far from sixty. In the morning, one might say, his face was of a fine florid hue, but after twelve o'clock, meridian—his dinner hour—it blazed like a grate full of Christmas coals; and continued blazing—but, as it were, with a gradual wane—till six o'clock, P.M., or thereabouts; after which, I saw no more of the proprietor of the face, which, gaining its meridian with the sun, seemed to set with it, to rise, culminate, and decline the following day, with the like regularity and undiminished glory. There are many singular coincidences I have known in the course of my life, not the least among which was the fact, that, exactly when Turkey displayed his fullest beams from his red and radiant countenance, just then, too, at that critical moment, began the daily period when I considered his business capacities as seriously disturbed for the remainder of the twenty-four hours. Not that he was absolutely idle, or averse to business, then; far from it. The difficulty was, he was apt to be altogether too energetic. There was a strange, inflamed, flurried, flighty recklessness of activity about him. He would be incautious in dipping his pen into his inkstand. All his blots upon my documents were dropped there after twelve o'clock, meridian. Indeed, not only would he be reckless, and sadly given to making blots in the afternoon, but, some days, he went further, and was rather noisy. At such times, too, his face flamed with augmented blazonry,* as if cannel coal had been heaped on anthracite. He made an unpleasant racket with his chair; spilled his sandbox; in mending his pens, impatiently split them all to pieces, and threw them on the floor in a sudden passion; stood up, and leaned over his table, boxing his papers about in a most indecorous* manner, very sad to behold in an elderly man like him. Nevertheless, as he was in many ways a most valuable person to me, and all the time before twelve o'clock, meridian, was the quickest, steadiest creature, too, accomplishing a great deal of work in a style not easily to be matched—for these reasons, I was willing to overlook his eccentricities, though, indeed, occasionally, I remonstrated with him. I did this very gently, however, because, though the civilest, nay, the blandest and most reverential of men in the morning, yet, in the afternoon, he was disposed, upon provocation, to be slightly rash with his tongue—in fact, insolent.* Now, valuing his morning services as I did, and resolved not to lose them—yet, at the same time, made uncomfortable by his inflamed ways after twelve o'clock—and being a man of peace, unwilling by my admonitions to call forth unseemly retorts from him, I took upon me, one Saturday noon (he was always worse on Saturdays) to hint to him, very kindly, that, perhaps, now that he was growing old, it might be well to abridge his labors; in short, he need not come to my chambers after twelve o'clock, but, dinner over, had best go home to his lodgings, and rest himself till tea-time. But no; he insisted upon his afternoon devotions. His countenance became intolerably fervid,* as he oratorically assured me–gesticulating with a long ruler at the other end of the room–that if his services in the morning were useful, how indispensable, then, in the afternoon?

blazonry: showy display
indecorous: lacking good taste
insolent: insulting in manner or speech, arrogant
fervid: extremely zealous

"With submission, sir," said Turkey, on this occasion, "I consider myself your right-hand man. In the morning I but marshal and deploy my columns; but in the afternoon I put myself at their head, and gallantly charge the foe, thus"–and he made a violent thrust with the ruler.

"But the blots, Turkey," intimated I.

"True; but, with submission, sir, behold these hairs! I am getting old. Surely, sir, a blot or two of a warm afternoon is not to be severely urged against gray hairs. Old age–even if it blot the page–is honorable. With submission, sir, we *both* are getting old."

This appeal to my fellow-feeling was hardly to be resisted. At all events, I saw that go he would not. So, I made up my mind to let him stay, resolving, nevertheless, to see to it that, during the afternoon, he had to do with my less important papers.

Nippers, the second on my list, was a whiskered, sallow,* and, upon the whole, rather piratical-looking young man, of about five and twenty. I always deemed him the victim of two evil powers–ambition and indigestion. The ambition was evinced by a certain impatience of the duties of a mere copyist, an unwarrantable usurpation of strictly professional affairs, such as the original drawing up of legal documents. The indigestion seemed betokened in an occasional nervous tes-

tiness and grinning irritability, causing the teeth to audibly grind together over mistakes committed in copying; unnecessary maledictions, hissed, rather than spoken, in the heat of business; and especially by a continual discontent with the height of the table where he worked. Though of a very ingenious mechanical turn, Nippers could never get this table to suit him. He put chips under it, blocks of various sorts, bits of pasteboard, and at last went so far as to attempt an exquisite adjustment, by final pieces of folded blotting-paper. But no invention would answer. If, for the sake of easing his back, he brought the table lid at a sharp angle well up towards his chin, and wrote there like a man using the steep roof of a Dutch house for his desk, then he declared that it stopped the circulation in his arms. If now he lowered the table to his waistbands, and stooped over it in writing, then there was a sore aching in his back. In short, the truth of the matter was, Nippers knew not what he wanted. Or, if he wanted anything, it was to be rid of a scrivener's table altogether. Among the manifestations of his diseased ambition was a fondness he had for receiving visits from certain ambiguous-looking fellows in seedy coats, whom he called his clients. Indeed, I was aware that not only was he, at times, considerable of a ward-politician, but he occasionally did a little business at the Justices' courts, and was not unknown on the steps of the Tombs.* I have good reason to believe, however, that one individual who called upon him at my chambers, and who, with a grand air, he insisted was his client, was no other than a dun,* and the alleged title-deed, a bill. But, with all his failings, and the annoyances he caused me, Nippers, like his compatriot Turkey, was a very useful man to me; wrote a neat, swift hand; and, when he chose, was not deficient in a gentlemanly sort of deportment. Added to this, he always dressed in a gentlemanly sort of way; and so, incidentally, reflected credit upon my chambers. Whereas, with respect to Turkey, I had much ado to keep him from being a reproach to me. His clothes were apt to look oily, and smell of eating-houses. He wore his panta-loons very loose and baggy in summer. His coats were execrable;* his hat not to be handled. But while the hat was a thing of indifference to me, inasmuch as his natural civility and deference, as a dependent Englishman, always led him to doff it the moment he entered the room, yet his coat was another matter. Concerning his coats, I rea-soned with him; but with no effect. The truth was, I suppose, that a man with so small an income could not afford to sport such a lustrous face and a lustrous coat at one and the same time. As Nip-pers once observed, Turkey's money went chiefly for red ink. One winter day, I presented Turkey with a highly respectable-looking coat of my own—a padded gray coat, of a most comfortable warmth, and which buttoned straight up from the knee to the neck. I thought Turkey would appre-ciate the favor, and abate his rashness and ob-streperousness* of afternoons. But no; I verily believe that buttoning himself up in so downy and blanket-like a coat had a pernicious* effect upon him—upon the same principle that too much oats are bad for horses. In fact, precisely as a rash, restive horse is said to feel his oats, so Turkey felt his coat. It made him insolent. He was a man whom prosperity harmed.

sallow: of sickly, yellowish complexion
Tombs: a New York City jail
dun: one who persistently demands payment from a debtor
execrable: deserving loathing
obstreperousness: stubborn defiance
pernicious: destructive

Though, concerning the self-indulgent habits of Turkey, I had my own private surmises, yet, touching Nippers, I was well persuaded that, whatever might be his faults in other respects, he was, at least, a temperate young man. But, indeed, nature herself seemed to have been his vintner,* and, at his birth, charged him so thoroughly with an irritable, brandy-like disposition, that all sub-sequent potations were needless. When I consider how, amid the stillness of my chambers, Nippers would sometimes impatiently rise from his seat,

and stooping over his table, spread his arms wide apart, seize the whole desk, and move it, and jerk it, with a grim, grinding motion on the floor, as if the table were a perverse voluntary agent, intent on thwarting and vexing him, I plainly perceive that, for Nippers, brandy-and-water were alto-gether superfluous.*

vintner: one who makes wine
superfluous: beyond what is necessary

It was fortunate for me that, owing to its pe-culiar cause—indigestion—the irritability and con-sequent nervousness of Nippers were mainly ob-servable in the morning, while in the afternoon he was comparatively mild. So that, Turkey's par-oxysms* only coming on about twelve o'clock, I never had to do with their eccentricities at one time. Their fits relieved each other, like guards. When Nipper's was on, Turkey's was off; and vice versa. This was a good natural arrangement, under the circumstances.

paroxysms: sudden outbursts of emotions or actions

Ginger Nut, the third on my list, was a lad, some twelve years old. His father was a car-man, ambitious of seeing his son on the bench instead of a cart, before he died. So he sent him to my office, as student at law, errand-boy, cleaner and sweeper, at the rate of one dollar a week. He had a little desk to himself, but he did not use it much. Upon inspection, the drawer exhibited a great ar-ray of the shells of various sorts of nuts. Indeed, to this quick-witted youth, the whole noble sci-ence of the law was contained in a nutshell. Not the least among the employments of Ginger Nut, as well as one which he discharged with the most alacrity,* was his duty as cake and apple purveyor for Turkey and Nippers. Copying law-papers be-ing proverbially a dry, husky sort of business, my two scriveners were fain to moisten their mouths very often with Spitzenbergs,* to be had at the numerous stalls nigh the Custom House and Post Office. Also, they sent Ginger Nut very frequently for that peculiar cake—small, flat, round, and very spicy–after which he had been named by them. Of a cold morning, when business was but dull, Turkey would gobble up scores of these cakes, as if they were mere wafers–indeed, they sell them at the rate of six or eight for a penny–the scrape of his pen blending with the crunching of the crisp particles in his mouth. Of all the fiery afternoon blunders and flurried rashnesses of Turkey, was his once moistening a ginger-cake between his lips, and clapping it on to a mortgage for a seal. I came within an ace of dismissing him then. But he mollified me by making an oriental bow, and saying–

alacrity: eagerness
Spitzenbergs: a specific type of apple

"With submission, sir, it was generous of me to find you in stationery on my own account."

Now my original business–that of a conveyancer and title hunter, and drawer-up of recondite* documents of all sorts–was considerably increased by receiving the master's office. There was now great work for scriveners. Not only must I push the clerks already with me, but I must have additional help.

recondite: not easily understood

In answer to my advertisement, a motionless young man one morning stood upon my office threshold, the door being open, for it was summer. I can see that figure now–pallidly* neat, pitiably respectable, incurably forlorn! It was Bartleby.

pallidly: colorlessly

After a few words touching his qualifications, I engaged him, glad to have among my corps of copyists a man of so singularly sedate an aspect, which I thought might operate beneficially upon the flighty temper of Turkey, and the fiery one of Nippers.

I should have stated before that ground glass folding-doors divided my premises into two parts, one of which was occupied by my scriveners, the other by myself. According to my humor, I threw open these doors, or closed them. I resolved to assign Bartleby a corner by the folding-doors, but on my side of them, so as to have this quiet man within easy call, in case any trifling thing was to be done. I placed his desk close up to a small side-window in that part of the room, a window which originally had afforded a lateral view of certain grimy back-yards and bricks, but which, owing to subsequent erections, commanded at present no view at all, though it gave some light. Within three feet of the panes was a wall, and the light came down from far above, between two lofty buildings, as from a very small opening in a dome. Still further to a satisfactory arrangement, I procured a high green folding screen, which might entirely isolate Bartleby from my sight, though not remove him from my voice. And thus, in a manner, privacy and society were conjoined.

At first, Bartleby did an extraordinary quantity of writing. As if long famishing for something to copy, he seemed to gorge himself on my documents. There was no pause for digestion. He ran a day and night line, copying by sun-light and by candle-light. I should have been quite delighted with his application, had he been cheerfully industrious. But he wrote on silently, palely, mechanically.

It is, of course, an indispensable part of a scrivener's business to verify the accuracy of his copy, word by word. Where there are two or more scriveners in an office, they assist each other in this examination, one reading from the copy, the other holding the original. It is a very dull, wearisome, and lethargic* affair. I can readily imagine that, to some sanguine* temperaments, it would be altogether intolerable. For example, I cannot credit that the mettlesome poet, Byron, would have contentedly sat down with Bartleby to examine a law document of, say five hundred pages, closely written in a crimpy hand.

lethargic: characterized by sluggish indifference
sanguine: passionate

Now and then, in the haste of business, it had been my habit to assist in comparing some brief document myself, calling Turkey or Nippers for this purpose. One object I had, in placing Bartleby so handy to me behind the screen, was, to avail myself of his services on such trivial occasions. It was on the third day, I think, of his being with me, and before any necessity had arisen for having his own writing examined, that, being much hurried to complete a small affair I had in hand, I abruptly called to Bartleby. In my haste and natural expectancy of instant compliance, I sat with my head bent over the original on my desk, and my right hand sideways, and somewhat nervously extended with the copy, so that, immediately upon emerging from his retreat, Bartleby might snatch it and proceed to business without the least delay.

In this very attitude did I sit when I called him, rapidly stating what it was I wanted him to do–namely, to examine a small paper with me. Imagine my surprise, nay, my consternation, when, without moving from his privacy, Bartleby, in a singularly mild, firm voice, replied, "I would prefer not to."

I sat awhile in perfect silence, rallying my stunned faculties. Immediately it occurred to me that my ears had deceived me, or Bartleby had entirely misunderstood my meaning. I repeated my request in the clearest tone I could assume; but in quite as clear a one came the previous reply, "I would prefer not to."

"Prefer not to," echoed I, rising in high excitement, and crossing the room with a stride. "What do you mean? Are you moon-struck? I want you to help me compare this sheet here–take it," and I thrust it towards him.

"I would prefer not to," said he.

I looked at him steadfastly. His face was leanly composed; his gray eye dimly calm. Not a wrinkle of agitation rippled him. Had there been the least uneasiness, anger, impatience or impertinence in his manner; in other words, had there been any thing ordinarily human about him, doubtless I should have violently dismissed him from the premises. But as it was, I should have as soon thought of turning my pale plaster-of-paris bust of Cicero out of doors. I stood gazing at him awhile, as he went on with his own writing, and then reseated myself at my desk. This is very strange, thought I. What had one best do? But my business hurried me. I concluded to forget the matter for the present, reserving it for my future leisure. So calling Nippers from the other room, the paper was speedily examined.

A few days after this, Bartleby concluded four lengthy documents, being quadruplicates of a week's testimony taken before me in my High Court of Chancery. It became necessary to examine them. It was an important suit, and great accuracy was imperative. Having all things arranged, I called Turkey, Nippers, and Ginger Nut, from the next room, meaning to place the four copies in the hands of my four clerks, while I should read from the original. Accordingly, Turkey, Nippers, and Ginger Nut had taken their seats in a row, each with his document in his hand, when I called to Bartleby to join this interesting group.

"Bartleby! quick, I am waiting."

I heard a slow scrape of his chair legs on the uncarpeted floor, and soon he appeared standing at the entrance of his hermitage.

"What is wanted?" said he, mildly.

"The copies, the copies," said I, hurriedly. "We are going to examine them. There"–and I held towards him the fourth quadruplicate.

"I would prefer not to," he said, and gently disappeared behind the screen.

For a few moments I was turned into a pillar of salt, standing at the head of my seated column of clerks. Recovering myself, I advanced towards the screen, and demanded the reason for such extraordinary conduct.

"*Why* do you refuse?"

"I would prefer not to."

With any other man I should have flown outright into a dreadful passion, scorned all further words, and thrust him ignominiously* from my presence. But there was something about Bartleby that not only strangely disarmed me, but, in a wonderful manner, touched and disconcerted me. I began to reason with him.

---

ignominiously: disgracefully

"These are your own copies we are about to examine. It is labor saving to you, because one examination will answer for your four papers. It is common usage. Every copyist is bound to help examine his copy. Is it not so? Will you not speak? Answer!"

"I prefer not to," he replied in a flutelike tone. It seemed to me that, while I had been addressing him, he carefully revolved every statement that I made; fully comprehended the meaning; could not gainsay* the irresistible conclusion; but, at the same time, some paramount consideration prevailed with him to reply as he did.

---

gainsay: deny

"You are decided, then, not to comply with my request—a request made according to common usage and common sense?"

He briefly gave me to understand, that on that point my judgment was sound. Yes: his decision was irreversible.

It is not seldom the case that, when a man is browbeaten in some unprecedented and violently unreasonable way, he begins to stagger in his own plainest faith. He begins, as it were, vaguely to surmise that, wonderful as it may be, all the justice and all the reason is on the other side. Accordingly, if any disinterested persons are present, he turns to them for some reinforcement of his own faltering mind.

"Turkey," said I, "what do you think of this? Am I not right?"

"With submission, sir," said Turkey, in his blandest tone, "I think that you are."

"Nippers," said I, "what do *you* think of it?"

"I think I should kick him out of the office."

(The reader, of nice perceptions, will here perceive that, it being morning, Turkey's answer is couched in polite and tranquil terms, but Nippers replies in ill-tempered ones. Or, to repeat a previous sentence, Nippers's ugly mood was on duty, and Turkey's off.)

"Ginger Nut," said I, willing to enlist the smallest suffrage in my behalf, "what do *you* think of it?"

"I think, sir, he's a little *luny,*" replied Ginger Nut, with a grin.

"You hear what they say," said I, turning towards the screen, "come forth and do your duty."

But he vouchsafed no reply. I pondered a moment in sore perplexity. But once more business hurried me. I determined again to postpone the consideration of this dilemma to my future leisure. With a little trouble we made out to examine the papers without Bartleby, though at every page or two Turkey deferentially dropped his opinion, that this proceeding was quite out of the common; while Nippers, twitching in his chair with a dyspeptic nervousness, ground out, between his set teeth, occasional hissing maledictions against the stubborn oaf behind the screen. And for his (Nippers's) part, this was the first and the last time he would do another man's business without pay.

Meanwhile Bartleby sat in his hermitage, oblivious to everything but his own peculiar business there.

Some days passed, the scrivener being employed upon another lengthy work. His late remarkable conduct led me to regard his ways narrowly. I observed that he never went to dinner; indeed, that he never went anywhere. As yet I had never, of my personal knowledge, known him to be outside of my office. He was a perpetual sentry in the corner. At about eleven o'clock though, in the morning, I noticed that Ginger Nut would advance toward the opening in Bartleby's screen, as if silently beckoned thither by a gesture invisible to me where I sat. The boy would then leave the office, jingling a few pence, and reappear with a handful of ginger-nuts, which he delivered in the hermitage, receiving two of the cakes for his trouble.

He lives, then, on ginger-nuts, thought I; never eats a dinner, properly speaking; he must be a vegetarian, then; but no; he never eats even vegetables, he eats nothing but ginger-nuts. My mind then ran on in reveries concerning the probable effects upon the human constitution of living entirely on ginger-nuts. Ginger-nuts are so called, because they contain ginger as one of their peculiar constituents, and the final flavoring one. Now, what was ginger? A hot, spicy thing. Was Bartleby hot and spicy? Not at all. Ginger, then, had no effect upon Bartleby. Probably he preferred it should have none.

Nothing so aggravates an earnest person as a passive resistance. If the individual so resisted be of a not inhumane temper, and the resisting one perfectly harmless in his passivity, then, in the better moods of the former, he will endeavor charitably to construe to his imagination what proves impossible to be solved by his judgment. Even so, for the most part, I regarded Bartleby and his ways. Poor fellow! thought I, he means no mischief; it is plain he intends no insolence; his aspect sufficiently evinces that his eccentricities are involuntary. He is useful to me. I can get along with him. If I turn him away, the chances are he will fall in with some less-indulgent employer, and then he will be rudely treated, and perhaps driven forth miserably to starve. Yes. Here I can cheaply purchase a delicious self-approval. To befriend Bartleby; to humor him in his strange willfulness, will cost me little or nothing, while I lay up in my soul what will eventually prove a sweet morsel for my conscience. But this mood was not invariable with me. The passiveness of Bartleby sometimes irritated me. I felt strangely goaded on to encounter him in new opposition–to elicit some angry spark from him answerable to my own. But, indeed, I might as well have essayed to strike first with my knuckles against a bit of Windsor soap. But one afternoon the evil impulse in me mastered me, and the following little scene ensued:

"Bartleby," said I, "when those papers are all copied, I will compare them with you."

"I would prefer not to."

"How? Surely you do not mean to persist in that mulish vagary?"

No answer.

I threw open the folding-doors near by, and, turning upon Turkey and Nippers, exclaimed:

"Bartleby a second time says, he won't examine his papers. What do you think of it, Turkey?"

It was afternoon, be it remembered. Turkey sat glowing like a brass boiler; his bald head steaming; his hands reeling among his blotted papers.

"Think of it?" roared Turkey; "I think I'll just step behind his screen, and black his eyes for him!"

So saying, Turkey rose to his feet and threw his arms into a pugilistic position. He was hurrying away to make good his promise, when I detained him, alarmed at the effect of incautiously rousing Turkey's combativeness after dinner.

"Sit down, Turkey," said I, "and hear what Nippers has to say. What do you think of it, Nippers? Would I not be justified in immediately dismissing Bartleby?"

"Excuse me, that is for you to decide, sir. I think his conduct quite unusual, and, indeed, unjust, as regards Turkey and myself. But it may only be a passing whim."

"Ah," exclaimed I, "you have strangely changed your mind, then–you speak very gently of him now."

"All beer," cried Turkey; "gentleness is effects of beer–Nippers and I dined together to-day. You see how gentle *I* am, sir. Shall I go and black his eyes?"

"You refer to Bartleby, I suppose. No, not to-day, Turkey," I replied; "pray, put up your fists."

I closed the doors, and again advanced towards Bartleby. I felt additional incentives tempting me to my fate. I burned to be rebelled against again. I remembered that Bartleby never left the office.

"Bartleby," said I, "Ginger Nut is away; just step around to the Post Office, won't you? (it was but a three minutes' walk), and see if there is anything for me."

"I would prefer not to."

"You *will* not?"

"I *prefer* not."

I staggered to my desk, and sat there in a deep study. My blind inveteracy* returned. Was there any other thing in which I could procure myself to be ignominiously repulsed by this lean, penniless wight?–my hired clerk? What added thing is there, perfectly reasonable, that he will be sure to refuse to do?

---

inveteracy: persistent or firmly established habit

"Bartleby!"

No answer.

"Bartleby," in a louder tone.

No answer.

"Bartleby," I roared.

Like a very ghost, agreeably to the laws of magical invocation, at the third summons, he appeared at the entrance of his hermitage.

"Go to the next room, and tell Nippers to come to me."

"I prefer not to," he respectfully and slowly said, and mildly disappeared.

"Very good, Bartleby," said I, in a quiet sort of serenely-severe self-possessed tone, intimating the unalterable purpose of some terrible retribution very close at hand. At the moment I half intended something of the kind. But upon the whole, as it was drawing towards my dinner-hour, I thought it best to put on my hat and walk home for the day, suffering much from perplexity and distress of mind.

Shall I acknowledge it? The conclusion of this whole business was, that it soon became a fixed fact of my chambers, that a pale young scrivener, by the name of Bartleby, had a desk there; that he copied for me at the usual rate of four cents a folio (one hundred words); but he was permanently exempt from examining the work done by him, that duty being transferred to Turkey and Nippers, out of compliment, doubtless, to their superior acuteness; moreover, said Bartleby was never, on any account, to be dispatched on the most trivial errand of any sort; and that even if entreated to take upon him such a matter, it was generally understood that he would "prefer not to"–in other words, that he would refuse point-blank.

As days passed on, I became considerably reconciled to Bartleby. His steadiness, his freedom from all dissipation, his incessant industry (except when he chose to throw himself into a standing revery behind his screen), his great stillness, his unalterableness of demeanor under all circumstances, made him a valuable acquisition. One prime thing was this—*he was always there*—first in the morning, continually through the day, and the last at night. I had a singular confidence in his honesty. I felt my most precious papers perfectly safe in his hands. Sometimes, to be sure, I could not, for the very soul of me, avoid falling into sudden spasmodic passions with him. For it was exceeding difficult to bear in mind all the time those strange peculiarities, privileges, and unheard of exemptions, forming the tacit* stipulations on Bartleby's part under which he remained in my office. Now and then, in the eagerness of dispatching pressing business, I would inadvertently summon Bartleby, in a short, rapid tone, to put his finger, say, on the incipient tie of a bit of red tape with which I was about compressing some papers. Of course, from behind the screen the usual answer, "I prefer not to," was sure to come; and then, how could a human creature, with the common infirmities of our nature, refrain from bitterly exclaiming upon such perverseness–such unreasonableness. However, every added repulse of this sort which I received only tended to lessen the probability of my repeating the inadvertence.

---
tacit: unspoken

Here it must be said, that according to the custom of most legal gentlemen occupying chambers in densely-populated law buildings, there were several keys to my door. One was kept by a woman residing in the attic, which person weekly scrubbed and daily swept and dusted my apartments. Another was kept by Turkey for convenience sake. The third I sometimes carried in my own pocket. The fourth I knew not who had.

Now, one Sunday morning I happened to go to Trinity Church, to hear a celebrated preacher, and finding myself rather early on the ground I thought I would walk around to my chambers for a while. Luckily I had my key with me; but upon applying it to the lock, I found it resisted by something inserted from the inside. Quite surprised, I called out; when to my consternation a key was turned from within; and thrusting his lean visage at me, and holding the door ajar, the apparition of Bartleby appeared, in his shirt sleeves, and otherwise in a strangely tattered deshabille, saying quietly that he was sorry, but he was deeply engaged just then, and–preferred not admitting me at present. In a brief word or two, he moreover added, that perhaps I had better walk around the block two or three times, and by that time he would probably have concluded his affairs.

Now, the utterly unsurmised appearance of Bartleby, tenanting my law-chambers of a Sunday morning, with his cadaverously* gentlemanly *nonchalance,* yet withal firm and self-possessed, had such a strange effect upon me, that incontinently I slunk away from my own door, and did as desired. But not without sundry twinges of impotent rebellion against the mild effrontery of this unaccountable scrivener. Indeed, it was his wonderful mildness chiefly, which not only disarmed me, but unmanned me as it were. For I consider that one, for the time, is a sort of unmanned when he tranquilly permits his hired clerk to dictate to

him, and order him away from his own premises. Furthermore, I was full of uneasiness as to what Bartleby could possibly be doing in my office in his shirt sleeves, and in an otherwise dismantled condition of a Sunday morning. Was anything amiss going on? Nay, that was out of the question. It was not to be thought of for a moment that Bartleby was an immoral person. But what could he be doing there?–copying? Nay again, whatever might be his eccentricities, Bartleby was an eminently decorous person. He would be the last man to sit down to his desk in any state approaching to nudity. Besides, it was Sunday; and there was something about Bartleby that forbade the supposition that he would by any secular occupation violate the proprieties of the day.

---
cadaverously: corpselike, deathly

Nevertheless, my mind was not pacified; and full of a restless curiosity, at last I returned to the door. Without hindrance I inserted my key, opened it, and entered. Bartleby was not to be seen. I looked round anxiously, peeped behind his screen; but it was very plain that he was gone. Upon more closely examining the place, I surmised that for an indefinite period Bartleby must have ate, dressed, and slept in my office, and that, too without plate, mirror, or bed. The cushioned seat of a ricketty old sofa in one corner bore the faint impress of a lean, reclining form. Rolled away under his desk, I found a blanket; under the empty grate, a blacking box and brush; on a chair, a tin basin, with soap and a ragged towel; in a newspaper a few crumbs of ginger-nuts and a morsel of cheese. Yes, thought I, it is evident enough that Bartleby has been making his home here, keeping bachelor's hall all by himself. Immediately then the thought came sweeping across me, what miserable friendlessness and loneliness are here revealed! His poverty is great; but his solitude, how horrible! Think of it. Of a Sunday, Wall Street is deserted as Petra;* and every night of every day it is an emptiness. This building, too, which of week-days hums with industry and life, at nightfall echoes with sheer vacancy, and all through Sunday is forlorn. And here Bartleby makes his home; sole spectator of a solitude which he has seen all populous–a sort of innocent and transformed Marius* brooding among the ruins of Carthage!

Petra: an ancient city of Edom (modern Jordan), whose ruins were unknown until rediscovered in 1812
Marius: Roman general (155?-86 B.C.) who was banished from Rome for political reasons

---

For the first time in my life a feeling of overpowering stinging melancholy seized me. Before, I had never experienced aught but a not unpleasing sadness. The bond of a common humanity now drew me irresistibly to gloom. A fraternal melancholy! For both I and Bartleby were sons of Adam. I remembered the bright silks and sparkling faces I had seen that day, in gala trim, swanlike sailing down the Mississippi of Broadway; and I contrasted them with the pallid copyist, and thought to myself, Ah, happiness courts the light, so we deem the world is gay; but misery hides aloof, so we deem that misery there is none. These sad fancyings–chimeras,* doubtless, of a sick and silly brain–led on to other and more special thoughts, concerning the eccentricities of Bartleby. Presentiments of strange discoveries hovered round me. The scrivener's pale form appeared to me laid out, among uncaring strangers, in its shivering winding sheet.

---

chimeras: derived from the Greek mythological monsters, meaning a terrifying or absurd imagining

---

Suddenly I was attracted by Bartleby's closed desk, the key in open sight left in the lock.

I mean no mischief, seek the gratification of no heartless curiosity, thought I; besides, the desk is mine, and its contents, too, so I will make bold to look within. Everything was methodically arranged, the papers smoothly placed. The pigeon holes were deep, and removing the files of documents, I groped into their recesses. Presently I felt something there, and dragged it out. It was

an old bandanna handkerchief, heavy and knotted. I opened it, and saw it was a savings's bank.

I now recalled all the quiet mysteries which I had noted in the man. I remembered that he never spoke but to answer; that, though at intervals he had considerable time to himself, yet I had never seen him reading–no, not even a newspaper; that for long periods he would stand looking out, at his pale window behind the screen, upon the dead brick wall; I was quite sure he never visited any refectory or eating house; while his pale face clearly indicated that he never drank beer like Turkey, or tea and coffee even, like other men; that he never went anywhere in particular that I could learn; never went out for a walk, unless, indeed, that was the case at present; that he had declined telling who he was, or whence he came, or whether he had any relatives in the world; that though so thin and pale, he never complained of ill health. And more than all, I remembered a certain unconscious air of pallid–how shall I call it?–of pallid haughtiness, say, or rather an austere reserve about him, which had positively awed me into my tame compliance with his eccentricities, when I had feared to ask him to do the slightest incidental thing for me, even though I might know, from his long-continued motionlessness, that behind his screen he must be standing in one of those dead-wall reveries of his.

Revolving all these things, and coupling them with the recently discovered fact, that he made my office his constant abiding place and home, and not forgetful of his morbid moodiness; revolving all these things, a prudential feeling began to steal over me. My first emotions had been those of pure melancholy and sincerest pity; but just in proportion as the forlornness of Bartleby grew and grew to my imagination, did that same melancholy merge into fear, that pity into repulsion. So true it is, and so terrible, too, that up to a certain point the thought or sight of misery enlists our best affections; but, in certain special cases, beyond that point it does not. They err who would assert that invariably this is owing to the inherent selfishness of the human heart. It rather proceeds from a certain hopelessness of remedying excessive and organic ill. To a sensitive being, pity is not seldom pain. And when at last it is perceived that such pity cannot lead to effectual succor, common sense bids the soul be rid of it. What I saw that morning persuaded me that the scrivener was the victim of innate and incurable disorder. I might give alms to his body; but his body did not pain him; it was his soul that suffered, and his soul I could not reach.

I did not accomplish the purpose of going to Trinity Church that morning. Somehow, the things I had seen disqualified me for the time from church-going. I walked homeward, thinking what I would do with Bartleby. Finally, I resolved upon this—I would put certain calm questions to him the next morning, touching his history, etc., and if he declined to answer them openly and unreservedly (and I supposed he would prefer not), then to give him a twenty dollar bill over and above whatever I might owe him, and tell him his services were no longer required; but that if in any other way I could assist him, I would be happy to do so, especially if he desired to return to his native place, wherever that might be, I would willingly help to defray the expenses. Moreover, if, after reaching home, he found himself at any time in want of aid, a letter from him would be sure of a reply.

The next morning came.

"Bartleby," said I, gently calling to him behind the screen. No reply.

"Bartleby," said I, in a still gentler tone, "come here; I am not going to ask you to do anything you would prefer not to do—I simply wish to speak to you."

Upon this he noiselessly slid into view.

"Will you tell me, Bartleby, where you were born?"

"I would prefer not to."

"Will you tell me *anything* about yourself?"

"I would prefer not to."

"But what reasonable objection can you have to speak to me? I feel friendly towards you."

He did not look at me while I spoke, but kept his glance fixed upon my bust of Cicero, which, as I then sat, was directly behind me, some six inches above my head.

"What is your answer, Bartleby?" said I, after waiting a considerable time for a reply, during which his countenance remained immovable, only there was the faintest conceivable tremor of the white attenuated mouth.

"At present I prefer to give no answer," he said, and retired into his hermitage.

It was rather weak in me I confess, but his manner, on this occasion, nettled me. Not only did there seem to lurk in it a certain calm disdain, but his perverseness seemed ungrateful, considering the undeniable good usage and indulgence he had received from me.

Again I sat ruminating what I should do. Mortified as I was at his behavior, and resolved as I had been to dismiss him when I entered my office, nevertheless I strangely felt something superstitious knocking at my heart, and forbidding me to carry out my purpose, and denouncing me for a villain if I dared to breathe one bitter word against this forlornest of mankind. At last, familiarly drawing my chair behind his screen, I sat down and said: "Bartleby, never mind, then, about revealing your history; but let me entreat you, as a friend, to comply as far as may be with the usages of this office. Say now, you will help to examine papers to-morrow or next day: in short, say now, that in a day or two you will begin to be a little reasonable:—say so, Bartleby."

"At present I would prefer not to be a little reasonable," was his mildly cadaverous reply.

Just then the folding-doors opened, and Nippers approached. He seemed suffering from an unusually bad night's rest, induced by severer indigestion than common. He overheard those final words of Bartleby.

"*Prefer not,* eh?" gritted Nippers—"I'd *prefer* him, if I were you, sir," addressing me—"I'd *prefer* him; I'd give him preferences, the stubborn mule! What is it, sir, pray, that he *prefers* not to do now?''

Bartleby moved not a limb.

"Mr. Nippers," said I, "I'd prefer that you would withdraw for the present."

Somehow, of late, I had got into the way of involuntarily using this word "prefer" upon all sorts of not exactly suitable occasions. And I trembled to think that my contact with the scrivener had already and seriously affected me in a mental way. And what further and deeper aberration might it not yet produce? This apprehension had not been without efficacy in determining me to summary measures.

As Nippers, looking very sour and sulky, was departing, Turkey blandly and deferentially approached.

"With submission, sir," said he, "yesterday I was thinking about Bartleby here, and I think that if he would but prefer to take a quart of good ale every day, it would do much towards mending him, and enabling him to assist in examining his papers."

"So you have got the word, too," said I, slightly excited.

"With submission, what word, sir?" asked Turkey, respectfully crowding himself into the contracted space behind the screen, and by so doing, making me jostle the scrivener. "What word, sir?"

"I would prefer to be left alone here," said Bartleby, as if offended at being mobbed in his privacy.

"*That's* the word, Turkey," said I–"*that's* it."

"Oh, *prefer?* oh yes–queer word. I never use it myself. But, sir, as I was saying, if he would but prefer–"

"Turkey," interrupted I, "you will please withdraw."

"Oh, certainly, sir, if you prefer that I should."

As he opened the folding-door to retire, Nippers at his desk caught a glimpse of me, and asked whether I would prefer to have a certain paper copied on blue paper or white. He did not in the least roguishly accent the word prefer. It was plain that it involuntarily rolled from his tongue. I thought to myself, surely I must get rid of a demented man, who already has in some degree turned the tongues, if not the heads of myself and clerks. But I thought it prudent not to break the dismission at once.

The next day I noticed that Bartleby did nothing but stand at his window in his dead-wall revery. Upon asking him why he did not write, he said that he had decided upon doing no more writing.

"Why, how now? what next?" exclaimed I, "do no more writing?"

"No more."

"And what is the reason?"

"Do you not see the reason for yourself," he indifferently replied.

I looked steadfastly at him, and perceived that his eyes looked dull and glazed. Instantly it occurred to me, that his unexampled diligence in copying by his dim window for the first few weeks of his stay with me might have temporarily impaired his vision.

I was touched. I said something in condolence with him. I hinted that of course he did wisely in abstaining from writing for a while; and urged him to embrace that opportunity of taking wholesome exercise in the open air. This, however, he did not do. A few days after this, my other clerks being absent, and being in a great hurry to dispatch certain letters by the mail, I thought that, having nothing else earthly to do, Bartleby would surely be less inflexible than usual, and carry these letters to the post-office. But he blankly declined. So, much to my inconvenience, I went myself.

Still added days went by. Whether Bartleby's eyes improved or not, I could not say. To all appearance, I thought they did. But when I asked him if they did, he vouchsafed no answer. At all events, he would do no copying. At last, in reply to my urgings, he informed me that he had permanently given up copying.

"What!" explained I; "suppose your eyes should get entirely well–better than ever before–would you not copy then?"

"I have given up copying," he answered, and slid aside.

He remained as ever, a fixture in my chamber. Nay–if that were possible–he became still more of a fixture than before. What was to be done? He would do nothing in the office; why should he stay there? In plain fact, he had now become

a millstone to me, not only useless as a necklace, but afflictive to bear. Yet I was sorry for him. I speak less than truth when I say that, on his own account, he occasioned me uneasiness. If he would but have named a single relative or friend, I would instantly have written, and urged their taking the poor fellow away to some convenient retreat. But he seemed alone, absolutely alone in the universe. A bit of wreck in the mid Atlantic. At length, necessities connected with my business tyrannized over all other considerations. Decently as I could, I told Bartleby that in six days time he must unconditionally leave the office. I warned him to take measures, in the interval, for procuring some other abode. I offered to assist him in this endeavor, if he himself would but take the first step towards a removal. "And when you finally quit me, Bartleby," added I, "I shall see that you go not away entirely unprovided. Six days from this hour, remember."

At the expiration of that period, I peeped behind the screen, and lo! Bartleby was there.

I buttoned up my coat, balanced myself; advanced slowly towards him, touched his shoulder, and said, "The time has come; you must quit this place; I am sorry for you; here is money; but you must go."

"I would prefer not," he replied, with his back still towards me.

"You *must*."

He remained silent.

Now I had an unbounded confidence in this man's common honesty. He had frequently restored to me sixpences and shillings carelessly dropped upon the floor, for I am apt to be very reckless in such shirt-button affairs. The proceeding, then, which followed will not be deemed extraordinary.

"Bartleby," said I, "I owe you twelve dollars on account; here are thirty-two; the odd twenty are yours–Will you take it?" and I handed the bills towards him.

But he made no motion.

"I will leave them here, then," putting them under a weight on the table. Then taking my hat and cane and going to the door, I tranquilly turned and added–"After you have removed your things from these offices, Bartleby, you will of course lock the door–since every one is now gone for the day but you–and if you please, slip your key underneath the mat, so that I may have it in the morning. I shall not see you again, so good-by to you. If, hereafter, in your new place of abode, I can be of any service to you, do not fail to advise me by letter. Good-by, Bartleby, and fare you well."

But he answered not a word; like the last column of some ruined temple, he remained standing mute and solitary in the middle of the otherwise deserted room.

As I walked home in a pensive mood, my vanity got the better of my pity. I could not but highly plume myself on my masterly management in getting rid of Bartleby. Masterly I call it, and such it must appear to any dispassionate thinker. The beauty of my procedure seemed to consist in its perfect quietness. There was no vulgar bullying, no bravado of any sort, no choleric hectoring,* and striding to and fro across the apartment, jerking out vehement commands for Bartleby to bundle himself off with his beggarly traps. Nothing of the kind. Without loudly bidding Bartleby depart–as an inferior genius might have done–I *assumed* the ground that depart he must; and upon that assumption built all I had to say. The more I thought over my procedure, the more I was charmed with it. Nevertheless, next morning, upon awakening, I had my doubts–I had somehow slept off the fumes of vanity. One of the coolest and wisest hours a man has, is just after he awakes in the morning. My procedure seemed as sagacious as ever–but only in theory. How it would prove in practice–there was the rub. It was truly a beautiful thought to have assumed Bartleby's departure; but, after all, that assumption was simply my own, and none of Bartleby's. The great point was, not whether I had assumed that he

would quit me, but whether he would prefer so to do. He was more a man of preferences than assumptions.

choleric hectoring: angry ravings

After breakfast, I walked down town, arguing the probabilities *pro* and *con*. One moment I thought it would prove a miserable failure, and Bartleby would be found all alive at my office as usual; the next moment it seemed certain that I should find his chair empty. And so I kept veering about. At the corner of Broadway and Canal Street, I saw quite an excited group of people standing in earnest conversation.

"I'll take odds he doesn't," said a voice as I passed.

"Doesn't go?–done!" said I, "put up your money."

I was instinctively putting my hand in my pocket to produce my own, when I remembered that this was an election day. The words I had overheard bore no reference to Bartleby, but to the success or non-success of some candidate for the mayoralty. In my intent frame of mind, I had, as it were, imagined that all Broadway shared in my excitement, and were debating the same question with me. I passed on, very thankful that the uproar of the street screened my momentary absent-mindedness.

As I had intended, I was earlier than usual at my office door. I stood listening for a moment. All was still. He must be gone. I tried the knob. The door was locked. Yes, my procedure had worked to a charm; he indeed must be vanished. Yet a certain melancholy mixed with this: I was almost sorry for my brilliant success. I was fumbling under the door mat for the key, which Bartleby was to have left there for me, when accidentally my knee knocked against a panel, producing a summoning sound, and in response a voice came to me from within–"Not yet; I am occupied."

It was Bartleby.

I was thunderstruck. For an instant I stood like the man who, pipe in mouth, was killed one cloudless afternoon long ago in Virginia, by summer lightning; at his own warm open window he was killed, and remained leaning out there upon the dreamy afternoon, till some one touched him, when he fell.

"Not gone!" I murmured at last. But again obeying that wondrous ascendancy which the inscrutable scrivener had over me, and from which ascendancy, for all my chafing, I could not completely escape, I slowly went down stairs and out into the street, and while walking round the block, considered what I should next do in this unheard-of perplexity. Turn the man out by an actual thrusting I could not; to drive him away by calling him hard names would not do; calling in the police was an unpleasant idea; and yet, permit him to enjoy his cadaverous triumph over me–this, too, I could not think of. What was to be done? or, if nothing could be done, was there anything further that I could *assume* in the matter? Yes, as before I had prospectively assumed that Bartleby would depart, so now I might retrospectively assume that departed he was. In the legitimate carrying out of this assumption, I might enter my office in a great hurry, and pretending not to see Bartleby at all, walk straight against him as if he were air. Such a proceeding would in a singular degree have the appearance of a home-thrust. It was hardly possible that Bartleby could withstand such an application of the doctrine of assumptions. But upon second thoughts the success of the plan seemed rather dubious. I resolved to argue the matter over with him again.

"Bartleby," said I, entering the office, with a quietly severe expression, "I am seriously displeased. I am pained, Bartleby. I had thought better of you. I had imagined you of such a gentlemanly organization, that in any delicate dilemma a slight hint would suffice–in short, an assumption. But it appears I am deceived. Why," I added, unaffectedly starting, "you have not even touched that money yet," pointing to it, just where I had left it the evening previous.

He answered nothing.

"Will you, or will you not, quit me?" I now demanded in a sudden passion, advancing close to him.

"I would prefer *not* to quit you," he replied, gently emphasizing the *not*.

"What earthly right have you to stay here? Do you pay any rent? Do you pay my taxes? Or is this property yours?"

He answered nothing.

"Are you ready to go on and write now? Are your eyes recovered? Could you copy a small paper for me this morning? or help examine a few lines? or step round to the post-office? In a word, will you do anything at all, to give a coloring to your refusal to depart the premises?"

He silently retired into his hermitage.

I was now in such a state of nervous resentment that I thought it but prudent to check myself at present from further demonstrations. Bartleby and I were alone. I remembered the tragedy of the unfortunate Adams and the still more unfortunate Colt in the solitary office of the latter; and how poor Colt, being dreadfully incensed by Adams, and imprudently permitting himself to get wildly excited, was at unawares hurried into his fatal act–an act which certainly no man could possibly deplore more than the actor himself. Often it had occurred to me in my ponderings upon the subject, that had that altercation taken place in the public street, or at a private residence, it would not have terminated as it did. It was the circumstance of being alone in a solitary office, up stairs, of a building entirely unhallowed by humanizing domestic associations–an uncarpeted office, doubtless, of a dusty, haggard sort of appearance–this it must have been, which greatly helped to enhance the irritable desperation of the hapless Colt.

But when this old Adam of resentment rose in me and tempted me concerning Bartleby, I grappled him and threw him. How? Why, simply by recalling the divine injunction: "A new commandment give I unto you, that ye love one another." Yes, this it was that saved me. Aside from higher considerations, charity often operates as a vastly wise and prudent principle—a great safeguard to its possessor. Men have committed murder for jealousy's sake, and anger's sake, and hatred's sake, and selfishness' sake, and spiritual pride's sake; but no man, that ever I heard of, ever committed a diabolical murder for sweet charity's sake. Mere self-interest, then, if no better motive can be enlisted, should, especially with high-tempered men, prompt all beings to charity and philanthropy. At any rate, upon the occasion in question, I strove to drown my exasperated feelings towards the scrivener by benevolently construing his conduct. Poor fellow, poor fellow! thought I, he don't mean anything; and besides, he has seen hard times, and ought to be indulged.

I endeavored, also, immediately to occupy myself, and at the same time to comfort my despondency. I tried to fancy, that in the course of the morning, at such time as might prove agreeable to him, Bartleby, of his own free accord, would emerge from his hermitage and take up some decided line of march in the direction of the door. But no. Half-past twelve o'clock came; Turkey began to glow in the face, overturn his inkstand, and become generally obstreperous; Nippers abated down into quietude and courtesy; Ginger Nut munched his noon apple; and Bartleby remained standing at his window in one of his profoundest dead-wall reveries. Will it be credited? Ought I to acknowledge it? That afternoon I left the office without saying one further word to him.

Some days now passed, during which, at leisure intervals I looked a little into "Edwards on the Will,"* and "Priestley on Necessity."* Under the circumstances, those books induced a salutary* feeling. Gradually I slid into the persuasion that these troubles of mine, touching the scrivener, had been all predestinated from eternity, and Bartleby was billeted upon me for some myste-

rious purpose of an allwise Providence, which it was not for a mere mortal like me to fathom. Yes, Bartleby, stay there behind your screen, thought I; I shall persecute you no more; you are harmless and noiseless as any of these old chairs; in short, I never feel so private as when I know you are here. At last I see it, I feel it; I penetrate to the predestinated purpose of my life. I am content. Others may have loftier parts to enact; but my mission in this world, Bartleby, is to furnish you with office-room for such period as you may see fit to remain.

Edwards . . . Will: reference to Jonathan Edwards's work, *The Freedom of the Will*
Priestley on Necessity: reference to late seventeenth century chemist and clergyman who discovered oxygen
salutary: designed to bring about improvement

I believe that this wise and blessed frame of mind would have continued with me, had it not been for the unsolicited and uncharitable remarks obtruded upon me by my professional friends who visited the rooms. But thus it often is, that the constant friction of illiberal minds wears out at last the best resolves of the more generous. Though to be sure, when I reflected upon it, it was not strange that people entering my office should be struck by the peculiar aspect of the unaccountable Bartleby, and so be tempted to throw out some sinister observations concerning him. Sometimes an attorney, having business with me, and calling at my office, and finding no one but the scrivener there, would undertake to obtain some sort of precise information from him touching my whereabouts; but without heeding his idle talk, Bartleby would remain standing immovable in the middle of the room. So after contemplating him in that position for a time, the attorney would depart, no wiser than he came.

Also, when a reference was going on, and the room full of lawyers and witnesses, and business driving fast, some deeply-occupied legal gentleman present, seeing Bartleby wholly unemployed, would request him to run round to his (the legal gentleman's) office and fetch some papers for him. Thereupon, Bartleby would tranquilly decline, and yet remain idle as before. Then the lawyer would give a great stare, and turn to me. And what could I say? At last I was made aware that all through the circle of my professional acquaintance, a whisper of wonder was running round, having reference to the strange creature I kept at my office. This worried me very much. And as the idea came upon me of his possibly turning out a long-lived man, and keep occupying my chambers, and denying my authority; and perplexing my visitors; and scandalizing my professional reputation; and casting a general gloom over the premises; keeping soul and body together to the last upon his savings (for doubtless he spent but half a dime a day), and in the end perhaps outlive me, and claim possession of my office by right of his perpetual occupancy: as all these dark anticipations crowded upon me more and more, and my friends continually intruded their relentless remarks upon the apparition in my room; a great change was wrought in me. I resolved to gather all my faculties together, and forever rid me of his intolerable incubus.*

---

incubus: something that is nightmarishly burdensome

Ere revolving any complicated project, however, adapted to this end, I first simply suggested to Bartleby the propriety of his permanent departure. In a calm and serious tone, I commended the idea to his careful and mature consideration. But, having taken three days to meditate upon it, he apprised me, that his original determination remained the same; in short, that he still preferred to abide with me.

What shall I do? I now said to myself, buttoning up my coat to the last button. What shall I do? what ought I to do? what does conscience say I *should* do with this man, or, rather, ghost. Rid myself of him, I must; go, he shall. But how? You will not thrust him, the poor, pale, passive mortal–you will not thrust such a helpless creature out of your door? you will dishonor yourself by such cruelty? No, I will not, I cannot do that.

Rather would I let him live and die here, and then mason up his remains in the wall. What, then, will you do? For all your coaxing, he will not budge. Bribes he leaves under your own paperweight on your table; in short, it is quite plain that he prefers to cling to you.

Then something severe, something unusual must be done. What! surely you will not have him collared by a constable, and commit his innocent pallor to the common jail? And upon what ground could you procure such a thing to be done?–a vagrant, is he? What! he a vagrant, a wanderer, who refuses to budge? It is because he will *not* be a vagrant, then, that you seek to count him *as* a vagrant. That is too absurd. No visible means of support: there I have him. Wrong again: for indubitably he *does* support himself, and that is the only unanswerable proof that any man can show of his possessing the means so to do. No more, then. Since he will not quit me, I must quit him. I will change my offices; I will move elsewhere, and give him fair notice, that if I find him on my new premises I will then proceed against him as a common trespasser.

Acting accordingly, next day I thus addressed him: "I find these chambers too far from the City Hall; the air is unwholesome. In a word, I propose to remove my offices next week, and shall no longer require your services. I tell you this now, in order that you may seek another place."

He made no reply, and nothing more was said.

On the appointed day I engaged carts and men, proceeded to my chambers, and, having but little furniture, everything was removed in a few hours. Throughout, the scrivener remained standing behind the screen, which I directed to be removed the last thing. It was withdrawn; and, being folded up like a huge folio, left him the motionless occupant of a naked room. I stood in the entry watching him a moment, while something from within me upbraided me.

I re-entered, with my hand in my pocket–and–and my heart in my mouth.

"Good-by, Bartleby; I am going–good-by, and God some way bless you; and take that," slipping something in his hand. But it dropped upon the floor, and then–strange to say–I tore myself from him whom I had so longed to be rid of.

Established in my new quarters, for a day or two I kept the door locked, and started at every footfall in the passages. When I returned to my rooms, after any little absence, I would pause at the threshold for an instant, and attentively listen, ere applying my key. But these fears were needless. Bartleby never came nigh me.

I thought all was going well, when a perturbed-looking stranger visited me, inquiring whether I was the person who had recently occupied rooms at No. – Wall Street.

Full of forebodings, I replied that I was.

"Then, sir," said the stranger, who proved a lawyer, "you are responsible for the man you left there. He refuses to do any copying; he refuses to do anything, he says he prefers not to; and he refuses to quit the premises."

"I am very sorry, sir," said I, with assumed tranquility, but an inward tremor, "but, really, the man you allude to is nothing to me–he is no relation or apprentice of mine, that you should hold me responsible for him."

"In mercy's name, who is he?"

"I certainly cannot inform you. I know nothing about him. Formerly I employed him as a copyist; but he has done nothing for me now for some time past."

"I shall settle him, then–good morning, sir."

Several days passed, and I heard nothing more; and, though I often felt a charitable prompting to call at the place and see poor Bartleby, yet a certain squeamishness, of I know not what, withheld me.

All is over with him, by this time, thought I, at last, when, through another week, no further intelligence reached me. But, coming to my room the day after, I found several persons waiting at my door in a high state of nervous excitement.

"That's the man–here he comes," cried the foremost one, whom I recognized as the lawyer who had previously called upon me alone.

"You must take him away, sir, at once," cried a portly person among them, advancing upon me, and whom I knew to be the landlord of No. – Wall Street. "These gentlemen, my tenants, cannot stand it any longer; Mr. B—," pointing to the lawyer, "has turned him out of his room, and he now persists in haunting the building generally, sitting upon the banisters of the stairs by day, and sleeping in the entry by night. Everybody is concerned; clients are leaving the offices; some fears are entertained of a mob; something you must do, and that without delay."

Aghast at this torrent, I fell back before it, and would fain have locked myself in my new quarters. In vain I persisted that Bartleby was nothing to me–no more than to any one else. In vain–I was the last person known to have anything to do with him, and they held me to the terrible account. Fearful, then, of being exposed in the papers (as one person present obscurely threatened), I considered the matter, and, at length, said, that if the lawyer would give me a confidential interview with the scrivener, in his (the lawyer's) own room, I would, that afternoon, strive my best to rid them of the nuisance they complained of.

Going up stairs to my old haunt, there was Bartleby silently sitting upon the banister at the landing.

"What are you doing here, Bartleby?" said I.

"Sitting upon the banister," he mildly replied.

I motioned him into the lawyer's room, who then left us.

"Bartleby," said I, "are you aware that you are the cause of great tribulation to me, by persisting in occupying the entry after being dismissed from the office?"

No answer.

"Now one of two things must take place. Either you must do something, or something must be done to you. Now what sort of business would you like to engage in? Would you like to re-engage in copying for some one?''

''No; I would prefer not to make any change.''

''Would you like a clerkship in a dry-goods store?''

''There is too much confinement about that. No, I would not like a clerkship; but I am not particular.''

''Too much confinement,'' I cried, ''why you keep yourself confined all the time!''

''I would prefer not to take a clerkship,'' he rejoined, as if to settle that little item at once.

''How would a bar-tender's business suit you? There is no trying of the eye-sight in that.''

''I would not like it at all; though, as I said before, I am not particular.''

His unwonted wordiness inspirited me. I returned to the charge.

''Well, then, would you like to travel through the country collecting bills for the merchants? That would improve your health.''

''No, I would prefer to be doing something else.''

''How, then, would going as a companion to Europe, to entertain some young gentleman with your conversation–how would that suit you?''

''Not at all. It does not strike me that there is anything definite about that. I like to be stationary. But I am not particular.''

''Stationary you shall be, then,'' I cried, now losing all patience, and, for the first time in all my exasperating connection with him, fairly flying into a passion. ''If you do not go away from these premises before night, I shall feel bound–indeed, I *am* bound–to–to–to quit the premises myself!'' I rather absurdly concluded, knowing not with what possible threat to try to frighten his immobility into compliance. Despairing of all further efforts, I was precipitately leaving him, when a final thought occurred to me–one which had not been wholly unindulged before.

''Bartleby,'' said I, in the kindest tone I could assume under such exciting circumstances, ''will

you go home with me now–not to my office, but my dwelling–and remain there till we can conclude upon some convenient arrangement for you at our leisure? Come, let us start now, right away.''

''No: at present I would prefer not to make any change at all.''

I answered nothing; but, effectually dodging every one by the suddenness and rapidity of my flight, rushed from the building, ran up Wall Street towards Broadway, and, jumping into the first omnibus, was soon removed from pursuit. As soon as tranquillity returned, I distinctly perceived that I had now done all that I possibly could, both in respect to the demands of the landlord and his tenants, and with regard to my own desire and sense of duty, to benefit Bartleby, and shield him from rude persecution. I now strove to be entirely care-free and quiescent;* and my conscience justified me in the attempt; though, indeed, it was not so successful as I could have wished. So fearful was I of being again hunted out by the incensed landlord and his exasperated tenants, that, surrendering my business to Nippers, for a few days, I drove about the upper part of the town and through the suburbs, in my rockaway;* crossed over to Jersey City and Hoboken, and paid fugitive visits to Manhattanville and Astoria. In fact, I almost lived in my rockaway for the time.

quiescent: inactive or still
rockaway: an old four-wheeled carriage named for the town in New Jersey where it was first made

When again I entered my office, lo, a note from the landlord lay upon the desk. I opened it with trembling hands. It informed me that the writer had sent to the police, and had Bartleby removed to the Tombs as a vagrant. Moreover, since I knew more about him than any one else, he wished me to appear at that place, and make a suitable statement of the facts. These tidings had a conflicting effect upon me. At first I was indignant; but, at last, almost approved. The landlord's energetic, summary disposition, had led him to adopt a procedure which I do not think I would have decided upon myself; and yet, as a last resort, under such peculiar circumstances, it seemed the only plan.

As I afterwards learned, the poor scrivener, when told that he must be conducted to the Tombs, offered not the slightest obstacle, but, in his pale, unmoving way, silently acquiesced.

Some of the compassionate and curious bystanders joined the party; and headed by one of the constables arm in arm with Bartleby, the silent procession filed its way through all the noise, and heat, and joy of the roaring thoroughfares at noon.

The same day I received the note, I went to the Tombs, or, to speak more properly, the Halls of Justice. Seeking the right officer, I stated the purpose of my call, and was informed that the individual I described was, indeed, within. I then assured the functionary that Bartleby was a perfectly honest man, and greatly to be compassionated, however unaccountably eccentric. I narrated all I knew, and closed by suggesting the idea of letting him remain in as indulgent confinement as possible, till something less harsh might be done—though, indeed, I hardly knew what. At all events, if nothing else could be decided upon, the alms-house must receive him. I then begged to have an interview.

Being under no disgraceful charge, and quite serene and harmless in all his ways, they had permitted him freely to wander about the prison, and, especially, in the inclosed grass-platted yards thereof. And so I found him there, standing all alone in the quietest of the yards, his face towards a high wall, while all around, from the narrow slits of the jail windows, I thought I saw peering out upon him the eyes of murderers and thieves.

"Bartleby!"

"I know you," he said, without looking round— "and I want nothing to say to you."

"It was not I that brought you here, Bartleby," said I, keenly pained at his implied suspicion. "And to you, this should not be so vile a place. Nothing reproachful attaches to you by being here. And see, it is not so sad a place as one might think. Look, there is the sky, and here is the grass."

"I know where I am," he replied, but would say nothing more, and so I left him.

As I entered the corridor again, a broad meat-like man, in an apron, accosted me, and, jerking his thumb over his shoulder, said—"Is that your friend?"

"Yes."

"Does he want to starve? If he does, let him live on the prison fare, that's all."

"Who are you?" asked I, not knowing what to make of such an unofficially speaking person in such a place.

"I am the grub-man. Such gentlemen as have friends here, hire me to provide them with something good to eat."

"Is this so?" said I, turning to the turnkey.*

turnkey: jailer

He said it was.

"Well, then," said I, slipping some silver into the grub-man's hands (for so they called him), "I want you to give particular attention to my friend there; let him have the best dinner you can get. And you must be as polite to him as possible."

"Introduce me, will you?" said the grub-man, looking at me with an expression which seemed to say he was all impatience for an opportunity to give a specimen of his breeding.

Thinking it would prove of benefit to the scrivener, I acquiesced; and, asking the grub-man his name, went up with him to Bartleby.

"Bartleby, this is a friend; you will find him very useful to you."

"Your sarvant, sir, your sarvant," said the grub-man, making a low salutation behind his apron. "Hope you find it pleasant here, sir; nice grounds—cool apartments—hope you'll stay with us sometime—try to make it agreeable. What will you have for dinner to-day?"

"I prefer not to dine to-day," said Bartleby, turning away. "It would disagree with me; I am unused to dinners." So saying, he slowly moved to the other side of the inclosure, and took up a position fronting the dead-wall.

"How's this?" said the grub-man, addressing me with a stare of astonishment. "He's odd, ain't he?"

"I think he is a little deranged," said I, sadly.

"Deranged? deranged is it? Well, now, upon my word, I thought that friend of yourn was a gentleman forger; they are always pale and genteel-like, them forgers. I can't help pity 'em—can't help it, sir. Did you know Monroe Edwards?" he added, touchingly, and paused. Then, laying his hand piteously on my shoulder, sighed, "he died of consumption at Sing-Sing. So you weren't acquainted with Monroe?"

"No, I was never socially acquainted with any forgers. But I cannot stop longer. Look to my friend yonder. You will not lose by it. I will see you again."

Some few days after this, I again obtained admission to the Tombs, and went through the corridors in quest of Bartleby; but without finding him.

"I saw him coming from his cell not long ago," said a turnkey, "may be he's gone to loiter in the yards."

So I went in that direction.

"Are you looking for the silent man?" said another turnkey, passing me. "Yonder he lies—sleeping in the yard there. 'Tis not twenty minutes since I saw him lie down."

The yard was entirely quiet. It was not accessible to the common prisoners. The surrounding walls, of amazing thickness, kept off all sounds behind them. The Egyptian character of the masonry weighed upon me with its gloom. But a soft imprisoned turf grew under foot. The heart of the eternal pyramids, it seemed, wherein, by some strange magic, through the clefts, grass-seed, dropped by birds, had sprung.

Strangely huddled at the base of the wall, his knees drawn up, and lying on his side, his head touching the cold stones, I saw the wasted Bartleby. But nothing stirred. I paused; then went close up to him; stooped over, and saw that his dim eyes were open; otherwise he seemed profoundly sleeping. Something prompted me to touch him. I felt his hand, when a tingling shiver ran up my arm and down my spine to my feet.

The round face of the grub-man peered upon me now. "His dinner is ready. Won't he dine to-day, either? Or does he live without dining?"

"Lives without dining," said I, and closed the eyes.

"Eh!—He's asleep, ain't he?"

"With kings and counselors,"* murmured I.

With . . . counselors: see Job 3:13-14

There would seem little need for proceeding further in this history. Imagination will readily supply the meagre recital of poor Bartleby's interment. But, ere parting with the reader, let me say, that if this little narrative has sufficiently interested him, to awaken curiosity as to who Bartleby was, and what manner of life he led prior to the present narrator's making his acquaintance, I can only reply, that in such curiosity I fully share, but am wholly unable to gratify it. Yet here I hardly know whether I should divulge one little item of rumor, which came to my ear a few months after the scrivener's decease. Upon what basis it rested, I could never ascertain; and hence, how true it is I cannot now tell. But, inasmuch as this vague report has not been without a certain suggestive interest to me, however sad, it may prove the same with some others; and so I will briefly mention it. The report was this: that Bartleby had been a subordinate clerk in the Dead Letter Office at Washington, from which he had been suddenly removed by a change in the administration. When I think over this rumor, hardly can I express the emotions which seize me. Dead letters! does it not sound like dead men? Conceive a man by nature and misfortune prone to pallid hopelessness, can any business seem more fitted to heighten it than that of continually handling these dead letters, and assorting them for the flames? For by the cart-load they are annually burned. Sometimes from out the folded paper the pale clerk takes a ring–the finger it was meant for, perhaps, moulders in the grave; a bank-note sent in swiftest charity–he whom it would relieve, nor eats nor hungers any more; pardon for those who died despairing; hope for those who died unhoping; good tidings for those who died stifled by unrelieved calamities. On errands of life, these letters speed to death.

Ah, Bartleby! Ah, humanity!

For Thought and Discussion

1. Discuss Melville's characterization of the narrator of the story using the questions which you find most revealing.
   a. Can you accept all of his judgments as reliable?
   b. Is he a noble character? Why or why not?
   c. What kind of employer is he?
   d. Whom does he come to tolerate better as employees, Turkey and Nippers or Bartleby? Why?
   e. Is he ever unreasonable in his demands on his employees?
   f. What is the narrator's attitude toward public opinion and the reaction of his clients and colleagues?
   g. In your opinion, is he ultimately charitable toward Bartleby? If so, what motivates his charity? Why does his charity finally fail?
   h. Carefully consider and discuss the meaning of the final three sentences of the story.
2. What does the narrator believe that he has learned as a result of his experiences with Bartleby?

3. What do you believe to be the major theme of Melville's story? Evaluate the soundness of this theme in terms of Biblical teaching. (What does Melville say about human nature? What does the Bible say about human nature?) At what point in the story does Melville quote the Bible? For what purpose?
4. Discuss Melville's characterization of Turkey, Nippers, and Ginger Nut. What is the significance of their names? What do Turkey and Nippers have in common? What kind of employees are they? What is their function in terms of Melville's theme? In what sense are they comic figures? Is there any sense in which they are to be pitied? Why?
5. Discuss Melville's characterization of Bartleby using the questions which you find most revealing. Is he a noble character? What do you know about his past? For what job does the narrator hire him? How well does he perform his job? What jobs in the offices does he "prefer not to" perform? Do you consider Bartleby's refusals polite? List Bartleby's earthly possessions. What does he eat? What adjectives and nouns does Melville use to describe Bartleby? Do you pity him? Why or why not? Do you believe that he is insane? Why or why not? To which of his character traits and actions do you react most negatively? Why or why not?
6. Discuss the significance of Melville's subtitle, "A Story of Wall Street." Read carefully the description of walls in the narrator's office and in the Tombs. (Notice that the narrator describes the green screen behind which Bartleby works as a movable wall.) How do walls function throughout the work? What is the significance of walls in the scene of Bartleby's death?

3

PART THREE

Sketch for Hound and Hunter; Winslow Homer; National Gallery of Art, Washington; Gift of Ruth K. Henschel in memory of her husband, Charles R. Henschel.

American Realism and Naturalism

An Era of New Beginnings

The half century following the Civil War was the most unsettling period that Americans had yet experienced. During this time the United States greatly changed not just in its standard of living but, more importantly, in its spiritual values. Gradually, as former beliefs became unpopular, the nation witnessed the birth of modern thought. Also during this period, which lasted from the end of the Civil War (1865) to the outbreak of World War I (1914), realism and naturalism triumphed in American literature.

SIGNS OF NEW BEGINNINGS

The Passing of the Frontier

By 1890 far-reaching changes were transforming the country. According to the 1890 census, the fabled American frontier had disappeared beneath the steadily growing Western population. But more than the frontier had vanished. Because of the growth of railroads, the long cattle drives from Texas to railroad centers in Montana and Kansas had virtually ceased. The awesome herds of buffalo that had once thundered across the prairie were also gone. Millions had been slaughtered to feed the work crews laying railroad tracks. Many others had been killed just for sport. In 1850 there were estimated to be twenty million buffalo, but forty years later there were fewer than six hundred.

By 1890 the last rebels among the Western Indians—weakened by war, disease, and starvation—finally surrendered to the army. Even in 1876, when the mighty Sioux nation under Chief Sitting Bull massacred General Custer and his soldiers at Little Big Horn, the end was already in sight. Ten years after Custer's last stand the capture of the wily Apache chief Geronimo ended Indian resistance in the Southwest. In December 1890 the last rebellious remnant of the Sioux nation was itself massacred at the Battle of Wounded Knee, South Dakota. The white man had unquestionably won the war of the West.

The Coming of Modern Transportation

As the frontier passed from the American scene, the modern age emerged. Air travel, one of the dominant symbols of modern life, began in 1903. In this year Or-

ville and Wilbur Wright successfully flew the first heavier-than-air machine at Kitty Hawk, North Carolina. But even before the Wright brothers' flight, the *horse-drawn* carriage had given way to the *horseless* carriage, or automobile. Through American ingenuity in the twentieth century, the automobile has been inexpensively mass-produced. As a result, the United States has become virtually a nation on wheels.

Difficulties Within the Nation

The years from 1865 to 1914 were not easy ones for the country. The nation had to live through the dark days of Reconstruction. Political and financial scandals greatly weakened Americans' trust in their national leaders. In the decade of its one-hundredth birthday, nothing seemed to go right for the United States. In 1870 the *New York Times* revealed the political corruption of the notorious Boss Tweed, who virtually ruled New York City. In 1871 a disastrous fire destroyed most of Chicago. In 1872 the *Baltimore Sun* revealed extensive corruption underlying the building of the Union Pacific Railroad. In 1873 a financial panic began a five-year depression. In 1877 federal troops were called out to put down a series of railroad strikes. It is no wonder that thoughtful citizens, particularly writers, had difficulty understanding this post-Civil War era.

NEW FORCES CHANGING AMERICAN SOCIETY

Underlying the swiftly occurring changes in this half century were two major forces. One was the nation's rapid industrialization. Between the end of the Civil War and the outbreak of World War I, the United States changed from a basically agricultural country to the most highly industrialized country in the world. This change raised the American standard of living to the world's highest.

The other major force was Charles Darwin's theory of biological evolution. This theory, which portrayed man as nothing more than an animal, dramatically affected the intellectual life of Americans. Darwin's supposedly scientific explanation of man's origin directly contradicted the Biblical account. Numerous Americans, accepting Darwin's theory as truth, abandoned their religious faith. As the forces of evolution and industrialism confronted American values and beliefs, the nation entered a period justifiably described as an era of new beginnings.

Industrialism

The Civil War (1861-65) cut this nation loose economically from its past and launched it into the industrial age. During the war Northern factories greatly expanded because of the demand for their products. After the war these factories turned to manufacturing peacetime goods. New technology made the production of goods increasingly easier and less expensive. As these goods became more accessible to consumers, the demand for them grew; mass production lowered the cost even more and further stimulated the demand.

The sewing machine is an interesting example of the role industry played in the development of American society. Prior to the Civil War, most Americans wore clothes made in the home or by professional tailors. During the war, because of the demand for military uniforms and ready-made clothing, manufacturers became interested in the sewing machine. When Isaac Merritt Singer (1811-75) obtained the legal rights to make sewing machines, the clothing industry rapidly expanded. By 1900 almost everyone wore ready-made clothing. As a result, nearly all Americans dressed alike no matter what their nationality or income. The sewing machine, both in the home and in the garment factory, helped produce uniformity among the American people. An American thus offered a striking contrast to the European, whose clothes usually reflected the wearer's racial, social, and economic background.

Industrialism was helped, of course, by the country's rich supply of natural resources. Iron ore (for manufacturing steel) and coal (for supplying energy) encouraged the growth of industry. Also available in the rapidly expanding cities of the East and Midwest was an ample supply of manpower, drawn both from American farms and from abroad. In fact, industrialism strongly supported the continued growth of the nation's cities.

Influence on population After the war thousands yielded to the spirit of national restlessness. Many uprooted their families and headed for the inexpensive and seemingly limitless land out West. Motivated by dreams of personal freedom and wealth, they tamed the land. In them the hardy pioneering spirit was yet very much alive. Some even struck it rich in mining and oil; others like Philip Armour (1832-1901) and Gustavus Swift (1839-1903) made fantastic fortunes in the newly developed meat industry.

Many other Americans, however, fled to the developing industrial cities. They abandoned the farmers' constant war against weather, disease, insects, and unstable markets. Some farmers were squeezed out by business deals between railroad offi-

cials and speculators, who undercut the prices farmers needed for economic survival. Later as factory workers began joining labor unions, farmers also started forming organizations for influencing business and government.

Most of the workers moving near the factories were immigrants newly arrived from Europe. Many were skilled or semiskilled workers driven out of their homelands by economic or political pressure. From 1860 to 1890 approximately ten million immigrants poured into the United States. Twenty million more (most of whom were Roman Catholic) came between 1890 and 1930. Most of those who arrived before 1896 were part of the "old immigration" (from European countries like Great Britain and Germany). Most of those who arrived after 1896 were part of the "new immigration" (from such countries as Italy, Austria-Hungary, Poland, the Balkans, and Russia).

The shifting population and the waves of immigrants dramatically enlarged the nation's cities. Many Southern blacks, leaving the rural South, also helped to swell the industrial centers. By the end of the nineteenth century, almost forty per cent of all Americans lived in cities—an increase of thirty per cent in a hundred years.

Influence of the financial leaders The industrialization of the nation could not have happened without the leadership of remarkable businessmen. These men organized the processes of industry and applied the developing technology. They obtained the money necessary for day-to-day operation and for expansion. They created markets for the products pouring from the plants. Among the most prominent of these businessmen were Andrew Carnegie (1835-1919) in the steel industry, John D. Rockefeller (1839-1937) in the oil refining industry, and J. Pierpont Morgan (1837-1913) in the banking industry.

Not always, however, did American business leaders act morally in their financial dealings. In fact, historians use the term "robber barons" to describe those who gained their money dishonestly. To achieve wealth, unscrupulous businessmen often manipulated the stock market, deliberately exploited their workers, or secured favorable government rulings through bribes and influence peddling. What motivated their actions was the belief that the end justifies the means. By unethically squeezing out their competition, they became rulers of extensive business empires.

In spite of notorious "robber barons," the success and prominence of the business tycoons brought them both national and international admiration. They were consulted by government officials on matters of national policy. They were courted by members of the European nobility. The country increasingly turned to businessmen for leadership rather than to lawyers, judges, and soldiers as it had before.

This rise of business leaders from stockboys to millionaires was popularized by national magazines and fictionalized in the Horatio Alger stories. Alger, a Unitarian minister from Massachusetts, worked with homeless boys at the Newsboy's Lodging House in New York City. To pass on to them the philosophy he had himself learned from such masters as Benjamin Franklin and Cotton Mather, Alger wrote over 130 novels about young men who succeeded by hard work, virtue, frugality, and timely response to opportunity. Such works as *Luck and Pluck* and *Strive and Succeed* helped to establish the legend which many later writers would refer to as "the great

American dream.'' In the era of urbanization and industrialization even a poor boy could by hard work and honesty, in the manner of Alger's Ragged Dick or Tattered Tom, become a millionaire or president of the United States. Later writers, particularly modern American dramatists, would attack "the great American dream" as a hollow notion. Their characters are either frustrated because they are not naturally gifted, or they sacrifice integrity to gain affluence and position, neither of which brings them true happiness.

As the nation's wealth increased, so did the fever for individual wealth. Many tried to make quick fortunes by playing the stock market, speculating in real estate, or by controlling the raw materials for a given product. Some were very successful. By 1883 there were approximately four thousand people worth a million dollars or more. But as the country became industrialized, its economy became more susceptible to severe depressions. In 1873 and 1893 high unemployment, reduced wages, and declining output brought economic disaster to hundreds of thousands. One result was the creation and growth of labor unions like the Knights of Labor and the American Federation of Labor (AFL) as well as farmers' organizations like the Grange.

Darwinism

While industrialism was profoundly changing Americans' values and standard of living, Darwinism was greatly influencing virtually every part of the nation's intellectual life. What Darwinism actually taught was not new, for the theory of evolution had existed in some form or another for over two thousand years. Darwinism's contribution to the existing theories of evolutionary development was so-called biological proof.

In his *Origin of Species,* Charles Darwin (1809-92) argued that animal forms are not fixed as unchangeable species. One kind of animal can develop into another type. Through the process of natural selection, he said, animals that develop superior traits survive and those that do not simply die out. As animals abundantly multiply, they fiercely compete for existing food, nesting sites, territorial range, and so forth. Those with some biological advantage win the struggle for survival. They then transmit that trait to their offspring and eventually a new species emerges. The process of developing the forms now existing, Darwin theorized, had taken millions of years. In his *Origin of Species* Darwin offered only a hint that his theory applied also to man's evolution. A dozen years later, in his *Descent of Man,* he proposed that man too had evolved, probably from something very much like an ape.

Influence upon science Darwin's theory electrified scientists who already wanted to throw out the Biblical account of creation. Their ready acceptance of this position doubtless rested on the eighteenth-century notion that man's reason can search out all truth. What is curious is that many scientists so quickly abandoned the principle of scientific objectivity. This principle demands that the scientist observe and test a new theory before he accepts it. No scientist—or anyone else, for that matter—has ever observed the process of change that Darwinism claims has happened and indeed is still going on.

Soon scientists from various disciplines extended Darwin's theory into anthropology, psychology, and other social sciences. Some, it is true, tried to adapt the Biblical account of creation to evolution. These argued essentially that after God created the first spark of life, He caused it to evolve into its present forms. The widespread belief in progress had prepared the way for rapid acceptance of Darwinism and for its adaptation to other fields. Significantly, Karl Marx (1818-83), the father of communism, wanted to dedicate his book *Das Kapital* (the Bible of communism) to Darwin but did not because of Darwin's wish that his religious relatives not be scandalized.

Influence on religion The most destructive influence of Darwinism was its effect on Americans' faith in God and His Word. The battle lines between the Bible and evolution were sharply drawn. There was no middle ground, although some–as we shall see later–tried to create one. Darwinism forced people to make a choice between two incompatible explanations for the origin of life, and it raised some monumental questions. If the Genesis account of creation is not accurate, then can any part of the Bible be trusted? If man has merely evolved from animals, does he have a soul or spirit responsive to God? If he is not conscious of God and feels no debt to Him, then why should man not live as he wishes? Is man not just an accident in a whole universe of accidents? Should he not live for whatever values he can discover or invent?

NEW ALIGNMENTS WITHIN AMERICAN CHRISTIANITY

The Attack by Disbelief

Assault against the Bible Simultaneous with this attack by Darwinism was the assault by the so-called higher criticism, which originated in German seminaries and universities. The higher critics assumed that the Bible is no different from other books and that it can therefore be best understood through the methods of scientific investigation. As a result, scholars tried to study the Bible in order to understand what they called the "real history" of the Biblical books. They soon denied the inspiration, the uniqueness, and the historical accuracy of the Word of God.

Effect of the assault The negative effects of the attack by Darwinism and higher criticism were alarming. For some, Christianity was either indefensible or not worth defending. These people became either agnostics (who believe that we cannot know whether there is a God) or atheists (who believe that there is no God). Others within American churches became liberals, or modernists. By trying to make the Bible agree with erroneous scientific theories, they denied the essential truths of Christianity. In fact, they created what amounted to a new religion with three key doctrines: (1) that God is the father of all men, (2) that all men are brothers, and (3) that all religions are true. For the liberals, man is not a sinner; the Bible is not divinely, verbally, and inerrantly inspired; Christ is not the divine Son of God; and salvation is not an individual matter but a communal one. Liberalism came to dominate the seminaries, the most prominent churches, the Sunday school materials, and the religious press. The liberals offered, however, only human opinions about contemporary social and moral problems. They gave easy, psychological solutions to the universal problem of sin.

A special form of their departure from God's Word was the social-gospel movement, founded in the late nineteenth century largely as a result of the writings of Walter Rauschenbusch (1861-1918). Most supporters of this movement believed that evil lies essentially in society's corrupt institutions. Men therefore should try to change society in order to make mankind better. Some agencies, like the Salvation Army (founded in 1878 in England), combined social concern with orthodox doctrine and evangelistic zeal. Most, however, were mere social-reform organizations disguised as religious agencies. By ignoring the fact of sin, the social-gospel movement attacked only a symptom of the disease within man. It ignored the disease itself–man's depraved nature. The supporters of this movement disregarded the fact that even in a perfect environment, the Garden of Eden, man had fallen into sin.

The Reaffirmation by Belief

Efforts of revivalists Not everyone within American Christianity yielded to the twin assaults of evolution and higher criticism. Thousands affirmed their faith in God's Word during the revival movements of the late nineteenth and early twentieth centuries. Two evangelists were especially instrumental in calling Americans back to God. Dwight L. Moody (1837-99), converted in his adolescent years through the efforts of his Sunday school teacher, untiringly preached to more than one million people in his lifetime. He held campaigns in nearly every major city from the East

Coast to the West. During the period from 1879 to 1886, he created two schools: one for girls (Northfield Seminary) and one for boys (Mount Herman School). Also during this time he established a summer Bible conference program at Northfield as well as the institution that later became known as Moody Bible Institute. Billy Sunday (1862-1935), converted in 1886 while a professional baseball player, became prominent as an evangelist during the latter part of Moody's life. Sunday conducted his campaigns in huge wooden tabernacles built especially for his evangelistic meetings. His well-organized campaigns saw over one million converts "hit the sawdust trail."

Rise of fundamentalism These revivals under Moody and Sunday had an immense spiritual impact on the American public. But within the churches and seminaries all was not well. Modernism was taking over the leadership in American Christianity. During the last quarter of the nineteenth century a religious movement emerged that would openly challenge American modernism.

This movement, later known as fundamentalism, arose in response to the liberal attacks against the Bible. In Bible conferences, which became especially important after 1875, leading preachers and laymen from various denominations counterattacked modernism. They jointly reaffirmed their belief in the doctrines that had always been the heart of Christianity: (1) the inerrancy of Scripture, (2) the virgin birth of Christ, (3) His substitutionary death, (4) His physical resurrection, and (5) His miracle-working power. In addition, these Bible conferences (the most significant of which met annually at a summer resort at Niagara Falls) stressed a doctrine previously overlooked in American preaching: the premillennial return of Christ (i.e., that Christ will return *before* the thousand year period described in Rev. 20:1-10). This teaching directly contradicted the evolutionary belief in man's steady progress toward perfection, for it affirmed that only Christ can create the reign of peace.

The premillennial conferences helped lay the groundwork for fundamentalism. But the actual birth of the movement appears to have occurred in the prophetical Bible conferences held in 1878 at New York City's Holy Trinity Episcopal Church and in Chicago eight years later. These conferences stressed the Biblical teaching of the imminence of the the Lord's Second Coming. The diversity of the speakers and delegates–drawn from the ranks of Presbyterians, Baptists, Episcopalians, Congregationalists, and Methodists–heralded the strongly interdenominational nature of the movement developing into fundamentalism

In the early twentieth century, the conflict within American Protestantism became intense. A series of twelve pamphlets entitled *The Fundamentals* clarified the issues dividing the two factions. Not all of the sixty-four European and American authors of these pamphlets were fully in agreement on every theological point or denominational teaching. Among the American authors were fifteen Presbyterians, eleven Baptists, four Methodists, three Dutch Reformed, three Congregationalists, two Episcopalians, and one Plymouth Brethren. Despite their denominational differences, they united to erect a wall of defense against modern unbelief on the common ground of historic Biblical Christianity.

Following World War I, the fundamentalist-modernist controversy rocked the major denominations. In every major denomination, however, the fundamentalists failed to dislodge the entrenched modernistic leadership. As a result, numerous pastors and laymen separated from their denominations to establish independent churches and groups of churches–the backbone of today's fundamentalist movement.

The term *fundamentalism* has been used in various ways since it was first applied to the movement in the 1920s. The term historically may designate the conservative theological reaction against the religious liberalism of the late nineteenth and early twentieth centuries. In a more universal theological sense, it may refer to the militant defense of the central doctrines of Biblical Christianity–especially those emphasized by Protestantism–in all ages of the church. The term also has been applied, or misapplied, to all nonliberal religious groups. As a result of the last usage, today's genuine fundamentalists often find themselves grouped in both the secular and the religious press with snake handlers from the Appalachian Mountains, Jehovah's Witnesses, and followers of cult leaders such as Sun Myung Moon or Jim Jones. A reasonable and useful way to think of American fundamentalism is as a modern historical expression of an age-old stance of God's people when their basic beliefs are threatened by unbelief within or without the professing church.

American literature of the post-Civil War era virtually ignored the important theological controversy that produced fundamentalism. Late-nineteenth-century writers of serious fiction and poetry only occasionally touched on general religious issues. When they did, they tended to side with religious liberalism. One of the most popular novels with a religious theme was *In His Steps* by Charles M. Sheldon (1857-1946). This stirring novel especially appealed to readers sympathetic with the emphases of the social gospel. Its characters decide to act on a new principle of Christian living. Before making any decision, they stop to ask, ''What would Jesus do?'' As a result, they dramatically change their midwestern city, particularly the section lying on ''the other side of the tracks.'' What this novel unfortunately omits, like other religious best sellers of the age, is a clear-cut presentation of the gospel. It does not force readers to confront the reality of their sinful condition before God and their need for personal forgiveness of sin.

NEW DIRECTIONS WITHIN AMERICAN LITERATURE

The development of American literature from after the Civil War until 1900 is, according to one noted literary historian, ''that of a vast adjustment to a new set of conditions for living.'' As writers grappled with the new conditions of this period, they were especially influenced by the forces of Darwinism, which encouraged atheism and industrialism with its accompanying materialism. In their subject matter and themes, writers quite naturally reflected the problems and values of their age. In their literary method, many writers mirrored the impact of science. These writers tried to study their characters and settings with the objectivity of a scientist. As a result, they often omitted the moral considerations that had guided most earlier writers. In short, they became realistic writers.

Domination of Realism

The spirit of realism Realism, of course, was not a new attitude in literature. Writers of all literary periods since classical times have used realistic settings and characters. In fact, almost all writers employ realistic description and themes. Still, some works are more realistic than others. That is, some works are more down-to-earth or matter-of-fact in depicting everyday life. They portray what generally lies within the common man's experiences. As a distinct literary movement, realism began in Europe in the 1830s. Writers like the Frenchmen Honoré de Balzac (1799-1850) and Gustave Flaubert (1821-80) tried to present the world not as it once had been nor as they wished it might be but exactly as they believed it was.

What a person regards as realism depends, of course, on his view of the world. The beliefs of a writer unquestionably influence what he sees or thinks he sees. For instance, because the Puritans believed that God controls everything, they saw God's hand revealed in everything. The Puritan writers, as a consequence, tried to reveal how and for what purposes God acts in the world. After a strong, young, but blasphemous sailor died aboard the *Mayflower*, Governor Bradford recorded the death as God's direct act of judgment on the sailor for his sin. But after a Christian man was swept overboard in the Atlantic, Bradford portrayed his stirring rescue as an act of God's mercy.

Many writers of the late nineteenth century did not believe in God. They therefore pictured the world as controlled by nature or fate or blind chance. Their realistic vision of the world was thus much different from the Puritans' realistic vision. Oftentimes what secular literary historians call realistic fiction will seem, in fact, quite unrealistic to Christians. A truly Christian realism emphasizes as a major theme the wisdom and goodness of God and the purpose and order of His universe. It includes as a minor theme the failure and misery of rebellious man. It affirms finally the possibility, though not the necessity, of human happiness.

Post-Civil War American writers, for the most part, agreed on certain basic artistic principles. They usually wrote about what they saw around them, especially the scenery and the people (their problems, their habits, and so forth). A small group of writers at the turn of the century reshaped the basic principles of realism. These naturalists, as they are called, tended to portray characters as mere brutes, more beast than human. Although the post-Civil War writers were a broad, heterogeneous lot, most of them belonged to one of three groups: the regionalists, the master realists, or the naturalists.

The divisions within realism The first clearly distinct group of writers following the Civil War was the regionalists. Like American writers before and after them, the regionalists located their fiction and poetry in a specific geographical section of the country. What partly distinguished these writers was their use of two sections almost untouched by earlier writers: the West and the Midwest. (The South and the Northeast dominated the work of other regionalists.) The regional writers also, to a greater extent than most previous writers, emphasized such details as the landscape, customs, people, dialect, dress, and beliefs of their chosen region. In fact, a regional work is so firmly rooted in its part of the country that transplanting the story or poem anywhere else seriously weakens it effect.

The regionalists, for the most part, were transitional writers standing between the major romantics of the middle of the century and the major realists of the last third. Writers such as Bret Harte concentrated on exotic characters (a romantic trait). Writers such as Sarah Orne Jewett depicted more representative figures (a realistic trait). One group of regionalists, the local colorists, were actually more romantic than realistic. They used realistic details primarily for decoration. The regionalists (especially the local colorists) helped greatly to popularize the short story among American readers. Yet generally their works lack the depth of **characterization** and seriousness of **theme** found in works by the major American realists.

The three most significant American realists, often called the "masters of realism," are William Dean Howells, Henry James, and Samuel Langhorne Clemens (who used the pen name "Mark Twain"). These three raised the realistic method to its highest artistic level. All three worked primarily in fiction, writing numerous novels and short stories. Each, however, reflects a different spirit, or literary force, working within American realism. Howells (who moved to Boston after spending his youth in the Midwest) embodies the middle-class spirit. James (who lived abroad for most of his youth and adult life) embodies the cosmopolitan, or international, spirit. Clemens (who spent his youth along the Mississippi River) embodies the frontier spirit. These three writers were major influences on American realism, particularly through their treatment of the physical world and their revelation of the inner workings of the human mind.

Emergence of Naturalism

Although often viewed as a mere continuation of realism, American naturalism is in many respects an altogether different movement. Fundamentally, it is the application of Darwinism to literature. The naturalist, instead of merely trying to report what he sees around him, portrays life as controlled by forces that no one can change or even understand. He argues the thesis that all life is an illustration of the laws of evolution. As a result, a naturalist rarely gives his characters an opportunity to control their lives.

A few American writers resisted the naturalistic movement by maintaining traditional social, literary, or religious values. The optimism of anti-naturalists like Edwin Markham, William Sydney Porter (who used the pen name "O. Henry"), and the hymnologist Fanny Crosby revealed that not all American writers had flocked to the naturalists' banner. Their influence, however, proved not so great as that of the naturalists, whose influence continues to the present day.

These changes affected nearly every aspect of American life and thought. The saddest change of all—and the one felt most strongly today—was the growing confidence of the American people in the words of men rather than in the Word of God. Their trust in mere human theory produced the drastic intellectual changes occurring in the half century following the Civil War. Some historians, impressed by these changes, call this period "the Second Republic" ("the First Republic" being the period between the War of Independence and the Civil War).

In 1914 this era ended. As World War I engulfed the world, it shook the nation's and the world's belief in the myth of human progress. Mankind, it seemed, had retrogressed, not progressed. As modern writers responded to the new mood, a deep sense of pessimism crept into their writing. To explain the attitudes of today's writers, we must understand those expressed in the literature of the post-Civil War period. A Christian view of the late nineteenth-century American writers is the key to a true understanding of the modern age.

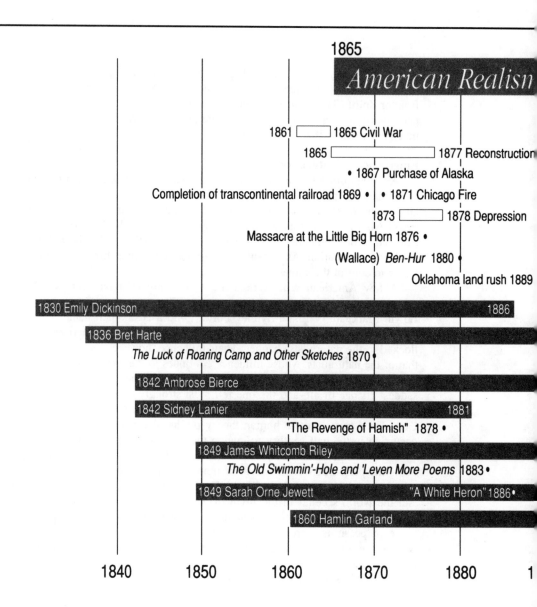

1865

American Realism

1861 ☐ 1865 Civil War

1865 ☐ 1877 Reconstruction

• 1867 Purchase of Alaska

Completion of transcontinental railroad 1869 • | • 1871 Chicago Fire

1873 ☐ 1878 Depression

Massacre at the Little Big Horn 1876 •

(Wallace) *Ben-Hur* 1880 •

Oklahoma land rush 1889

1830 Emily Dickinson   1886

1836 Bret Harte

The Luck of Roaring Camp and Other Sketches 1870 •

1842 Ambrose Bierce

1842 Sidney Lanier   1881

"The Revenge of Hamish" 1878 •

1849 James Whitcomb Riley

The Old Swimmin'-Hole and 'Leven More Poems 1883 •

1849 Sarah Orne Jewett   "A White Heron" 1886 •

1860 Hamlin Garland

1840   1850   1860   1870   1880   1

1914

and Naturalism

8 Regionalists

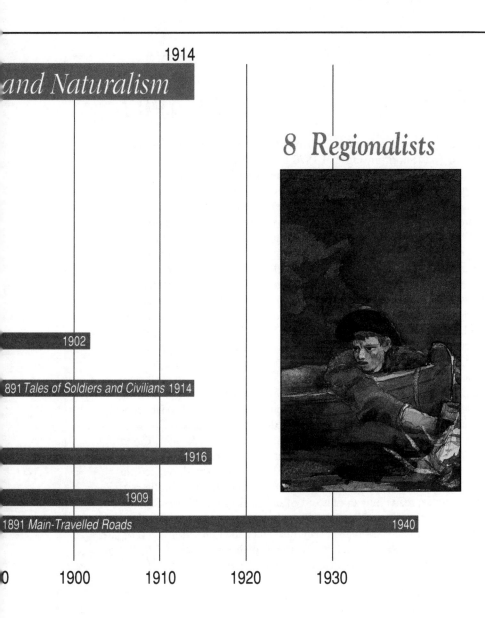

1902

891 *Tales of Soldiers and Civilians* 1914

1916

1909

1891 *Main-Travelled Roads* 1940

0   1900   1910   1920   1930

Bret Harte   1836-1902

Bret Harte was the first writer after the Civil War to win a large public following in the United States. For a short time around 1870 he was regarded as the most important of all living American writers. His stories about the West made him popular both in the eastern part of this country and in England. He spent the last part of his life in London, still writing the same type of story that had made him popular earlier.

Harte was born in Albany, New York, and spent his early years in New York City and Brooklyn. When his father died in 1845, the Harte family fell on hard times. In 1854 seventeen-year-old Bret sailed by way of Nicaragua to San Francisco to join his widowed mother, who had moved out West the year before to remarry. He arrived just five years after the Gold Rush of 1849 had brought hordes of people into the territory. He tried a number of jobs, including teaching, printing, journalism, and (according to some) gold mining. After working for the *Northern Californian* and the *Golden Era,* he was appointed editor of the *Overland Monthly* in 1858. The second issue of this magazine included ''The Luck of Roaring Camp,'' the tale that brought Harte to the nation's attention. This story, set in California in 1850-51, shows the rough men of a mining camp changed from evil to virtuous characters as they care for an orphaned, illegitimate half-breed baby they call Tommy Luck. When a flash flood destroys the camp, both the baby and the two miners who have given him a home drown. This sentimental twist touched the emotions of many nineteenth-century readers.

In 1870 Harte published his first collection of stories, *The Luck of Roaring Camp and Other Sketches*. These tales made Harte an immediate literary success. They owed enough to the famous English novelist Charles Dickens to earn Harte the title ''The American Dickens.'' The editors of the *Atlantic Monthly,* the leading literary publication in the country, made him an unheard-of offer. They would pay $10,000 for the exclusive rights to whatever Harte would write for one year. He accepted the offer and returned East in 1871. But his career soon turned downward. He plunged into debt and alienated many of his friends, among them Samuel Clemens. The works Harte wrote at this time were generally inferior to his earlier ones.

In 1878 he sailed to Europe to serve as United States consul, in Germany and then in Scotland. He never returned to the States. After 1885 he lived in London, writing Western stories that imitated those he had written in the late 1860s. Because he continued writing only what his reading public demanded, he never developed as a writer. Even though his works began the local-color movement in the States, they lost favor in literary circles long before his death in 1902.

Harte's stories about the West became successful for several reasons. They were written in a clean, disciplined style. Their

plots move crisply to climactic endings, often of surprise. Harte seasoned these stories with humor and unexpected turns. He skillfully used Western dialects in both his poetry and his fiction. He also blended two widely accepted views of the West. One represented the region as a barbaric land with half-civilized, immoral people. The other portrayed it as an American Eden where dreams could become realities.

As a writer, Harte had an important influence on the trend of American fiction in the post-Civil War era. Many today regard him as the father of the modern short story. His style, choice of subject matter, and attitude toward his characters helped prepare the way for the explosion of local-color writing after 1870. Harte failed, however, as a moral guide. His fiction lacks a moral framework that implies judgments on characters and their actions. In fact, his popularity was undoubtedly aided by the country's accelerating departure from traditional moral values. The twentieth-century literary critic Floyd Stovall finds that Harte's work has significantly influenced modern society. Stovall writes in *American Idealism* that Harte's "sentimental confusion of evil with good has been partly responsible for the spread of vice and crime and the laxity of courts of justice in this country." If Stovall is right, Harte was the source of much more than just the explosion of local-color writing. His work signaled the beginning of the modern tradition in American literature.

The Boom in the *Calaveras Clarion*

In some respects this story is not typical of Harte's most popular tales. It lacks the moral vagueness and tolerance of frequently reprinted stories like "The Luck of Roaring Camp," "The Outcasts of Poker Flat," and "Tennessee's Partner." It is, however, artistically representative of Harte's popular works. The story was not published until 1899, when it appeared in Mr. Jack Hamlin's Meditation and Other Stories. *It shows that Harte, near the end of his life, was still mining the same vein that had created his popularity thirty years before.*

In this tale Harte looks back at least in part to his experiences as a newspaperman in the California of the 1860s. The **setting,** *which appears in several of Harte's stories, is Calaveras County. This is an actual county about one hundred miles inland from San Francisco. It also provided the locale for Samuel Clemens's first famous tall tale, "The Celebrated Jumping Frog of Calaveras County" (1865).*

Harte fully describes both the surroundings and the characters. The story centers on three meetings between one or both of the Dimmidges and the acting editor of the Clarion. *Notice that the story ends with an unexpected twist. Notice also the humor in the tale. The Dimmidges are humorous figures and their newspaper advertisements are humorously appropriate to the way each views himself and his spouse.*

The editorial sanctum* of the *Calaveras Clarion* opened upon the ''composing-room'' of the paper on the one side, and gave* apparently upon the rest of Calaveras County upon the other. For, situated on the very outskirts of the settlement and the summit of a very steep hill, the pines sloped away from the editorial windows to the long valley of the South Fork and–infinity. The little wooden building had invaded Nature without subduing it. It was filled night and day with the murmur of pines and their fragrance. Squirrels scampered over its roof when it was not preoccupied by woodpeckers, and a printer's devil* had once seen a nest-building blue jay enter a window in the composing room, flutter before one of the slanting type-cases with an air of deliberate selection, and then fly off with a vowel in its bill.

sanctum: a private office free from intrusion
gave: looked out
printer's devil: an apprentice to a printer

Amidst these sylvan* surroundings the temporary editor of the *Clarion* sat at his sanctum, reading the proofs of an editorial. As he was occupying that position during a six week's absence of the *bona fide** editor and proprietor, he was consequently reading the proof with some anxiety and responsibility. . . . In that occupation he became oblivious of the next room, of a silence, a whispered conversation, which ended with a rapping at the door and the appearance of the foreman in the doorway.

sylvan: relating to the forest
bona fide: genuine, Lat., good faith

''There's a man in the office who wants to see the editor,'' he said.

''Show him in,'' replied the editor briefly. He was, however, conscious that there was a singular significance in his foreman's manner, and an eager apparition of the other printer over the foreman's shoulder.

''He's carryin' a shot-gun, and is a man twice as big as you be,'' said the foreman gravely.

The editor quickly recalled his own brief and as yet blameless record in the *Clarion*. ''Perhaps,'' he said tentatively,* with a gentle smile, ''he's looking for Captain Brush'' (the absent editor).

tentatively: hesitantly

''I told him all that,'' said the foreman grimly, ''and he said he wanted to see the man in charge.''

In proportion as the editor's heart sank his outward crest arose.* ''Show him in,'' he said loftily.

his . . . arose: i.e., he became outwardly brave

''We *kin* keep him out,'' suggested the foreman, lingering a moment; ''me and him,'' indicating the expectant printer behind him, ''is enough for that.''

''Show him up,'' repeated the editor firmly.

The foreman withdrew; the editor seated himself and again took up his proof. The doubtful word ''ignominious''* seemed to stand out of the paragraph before him; it certainly *was* a strong expression! He was about to run his pencil through it when he heard the heavy step of his visitor approaching. A sudden instinct of belligerency* took possession of him, and he wrathfully threw the pencil down.

ignominious: dishonorable
belligerency: aggressiveness, hostility

The burly form of the stranger blocked the doorway. He was dressed like a miner, but his build and general physiognomy* were quite distinct from the local variety. His upper lip and chin were clean-shaven, still showing in the blue-black roots of the beard which covered the rest of his face and deepened in a thick fleece* under his throat. He carried a small bundle tied up in a silk handkerchief in one hand, and a ''shot-gun'' in the other, perilously* at half-cock. Entering the sanctum, he put down his bundle and quietly closed the door behind him. He then drew an empty chair towards him and dropped heavily into it with his gun on his knees. The editor's heart dropped almost as heavily, although he quite composedly held out his hand.

physiognomy: external appearance
fleece: a soft woolly mass
perilously: dangerously

"Shall I relieve you of your gun?"

"Thank ye, lad–noa. It's moor coomfortable wi' me, and it's main dangersome to handle on the half-cock. That's why I didn't leave 'im on the horse outside!"

At the sound of his voice and occasional accent a flash of intelligence relieved the editor's mind. He remembered that twenty miles away, in the illimitable* vista* from his windows, lay a settlement of English north-country miners, who, while faithfully adopting the methods, customs, and even slang of the Californians, retained many of their native peculiarities. The gun he carried on his knee, however, was evidently part of the Californian imitation.

illimitable: measureless
vista: a distant view

"Can I do anything for you?" said the editor blandly.*

blandly: soothingly

"Ay! I've coom here to bill ma woife."

"I–don't think I understand," hesitated the editor, with a smile.

"I've coom here to get ye to put in your paper a warnin', a notiss, that onless she returns to my house in four weeks, I'll have nowt to do wi' her again."

"Oh!" said the editor, now perfectly reassured, "you want an advertisement? That's the business of the foreman; I'll call him." He was rising from his seat when the stranger laid a heavy hand on his shoulder and gently forced him down again.

"Noa, lad! I don't want noa foreman nor understrappers* to take this job, I want to talk it over wi' you. *Sabe?* My woife she bin up and awaa these six months. We had a bit of difference, that ain't here nor there, but she skedaddled* outer my house. I want to give her fair warning, and let her know I ain't paying any debt o' hers, arter this notiss, and I ain't takin' her back arter four weeks from date."

understrappers: underlings
Sabe: Sp., "Do you understand?"
skedaddled: ran away

"I see," said the editor glibly.* "What's your wife's name?"

glibly: smoothly, nonchalantly

"Eliza Jane Dimmidge."

"Good," continued the editor, scribbling on the paper before him; "something like this will do: 'Whereas my wife, Eliza Jane Dimmidge having left my bed and board without just cause or provocation, this is to give notice that I shall not be responsible for any debts of her contracting on or after this date.' "

"Ye must be a lawyer," said Mr. Dimmidge admiringly.

It was an old enough form of advertisement, and the remark showed incontestably* that Mr. Dimmidge was not a native; but the editor smiled patronizingly* and went on: " 'And I further give notice that if she does not return within the period of four weeks from this date, I shall take such proceedings for relief as the law affords.' "

incontestably: unquestionably
patronizingly: acting with an air of superiority

"Coom, lad, I didn't say *that*."

"But you said you wouldn't take her back."

"Ay."

"And you can't prevent her without legal proceedings. She's your wife. But you needn't take proceedings, you know. It's only a warning."

Mr. Dimmidge nodded approvingly, "That's so."

"You'll want it published for four weeks, until date?" asked the editor.

"Mebbe longer, lad."

The editor wrote "till forbid" in the margin of the paper and smiled.

"How big will it be?" said Mr. Dimmidge.

The editor took up a copy of the *Clarion* and indicated about an inch of space. Mr. Dimmidge's face fell.

"I want it bigger,–in large letters, like a play-card,"* he said. "That's no good for a warning."

---

play-card: i.e., poster

"You can have half a column or a whole column if you like," said the editor airily.

"I'll take a whole one," said Mr. Dimmidge simply.

The editor laughed. "Why! It would cost you a hundred dollars."

"I'll take it," repeated Mr. Dimmidge.

"But," said the editor gravely, "the same notice in a small space will serve your purpose and be quite legal."

"Never you mind that, lad! It's the looks of the thing I'm arter, and not the expense. I'll take that column."

The editor called in the foreman and showed him the copy. "Can you display that so as to fill a column."

The foreman grasped the situation promptly. It would be big business for the paper. "Yes," he said meditatively, "that bold-faced election type will do it."

Mr. Dimmidge's face brightened. The expression "bold-faced" pleased him. "That's it! I told you. I want to bill her in a portion of the paper."

"I might put in a cut," said the foreman suggestively; "something like this." He took a venerable woodcut from the case. I grieve to say it was one which, until the middle of the present century, was common enough in the newspaper offices in the Southwest. It showed the running figure of a Negro woman carrying her personal property in a knotted handkerchief slung from a stick over her shoulder, and was supposed to represent "a fugitive slave."

Mr. Dimmidge's eyes brightened. "I'll take that, too. It's a little dark-complected for Mrs. D., but it will do. Now roon away, lad," he said to the foreman, as he quietly pushed him into the outer office again and closed the door. Then, facing the surprised editor, he said, "Theer's another notiss I want ye to put in your paper; but's that's atween *us*. Not a word to *them*," he indicated the banished foreman with a jerk of his thumb. "*Sabe?* I want you to put this in another part o' your paper, quite innocent-like, ye know." He drew from his pocket a gray wallet, and taking a slip of paper read from it gravely. " 'If this should meet the eye of R. B., look out for M. J. D. He is on your track. When this you see write a line to E. J. D., Elktown Post Office.' I want this to go in as 'Personal and Private'–*sabe?* like them notisses in the big 'Frisco papers."

"I see," said the editor, laying it aside. "It shall go in the same issue in another column."

Apparently Mr. Dimmidge expected something more than this reply, for after a moment's hesitation he said with an odd smile:–

"Ye ain't seein' the meanin' o' that, lad?"

"No," said the editor lightly, "but I suppose R. B. does, and it isn't intended that any one else should."

"Mebbe it is, and mebbe it isn't," said Mr. Dimmidge, with a self-satisfied air. "I don't mind saying atween us that R. B. is the man as I've suspicioned as havin' something to do with my wife goin' away; and ye see, if he writes to E. J. D.–that's my wife's initials–at Elktown, *I'll* get that letter and so make sure."

"But suppose your wife goes there first, or sends?"

"Then I'll ketch her or her messenger. Ye see?"

The editor did not see fit to oppose any argument to this phenomenal simplicity, and Mr. Dimmidge, after settling his bill with the foreman, and enjoining the editor to the strictest secrecy regarding the origin of the "personal notice," took up his gun and departed, leaving the treasury

WHEREAS MY WIFE,

ELIZA JANE DIMMIDGE

HAVING LEFT MY BED AND BOARD WITHOUT JUST CAUSE OR PROVOCATION, THIS IS TO GIVE NOTICE THAT I SHALL NOT BE RESPONSIBLE FOR ANY DEBTS OF HER CONTRACTING ON OR AFTER THIS DATE.

AND I FURTHER GIVE NOTICE THAT IF SHE DOES NOT RETURN WITHIN THE PERIOD OF FOUR WEEKS FROM THIS DATE, I SHALL TAKE SUCH PROCEEDINGS FOR RELIEF AS THE LAW AFFORDS.

of the *Clarion* unprecedentedly* enriched, and the editor to his proofs.

unprecedentedly: new, as not seen before

The paper duly appeared the next morning with the column advertisement, the personal notice, and the weighty editorial on the wagon road. There was a singular demand for the paper, the edition was speedily exhausted, and the editor was proportionately flattered, although he was surprised to receive neither praise nor criticism from his subscribers. Before evening, however, he learned to his astonishment that the excitement was caused by the column advertisement. Nobody knew Mr. Dimmidge, nor his domestic infelicities,* and the editor and foreman, being equally in the dark, took refuge in a mysterious and impressive evasion of all inquiry.

domestic infelicities: family quarrels

Never since the last San Francisco Vigilance Committee had the office been so besieged. The editor, foreman, and even the apprentice were buttonholed and "treated" at the bar, but to no effect. All that could be learned was that it was a *bona fide* advertisement, for which one hundred dollars had been received! There were great discussions and conflicting theories as to whether the value of the wife, or the husband's anxiety to get rid of her, justified the enormous expense and ostentatious* display. She was supposed to be an exceedingly beautiful woman by some, by others a perfect Sycorax;* in one breath Mr. Dimmidge was a weak, uxorious spouse,* wasting his substance on a creature who did not care for him, and in another a maddened, distracted, henpecked man, content to purchase peace and rest at any price.

ostentatious: showy
Sycorax: an ugly witch from Shakespeare's *The Tempest*
uxorious spouse: one excessively fond of his wife

Certainly, never was an advertisement more effective in its publicity, or cheaper in proportion to the circulation it commanded. It was copied throughout the whole Pacific slope; mighty San Francisco papers described its size and setting under the attractive headline, "How they Advertise a Wife in the Mountains!" It reappeared in the Eastern journals, under the title of "Whimsicalities* of the Western Press." It was believed to have crossed to England as a specimen of "Transatlantic Savagery." The real editor of the *Clarion* awoke one morning, in San Francisco, to find his paper famous. Its advertising columns were eagerly sought for; he at once advanced the rates. People bought excessive issues to gaze upon this monumental record of extravagance.

Whimsicalities: playfulness, pranks

A singular idea, which, however, brought further fortune to the paper, was advanced by an astute* critic at the Eureka Saloon. "My opinion, gentlemen, is that the whole blamed thing is a bluff! There ain't no Mr. Dimmidge; there ain't no Mrs. Dimmidge; there ain't no desertion! The whole rotten thing is an *advertisement* o' suthin'! Ye'll find afore ye get through with it that that there wife won't come back until that blamed husband buys Somebody's Soap, or treats her to Somebody's particular Starch or Patent Medicine! Ye jest watch and see!" The idea was startling, and seized upon the mercantile* mind. The principal merchant of the town, and the purveyor* to the mining settlements beyond, appeared next morning at the office of the *Clarion*. "Ye wouldn't mind putting this 'ad' in a column alongside o' the Dimmidge one, would ye?" The young editor glanced at it, and then, with a serpent-like sagacity, veiled, however, by the suavity, of the dove, pointed out that the original advertiser might think it called his *bona fides* into question and withdraw his advertisement. "But if we secured you by an offer of double the amount per column?" urged the merchant. "That," responded the *locum tenens,** "was for the actual editor and proprietor in San Francisco to determine. He would telegraph." He did so. The response was, "Put it in."

astute: shrewd
mercantile: commercial, business
purveyor: provider
locum tenens: Lat., temporary substitute

Whereupon in the next issue, side by side with Mr. Dimmidge's protracted* warning, appeared a column with the announcement, in large letters, WE HAVEN'T LOST ANY WIFE, but WE are prepared to furnish the following goods at a lower rate than any other advertiser in the country,'' followed by the usual price list of the merchant's wares. There was an unprecedented demand for that issue. The reputation of the *Clarion,* both as a shrewd advertising medium and a comic paper, was established at once. For a few days the editor waited with some apprehension for a remonstrance* from the absent Dimmidge, but none came. Whether Mr. Dimmidge recognized that this new advertisement gave extra publicity to his own, or that he was already on the track of the fugitive, the editor did not know. The few curious citizens who had, early in the excitement, penetrated the settlement of the English miners twenty miles away in search of information, found that Mr. Dimmidge had gone away, and that Mrs. Dimmidge had *never* resided there with him!

protracted: drawn out, prolonged
remonstrance: reproof, objection

Six weeks passed. The limit of Mr. Dimmidge's advertisement had been reached, and, as it was not renewed, it had passed out of the pages of the *Clarion,* and with it the merchant's advertisement in the next column. The excitement had subsided, although its influence was still felt in the circulation of the paper and its advertising popularity. The temporary editor was also nearing the limit of his incumbency,* but had so far participated in the good fortune of the *Clarion* as to receive an offer from one of the San Francisco dailies.*

incumbency: period of office
dailies: newspapers

It was a warm night, and he was alone in his sanctum. The rest of the building was dark and deserted, and his solitary light, flashing out through the open window, fell upon the nearer pines and was lost in the dark, indefinable slope below. He had reached the sanctum by the rear, and a door which he also left open to enjoy the freshness of the aromatic air. Nor did it in the least mar his privacy. Rather the solitude of the great woods without seemed to enter through that door and encompassed him with its protecting loneliness. There was occasionally a faint ''peep'' in the scant eaves, or a ''pat-pat,'' ending in a frightened scurry across the roof, or the slow flap of a heavy wing in the darkness below. These gentle disturbances did not, however, interrupt his work on ''The True Functions of the County Newspaper,'' the editorial on which he was engaged.

Presently a more distinct rustling against the straggling blackberry bushes beside the door attracted his attention. It was followed by a light tapping against the side of the house. The editor started and turned quickly towards the open door. Two outside steps led to the ground. Standing upon the lower one was a woman. The upper part of her figure, illuminated by the light from the door, was thrown into greater relief by the dark background of the pines. Her face was unknown to him, but it was a pleasant one, marked by a certain good-humored determination.

''May I come in?'' she said confidently.

''Certainly,'' said the editor. ''I am working here alone because it is so quiet.'' He thought he would precipitate* some explanation from her by excusing himself.

precipitate: cause to happen

''That's the reason why I came,'' she said, with a quiet smile.

She came up the next step and entered the room. She was plainly but neatly dressed, and now that her figure was revealed he saw that she was wearing a linsey-woolsey* riding skirt, and carried a serviceable raw-hide whip in her cotton-gauntleted hand. She took the chair he offered her and sat down sideways on it, her whip hand now also holding up her skirt, and permitting a hem of clean white petticoat and a smart, well-shaped boot to be seen.

linsey-woolsey: a coarse fabric of wool and cotton or linen

"I don't remember to have had the pleasure of seeing you in Calaveras before," said the editor tentatively.

"No. I never was here before," she said composedly, "but you've heard enough of me, I reckon. I'm Mrs. Dimmidge." She threw one hand over the back of the chair, and with the other tapped her riding-whip on the floor.

The editor started. Mrs. Dimmidge! Then she was not a myth. An absurd similarity between her attitude with the whip and her husband's entrance with his gun six weeks before forced itself upon him and made her an invincible* presence.

invincible: unconquerable

"Then you have returned to your husband?" he said hesitatingly.

"Not much!" she returned with a slight curl of her lip.

"But you read his advertisement?"

"I saw the column of fool nonsense he put in your paper–ef that's what you mean," she said with decision, "but I didn't come here to see *him*–but *you.*"

The editor looked at her with a forced smile, but vague misgiving. He was alone at night in a deserted part of the settlement, with a plump, self-possessed woman who had a contralto* voice, a horsewhip, and–he could not help feeling–an evident grievance.

contralto: the lowest female voice

"To see me?" he repeated, with a faint attempt at gallantry. "You are paying me a great compliment, but really–"

"When I tell you I've come three thousand miles from Kansas straight here without stopping, ye kin reckon it's so," she replied firmly.

"Three thousand miles!" echoed the editor wonderingly.

"Yes. Three thousand miles from my own folk's home in Kansas, where six years ago I married Mr. Dimmidge,–a British furriner* as could scarcely make himself understood in any Christian language! Well, he got round me and dad, allowin' he was a reg'lar out-and-out profeshnal miner,–had lived in mines ever since he was a boy; and so, not knowin' what kind o' mines, and dad just bilin' over with the gold fever, we were married and kem across the plains to Californy. He was a good enough man to look at, but it warn't three months before I discovered that he allowed a wife was no better nor a slave, and he the master. That made me open my eyes; but then, as he didn't drink, and didn't gamble, and didn't swear, and was a good provider and laid by money, why, I shifted along with him as best I could. We drifted down the first year to Sonora, at Red Dog, where there wasn't another woman. Well, I did the slave business,–never stirring out o' the settlement, never seein' a town or a crowd o' decent people,–and he did the lord and master! We played that game for two years, and I got tired. But when at last he allowed he'd go up to Elktown Hill, where there was a passel* o' his countrymen at work, with never a sign o' any other folks, and leave me alone at Red Dog until he fixed up a place for me at Elktown Hill,–I kicked! I gave him fair warning! I did as other slaves did,–I ran away!"

furriner: foreigner
passel: a large number

A recollection of the wretched woodcut which Mr. Dimmidge had selected to personify his wife flashed upon the editor with a new meaning. Yet perhaps she had not seen it, and had only read a copy of the advertisement. What could she want? The *Calaveras Clarion,* although a "Palladium"* and a "Sentinel upon the Heights of Freedom'' in reference to wagon roads, was not a redresser* of domestic wrongs,–except through its advertising columns! Her next word intensified that suggestion.

Palladium: a safeguard
redresser: an avenger, one who compensates for wrongs

"I've come here to put an advertisement in your paper.''

The editor heaved a sigh of relief, as once before. "Certainly,'' he said briskly. "But that's another department of the paper, and the printers have gone home. Come to-morrow morning early.''

"To-morrow morning I shall be miles away,'' she said decisively, "and what I want done has got to be done *now!* I don't want to see no printers; I don't want *anybody* to know I've been here but you. That's why I kem here at night, and rode all the way from Sawyer's Station, and wouldn't take the stagecoach. And when we've settled about the advertisement, I'm going to mount my horse, out thar in the bushes, and scoot outer the settlement.''

"Very good,'' said the editor resignedly. "Of course I can deliver your instruction to the foreman. And now–let me see–I suppose you wish to intimate in a personal notice to your husband that you've returned.''

"Nothin' o' the kind!'' said Mrs. Dimmidge cooley. "I want to placard him as he did me. I've got it all written out here. *Sabe?*''

She took from her pocket a folded paper, and spreading it out on the editor's desk with a certain pride of authorship, read as follows:–

"Whereas my husband, Micah J. Dimmidge, having given out that I have left his bed and board,–the same being a bunk in a log cabin and pork and molasses three times a day,–and having advertised that he'd pay no debts of *my* contractin',–which, as thar ain't any, might be easier collected than debts of his own contractin',–this is to certify that unless he returns from Elktown Hill to his only home in Sonora in one week from

date, payin' the cost of this advertisement, I'll know the reason why.–Eliza Jane Dimmidge.

"Thar,'' she added, drawing a long breath, "put that in a column of the *Clarion,* same size as the last, and let it work, and that's all I want of you.''

"A column?'' repeated the editor. "Do you know the cost is very expensive, and I *could* put it in a single paragraph?''

"I reckon I kin pay the same as Mr. Dimmidge did for *his,*'' said the lady complacently. "I didn't see your paper myself, but the paper as copied it–one of them New York dailies–said it took up a whole column.''

The editor breathed more freely; she had not seen the infamous woodcut which her husband had selected. At the same moment he was struck with a sense of retribution,* justice, and compensation.

retribution: punishment, recompense

"Would you,'' he asked hesitatingly,–"would you like it illustrated–by a cut?''

"With which?''

"Wait a moment; I'll show you.''

He went into the dark composing-room, lit a candle, and rummaging in a drawer sacred to weather-beaten, old-fashioned electrotyped advertising symbols of various trades, finally selected one and brought it to Mrs. Dimmidge. It represented a bare and exceedingly stalwart arm wielding a large hammer.

"Your husband being a miner,–a quartz miner,–would that do?'' he asked. (It had been previously used to advertise a blacksmith, a gold-beater, and a stone-mason.)

The lady examined it critically.

"It does look a little like Micah's arm,'' she said meditatively. "Well–you kin put it in.''

The editor was so pleased with his success that he must needs make another suggestion. "I suppose,'' he said ingenuously,* that you don't want to answer the 'Personal'?''

ingenuously: simply, candidly

" 'Personal?' " she repeated quickly, "what's that? I aint' seen no 'Personal.' "

The editor saw his blunder. She, of course, had never seen Mr. Dimmidge's artful "Personal"; *that* the big dailies naturally had not noticed nor copied. But it was too late to withdraw now. He brought out a file of the *Clarion,* and snipping out the paragraph with his scissors, laid it before the lady.

She stared at it with wrinkled brows and a darkening face.

"And *this* was in the same paper?–put in by Mr. Dimmidge? she asked breathlessly.

The editor, somewhat alarmed, stammered "Yes." But the next moment he was reassured. The wrinkles disappeared, a dozen dimples broke out where they had been, and the determined, matter-of-fact Mrs. Dimmidge burst into a fit of rosy merriment. Again and again she laughed, shaking the building, startling the sedate, melancholy woods beyond, until the editor himself laughed in sheer vacant sympathy.

"I never thought of *that,*" she said at last, gasping, and wiping the laughter from her wet eyes.

"No," explained the editor smilingly; "of course you didn't. Don't you see, the papers that copied the big advertisement never saw that little paragraph, or if they did, they never connected the two together."

"Oh, it ain't that," said Mrs. Dimmidge, trying to regain her composure and holding her sides. "It's that blessed *dear* old dunderhead of a Dimmidge I'm thinking of. That gets me. I see it all now. Only, sakes alive! I never thought *that* of him. Oh, it's just too much!" and she again relapsed behind her handkerchief.

"Then I suppose you don't want to reply to it," said the editor.

Her laughter instantly ceased. "Don't I?" she said, wiping her face into its previous complacent determination. "Well, young man, I reckon that's

just what I *want* to do! Now wait a moment; let's see what he said," she went on, taking up and reperusing the "Personal" paragraph. "Well, then," she went on, after a moment's silent composition with moving lips, "you just put these lines in."

The editor took up his pencil.

"To Mr. M. J. Dimmidge.–Hope you're still on R. B.'s tracks. Keep there!–E. J. D.

The editor wrote down the line, and then, remembering Mr. Dimmidge's voluntary explanation of *his* "Personal," waited with some confidence for a like frankness from Mrs. Dimmidge. But he was mistaken.

"You think that he–R. B.–or Mr. Dimmidge–will understand this?" he at last asked tentatively. "Is it enough?"

"Quite enough," said Mrs. Dimmidge emphatically. She took a roll of greenbacks from her pocket, selected a hundred-dollar bill and then a five, and laid them before the editor. "Young man," she said, with a certain demure* gravity, "you've done me a heap o' good. I never spent money with more satisfaction than this. I never thought much o' the 'power o' the Press' as you call it, afore. But this has been a right comfortable visit, and I'm glad I ketched you alone. But you understand one thing; this yer visit, and *who* I am, is betwixt you and me only."

demure: reserved, serious

"Of course I must say that the advertisement was *authorized,*" returned the editor. "I'm only the temporary editor. The proprietor is away."

"So much the better," said the lady complacently. "You just say you found it on your desk with the money; but don't you give me away."

"I can promise you that the secret of your personal visit is safe with me," said the young man, with a bow, as Mrs. Dimmidge rose. "Let me see you to your horse," he added. "It's quite dark in the woods."

"I can see well enough alone, and it's just as well you shouldn't know *how* I kem or *how* I went away. Enough for you to know that I'll be miles away before that paper comes out. So stay where you are.''

She pressed his hand frankly and firmly, gathered up her riding-skirt, slipped backwards to the door, and the next moment rustled away into the darkness.

Early the next morning the editor handed Mrs. Dimmidge's advertisement, and the woodcut he had selected, to his foreman. He was purposely brief in his directions, so as to avoid inquiry, and retired to his sanctum. In the space of a few moments the foreman entered with a slight embarrassment of manner.

''You'll excuse my speaking to you, sir,'' he said, with a singular mixture of humility and cunning. ''It's no business of mine, I know; but I thought I ought to tell you that this yer kind o' thing won't pay anymore,–it's about played out!''

''I don't think I understand you,'' said the editor loftily, but with an inward misgiving. ''You don't mean to say that a regular, actual advertisement''–

''Of course, I know all that,'' said the foreman, with a peculiar smile; ''and I'm ready to back you up in it, and so's the boy; but it won't pay.''

''It *has* paid a hundred and five dollars,'' said the editor. Taking the notes from his pocket; ''so I'd advise you to simply attend to your duty and set it up.''

A look of surprise, followed, however, by a kind of pitying smile, passed over the foreman's face. ''Of course, sir, *that's* all right, and you know your own business; but if you think that the new advertisement will pay this time as the other one did, and whoop up another column from an advertiser, I'm afraid you'll slip up. It's a little 'off color' now,–not 'up to date,'–if it ain't a regular 'back number,' as you'll see.''

''Meantime I'll dispense with your advice,'' said the editor curtly, ''and I think you had better let our subscribers and advertisers do the same,

or the *Clarion* might also be obliged to dispense with your *services*.''

''I ain't no blab,'' said the foreman, in an aggrieved* manner, ''and I don't intend to give the show away even if it don't *pay*. But I thought I'd tell you, because I know the folks round here better than you do.''

aggrieved: offended, distressed

He was right. No sooner had the advertisement appeared than the editor found that everybody believed it to be a sheer invention of his own to ''once more boom'' the *Clarion*. If they had doubted *Mr.* Dimmidge, they utterly rejected *Mrs.* Dimmidge as an advertiser! It was a stale joke that nobody would follow up; and on the heels of this came a letter from the editor-in-chief.

My dear Boy,–You meant well, I know, but the second Dimmidge ''ad'' was a mistake. Still, it was a big bluff of yours to show the money, and I send you back your hundred dollars, hoping you won't ''do it again.'' Of course you'll have to keep the advertisement in the paper for two issues, just as if it were a real thing, and it's lucky that there's just now no pressure in our columns. You might have told a better story than that hogwash about your finding the ''ad'' and a hundred dollars lying loose on your desk one morning. It was rather thin, and I don't wonder the foreman kicked.

The young editor was in despair. At first he thought of writing to Mrs. Dimmidge at the Elktown Post-Office, asking her to relieve him of his vow of secrecy; but his pride forbade. There was a humorous concern, not without a touch of pity, in the faces of his contributors as he passed; a few affected to believe in the new advertisement, and asked him vague, perfunctory* questions about it. His position was trying, and he was not sorry when the term of his engagement expired the next week, and he left Calaveras to take his new position on the San Francisco paper.

perfunctory: routine, superficial

He was standing in the saloon* of the Sacramento boat when he felt a sudden heavy pressure on his shoulder, and looking round sharply, beheld not only the black-bearded face of Mr. Dimmidge, lit up by a smile, but beside it the beaming, buxom face of Mrs. Dimmidge, overflowing with good-humor. Still a little sore from his past experience, he was about to address them abruptly, when he was utterly vanquished by the hearty pressure of their hands and the unmistakable look of gratitude in their eyes.

saloon: main cabin or lounge

"I was just saying to 'Lizy Jane," began Mr. Dimmidge breathlessly, "if I could only meet that young man o' the *Clarion* what brought us together again—"

"You'd be willin' to pay four times the amount we both paid him," interpolated* the laughing Mrs. Dimmidge.

interpolated: inserted

"But I didn't bring you together," burst out the dazed young man, "and I'd like to know, in the name of Heaven, what brought you together now?"

"Don't you see, lad," said the imperturbable* Mr. Dimmidge, " 'Lizy Jane and myself had qua'led, and we just unpacked our fool nonsense in your paper and let the hull world know it! And we both felt kinder skeert and shamed like, and it looked such small hogwash, and of so little account, for all the talk it made, that we kinder felt lonely as two separated fools that really ought to share their foolishness together."

imperturbable: unable to be disturbed, calm

"And that ain't all," said Mrs. Dimmidge, with a sly glance at her spouse, "for I found out

from that 'Personal' you showed me that this particular old fool was actooally jealous!—*jealous!*"

"And then?" said the editor impatiently.

"And then I *knew* he loved me all the time."

For Thought and Discussion

1. Bret Harte, a significant local-color writer, combines both realistic and romantic elements in his writing. Using specific passages from the story, show how Harte establishes a realistic sense of locale in "The Boom in the *Calaveras Clarion.*" Next discuss his romantic characterizations of the Dimmidges.

2. Describe the two woodcuts mentioned in the story. What does the choice of these particular items reveal about Mr. and Mrs. Dimmidge, the acting editor, and the author as a realist?

3. Why do you think Harte chose the acting editor instead of the *bona fide* editor as the foil for the Dimmidges? How would the story have been different if the actual editor had been present?

4. One of the literary characteristics for which Harte is famous is his use of paradox. Discuss the apparent contradiction between appearance and reality in the following: Mr. Dimmidge's physical appearance and his mission, the townspeople's reaction to Mrs. Dimmidge's advertisement, and the advertisements as the means of reconciling the Dimmidges.

5. What specific incidents in the story prepare the reader for the unexpected twist at the end? Is the ending consistent with the rest of the story? Why or why not? How does the ending contribute to the humorous tone Harte establishes?

Ambrose Bierce   1842-1914

Ambrose Bierce is generally numbered among the Western writers of the late nineteenth century. Like the local-color writers of his day, he often used details of specific geographical locales in his stories. Unlike his contemporaries, he usually wrote gruesome tales of destruction and of the dying. Because of his pessimistic tone, he is regarded by many as the first writer of **black humor** in American literature.

Bierce's early years were somber. He was born on a farm in Meigs County, Ohio, into a family that was both poor and large. He left his home at the age of fifteen and served as a printer's apprentice for two years. He then attended Kentucky Military Institute for a year, receiving there his only formal education. When the Civil War broke out in 1861, he immediately enlisted, joining the Ninth Indiana Volunteers as a private (some say as a drummer boy). During the next four years he reenlisted several times, fought in some of the bloodiest battles of the war, and received a severe head wound in the Battle of Kennesaw Mountain, Georgia. He was commended or mentioned for bravery over a dozen times by his superiors. He also steadily earned promotions in military rank, becoming a major after the war ended.

Following the war, he moved to San Francisco and became a professional journalist. During the next two decades, he was a popular columnist on the West Coast and the area's literary dictator. As his experience grew broader, so did his distrust of men. He became especially angry over the widespread business and political corruption he saw around him. On one occasion he revealed that the Southern Pacific Railroad planned to establish a monopoly over the Western railroads. One of its officials asked him his price for silence about the plan. Bierce replied in print: "My price is about seventy-five million dollars, to be handed to the Treasurer of the United States."

The last two decades of his life were the most productive of his literary career. But they were not happy years. Divorced from his wife and sorrowing over the deaths of his two sons, he became increasingly pessimistic in his writing. His nickname "Bitter Bierce" dates from this period. In the 1890s he published his best stories. The first collection (1891) was entitled *Tales of Soldiers and Civilians.* In its ten stories about soldiers, the chief character always dies. In 1898 he published *In the Midst of Life,* another volume of short stories. This one included among its twenty-six stories some of Bierce's most famous tales: "Chickamauga," "A Horseman in the Sky," "One of the Missing," and "An Occurrence at Owl Creek Bridge."

Bierce's dismal outlook worsened, and in 1906 he published *The Cynic's Wordbook,* which in 1911 he retitled *The Devil's Dictionary.* This work includes definitions that reflect the pessimism, cynicism, and nihilism possessing him. Some are relatively tame: "BORE, n. A person who talks when you wish him to listen"; "POSITIVE, adj. Mistaken at the top of one's voice." Others are much more bitter:

"YEAR, n. A period of three hundred and sixty-five disappointments"; "PRAY, v. To ask that the laws of the universe be annulled in behalf of a single petitioner confessedly unworthy."

In 1913 a chain of circumstances began that made Bierce's death puzzling. He first revisited some of the Civil War battlefields where he had fought. The seventy-one-year-old journalist then entered Mexico to report on the revolution. He evidently joined up with Pancho Villa's revolutionaries. He was probably killed by government troops in a battle fought in January 1914. Just before leaving the States, Bierce had written a friend: "Goodbye. If you hear of my being stood up against a Mexican stone wall and shot to rags please know that I think it a pretty good way to depart this life. It beats old age, disease, or falling down the cellar stairs. To be a Gringo in Mexico—ah, that is euthanasia!"

Bierce's stories are not altogether typical of the local-color movement. Although associated with the West, Bierce wrote his best stories about the South. In many of these he drew from his wartime experiences. His Civil War fiction shows his obsession with the mental as well as the physical horrors of war. His characters reflect the confusion that dying soldiers apparently undergo. As his characters experience terror, they become keenly, even abnormally, aware of what is happening around them. Time slows dramatically so that much may take place within a very short period of time. Usually for both character and reader, the twist is a moment of truth that reveals things to be different from what they have seemed. Like Edgar Allan Poe, to whom he is often compared, Bierce strongly moves readers with his unity of effect and startling climaxes.

Bierce's work reflects the strong undercurrent of bitterness in American writers at the turn of the century. The drift from the spiritual values of the earlier centuries was bringing only disillusionment. As man placed his faith in mankind rather than God, he was doomed to disappointment. By the end of his life, he denied all values except those that a person might display in battle: honesty and courage. Although his work is strongly regional in **setting** and situation, it reflects the universal problem of someone's trying to establish values and discover life's meaning apart from God.

An Occurrence at Owl Creek Bridge

The title of this story seems to indicate that the events are minor, of little importance, only an "occurrence." As the story unfolds, however, we see that the events are really of utmost importance. Consequently, the story's ending may startle readers unless they are carefully attentive to the details of the tale.

1

A man stood upon a railroad bridge in northern Alabama, looking down into the swift water twenty feet below. The man's hands were behind his back, the wrists bound with a cord. A rope loosely encircled his neck. It was attached to a stout cross-timber above his head, and slack fell to the level of his knees. Some loose boards laid upon the sleepers* supporting the metals of the railway supplied a footing for him and his executioners–two private soldiers of the Federal army, directed by a sergeant, who in civil life may have been a deputy sheriff. At a short remove upon the same temporary platform was an officer in the uniform of his rank, armed. He was a captain. A sentinel at each end of the bridge stood with his rifle in the position known as "support," that is to say, vertical in front of the left shoulder, the hammer resting on the forearm thrown straight across the chest–a formal and unnatural position, enforcing an erect carriage* of the body. It did not appear to be the duty of these two men to know what was occurring at the center of the bridge; they merely blockaded the two ends of the foot plank which traversed it.

sleepers: crossties
carriage: posture

Beyond one of the sentinels, nobody was in sight; the railroad ran straight away into a forest for a hundred yards, then, curving, was lost to view. Doubtless there was an outpost farther along. The other bank of the stream was open ground–a gentle acclivity* crowned with a stockade* of vertical tree trunks, loop-holed for rifles, with a single embrasure* through which protrud-

ed the muzzle of a brass cannon commanding the bridge. Midway of the slope between bridge and fort were the spectators–a single company of infantry in line, at "parade rest," the butts of the rifles on the ground, the barrels inclining slightly backward against the right shoulder, the hands crossed upon the stock. A lieutenant stood at the right of the line, the point of his sword upon the ground, his left hand resting upon his right. Excepting the group of four at the center of the bridge, not a man moved. The company faced the bridge, staring stonily, motionless. The sentinels, facing the banks of the stream, might have been statues to adorn the bridge. The captain stood with

folded arms, silent, observing the work of his subordinates, but making no sign. Death is a dignitary who when he comes announced is to be received with formal manifestations* of respect, even by those most familiar with him. In the code of military etiquette silence and fixity* are forms of deference.*

acclivity: sloping upward
stockade: an enclosure in which prisoners are kept, made of heavy
    posts driven upright side by side in the ground
embrasure: an opening in a wall for a gun
manifestations: demonstrations
fixity: the state of being unmoving
deference: respect

The man who was engaged in being hanged was apparently about thirty-five years of age. He was a civilian, if one might judge from his dress, which was that of a planter. His features were good—a straight nose, firm mouth, broad forehead, from which his long, dark hair was combed straight back, falling behind his ears to the collar of his well-fitting frock coat. He wore a mustache and pointed beard, but not whiskers; his eyes were large and dark gray, and had a kindly expression which one would hardly have expected in one whose neck was in the hemp.* Evidently this was no vulgar assassin. The liberal military code makes provision for hanging many kinds of people, and gentlemen are not excluded.

hemp: rope

The preparations being complete, the two private soldiers stepped aside and each drew away the plank upon which he had been standing. The sergeant turned to the captain, saluted, and placed himself immediately behind that officer, who in turn moved apart one pace. These movements left the condemned man and the sergeant standing on the two ends of the same plank, which spanned three of the crossties of the bridge. The end upon which the civilian stood almost, but not quite, reached a fourth. This plank had been held in place by the weight of the captain; it was now held by that of the sergeant. At a signal from the former, the latter would step aside, the plank would

tilt, and the condemned man go down between two ties. The arrangement commended itself to his judgment as simple and effective. His face had not been covered nor his eyes bandaged. He looked a moment at his "unsteadfast footing," then let his gaze wander to the swirling water of the stream racing madly beneath his feet. A piece of dancing driftwood caught his attention and his eyes followed it down the current. How slowly it appeared to move! What a sluggish stream!

He closed his eyes in order to fix his last thoughts upon his wife and children. The water, touched to gold by the early sun, the brooding mists under the banks at some distance down the stream, the fort, the soldiers, the piece of drift—all had distracted him. And now he became conscious of a new disturbance. Striking through the thought of his dear ones was a sound which he could neither ignore nor understand, a sharp, distinct, metallic percussion* like the stroke of a blacksmith's hammer upon the anvil; it had the same ringing quality. He wondered what it was and whether immeasurably distant or near by—it seemed both. Its recurrence was regular, but as slow as the tolling of a death knell.* He awaited each stroke with impatience and—he knew not why—apprehension. The intervals of silence grew progressively longer; the delays became maddening. With their greater infrequency the sounds increased in strength and sharpness. They hurt his ear like the thrust of a knife; he feared he would shriek. What he heard was the ticking of his watch.

percussion: the sound made by striking two objects together
knell: the slow solemn sounding of a bell

He unclosed his eyes and saw again the water below him. "If I could free my hands," he thought, "I might throw off the noose and spring into the stream. By diving I could evade the bullets, and swimming vigorously, reach the bank, take to the woods, and get away home. My home, thank God, is as yet outside their lines; my wife and little ones are still beyond the invader's farthest advance.''

As these thoughts, which have here to be set down in words, were flashed into the doomed man's brain rather than evolved from it, the captain nodded to the sergeant. The sergeant stepped aside.

2

Peyton Farquhar was a well-to-do planter of an old and highly respected Alabama family. Being a slave owner and like other slave owners a politician, he was naturally an original secessionist* and ardently devoted to the Southern cause. Circumstances of an imperious* nature, which it is unnecessary to relate here, had prevented him from taking service with the gallant army which had fought the disastrous campaigns ending with the fall of Corinth,* and he chafed* under the inglorious restraint, longing for the release of his energies, the larger life of the soldier, the opportunity for distinction. That opportunity, he felt, would come, as it comes to all in war time. Meanwhile he did what he could. No service was too humble for him to perform in aid of the South, no adventure too perilous for him to undertake if consistent with the character of a civilian who was at heart a soldier, and who in good faith and without too much qualifications assented to at least a part of the frankly villainous dictum* that all is fair in love and war.

secessionist: one who withdrew from the Union during the Civil War
imperious: urgent
Corinth: important Confederate railway center captured by Grant's troops in May 1862
chafed: became annoyed, irritated, or impatient
dictum: authoritative or dogmatic statement

One evening while Farquhar and his wife were sitting on a rustic bench near the entrance to his grounds, a gray-clad soldier* rode up to the gate and asked for a drink of water. Mrs. Farquhar was only too happy to serve him with her own white hands. While she was gone to fetch the water, her husband approached the dusty horseman and inquired eagerly for news from the front.

gray-clad soldier: one dressed as a Confederate soldier

"The Yanks are repairing the railroads," said the man, "and are getting ready for another advance. They have reached the Owl Creek bridge, put it in order, and built a stockade on the north bank. The commandant has issued an order, which is posted everywhere, declaring that any civilian caught interfering with the railroad, its bridges, tunnels, or trains will be summarily* hanged. I saw the order.''

summarily: speedily

"How far is it to the Owl Creek bridge?'' Farquhar asked.

"About thirty miles.''

"Is there no force on this side of the creek?''

"Only a picket* post half a mile out, on the railroad, and a single sentinel at this end of the bridge.''

picket: an advance detachment of soldiers who give warning of the approach of the enemy

"Suppose a man—a civilian and student of hanging—should elude* the picket post and perhaps get the better of the sentinel," said Farquhar, smiling, "what could he accomplish?''

elude: escape

The soldier reflected. "I was there a month ago," he replied. "I observed that the flood of last winter had lodged a great quantity of driftwood against the wooden pier at this end of the bridge. It is now dry and would burn like tow.''*

tow: flax or hemp fiber

The lady had now brought the water, which the soldier drank. He thanked her ceremoniously, bowed to her husband, and rode away. An hour later, after nightfall, he repassed the plantation, going northward in the direction from which he had come. He was a Federal scout.

3

As Peyton Farquhar fell straight downward

through the bridge he lost consciousness and was as one already dead. From this state he was awakened—ages later, it seemed to him—by the pain of a sharp pressure upon his throat, followed by a sense of suffocation. Keen, poignant* agonies seemed to shoot from his neck downward through every fiber of his body and limbs. These pains appeared to flash along well-defined lines a ramification* and to beat with an inconceivably rapid periodicity.* They seemed like streams of pulsating fire heating him to an intolerable temperature. As to his head, he was conscious of nothing but a feeling of fullness—of congestion. These sensations were unaccompanied by thought. The intellectual part of his nature was already effaced;* he had power only to feel, and feeling was torment. He was conscious of motion. Encompassed in a luminous* cloud, of which he was now merely the fiery heart, without material substance, he swung through unthinkable arcs of oscillation,* like a vast pendulum. Then all at once, with terrible suddenness, the light about him shot upward with the noise of a loud plash; a frightful roaring in his ears, and all was cold and dark. The power of thought was restored; he knew that the rope had broken and he had fallen into the stream. There was no additional strangulation; the noose about his neck was already suffocating him and kept the water from his lungs. To die of hanging at the bottom of a river!—the idea seemed to him ludicrous.* He opened his eyes in the darkness and saw above him a gleam of light, but how distant, how inaccessible! He was still sinking, for the light became fainter and fainter until it was a mere glimmer. Then it began to grow and brighten, and he knew that he was rising toward the surface—knew it with reluctance, for he was now very comfortable. "To be hanged and drowned," he thought, "that is not so bad; but I do not wish to be shot. No, I will not be shot, that is not fair."

poignant: extremely painful
ramification: consequence
periodicity: the quality of recurring at regular intervals
effaced: erased or rubbed out
luminous: bright, full of light
oscillation: to swing steadily back and forth
ludicrous: absurd, ridiculous

He was not conscious of an effort, but a sharp pain in his wrist apprised him that he was trying to free his hands. He gave the struggle his attention, as an idler might observe the feat of a juggler, without interest in the outcome. What splendid effort!—what magnificent, what super-human strength! Ah, that was a fine endeavor! Bravo! The cord fell away; his arms parted and floated upward, the hands dimly seen on each side in the growing light. He watched them with a new interest as first one and then the other pounced upon the noose at his neck. They tore it away and thrust it fiercely aside, its undulations* resembling those of a water snake. "Put it back, put it back!" He thought he shouted these words to his hands, for the undoing of the noose had been succeeded by the direst* pang that he had yet experienced. His neck ached horribly; his brain was on fire; his heart, which had been fluttering faintly, gave a great leap, trying to force itself out at his mouth. His whole body was racked and wrenched with an insupportable anguish! But his disobedient hands gave no heed to the command. They beat the water vigorously with quick, downward strokes, forcing him to the surface. He felt his head emerge; his eyes were blinded by the sunlight; his chest expanded convulsively, and with a supreme and crowning agony his lungs engulfed a great draught* of air, which instantly he expelled in a shriek!

undulations: wavelike movements
direst: most dreadful
draught: gulp: i.e., a breath of air

He was now in full possession of his physical senses. They were, indeed, preternaturally* keen and alert. Something in the awful disturbance of his organic system had so exalted and refined them that they made record of things never before perceived. He felt the ripples upon his face and heard their separate sounds as they struck. He looked at the forest on the bank of the stream, saw the individual trees, the leaves and the veining of each leaf—saw the very insects upon them; the locusts, the brilliant-bodied flies, the gray spiders stretching their webs from twig to twig. He noted the prismatic colors in all the dewdrops upon a million blades of grass. The humming of the gnats that danced above the eddies* of the stream, the beating of the dragonflies' wings, the strokes of the water spiders' legs, like oars which had lifted their boat—all these made audible music. A fish slid along beneath his eyes and he heard the rush of its body parting the water.

preternaturally: unnaturally
eddies: currents moving contrary to the main current of a stream

He had come to the surface facing down the stream; in a moment the visible world seemed to wheel slowly round, himself the pivotal point, and he saw the bridge, the fort, the soldiers upon the bridge, the captain, the sergeant, the two privates, his executioners. They were in silhouette against the blue sky. They shouted and gesticulated,* pointing at him. The captain had drawn his pistol, but did not fire; the others were unarmed. Their movements were grotesque and horrible, their forms gigantic.

gesticulated: gestured vigorously

Suddenly he heard a sharp report and something struck the water smartly within a few inches of his head, spattering his face with spray. He heard the second report, and saw one of the sentinels with his rifle at his shoulder, a light cloud of blue smoke rising from the muzzle. The man in the water saw the eye of the man on the bridge gazing into his own through the sights of the rifle. He observed that it was a gray eye and remembered having read that gray eyes were keenest, and that all famous marksmen had them. Nevertheless, this one had missed.

A counterswirl had caught Farquhar and turned him half round; he was again looking into the forest on the bank opposite the fort. The sound of a clear, high voice in a monotonous singsong now rang out behind him and came across the water with distinctness that pierced and subdued all other sounds, even the beating of the ripples in his ears. Although no soldier, he had frequented camps enough to know the dread significance of that deliberate, drawling, aspirated chant;* the lieutenant on shore was taking part in the morning's work. How coldly and pitilessly—with what an even, calm intonation,* presaging and enforcing tranquillity in the men—with what accurately measured intervals fell those cruel words:

chant: i.e., deliberately spoken
intonation: a singing or monotone utterance

"Attention, company! . . . Shoulder arms! . . . Ready! . . . Aim! . . . Fire!"

Farquhar dived—dived as deeply as he could. The water roared in his ears like the voice of Niagara, yet he heard the dulled thunder of the volley and, rising again toward the surface, met shining bits of metal, singularly flattened, oscillating slowly downward. Some of them touched him on the face and hands, then fell away, continuing their descent. One lodged between his collar and his neck; it was uncomfortably warm and he snatched it out.

As he rose to the surface, gasping for breath, he saw that he had been a long time under water; he was perceptibly farther downstream—nearer to safety. The soldiers had almost finished reloading; the metal ramrods flashed all at once in the sunshine as they were drawn from the barrels, turned in the air, and thrust into their sockets. The two sentinels fired again, independently and ineffectually.

The hunted man saw all this over his shoulder; he was now swimming vigorously with the current. His brain was as energetic as his arms and legs; he thought with the rapidity of lightning.

"The officer," he reasoned, "will not make that martinet's error a second time. It is as easy to dodge a volley as a single shot. He has probably already given the command to fire at will. God help me, I cannot dodge them all!"

An appalling plash within two yards of him was followed by a loud, rushing sound, diminuendo,* which seemed to travel back through the air to the fort and died in an explosion which stirred the very river to its deeps! A rising sheet of water, which curved over him, fell down upon him, blinded him, strangled him! The cannon had taken a hand in the game. As he shook his head free from the commotion of the smitten water, he heard the deflected shot humming through the air ahead, and in an instant it was cracking and smashing the branches in the forest beyond.

diminuendo: Ital., with gradually diminishing volume

"They will not do that again," he thought; "the next time they will use a charge of grape.*

I must keep my eye upon the gun; the smoke will apprise* me–the report arrives too late; it lags behind the missile. That is a good gun."

grape: small iron balls
apprise: inform

Suddenly he felt himself whirled round and round–spinning like a top. The water, the banks, the forests, the now distant bridge, fort, and men–all were commingled* and bluffed. Objects were represented by their colors only; circular horizontal streaks of color–that was all he saw. He had been caught in a vortex* and was being whirled on with a velocity of advance and gyration* which made him giddy and sick. In a few moments he was flung upon the gravel at the foot of the left bank of the stream–the southern bank–and behind a projecting point which concealed him from his enemies. The sudden arrest of his motion, the abrasion* of one of his hands on the gravel, restored him, and he wept with

delight. He dug his fingers in the sand, threw it over himself in handfuls, and audibly blessed it. It looked like gold, like diamonds, rubies, emeralds; he could think of nothing beautiful which it did not resemble. The trees upon the bank were giant garden plants; he noted a definite order in their arrangement, inhaled the fragrance of their blooms. A strange, roseate* light shone through the spaces among their trunks and the wind made in their branches the music of aeolian harps.* He had no wish to perfect his escape—was content to remain in that enchanting spot until retaken.

commingled: blended together
vortex: whirlpool
gyration: a revolution around the center
abrasion: a scraped area
roseate: rose-colored
aeolian harps: boxes with strings stretched over them to produce sound when the wind blows

A whiz and rattle of grapeshot among the branches high above his head roused him from his dream. The baffled cannoneer had fired him a random farewell. He sprang to his feet, rushed up the sloping bank, and plunged into the forest.

All that day he traveled, laying his course by the rounding sun. The forest seemed interminable;* nowhere did he discover a break in it, not even a woodman's road. He had not known he lived in so wild a region. There was something uncanny in the revelation.

interminable: endless

By nightfall he was fatigued, footsore, famishing. The thought of his wife and children urged him on. At last he found a road which led him in what he knew to be the right direction. It was wide as a city street, yet it seemed untraveled. No fields bordered it, no dwelling anywhere. Not so much as the barking of a dog suggested human habitation. The black bodies of the great trees formed a straight wall on both sides, terminating on the horizon in a point, like a diagram in a lesson in perspective. Overhead, as he looked up through this rift in the wood, shone great golden stars looking unfamiliar and grouped in strange constellations.

He was sure they were arranged in some order which had a great secret and malign* significance. The wood on either side was full of singular noises, among which—once, twice, and again—he distinctly heard whispers in an unknown tongue.

malign: evil

His neck was in pain and lifting his hand to it he found it horribly swollen. He knew that it had a circle of black where the rope had bruised it. His eyes felt congested; he could no longer close them. His tongue was swollen with thirst; he relieved its fever by thrusting it forward from between his teeth into the cool air. How softly the turf had carpeted the untraveled avenue—he could no longer feel the roadway under his feet!

Doubtless, despite his suffering, he had fallen asleep while walking, for now he sees another scene—perhaps he has merely recovered from a delirium.* He stands at the gate of his own home. All is as he left it, and all bright and beautiful in the morning sunshine. He must have traveled the entire night. As he pushes open the gate and passes up the wide white walk, he sees a flutter of female garments; his wife, looking fresh and cool and sweet, steps down from the veranda to meet him. At the bottom of the steps she stands waiting, with a smile of ineffable* joy, an attitude of matchless grace and dignity. Ah, how beautiful she is! He springs forward with extended arms. As he is about to clasp her, he feels a stunning blow upon the back of the neck; a blinding white light blazes all about him with a sound like the shock of a cannon—then all is darkness and silence!

delirium: temporary mental confusion
ineffable: unspeakable

Peyton Farquhar was dead; his body, with a broken neck, swung gently from side to side beneath the timbers of the Owl Creek bridge.

Thought and Discussion

1. How does Bierce set the stage in part 1 for the hanging to follow? Does Bierce's de-

scription in part 1 evoke any sympathy from the reader for the condemned man? Support your answers with specific passages from the story.

2. How does Bierce prepare us at the end of part 1 for his use of flashback in part 2? Why do you think Bierce chose to employ the technique of flashback, and does this technique enhance or detract from the story? Explain your answer.

3. What is ironic about the fact that part 3 is the longest part of the story? What ideas about the experience of dying are presented in this section?

4. Bierce ends his story with a one-sentence paragraph confirming Farquhar's death. What details prior to this point led you to believe Farquhar really had escaped? Did Bierce prepare you in any way for the sudden reversal in plot? Did you find the resolution of the story satisfactory? Why or why not?

5. How is Bierce's bitterness, a trait not shared by most other regionalists, evident in his title "An Occurrence at Owl Creek Bridge"? Point out passages in the story which illustrate the bitterness and pessimism characteristic of Bierce.

Sidney Lanier   1842-1881

Sidney Lanier was considered the best Southern poet during the last half of the nineteenth century. Although he wrote his poetry outside the South, he remained sensitive to the effects that economic forces and intellectual currents of his day were having on that region. He believed, for instance, that the South should not imitate the industrial development of the North, as some influential Southerners recommended. He also reacted against the tendency of his fellow poets to avoid religion and nature in their poetry. As a result, his poems often call Americans to return to values they once held.

Lanier early showed himself to be unusually gifted. As a child in Macon, Georgia, he learned (according to reports) to play the flute, violin, organ, piano, and guitar nearly as early as he learned to read. In 1857 he entered Oglethorpe College, a small, religious Georgia college, and graduated with highest honors in 1860. When the Civil War broke out the next year, he immediately enlisted, along with his younger brother Clifford. (Both brothers refused promotions that would have separated them.) In late 1864, while serving as a signal officer aboard a Confederate blockade runner, Lanier was captured by Union forces and imprisoned at Point Lookout, Maryland. It is likely that here he contracted tuberculosis, which claimed his life sixteen years later. Released from the prisoner-of-war camp in March 1865 Lanier returned home to Macon to recuperate. Two years later he published his only novel, *Tiger-Lilies*. Lanier had begun the manuscript of this rather unusual work during the war, keeping both it and his flute in his knapsack.

In the years immediately after the war, Lanier was unable to survive financially in the poverty-stricken South. Seeking a livelihood in the North, he was named in 1873 as first flutist with the Peabody Orchestra in Baltimore, Maryland. About this time he turned seriously to writing poetry. In 1876, the year of the nation's one-hundredth birthday, the first edition of Lanier's poems appeared in print. Also in this year he wrote the poem that, set to music, opened the ceremonies at the Philadelphia Centennial. During the next five years, he devoted himself almost exclusively to his poetry while desperately fighting against the tuberculosis wasting his body. In 1879 he received an appointment as lecturer in English literature at Johns Hopkins University. Although he was becoming a better poet in these last years, his body was failing him. He wrote "Sunrise," one of his last poems, while fighting a 104-degree fever. In September 1881 in Lynn, North Carolina, where he had moved in an attempt to find a more healthful climate, the thirty-nine-year-old poet died.

The poems left by Lanier do not represent fully the literary developments of the post-Civil War period. Nevertheless, some have made their mark on American literary history. Believing that industrialization in the South would destroy the region's values, Lanier wrote "Corn" in an attempt to encourage Southern farmers to depend less on cotton for their staple crop. Lanier believed that King Cotton left the South at the whim of Northern manufacturers. Trade was something to fear; agriculture, he thought, should be the backbone of the Southern economy. In "The Symphony" the poet combined his interest in music with his poetry. Various sections of this poem attempt to duplicate the sounds of instruments in an orchestra. In "The Marshes of Glynn" and in "The Song of the Chattahoochee," Lanier showed his interest in nature. In "The Revenge of Hamish," he reflected his interest in medieval settings, situations, and forms. Finally, in "A Ballad of Trees and the Master," written near the end of his life, Lanier revealed his increasing dependence on religious subject matter.

Lanier died young; we have, therefore, only what would have been his early poetry had he lived longer. This verse is uneven in quality and sometimes unclear in content. Few poets build lasting reputations on just their early work. Yet Lanier's poetry is a significant attempt to arrest the nation's departure from traditional beliefs. While distinctively regional in themes and content, his work strove for universality through new musical forms. His spirit was romantic more than realistic, it is true. Nevertheless, he remained responsive to key issues of his day—attacking, for instance, the atheistic theory of evolution and the demoralizing dominance of business. His poems thus reveal literary resistance in the South to the country's adoption of new ideals and values.

The Revenge of Hamish

Published in 1878, this poem tells the story of Hamish's revenge against his lord. The **setting** *is Scotland during the Middle Ages, when noblemen ruled and the majority of people lived to serve them. The cruelty of Maclean begets cruelty from Hamish. Although other writers had used this incident in various works, Lanier may very well be using it to suggest the revolt of the South against the North in the Civil War. Notice Hamish's pride and almost immediate retaliation for the wrong done to him. Notice also that Hamish reacts without any consideration for his own life.*

This poem has been called one of the best modern **ballads.** *Like many other ballads, the poem focuses on a single episode or situation, portrays the events as they supposedly happened, and conceals the narrator's feelings about the events.*

It was three slim does and a ten-tined* buck in the bracken* lay;
    And all of a sudden the sinister smell of a man,
    Awaft* on a wind-shift, wavered and ran
Down the hill-side, and sifted along through the bracken and passed that way.

ten-tined: ten branches of antlers/*bracken:* an area overgrown with ferns
Awaft: carried

Then Nan got a-tremble at nostril; she was the daintiest doe;   5
    In the print of her velvet flank on the velvet fern*
    She reared, and rounded her ears in turn.
Then the buck leaped up, and his head as a king's to a crown did go

her . . . fern: The doe was lying down in the ferns.

Full high in a breeze, and he stood as if Death had the form of a deer;
    And the two slim does long lazily stretching arose,   10
    For their day-dream slowlier came to a close,
Till they woke and were still, breath-bound with waiting and wonder and fear.

Then Alan the huntsman sprang over the hillock,* the hounds shot by,
    The does and the ten-tined buck made a marvelous bound,
    The hounds swept after with never a sound,   15
But Alan loud winded his horn in sign that the quarry* was nigh.

hillock: a small hill

quarry: prey: i.e., the deer

For at dawn of that day proud Maclean of Lochbury to the hunt had waxed* wild,
    And he cursed at Old Alan till Alan fared off with the hounds
    For to drive him the deer to the lower glen*-grounds:
"I will kill a red deer," quoth Maclean, "in sight of the wife and the child."   20

waxed: grown, become

glen: valley

So gayly he paced with the wife and the child to his chosen stand;
  But he hurried tall Hamish the henchman* ahead: "Go turn,"–
  Cried Maclean–"if the deer seek to cross to the burn,*
Do thou turn them to me: nor fail, lest thy back be red as thy hand!"

henchman: a follower

burn: a small stream

Now hard-fortuned Hamish, half blown of his breath* with the height of the hill,   25
  Was white in the face when the ten-tined buck and the does
  Drew leaping to burn-ward; huskily rose
His shouts, and the nether* lip twitched, and his legs were o'er weak for his will.

half . . . breath: i.e., half out of breath

nether: bottom

So the deer darted lightly by Hamish and bounded away to the burn.
  But Maclean never bating* his watch tarried waiting below.   30
  Still Hamish hung heavy with fear for to go
All the space of an hour; then he went, and his face was greenish and stern,

bating: lessening

And his eye sat back in the socket, and shrunken the eyeballs shone,
  As withdrawn from a vision of deeds it were shame to see.
  "Now, now, grim henchman, what is't with thee?"   35
Brake Maclean, and his wrath rose red as a beacon the wind hath upblown.

"Three does and a ten-tined buck made out," spoke Hamish, full mild,
  "And I ran for to turn, but my breath it was blown, and they passed;
  I was weak, for ye called ere* I broke my fast."*
Cried Maclean: "Now a ten-tined buck in the sight of the wife and the child   40

ere: before//I . . . fast: i.e., before I had breakfast

I had killed if the gluttonous kern* had not wrought me a snail's own wrong!"*
  Then he sounded,* and down came kinsmen and clansmen all:
  "Ten blows, for ten tine, on his back let fall,
And reckon no stroke if the blood follow not at the bite of the thong!"*

kern: a lout, a stupid person

snail's . . . wrong: i.e., done me wrong by being slow

sounded: i.e., blew his horn

thong: a strip of leather

So Hamish made bare, and took him his strokes; at the last he smiled.   45
  "Now I'll to the burn," quoted Maclean, "for it still may be
  If a slimmer-paunched* henchman will hurry with me
I shall kill me the ten-tined buck for a gift to the wife and the child!"

slimmer-paunched: i.e., faster

Then the clansmen departed, by this path and that; and over the hill
    Sped Maclean with an outward wrath for an inward shame;   50
    And that place of the lashing full quiet became;
And the wife and the child stood sad; and bloody-backed Hamish sat still.

But look! red Hamish has risen; quick about and about turns he.
    "There is none betwixt me and the crag-top!" he screams under breath.
    Then, livid as Lazarus lately from death,   55
He snatches the child from the mother, and clambers the crag* toward the sea.

crag: a steeply projecting mass of rock

Now the mother drops breath; she is dumb, and her heart goes dead for space,
    Till the motherhood, mistress of death, shrieks, shrieks through the glen,
    And that place of the lashing is live with men,
And Maclean, and the gillie* that told him, dash up in a desperate race.   60

gillie: a servant or guide of a hunter

Not a breath's time for asking; an eye-glance reveals all the tale untold.
    They follow mad Hamish afar up the crag toward the sea,
    And the lady cries: "Clansmen, run for a fee!*
Yon castle and lands to the two first hands that shall hook him and hold

fee: reward

Fast Hamish back from the brink"–and ever she flies up the steep,   65
    And the clansmen pant, and they sweat, and they jostle and strain.
    But, mother, 'tis vain; but, father, 'tis vain;
Stern Hamish stands bold on the brink, and dangles the child o'er the deep.

Now a faintness falls on the men that run, and they all stand still.
    And the wife prays Hamish as if he were God, on her knees,   70
    Crying: "Hamish! O Hamish! but please, but please
For to spare him!" and Hamish still dangles the child, with a wavering will.

On a sudden he turns; with a sea-hawk scream, and a gibe,* and a song,
    Cries: "So; I will spare ye the child, if, in sight of ye all,
    Ten blows on Maclean's bare back shall fall,   75
And ye reckon no stroke if the blood follow not at the bite of the thong!"

gibe: a taunt or mocking remark

Then Maclean he set hardly* his tooth to his lip that his tooth was red,
    Breathed short for a space, said: "Nay, but it never shall be!
    Let me hurl off the damnable hound in the sea!"
But the wife: "Can Hamish go fish us the child from the sea, if dead?   80

hardly: harshly

Say yea!–Let them lash *me*, Hamish?''–''Nay!''–''Husband, the lashing will heal;
    But, oh, who will heal me the bonny sweet bairn* in his grave?
    Could ye cure me my heart with the death of a knave?
Quick! Love! I will bare thee*–so–kneel!'' Then Maclean 'gan slowly to kneel

With never a word, till presently downward he jerked to the earth.   85
    Then the henchman–he that smote Hamish–would tremble and lag;
    ''Strike, hard!'' quoth Hamish, full stern, from the crag;
Then he struck him, and ''One!'' sang Hamish, and danced with the child in his mirth.

And no man spake beside Hamish; he counted each stroke with a song.
    When the last stroke fell, then he moved him a pace down the height,   90
    And he held forth the child in the heart-aching sight
Of the mother, and looked all pitiful grave, as repenting a wrong.

And there as the motherly arms stretched out with the thanksgiving prayer–
    And there as the mother crept up with the fearful swift pace,
    Till her finger nigh felt of the bairnie's face–   95
In a flash fierce Hamish turned round and lifted the child in the air,

And sprang with the child in his arms from the horrible height in the sea,
    Shrill screeching, ''Revenge!'' in the wind-rush; and pallid* Maclean,
    Age-feeble with anger and impotent pain,*
Crawled up on the crag, and lay flat, and locked hold of dead roots of a tree–   100

And gazed hungrily o'er, and the blood from his back drip-dripped in the brine,*
    And a sea-hawk flung down a skeleton fish as he flew,
    And the mother stared white on the waste of blue,
And the wind drove a cloud to seaward, and the sun began to shine.

bairn: child

bare thee: i.e., she removes his shirt

pallid: pale

Age . . . pain: He has been made powerless by the pain from the lashing.

brine: salt water: i.e., the sea

The Song of the Chattahoochee

This poem, published in 1877, is Lanier's best-known work. The Chattahoochee River is one of the largest Georgia rivers. It flows out of Habersham and Hall counties in northeastern Georgia and eventually reaches the Gulf of Mexico. In the final stanza Lanier reveals that the river is responding to the call of duty. Its story, the poem, exemplifies obedience to the call of conscience and purpose. As the river journeys to the sea, it must resist the alluring voices and activities of many things that would keep it from fulfilling its duty. Notice that the **onomatopoeia** *(see glossary) and verse form suggest both the fluid movement of the river and the obstructions seeking to hold it back.*

Out of the hills of Habersham,
   Down the valleys of Hall,
I hurry amain* to reach the plain,   *amain:* at full speed
Run the rapid and leap the fall,
Split at the rock and together again,   5
Accept my bed, or* narrow or wide,   *or:* whether
And flee from folly on every side
With a lover's pain to attain the plain
    Far from the hills of Habersham,
    Far from the valleys of Hall.   10

All down the hills of Habersham,
    All through the valleys of Hall,
The rushes cried *Abide, abide,*
The wilful water weeds held me thrall,*   *thrall:* slave
The laving laurel* turned my tide,   15   *laurel:* i.e., the branch-
The ferns and the fondling* grass said *Stay,*   es bathing in the water
The dewberry dipped for to work delay,   *fondling:* caressing
And the little reeds sighed *Abide, abide,*
    Here in the hills of Habersham,
    Here in the valleys of Hall.   20

High o'er the hills of Habersham,
    Veiling the valleys of Hall,
The hickory told me manifold
Fair tales of shade, the poplar tall
Wrought me her shadowy self to hold,*   25   *hold:* i.e., worked her
The chestnut, the oak, the walnut, the pine,   shadowy self to hold me
Overleaning, with flickering meaning and sign,
Said, *Pass not, so cold, these manifold*
    Deep shades of the hills of Habersham,
    These glades in the valleys of Hall.*   30   *glades:* open spaces in the forest

And oft in the hills of Habersham,
And oft in the valleys of Hall,
The white quartz shone, and the smooth brook-stone
Did bar me of passage with friendly brawl,
And many a luminous jewel lone   35
—Crystals clear or a-cloud with mist,
Ruby, garnet, and amethyst—
Made lures* with the lights of streaming stone   *lures:* decoys
In the clefts of the hills of Habersham
In the beds of the valleys of Hall.   40

But oh, not the hills of Habersham,
And oh, not the valleys of Hall
Avail:* I am fain for* to water the plain.   *Avail:* serve / *fain for:*
Downward the voices of Duty call—   obliged
Downward, to toil and be mixed with the main,*   45   *main:* the ocean
The dry fields burn, and the mills are to turn,
And a myriad* flowers mortally yearn,   *myriad:* a very large
And the lordly main from beyond the plain   number
Calls o'er the hills of Habersham,
Calls through the valleys of Hall.   50

A Ballad of Trees and the Master

This brief poem, one of Lanier's last, portrays the Saviour being fortified for His experience in the judgment hall and on Calvary by His time in the Garden of Gethsemane. Notice that the poem falls into two parts. The olives, leaves, and thorn-tree of the first stanza show a different reaction to Him from that of the people implied in the second stanza. Notice Lanier's careful attention to the sound of words and to the value of repetition.

Into the woods
   my Master went,
Clean* forspent,* forspent.
Into the woods my Master came,
Forspent with love and shame.
But the olives they were not blind to Him,
The little gray leaves were kind to Him:
The thorn-tree had a mind to Him
When into the woods He came.

Clean: completely / *forspent:* exhausted

Out of the woods my Master went,
  And He was well content.
Out of the woods my Master came,
Content with death and shame.
When Death and Shame would woo Him last,
From under the trees they drew Him last:
'Twas on a tree they slew Him – last
When out of the woods He came.

For Thought and Discussion

1. Briefly relate the narrative of Lanier's ballad ''The Revenge of Hamish.'' Identify other ballad devices that Lanier employs in the poem, and discuss the elements that make the poem more romantic than realistic.

2. Which lines in the poem foreshadow the fact that Hamish will seek revenge? Discuss why you think Hamish is not satisfied with his first act of revenge and whether his initial desire for revenge is justified. What does Romans 12:19 say about vengeance? What character flaw do Hamish and Maclean have in common, and what is the significance of this flaw in the narrative?

3. Identify or give an example of the following elements in the first stanza of ''The Song of the Chattahoochee'':
   a. rhyme scheme
   b. metrical pattern
   c. internal rhyme
   d. alliteration
   e. musical effects
   f. personification

4. According to the last stanza of the poem, what does the Chattahoochee consider to be its duty? In stanzas 2, 3, and 4, what are some of the objects of nature that attempt to keep the river from doing its duty? In your own words, state the theme of the poem and tell how you can make a personal application of the theme.

5. The two stanzas of ''A Ballad of Trees and the Master'' are parallel in structure and content. Give specific examples of this parallelism. Describe the change that takes place while Christ is in the Garden of Gethsemane, and tell what additions Lanier makes to the Biblical account given in Matthew 26:36-46.

Hamlin Garland 1860-1940

Hamlin Garland wrote extensively about life in the Midwest. His most powerful short stories portray the plight of the farmer. They also reveal the two sides of Garland's literary creed. They show, first, that he was a local colorist who used realistic details to make his work concrete. They show, second, that he was an idealist who tried to bring about reforms through his writing.

Garland's early life in the Midwest provided the materials for his best work. He lived nine years in Wisconsin and then twelve in Iowa. After graduation in 1881 from Cedar Valley Seminary (Osage, Iowa), he taught school in Illinois for a year and then settled in South Dakota. In 1884 he moved to Boston, planning to receive training in teaching. While in the East, he fell under the influence of several realistic writers who encouraged him to write and who shaped his literary principles.

In 1887, having already published his first book, Garland returned to his boyhood home. What he found in the Midwest shocked him. "All the gilding of farm life melted away," he recorded. "The hard and bitter realities came back on me in a flood. Nature was as beautiful as ever . . . but no splendor of cloud, no grace of sunset, could conceal the poverty of these people. I perceived life without its glamour." The lack of culture, the tasteless houses, the barren lives, but especially the poverty of the farmers appalled him. Over the next four years he wrote a series of stories that reflected his emotional reaction. These stories he published as *Main-Travelled Roads* (1891), his first and most famous short-story collection. Previous writers had presented farm life as ennobling and glorious. Garland described it as dehumanizing and brutal. After publishing this 1891 collection, he never again painted quite so dreary a picture of Midwestern rural life.

In *Crumbling Idols* (1894), a book of essays on literature, Garland described his brand of realism as *veritism*. Evidently he wished to write a new kind of regional work that remained hopeful yet used realistic details. He rejected the pessimistic realism that characterized many works published at the turn of the century. In his works environment plays a major role. The long hours, grueling work, and spiritual deadness of the farmers show the fundamental poverty of their existence. Yet his characters often display inner nobility and courage. Frequently Garland aimed at reforming what he considered evil in society (e.g., the contemporary scheme of taxation, as in "Under the Lion's Paw"). As a result, many of his stories advocate solutions to problems within society.

The works that gave Garland his greatest reputation in the United States were a series of autobiographical novels that began appearing in 1917. The second work in this series, *A Daughter of the Middle Border,* earned him a Pulitzer Prize in 1921. During the last forty years of his life, Garland lived in various urban centers such as Chicago, New York, and Los Angeles. These years saw Garland's increasing interest in spiritualism and psychic research.

In the last two decades of his life, his work brought sharp criticism from the more radical among his fellow writers. They claimed that Garland had fallen out of step with his own times and therefore had abandoned the radical values stressed in his early work. His growing conservatism may have come, however, not because of his advancing age or his growing timidity in literary matters. It may have been due to his groping for what is most important in life.

The Return of a Private

In this story from Main-Travelled Roads, *Garland explores the plight of a Civil War veteran returning to his Wisconsin farm. As in his other novels and short stories, he illustrates a writer's use of fiction to arouse the emotions of the reader. What the character does not find (the welcome of the townspeople) and what he does find (the condition of his farm) are major parts of the emotional appeal of this story.*

The story falls into two parts. In the first part Garland depicts the arrival of four Civil War veterans in La Crosse, a town on the western edge of Wisconsin. In the second part he depicts the actions of the Smith family both before and after Private Smith's arrival home. The final paragraph establishes the **theme** *developed by the two parts of the story. Although lacking Christian elements, "The Return of a Private" is a moving portrait of an American whose spirit, though bent, is not broken.*

1

The nearer the train drew toward La Crosse, the soberer* the little group of "vets" became. On the long way from New Orleans, they had beguiled* tedium* with jokes and friendly chaff;* or with planning with elaborate detail what they were going to do now, after the war. A long journey, slowly, irregularly, yet persistently pushing northward. When they entered on Wisconsin territory they gave a cheer, and another when they reached Madison, but after that they sank into a dumb expectancy. Comrades dropped off at one or two points beyond, until there were only four or five left who were bound for La Crosse County.

soberer: more serious
beguiled: turned away
tedium: boredom
chaff: jesting, teasing

Three of them were gaunt* and brown, the fourth was gaunt and pale, with signs of fever and ague* upon him. One had a great scar down his temple, one limped, and they all had unnaturally large, bright eyes, showing emaciation.* There were no bands greeting them at the station, no banks of gayly dressed ladies waving handkerchiefs and shouting "Bravo!" as they came in on the caboose of a freight train into the towns that had cheered and blared at them on their way to war. As they looked out or stepped upon the platform for a moment, while the train stood at the station, the loafers looked at them indifferently. Their blue coats, dusty and grimy, were too familiar now to excite notice, much less a friendly word. They were the last of the army to return, and the loafers were surfeited with such sights.

gaunt: lean, haggard
ague: chills
emaciation: thinness as a result of starvation or illness

The train jogged forward so slowly that it seemed likely to be midnight before they should reach La Crosse. The little squad grumbled and swore, but it was no use; the train would not hurry, and, as a matter of fact, it was nearly two o'clock when the engine whistled "down brakes."

All of the group were farmers, living in districts several miles out of the town, and all were poor.

"Now, boys," said Private Smith, he of the fever and ague, "we are landed in La Crosse in the night. We've got to stay somewhere till mornin'. Now I ain't got no two dollars to waste on a hotel. I've got a wife and children, so I'm goin' to roost on a bench and take the cost of a bed out of my hide."

"Same here," put in one of the other men. "Hide'll grow on again, dollars'll come hard. It's

goin' to be mighty hot skirmishin'* to find a dollar these days.''

skirmishin': fighting

''Don't think they'll be a deputation* of citizens waitin' to 'scort* us to a hotel, eh?'' said
another. His sarcasm was too obvious to require
an answer.

deputation: a group representing others
'scort: escort

Smith went on. ''Then at daybreak we'll start
for home—at least, I will.''

''Well, I'll be dummed if I'll take two dollars
out o' *my* hide,'' one of the younger men said.
''I'm goin' to a hotel, ef I don't never lay up a
cent.''

''That'll do f'r you,'' said Smith; ''but if you
had a wife an' three young uns dependin' on
yeh—''

''Which I ain't, thank the Lord! and don't
intend havin' while the court knows itself.''*

while . . . itself: i.e., while he's in control of his mind

The station was deserted, chill, and dark, as
they came into it at exactly a quarter to two in
the morning. Lit by the oil lamps that flared a dull
red light over the dingy benches, the waiting room
was not an inviting place. The younger man went
off to look up a hotel, while the rest remained and
prepared to camp down on the floor and benches.
Smith was attended to tenderly by the other men,
who spread the blankets on the bench for him,
and, by robbing themselves, made quite a comfortable bed, though the narrowness of the bench
made his sleeping precarious.*

precarious: dangerous

It was chill, though August, and the two men,
sitting with bowed heads, grew stiff with cold and
weariness, and were forced to rise now and again
to walk about to warm their stiffened limbs. It did
not occur to them, probably, to contrast their coming home with their going forth, or with the coming home of the generals, colonels, or even cap-
tains—but to Private Smith, at any rate, there came
a sickness at heart almost deadly as he lay there
on his hard bed and went over his situation.

In the deep of night, lying on a board in the
town where he had enlisted three years ago, all
elation* and enthusiasm gone out of him, he faced
the fact that with the joy of home-coming was
already mingled the bitter juice of care. He saw
himself sick, worn out, taking up the work on his
half-cleared farm, the inevitable mortgage standing ready with open jaw to swallow half his earnings. He had given three years of his life for a
mere pittance* of pay, and now!—

elation: happiness
pittance: a very small amount

Morning dawned at last, slowly, with a pale
yellow dome of light rising silently above the
bluffs, which stand like some huge storm-devas-
tated castle, just east of the city. Out to the left
the great river* swept on its massive yet silent
way to the south. Bluejays called across the water
from hillside to hillside through the clear, beautiful air, and hawks began to skim the tops of the
hills. The older men were astir early, but Private
Smith had fallen at last into a sleep, and they
went out without waking him. He lay on his knapsack, his gaunt face turned toward the ceiling, his
hands clasped on his breast, with a curious pathetic effect of weakness and appeal.

great river: the Mississippi

An engine switching near woke him at last,
and he slowly sat up and stared about. He looked
out the window and saw that the sun was light-
ening the hills across the river. He rose and
brushed his hair as well as he could, folded his
blankets up, and went out to find his companions.
They stood gazing silently at the river and at the
hills.

''Looks natcher'l, don't it?'' they said, as he
came out.

''That's what it does,'' he replied. ''An' it
looks good. D' yeh see that peak?'' He pointed

at a beautiful symmetrical* peak, rising like a slightly truncated* cone, so high that it seemed the very highest of them all. It was touched by the morning sun and it glowed like a beacon, and a light scarf of gray morning fog was rolling up its shadowed side.

symmetrical: balanced, evensided in arrangement
truncated: having the top cut off

"My farm's just beyond that. Now, if I can only ketch a ride, we'll be home by dinner-time."

"I'm talkin' about breakfast," said one of the others.

"I guess it's one more meal o' hardtack* f'r me," said Smith.

hardtack: a very hard biscuit made with only flour and water

They foraged* around, and finally found a restaurant with a sleepy old German behind the counter, and procured some coffee, which they drank to wash down their hardtack.

foraged: searched

"Time'll come," said Smith, holding up a piece by the corner, "when this'll be a curiosity."

"I hope to God it will! I bet I've chawed hardtack enough to shingle every house in the coolly.* I've chawed it when my lampers was down,* and when they wasn't. I've took it dry, soaked, and mashed. I've had it wormy, musty, sour, and blue-moldy. I've had it in little bits and big bits; 'fore coffee an' after coffee. I'm ready f'r a change. I'd like t' git holt just about now o' some of the hot biscuits my wife c'n make when she lays herself out f'r company."

coolly: coulee, a deep gully or valley
lampers . . . down: said of a horse when it has a sore mouth

"Well, if you set there gabblin', you'll never *see* yer wife."

"Come on," said Private Smith. "Wait a moment, boys; less take suthin'.* It's on me." He led them to the rusty tin dipper which hung on a nail beside the wooden water-pail, and they grinned and drank. Then shouldering their blan-

kets and muskets, which they were "takin' home to the boys," they struck out on their last march.

less . . . suthin': let's take something

"They called that coffee Jayvy,"* grumbled one of them, "but it never went by the road where government Jayvy resides. I reckon I know coffee from peas."*

Jayvy: Java
coffee . . . peas: i.e., coffee made from peas

They kept together on the road along the turnpike,* and up the winding road by the river, which they followed for some miles. The river was very lonely, curving down along its sandy beds, pausing now and then under broad basswood trees, or running in dark, swift, silent currents under tangles of wild grapevines, and drooping alders, and haw trees. At one of these lovely spots the three vets sat down on the thick green sward* to rest, "on Smith's account." The leaves of the trees were as fresh and green as in June, the jays called cheery greetings to them, and kingfishers darted to and fro with swooping, noiseless flight.

turnpike: toll road
sward: turf, meadow

"I tel yeh, boys, this knocks the swamps of Loueesiana into kingdom come." . . .

"I guess we'd better be crawlin' along," interrupted Smith, rising and shouldering his knapsack, with considerable effort, which he tried to hide.

"Say, Smith, lemme give you a lift on that."

"I guess I c'n manage," said Smith, grimly.

"Course. But, yo' see, I may not have a chance right off to pay yeh back for the times you've carried my gun and hull caboodle.* Say, now, gimme that gun, anyway."

hull caboodle: i.e., the rest of his equipment

"All right, if yeh feel like it, Jim." Smith replied, and they trudged along doggedly in the sun, which was getting higher and hotter each half-mile.

"Ain't it queer there ain't no teams comin' along," said Smith, after a long silence.

"Well, no, seein' it's Sunday."

"By jinks, that's a fact. It *is* Sunday. I'll git home in time f'r dinner, sure!" he exulted. "She don't hev dinner usually till about *one* on Sundays." And he fell into a muse, in which he smiled.

"Well, I'll git home jest about six o'clock, jest about when the boys are milkin' the cows," said old Jim Cranby. "I'll step into the barn, an' then I'll say: *Heah!* why ain't this milkin' done before this time o' day?" An' then won't they yell!" he added, slapping his thigh in great glee.

Smith went on. "I'll jest go up the path. Old Rover'll come down the road to meet me. He won't bark; he'll know me, an' he'll come down waggin' his tail an' showin' his teeth. That's his way of laughin'. An' so I'll walk up to the kitchen door, an' I'll say, '*Dinner* f'r a hungry man!' An' then she'll jump up, an'–"

He couldn't go on. His voice choked at the thought of it. Saunders, the third man, hardly uttered a word, but walked silently behind the others. He had lost his wife the first year he was in the army. She died of pneumonia, caught in the autumn rains while working in the fields in his place.

They plodded along till at last they came to a parting of the ways. To the right the road continued up the main valley; to the left it went over the big ridge.

"Well, boys," began Smith, as they grounded their muskets and looked away up the valley, "here's where we shake hands. We've marched together a good many miles, an' now I s'pose we're done."

"Yes, I don't think we'll do any more of it f'r a while. I don't want to, I know."

"I hope I'll see yeh once in a while, boys, to talk over old times."

"Of course," said Saunders, whose voice trembled a little, too. "It ain't *exactly* like dyin'." They all found it hard to look at each other.

"But we'd ought'r go home with you," said Cranby. "You'll never climb that ridge with all them things on yer back."

"Oh, I'm all right! Don't worry about me. Every step takes me nearer home, yeh see. Well, good-by, boys."

They shook hands. "Good-by. Good luck!"

"Same to you. Lemme know how you find things at home."

"Good-by."

"Good-by."

He turned once before they passed out of sight, and waved his cap, and they did the same, and all yelled. Then all marched away with their long, steady, loping* veteran step. The solitary climber in blue walked on for a time, with his mind filled with the kindness of his comrades, and musing upon the many wonderful days they had had together in camp and field.

loping: easy gait

He thought of his chum, Billy Tripp. Poor Billy! A "minié" ball* fell into his breast one day, fell wailing like a cat, and tore a great ragged hole in his heart. He looked forward to a sad scene with Billy's mother and sweetheart. They would want to know all about it. He tried to recall all that Billy had said, and the particulars of it but there was little to remember, just that wild wailing sound high in the air, a dull slap, a short, quick, expulsive groan, and the boy lay with his face in the dirt in the ploughed field they were marching across.

minié ball: rifle bullet named for its nineteenth century French inventor, Claude Etienne Minié

That was all. But all the scenes he had since been through had not dimmed the horror, the terror of that moment, when his boy comrade fell, with only a breath between a laugh and a death-groan. Poor handsome Billy! Worth millions of dollars was his young life.

These sombre* recollections gave way at length to more cheerful feelings as he began to approach his home coolly. The fields and houses grew familiar, and in one or two he was greeted by people seated in the doorways. But he was in no mood to talk, and pushed on steadily, though he stopped and accepted a drink of milk once at the well-side of a neighbor.

sombre: gloomy

The sun was burning hot on that slope, and his steps grew slower, in spite of his iron resolution. He sat down several times to rest. Slowly he crawled up the rough, reddish-brown road, which wound along the hillside, under great trees, through dense groves of jack oaks, with tree-tops far below him on his left hand, and the hill far above him on his right. He crawled along like some minute, wingless variety of fly.

He ate some hardtack, sauced with wild berries, when he reached the summit of the ridge, and sat there for some time, looking down into his home coolly.

Sombre, pathetic figure! His wide, round gray eyes gazing down into the beautiful valley, seeing and not seeing, the splendid cloud-shadows sweeping over the western hills and across the green and yellow wheat far below. His head drooped forward on his palm, his shoulders took on a tired stoop, his cheekbones showed painfully. An observer might have said, ''He is looking down upon his own grave.''

2

[On the Sunday afternoon when Private Smith finally reaches his home, his wife and children are away visiting at a neighbor's house. Emma, his wife, catches a glimpse of him as he passes. But when she calls to him, he does not hear her. She hurriedly gathers up the children—Mary, nine; Tommy, six; and Teddy, four—and rushes home. But Private Smith had already arrived.]

A man in a blue coat, with a musket on his back, was toiling slowly up the hill on the sun-bright, dusty road, toiling slowly, with bent head half hidden by a heavy knapsack. So tired it

seemed that walking was indeed a process of falling. So eager to get home he would not stop, would not look aside, but plodded on, amid the cries of the locust, the welcome of the crickets, and the rustle of the yellow wheat. Getting back to God's country, and his wife and babies!

Laughing, crying, trying to call to him and the children at the same time, the little wife, almost hysterical, snatched her hat and ran out into the yard.* But the soldier had disappeared over the hill into the hollow beyond, and, by the time she had found the children, he was too far away for her voice to reach him. And, besides, she was not sure it was her husband, for he had not turned his head at their shouts. This seemed strange. Why didn't he stop to rest at his old neighbor's house? Tortured by hope and doubt, she hurried up the coolly as fast as she could push the baby wagon, the blue-coated figure just ahead pushing steadily, silently forward up the coolly.

the yard: i.e., the neighbor's yard where she had been visiting

When the excited, panting little group came in sight of the gate they saw the blue-coated figure standing, leaning upon the rough rail fence, his chin on his palms, gazing at the empty house. His knapsack, canteen, blankets, and musket lay upon the dusty grass at his feet.

He was like a man lost in a dream. His wide, hungry eyes devoured the scene. The rough lawn, the little unpainted house, the field of clear yellow wheat behind it, down across which streamed the sun, now almost ready to touch the high hill to the west, the crickets crying merrily, a cat on the fence near by, dreaming, unmindful of the stranger in blue—

How peaceful it all was. . . . How far removed from all camps, hospitals, battle lines. A little cabin in a Wisconsin coolly, but it was majestic in its peace. How did he ever leave it for those years of tramping, thirsting, killing?

Trembling, weak with emotion, her eyes on the silent figure, Mrs. Smith hurried up to the fence. Her feet made no noise in the dust and

grass, and they were close upon him before he knew of them. The oldest boy ran a little ahead. He will never forget that figure, that face. It will always remain as something epic,* that return of the private. He fixed his eyes on the pale face covered with a ragged beard.

epic: heroic

"Who *are* you, sir?" asked the wife, or rather, started to ask, for he turned, stood a moment, and then cried:

"Emma!"

"Edward!"

The children stood in a curious row to see their mother kiss this bearded, strange man, the elder girl sobbing sympathetically with her mother. Illness had left the soldier partly deaf, and this added to the strangeness of his manner.

But the youngest child stood away, even after the girl had recognized her father and kissed him. The man turned then to the baby, and said in a curiously unpaternal* tone:

unpaternal: unfatherlike

"Come here, my little man; don't you know me?" But the baby backed away under the fence and stood peering at him critically.

"My little man!" What meaning in those words! This baby seemed like some other woman's child, and not the infant he had left in his wife's arms. The war had come between him and his baby–he was only a stranger man to him, with big eyes; a soldier, with mother hanging to his arm, and talking in a loud voice.

"And this is Tom," the private said, drawing the oldest boy to him. *He'll* come and see me. *He* knows his poor old pap when he comes home from the war."

The mother heard the pain and reproach* in his voice and hastened to apologize.

reproach: blame

"You've changed so, Ed. He can't know yeh. This is papa, Teddy; come and kiss him–Tom and Mary do. Come, won't you?" But Teddy still peered through the fence with solemn eyes, well out of reach. He resembled a half-wild kitten that hesitates, studying the tones of one's voice.

''I'll fix him,'' said the soldier, and sat down to undo his knapsack, out of which he drew three enormous and very red apples. After giving one to each of the older children, he said:

''*Now* I guess he'll come. Eh, my little man? Now come see your pap.''

Teddy crept slowly under the fence assisted by the over-zealous Tommy, and a moment later was kicking and squalling in his father's arms. Then they entered the house, into the sitting room, poor, bare, art-forsaken little room, too, with its rag carpet, its square clock, and its two or three chromos* from *Harper's Weekly* pinned about.

---

chromos: colored pictures

''Emma, I'm all tired out,'' said Private Smith, as he flung himself down on the carpet as he used to do, while his wife brought a pillow to put under his head, and the children stood about munching their apples.

''Tommy, you run and get me a pan of chips,* and Mary, you get the tea-kettle on, and I'll go and make some biscuit.''

---

chips: wood or dried pieces of animal dung used for fuel

And the soldier talked. Question after question he poured forth about the crops, the cattle, the renter, the neighbors. He slipped his heavy government brogan shoes* off his poor tired, blistered feet, and lay out with utter, sweet relaxation. He was a free man again, no longer a soldier under command. At supper he stopped once, listened and smiled. ''That's old Spot. I know her voice. I s'pose that's her calf out there in the pen. I can't milk her to-night, though. I'm too tired. But I tell you, I'd like a drink o' her milk. What's become of old Rove?''

---

brogan shoes: heavy, ankle-high boots

''He died last winter. Poisoned, I guess.'' There was a moment of sadness for them all. It was some time before the husband spoke again in a voice that trembled a little.

''Poor old feller! He'd 'a' known me half a mile away. I expected him to come down the hill to meet me. It 'ud 'a' been more like comin' home if I could 'a' seen him comin' down the road an' waggin' his tail, an' laughin' that way he has. I tell yeh, it kind o' took hold o' me to see the blinds down an' the house shut up.''

''But, yeh see, we–expected you'd write again 'fore you started. And then we thought we'd see you if you *did* come,'' she hastened to explain.

''Well, I ain't worth a cent on writin'. Besides, it's just as well yeh didn't know when I was comin'. I tell you, it sounds good to hear them chickens out there, an' turkeys, an' the crickets. Do you know they don't have just the same kind o' crickets down South? Who's Sam hired t' help cut yer grain?''

''The Ramsey boys.''

''Looks like a good crop; but I'm afraid I won't do much gettin' it cut. This cussed fever an' ague has got me down pretty low. I don't know when I'll get rid of it. I'll bet I've took twenty-five pounds of quinine* if I've taken a bit. Gimme another biscuit. I tell yeh, they taste good, Emma. I ain't had anything like it–Say, if you'd 'a' hear'd me braggin' to th' boys about your butter 'n' biscuits I'll bet your ears 'ud 'a' burnt.''

---

quinine: medicine used to treat malaria

The private's wife colored with pleasure. ''Oh, you're always a-braggin' about your things. Everybody makes good butter.''

''Yes, old Lady Snyder, for instance.''

''Oh, well, she ain't to be mentioned. She's Dutch.''

''Or old Mis' Snively. One more cup o' tea, Mary. That's my girl! I'm feeling better already. I just b'lieve the matter with me is I'm *starved*.''

This was a delicious hour, one long to be remembered. They were like lovers again. But their tenderness, like that of a typical American family, found utterance in tones, rather than in words. He was praising her when praising her biscuit, and she knew it. They grew soberer when he showed where he had been struck, one ball burning the back of his hand, one cutting away a lock of hair from his temple, and one passing through the calf of his leg. The wife shuddered to think how near she had come to being a soldier's widow. Her waiting no longer seemed hard. This sweet, glorious hour effaced* it all.

---

effaced: erased

Then they rose, and all went out into the garden and down to the barn. He stood beside her while she milked old Spot. They began to plan fields and crops for next year.

His farm was weedy and encumbered,* a rascally renter had run away with his machinery (departing between two days),* his children needed clothing, the years were coming upon him, he was sick and emaciated, but his heroic soul did not quail.* With the same courage with which he had faced his Southern march he entered upon a still more hazardous future.

---

encumbered: i.e., burdened with a mortgage
between . . . days: i.e., during the night
quail: lose courage

Oh, that mystic* hour! The pale man with big eyes standing there by the well, with his young wife by his side. The vast moon swinging above the eastern peaks, the cattle winding down the pasture slopes with jangling bells, the crickets singing, the stars blooming out sweet and far and serene; the katydids* rhythmically calling, the little turkeys crying querulously,* as they settled to roost in the poplar tree near the open gate. The voices at the well drop lower, the little ones nestle in their father's arms at last, and Teddy falls asleep there.

---

mystic: inspiring a sense of wonder
katydids: grasshopperlike insects
querulously: grumbling, complaining

The common soldier of the American volunteer army had returned. His war with the South was over, and his fight, his daily running fight with nature and against the injustice of his fellowmen, was begun again.

For Thought and Discussion

1. Which sentences in the second paragraph of part 1 explain the lack of enthusiasm with which the soldiers were met at the train station? Do the men express any disappointment at this lack of a welcoming reception? What do you think sustains the men as they complete the journey home?

2. What effect do you think Garland intended sentences like the following to have on the reader: "He lay on his knapsack, his gaunt face turned toward the ceiling, his hands clasped on his breast, with a curious pathetic effect of weakness and appeal"? Find additional words or phrases from the last paragraph of part 1 that produce the same effect.

3. In part 2, the point of view alternates between that of Private Smith and that of his wife and children. Why do you think Garland chose to alternate his point of view in the scene? What are some realistic details that make each point of view poignant?

4. How do Private Smith's visualizations in part 1 concerning his arrival home differ from his actual arrival in part 2? What conclusion about appearance and reality can you draw from this comparison?

5. After stating in the last paragraph that Private Smith, a "common soldier of the American volunteer army" was finally at home, the narrator continues: "His war with the South was over, and his fight, his daily running fight with nature and against the injustice of his fellowmen, was begun again." Give lines from the paragraphs immediately preceding this statement that help to shape your opinion as to whether Private Smith will win this second "war." Then state the story's theme in one or two sentences.

James Whitcomb Riley
1849-1916

James Whitcomb Riley was probably the most popular midwestern poet of the late nineteenth century. His poems often treated homely subjects such as the old swimming hole and the coming of fall. This type of poetry raised memories that Americans found much more pleasant than the changes swiftly taking place around them. Although his subject matter and style brought immediate popularity, his reputation among literary critics has greatly declined since his death.

Riley, the son of an Indiana lawyer, rebelled against his parents' wish that he pursue a career in law and ran away to join a patent-medicine show. Before he found his niche as a journalist, he worked as a house painter and an actor. After writing for two small newspapers, he joined the staff of the *Indianapolis Journal* in 1887. Here he began writing pieces in the dialect of Hoosier farmers. He produced a series of lighthearted poems attributed to "Benjamin F. Johnson, of Boone." In 1883 he collected these rustic poems into a volume entitled *The Old Swimmin'-Hole and 'Leven More Poems*. This was the first of some twenty volumes he published before his death.

In his later years Riley often gave public readings of his poetry, a practice that helped greatly to increase his popularity. His genial humor and cheerful attitude about rural life won the hearts of thousands of Americans, many of whom had lived on the farm in their youth. Riley died in 1916, a year before the United States entered the war that would signal the end of the America he had lovingly described.

Although he wrote much verse in conventional English, Riley was one of the chief practitioners of the dialect poem. His travels throughout the Midwest during his youth apparently helped him capture the way that country people actually spoke. His poems often express the homely values that he found in the Midwesterners of his day. His witty and folksy philosophy, the happy endings, the celebration of the simple virtues fading from American life–all are part of what one critic has called the "triumphantly common" in Riley's work.

Poems like "When the Frost Is on the Punkin" illustrate one major trend within regional writing: the tendency to look backward with nostalgia to simpler days. Riley's contemporary Hamlin Garland, also writing about the Midwest, described a quite different world. Where Riley omitted harsh actualities, Garland dragged them in. Because Riley depicted the pleasure of ordinary life, to cynical moderns his verse has seemed to offer relatively limited value.

When the Frost Is on the Punkin

When the frost is on the punkin and the fodder's* in the shock,*
And you hear the kyouck* and gobble of the struttin' turkey-cock,
And the clackin' of the guineys,* and the cluckin' of the hens,
And the rooster's hallylooyer* as he tiptoes on the fence;
O, it's then's the times a feller is a-feelin' at his best   5
With the risin' sun to greet him from a night of peaceful rest,
As he leaves the house, bareheaded, and goes out to feed the stock,
When the frost is on the punkin and the fodder's in the shock.

They's something kindo' harty*-like about the atmusfere
When the heat of summer's over and the coolin' fall is here—   10
Of course we miss the flowers, and the blossums on the trees,
And the mumble of the hummin'-birds and buzzin' of the bees;
But the air's so appetizin'; and the landscape through the haze
Of a crisp and sunny morning of the airly* autumn days
Is a pictur' that no painter has the colorin' to mock —*   15
When the frost is on the punkin and the fodder's in the shock.

The husky, rusty russel of the tossels* of the corn,
And the raspin' of the tangled leaves, as golden as the morn;
The stubble in the furries*–kindo' lonesome-like, but still
A-preachin' sermuns to us of the barns they growed to fill;   20
The strawstack in the medder,* and the reaper in the shed;
The hosses in theyr stalls below–the clover overhead!–
O, it sets my hart a-clickin' like the tickin' of a clock,
When the frost is on the punkin and the fodder's in the shock!

Then your apples all is getherd,* and the ones a feller keeps   25
Is poured around the cellar-floor in red and yeller heaps;
And your cider-makin' 's over, and your wimmern-folks* is through
With their mince and apple-butter, and theyr souse* and saussage, too! . . .
I don't know how to tell it–but ef sich a thing could be
As the Angels wantin' boardin', and they'd call around on *me*—   30
I'd want to 'commodate 'em–all the whole-indurin' flock–
When the frost is on the punkin and the fodder's in the shock!

fodder's: feed for live-
stock/*shock:* grain
stalks stacked for
drying
kyouck: onomatopoetic
word for the sound a
turkey makes
guineys: guinea hens
hallylooyer: hallelujah

harty: hearty

airly: early
mock: i.e., imitate

tossels: tassels

furries: furrows

medder: meadow

getherd: gathered

wimmern-folks: wom-
en-folk

souse: pickled pork
trimming

For Thought and Discussion

1. Give examples of the poet's appeal to the senses of seeing, hearing, smelling, and tasting. Identify any imaginative comparisons in the examples you choose (e.g., metaphor, simile, personification).
2. The midwestern farmer is the subject of both Hamlin Garland's and James Whitcomb Riley's writing. How does the tone of ''The Return of a Private'' and ''When the Frost Is on the Punkin'' differ? What are some clues that help you discern that Garland and Riley are regionalists from the same area? Does Garland's or Riley's selection seem more realistic to you? Why?

Sarah Orne Jewett
1849-1909

The stories of Sarah Orne Jewett are regarded as the finest fiction written in the late nineteenth century. Like Nathaniel Hawthorne, who had died just four years before her first short story appeared in print, Jewett wrote about the New England she knew. Unlike Hawthorne, she tended to concentrate on the positive side of her characters rather than to reveal the suffering or tragedy of their lives.

Jewett's childhood experiences strongly affected her fiction. She was a sickly child, often kept out of school. As a result, she was free to accompany her gifted physician-father as he made his house calls. It was he who opened her eyes to the potential stories around her in southeastern Maine. His advice shaped her own approach to writing. ''Great writers don't try to write *about* people and things,'' he told her; ''they tell them just as they are.'' Jewett was only fifteen when she first sensed a purpose for her writing. Later she recalled how the experience had inspired her career. ''The first 'city boarders' began to make their appearance near Berwick; and the way they misconstrued the country people and made game of their peculiarities fired me with indignation. I determined to teach the world that country people were not the awkward, ignorant set those people seemed to think. I wanted the world to know their grand, simple lives; and, so far as I had a mission, when I first began to write, I think that was it.'' Four years later, the nineteen-year-old girl published her first short story.

By 1877, less than ten years after her first story, Jewett had published enough material to follow William Dean Howell's advice to her to collect it and publish it as a novel. In the preface to *Deephaven,* the work that resulted, she wrote that Harriet Beecher Stowe's novel *The Pearl of Orr's Island* (1862) had shown her the value of writing about Maine locale. (Mrs. Stowe's novel, one of the first of the local-color novels in American literary history, sympathetically portrays the lives of fishermen and their families along the Maine coast.) In 1884 Jewett published *A Country Doctor,* which is a fictional portrayal of her beloved father and her childhood. Interestingly, the central figure of this novel is a woman doctor modeled on Jewett's father, who had died six years before the book appeared.

Jewett continued to publish stories in the leading magazines of her day to enlarge her literary reputation. From 1885 to 1899 she published the short stories regarded as the most successful part of her literary achievement. In 1901 Bowdoin College (Maine) awarded her an honorary doctorate, the first such degree granted by that college to a woman. An accident on her birthday in 1902, however, cut short her writing career. Thrown from her carriage when her horse fell, she seriously injured her head and spine. After this accident she could still write but only with great physical difficulty. Although she kept up her voluminous personal correspondence, she published no more fiction. When she experienced a stroke in March, 1909, she asked to return home to Maine. Three months later on June 24, she died in the same house in which she had been born.

Jewett's stories tend to focus on **character** rather than on **plot** or **setting.** She once defined her goal for writing as acquainting the people of her region with one another. As a result, a Jewett story is usually a "sympathetic study in individuality." Her central figures are stalwart individuals living commonplace lives. Although she tended to ignore the harsh, brutal aspects of life, her works at times portray the negative side of life, the bittersweet sense of loss, of isolation, of life turned back on itself. This passage from *Deephaven* paints a deserted farmhouse: "That fireless, empty, forsaken house, where the winter sun shines in and creeps slowly along the floor; the bitter cold is in and around the house, and the snow has sifted in at every crack; outside it is untrodden by any living creature's footstep. The wind blows and rushes and shakes the loose window-sashes in their frames, while the padlock knocks–knocks against the door." On the whole, Jewett's best work tenderly and convincingly depicts the inhabitants of her native region. Her touch with the pen is so sure that outsiders wanting to understand New Englanders are often advised to begin their study by reading her fiction.

Jewett clothed even her simplest characters with dignity. Though she seldom draws an explicit moral, she often leads a reader to believe that the lives of her major characters have lessons for him. It is true that Jewett's God seems little more than the romantic, pantheistic deity of Emerson and other New England writers of the nineteenth century. Her character studies, as a result, seldom reflect the reality of sin and guilt seen in the work of her predecessor Nathaniel Hawthorne. Yet in her study of characters like Sylvia, who is the **protagonist** of "A White Heron," Jewett's view of people reminds us of God's: even the least regarded is of inestimable value.

A White Heron

*This 1886 story, like many of Jewett's stories, is set in New England, specifically in Maine. The **protagonist,** Sylvia, is a young girl who faces a major decision. Her conflict and final decision initiate her into a life of responsibility where she must carefully consider the effects of her acts.*

*Although this story is one of the most often reprinted of Jewett's tales, it is not perfect. Notice that the author shifts from one tense to another in the story and, like many of her contemporary writers, even enters the story herself. These problems, however, remain minor in comparison to the convincing portrayal of **setting, character,** and **conflict.***

1

The woods were already filled with shadows one June evening, just before eight o'clock, though a bright sunset still glimmered faintly among the trunks of the trees. A little girl was driving home her cow, a plodding, dilatory,* provoking creature in her behavior, but a valued companion for all that. They were going away from the western light, and striking deep into the dark woods, but their feet were familiar with the path, and it was no matter whether their eyes could see it or not.

---

dilatory: dawdling

There was hardly a night the summer through when the old cow could be found waiting at the pasture bars;* on the contrary, it was her greatest pleasure to hide herself away among the high huckleberry bushes, and though she wore a loud bell she had made the discovery that if one stood perfectly still it would not ring. So Sylvia had to hunt for her until she found her, and call Co'! Co'! with never an answering Moo, until her childish patience was quite spent. If the creature had not given good milk and plenty of it, the case would have seemed very different to her owners. Besides, Sylvia had all the time there was, and very little use to make of it. Sometimes in pleasant weather it was a consolation to look upon the cow's pranks as an intelligent attempt to play hide and seek, and as the child had no playmates she lent herself to this amusement with a good deal of zest. Though this chase had been so long that the wary* animal herself had given an unusual signal to her whereabouts, Sylvia had only laughed when she came upon Mistress Moolly at the swamp-side, and urged her affectionately homeward with a twig of birch leaves. The old cow was not inclined to wander farther; she even turned in the right direction for once as they left the pasture, and stepped along the road at a good pace. She was quite ready to be milked now, and seldom stopped to browse. Sylvia wondered what her grandmother would say because they were so late. It was a great while since she had left home at half past five o'clock, but everybody knew the difficulty of making this errand a short one. Mrs. Tilley had chased the hornéd torment* too many summer evenings herself to blame any one else for lingering, and was only thankful as she waited that she had Sylvia, nowadays, to give such valuable assistance. The good woman suspected that Sylvia loitered occasionally on her own account; there never was such a child for straying about out-of-doors since the world was made! Everybody said that it was a good change for a little maid who had tried to grow for eight years in a crowded manufacturing town, but, as for Sylvia herself, it seemed as if she never had been alive before she came to live at the farm. She thought often with wistful* compassion of a wretched dry geranium that belonged to a town neighbor.

---

pasture bars: i.e., by the fence
wary: cautious
hornéd torment: i.e., the cow
wistful: wishful

" 'Afraid of folks,' " old Mrs. Tilley said to herself, with a smile, after she had made the unlikely choice of Sylvia from her daughter's houseful of children, and was returning to the farm. " 'Afraid of folks,' they said! I guess she won't be troubled no great with 'em up to the old place!" When they reached the door of the lonely house and stopped to unlock it, and the cat came to purr loudly, and rub against them, a deserted pussy, indeed, but fat with young robins, Sylvia whispered that this was a beautiful place to live in, and she never should wish to go home.

The companions followed the shady wood-road, the cow taking slow steps, and the child very fast ones. The cow stopped long at the brook to drink, as if the pasture were not half a swamp, and Sylvia stood still and waited, letting her bare feet cool themselves in the shoal* water, while the great twilight moths struck softly against her. She waded on through the brook as the cow moved away, and listened to the thrushes with a heart that beat fast with pleasure. There was a stirring in the great boughs overhead. They were full of little birds and beasts that seemed to be wide-awake, and going about their world, or else saying good-night to each other in sleepy twitters. Sylvia herself felt sleepy as she walked along. However, it was not much farther to the house, and the air was soft and sweet. She was not often in the woods so late as this, and it made her feel as if she were a part of the gray shadows and the moving leaves. She was just thinking how long it seemed since she first came to the farm a year ago, and wondering if everything went on in the noisy town just the same as when she was there;

the thought of the great red-faced boy who used to chase and frighten her made her hurry along the path to escape from the shadow of the trees.

shoal: shallow

Suddenly this little woods-girl is horror-stricken to hear a clear whistle not very far away. Not a bird's whistle, which would have a sort of friendliness, but a boy's whistle, determined, and somewhat aggressive. Sylvia left the cow to whatever sad fate might await her, and stepped discreetly* aside into the bushes, but she was just too late. The enemy had discovered her, and called out in a very cheerful and persuasive tone, "Halloa, little girl, how far is it to the road?" and trembling Sylvia answered almost inaudibly, "A good ways."

discreetly: quietly

She did not dare to look boldly at the tall young man who carried a gun over his shoulder, but she came out of her bush and again followed the cow while he walked alongside.

"I have been hunting for birds," the stranger said kindly, "and I lost my way, and need a friend very much. Don't be afraid," he added gallantly. "Speak up and tell me what your name is, and whether you think I can spend the night at your house, and go out gunning early in the morning."

Sylvia was more alarmed than before. Would not her grandmother consider her much to blame? But who could have foreseen such an accident as this? It did not appear to be her fault, and she hung her head as if the stem of it were broken but managed to answer "Sylvy," with much effort when her companion again asked her name.

Mrs. Tilley was standing in the doorway when the trio came into view. The cow gave a loud moo by way of explanation.

"Yes, you'd better speak up for yourself, you old trial! Where'd she tuck herself away this time, Sylvy?" Sylvia kept an awed silence; she knew by instinct that her grandmother did not comprehend the gravity* of the situation. She must be mistaking the stranger for one of the farmer-lads of the region.

gravity: seriousness

The young man stood his gun beside the door, and dropped a heavy game-bag beside it; then he bade Mrs. Tilley good-evening, and repeated his wayfarer's story, and asked if he could have a night's lodging.

"Put me anywhere you like," he said. "I must be off early in the morning, before day; but I am very hungry, indeed. You can give me some milk at any rate, that's plain."

"Dear sakes, yes," responded the hostess, whose long slumbering hospitality seemed to be easily awakened. "You might fare better if you went out on the main road a mile or so, but you're welcome to what we've got. I'll milk right off, and you make yourself at home. You can sleep on husks* or feathers," she proffered* graciously. "I raised them all myself. There's good pasturing for geese just below here towards the ma'sh.* Now step round and set a plate for the gentleman, Sylvy!" and Sylvia promptly stepped. She was glad to have something to do, and she was hungry herself.

husks: mattress stuffed with cornhusks
proffered: offered
ma'sh: marsh

It was a surprise to find so clean and comfortable a little dwelling in this New England wilderness. The young man had known the horrors of its most primitive housekeeping, and the dreary squalor* of that level of society which does not rebel at the companionship of hens. This was the best thrift* of an old-fashioned farmstead, though on such a small scale that it seemed like a hermitage.* He listened eagerly to the old woman's quaint talk, he watched Sylvia's pale face and shining gray eyes with ever growing enthusiasm, and insisted that this was the best supper he had eaten for a month; then, afterwards, the new-made friends sat down in the doorway together while the moon came up.

squalor: filthy poverty
thrift: wise management so as to avoid waste
hermitage: lit., the home of a hermit: i.e., a secluded dwelling

Soon it would be berry-time, and Sylvia was a great help at picking. The cow was a good milker, though a plaguy* thing to keep track of, the hostess gossiped frankly, adding presently that she had buried four children, so that Sylvia's mother, and a son (who might be dead) in California were all the children she had left. "Dan, my boy, was a great hand to go gunning," she explained sadly. "I never wanted for pa'tridges or gray squer'ls while he was to home. He's been a great wand'rer, I expect, and he's no hand to write letters.* There, I don't blame him, I'd ha' seen the world myself if it had been so I could.

plaguy: troublesome
he's . . . letters: i.e., he does not like to write letters

"Sylvia takes after him," the grandmother continued affectionately, after a minute's pause. "There ain't a foot o' ground she don't know her way over, and the wild creatur's counts her one o' themselves. Squer'ls she'll tame to come an' feed right out o' her hands, and all sorts o' birds. Last winter she got the jay-birds to bangeing* here, and I believe she'd 'a' scanted herself of her own meals* to have plenty to throw out amongst 'em, if I hadn't kep' watch. Anything but crows, I tell her, I'm willin' to help support,—though Dan he went an' tamed one o' them that did seem to have reason same as folks. It was round here a good spell after he went away. Dan an' his father they didn't hitch*—but he never held up his head ag'in* after Dan had dared* him an' gone off.

bangeing: banqueting?
she'd . . . meals: she would not have eaten
hitch: get along
he . . . ag'in: i.e., he was ashamed and sad
dared: defied

The guest did not notice this hint of family sorrows in his eager interest in something else.

"So Sylvy knows all about birds, does she?" he exclaimed, as he looked round at the little girl who sat, very demure* but increasingly sleepy, in the moonlight. "I am making a collection of birds myself. I have been at it ever since I was a boy." (Mrs. Tilley smiled.) "There are two or three very rare ones I have been hunting for these five years. I mean to get them on my own grounds if they can be found."

demure: reserved, serious

"Do you cage 'em up?" asked Mrs. Tilley doubtfully, in response to this enthusiastic announcement.

"Oh, no, they're stuffed and preserved, dozens and dozens of them," said the ornithologist,* "and I have shot or snared* every one myself. I caught a glimpse of a white heron three miles from here on Saturday, and I have followed it in this direction. They have never been found in this district at all. The little white heron, it is," and he turned again to look at Sylvia with the hope of discovering that the rare bird was one of her acquaintances.

ornithologist: one who studies birds
snared: trapped

But Sylvia was watching a hop-toad in the narrow footpath.

"You would know the heron if you saw it," the stranger continued eagerly. "A queer tall white bird with soft feathers and long thin legs.

"And it would have a nest perhaps in the top of a high tree, made of sticks, something like a hawk's nest."

Sylvia's heart gave a wild beat; she knew that strange white bird, and had once stolen softly near where it stood in some bright green swamp grass, away over at the other side of the woods. There was an open place where the sunshine always seemed strangely yellow and hot, where tall, nodding rushes grew, and her grandmother had warned her that she might sink in soft black mud underneath and never be heard of more. Not far

beyond were the salt marshes and beyond those was the sea, the sea which Sylvia wondered and dreamed about, but never had looked upon, though its great voice could often be heard above the noise of the woods on stormy nights.

"I can't think of anything I should like so much as to find the heron's nest," the handsome stranger was saying. "I would give ten dollars to anybody who could show it to me," he added desperately, "and I mean to spend my whole vacation hunting for it if need be. Perhaps it was only migrating, or had been chased out of its own region by some bird of prey."

Mrs. Tilley gave amazed attention to all this, but Sylvia still watched the toad, not divining,* as she might have done at some calmer time, that the creature wished to get to its hole under the doorstep, and was much hindered by the unusual spectators at that hour of the evening. No amount of thought, that night, could decide how many wished-for treasures the ten dollars so lightly spoken of, would buy.

divining: understanding

The next day the young sportsman hovered about the woods, and Sylvia kept him company, having lost her first fear of the friendly lad, who proved to be most kind and sympathetic. He told her many things about the birds and what they knew and where they lived and what they did with themselves. And he gave her a jack-knife, which she thought as great a treasure as if she were a desert-islander. All day long he did not once make her troubled or afraid except when he brought down some unsuspecting singing creature from its bough. Sylvia would have liked him vastly better without his gun; she could not understand why he killed the very birds he seemed to like so much. But as the day waned, Sylvia still watched the young man with loving admiration. She had never seen anybody so charming and delightful; the woman's heart, asleep in the child, was vaguely thrilled by a dream of love. Some premonition of that great power stirred and

swayed these young foresters who traversed the solemn woodlands with soft-footed silent care. They stopped to listen to a bird's song; they pressed forward again eagerly, parting the branches—speaking to each other rarely and in whispers; the young man going first and Sylvia following, fascinated, a few steps behind, with her gray eyes dark with excitement.

She grieved because the longed-for white heron was elusive, but she did not lead the guest, she only followed, and there was no such thing as speaking first. The sound of her own unquestioned voice would have terrified her—it was hard enough to answer yes or no when there was need of that. At last, evening began to fall, and they drove the cow home together, and Sylvia smiled with pleasure when they came to the place where she heard the whistle and was afraid only the night before.

2

Half a mile from home, at the farther edge of the woods, where the land was highest, a great pine-tree stood, the last of its generation. Whether it was left for a boundary mark, or for what reason, no one could say; the wood-choppers who had felled* its mates were dead and gone long ago, and a whole forest of sturdy trees, pines and oaks and maples, had grown again. But the stately head of this old pine towered above them all and made a landmark for sea and shore miles and miles away. Sylvia knew it well. She had always believed that whoever climbed to the top of it could see the ocean; and the little girl had often laid her hands on the great rough trunk and looked up wistfully at those dark boughs that the wind always stirred, no matter how hot and still the air might be below. Now she thought of the tree with a new excitement, for why, if one climbed it at break of day, could not one see all the world, and easily discover from whence the white heron flew, and mark the place, and find the hidden nest?

felled: cut down

What a spirit of adventure, what wild ambition! What fancied* triumph and delight and glory for the later morning when she could make known the secret! It was almost too real and too great for the childish heart to bear.

fancied: imagined

All night the door of the little house stood open, and the whippoorwills came and sang upon the very step. The young sportsman and his old hostess were sound asleep, but Sylvia's great design kept her broad awake and watching. She forgot to think of sleep. The short summer night seemed as long as the winter darkness, and at last when the whippoorwills ceased, and she was afraid the morning would after all come too soon, she stole out of the house and followed the pasture path through the woods, hastening toward the open ground beyond, listening with a sense of comfort and companionship to the drowsy twitter of a half-awakened bird, whose perch she had jarred in passing. Alas, if the great wave of human interest which flooded for the first time this dull little life should sweep away the satisfactions of an existence heart to heart with nature and the dumb life of the forest!

There was the huge tree asleep yet in the paling moonlight, and small and hopeful Sylvia began with utmost bravery to mount to the top of it, with tingling, eager blood coursing the channels of her whole frame, with her bare feet and fingers, that pinched and held like bird's claws to the monstrous ladder* reaching up, up, almost to the sky itself. First she must mount the white oak tree that grew alongside, where she was almost lost among the dark branches and green leaves heavy and wet with dew; a bird fluttered off its nest, and a red squirrel ran to and fro and scolded pettishly* at the harmless housebreaker. Sylvia felt her way easily. She had often climbed there, and knew that higher still one of the oak's upper branches chafed* against the pine trunk, just where its boughs were set close together. There, when she

made the dangerous pass from one tree to the other, the great enterprise would really begin.

monstrous ladder: i.e., the tree
pettishly: fretfully
chafed: rubbed

She crept out along the swaying oak limb at last, and took the daring step across into the old pine-tree. The way was harder than she thought; she must reach far and hold fast, the sharp dry twigs caught and held her and scratched her like angry talons,* the pitch made her thin little fingers clumsy and stiff as she went round and round the tree's great stem, higher and higher upward. The sparrows and robins in the woods were beginning to wake and twitter to the dawn, yet it seemed much lighter there aloft in the pine-tree, and the child knew that she must hurry if her project were to be of any use.

talons: claws

The tree seemed to lengthen itself out as she went up to reach farther and farther upward. It was like a great main-mast to the voyaging earth; it must truly have been amazed that morning through all its ponderous* frame as it felt this determined spark of human spirit creeping and climbing from high branch to branch. Who knows how steadily the least twigs held themselves to advantage* this light, weak creature on her way! The old pine must have loved his new dependent. More than all the hawks, and bats, and moths, and even the sweet-voiced thrushes, was the brave beating heart of the solitary gray-eyed child. And the tree stood still and held away the winds that June morning while the dawn grew bright in the east.

ponderous: clumsy, heavy
advantage: help

Sylvia's face was like a pale star, if one had seen it from the ground, when the last thorny bough was past, and she stood trembling and tired but wholly triumphant, high in the tree-top. Yes, there was the sea with the dawning sun making a golden dazzle over it, and toward that glorious east flew two hawks with slow-moving pinions.* How low they looked in the air from that height when before one had only seen them far up, and dark against the blue sky. Their gray feathers were as soft as moths; they seemed only a little way from the tree; and Sylvia felt as if she too could go flying away among the clouds. Westward, the woodlands and farms reached miles and miles into the distance; here and there were church steeples, and white villages; truly it was a vast and awesome world.

pinions: wings

The birds sang louder and louder. At last the sun came up bewilderingly bright. Sylvia could see the white sails of ships out at sea, and the clouds that were purple and rose-colored and yellow at first began to fade away. Where was the white heron's nest in the sea of green branches, and was this wonderful sight and pageant of the world the only reward for having climbed to such a giddy height?* Now look down again, Sylvia, where the green marsh is set among the shining birches and dark hemlocks; there where you saw the white heron once you will see him again; look, look! a white spot of him like a single floating feather comes up from the dead hemlock and grows larger and rises, and comes close at last, and goes by the landmark pine with steady sweep of wing and outstretched slender neck and crested head. And wait, wait! do not move a foot or a finger, little girl, do not send an arrow of light and consciousness from your two eager eyes, for the heron has perched on a pine bough not far below yours, and cries back to his mate on the nest, and plumes* his feathers for the new day!

giddy height: height that makes one faint
plumes: smooths

The child gives a long sigh a minute later when a company of shouting cat-birds comes also to the tree, and vexed* by their fluttering and lawlessness the solemn heron goes away. She knows his secret now, the wild light slender bird that floats and wavers, and goes back like an arrow presently to his home in the green world beneath. Then Sylvia, well satisfied, makes her perilous way down again, not daring to look far below the branch she stands on, ready to cry sometimes because her fingers ache and her lamed feet slip. Wondering over and over again what the stranger would say to her, and what he would think when she told him how to find his way straight to the heron's nest.

vexed: disturbed

"Sylvy, Sylvy!" called the busy old grandmother again and again, but nobody answered, and the small husk bed was empty, and Sylvia had disappeared.

The guest waked from a dream, and remembering his day's pleasure hurried to dress himself that it might sooner begin. He was sure from the way the shy little girl looked once or twice yesterday that she had at least seen the white heron, and now she must really be persuaded to tell. Here she comes now, paler than ever, and her worn old frock is torn and tattered, and smeared with pine pitch. The grandmother and the sportsman stand in the door together and question her, and the splendid moment has come to speak of the dead hemlock-tree by the green marsh.

But Sylvia does not speak after all, though the old grandmother fretfully rebukes her, and the young man's kind appealing eyes are looking straight in her own. He can make them rich with money; he has promised it, and they are poor now. He is so well worth making happy, and he waits to hear the story she can tell.

No, she must keep silence! What is it that suddenly forbids her and makes her dumb? She has been nine years growing, and now, when the great world for the first time puts out a hand to her, must she thrust it aside for a bird's sake? The murmur of the pine's green branches is in her ears, she remembers how the white heron came flying through the golden air and how they watched the sea and the morning together, and

Sylvia cannot speak; she cannot tell the heron's secrets and give its life away.

Dear loyalty, that suffered a sharp pang as the guest went away disappointed later in the day, that could have served and followed him and loved him as a dog loves! Many a night Sylvia heard the echo of his whistle haunting the pasture path as she came home with the loitering cow. She forgot even her sorrow at the sharp report of his gun and the piteous sight of thrushes and sparrows dropping silent to the ground, their songs hushed and their pretty feathers stained and wet with blood. Were the birds better friends than their hunter might have been—who can tell? Whatever treasures were lost to her, woodlands and summer-time, remember! Bring your gifts and graces and tell your secrets to this lonely country child!

For Thought and Discussion

1. Although Jewett does deal with universal themes and her story would still be effective if it were removed from its setting, she is nevertheless a successful local colorist who realistically represents her native New England in landscape, customs, characters, dialect, and dress. Find at least one sentence from the story to illustrate each of the above areas.

2. Tell what the following incidents reveal about Sylvia, the central character in the story: her reaction when first entering her grandmother's home after leaving the city, her patience with the cow, her first reaction to the young stranger she met in the woods, and her experience climbing the tree.

3. What is the central conflict in the story? What makes Sylvia's decision so difficult? What experience helps her make the decision she makes? Do you think the author of the story is positive, negative, or neutral about the decision? Explain your answer.

4. Find specific examples from the second part of the story to illustrate the following techniques: change of tense, use of rhetorical questions, shifts in point of view, and authorial intrusion into the story. Do you think these stylistic shortcomings detract from Jewett's ability as an effective storyteller?

5. Compare and contrast Sylvia and the ornithologist. Which character does Jewett develop more fully? Does she treat both characters sympathetically? Support your answer with incidents from the story.

Emily Dickinson 1830-1886

Emily Dickinson was unquestionably the best of the regionalists writing during the post-Civil War era. Because only seven of her poems were published before her death, her splendid achievement was unknown during her lifetime. In 1955 the publication of her verse was finally completed. Since then she has ranked as one of America's best poets. Dickinson's verse expresses themes that poets have always treated, but it does so in very unusual ways. Like other American writers of this period, she reevaluated beliefs that earlier Americans had taken for granted. As a result, in both attitude and poetic form, her work signals the beginning of modern American poetry.

The external details of Dickinson's life are soon told. Her roots were sunk deep in Amherst, Massachusetts, where she was born and resided until her death. After graduation from Amherst Academy in 1847, she entered Mount Holyoke Female Seminary, a private girl's school. Illness forced her to withdraw from school during her freshman year. By modern standards Dickinson's life thereafter seems incredibly narrow. Even in her youth she almost never left Amherst (except for an extended trip to Washington and Philadelphia and for several trips to Boston). After 1865 she seems never to have left Amherst again.

Although Dickinson was to become a local legend because of her eccentric behavior, her girlhood seemed normal enough. Letters she wrote at the time tell of sledding and other parties with both girl and boy friends. As she grew older, her shyness became more intense. She increasingly withdrew from life around her. In her later years, according to contemporary accounts, she often ran to hide from visitors. She talked with friends while sitting behind a nearly closed door. She dressed entirely in white, as if she were ready to marry at a moment's notice. Her sister, Lavinia, stood as a buffer between her and the world. Nevertheless, out of her seemingly limited experience, Dickinson mined riches. She scrutinized familiar objects with far-seeing eyes. She saw the uncommon in even the most ordinary things.

As Dickinson turned inward, she wrote poetry. The year 1862 was a climactic point in her life, for she evidently underwent some traumatic experience. She may have been coming to grips with the fact that she had passed thirty and would likely never marry. Or she may have been reacting to the loss of someone she loved. During this year she began dressing in white. She also began corresponding with literary critic Thomas Wentworth Higginson. What she wrote to him in April may explain why she wrote more poems in 1862 than in any other year: "I had a terror–since September–I could tell to none–and so I sing, as the Boy does by the Burying Ground–because I am afraid."

After 1874 the poet seemed constantly to be preoccupied with death. In that year her father suddenly died. Almost exactly a year later her mother suffered a stroke that left her an invalid for the last seven years of her life. In 1877 and 1882, two of Dickinson's most valued friends died. In 1883 her favorite nephew, only eight years old, died unexpectedly. In 1884 Dickinson suffered a nervous breakdown and late the next year became confined to her bed. During these two years of illness, two more close friends died. Shortly before her own death on May 15, 1886, she wrote a cryptic letter to two young cousins. Its message was simply, "Called back, Emily."

After Dickinson's death Lavinia discovered numerous packets of manuscript poems carefully tied with ribbon and hidden among the poet's belongings. Within ten years four volumes of these poems were published but only in a somewhat garbled form. Because Dickinson's verse deviated so much from contemporary practice, her first editors thought they could improve her poetry by regularizing it. As a result, what people read was not what Dickinson had actually written. In 1955 Thomas H. Johnson (who had also edited in the late 1930s the poems of the best Puritan poet, Edward Taylor) published the complete poems of Dickinson in a form true to the original manuscripts.

Critics view Dickinson's work from several different angles. One of their most illuminating perspectives is to see her as a regionalist. She was a New England poet writing about her native region, New England. "I see," she wrote, "New England-ly." According to George Frisbie Whicher, one of her first biographers, Dickinson's poetry reflects New England's "Puritan tradition," "Yankee . . . humor," and "spiritual unrest." Her favorite subjects include nature, love, death, and immortality. But her approach to these universal subjects is not at all what a reader might expect. For one thing Dickinson rebelled against God. As a result, her verse reveals the modern attitudes of doubt and denial. Her poetry is also strikingly individualistic in its original form.

Dickinson's verse directly anticipated twentieth-century poetry. By altering traditional patterns of form and thought, her work has encouraged modern poets to experiment with language and form. Her poems have also encouraged modern writers to express their doubt, irreverence, bitterness, and even outright rebellion. Dickinson prefigures the twentieth century in both what she says and how she says it.

Dickinson was a very private person. When Higginson asked her for a portrait after she had begun corresponding with him in 1862, she replied: "I had no portrait, but am small, like the wren; and my hair is bold like the chestnut bur; and my eyes, like the sherry in the glass, that the guest leaves. Would this do just as well?" Almost all of his requests for information brought replies as enigmatic as this. Their correspondence reveals, moreover, that he never did understand the Amherst poet.

In her poetry, however, Dickinson often seemed more open. In fact, her poems serve as a diary in which she notes her passing thoughts and reflects on the world around her. The clusters of poems that follow are grouped around several of her most common themes. Incidentally, since Dickinson did not give titles to her poems, these titles are editorial additions.

The Poet's Self

In these poems Dickinson reveals the very special nature of her mind. Notice her view of her own poetry ("Prologue") and her attitude toward people who crave public attention ("I'm Nobody! Who Are You?"). Notice, too, how she reveals her link to Emerson, another New England poet, in her view of sanity and success.

Prologue (441)

This is my letter to the World
That never wrote to Me—
The simple News that Nature told—
With tender Majesty

Her Message is committed
To Hands I cannot see—
For love of Her—Sweet—countrymen—
Judge tenderly—of Me

I'm Nobody! Who Are You? (288)

I'm Nobody! Who are you?
Are you—Nobody—Too?
Then there's a pair of us!
Don't tell! they'd advertise—you know!

How dreary—to be—Somebody!
How public—like a Frog—
To tell one's name—the livelong June—
To an admiring Bog*!

Bog: swamp

Much Madness Is Divinest Sense (435)

Much Madness is divinest Sense—
To a discerning* Eye—
Much Sense—the starkest* Madness—
'Tis the Majority
In this, as All, prevail—*   5
Assent—and you are sane—
Demur*—you're straightway dangerous—
And handled with a Chain—*

discerning: under-
standing, perceptive
starkest: most utter

prevail: wins

Demur: to object
handled . . . chain:
standard care of the
insane in Dickinson's
day

Success (67)

Success is counted sweetest
By those who ne'er succeed.
To comprehend a nectar*
Requires sorest* need.

Not one of all the purple Host*   5
Who took the Flag today
Can tell the definition
So clear of Victory

As he defeated–dying–
On whose forbidden ear   10
The distant strains of triumph
Burst agonized and clear!

nectar: a delicious beverage: cf. the nectar of a flower
sorest: extreme
purple Host: i.e., the victorious soldiers

Aspiration (1176)

We never know how high we are
Till we are called to rise
And then if we are true to plan
Our statures* touch the skies–

The Heroism we recite   5
Would be a normal thing
Did not ourselves the Cubits* warp*
For fear to be a King–

statures: heights
Cubits: measurement of height (orig. the distance from the elbow to the tip of the middle finger)/*warp:* twist out of shape

I Never Saw a Moor (1052)

I never saw a Moor*–
I never saw the Sea–
Yet know I how the Heather looks
And what a Billow be.

I never spoke with God   5
Nor visited in Heaven–
Yet certain am I of the spot
As if the Checks were given–

Moor: a broad tract of open land with patches of heather and peat bogs

The Power of Imagination

Although she rarely left Amherst, Dickinson traveled much in her imagination. In these poems she shows the liberating power of the imagination through words and reverie. She also illustrates her imaginative power in the figurative definition of hope (cf. a dictionary definition: "a wish or desire supported by some confidence of its fulfillment").

A Word (1212)

A word is *dead*
When it is said,
Some say.
I say it just
Begins to live
That day.

To Make a Prairie It Takes a Clover (1755)

To make a prairie it takes a clover and one bee,
One clover, and a bee,
And revery.*
The revery alone will do,
If bees are few.

revery: imagination, daydreaming

Hope (254)

"Hope" is the thing with feathers–
That perches in the soul–
And sings the tune without the words–
And never stops–at all–

And sweetest–in the Gale*–is heard–   5   *Gale:* storm
And sore must be the storm–
That could abash* the little Bird   *abash:* destroy the
That kept so many warm–   self-confidence of

I've heard it in the chillest land–
And on the strangest Sea–
Yet, never, in Extremity,*   *Extremity:* distress
It asked a crumb–of Me.

A Book (1263)

There is no Frigate* like a Book   *Frigate:* sailing ship
To take us Lands away
Nor any Coursers* like a Page   *Coursers:* swift horses
Of prancing Poetry–
This Traverse* may the poorest take   *Traverse:* journey
Without oppress of Toll–
How frugal is the Chariot*   *Chariot:* i.e, the imagina-
That bears the Human soul.   tion or the mind

The Lackawanna Valley; George Inness; National Gallery of Art, Washington; Gift of Mrs. Huttleston Rogers.

The Railway Train (585)

I like to see it lap the Miles–
And lick the Valleys up–
And stop to feed itself at Tanks–
And then–prodigious* step

prodigious: enormous

Around a Pile of Mountains–   5
And supercilious* peer
In Shanties–by the sides of Roads–
And then a Quarry* pare*

supercilious: proud

Quarry: an open pit from which stone is digged/*pare:* peel

To fit its Ribs
And crawl between   10
Complaining all the while
In horrid–hooting stanza–
Then chase itself down Hill–

And neigh like Boanerges*
Then–punctual as a Star   15
Stop–docile and omnipotent
At its own stable door–

Boanerges: i.e., a loud preacher or orator: from Heb. for "sons of thunder": See Mark 3:17.

Glimpses of Nature

Dickinson often saw "New Englandly" in her pictures of nature. Notice that the first and second poems deliberately involve the process of poetic creation. Rather than directly stating what she is describing, Dickinson imaginatively depicts the objects. As a result, the reader has to infer the poet's subject from the description.

She Sweeps with Many-Colored Brooms (219)

She sweeps with many-colored Brooms–
And leaves the Shreds behind–
Oh Housewife in the Evening West–
Come back, and dust the Pond!

You dropped a Purple Ravelling* in–   5   *Ravelling:* thread
You dropped an Amber* thread–   *Amber:* brownish yellow
And now you've littered all the East
With Duds* of Emerald!   *Duds:* clothes

And still, she plies* her spotted Brooms,   *plies:* uses vigorously
And still the Aprons fly,   10
Till Brooms fade softly into stars–
And then I come away–

The Snake (986)

A narrow Fellow in the Grass
Occasionally rides–
You may have met Him–did you not
His notice sudden is–

The Grass divides as with a Comb–   5
A spotted shaft* is seen–
And then it closes at your feet
And opens further on–

shaft: a long, narrow object like an arrow

He likes a Boggy Acre
A Floor too cool for Corn–   10
Yet when a Boy, and Barefoot–
I more than once at Noon
Have passed, I thought, a Whip lash*
Unbraiding in the Sun
When stooping to secure it   15
It wrinkled, and was gone–

Whip lash: a thong of a whip

Several of Nature's People
I know, and they know me–
I feel for them a transport*
Of cordiality–   20

transport: a feeling of strong emotion

But never met this Fellow
Attended, or alone
Without a tighter breathing
And Zero at the Bone–

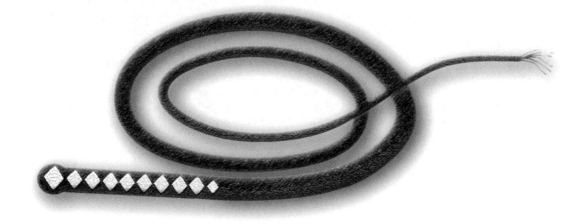

Simplicity (1510)

How happy is the little Stone
That rambles* in the Road alone,
And doesn't care about Careers
And Exigencies* never fears–
Whose Coat of elemental* Brown   5
A passing Universe put on,
And independent as the Sun
Associates or glows alone,
Fulfilling absolute Decree*
In casual simplicity–   10

rambles: wanders aimlessly

Exigencies: pressing needs
elemental: lit., of the elements

absolute Decree: i.e.,God's or Nature's Law

The Poet and Death

Many poets, of course, have written about death, but none with the same slant as Dickinson. She describes the suffering and pain that go before death. (Separation, as she reveals in the first poem below, is much like death.) She also depicts what family members undergo after a loved one has died.

Part of Dickinson's preoccupation with death stems doubtlessly from her rejection of Christ. She grew up in a strongly religious home. Her father conducted family worship. The godly influence of the Puritans and of Jonathan Edwards was still felt in her community. Nevertheless, she apparently refused to place her faith in Christ, even though she knew the way of salvation. While a student at Mount Holyoke, she wrote to a friend: "I have neglected the one thing needful [Luke 10:42] when all were obtaining it, and I may never, never again pass through such a season as was granted us last winter. . . . I am not happy, and I regret that last term, when that golden opportunity was mine, that I did not give up and become a Christian. It is not now too late, so my friends tell me, so my offended conscience whispers, but it is hard for me to give up the world."

Dickinson evidently never did find it possible "to give up the world." Religious matters, however, remained on her mind. Her knowledge of the Bible–its words, stories, rhythms–is often visible in her verse. At times she seems orthodox; at other times she is blasphemous. She suggests, for instance, in several poems not included here that God created evil, that the Bible would be a better book if it did not condemn sin, and that God sadistically approves of and ordains suffering.

I Never Lost as Much but Twice (49)

I never lost as much but twice,
And that was in the sod.
Twice have I stood a beggar
Before the door of God!

Angels–twice descending   5
Reimbursed my store–
Burglar! Banker–Father!
I am poor once more!

Presentiment* Is That Long Shadow on the Lawn (764)

Presentiment*–is that long Shadow–on the Lawn–
Indicative that Suns go down–

Presentiment: sense of something about to happen

The Notice to the startled Grass
That Darkness–is about to pass–

The Bustle in a House (1078)

The Bustle* in a House
The Morning after Death
Is solemnest* of industries*
Enacted* upon Earth–

Bustle: lively activity

solemnest: most serious/*industries:* activities
Enacted: acted out

The Sweeping up the Heart   5
And putting Love away
We shall not want to use again
Until Eternity.

For Thought and Discussion

1. In her poems dealing with self, Dickinson succinctly reveals her thoughts and attitudes in various areas. Discuss the following aspects of this group of poems:
   a. According to "Prologue," what is the poet's task? What does the speaker reveal about her isolation from her audience?
   b. How does "I'm Nobody!" support the idea that a person's desire for privacy or isolation is acceptable? What simile does the speaker in the poem use to make this point?
   c. What paradoxical statements does the speaker use in lines 1 and 3 of "Much Madness Is Divinest Sense"? According to the majority, what makes a person dangerous? Do you agree or disagree?
   d. What ironies concerning success and heroism do you find in "Success" and "Aspiration"? Can you make any personal applications based on the central ideas expressed in the two poems? Although Dickinson clearly rejected traditional Christianity, what seemingly orthodox view of heaven and God does the speaker in "I Never Saw a Moor" express? How are the central ideas of the two stanzas related?
2. One of Dickinson's favorite themes is the power of imagination. In "A Word," the speaker states that a word begins to live only when it is spoken. In what ways do words live? What effect does the poet achieve by inverting the word order in the first sentence? What do you think the poet means in "To Make a Prairie" when she says that a prairie can be created by reverie alone "if bees are few"? Discuss the extended metaphors Dickinson uses in the poems "Hope" and "The Railway Train" and the similies in "A Book." Point out any other images you consider especially effective.
3. In her nature poetry, Dickinson again uses striking figurative devices to convey her impressions. In "She Sweeps with Many-Colored Brooms," what imaginative comparison does the poet use throughout the poem? Who is the "she" in stanza one, and what are her "brooms"? What time of day is being de-

scribed? Do you see another possible interpretation? In "The Snake" what is the main comparison the poet makes? Find a simile and specific words that describe the snake's movements. What type of relationship does the speaker have with other of "nature's people"? What terminology does she use to describe her reaction to encountering a snake? Do you think this is a realistic description? What comparison does the poet use in "Simplicity," and what point does she make by attributing the emotion of happiness to an inanimate object?

4. In her death poetry, as in much of her other poetry, Dickinson is often enigmatic. In what way could the speaker of "I Never Lost as Much but Twice" have been a "beggar" at God's door on two different occasions? What do you think she means by the terms "burglar," "banker," and "father" in line 7? In what way is she "poor once more"? What metaphor does Dickinson use and what mood does she create by the use of this comparison in "Presentiment"? In "The Bustle in a House" do you think the poet is referring to physical or emotional activity? Identify the metaphor in the second stanza, and tell whether you think it is realistic.

5. Find specific examples from the Dickinson poems to illustrate the following aspects of the poet's style: compactness; simple, precise language; traditional meter and variations in metrical form; unusual syntax; exact rhyme and approximate rhyme; and figurative language.

1865

American Realism

9 Masters of Realism

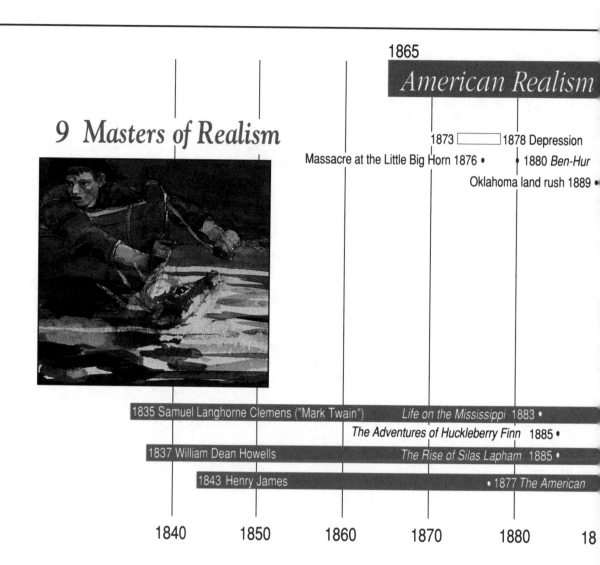

1873 ☐ 1878 Depression

Massacre at the Little Big Horn 1876 •

• 1880 *Ben-Hur*

Oklahoma land rush 1889 •

1835 Samuel Langhorne Clemens ("Mark Twain")   *Life on the Mississippi* 1883 •

The Adventures of Huckleberry Finn 1885 •

1837 William Dean Howells   *The Rise of Silas Lapham* 1885 •

1843 Henry James   • 1877 *The American*

1840   1850   1860   1870   1880   18

1914

and Naturalism

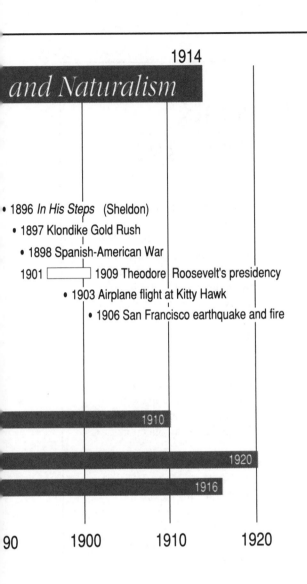

- 1896 *In His Steps* (Sheldon)
  - 1897 Klondike Gold Rush
    - 1898 Spanish-American War
  1901 ☐ 1909 Theodore Roosevelt's presidency
    - 1903 Airplane flight at Kitty Hawk
      - 1906 San Francisco earthquake and fire

1910

1920

1916

90   1900   1910   1920

William Dean Howells
1837-1920

From 1890 to 1910 William Dean Howells was unquestionably the nation's most influential author. He was an enormously productive writer and editor. He published at least twelve hundred short stories, reviews, essays, and other periodical pieces. He also authored or contributed to nearly two hundred books. Furthermore, he strongly shaped the literary principles underlying the American realistic movement. Through his criticism he set the literary standards of his day, and through his fiction he exemplified those standards. Although Howells's reputation declined in the last decade of his life, for nearly a quarter of a century he reigned as the undisputed dean of American letters.

Howells emerged from the Midwest to spend almost all his adult life in Boston and New York City. Born in 1837 in Martin's Ferry, Ohio, Howells knew few advantages during his youth. By the time he was nine, he was setting type in his father's printing shop. He received very little formal education but absorbed knowledge from printing and from his wide reading. In fact, the habit of avid reading and study that he began in his youth continued for the rest of his life. His early efforts at writing were in poetry. His first book, which appeared in 1860, was a collection of poems published jointly with a friend, J. J. Piatt.

Like many other writers Howells worked as a journalist during his apprenticeship period. From 1856 to 1861 he was employed by the *Ohio State Journal,* a Columbus, Ohio, newspaper. In 1860 he wrote a campaign biography of Abraham Lincoln, the presidential nominee of the recently organized Republican party. When Lincoln became president, he rewarded Howells by appointing him to the American consulate in Venice, Italy. (His four years in Italy furnished materials for three books published later.) In 1862, while abroad, Howells married Eleanor Mead, beginning a happy marriage that lasted nearly fifty years.

After Howells returned to the States in 1865, he became the assistant editor of Boston's prestigious *Atlantic Monthly.* In 1871 he was named its editor-in-chief, a position he held until he resigned in 1881. At this point he turned seriously to writing novels and during the rest of the 1880s produced his best work. The most praised novel of this decade is *The Rise of Silas Lapham* (1885), the first American novel to treat a businessman favorably. This novel rejects the post-Civil War notion that success in business is what truly matters. Howells's title, instead, points to the change in the *moral* fortune of Silas Lapham.

While the central character loses almost all his material possessions, he emerges at the end of the novel a clearly better man.

In 1886 Howells entered a new phase of his career. He began writing a regular column for *Harper's Magazine* and began reading widely in various reform and utopian works. His move to New York City in 1885 also helped change his perspective on American society and industry. Howells became increasingly sympathetic to socialist ideas, which he often illustrated in his later works. In his utopian novel *A Traveler from Altruria* (1894), for instance, he satirized the industrialization of America in the late nineteenth century. From this point on, his works became more and more liberal, reflecting the influence of numerous reform groups, including the social-gospel movement.

In his last three decades, Howells exerted considerable influence on American literary attitudes. His views appeared in his books on literary matters as well as in his regular columns: "Editor's Study" (1886-91) and "Editor's Easy Chair" (1900-20). He also encouraged young writers, no matter how much they differed from him in philosophical outlook. The extent of Howells's influence was measured by the public honors he received. He was the first president of the American Academy of Arts and Letters, serving in that office from 1909 to 1920. In 1912 two years after his wife's death, Howells's publishers recognized the writer on his seventy-fifth birthday. Numbered among the guests at the celebration were many of the nation's prominent leaders, including the twenty-seventh president of the United States, William Howard Taft. Howells was also honored in 1915 with a gold medal for fiction by the National Institute of Arts and Letters. He received honorary degrees from Princeton, Columbia, Harvard, Yale, and Oxford. In keeping with his lifelong practice of diligence, he continued actively writing until his death in 1920.

Perhaps Howells's greatest contribution to American literature is that he brought respectability to realism, which he defined as the truthful presentation of life. He strongly attacked romanticism, believing that it failed to paint life as it really was and thus distorted human relationships. Howells excelled in depicting characters. According to one noted literary critic, Howells's special role was "to discover the prosaic ordinary man of the middle class and make him tolerable in fiction." A Howells character is not larger than life but is rather like the ordinary people one passes on the sidewalk. "I don't believe in heroes and heroines," he once wrote, "and willingly avoid the heroic. . . . Nothing in a story can be better than life." Howells also avoided direct comment in his fiction. As a result, readers must interpret the hints within a work in order to evaluate the characters accurately. Unlike most of the American regionalists, who tended to concentrate on **plot** and **setting,** Howells emphasized **character** and **theme.**

Editha

"Editha" intensely explores its chief character and presents a propagandistic **theme.** *Since Howells does not make an explicit judgment of Editha, we must consider her words and actions thoroughly in order to see her as Howells wishes us to. In reality, Editha's fiancé, George, seems to deserve more sympathy from us; yet he proves too weak to resist Editha's crafty manipulation of him.*

This story, first published in 1905, portrays Howells's response to the Spanish-American War (1898), which was for many American intellectuals an unpopular war like the Mexican War (1846-48) and the Vietnam War (1964-73). Howells's growing pacificism appears in the way he condemns the war. Notice, however, that his condemnation of the war—like his evaluation of Editha—is implied rather than explicitly stated.

The air was thick with the war feeling, like the electricity of a storm which has not yet burst. Editha sat looking out into the hot spring afternoon, with her lips parted, and panting with the intensity of the question whether she could let him go. She had decided that she could not let him stay, when she saw him at the end of the still leafless avenue, making slowly up toward the house, with his head down, and his figure relaxed. She ran impatiently out on the veranda, to the edge of the steps, and imperatively* demanded greater haste of him with her will before she called aloud to him, "George!"

imperatively: urgently

He had quickened his pace in mystical* response to her mystical urgence, before he could have heard her; now he looked up and answered "Well?"

mystical: mysterious, not perceived by the senses

"Oh, how united we are!" she exulted, and then she swooped down the steps to him. "What is it?" she cried.

"It's war," he said, and he pulled her up to him, and kissed her.

She kissed him back intensely, but irrelevantly, as to their passion, and uttered from deep in her throat, "How glorious!"

"It's war," he repeated, without consenting to her sense of it; and she did not know just what to think at first. She never knew what to think of him; that made his mystery, his charm. All through their courtship, which was contemporaneous* with the growth of the war feeling, she had been puzzled by his want of seriousness about it. He seemed to despise it even more than he abhorred it. She could have understood his abhorring any sort of bloodshed; that would have been a survival of his old life when he thought he would be a minister, and before he changed and took up the law. But making light of a cause so high and noble seemed to show a want of earnestness at the core of his being. Not but that she felt herself able to cope with a congenital defect of that sort, and make his love for her save him from himself. Now perhaps the miracle was already wrought in him. In the presence of the tremendous fact that he announced, all triviality seemed to have gone out of him; she began to feel that. He sank down on the top step, and wiped his forehead with his handkerchief, while she poured out upon him her question of the origin and authenticity of his news.

contemporaneous: existing at the same time

All the while, in her duplex* emotioning, she was aware that now at the very beginning she must put a guard upon herself against urging him, by any word or act, to take the part that her whole soul willed him to take, for the completion of her ideal of him. He was very nearly perfect as he was, and he must be allowed to perfect himself. But he was peculiar, and he might very well be reasoned out of his peculiarity. Before her reasoning went her emotioning: her nature pulling upon his nature, her womanhood upon his manhood, without her knowing the means she was using to the end she was willing. She had always supposed that the man who won her would have done something to win her; she did not know what, but something. George Gearson had simply asked her for her love, on the way home from a concert, and she gave her love to him, without, as it were, thinking. But now, it flashed upon her, if he could do something worthy to *have* won her–be a hero, *her* hero–it would be even better than if he had done it before asking her; it would be grander. Besides, she had believed in the war from the beginning.

duplex: double, twofold

"But don't you see, dearest," she said, "that it wouldn't have come to this, if it hadn't been in the order of Providence? And I call any war glorious that is for the liberation of people who have been struggling for years against the cruelest oppression. Don't you think so too?"

"I suppose so," he returned, languidly.* "But war! Is it glorious to break the peace of the world?"

languidly: listlessly, without excitement

"That ignoble* peace! It was no peace at all, with that crime and shame at our very gates." She was conscious of parroting* the current phrases of the newspapers, but it was no time to pick and choose her words. She must sacrifice anything to the high ideal she had for him, and after a good deal of rapid argument she ended with the climax: "But now it doesn't matter about the how or why. Since the war has come, all that

is gone. There are no two sides, any more. There is nothing now but our country."

ignoble: base, degrading
parroting: repeating by rote

He sat with his eyes closed and his head leant back against the veranda, and he said with a vague smile, as if musing aloud, "Our country–right or wrong."

"Yes, right or wrong!" she returned fervidly.* "I'll go and get you some lemonade." She rose rustling, and whisked away; when she came back with two tall glasses of clouded liquid, on a tray, and the ice clucking in them, he still sat as she had left him, and she said as if there had been no interruption: "But there is no question of wrong in this case. I call it a sacred war. A war for liberty, and humanity, if ever there was one. And I know you will see it just as I do, yet."

fervidly: earnestly, zealously

He took half of the lemonade at a gulp, and he answered as he set the glass down: "I know you always have the highest idea. When I differ from you, I ought to doubt myself."

A generous sob rose in Editha's throat for the humility of a man, so very nearly perfect, who was willing to put himself below her.

Besides, she felt, more subliminally,* that he was never so near slipping through her fingers as when he took that meek way.

subliminally: without conscious awareness

"You shall not say that! Only, for once I happen to be right." She seized his hand in her two hands, and poured her soul from her eyes into his. "Don't you think so?" she entreated him.

He released his hand and drank the rest of his lemonade, and she added, "Have mine, too," but he shook his head in answering, "I've no business to think so, unless I act so, too."

Her heart stopped a beat before it pulsed on with leaps that she felt in her neck. She had noticed that strange thing in men; they seemed to feel bound to do what they believed, and not think a thing was finished when they said it, as girls did. She knew what was in his mind, but she pretended not, and she said, "Oh, I am not sure," and then faltered.

He went on as if to himself without apparently heeding her, "There's only one way of proving one's faith in a thing like this."

She could not say that she understood, but she did understand.

He went on again. "If I believed–if I felt as you do about this war–Do you wish me to feel as you do?"

Now she was really not sure; so she said, "George, I don't know what you mean."

He seemed to muse* away from her as before. "There is a sort of fascination in it. I suppose that at the bottom of his heart every man would like at times to have his courage tested; to see how he would act."

muse: think or meditate

"How can you talk in that ghastly way?"

"It *is* rather morbid. Still, that's what it comes to, unless you're swept away by ambition, or driven by conviction. I haven't the conviction or the ambition, and the other thing is what it comes to with me. I ought to have been a preacher, after all; then I couldn't have asked it of myself, as I must, now I'm a lawyer. And you believe it's a holy war, Editha?" he suddenly addressed her. "Or, I know you do! But you wish me to believe so, too?"

She hardly knew whether he was mocking or not, in the ironical* way he always had with her plainer mind. But the only thing was to be outspoken with him.

ironical: teasing by using words to mean something other than their literal meaning

"George, I wish you to believe whatever you think is true, at any and every cost. If I've tried to talk you into anything, I take it all back."

"Oh, I know that, Editha. I know how sincere you are, and how–I wish I had your undoubting spirit! I'll think it over; I'd like to believe as you do. But I don't, now; I don't indeed. It isn't this war alone; though this seems peculiarly wanton* and needless; but it's every war–so stupid; it makes me sick. Why shouldn't this thing have been settled reasonably?"

wanton: unjustified

"Because," she said, very throatily again, "God meant it to be war."

"You think it was God? Yes, I suppose that is what people will say."

"Do you suppose it would have been war if God hadn't meant it?"

"I don't know. Sometimes it seems as if God had put this world into men's keeping to work it as they pleased."

"Now, George, that is blasphemy."

"Well, I won't blaspheme. I'll try to believe in your pocket Providence," he said, and then he rose to go.

"Why don't you stay to dinner?" Dinner at Balcom's Works was at one o'clock.

"I'll come back to supper, if you'll let me. Perhaps I shall bring you a convert."

"Well, you may come back, on that condition."

"All right. If I don't come, you'll understand."

He went away without kissing her, and she felt it a suspension of their engagement. It all interested her intensely; she was undergoing a tremendous experience, and she was being equal to it. While she stood looking after him, her mother came out through one of the long windows, on to the veranda, with a catlike softness and vagueness.

"Why didn't he stay to dinner?"

"Because–because–war has been declared," Editha pronounced, without turning.

Her mother said, "Oh, my!" and then said nothing more until she had sat down in one of the large Shaker chairs, and rocked herself for some time. Then she closed whatever tacit* passage of thought there had been in her mind with the spoken words, "Well, I hope *he* won't go."

tacit: unexpressed

"And I hope he *will*," the girl said, and confronted her mother with a stormy exultation* that would have frightened any creature less unimpressionable than a cat.

exultation: triumph

Her mother rocked herself again for an interval of cogitation.* What she arrived at in speech was, "Well, I guess you've done a wicked thing, Editha Balcom."

cogitation: serious thinking

The girl said, as she passed indoors through the same window her mother had come out by, "I haven't done anything–yet."

In her room, she put together all her letters and gifts from Gearson, down to the withered petals of the first flower he had offered, with that timidity of his veiled in that irony of his. In the heart of the packet she enshrined her engagement ring which she had restored to the pretty box he had brought it her in. Then she sat down, if not calmly yet strongly, and wrote:

George: I understood–when you left me. But I think we had better emphasize your meaning that if we cannot be one in everything we had better be one in nothing. So I am sending these things for your keeping till you have made up your mind.

I shall always love you, and therefore I shall never marry anyone else. But the man I marry must love his country first of all, and be able to say to me,

I could not love thee, dear, so much,
Loved I not honor more.

There is no honor above America with me. In this great hour there is no other honor.

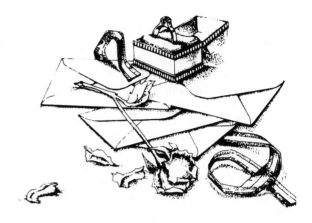

Your heart will make my words clear to you. I have never expected to say so much, but it had come upon me that I must say the utmost.

Editha

She thought she had worded her letter well, worded it in a way that could not be bettered: all had been implied and nothing expressed.

She had it ready to send with the packet she had tied with red, white, and blue ribbon, when it occurred to her that she was not just to him, she was not giving him a fair chance. He had said he would go and think it over, and she was not waiting. She was pushing, threatening, compelling. That was not a woman's part. She must leave him free, free, free. She could not accept for her country or herself a forced sacrifice.

In writing her letter she had satisfied the impulse from which it sprang; she could well afford to wait till he had thought it over. She put the packet and the letter by, and rested serene in the consciousness of having done what was laid upon her by her love itself to do, and yet used patience, mercy, justice.

She had her reward. Gearson did not come to tea, but she had given him till morning, when, late at night there came up from the village the sound of a fife and drum with a tumult of voices, in shouting, singing, and laughing. The noise drew nearer and nearer; it reached the street end of the avenue; there it silenced itself, and one voice, the voice she knew best, rose over the silence. It fell; the air was filled with cheers; the fife and drum struck up, with the shouting, singing, and laughing again, but now retreating; and a single figure came hurrying up the avenue.

She ran down to meet her lover and clung to him. He was very gay, and he put his arm around her with a boisterous laugh. "Well, you must call me Captain, now; Cap, if you prefer; that's what the boys call me. Yes, we've had a meeting at the town hall, and everybody has volunteered; and they selected me for captain, and I'm going to war, the big war, the glorious war, the holy war ordained by the pocket Providence that blesses butchery. Come along; let's tell the whole family about it. Call them from their downy beds, father, mother, Aunt Hitty, and all the folks!"

But when they mounted the veranda steps he did not wait for a larger audience; he poured the story out upon Editha alone.

"There was a lot of speaking, and then some of the fools set up a shout for me. It was all going one way, and I thought it would be a good joke to sprinkle a little cold water on them. But you can't do that with a crowd that adores you. The first thing I knew I was sprinkling hell-fire on them. 'Cry havoc, and let slip the dogs of war.' That was the style. Now that it had come to the fight, there were no two parties; there was one country, and the thing was to fight the fight to a finish as quick as possible. I suggested volunteering then and there, and I wrote my name first of all on the roster. Then they elected me—that's all. I wish I had some ice-water!"

She left him walking up and down the veranda, while she ran for the ice-pitcher and a goblet, and when she came back he was still walking up and down, shouting the story he had told her to her father and mother, who had come out more sketchily dressed than they commonly were by day. He drank goblet after goblet of the ice-water without noticing who was giving it, and kept on

talking, and laughing through his talk wildly. "It's astonishing," he said, "how well the worse reason looks when you try to make it appear the better. Why, I believe I was the first convert to the war in that crowd to-night! I never thought I should like to kill a man; but now, I shouldn't care; and the smokeless powder lets you see the man drop that you kill. It's all for the country! What a thing it is to have a country that *can't* be wrong, but if it is, is right anyway!"

Editha had a great, vital thought, and inspiration. She set down the ice-pitcher on the veranda floor, and ran up-stairs and got the letter she had written him. When at last he noisily bade her father and mother, "Well, good night. I forgot I woke you up; I sha'n't want any sleep myself," she followed him down the avenue to the gate. There, after the whirling words that seemed to fly away from her thoughts and refuse to serve them, she made a last effort to solemnize the moment that seemed so crazy, and pressed the letter she had written upon him.

"What's this?" he said, "Want me to mail it?"

"No, no. It's for you. I wrote it after you went this morning. Keep it–keep it–and read it some-time–" She thought, and then her inspiration came: "Read it if ever you doubt what you've done, or fear that I regret your having done it. Read it after you've started."

They strained each other in embraces that seemed as ineffective as their words, and he kissed her face with quick, hot breaths that were so unlike him, that made her feel as if she had lost her old lover and found a stranger in his place. The stranger said, "What a gorgeous flower you are, with your red hair, and your blue eyes that look black now, and your face with the color painted out by the white moonshine! Let me hold you under my chin, to see whether I love blood, you tiger-lily!" Then he laughed Gearson's laugh, and released her, scared and giddy.* Within her wilfulness she had been frightened by a sense of subtler force in him, and mystically mastered as she had never been before.

giddy: dizzy

She ran all the way back to the house, and mounted the steps panting. Her mother and father were talking of the great affair. Her mother said: "Wa'n't Mr. Gearson in rather of an excited state of mind? Didn't you think he acted curious?"

"Well, not for a man who'd just been elected captain and had to set 'em up for the whole Company A," her father chuckled back.

"What in the world do you mean, Mr. Balcom? Oh! There's Editha!" She offered to follow the girl indoors.

"Don't come, mother!" Editha called, vanishing.

Mrs. Balcom remained to reproach her husband. "I don't see much of anything to laugh at."

"Well, it's catching. Caught it from Gearson. I guess it won't be much of a war, and I guess Gearson don't think so, either. The other fellows will back down as soon as they see we mean it. I wouldn't lose any sleep over it. I'm going back to bed, myself."

Gearson came again next afternoon, looking pale, and rather sick, but quite himself even to his languid irony. "I guess I'd better tell you, Editha, that I consecrated* myself to your god of battles last night by pouring too many libations* to him down my own throat. But I'm all right, now. One has to carry off the excitement, somehow."

consecrated: dedicated
libations: drinks (usually poured in sacrifice to a god)

"Promise me," she commanded, "that you'll never touch it again!"

"What! Not let the cannikin clink?* Not let the soldier drink? Well, I promise."

cannikin clink: reference to the clinking of drinking vessels

"You don't belong to yourself now; you don't even belong to *me.* You belong to your country, and you have a sacred charge to keep yourself strong and well for your country's sake. I have been thinking, thinking all night and all day long."

"You look as if you had been crying a little, too," he said with his queer smile.

"That's all past. I've been thinking, and worshipping *you.* Don't you suppose I know all that you've been through, to come to this? I've followed you every step from your old theories and opinions."

"Well, you've had a long row to hoe."

"And I know you've done this from the highest motives—"

"Oh, there won't be much pettifogging* to do till this cruel war is—"

pettifogging: arguing over insignificant matters

"And you haven't simply done it for my sake. I couldn't respect you if you had."

"Well, then we'll say I haven't. A man that hasn't got his own respect intact wants the respect of all the other people he can corner. But we won't go into that. I'm in for the thing now, and we've got to face our future. My idea is that this isn't going to be a very protracted* struggle; we shall just scare the enemy to death before it comes to a fight at all. But we must provide for contingencies,* Editha. If anything happens to me—"

protracted: drawn out
contingencies: possibilities of unexpected occurrences

"Oh, George!" She clung to him sobbing.

"I don't want you to feel foolishly bound to my memory. I should hate that, wherever I happened to be."

"I am yours, for time and eternity—time and eternity." She liked the words; they satisfied her famine for phrases.

"Well, say eternity; that's all right; but time's another thing; and I'm talking about time. But there is something! My mother! If anything happens—"

She winced, and he laughed. "You're not the bold soldier-girl of yesterday!" Then he sobered.

"If anything happens, I want you to help my
mother out. She won't like my doing this thing.
She brought me up to think war a fool thing as
well as a bad thing. My father was in the civil
war; all through it; lost his arm in it." She thrilled
with the sense of the arm round her; what if that
should be lost? He laughed as if divining* her:
"Oh, it doesn't run in the family, as far as I
know!" Then he added gravely, "He came home
with misgivings about war, and they grew on him.
I guess he and mother agreed between them that
I was to be brought up in his final mind about it;
but that was before my time. I only knew him
from my mother's report of him and his opinions;
I don't know whether they were hers first; but
they were hers last. This will be a blow to her. I
shall have to write and tell her—"

divining: perceiving intuitively

He stopped, and she asked, "Would you like
me to write too, George?"

"I don't believe that would do. No, I'll do the
writing. She'll understand a little if I say that I
thought the way to minimize it was to make war
on the largest possible scale at once—that I felt I
must have been helping on the war somehow if I
hadn't helped keep it from coming, and I knew I
hadn't; when it came, I had no right to stay out
of it."

Whether his sophistries* satisfied him or not,
they satisfied her. She clung to his breast, and
whispered, with closed eyes and quivering lips,
"Yes, yes, yes!"

sophistries: subtle or cunning but misleading reasonings

"But if anything should happen, you might
go to her, and see what you could do for her. You
know? It's rather far off; she can't leave her
chair—"

"Oh, I'll go, if it's the ends of the earth! But
nothing will happen! Nothing *can!* I—"

She felt herself lifted with his rising, and
Gearson was saying, with his arm still around her,
to her father: "Well, we're off at once, Mr. Bal-

com. We're to be formally accepted at the capital,
and then bunched up with the rest somehow, and
sent into camp somewhere, and got to the front
as soon as possible. We all want to be in the van,*
of course; we're the first company to report to the
Governor. I came to tell Editha, but I hadn't got
round to it."

van: i.e., vanguard, the front position

She saw him again for a moment at the capital,
in the station, just before the train started southward with his regiment. He looked well, in his
uniform, and very soldierly, but somehow girlish,
too, with his clean-shaved face and slim figure.
The manly eyes and the strong voice satisfied her,
and his preoccupation with some unexpected details of duty flattered her. Other girls were weeping and bemoaning themselves, but she felt a sort
of noble distinction in the abstraction,* the almost
unconsciousness, with which they parted. Only at
the last moment he said, "Don't forget my

mother. It mayn't be such a walkover as I supposed,'' and he laughed at the notion.

He waved his hand to her, as the train moved
off–she knew it among a score of hands that were
waved to other girls from the platform of the car,
for it held a letter which she knew was hers. Then
he went inside the car to read it, doubtless, and
she did not see him again. But she felt safe for
him through the strength of what she called her
love. What she called her God, always speaking
the name in a deep voice and with the implication
of a mutual understanding, would watch over him
and keep him and bring him back to her. If with
an empty sleeve, then he should have three arms
instead of two, for both of hers should be his for
life. She did not see, though, why she should
always be thinking of the arm his father had lost.

There were not many letters from him, but
they were such as she could have wished, and she
put her whole strength into making hers such as
she imagined he could have wished, glorifying
and supporting him. She wrote to his mother glorifying him as their hero, but the brief answer she
got was merely to the effect that Mrs. Gearson
was not well enough to write herself, and thank-
ing her for her letter by the hand of some one
who called herself ''Yrs truly, Mrs. W. J.
Andrews.''

Editha determined not to be hurt, but to write
again quite as if the answer had been all she expected. But before it seemed as if she could have
written, there came news of the first skirmish, and
in the list of the killed which was telegraphed as a
trifling loss on our side, was Gearson's name.
There was a frantic time of trying to make out that
it might be, must be, some other Gearson; but the
name, and the company and the regiment, and the
State were too definitely given.

Then there was a lapse into depths of which
it seemed as if she never could rise again; then a
lift into clouds far above all grief, black clouds,
that blotted out the sun, but where she soared with

him, with George, George! She had the fever that
she expected of herself, but she did not die in it;
she was not even delirious, and it did not last
long. When she was well enough to leave her bed,
her one thought was of George's mother, of his
strangely worded wish that she should go to her
and see what she could do for her. In the exultation of the duty laid upon her–it buoyed her up
instead of burdening her–she rapidly recovered.

Her father went with her on the long railroad
journey from northern New York to western
Iowa; he had business out at Davenport, and he
said he could just as well go then as any other
time; and he went with her to the little country
town where George's mother lived in a little
house on the edge of illimitable* corn-fields, under trees pushed to a top of a rolling prairie.
George's father had settled there after the civil
war, as so many other old soldiers had done; but
they were Eastern people, and Editha fancied
touches of the East in the June rose overhanging
the front door, and the garden with early summer
flowers stretching from the gate of the paling
fence.

It was very low inside the house, and so dim,
with the closed blinds, that they could scarcely
see one another: Editha tall and black in her
crapes* which filled the air with the smell of their
dyes; her father standing decorously* apart with
his hat on his forearm, as at funerals; a woman
rested in a deep armchair, and the woman who
had let the strangers in stood behind the chair.

The seated woman turned her head round and
up, and asked the woman behind her chair, ''*Who
did you say?*''

Editha, if she had done what she expected of
herself, would have gone down on her knees at
the feet of the seated figure and said, ''I am
George's Editha,'' for answer.

But instead of her own voice she heard that other woman's voice, saying, "Well, I don't know as I *did* get the name just right. I guess I'll have to make a little more light in here," and she went and pushed two of the shutters ajar.

Then Editha's father said in his public will-now-address-a-few-remarks tone, "My name is Balcom, ma'am; Junius H. Balcom, of Balcom's Works, New York; my daughter–"

"Oh!" The seated woman broke in, with a powerful voice, the voice that always surprised Editha from Gearson's slender frame. "Let me see you! Stand round where the light can strike on your face," and Editha dumbly obeyed. "So, you're Editha Balcom," she sighed.

"Yes," Editha said, more like a culprit than a comforter.

"What did you come for?" Mrs. Gearson asked.

Editha's face quivered, and her knees shook. "I came–because–because George–" She could go not farther.

"Yes," the mother said, "he told me he had asked you to come if he got killed. You didn't expect that, I suppose, when you sent him."

"I would rather have died myself than done it!" Editha said with more truth in her deep voice than she ordinarily found in it. "I tried to leave him free–"

"Yes, that letter of yours, that came back with his other things, left him free."

Editha saw now where George's irony came from.

"It was not to be read before–unless–until–I told him so," she faltered.

"Of course, he wouldn't read a letter of yours, under the circumstances, till he thought you wanted him to. Been sick?" the woman abruptly demanded.

"Very sick," Editha said, with self-pity.

"Daughter's life," her father interposed,* "was almost despaired of, at one time."

---

interposed: interrupted

Mrs. Gearson gave him no heed. "I suppose you would have been glad to die, such a brave person as you! I don't believe *he* was glad to die. He was always a timid boy, that way; he was afraid of a good many things; but if he was afraid he did what he made up his mind to. I suppose he made up his mind to go, but I knew what it cost him, by what it cost me when I heard of it. I had been through *one* war before. When you sent him you didn't expect he would get killed."

The voice seemed to compassionate* Editha, and it was time. "No," she huskily murmured.

---

to compassionate: to pity

"No, girls don't; women don't, when they give their men up to their country. They think they'll come marching back, somehow, just as gay as they went, or if it's an empty sleeve, or even an empty pantaloon,* it's all the more glory, and they're so much the prouder of them, poor things."

---

pantaloon: trouser leg

The tears began to run down Editha's face; she had not wept till then; but it was now such a relief to be understood that the tears came.

"No, you didn't expect him to get killed," Mrs. Gearson repeated in a voice which was startlingly like George's again. "You just expected him to kill some one else, some of those foreigners, that weren't there because they had any say about it, but because they had to be there, poor wretches–conscripts, or whatever they call 'em. You thought it would be all right for my George, *your* George, to kill the sons of those miserable mothers and the husbands of those girls that you would never see the faces of." The woman lifted her powerful voice in a psalmlike note. "I thank my God he didn't live to do it. I thank my God they killed him first, and that he ain't livin' with their blood on his hands!" She dropped her eyes which she had raised with her voice, and glared at Editha. "What you got that black on for?" She lifted herself by her powerful arms so high that her helpless body seemed to hang limp its full length. "Take it off, take it off, before I tear it from your back!"

The lady who was passing the summer near Balcom's Works was sketching Editha's beauty, which lent itself wonderfully to the effects of a colorist.* It had come to that confidence which is rather apt to grow between artist and sitter, and Editha had told her everything.

---

colorist: painter

"To think of your having such a tragedy in your life!" the lady said. She added: "I suppose there are people who feel that way about war. But when you consider the good this war has done–how much it has done for the country! I can't understand such people, for my part. And when you had come all the way out there to console her–got up out of a sick bed! Well!"

"I think," Editha said, magnanimously,* "she wasn't quite in her right mind; and so did papa."

---

magnanimously: generously

"Yes," the lady said, looking at Editha's lips in nature and then at her lips in art, and giving an empirical* touch to them in the picture. "But how dreadful of her! How perfectly–excuse me–how *vulgar!*"

---

empirical: based on observation

A light broke upon Editha in the darkness which she felt had been without a gleam of brightness for weeks and months. The mystery that had bewildered her was solved by the word; and from that moment she rose from grovelling* in shame and self-pity, and began to live again in the ideal.

---

grovelling: cringing, demeaning

For Thought and Discussion

1. Howells, a master of characterization, does not comment directly on his characters; instead, he forces the reader to draw his own conclusions. How would you describe Editha, the title character? How does Howells succeed in making the reader feel unsympathetic toward her without explicitly condemning her? Discuss how you arrived at your conclusion, using specific quotations from the story. Also, discuss Editha's reactions to the following characters: George, Editha's mother, George's mother, and the painter. Does Editha undergo a change in the story? Find specific quotations to justify your answer.

2. How would you describe Editha's fiancé, George? How does Howells make you feel more sympathetic to George than to Editha? What weaknesses do you see in George's character? How do his mother's comments to Editha after George's death confirm his weaknesses? Do you think that George displayed a greater degree of love than Editha? Why or why not?

3. What opposing ideas concerning war do the two main characters express? What circumstances have shaped their ideas? Which minor characters support each of these two views? Which of the two views do you think the author supports? Do you agree with his view? Why or why not?

4. Just as Howells does not directly comment on his characters, he also does not state his theme explicitly. Through his artful presentation of character, however, he conveys his own propagandistic ideas to the reader. Having already discussed Howells's theme in reference to war, now discuss his theme in light of romantic idealism.

5. How does "Editha" differ from the stories of the regionalists? How does the story support the statement in the introduction that Howells brought respectability to realism?

Henry James 1843-1916

Henry James was one of the most prolific major American authors of the post-Civil War period. He published 22 novels, 112 short stories, 15 plays, and 7 books of literary criticism. In addition, he wrote more than a dozen books of various types and over a thousand letters. Noted for his psychological realism, James minutely explored the minds of his characters. He often placed his major figures in settings that allowed him to develop the "international theme." Works with this theme set the values of the New World (particularly of the Americans) against those of the Old World (especially of the French and English).

James's **settings** and **themes** grew, to a great extent, out of his early experiences. He was born into a wealthy, unusually gifted New York family. Named after his father, he was the second child in a family of four sons and one daughter. (The oldest child, William, was later to become one of America's most influential philosophers and psychologists.) When James was only six months old, his parents first took him to Europe. During his formative years he repeatedly returned because his father fervently believed in education through travel abroad. Because of the family's travels, much of James's early education was haphazard. It was, however, not narrow, for Henry James, Sr., reported his son to be a "devourer of libraries."

In 1865, when James was twenty-two, his first signed short story appeared in print. By this time he was certain that he wanted to be a writer. For a brief time, though, he had studied painting in London and, in 1862, had even entered Harvard Law School for a year. (James, incidentally, is the only major American writer who never had to work at something other than writing in order to support himself.) Because of a back injury received while fighting in 1861, James did not enlist in the Civil War. Through his literary activity during the war years, he became recognized as one of America's brightest young writers.

In 1875, after a decade of writing short stories and reviews, James appeared ready to enter seriously into the writing profession. In this year—as though to signal his intention to separate himself from his family and his country—James moved to Europe. He soon settled in England, which became his home for the rest of his life and eventually his adopted country. During the first portion (1875-85) of his subsequent career, James wrote about American or European settings. In this period James introduced the "international theme," which he once described as "a general theme dealing for the most part with the bewilderment of the good American, of either sex and of almost any age, in presence of the 'European' order." In *The American* (1877), the second novel of this first period, James clearly defined the conflicts he was repeatedly to develop over the next forty years.

In the second portion (1885-1901) of his career, James concentrated almost exclusively on picturing English characters in English settings. From 1890 to 1895 he also wrote plays for the English stage. Although technically good, they were not popular. What turned James away from writing drama occurred on January 5, 1895, at the opening-night performance in London of *Guy Domville*. When he came on stage in response to the audience's cries of ''Author! Author!'' those in the gallery (the cheaper seats) jeered and hissed him. This experience, although humiliating, fortunately turned James back to fiction. He was yet to write most of his greatest works.

In the final phase (1901-16) of his career, James wrote such highly regarded novels as *The Wings of the Dove* (1902), *The Ambassadors* (1903), and *The Golden Bowl* (1904). Because of his artistic success, this portion of his career is called his ''major phase.'' He returned during this time to the ''international theme,'' presenting American characters in European settings. He also prepared the New York Edition of his works by writing a series of prefaces for its eighteen novels and by extensively revising most of the novels and stories making up the original twenty-four volumes of the edition.

By living abroad for most of his career, James became the most famous nineteenth-century American expatriate. In 1915, unhappy about the United States' delay in entering World War I, he renounced his American citizenship and became a British subject. He reminded those critical of his decision that he had already lived in his adopted country forty years. His works show, however, that he never forgot his native land. They help answer the question that has frequently challenged American writers: What is the American? In other words, how is he different from citizens of other countries? Late in 1915 James, who suffered from a deteriorating heart, experienced first one stroke, then another. On February 28, 1916, he died. His sister-in-law, honoring his request, returned his ashes to the States to be buried in the family burial plot.

James's experience abroad gave his works a cosmopolitan spirit uncharacteristic of the other major American realists. While William Dean Howells reflected a middle-class spirit in his works, James wrote about the lives and experiences of the wealthy, about those who traveled abroad, about those sensitive to art and culture.

In James's works the Europeans generally appear world-weary, preoccupied with social conventions, and often lacking in moral backbone. The Americans, in contrast, are frequently naive and sometimes even crude. Nevertheless, in their conflict with more sophisticated Europeans, the Americans almost always emerge as morally superior.

James is the acknowledged master of nineteenth-century psychological realism. His works explore in detail the complex relationships between characters. He shows the subtleties of these relationships, probing both thought processes and unconscious motivation. For James, studying characters is more important than developing plots. As a consequence, little external action (in the sense of adventure) appears in his works. What does appear is a great amount of internal action with thoughts and feelings laid bare.

As a literary artist, James took fiction to new heights. He raised the novel to an art form, seeing it as a "picture of life, capable of deriving a high value from its form." He insisted on a writer's freedom to choose any subject but reacted against the use of fiction to teach a philosophy or moral. His antididactic emphasis set his work apart from that of many of his peers and most of his predecessors in American literature.

James's works thus give little insight into the spiritual realities of life. Perhaps the root of the author's spiritual complacency lies in his family history. James's grandfather was an Irish immigrant to the United States, a very successful businessman, and a devout Presbyterian who brought up his large family in the doctrines and practices of his church. James's father, however, rebelled against what he felt was a joyless religion and, in time, became a follower of Emanuel Swedenborg (1688-1772). (This Swedish scientist-theologian rejected the doctrines of the Trinity, original sin, the vicarious atonement of Christ, and eternal punishment for sin.) Henry James, the writer–professing no religious beliefs at all–substituted the worship of beauty and art for the worship of God. These three generations show in miniature the religious history of the nineteenth-century American society, which in large part shifted from orthodoxy to heterodoxy and then to indifference.

The American

The American *is the best place to begin a study of the celebrated "international theme." The idea for the novel came, James later remembered, in this fashion: "I was seated in an American 'horsecar' when I found myself, of a sudden, considering with enthusiasm as the theme of a 'story,' the situation, in another country and an aristocratic society, of some robust but insidiously beguiled and betrayed, some cruelly wronged, compatriot; the point being in especial that he should suffer at the hands of persons pretending to represent the highest possible civilization. . . . What would he 'do' in that predicament, how would he right himself, or how, failing a remedy, would he conduct himself under his wrong?"*

The following excerpts describe Christopher Newman and his background. Newman, the protagonist, is a rich but uncorrupted, self-made businessman. He has come to realize that money is not all he really wants from life. Freeing himself from his business, he has travelled to Europe to seek the finer things of life and to find a wife.

Chapter 1

On a brilliant day in May, in the year 1868, a gentleman was reclining at his ease on the great circular divan* which at that period occupied the centre of the Salon Carré, in the Museum of the Louvre.* This commodious* ottoman has since been removed, to the extreme regret of all weak-kneed lovers of the fine arts; but the gentleman in question had taken serene possession of its softest spot, and, with his head thrown back and legs outstretched, was staring at Murillo's* beautiful moon-borne Madonna in profound enjoyment of his posture. He had removed his hat, and flung down beside him a little red guide-book and an opera-glass. The day was warm; he was heated with walking, and he repeatedly passed his handkerchief over his forehead, with a somewhat wearied gesture. And yet he was evidently not a man to whom fatigue was familiar; long, lean, and muscular, he suggested the sort of vigour that is commonly known as "toughness."

divan: long couch without a back
Louvre: the most famous Paris museum, noted for its art collection
commodious: spacious
Murillo: Spanish religious and portrait painter (1617?-82)

But his exertions on this particular day had been of an unwonted* sort, and he had often performed great physical feats which left him less jaded* than his tranquil stroll through the Louvre. He had looked out all the pictures to which an asterisk was affixed in those formidable* pages of fineprint in his Bädeker;* his attention had been trained and his eyes dazzled, and he had sat down with an aesthetic* headache. He had looked, moreover, not only at all the pictures, but at all the copies that were going forward around them, in the hands of those innumerable young women in irreproachable* toilets* who devote themselves, in France, to the propagation of masterpieces; and if the truth must be told, he had often admired the copy much more than the original. His physiognomy* would have sufficiently indicated that he was a shrewd and capable fellow, and in truth he had often sat up all night over a bristling bundle of accounts, and heard the cock crow without a yawn. But Raphael and Titian and Rubens* were a new kind of arithmetic, and they inspired our friend, for the first time in his life, with a vague self-mistrust.

unwonted: unusual
jaded: wearied
formidable: difficult
Bädeker: travel guide, named for the publisher who developed it
aesthetic: artistic
irreproachable: beyond criticism
toilets: costumes, gowns
physiognomy: facial features
Raphael . . . Rubens: old masters whose works are in the Louvre:
    Raphael (1483-1520), Titian (1490-1576), Rubens (1577-1640)

An observer, with anything of an eye for national types, would have had no difficulty in determining the local origin of this undeveloped connoisseur,* and indeed such an observer might have felt a certain humorous relish* of the almost ideal completeness with which he filled out the national mould. The gentleman on the divan was a powerful specimen of an American. But he was not only a fine American; he was in the first place, physically, a fine man. He appeared to possess that kind of health and strength which, when found in perfection, are the most impressive–the physical capital* which the owner does nothing to "keep up." If he was a muscular Christian, it was quite without knowing it. If it was necessary to walk to a remote spot, he walked, but he had never known himself to "exercise." He had no theory with regard to cold bathing or the use of Indian clubs; he was neither an oarsman, a rifleman, nor a fencer–he had never had time for these amusements–and he was quite unaware that the saddle is recommended for certain forms of indigestion. He was by inclination a temperate man; but he had supped the night before his visit to the Louvre at the Café Anglais–someone had told him it was an experience not to be omitted–and he had slept none the less the sleep of the just. His usual attitude and carriage were of a rather relaxed and lounging kind, but when, under a special inspiration, he straightened himself, he looked like a grenadier* on parade. He never smoked. He had been assured–such things are said–that cigars were excellent for the health, and he was quite capable of believing it; but he knew as little about tobacco as about homeopathy.* He had a very well-formed head, with a shapely, symmetrical balance of the frontal and occipital* development, and a good deal of straight, rather dry brown hair. His complexion was brown, and his nose had a bold, well-marked arch. His eye was of a clear, cold gray, and, save for a rather abundant moustache, he was clean-shaved. He had the flat jaw and sinewy neck which are frequent in the American type; but the traces of national origin are a matter of expression even more than of feature, and it was in this respect that our friend's countenance was supremely eloquent.

connoisseur: an informed and discriminating person
relish: pleasure
capital: accumulated wealth
grenadier: member of a regiment of the British royal household infantry
homeopathy: treatment of a disease by giving small doses of a remedy which in larger doses would produce symptoms of the disease
occipital: relating to the back part of the head or skull

The discriminating observer we have been supposing might, however, perfectly have measured its expressiveness, and yet have been at a loss to describe it. It had that typical vagueness which is not vacuity,* that blankness which is not simplicity, that look of being committed to nothing in particular, of standing in an attitude of general hospitality to the chances of life, of being very much at one's own disposal, so characteristic of many American faces. It was our friend's eye that chiefly told his story; an eye in which innocence and experience were singularly blended. It was full of contradictory suggestions; and though it was by no means the glowing orb of a hero of romance, you could find in it almost anything you looked for. Frigid and yet friendly, frank yet cautious, shrewd yet credulous, positive yet sceptical, confident yet shy, extremely intelligent and extremely good-humoured, there was something vaguely defiant in its concessions, and something

profoundly reassuring in its reserve. The cut of this gentleman's moustache, with the two premature wrinkles in the cheek above it, and the fashion of his garments, in which an exposed shirt-front and a cerulean* cravat played perhaps an obtrusive* part, completed the conditions of his identity.

vacuity: emptiness
cerulean: sky blue
obtrusive: undesirably noticeable

We have approached him, perhaps, at a not especially favourable moment; he is by no means sitting for his portrait. But listless as he lounges there, rather baffled on the aesthetic question, and guilty of the damning fault (as we have lately discovered it to be) of confounding the merit of the artist with that of his work (for he admires the squinting Madonna of the young lady with the boyish coiffure,* because he thinks the young lady herself uncommonly taking*), he is a sufficiently promising acquaintance. Decision, salubrity,* jocosity,* prosperity, seem to hover within his call; he is evidently a practical man, but the idea, in his case, has undefined and mysterious boundaries, which invite the imagination to bestir itself on his behalf. . . .

coiffure: hairstyle
taking: attractive
salubrity: healthfulness
jocosity: merriment

Chapter 2

He wandered back to the divan and seated himself on the other side, in view of the great canvas on which Paul Veronese had depicted the marriage feast of Cana. Wearied as he was he found the picture entertaining; it had an illusion for him; it satisfied his conception, which was ambitious, of what a splendid banquet should be. In the left-hand corner of the picture is a young woman with yellow tresses confined in a golden head-dress; she is bending forward and listening, with the smile of a charming woman at a dinner-party, to her neighbour. Newman detected her in the crowd, admired her, and perceived that she too had her votive copyist—a young man with his hair standing on end. Suddenly he became conscious of the germ of the mania of the "collector;" he had taken the first step; why should he not go on? It was only twenty minutes before that he had bought the first picture of his life, and now he was already thinking of art-patronage as a fascinating pursuit. His reflections quickened his good-humour. . . . At this moment, however, his attention was attracted by a gentleman who had come from another part of the room, and whose manner was that of a stranger in the gallery, although he was equipped with neither guide-book nor opera-glass. He carried a white sun-umbrella, lined with blue silk, and he strolled in front of the Paul Veronese, vaguely looking at it, but much too near to see anything but the grain of the canvas. Opposite to Christopher Newman he paused and turned, and then our friend, who had been observing him, had a chance to verify a suspicion aroused by an imperfect view of his face. The result of this larger scrutiny was that he presently sprang to his feet, strode across the room, and, with an outstretched hand, arrested the gentleman with the blue-lined umbrella. The latter stared, but put out his hand at a venture. He was corpulent and rosy; and though his countenance, which was ornamented with a beautiful flaxen beard, carefully divided in the middle and brushed outward at both sides, was not remarkable for intensity of expression, he looked like a person who would willingly shake hands with anyone. I know not what Newman thought of his face, but he found a want of response in his grasp.

"Oh, come, come," he said laughing; "don't say, now, you don't know me—if I have *not* got a white parasol!"

The sound of his voice quickened the other's memory, his face expanded to its fullest capacity, and he also broke into a laugh.

"Why, Newman—I'll be blowed! Where in the world—I declare—who would have thought? You know you have changed."

"You haven't," said Newman.

"Not for the better, no doubt. When did you get here?"

"Three days ago."

"Why didn't you let me know?"

"I had no idea *you* were here."

"I have been here for six years."

"It must be eight or nine since we met."

"Something of the sort. We were very young."

"It was in St. Louis, during the war. You were in the army."

"Oh no, not I. But you were."

"I believe I was."

"You came out all right?"

"I came out with my legs and arms—and with satisfaction. All that seems very far away."

"And how long have you been in Europe?"

"Seventeen days."

"First time?"

"Yes, very much so."

"Made your everlasting fortune?"

Christopher Newman was silent a moment, and then, with a tranquil smile, he answered: "Yes."

"And come to Paris to spend it, eh?"

"Well, we shall see. So they carry those parasols here—the men-folk?"

"Of course they do. They're great things. They understand comfort out here."

"Where do you buy them?"

"Anywhere, everywhere."

"Well, Tristram, I'm glad to get hold of you. You can show me the ropes. I suppose you know Paris inside out."

Mr. Tristram gave a mellow smile of self-congratulation. "Well, I guess there are not many men that can show me much. I'll take care of you. . . ."

Tristram looked at him for some moments, and allowed his placid eyes to measure his friend's generous longitude and rest upon his comfortably contemplative face. "What have you worked at?" he asked.

"Oh, at several things."

"I suppose you're a smart fellow, eh?"

"Yes," he said at last, "I suppose I am." And then, in answer to his companion's inquiries, he related briefly his history since their last meeting. It was an intensely Western story, and it dealt with enterprises which it will be needless to introduce to the reader in detail. Newman had come out of the war with a brevet* of brigadier-general, an honour which in this case—with invidious* comparisons—had lighted upon shoulders amply competent to bear it. But though he could manage a fight, when need was, Newman heartily disliked the business; his four years in the army had left him with an angry, bitter sense of the waste of precious things—life and time and money and "smartness" and the early freshness of purpose; and he had addressed himself to the pursuits of peace with passionate zest and energy. He was of course as penniless when he plucked off his shoulder-straps as when he put them on, and the only capital at his disposal was his dogged resolution and his lively perception of ends and means. Exertion and action were as natural to him as respiration; a more completely healthy mortal had never trod the elastic soil of the West.

brevet: a commission of higher rank than the officer receives pay for
invidious: offensive

His experience, moreover, was as wide as his capacity; when he was fourteen years old, necessity had taken him by his slim young shoulders and pushed him into the street, to earn that night's supper. He had not earned it; but he had earned the next night's, and afterwards, whenever he had had none, it was because he had gone without it to use the money for something else, a keener pleasure or a finer profit. He had turned his hand, with his brain in it, to many things; he had been enterprising, in an eminent sense of the term; he had been adventurous and even reckless, and he had known bitter failure as well as brilliant success; but he was a born experimentalist, and he had always found something to enjoy in the pres-

sure of necessity, even when it was as irritating as the haircloth shirt of the mediaeval monk.

At one time failure seemed inexorably* his portion; ill-luck became his bed-fellow, and whatever he touched he turned, not to gold, but to ashes. His most vivid conception of a supernatural element in the world's affairs had come to him once his pertinacity* of misfortune was at its climax; there seemed to him something stronger in life than his own will. But the mysterious something could only be the devil, and he was accordingly seized with an intense personal enmity to this impertinent force. He had known what it was to have utterly exhausted his credit, to be unable to raise a dollar, and to find himself at nightfall in a strange city, without a penny to mitigate* its strangeness.

inexorably: unyieldingly
pertinacity: persistency, stubbornness
mitigate: to make less intense

It was under these circumstances that he made his entrance into San Francisco, the scene, subsequently, of his happiest strokes of fortune. If he did not, like Dr. Franklin in Philadelphia, march along the street munching a penny loaf, it was only because he had not the penny loaf necessary to the performance. In his darkest days he had had but one simple practical impulse—the desire, as he would have phrased it, to see the thing through. He did so at last, buffeted his way into smooth waters, and made money largely. It must be admitted, rather nakedly, that Christopher Newman's sole aim in life had been to make money; what he had been placed in the world for was, to his own perception, simply to wrest a fortune, the bigger the better, from defiant opportunity. This idea completely filled his horizon and satisfied his imagination. Upon the uses of money, upon what one might do with a life into which one had succeeded in injecting the golden stream, he had up to his thirty-fifth year very scantily reflected. Life had been for him an open game, and he had played for high stakes. He had won at last and carried off his winnings; and now what was he to do with them? He was a man to whom, sooner or later, the question was sure to present itself, and the answer to it belongs to our story. A vague sense that more answers were possible than his philosophy had hitherto dreamt of had already taken possession of him, and it seemed softly and agreeably to deepen as he lounged in this brilliant corner of Paris with his friend.

"I must confess," he presently went on, "that here I don't feel at all smart. My remarkable talents seem of no use. I feel as simple as a little child, and a little child might take me by the hand and lead me about."

"Oh, I'll be your little child," said Tristram, jovially; "I'll take you by the hand. Trust yourself to me."

"I am a good worker," Newman continued, "but I rather think I am a poor loafer. I have come abroad to amuse myself, but I doubt whether I know how."

"Oh, that's easily learned."

"Well, I may perhaps learn it, but I am afraid I shall never do it by rote. I have the best will in the world about it, but my genius doesn't lie in that direction. As a loafer I shall never be original, as I take it that you are."

"Yes," said Tristram, "I suppose I am original; like all those immoral pictures in the Louvre."

"Besides," Newman continued, "I don't want to work at pleasure, any more than I played at work. I want to take it easily. I feel deliciously lazy, and I should like to spend six months as I am now, sitting under a tree and listening to a band. There's only one thing; I want to hear some good music." . . .

Tristram seemed restless and suspicious; he eyed his friend askance, and then: "What are you up to, anyway?" he demanded. "Are you going to write a book?"

Christopher Newman twisted one end of his moustache awhile, in silence, and at last he made answer. "One day, a couple of months ago, something very curious happened to me. I had come on to New York on some important business; it was rather a long story—a question of getting ahead of another party, in a certain particular way, in the stock-market. This other party had once played me a very mean trick. I owed him a grudge. I felt awfully savage at the time, and I vowed that, when I got a chance, I would, figuratively speaking, put his nose out of joint. There was a matter of some sixty thousand dollars at stake. If I put it out of his way, it was a blow the fellow would feel, and he really deserved no quarter. I jumped into a hack and went about my business, and it was in this hack—this immortal, historical hack—that the curious thing I speak of occurred. It was a hack like any other, only a trifle dirtier, with a greasy line along the top of the drab cushions, as if it had been used for a great many Irish funerals. It is possible I took a nap; I had been travelling all night, and though I was excited with my errand, I felt the want of sleep. At all events I woke up suddenly, from a sleep or from some kind of a reverie, with the most extraordinary feeling in the world—a mortal disgust for the thing I was going to do. It came upon me like *that!*"—and he snapped his fingers—"as abruptly as an old wound that begins to ache. I couldn't tell the meaning of it; I only felt that I loathed the whole business and wanted to wash my hands of it. The idea of losing that sixty thousand dollars, of letting it utterly slide and scuttle and never hearing of it again, seemed the sweetest thing in the world. And all this took place quite independently of my will, and I sat watching it as if it were a play at the theatre. I could feel it going on inside of me. You may depend upon it that there are things going on inside of us that we understand mighty little about."

"Jupiter! you make my flesh creep!" cried Tristram. "And while you sat in your hack, watching the play, as you call it, the other man marched in and bagged your sixty thousand dollars?"

"I have not the least idea. I hope so, poor devil! but I never found out. We pulled up in front of the place I was going to in Wall Street, but I sat still in the carriage, and at last the driver scrambled down off his seat to see whether his carriage had not turned into a hearse. I couldn't have got out, any more than if I had been a corpse. What was the matter with me? Momentary idiocy, you'll say. What I wanted to get out of was Wall Street. I told the man to drive down to the Brooklyn ferry and to cross over. When we were over, I told him to drive me out into the country. As I had told him originally to drive for dear life down town, I suppose he thought me insane. Perhaps I was, but in that case I am insane still. I spent the morning looking at the first green leaves on Long Island. I was sick of business; I wanted to throw it all up and break off short; I had money enough, or if I hadn't I ought to have. I seemed to feel a new man inside my old skin, and I longed for a new world. When you want a thing so very badly you had better treat yourself to it. I didn't understand the matter, not in the least; but I gave the old horse the bridle and let him find his way. As soon as I could get out of the game I sailed for Europe. That is how I come to be sitting here.''

''You ought to have bought up the hack,'' said Tristram; ''it isn't a safe vehicle to have about. And you have really sold out, then; you have retired from business?''

''I have made over my hand to a friend; when I feel disposed, I can take up the cards again. I daresay that a twelvemonth hence the operation will be reversed. The pendulum will swing back again. I shall be sitting in the gondola or on the dromedary,* and all of a sudden I shall want to clear out. But for the present I am perfectly free. I have even bargained that I am to receive no business letters.''

---

dromedary: a camel trained especially for riding

''Oh, it's a real *caprice de prince,*''* said Tristram. ''I back out; a poor devil like me can't help you to spend such very magnificent leisure as that. You should get introduced to the crowned heads.''

---

caprice de prince: princely whim

Newman looked at him a moment, and then, with his easy smile: ''How does one do it?'' he asked.

''Come, I like that!'' cried Tristram. ''It shows you are in earnest.''

''Of course I am in earnest. Didn't I say I wanted the best? I know the best can't be had for mere money, but I rather think money will do a good deal. In addition, I am willing to take a good deal of trouble.''

''You are not bashful, eh?''

''I haven't the least idea. I want the biggest kind of entertainment a man can get. People, places, art, nature, everything! I want to see the tallest mountains, and the bluest lakes, and the finest pictures, and the handsomest churches, and the most celebrated men, and the most beautiful women.''

''Settle down in Paris, then. There are no mountains that I know of, and the only lake is the Bois de Boulogne, and not particularly blue. But there is everything else: plenty of pictures and churches, no end of celebrated men, and several beautiful women.''

''But I can't settle down in Paris at this season, just as summer is coming on.''

''Oh, for the summer go up to Trouville.''

''What is Trouville?''

''The French Newport. Half the Americans go.''

''Is it anywhere near the Alps?''

''About as near as Newport is to the Rocky Mountains.''

''Oh, I want to see Mont Blanc,'' said Newman, ''and Amsterdam, and the Rhine, and a lot of places. Venice in particular. I have great ideas about Venice.''

''Ah,'' said Mr. Tristram, rising, ''I see I shall have to introduce you to my wife!''

Chapter Twenty-two

While in Europe Newman meets Claire, the widowed daughter of the Bellegarde family. He falls in love with her and proposes marriage. Newman soon learns, however, that Europeans have a special set of social customs he cannot penetrate. The ruling members of the family–Madame de Bellegarde (the mother) and Urbain (the older son)–refuse to consent to the marriage because of their aristocratic pride. They believe that they will be lowering themselves socially if the family becomes connected with a mere American businessman, no matter how rich he is.

For the first time Newman faces a situation in which money cannot buy him what he seeks. But in Chapter 22 Newman learns the family secret from Mrs. Bread, the Bellegardes' maid. With this secret, Newman believes he can force the Belle-gardes into relenting and allowing Claire to marry him.

At last she [Mrs. Bread] appeared to have set her memories in order. "It was when the late marquis* was an old man and his eldest son had been two years married. It was when the time came on for marrying Mademoiselle Claire; that's the way they talk of it here, you know, sir. The marquis's health was bad; he was very much bro-ken down. My lady had picked out M. de Cintré, for no good reason that I could see. But there are reasons, I very well know, that are beyond me, and you must be high in the world to understand them. Old M. de Cintré was very high, and my lady thought him almost as good as herself; that's saying a good deal. Mr. Urbain took sides with his mother, as he always did. The trouble, I believe, was that my lady would give very little money, and all the other gentlemen asked more. It was only M. de Cintré that was satisfied. The Lord willed it he should have that one soft spot; it was the only one he had. He may have been very grand in his birth, and he certainly was very grand in his bows and speeches; but that was all the grandeur he had. I think he was like what I have heard of comedians; not that I have ever seen one. But I know he painted his face. He might paint it all he would; he could never make me like it! The marquis couldn't abide him, and declared that sooner than take such a husband as that, Mademoiselle Claire should take none at all.

---

marquis: a nobleman ranking below a duke and above a count

"He and my lady had a great scene; it came even to our ears in the servant's hall. It was not their first quarrel, if the truth must be told. They were not a loving couple, but they didn't often come to words, because, I think, neither of them thought the other's doings worth the trouble. My lady had long ago got over her jealousy, and she had taken to indifference. In this, I must say, they were well matched. The marquis was very easy-going; he had a most gentlemanly temper. He got angry only once a year, but then it was very bad. He always took to bed directly afterwards. This time I speak of he took to bed as usual, but he never got up again. I'm afraid the poor gentleman was paying for his dissipation;* isn't it true they mostly do, sir, when they get old? My lady and Mr. Urbain kept quiet, but I know my lady wrote letters to M. de Cintré. The marquis got worse and the doctors gave him up. My lady she gave him up too, and if the truth must be told, she gave him up gladly. When once he was out of the way she could do what she pleased with her daughter,

and it was all arranged that my poor innocent child should be handed over to M. de Cintré.

---

dissipation: unrestrained indulgence in pleasure

"You don't know what mademoiselle was in those days, sir; she was the sweetest young creature in France, and knew as little of what was going on around her as the lamb does of the butcher. I used to nurse the marquis, and I was always in his room. It was here at Fleurières, in the autumn. We had a doctor from Paris, who came and stayed two or three weeks in the house. Then there came two others, and there was a consultation, and these two others, as I said, declared that the marquis couldn't be saved. After this they went off, pocketing their fees, but the other one stayed and did what he could. The marquis himself kept crying out that he wouldn't die, that he didn't want to die, that he would live and look after his daughter. Mademoiselle Claire and the viscount*–that was Mr. Valentin, you know–were both in the house. The doctor was a clever man–that I could see myself–and I think he believed that the marquis might get well.

---

viscount: a nobleman ranking below an earl and above a baron

"We took good care of him, he and I, between us, and one day when my lady had almost ordered her mourning, my patient suddenly began to mend. He got better and better, till the doctor said he was out of danger. What was killing him was the dreadful fits of pain in his stomach. But little by little they stopped, and the poor marquis began to make his jokes again. The doctor found something that gave him great comfort–some white stuff that we kept in a great bottle on the chimney-piece. I used to give it to the marquis through a glass tube; it always made him easier. Then the doctor went away, after telling me to keep on giving him the mixture whenever he was bad. After that there was a little doctor from Poitiers, who came every day. So we were alone in the house–my lady and her poor husband and their three children. Young Madame de Bellegarde had gone away, with her little girl, to her mother's. You know she is very lively, and her maid told me that she didn't like to be where people were dying.'' Mrs. Bread paused a moment, and then she went on with the same quiet consistency. ''I think you have guessed, sir, that when the marquis began to turn my lady was disappointed.'' And she paused again, bending upon Newman a face which seemed to grow whiter as the darkness settled down upon them.

Newman had listened eagerly—with an eagerness greater even than that with which he had bent his ear to Valentin de Bellegarde's last words. Every now and then, as his companion looked up at him, she reminded him of an ancient tabby cat, protracting* the enjoyment of a dish of milk. Even her triumph was measured and decorous;* the faculty* of exultation had been chilled by disuse. She presently continued. ''Late one night I was sitting by the marquis in his room, the great red room in the west tower. He had been complaining a little, and I gave him a spoonful of the doctor's dose. My lady had been there in the early part of the evening; she sat for more than an hour by his bed. Then she went away and left me alone. After midnight she came back, and her eldest son was with her. They went to the bed and looked at the marquis, and my lady took hold of his hand. Then she turned to me and said he was not so well; I remember how the marquis, without saying anything, lay staring at her. I can see his white face, at this moment, in the great black square between the bed-curtains. I said I didn't think he was very bad; and she told me to go to bed—she would sit a while with him.

protracting: drawing out
decorous: proper
faculty: power

''When the marquis saw me going he gave a sort of groan, and called out to me not to leave him; but Mr. Urbain opened the door for me and pointed the way out. The present marquis—perhaps you have noticed, sir—has a very proud way of giving orders, and I was there to take orders. I went to my room, but I wasn't easy; I couldn't tell you why. I didn't undress; I sat there waiting and listening. For what would you have said, sir? I couldn't have told you; for surely a poor gentleman might be comfortable with his wife and his son. It was as if I expected to hear the marquis moaning after me again. I listened, but I heard nothing. It was a very still night; I never knew a night so still. At last the very stillness itself seemed to frighten me, and I came out of my room and went very softly downstairs. In the anteroom, outside of the marquis's chamber, I found Mr. Urbain walking up and down. He asked me what I wanted, and I said I came back to relieve my lady. He said *he* would relieve my lady, and ordered me back to bed; but as I stood there, unwilling to turn away, the door of the room opened and my lady came out. I noticed she was very pale; she was very strange.

''She looked a moment at the count and at me, and then she held out her arms to the count. He went to her, and she fell upon him and hid her face. I went quickly past her into the room, and to the marquis's bed. He was lying there, very white, with his eyes shut, like a corpse. I took hold of his hand and spoke to him, and he felt to me like a dead man. Then I turned round; my lady and Mr. Urbain were there. 'My poor Bread,' said my lady, 'M. le Marquis is gone,' Mr. Urbain knelt down by the bed and said softly, *'Mon père, mon père.'** I thought it wonderful strange, and asked my lady what in the world had happened, and why she hadn't called me. She said nothing had happened; that she had only been sitting there with the marquis, very quiet. She had closed her eyes, thinking she might sleep, and she had slept she didn't know how long. When she woke up he was dead. 'It's death, my son, it's death,' she said to the count. Mr. Urbain said they must have the doctor immediately, from Poitiers, and that he would ride off and fetch him. He kissed his father's face, and then he kissed his mother and went away. My lady and I stood there at the bedside.

Mon père, mon père: Fr. for my father, my father

"As I looked at the poor marquis it came into my head that he was not dead, that he was in a kind of a swoon. And then my lady repeated, 'My poor Bread, it's death, it's death'; and I said, 'Yes, my lady, it's certainly death.' I said just the opposite to what I believed; it was my notion. Then my lady said we must wait for the doctor, and we sat there and waited. It was a long time; the poor marquis neither stirred nor changed. 'I have seen death before,' said my lady, 'and it's terribly like this.' 'Yes, please, my lady,' said I; and I kept thinking. The night wore away without the count's coming back, and my lady began to be frightened. She was afraid he had had an accident in the dark, or met with some wild people. At last she got so restless that she went below to watch in the court for her son's return. I sat there alone and the marquis never stirred."

Here Mrs. Bread paused again, and the most artistic of romancers could not have been more effective. Newman made a movement as if he were turning over the page of a novel. "So he *was* dead!" he exclaimed.

"Three days afterwards he was in his grave," said Mrs. Bread sententiously.* "In a little while I went away to the front of the house and looked out into the court, and there, before long, I saw Mr. Urbain ride in alone. I waited a bit, to hear him come upstairs with his mother, but they stayed below, and I went back to the marquis's room. I went to the bed and held up the light to him, but I don't know why I didn't let the candlestick fall. The marquis's eyes were open—open wide! They were staring at me."

sententiously: pithy: i.e., making a long story short

"I knelt down beside him and took his hands, and begged him to tell me, in the name of wonder, whether he was alive or dead. Still he looked at me a long time, and then he made a sign to put my ear close to him: 'I am dead,' he said, 'I am dead. The marquise has killed me.' I was all in a

tremble. I didn't understand him. I didn't know what had become of him. He seemed both a man and a corpse if you can fancy, sir. 'But you'll get well, now, sir,' I said. And then he whispered again, ever so weak: 'I wouldn't get well, for a kingdom. I wouldn't be that woman's husband again.' And then he said more; he said she had murdered him. I asked him what she had done to him, but he only replied: 'Murder, murder. And she'll kill my daughter,' he said: 'my poor unhappy child.' And he begged me to prevent that, and then he said that he was dying, that he was dead. I was afraid to move or to leave him; I was almost dead myself.

"All of a sudden he asked me to get a pencil and write for him; and then I had to tell him that I couldn't manage a pencil. He asked me to hold him up in bed while he wrote himself, and I said he could never, never do such a thing. But he seemed to have a kind of terror that gave him strength. I found a pencil in the room and a piece of paper and a book, and I put the paper on the book and the pencil into his hand, and moved the candle near him. You will think all this very strange, sir; and very strange it was. The strangest part of it was that I believed he was dying, and that I was eager to help him to write. I sat on the bed and put my arm round him, and held him up. I felt very strong; I believe I could have lifted him and carried him.

"It was a wonder how he wrote, but he did write, in a big scratching hand; he almost covered one side of the paper. It seemed a long time; I suppose it was three or four minutes. He was groaning, terribly, all the while. Then he said it was ended, and I let him down upon his pillows, and he gave me the paper and told me to fold it, and hide it, and to give it to those who would act upon it. 'Whom do you mean?' I said. 'Who are those who will act upon it?' But he only groaned, for an answer; he couldn't speak, for weakness. In a few minutes he told me to go and look at the bottle on the chimney-piece. I knew the bottle he meant; the white stuff that was good for his stomach. I went and looked at it, but it was empty. When I came back his eyes were open and he was staring at me; but soon he closed them and he said no more. I hid the paper in my dress; I didn't look at what was written upon it, though I can read very well, sir, if I haven't any handwriting.

"I sat down near the bed, but it was nearly half an hour before my lady and the count came in. The marquis looked as he did when they left him, and I never said a word about his having been otherwise. Mr. Urbain said that the doctor had been called to a person in childbirth, but that he promised to set out for Fleurières immediately. In another half hour he arrived, and as soon as he had examined the marquis he said that we had had a false alarm. The poor gentleman was very low, but he was still living. I watched my lady and her son when he said this, to see if they looked at each other, and I am obliged to admit that they didn't. The doctor said there was no reason he should die; he had been going on so well. And then he wanted to know how he had suddenly fallen off; he had left him so very hearty. My lady told her little story again—what she had told Mr. Urbain and me—and the doctor looked at her and said nothing. He stayed all the next day at the château, and hardly left the marquis. I was always there. Mademoiselle and Mr. Valentin came and looked at their father, but he never stirred. It was a strange, deathly stupor. My lady was always about; her face was as white as her husband's, and she looked very proud, as I had seen her look when her orders or her wishes had been disobeyed. It was as if the poor marquis had defied her; and the way she took it made me afraid of her.

"The apothecary from Poitiers kept the marquis along through the day, and we waited for the other doctor from Paris, who, as I told you, had been staying at Fleurières. They had telegraphed for him early in the morning, and in the evening he arrived. He talked a bit outside with the doctor from Poitiers, and then they came in to see the marquis together. I was with him, and so was Mr. Urbain. My lady had been to receive the doctor from Paris, and she didn't come back with him into the room. He sat down by the marquis—I can see him there now, with his hand on the marquis's wrist, and Mr. Urbain watching him with a little looking-glass in his hand. 'I'm sure he's better,' said the little doctor from Poitiers; 'I'm sure he'll come back.' A few moments after he had said this the marquis opened his eyes, as if he were waking up, and looked at us, from one to the other. I saw him look at me very softly, as you'd say. At the same moment my lady came in on tiptoe; she came up to the bed and put in her head between me and the count. The marquis saw her and gave a long, most wonderful moan. He said something we couldn't understand, and he seemed to have a kind of spasm. He shook all over and then closed his eyes, and the doctor jumped up and took hold of my lady. He held her for a moment a bit roughly. The marquis was stone dead! This time there were those there that knew."

Newman felt as if he had been reading by starlight the report of a highly important evidence in a great murder case. "And the paper—the paper!" he said, excitedly. "What was written upon it?"

"I can't tell you, sir," answered Mrs. Bread. "I couldn't read it; it was in French."

"But could no one else read it?"

"I never asked a human creature."

"No one has ever seen it?"

"If you see it you'll be the first."

Newman seized the old woman's hand in both his own and pressed it vigorously. "I thank you ever so much for that," he cried. "I want to be the first; I want it to be my property and no one else's! You're the wisest old woman in Europe. And what did you do with the paper?" This information had made him feel extraordinarily strong. "Give it to me quick!"

Mrs. Bread got up with a certain majesty. "It is not so easy as that, sir. If you want the paper, you must wait."

"But waiting is horrible, you know," urged Newman.

"I'm sure *I* have waited; I have waited these many years," said Mrs. Bread.

"That is very true. You have waited for me. I won't forget it. And yet, how comes it you didn't do as M. de Bellegarde said, show the paper to someone?"

"To whom should I show it?" answered Mrs. Bread mournfully. "It was not easy to know, and many's the night I have lain awake thinking of it. Six months afterwards, when they married Mademoiselle to her vicious old husband, I was very near bringing it out. I thought it was my duty to do something with it, and yet I was mightily afraid. I didn't know what was written on the paper, or how bad it might be, and there was no one I could trust enough to ask. And it seemed to me a cruel kindness to do that sweet young creature, letting her know that her father had written her mother down so shamefully; for that's what he did I suppose. I thought she would rather be unhappy with her husband than be unhappy that way. It was for her and for my dear Mr. Valentin I kept quiet. Quiet I call it, but for me it was a weary quietness. It worried me terribly, and it changed me altogether. But for others I held my tongue, and no one, to this hour, knows what passed between the poor marquis and me."

"But evidently there were suspicions," said Newman. "Where did Mr. Valentin get his ideas?"

"It was the little doctor from Poitiers. He was very ill-satisfied, and he made a great talk. He was a sharp Frenchman, and coming to the house, as he did, day after day, I suppose he saw more than he seemed to see. And indeed the way the poor marquis went off as soon as his eyes fell on my lady was a most shocking sight for anyone. The medical gentleman from Paris was much more accommodating, and he hushed up the other. But for all he could do Mr. Valentin and Mademoiselle heard something; they knew their father's death was somehow against nature. Of course they couldn't accuse their mother, and, as I tell you, I was as dumb as that stone.

"Mr. Valentin used to look at me sometimes, and his eyes seemed to shine, as if he were thinking of asking me something. I was dreadfully afraid he would speak, and I always looked away and went about my business. If I were to tell him, I was sure he would hate me afterwards, and that I could never have borne. Once I went up to him and took a great liberty; I kissed him, as I had kissed him when he was a child. 'You oughtn't to look so sad, sir,' I said; 'believe your poor old Bread. Such a gallant, handsome young man can have nothing to be sad about.' And I think he understood me; he understood that I was begging off, and he made up his mind in his own way. He went about with his unasked question in his mind, as I did with my untold tale; we were both afraid of bringing dishonour on a great house. And it was the same with Mademoiselle. She didn't know what had happened; she wouldn't know. My lady and Mr. Urbain asked me no questions because they had no reason. I was as still as a mouse. When I was younger my lady thought me a hussy,* and now she thought me a fool. How should I have any ideas?"

hussy: a saucy girl

"But you say the little doctor from Poitiers made talk," said Newman. "Did no one take it up?"

"I heard nothing of it, sir. They are always talking scandal in these foreign countries—you may have noticed—and I suppose they shook their heads over Madame de Bellegarde. But after all, what could they say? The marquis had been ill, and the marquis had died; he had as good a right to die as anyone. The doctor couldn't say he had not come honestly by his cramps. The next year the little doctor left the place and bought a practice in Bordeaux, and if there has been any gossip it died out. And I don't think there could have been much gossip about my lady that anyone would listen to. My lady is so very respectable."

Newman, at this last affirmation, broke into an immense, resounding laugh. Mrs. Bread had begun to move away from the spot where they were sitting, and he helped her through the aperture* in the wall and along the homeward path. "Yes," he said, "my lady's respectability is delicious; it will be a great crash!" They reached the empty space in front of the church, where they stopped a moment, looking at each other with something of an air of closer fellowship–like two sociable conspirators. "But what was it," said Newman, "what was it she did to her husband? She didn't stab him or poison him."

aperture: opening

"I don't know, sir, no one saw it."

"Unless it was Mr. Urbain. You say he was walking up and down, outside the room. Perhaps he looked through the keyhole. But no; I think that with his mother he would take it on trust."

"You may be sure I have often thought of it," said Mrs. Bread. "I am sure she didn't touch him with her hands. I saw nothing on him, anywhere. I believe it was in this way. He had a fit of his great pain, and he asked her for his medicine. Instead of giving it to him she went and poured it away, before his eyes. Then he saw what she meant, and, weak and helpless as he was, he was frightened, he was terrified. 'You want to kill me,' he said. 'Yes, M. le Marquis, I want to kill you,' says my lady, and sits down and fixes her eyes upon him. You know my lady's eyes, I think, sir; it was with them she killed him; it was with the terrible strong will she put into them. It was like a frost on flowers."

"Well, you are a very intelligent woman; you have shown great discretion," said Newman. "I shall value your services as housekeeper extremely."

They had begun to descend the hill, and Mrs. Bread said nothing until they reached the foot. Newman strolled lightly beside her; his head was thrown back as he was gazing at all the stars; he seemed to himself to be riding his vengeance along the Milky Way. "So you are serious, sir, about that?" said Mrs. Bread, softly.

"About your living with me? Why of course I take care of you to the end of your days. You can't live with those people any longer. And you oughtn't to, you know, after this. You give me the paper, and you move away."

"It seems very flighty in me to be taking a new place at this time of life," observed Mrs. Bread lugubriously.* "But if you are going to turn the house upside down, I would rather be out of it."

lugubriously: mournfully

"Oh," said Newman, in the cheerful tone of a man who feels rich in alternatives, "I don't think I shall bring in the constables, if that's what you mean. Whatever Madame de Bellegarde did, I am afraid the law can't take hold of it. But I am glad of that; it leaves it altogether to me!"

"You are a mighty bold gentleman, sir." murmured Mrs. Bread, looking at him round the edge of her great bonnet.

He walked with her back to the château; the curfew had tolled for the laborious villagers of Fleurières, and the street was unlighted and empty. She promised him that he should have the marquis's manuscript in half an hour. Mrs. Bread choosing not to go in by the great gate, they passed round by a winding lane to a door in the wall of the park, of which she had the key, and which would enable her to enter the château from behind. Newman arranged with her that he should await outside the wall her return with the coveted document.

She went in, and his half hour in the dusky land seemed very long. But he had plenty to think about. At last the door in the wall opened and Mrs. Bread stood there, with one hand on the latch and the other holding out a scrap of white paper, folded small. In a moment he was master of it, and it had passed into his waistcoat-pocket. "Come and see me in Paris," he said; "we are to settle your future, you know; and I will translate poor M. de Bellegarde's French to you.". . .

Mrs. Bread's dull eyes had followed the disappearance of the paper, and she gave a heavy sigh. "Well, you have done what you would with me, sir, and I suppose you will do it again. You *must* take care of me now. You are a terribly positive gentleman."

"Just now," said Newman, "I'm a terribly impatient gentleman!" And he bade her goodnight and walked rapidly back to the inn. He ordered his vehicle to be prepared for his return to Poitiers, and then he shut the door of the common salle* and strode towards the solitary lamp on the chimney-piece. He pulled out the paper and quickly unfolded it. It was covered with pencil-marks, which at first, in the feeble light, seemed indistinct. But Newman's fierce curiosity forced a meaning from the tremulous* signs. The English of them was as follows:

---

salle: lobby
tremulous: caused by trembling

"My wife has tried to kill me, and she has done it; I am dying, dying horribly. It is to marry my dear daughter to M. de Cintré. With all my soul I protest–I forbid it. I am not insane–ask the doctors, ask Mrs. B–. It was alone with me here, to-night; she attacked me and put me to death. It is murder, if murder ever was. Ask the doctors.

"*Henri-Urbain de Bellegarde.*"

Chapter 26

Despite Newman's threat to expose the family's secret, Urbain and Madame de Bellegarde refuse to reconsider their decision to allow Claire to marry Newman. In retaliation to the family's cruel and unrelenting position, Claire enters a convent. Newman leaves Paris but returns several months later for a final visit.

He walked away through the city, beside the Seine and over it, and took the direction of the Rue d'Enfer. The day had the softness of early spring; but the weather was gray and humid. Newman found himself in a part of Paris which he little knew–a region of convents and prisons, of streets bordered by long dead walls and traversed by few wayfarers. At the intersection of two of these streets stood the house of the Carmelites*–a dull, plain edifice, with a high-shouldered blank wall all round it. From without Newman could see its upper windows, its steep roof and its chimneys. But these things revealed no symptoms of human life; the place looked dumb, deaf, inanimate. The pale, dead, discoloured wall stretched beneath it far down the empty side street–a vista without a human figure.

Carmelites: an order of nuns

Newman stood there a long time; there were no passers; he was free to gaze his fill. This seemed the goal of his journey; it was what he had come for. It was a strange satisfaction, and yet it was a satisfaction; the barren stillness of the place seemed to be his own release from ineffectual longing. It told him that the woman within was lost beyond recall, and that the days and years of the future would pile themselves above her like the huge immovable slab of a tomb. These days and years, in this place, would always be just so gray and silent. Suddenly, from the thought of their seeing him stand there, again the charm utterly departed. He would never stand there again; it was gratuitous* dreariness. He turned away with a heavy heart, but a heart lighter than the one he had brought.

---

gratuitous: unnecessary

Everything was over, and he too at last could rest. He walked down through narrow, winding streets to the edge of the Seine again, and there he saw, close above him, the soft, vast towers of

Notre Dame. He crossed one of the bridges and stood a moment in the empty place before the great cathedral; then he went in beneath the grossly-imaged portals. He wandered some distance up the nave and sat down in the splendid dimness. He sat a long time; he heard far-away bells chiming off, at long intervals, to the rest of the world. He was very tired; this was the best place he could be in. He said no prayers; he had no prayers to say. He had nothing to be thankful for, and he had nothing to ask; nothing to ask, because now he must take care of himself. But a great cathedral offers a very various hospitality, and Newman sat in his place, because while he was there he was out of the world.

The most unpleasant thing that had ever happened to him had reached its formal conclusion, as it were; he could close the book and put it away. He leaned his hand for a long time on the chair in front of him; when he took it up he felt that he was himself again. Somewhere in his mind, a tight knot seemed to have loosened. He thought of the Bellegardes; he had almost forgotten them. He remembered them as people he had meant to do something to. He gave a groan as he remembered what he had meant to do; he was annoyed at having meant to do it; the bottom, suddenly, had fallen out of his revenge. Whether it was Christian char-ity or unregenerate good nature—what it was, in the background of his soul—I don't pretend to say; but Newman's last thought was that of course he would let the Bellegardes go.

If he had spoken it aloud he would have said that he didn't want to hurt them. He was ashamed of having wanted to hurt them. They had hurt him, but such things were really not his game. At last he got up and came out of the darkening church; not with the elastic step of a man who has won a victory or taken a resolve, but strolling soberly, like a good-natured man who is still a little ashamed.

Going home, he said to Mrs. Bread that he must trouble her to put his things into the portmanteau she had had unpacked the evening before. His gentle stewardess* looked at him through eyes a trifle bedimmed. "Dear me, Sir," she exclaimed, "I thought you said that you were going to stay forever."

stewardess: one who cares for another

"I meant that I was going to stay away forever," said Newman kindly. And since his departure from Paris on the following day he has certainly not returned. The gilded apartments I have so often spoken of stand ready to receive him; but they serve only as a spacious residence for Mrs. Bread, who wanders eternally from room to room, adjusting the tassels of the curtains, and keeps her wages, which are regularly brought her by a banker's clerk, in a great pink Sèvres vase on the drawing-room mantel-shelf.

Late in the evening Newman went to Mrs. Tristram's and found Tom Tristram by the domestic fireside. "I'm glad to see you back in Paris," this gentleman declared. Mr. Tristram made his friend welcome, according to his own rosy light, and offered him a convenient *résumé* of the Franco-American gossip of the last six months. Then at last he got up and said he would go for half an hour to the club. "I suppose a man who has been for six months in California wants a little intellectual conversation. I'll let my wife have a go at you."

Newman shook hands heartily with his host, but did not ask him to remain; and then he relapsed into his place on the sofa, opposite to Mrs. Tristram. She presently asked him what he had done after leaving her. "Nothing particular," said Newman.

"You struck me," she rejoined, "as a man with a plot in his head. You looked as if you were bent on some sinister errand, and after you had left me I wondered whether I ought to have let you go."

"I only went over to the other side of the river–to the Carmelites," said Newman.

Mrs. Tristram looked at him a moment and smiled. "What did you do there? Try to scale the wall?"

"I did nothing. I looked at the place for a few minutes and then came away."

Mrs. Tristram gave him a sympathetic glance. "You didn't happen to meet M. de Bellegarde," she asked, "staring hopelessly at the convent-wall as well? I am told he takes his sister's conduct very hard."

"No, I didn't meet him, I am happy to say," Newman answered, after a pause.

"They are in the country," Mrs. Tristram went on; "at–what is the name of the place?–Fleurières. They returned there at the time you left Paris and have been spending the year in extreme seclusion. The little marquise must enjoy it; I expect to hear that she has eloped with her daughter's music-master!"

Newman was looking at the light wood-fire; but he listened to this with extreme interest. At last he spoke; "I mean never to mention the name of those people again, and I don't want to hear anything more about them." And then he took out his pocketbook and drew forth a scrap of paper. He looked at it in an instant, then got up and stood by the fire. "I am going to burn them up," he said. "I am glad to have you as a witness. There they go!" And he tossed the paper into the flame.

Mrs. Tristram sat with her embroidery-needle suspended. "What is that paper?" she asked.

Newman, leaning against the fireplace, stretched his arms and drew a longer breath than usual. Then after a moment, "I can tell you now," he said. "It was a paper containing a secret of the Bellegardes–something which would damn them if it were known."

Mrs. Tristram dropped her embroidery with a reproachful moan. "Ah, why didn't you show it to me?"

"I thought of showing it to you–I thought of showing it to everyone. I thought of paying my debt to the Bellegardes that way. So I told them, and I frightened them. They have been staying in the country, as you tell me, to keep out of the explosion. But I have given it up."

Mrs. Tristram began to take slow stitches again. "Have you quite given it up?"

"Oh yes."

"Is it very bad, this secret?"

"Yes, very bad."

"For myself," said Mrs. Tristram, "I am sorry you have given it up. I should have liked immensely to see your paper. They have wronged me too, you know, as your sponsor and guarantee, and it would have served for my revenge as well. How did you come into possession of your secret?"

"It's a long story. But honestly, at any rate."

"And they knew you were master of it?"

"Oh, I told them."

"Dear me, how interesting!" cried Mrs. Tristram. "And you humbled them at your feet?"

Newman was silent a moment. "No, not at all. They pretended not to care–not to be afraid. But I know they did care–they were afraid."

"Are you very sure?"

Newman stared a moment. "Yes, I'm sure."

Mrs. Tristram resumed her slow stitches. "They defied you, eh?"

"Yes," said Newman, "it was about that."

"You tried by the threat of exposure to make them retract?" Mrs. Tristram pursued.

"Yes, but they wouldn't. I gave them their choice, and they chose to take their chance of bluffing off the charge and convicting me of fraud. But they *were* frightened," Newman added, "and I have had all the vengeance I want."

"It is most provoking," said Mrs. Tristram, "to hear you talk of the 'charge' when the charge is burnt up. Is it quite consumed?" she asked, glancing at the fire.

Newman assured her that there was nothing left of it.

"Well then," she said, "I suppose there is no harm in saying that you probably did not make them so very uncomfortable. My impression would be that since, as you say, they defied you, it was because, they believed that, after all, you would never really come to the point. Their confidence, after counsel taken of each other, was not in their innocence, nor in their talent for bluffing things off; it was in your remarkable good nature! You see they were right."

Newman instinctively turned to see if the little paper was in fact consumed; but there was nothing left of it.

For Thought and Discussion

1. In Chapters 1 and 2 James creates the international theme for which he is famous by placing Christopher Newman in a European setting. According to the narrator, what distinguishes Newman as an American? In what aspects is he less sophisticated than the Europeans, and in what way does he prove to be superior? What does he reveal to Tom Tristram in Chapter 2 about his early life of poverty? What does Newman say became the most important thing in his life, and what made him decide to escape to Europe and become a "new man"? Find specific sentences in Newman's description of the scene in the New York City hack which illustrate James's use of psychological realism.

2. What method does James use in Chapter 22 to build suspense? How did Mrs. Bread find out about the murder? Why does she say she has not shown the note to anyone? Why do you think she decides to give it to Christopher Newman?

3. Throughout the story, James carefully portrays his American hero as morally superior to the corrupt European aristocracy. In what ways does Christopher Newman's burning of the note illustrate his moral superiority? The narrator states that he does not pretend to say whether Newman's decision not to seek revenge stemmed from "Christian charity or unregenerate good nature." Find quotations from Chapters 2 and 26 which show that Newman's motivation is not the result of a Christian perspective.

4. Why do you think many readers have been dissatisfied with the ending of James's story? Would you like to change the ending? Why or why not? Is the ending realistically consistent with what you have read of the novel?

5. How do these excerpts from *The American,* which had been praised by some twentieth-century critics as one of James's best novels, reveal the following Jamesian characteristics: a deep interest in character development, a tendency to make the reader carefully analyze the characters' words and actions, and a dependence on conversation for plot development?

Samuel Langhorne Clemens
1835-1910

Samuel Langhorne Clemens—better known as "Mark Twain"—is one of America's all-time favorite authors whose writings have brought laughter to countless readers. But Clemens was not just a humorist; he was also a satirist. A careful reading of his works, especially his later writings, reveals a darkly pessimistic outlook on life. His picture of his fellow men and of God is not at all attractive. Indeed, in numerous ways Clemens's later works reflect the despair of the naturalists and of many recent twentieth-century writers.

Clemens was born November 30, 1835, in the small frontier town of Florida, Missouri. When he was four, his family moved to Hannibal, Missouri, on the west bank of the Mississippi River. This is the town his novels later made famous as the fictional St. Petersburg. His father's death when Clemens was twelve ended the boy's formal schooling, but it did not end his education. To help support the family, he was apprenticed to a country newspaper printer. When eighteen, Clemens left Hannibal to spend the next four years working as a printer in St. Louis, New York, Philadelphia, and Cincinnati.

In 1857, having returned home but eager for wealth and adventure, Clemens became a riverboat pilot on the Mississippi. For one and a half years he was a cub pilot, learning his craft from the famous Horace Bixby. For the next two years Clemens was himself one of the highly regarded pilots he had admired in his youth. These years on the river were rich ones for Clemens. "In that brief, sharp schooling," he said, "I got personally and familiarly acquainted with about all the different types of human nature that are to be found in fiction, biography, or history."

In 1861, as the Civil War stopped traffic on the Mississippi and thus ended his pilot days, Clemens moved to the West. Although he failed to become rich from mining or lumbering, he learned techniques and gathered materials for the trade that eventually made him both rich and famous: writing. He became especially skillful in writing and telling the tall tale; in fact, his first popular work was a tall tale, "The Celebrated Jumping Frog of Calaveras County." This work caught the nation's attention and made Clemens an almost instant celebrity. While in the West, he began regularly using the pen name "Mark Twain," probably the most famous American pseudonym, or pen name. ("Mark Twain" is a river term for two fathoms, or twelve feet. It meant that the water was deep enough for safe passage of a steamboat.) Also while out West, Clemens began lecturing. His lectures, which promoted book sales, endeared him to audiences around the world, improved his "ear" for fiction, and later helped him recover from bankruptcy.

In 1870 Clemens married Olivia Langdon, the daughter of a wealthy New York coal dealer. His marriage marked the beginning of nearly a quarter century of happiness and productive writing. During this period he settled in a specially built $100,000 mansion in Hartford, Connecticut. Here he enjoyed his role as husband and father, wrote his most famous works, and basked in his growing international fame. With the business panic of 1893, however, his fortunes turned downward. Always looking for ways to make money, Clemens had invested hundreds of thousands of dollars in dozens of inventions, in a publishing company, and in the Paige typesetting machine. In 1894 the publishing company went bankrupt and the typesetter lost out to a superior competitor. As a result, Clemens suffered disastrous financial losses.

These financial setbacks were the start of a series of personal losses. While on a world lecture tour (1895-96) to raise money to pay off his debts (an honorable undertaking since the law excused him from repayment), he received word that his favorite daughter, Susy, had died of meningitis. He never recovered from this bitter grief. In 1904 his wife died, after years of worsening invalidism. In 1909 another daughter, Jean, also died. His own health had some time earlier begun to decline, and with the weakening of his creative powers, his frustration grew.

But as his sorrows increased, so did the world's acclaim. His birthday became a national event. He received honorary degrees from Yale, Missouri, and Oxford. Dressing entirely in white, he made an impressive sight for the thousands who flocked to his lectures. As Clemens neared his death, he harbored a personal superstition. Since Halley's comet had appeared in the skies in the year of his birth (1835), he believed that when it reappeared, he would die. In 1910, the year of his death, the comet again streaked across the heavens.

Clemens left a literary legacy equaled by few other American writers. Regarded as one of the three greatest American realists, he represents in his works the frontier spirit of the American people. His writings reflect the tradition of native American humor (especially in oral form) and the ideals of frontier democracy. Clemens's special contribution is his style. In his masterpiece, *Huckleberry Finn* (1885), Clemens made the colloquial speech of the frontier into an artistic form. In this novel he also fused poetry, symbolism, personal memory, romance, and realism.

Many of Clemens's works relive the author's personal experiences. In *Roughing It* (1872) Clemens tells of his adventures out West during the Civil War. In *Life on the Mississippi* (1883) he recounts his experiences as a riverboat pilot, first as a cub and then as a veteran. In *Tom Sawyer* and *Huckleberry Finn*, his two most famous novels, he draws extensively from his memories of life in Hannibal and along the Mississippi.

But Clemens was never satisfied merely to entertain readers with tales from his past. As a satirist he criticized traditions, attitudes, and actions in order to prod people into changing. Hypocrisy, slavery, sentimentality, aristocratic pride, and religion are all major targets of his satiric pen. Sometimes his **satire** is gentle mockery; at other times it is sharp, bitter ridicule.

As Clemens grew older, his works became increasingly stronger expressions of his own growing bitterness and despair. Some believe that his pessimism grew out of his personal experiences with sickness and death in his family and out of his failures in both finances and artistic creativity. Others believe that it grew out of the disappointment and disillusionment he had experienced from dealings with people. "If you pick up a starving dog and make him prosperous," he wrote in *Pudd'nhead Wilson,* "he will not bite you. This is the principal difference between a dog and a man."

There is, however, another reason for Clemens's pessimism. During his lifetime Clemens deliberately rejected God. Even in a relatively early work like *Huckleberry Finn,* Clemens showed his own rebellion through the character of Huck Finn, who mocks prayer, sees all religious people as naive or hypocritical, and rejects traditional standards of right and wrong. Clemens wrote in the mid-1890s, "Whoever has lived long enough to find out what life is, knows how deep a debt of gratitude we owe to Adam, the first great benefactor of our race. He brought death into the world." At the turn of the century, Clemens published "The Man That Corrupted Hadleyburg," in which a mysterious stranger strips from a small town its mask of hypocrisy. Although the townspeople in this story have prided themselves on their honesty, they reveal themselves as mere crooks hiding behind religious pretense. The story implies that even a good man is morally too weak to resist temptation.

In *The Mysterious Stranger,* published six years after his death, Clemens gave his own conclusion: "There is no God, no universe, no human race, no earthly life, no heaven, no hell. It is all a dream—a grotesque and foolish dream." For Clemens, life is a nasty trick played on man. He gained some comfort from believing that life would end in death, which he vainly hoped meant extinction. His works, individually often pleasant, together reveal the sad history of man's stubborn rebellion against God.

Life on the Mississippi

In 1875 Clemens published "Old Times on the Mississippi" in the Atlantic Monthly. *He was forty years old when he wrote about his steamboat experiences, which had occurred in his early twenties. Eight years later Clemens added thirty-nine chapters and published the whole as* Life on the Mississippi.

In this work Clemens gives us much more than just a biographical account of his learning to become a riverboat pilot. He tells a story of initiation. As the young Clemens comes face to face with the realities of life on the river, he learns that piloting is quite different from what he had imagined it to be.

Chapter Four
The Boys' Ambition

When I was a boy, there was but one permanent ambition among my comrades in our village* on the west bank of the Mississippi River. That was, to be a steamboatman. We had transient* ambitions of other sorts, but they were only transient. When a circus came and went, it left us all burning to become clowns; the first negro minstrel show that ever came to our section left us all suffering to try that kind of life; now and then we had a hope that, if we lived and were good, God would permit us to be pirates. These ambitions faded out, each in its turn; but the ambition to be a steamboatman always remained. . . .

our village: Hannibal, Missouri
transient: fleeting

My father was a justice of the peace, and I supposed he possessed the power of life and death over all men, and could hang anybody that offended him. This was distinction enough for me as a general thing; but the desire to be a steamboatman kept intruding nevertheless. I first wanted to be a cabin-boy, so that I could come out with a white apron on and shake a table-cloth over the side, where all my old comrades could see me; later I thought I would rather be the deckhand who stood on the end of the stage-plank with the coil of rope in his hand, because he was particularly conspicuous. But these were only day-dreams–they were too heavenly to be contemplated as real possibilities. By and by one of our boys went away. He was not heard of for a long time. At last he turned up as apprentice engineer or "striker" on a steamboat. This thing shook the bottom out of all my Sunday-school teachings. That boy had been notoriously worldly, and I just the reverse; yet he was exalted to this eminence, and I left in obscurity and misery. There was nothing generous about this fellow in

his greatness. He would always manage to have a rusty bolt to scrub while his boat tarried at our town, and he would sit on the inside guard and scrub it, where we all could see him and envy him and loathe him. And whenever this boat was laid up he would come home and swell* around the town in his blackest and greasiest clothes, so that nobody could help remembering that he was a steamboatman; and he used all sorts of steamboat technicalities in his talk, as if he were so used to them that he forgot common people could not understand them. He would speak of the "labboard"* side of a horse in an easy, natural way that would make one wish he was dead. And he was always talking about "St. Looy" like an old citizen; he would refer casually to occasions when he was "coming down Fourth Street," or when he was "passing by the Planter's House," or when there was a fire and he took a turn on the brakes* of the "old Big Missouri"; and then he would go on and lie about how many towns the size of ours were burned down there that day. Two or three of the boys had long been persons of consideration among us because they had been to St. Louis once and had a vague general knowledge of its wonders, but the day of their glory was over now. They lapsed into a humble silence, and learned to disappear when the ruthless "cub"-engineer approached. This fellow had money, too, and hair-oil. Also an ignorant* silver watch and a showy brass watch-chain. He wore a leather belt and used no suspenders. If ever a youth was cordially admired and hated by his comrades, this one was. No girl could withstand his charms. He "cut out" every boy in the village. When his boat blew up at last, it diffused a tranquil contentment among us such as we had not known for months. But when he came home the next week, alive, renowned, and appeared in church all battered up and bandaged, a shining hero, stared at and wondered over by everybody, it seemed to us that the partiality of Providence for an undeserving reptile had reached a point where it was open to criticism.

swell: i.e., proudly walk
labboard: larboard: i.e., left
brakes: pump handles
ignorant: i.e., nonworking

This creature's career could produce but one result, and it speedily followed. Boy after boy managed to get on the river. The minister's son became an engineer. The doctor's and the postmaster's sons became "mud clerks";* the wholesale liquor dealer's son became a bar-keeper on a boat; four sons of the chief merchant, and two sons of the county judge, became pilots. Pilot was the grandest position of all. The pilot, even in those days of trivial wages, had a princely salary–from a hundred and fifty to two hundred and fifty dollars a month, and no board to pay. Two months of his wages would pay a preacher's salary for a year. Now some of us were left disconsolate. We could not get on the river–at least our parents would not let us.

mud clerks: assistants to a steamboat's purser, who keeps accounts

So, by and by, I ran away. I said I would never come home again till I was a pilot and could come in glory. But somehow I could not manage it. I went meekly aboard a few of the boats that lay packed together like sardines at the long St. Louis wharf, and humbly inquired for the pilots, but got only a cold shoulder and short words from mates and clerks. I had to make the best of this sort of treatment for the time being, but I had comforting day-dreams of a future when I should be a great and honored pilot, with plenty of money, and could kill some of these mates and clerks and pay for them.

Chapter Six
A Cub-pilot's Experience

. . . I entered upon the small enterprise of "learning" twelve or thirteen hundred miles of the great Mississippi River with the easy confidence of my time of life. If I had really known what I was about to require of my faculties, I should not have had the courage to begin. I supposed that all a pilot had to do was to keep his boat in the river, and I did not consider that that could be much of a trick, since it was so wide.

The boat backed out from New Orleans at four in the afternoon, and it was "our watch" until eight. Mr. Bixby, my chief, "straightened her up," plowed her along past the sterns of the other boats that lay at the Levee, and then said, "Here, take her; shave those steamships as close as you'd peel an apple." I took the wheel, and my heartbeat fluttered up into the hundreds; for it seemed to me that we were about to scrape the side off every ship in the line, we were so close. I held my breath and began to claw the boat away from the danger; and I had my own opinion of the pilot who had known no better than to get us into such peril, but I was too wise to express it. In half a minute I had a wide margin of safety intervening between the *Paul Jones* and the ships; and within ten seconds more I was set aside in disgrace, and Mr. Bixby was going into danger again and flaying me alive with abuse of my cowardice. I was stung, but I was obliged to admire the easy confidence with which my chief loafed from side to side of his wheel, and trimmed the ships so closely that disaster seemed ceaselessly imminent. When he had cooled a little he told me that the easy water was close ashore and the current outside, and therefore we must hug the bank, upstream, to get the benefit of the former, and stay well out, down-stream, to take advantage of the latter. In my own mind I resolved to be a downstream pilot and leave the up-streaming to people dead to prudence.

Now and then Mr. Bixby called my attention to certain things. Said he, "This is Six-Mile Point." I assented. It was pleasant enough information, but I could not see the bearing of it. I was not conscious that it was a matter of any interest to me. Another time he said, "This is Nine-Mile Point." Later he said, "This is Twelve-Mile

Point.'' They were all about level with the water's edge; they all looked about alike to me; they were monotonously unpicturesque. I hoped Mr. Bixby would change the subject. But no; he would crowd up around a point, hugging the shore with affection, and then say: ''The slack water* ends here, abreast this bunch of China trees; now we cross over.'' So he crossed over. He gave me the wheel once or twice, but I had no luck. I either came near chipping off the edge of a sugar-plantation, or I yawed* too far from shore, and so dropped back into disgrace again and got abused.

slack water: still water
yawed: changed from an intended course

The watch was ended at last, and we took supper and went to bed. At midnight the glare of a lantern shone in my eyes, and the night watchman said:

''Come, turn out!''

And then he left. I could not understand this extraordinary procedure; so I presently gave up trying to, and dozed off to sleep. Pretty soon the watchman was back again, and this time he was gruff. I was annoyed. I said:

''What do you want to come bothering around here in the middle of the night for? Now, as like as not, I'll not get to sleep again to-night.''

''Well, if this ain't good, I'm blessed.''

The ''off-watch'' was just turning in, and I heard some brutal laughter from them, and such remarks as ''Hello, watchman! ain't the new cub turned out yet? He's delicate, likely. Give him some sugar in a rag, and send for the chambermaid to sing 'Rock-a-by Baby,' to him.''

About this time Mr. Bixby appeared on the scene. Something like a minute later I was climbing the pilot-house steps with some of my clothes on and the rest in my arms. Mr. Bixby was close behind, commenting. Here was something fresh–this thing of getting up in the middle of the night to go to work. It was a detail in piloting that had never occurred to me at all. I knew that boats ran all night, but somehow I had never happened to reflect that somebody had to get up out of a warm bed to run them. I began to fear that piloting was not quite so romantic as I had imagined it was; there was something very real and worklike about this new phase of it.

. . . Presently he turned on me and said:

''What's the name of the first point above New Orleans?''

I was gratified to be able to answer promptly, and I did. I said I didn't know.

''Don't know?''

This manner jolted me. I was down at the foot again, in a moment. But I had to say just what I had said before.

''Well, you're a smart one!'' said Mr. Bixby. ''What's the name of the next point?''

Once more I didn't know.

"Well, this beats anything. Tell me the name of *any* point or place I told you."

I studied awhile and decided that I couldn't.

"Look here! What do you start out from, above Twelve-Mile Point, to cross over?"

"I–I–don't know."

"You–you–don't know?" mimicking my drawling manner of speech. "What *do* you know?"

"I–I–nothing, for certain."

"By the great Caesar's ghost, I believe you! You're the stupidest dunderhead I ever saw or ever heard of! The idea of *you* being a pilot–*you!* Why, you don't know enough to pilot a cow down a lane."

Oh, but his wrath was up! He was a nervous man, and he shuffled from one side of his wheel to the other as if the floor was hot. He would boil awhile to himself, and then overflow and scald me again.

"Look here! What do you suppose I told you the names of those points for?"

I tremblingly considered a moment, and then the devil of temptation provoked me to say:

"Well, to–to–be entertaining, I thought."

This was a red rag to the bull. He raged and stormed so (he was crossing the river at the time) that I judged it made him blind, because he ran over the steering-oar of a trading-scow.* . . . Presently he said to me in the gentlest way:

---

trading-scow: a large flat-bottomed boat

"My boy, you must get a little memorandum-book; and every time I tell you a thing, put it down right away. There's only one way to be a pilot, and that is to get this entire river by heart. You have to know it just like A B C."

That was a dismal revelation to me; for my memory was never loaded with anything but blank cartridges. . . .

By the time we had gone seven or eight hundred miles up the river, I had learned to be a tolerably plucky up-stream steersman, in daylight; and before we reached St. Louis I had made a trifle of progress in night work, but only a trifle. I had a note-book that fairly bristled with the names of towns, "points," bars, islands, bends, reaches, etc.; but the information was to be found only in the note-book–none of it was in my head. It made my heart ache to think I had only got half of the river set down; for as our watch was four hours off and four hours on, day and night, there was a long four-hour gap in my book for every time I had slept since the voyage began. . . .

Chapter Nine
Continued Perplexities

. . . The face of the water, in time, became a wonderful book–a book that was a dead language to the uneducated passenger, but which told its mind to me without reserve, delivering its most cherished secrets as clearly as if it uttered them with a voice. And it was not a book to be read once and thrown aside, for it had a new story to tell every day. Throughout the long twelve hundred miles there was never a page that was void of interest, never one that you could leave unread without loss, never one that you would want to skip, thinking you could find higher enjoyment in some other thing. There never was so wonderful a book written by man; never one whose interest was so absorbing, so unflagging, so sparklingly renewed with every reperusal. The passenger who could not read it was charmed with a peculiar sort of faint dimple on its surface (on the rare occasions when he did not overlook it altogether); but to the pilot that was an *italicized* passage; indeed, it was more than that, it was a legend* of the largest capitals, with a string of shouting exclamation-points at the end of it, for it meant that a wreck or a rock was buried there that could tear the life out of the strongest vessel that ever floated. It is the faintest and simplest expression the water ever makes, and the most hideous to a pilot's eye. In truth, the passenger who could not read this book saw nothing but all manner of pretty pictures in it, painted by the sun and shaded by the clouds, whereas to the trained eye these were not pictures at all, but the grimmest and most dead-earnest of reading-matter.

legend: title or caption

Now when I had mastered the language of this water, and had come to know every trifling feature that bordered the great river as familiarly as I knew the letters of the alphabet, I had made a valuable acquisition. But I had lost something, too. I had lost something which could never be restored to me while I lived. All the grace, the beauty, the poetry, had gone out of the majestic river! I still kept in mind a certain wonderful sunset which I witnessed when steamboating was new to me. A broad expanse of the river was turned to blood; in the middle distance the red hue brightened into gold, through which a solitary log came floating, black and conspicuous; in one place a long, slanting mark lay sparkling upon the water; in another the surface was broken by boiling, tumbling rings, that were as many-tinted as an opal; where the ruddy flush was faintest, was a smooth spot that was covered with graceful circles and radiating lines, ever so delicately traced; the shore on our left was densely wooded, and the sombre shadow that fell from this forest was broken in one place by a long, ruffled trail that shone like silver; and high above the forest wall a clean-stemmed dead tree waved a single leafy bough that glowed like a flame in the unobstructed splendor that was flowing from the sun. There were graceful curves, reflected images, woody heights, soft distances; and over the whole scene, far and near, the dissolving lights drifted steadily, enriching it every passing moment with new marvels of coloring.

I stood like one bewitched. I drank it in, in a speechless rapture. The world was new to me, and I had never seen anything like this at home. But as I have said, a day came when I began to cease from noting the glories and the charms which the moon and the sun and the twilight wrought upon the river's face; another day came when I ceased altogether to note them. Then, if that sunset scene had been repeated, I should have looked upon it without rapture, and should have commented upon it, inwardly, after this fashion; "This sun means that we are going to have wind to-morrow; that floating log means that the river is rising, small thanks to it; that slanting mark on the water refers to a bluff reef* which is going to kill somebody's steamboat one of these nights, if it keeps on stretching out like that; those tumbling 'boils' show a dissolving bar and a changing channel there; the lines and circle in the slick water over yonder are a warning that that trouble-some place is shoaling up dangerously;* that silver streak in the shadow of the forest is the 'break' from a new snag, and he has located himself in the very best place he could have found to fish for steamboats; that tall dead tree, with a single living branch, is not going to last long, and then how is a body ever going to get through this blind place at night without the friendly old landmark?"

bluff reef: a concealed ridge of sand just below the water and extending out from a high river bank
shoaling . . . dangerously: i.e., becoming dangerously shallow

No, the romance and beauty were all gone from the river. All the value any feature of it had for me now was the amount of usefulness it could furnish toward compassing the safe piloting of a steamboat. Since those days, I have pitied doctors from my heart. What does the lovely flush in a beauty's cheek mean to a doctor but a "break" that ripples above some deadly disease? Are not all her visible charms sown thick with what are to him the signs and symbols of hidden decay? Does he ever see her beauty at all, or doesn't he simply view her professionally, and comment upon her unwholesome condition all to himself? And doesn't he sometimes wonder whether he has gained most or lost most by learning his trade?

The Adventures of Huckleberry Finn

Huckleberry Finn (1885) is one of the most influential books in American literary history. Ernest Hemingway declared in 1935 that "all modern American literature comes from one book by Mark Twain called Huckleberry Finn. . . . *It's the best book we've had. All American writing comes from that. There was nothing before. There has been nothing as good since."*

Although Hemingway's claim is doubtlessly exaggerated, Clemens's novel certainly helped change the way American authors wrote. Some critics have even made the point that in this novel Clemens succeeded in doing away with the standard literary language used by earlier authors. Notice that since Huck tells his own story, the novel is full of mispronunciations, misspellings, and ungrammatical sentences. Clemens's style fits Huck's character.

Huck, said Clemens, is a boy with a "sound heart and a deformed conscience." By this description Clemens meant that although fourteen-year-old Huck instinctively does what the author believes to be the right thing, he is so conditioned by society that his conscience tells him his actions are wrong. Huck is clearly on the fringes of society. As the son of the town drunkard, he is an outcast socially. By not believing in the values and institutions of society (in religion, slavery, education, and so forth), Huck is an outcast intellectually. Because almost all readers feel a strong attraction toward Huck, his attitudes and experiences are a powerful way of criticizing what Clemens regards as weaknesses in society.

Chapter Seven

The opening chapters of Huckleberry Finn *tell of Huck's involvement in an escape from two difficult situations. At the beginning Huck is in the village under the care of the Widow Douglas and Miss Watson, her sister. Here he is being civilized: he attends school, wears proper clothing, and learns proper social behavior. Then Pap, Huck's father, kidnaps Huck and takes him three miles up the Mississippi River to the Illinois side, where they live in a previously deserted cabin. Pap regularly beats Huck, locks him in the cabin whenever he goes to town, and under the influence of liquor actually tries to kill the boy. Hearing Pap threaten to move him to another place where no one can find him, Huck decides to escape. He has already escaped the attempt to civilize him (thanks to Pap's kidnapping). Now he needs to escape from Pap if he is to survive.*

As Chapter 7 opens, Huck is awakened by Pap, who while drunk the previous night had tried to kill him. Pap had imagined that Huck was the Angel of Death. Huck had finally managed to get Pap's gun, afraid that when Pap awakened from his drunken stupor, he would again try to kill him.

Notice how this chapter reveals the quality of Huck's mind. He engineers a successful escape from Pap by carefully managing every detail. Also, he plans the escape in such a way that the townspeople believe he has been killed. They, therefore, do not continue looking for him once they have tried, and failed, to find his body.

ADVENTURES OF HUCKLEBERRY FINN

(Tom Sawyer's Comrade)

SCENE: THE MISSISSIPPI VALLEY
TIME: FORTY TO FIFTY YEARS AGO

by

MARK TWAIN

✎ Notice ✐

Persons attempting to find a motive in this narrative will be prosecuted; persons attempting to find a moral in it will be banished; persons attempting to find a plot in it will be shot.

"Git up! what you 'bout!"

I opened my eyes and looked around, trying to make out where I was. It was after sun-up, and I had been sound asleep. Pap was standing over me, looking sour–and sick, too. He says–

"What you doin' with this gun?"

I judged he didn't know nothing about what he had been doing, so I says:

"Somebody tried to get in, so I was laying for him."

"Why didn't you roust me out?"*

roust me out: awaken me roughly

"Well I tried to, but I couldn't; I couldn't budge you."

"Well, all right. Don't stand there palavering* all day, but out with you and see if there's a fish on the lines for breakfast. I'll be along in a minute."

palavering: idly chattering

He unlocked the door and I cleared out, up the river bank. I noticed some pieces of limbs and such things floating down, and a sprinkling of bark; so I know the river had begun to rise. I reckoned I would have great times, now, if I was over at the town. The June rise used to be always luck for me; because as soon as that rise begins, here comes cord-wood floating down, and pieces of log rafts–sometimes a dozen logs together; so all you have to do is to catch them and sell them to the wood yards and the sawmill.

I went along up the bank with one eye out for pap and 'tother one out for what the rise might fetch along. Well, all at once, here comes a canoe; just a beauty, too, about thirteen or fourteen foot long, riding high like a duck. I shot head first off of the bank, like a frog, clothes and all on, and struck out for the canoe. I just expected there'd be somebody laying down in it, because people often done that to fool folks, and when a chap had pulled a skiff* out most to it they'd raise up and laugh at him. But it warn't so this time. It was a drift-canoe, sure enough, and I clumb in and paddled her ashore. Thinks I the old man will be glad when he sees this–she's worth ten dollars. But when I got to shore pap wasn't in sight yet, and as I was running her into a little creek like a gully, all hung over with vines and willows, I struck another idea; I judged I'd hide her good, and then, stead of taking to the woods when I run off, I'd go down the river about fifty mile and camp in one place for good, and not have such a rough time tramping on foot.

skiff: a flat-bottomed open boat

It was pretty close to the shanty, and I thought I heard the old man coming, all the time; but I got her hid; and then I out and looked around a bunch of willows, and there was the old man down the path apiece just drawing a bead on a bird with his gun. So he hadn't seen anything.

When he got along, I was hard at it taking up a "trot" line.* He abused me a little for being so slow, but I told him I fell in the river and that was what made me so long. I knowed he would see I was wet, and then he would be asking questions. We got five catfish off of the lines and went home.

"trot" line: a long fishing line (to be set in a stream) from which hooks are suspended at intervals

While we laid off, after breakfast, to sleep up, both of us being about wore out, I got to thinking that if I could fix up some way to keep pap and the widow from trying to follow me, it would be a certainer thing than trusting to luck to get far enough off before they missed me; you see, all kinds of things might happen. Well, I didn't see no way for a while, but by-and-by pap raised up a minute, to drink another barrel of water, and he says:

"Another time a man comes a-prowling round here, you roust me out, you hear? That man warn't here for no good. I'd a shot him. Next time, you roust me out, you hear?"

Then he dropped down and went to sleep again—but what he had been saying give me the very idea I wanted. I says to myself, I can fix it now so nobody won't think of following me.

About twelve o'clock we turned out and went along up the bank. The river was coming up pretty fast, and lots of drift-wood going by on the rise. By-and-by, along comes part of a log raft—nine logs fast together. We went out with the skiff and towed it ashore. Then we had dinner. Anybody but pap would a waited and see the day through, so as to catch more stuff; but that warn't pap's style. Nine logs was enough for one time; he must shove right over to town and sell. So he locked me in and took the skiff and started off towing the raft about half-past three. I judged he wouldn't come back that night. I waited till I reckoned he had got a good start, then I out with my saw and went to work on that log again. Before he was 'tother side of the river I was out of the hole; him and his raft was just a speck on the water away off yonder.

I took the sack of corn meal and took it to where the canoe was hid, and shoved the vines and branches apart and put it in; then I done the same with the side of bacon; then the whisky jug; I took all the coffee and sugar there was, and all the ammunition; I took the wadding; I took the bucket and gourd, I took a dipper and a tin cup, and my old saw and two blankets, and the skillet and the coffee-pot. I took fish-lines and matches and other things—everything that was worth a cent. I cleaned out the place. I wanted an ax, but there wasn't any, only the one out at the wood pile, and I knowed why I was going to leave that. I fetched out the gun, and now I was done.

I had wore the ground a good deal, crawling out of the hole and dragging out so many things. So I fixed that as good as I could from the outside by scattering dust on the place, which covered up the smoothness and the sawdust. Then I fixed the piece of log back into its place, and put two rocks under it and one against it to hold it there,—for it was bent up at that place, and didn't quite touch ground. If you stood four or five foot away and didn't know it was sawed, you wouldn't ever notice it; and besides, this was the back of the cabin and it warn't likely anybody would go fooling around there.

It was all grass clear to the canoe; so I hadn't left a track. I followed around to see. I stood on the bank and looked out over the river. All safe. So I took the gun and went up a piece into the woods and was hunting around for some birds, when I see a wild pig; hogs soon went wild in them bottoms* after they had got away from the prairie farms. I shot this fellow and took him into camp.

bottoms: low land along a river

I took the ax and smashed in the door—I beat it and hacked it considerable, a-doing it. I fetched the pig in and took him back nearly to the table and hacked into his throat with the ax, and laid him down on the ground to bleed—I say ground, because it *was* ground—hard packed, and no boards. Well, next I took an old sack and put a lot of big rocks in it,–all I could drag–and I started it from the pig and dragged it to the door and through the woods down to the river and dumped it in, and down it sunk, out of sight. You could easy see that something had been dragged over the ground. I did wish Tom Sawyer was there, I know he would take an interest in this kind of business, and throw in the fancy touches. Nobody could spread himself like Tom Sawyer in such a thing as that.

Well, last I pulled out some of my hair, and bloodied the ax good, and stuck it on the back side, and slung the ax in the corner. Then I took up the pig and held him to my breast with my jacket (so he couldn't drip) till I got a good piece below the house and then dumped him into the river. Now I thought of something else. So I went and got the bag of meal and my old saw out of the canoe and fetched them to the house. I took the bag to where it used to stand, and ripped a hole in the bottom of it with the saw, for there warn't no knives and forks on the place–pap done everything with his clasp-knife, about the cooking. Then I carried the sack about a hundred yards across the grass and through the willows east of the house, to a shallow lake that was five mile wide and full of rushes–and ducks too, you might say, in the season. There was a slough or a creek leading out of it on the other side, that went miles away, I don't know where, but it didn't go to the river. The meal sifted out and made a little track all the way to the lake. I dropped pap's whetstone* there too, so as to look like it had been done by accident. Then I tied up the rip in the meal sack with a string, so it wouldn't leak no more, and took it and my saw to the canoe again.

whetstone: a stone for sharpening knives and other tools

It was about dark, now; so I dropped the canoe down the river under some willows that hung over the bank, and waited for the moon to rise. I made fast to a willow; then I took a bite to eat, and by-and-by laid down in the canoe to smoke a pipe and lay out a plan. I says to myself, they'll follow the track of that sackful of rocks to the shore and then drag the river for me. And they'll follow that meal track to the lake and go browsing down the creek that leads out of it to find the robbers that killed me and took the things. They won't ever hunt the river for anything but my dead carcass. They'll soon get tired of that, and won't bother no more about me. All right; I can stop anywhere I want to. Jackson's Island is good enough for me; I know that island pretty well, and nobody ever comes there. And then I can paddle over to town, nights, and slink around and pick up things I want. Jackson's Island's the place.

I was pretty tired, and the first thing I knowed, I was asleep. When I woke up I didn't know where I was, for a minute. I set up and looked around, a little scared. Then I remembered. The river looked miles and miles across. The moon was so bright I could a counted the drift logs that went a slipping along, black and still, hundred of yards out from the shore. Everything was dead quiet, and it looked late, and *smelt* late. You know what I mean–I don't know the words to put it in.

I took a good gap* and a stretch, and was just going to unhitch and start, when I heard a sound away over the water. I listened. Pretty soon I made it out. It was that dull kind of regular sound that comes from oars working in rowlocks when it's a still night. I peeped out through the willow branches, and there it was–a skiff, away across the water. I couldn't tell how many was in it. It kept a-coming, and when it was abreast of me I see there warn't but one man in it. Thinks I, maybe it's pap, though I warn't expecting him. He dropped below me, with the current, and by-and-by he come a-swinging up shore in the easy water, and he went by so close I could a reached out the gun and touched him. Well, it *was* pap, sure enough,–and sober, too, by the way he laid to the oars.

gap: yawn

I didn't lose no time. The next minute I was a-spinning down stream soft but quick in the shade of the bank. I made two mile and a half, and then struck out a quarter of a mile or more towards the middle of the river, because pretty soon I would be passing the ferry landing and people might see me and hail me. I got out amongst the drift-wood and then laid down in the bottom of the canoe and let her float. I laid there and had a good rest and a smoke out of my pipe, looking away into the sky, not a cloud in it. The sky looks ever so deep when you lay down on your back in the moon-shine; I never knowed it before. And how far a body can hear on the water such nights! I heard people talking at the ferry landing. I heard what they said, too, every word of it. One man said it was getting towards the long days and the short nights, now. 'Tother one said *this* warn't one of the short ones, he reckoned—and then they laughed, and he said it over again and they laughed again; then they waked up another fellow and told him, and laughed, but he didn't laugh; he ripped out something brisk and said let him alone. The first fellow said he 'lowed to tell it to his old woman—she would think it was pretty good; but he said that warn't nothing to some things he had said in his time. I heard one man say it was nearly three o'clock, and he hoped daylight wouldn't wait more than about a week longer. After that, the talk got further and further away, and I couldn't make out the words anymore, but I could hear the mumble; and now and then a laugh, too, but it seemed a long ways off.

I was away below the ferry now. I rose up and there was Jackson's Island, about two mile and a half down stream, heavy-timbered and standing up out of the middle of the river, big and dark and solid, like a steamboat without any lights. There warn't any signs of the bar at the head—it was all under water, now.

It didn't take me long to get there. I shot past the head at a ripping rate, the current was so swift, and then I got into the dead water and landed on the side towards the Illinois shore. I run the canoe into a deep dent in the bank that I knowed about; I had to part the willow branches to get in; and when I made fast nobody could a seen the canoe from the outside.

I went up and set down on a log at the head of the island and looked out on the big river and the black driftwood, and away over to the town, three miles away, where there was three or four lights twinkling. A monstrous big lumber raft was about a mile up stream, coming along down, with a lantern in the middle of it. I watched it come creeping down, and when it was most abreast of where I stood I heard a man say, "Stern oars, there! heave her head to stabboard!" I heard that just as plain as if the man was by my side.

There was a little gray in the sky, now; so I stepped into the woods and laid down for a nap before breakfast.

Chapter Seventeen

During nighttime fog and bad weather, a steamboat hits Huck and Jim's raft. Huck and his companion, Miss Watson's runaway slave Jim, dive into the water to escape the thirty-foot paddle wheel of the steamboat. When Huck comes to the surface, he calls for Jim (who also has escaped the near tragedy) but receives no answer. Finding a piece of driftwood, he swims across the river to the Kentucky side. Here he receives lodging with the Grangerfords, who are engaged in a deadly feud with the Shepherdsons. As this excerpt begins, Huck is describing the Grangerford household.

Notice that through Huck's naive praise of Emmeline's artistic accomplishments, Clemens satirizes the cultural values of the frontier. Readers, of course, are able to see through Huck's admiration and recognize that the pictures and poems are actually grotesque. Incidentally, there is some evidence that Clemens had a particular poet in mind as he described Emmeline's poetry. Julia Moore, called the "Sweet Singer of Michigan," wrote poetry that Clemens regarded as comparable to Emmeline's. In this chapter we see the more genial side of Clemens's satire.

. . . They [the Grangerfords] had pictures hung on the walls—mainly Washingtons and Lafayettes, and battles, and Highland Marys,* and one called "Signing the Declaration." There was some that they called crayons, which one of the daughters which was dead made her own self when she was only fifteen years old. They was different from any pictures I ever see before; blacker, mostly, than is common. One was a woman in a slim black dress, belted small under the arm-pits, with bulges like a cabbage in the middle of the sleeves, and a large black scoop-shovel bonnet with a black veil, and white slim ankles crossed about with black tape, and very wee black slippers, like a chisel, and she was leaning pensive on a tombstone on her right elbow, under a weeping willow, and her other hand hanging down her side holding a white handkerchief . . . , and underneath the picture it said "Shall I Never See Thee More Alas." Another one was a young lady with her hair all combed up straight to the top of her head, and knotted there in front of a comb like a chairback, and she was crying into a handkerchief and had a dead bird laying on its back in her other hand with its heels up, and underneath the picture it said "I Shall Never Hear Thy Sweet Chirrup More Alas." There was one where a young lady was at a window looking up at the moon, and tears running down her cheeks; and she had an open letter in one hand with black sealing-wax showing on one edge of it, and she was mashing* a locket with a chain to it against her mouth, and underneath the picture it said "And Art Thou Gone Yes Thou Art Gone Alas." These was all nice pictures, I reckon, but I didn't somehow

seem to take to them, because if ever I was down a little, they always give me the fan-tods.* Everybody was sorry she died, because she had laid out a lot more of these pictures to do, and a body could see by what she had done what they had lost. But I reckoned, that with her disposition,* she was having a better time in the graveyard. She was at work on what they said was her greatest picture when she took sick, and every day and every night it was her prayer to be allowed to live till she got it done, but she never got the chance. It was a picture of a young woman in a long white gown, standing on the rail of a bridge all ready to jump off, with her hair all down her back, and looking up to the moon, with tears running down her face, and she had two arms folded across her breast, and two arms stretched out in front and two more reaching up towards the moon—and the idea was, to see which pair would look best and then scratch out all the other arms; but, as I was saying, she died before she got her mind made up, and now they kept this picture over the head of the bed in her room, and every time her birthday come they hung flowers on it. Other times it was hid with a little curtain. The young woman in the picture had a kind of a nice sweet face, but there was so many arms it made her look too spidery, seemed to me.

Highland Marys: Mary Campbell was the subject of several elegies by the Scottish poet Robert Burns (1759-1796).
mashing: pressing
fan-tods: a state of irritability, the fidgets
disposition: frame of mind

This young girl kept a scrap-book when she was alive and used to paste obituaries and accidents and cases of patient sufferings in it out of the *Presbyterian Observer,* and write poetry after them out of her own head. It was very good poetry. This is what she wrote about a boy by the name of Stephen Dowling Bots that fell down a well and was drownded:

ODE TO STEPHEN DOWLING BOTS,
DEC'D [deceased].

And did young Stephen sicken,
    And did young Stephen die?
And did the sad hearts thicken,
    And did the mourners cry?

No; such was not the fate of
    Young Stephen Dowling Bots;
Though sad hearts round him thickened,
    'Twas not from sickness' shots.

No whooping-cough did rack his frame,
    Nor measles drear, with spots;
Not these impaired the sacred name
    Of Stephen Dowling Bots.

Despised loved struck not with woe
    That head of curly knots,
Nor stomach troubles laid him low,
    Young Stephen Dowling Bots.

O no. Then list with tearful eye,
    Whilst I his fate do tell.
His soul did from this cold world fly,
    By falling down a well.

They got him out and emptied him;
    Alas it was too late;
His spirit was gone for to sport aloft
    In the realm of the good and great.

If Emmeline Grangerford could make poetry like that before she was fourteen, there ain't no telling what she could a done by-and-by. Buck [Emmeline's brother] said she could rattle off poetry like nothing. She didn't ever have to stop to think. He said she would slap down a line, and if she couldn't find anything to rhyme with it she would just scratch it out and slap down another one and go ahead. She warn't particular, she could write about anything you choose to give her to write about, just so it was sadful. Every time a man died, or a woman died, or a child died, she would be on hand with her "tribute" before he was cold. She called them tributes. The neighbors said it was the doctor first, then Emmeline, then the undertaker—the undertaker never got in ahead of Emmeline but once, and then she hung fire* on a rhyme for the dead person's name, which was Whistler. She warn't ever the same, after that; she never complained, but she kind of pined away and did not live long. Poor thing, many's the time I made myself go up to the little room that used to be hers and get out her poor old scrap-book and read in it when her pictures had been aggravating me and I had soured on her a little. I liked all that family, dead ones and all, and warn't going to let anything come between us. Poor Emmeline made poetry about all the dead people when she was alive, and it didn't seem right that there warn't nobody to make some about her, now she was gone; so I tried to sweat out a verse or two myself, but I couldn't seem to make it go, somehow. . . .

hung fire: was temporarily delayed

Chapter Thirty-one

In this famous chapter Huck faces the major moral crisis of the novel. Should he write to Miss Watson, Jim's owner, to tell her the whereabouts of her escaped slave? Or should he try to help Jim escape? Notice Clemens sets Huck's awareness of society's values (e.g., that slavery is lawful and right: this novel is set before the Civil War) against his heartfelt beliefs. The conflict between society and the individual's conscience is clearly resolved in favor of individual conscience.

Notice that Clemens distorts the issues as he attacks society. He is dishonest in suggesting that there are only two ways to view the situation: Huck's way or society's way. He thus leads readers into a logical trap (the either-or fallacy). Because society's beliefs–whether in culture, religion, or whatever–are so clearly wrong, readers are strongly tempted to accept Huck's views as right. Clemens thus implies that readers have to believe either what society believes or what Huck believes. Readers tend to overlook the fact that at least in moral issues there is a third alternative: a belief based on the Bible. Because Huck is portrayed sympathetically, even Christian readers may be tempted to agree with Huck that his decision to free Jim and "go to hell" as a consequence is the right decision. Obviously this story that pretends to be an adventure book for children is really a work which provides an erroneous view of serious issues and themes.

. . . I went to the raft, and set down in the wigwam* to think. But I couldn't come to nothing. I thought till I wore my head sore, but I couldn't see no way out of the trouble. After all this long journey, and after all we'd done for them scoundrels,* here was it all come to nothing, everything all busted up and ruined, because they could have the heart to serve Jim such a trick as that, and make him a slave again all his life, and amongst strangers, too, for forty dirty dollars.

---

wigwam: a tentlike structure built on the raft
them scoundrels: The Duke and Dauphine are two unscrupulous con men working their trade along the Mississippi. After Huck and Jim have rescued them and allowed them to travel on the raft, they sell Jim back into slavery for the forty-dollar reward.

Once I said to myself it would be a thousand times better for Jim to be a slave at home where his family was, as long as he'd *got* to be a slave, and so I'd better write a letter to Tom Sawyer and tell him to tell Miss Watson where he was. But I soon give up that notion, for two things: she'd be mad and disgusted at his rascality and ungratefulness for leaving her, and so she'd sell him straight down the river again; and if she didn't, everybody naturally despises an ungrateful nigger, and they'd make Jim feel it all the time, and so he'd feel ornery and disgraced. And then think of *me!* It would get all around, that Huck Finn helped a nigger to get his freedom; and if I was to ever see anybody from that town again, I'd be ready to get down and lick his boots for shame.

That's just the way: a person does a low-down thing, and then he don't want to take no consequences of it. Thinks as long as he can hide it, it ain't no disgrace. That was my fix exactly. The more I studied about this, the more my conscience went to grinding me, and the more wicked and low-down and ornery I got to feeling. And at last, when it hit me all of a sudden that here was the plain hand of Providence slapping me in the face and letting me know my wickedness was being watched all the time from up there in heaven, whilst I was stealing a poor old woman's nigger that hadn't ever done me no harm, and now was showing me there's One that's always on the lookout, and ain't agoing to allow no such miserable doings to go only just so fur and no further, I most dropped in my tracks I was so scared. Well, I tried the best I could to kinder soften it up somehow for myself, by saying I was brung up wicked, and so I warn't so much to blame; but something inside of me kept saying, "There was the Sunday school, you could a gone to it; and if you'd a done it they'd a learnt you, there, that people that acts as I'd been acting about that nigger goes to everlasting fire."

It made me shiver. And I about made up my mind to pray; and see if I couldn't try to quit being the kind of a boy I was, and be better. So I kneeled down. But the words wouldn't come. Why wouldn't they? It warn't no use to try and hide it from Him. Nor from *me,* neither. I knowed very well why they wouldn't come. It was because my heart warn't right; it was because I warn't square; it was because I was playing double. I was letting *on* to give up sin, but away inside of me I was holding on to the biggest one of all.* I was trying to make my mouth *say* I would do the right thing and the clean thing, and go and write to that nigger's owner and tell where he was; but deep down in me I knowed it was a lie–and He knowed it. You can't pray a lie–I found that out.

---

biggest . . . all: i.e., hypocrisy

So I was full of trouble, full as I could be; and didn't know what to do. At last I had an idea; and I says, I'll go and write the letter–and *then* see if I can pray. Why, it was astonishing, the way I felt as light as a feather, right straight off, and my troubles all gone. So I got a piece of paper and a pencil, all glad and excited, and set down and wrote:

> Miss Watson your runaway nigger Jim is down here two mile below Pikesville and Mr. Phelps has got him and he will give him up for the reward if you send.
>
> Huck Finn

I felt good and all washed clean of sin for the first time I had ever felt so in my life, and I knowed I could pray now. But I didn't do it straight off, but laid the paper down and set there thinking–thinking how good it was all this happened so, and how near I come to being lost and going to hell. And went on thinking. And got to thinking over our trip down the river; and I see Jim before me, all the time, in the day, and in the night-time, sometimes moonlight, sometimes storms, and we a floating along, talking, and singing, and laughing. But somehow I couldn't seem to strike no places to harden me against him, but only the other kind. I'd see him standing my watch on top of his'n, stead of calling me, so I could go on sleeping; and see him how glad he was when I come back out of the fog; and when I come to him again in the swamp, up there where the feud was; and such-like times; and would always call me honey, and pet me, and do everything he could think of for me, and how good he always was; and at last I struck the time I saved him by telling the men we had small-pox aboard, and he was so grateful, and said I was the best friend old Jim ever had in the world, and the *only* one he's got now; and then I happened to look around, and see that paper.

It was a close place. I took it up, and held it in my hand. I was a trembling, because I'd got to decide, forever, betwixt two things, and I knowed it. I studied a minute, sort of holding my breath, and then says to myself:

"All right, then, I'll *go* to hell"–and tore it up.

It was awful thoughts, and awful words, but they was said. And I let them stay said; and never thought no more about reforming. I shoved the whole thing out of my head; and said I would take up wickedness again, which was in my line, being brung up to it, and the other warn't. And for a starter, I would go to work and steal Jim out of slavery again; and if I could think up anything worse, I would do that, too; because as long as I was in, and in for good, I might as well go the whole hog. . . .

Chapter Thirty-eight

After being captured, Jim is lodged in an old cabin on the farm of Silas Phelps (Tom Sawyer's uncle). After Tom unexpectedly appears, Huck no longer directs the action. Had Huck been engineering Jim's escape, Jim would have been quickly set free again. Tom, however, automatically takes over. He proceeds to put his book-learning into operation. The result is that Jim has to undergo the kind of imprisonment that romantic novelists had described for their heroes. Although Jim registers objections to Tom's plans, he nevertheless meekly submits to the humiliation and the inconvenience caused by Tom's romantic ideas. As this excerpt begins, Tom has just read aloud several inscriptions he believes a prisoner might carve on his cell walls.

... Tom's voice trembled, whilst he was reading them, and he most broke down. When he got done, he couldn't no way make up his mind which one for Jim to scrabble* onto the wall, they was all so good; but at last he allowed he would let him scrabble them all on. Jim said it would take him a year to scrabble such a lot of truck* onto the logs with a nail; and he didn't know how to make letters, besides; but Tom said he would block them out for him, and then he wouldn't have nothing to do but just follow the lines. Then pretty soon he says:

scrabble: scribble
truck: rubbish

"Come to think, the logs ain't agoing to do; they don't have log walls in a dungeon; we got to dig the inscriptions into a rock. We'll fetch a rock."

Jim said the rock was worse than the logs; he said it would take him such a long time to dig them into a rock, he wouldn't ever get out. But Tom said he would let me help him do it. Then he took a look to see how me and Jim was getting along with the pens.* It was most pesky tedious hard work and slow, and didn't give my hands no show to get well of the sores, and we didn't seem to make no headway, hardly. So Tom says:

pens: These "pens" were made from a pewter spoon and a brass candlestick; they were used for scratching inscriptions.

"I know how to fix it. We got to have a rock for the coat of arms and mournful inscriptions, and we can kill two birds with that same rock. There's a gaudy big grindstone down at the mill, and we'll smouch* it, and carve the things on it, and file out the pens and the saw on it, too."

smouch: steal

It warn't no slouch of an idea; and it warn't no slouch of a grindstone nuther; but we allowed we'd tackle it. It warn't quite midnight, yet, so we cleared out for the mill, leaving Jim at work. We smouched the grindstone, and set out to roll her home, but it was a most nation tough job.

Sometimes, do what we could, we couldn't keep her from falling over, and she come mighty near smashing us, every time. Tom said she was going to get one of us, sure, before we got through. We got her half way; and then we was plumb played out, and most drownded with sweat. We see it warn't no use, we got to go and fetch Jim, so he raised up his bed and slid the chain off of the bed-leg, and wrapt it round and round his neck,* and we crawled out through our hole and down there, and Jim and me laid into that grindstone and walked her along like nothing; and Tom superintended. He could out-superintend any boy I ever see. He knowed how to do everything.

raised . . . neck: By lifting up his bed, Jim could free the chain. Then, wrapping his chain around him, he could move about.

Our hole was pretty big, but it warn't big enough to get the grindstone through; but Jim he took the pick and soon made it big enough. Then Tom marked out them things on it with the nail, and set Jim to work on them, with the nail for a chisel and an iron bolt from the rubbage in the lean-to for a hammer, and told him to work till the rest of the candle quit on him, and then he could go to bed, and hide the grindstone under his straw tick and sleep on it. Then we helped him fix his chain back on the bed-leg, and was ready for bed ourselves. But Tom thought of something, and says:

"You got any spiders in here, Jim?"

"No, sah, thanks to goodness I hain't, Mars Tom."

"All right, we'll get you some."

"But bless you, honey, I doan' want none. I's afeard un um. I jis' 's soon have rattlesnakes aroun'."

Tom thought a minute or two, and says:

"It's a good idea. And I reckon, it's been done. It must a been done; it stands to reason. Yes, it's a prime good idea. Where could you keep it?"

"Keep what, Mars Tom?"

"Why, a rattlesnake."

"De goodness gracious alive, Mars Tom! Why, if dey was a rattlesnake to come in heah, I'd take en bust right out thoo dat log wall, I would, wid my head."

"Why, Jim, you wouldn't be afraid of it, after a little. You could tame it."

"*Tame* it!"

"Yes—easy enough. Every animal is grateful for kindness and petting, and they wouldn't *think* of hurting a person that pets them. Any book will tell you that. You try—that's all I ask; just try for two or three days. Why, you can get him so, in a little while, that he'll love you; and sleep with you; and won't stay away from you a minute; and will let you wrap him round your neck and put his head in your mouth."

"*Please,* Mars Tom—doan' talk so! I can't *stan*' it! He'd *let* me shove his head in my mouf—fer a favor, hain't it? I lay he'd wait a pow'ful long time 'fo' I *ast* him. En mo' en dat, I doan' *want* him to sleep with me."

"Jim, don't act so foolish. A prisoner's *got* to have some kind of a dumb pet, and if a rattlesnake hain't ever been tried, why, there's more glory to be gained in your being the first to ever try it than any other way you could ever think of to save your life."

"Why, Mars Tom, I doan' *want* no sich glory. Snake take'n bite Jim's chin off, den *whah* is de glory? No, sah, I doan't want no sich doin's."

"Blame it, can't you *try?* I only want you to try—you needn't keep it up if it don't work."

"But de trouble all *done,* ef de snake bite me while I's a tryin' him. Mars Tom, I's willin' to tackle mos' anything 'at ain't onreasonable, but ef you en Huck fetches a rattlesnake in heah for me to tame, I's gwyne to *leave,* dat's *shore.*"

"Well, then, let it go, let it go, if you're so bullheaded about it. We can get you some garter-snakes and you can tie some buttons on their tails, and let on they're rattlesnakes, and I reckon that'll have to do."

"I k'n stan' *dem,* Mars Tom, but blame' 'f I couldn't get along widout um, I tell you dat. I never knowed b'fo', 'twas so much bother and trouble to be a prisoner."

"Well, it *always* is, when it's done right. You got any rats around here?"

"No, sah, I hain't seed none."

"Well, we'll get you some rats."

"Why Mars Tom, I doan' *want* no rats. Dey's de dad-blamedest creturs to sturb a body, en rustle roun' over 'im, en bite his feet, when he's trying to sleep, I ever see. No, sah, gimme g'yarter-snakes, 'f I's got to have 'm, but doan' gimme no rats, I ain' got no use f'r um, skasely."*

---

skasely: scarcely

"But Jim, you *got* to have 'em—they all do. So don't make no more fuss about it. Prisoners ain't ever without rats. There ain't no instance of it. And they train them, and pet them, and learn them tricks, and they get to be as sociable as flies. But you got to play music to them. You got anything to play music on?"

"I ain' got nuffn but a coase comb en a piece o' paper, en a juice-harp;* but I reck'n dey wouldn' take no stock in a juice-harp."

---

juice-harp: jew's harp

"Yes they would. *They* don't care what kind of music 'tis. A jews-harp's plenty good enough for a rat. All animals likes music—in a prison they dote on* it. Specially, painful music; and you can't get no other kind out of a jews-harp. It always interests them; they come out to see what's the matter with you. Yes, you're all right; you're fixed very well. You want to set on your bed, nights, before you go to sleep, and early in the mornings, and play your jews-harp; play The Last Link Is Broken—that's the thing that'll scoop* a rat, quicker'n anything else: and when you've played about two minutes, you'll see all the rats, and the snakes, and spiders, and things begin to feel worried about you, and come. And they'll just fairly swarm over you, and have a noble good time."

dote on : are especially fond of
scoop : bring out

"Yes, *dey* will, I reck'n, Mars Tom, but what kine er* time is *Jim* havin'? Blest if I kin see de pint. But I'll do it ef I got to. I reck'n I better keep de animals satisfied, en not have no trouble in de house."

kine er: kind of

Tom waited to think over, and see if there wasn't nothing else; and pretty soon he says:

"Oh–there's one thing I forgot. Could you raise a flower here, do you reckon?"

"I doan' know but maybe I could, Mars Tom; but it's tolable dark in heah, en I ain' got no use f'r no flower, no how, en she'd be a pow'ful sight o' trouble."

"Well, you try it, anyway. Some other prisoners has done it."

"One er dem big cat-tail-lookin' mullen-stalks would grow in heah, Mars Tom, I reck'n, but she wouldn' be wuth half de trouble she'd coss."

"Don't you believe it. We'll fetch you a little one, and you plant it in the corner, over there, and raise it. And don't call it mullen, call it Pitchiola*–that's its right name, when it's in a prison. And you want to water it with your tears."

Pitchiola: In the romantic novel *Picciola,* by Joseph Boniface (1796-1865), a prisoner is kept alive by a plant growing in his cell.

"Why, I got plenty of spring water, Mars Tom."

"You don't *want* spring water; you want to water it with your tears. It's the way they always do."

"Why, Mars Tom, I lay I kin raise one er dem mullen-stalks twyste* wid spring water whiles another man's a *start'n* one wid tears."

twyste: twice

"That ain't the idea. You *got* to do it with tears."

"She'll die on my han's, Mars Tom, she sholy will; kase I doan' skasely ever cry."

So Tom was stumped. But he studied it over, and then said Jim would have to worry along the best he could with an onion. He promised he would go to the nigger cabins and drop one, private, in Jim's coffee-pot, in the morning. Jim said he would "jis' 's soon have tobacker in his coffee"; and found so much fault with it, and with the work and bother of raising the mullen, and jews-harping the rats, and petting and flattering up the snakes and spiders and things, on top of all the other work he had to do on pens, and inscriptions, and journals, and things, which made it more trouble and worry and responsibility to be a prisoner than anything he ever undertook, that Tom most lost all patience with him; and said he was just loadened down with more gaudier chances than a prisoner ever had in the world to make a name for himself, and yet he didn't know enough to appreciate them, and they was just about wasted on him. So Jim he was sorry, and said he wouldn't behave so no more, and then me and Tom shoved* for bed.

shoved: left

Chapter Thirty-nine

In the morning we went up to the village and bought a wire rat trap and fetched it down, and unstopped the best rat hole, and in about an hour we had fifteen of the bulliest kind of ones; and then we took it and put it in a safe place under Aunt Sally's bed. But while we was gone for spiders, little Thomas Franklin Benjamin Jefferson Elexander Phelps found it there, and opened the door of it to see if the rats would come out, and they did; and Aunt Sally she come in, and when we got back she was a standing on top of the bed raising Cain, and the rats was doing what they could to keep off the dull times for her. So she took and dusted* us both with the hickry, and we was as much as two hours catching another fifteen or sixteen, drat that meddlesome cub, and they warn't the likeliest, nuther, because the first haul was the pick of the flock. I never see a likelier lot of rats than what that first haul was.

dusted: spanked

We got a splendid stock of sorted spiders, and bugs, and frogs, and caterpillars, and one thing or another; and we like-to got a hornet's nest, but we didn't. The family was at home. We didn't give it right up, but staid with them as long as we could; because we allowed we'd tire them out or they'd got to tire us out, and they done it. Then we got allycumpain* and rubbed on the places, and was pretty near all right again, but couldn't set down convenient. And so we went for snakes, and grabbed a couple of dozen garters and house-snakes, and put them in a bag, and put it in our room, and by that time it was supper time, and a rattling good honest day's work; and hungry?—oh, no, I reckon not! And there warn't a blessed snake up there, when we went back—we didn't half tie the sack, and they worked out, somehow, and left. But it didn't matter much, because they was still on the premises somewhere. So we judged we could get some of them again. No, there warn't no real scarcity of snakes about the house for a considerable spell. You'd see them dripping from the rafters and places, every now and then; and they generly landed in your plate, or down the back of your neck, and most of the time where you didn't want them. Well, they was handsome, and striped, and there warn't no harm in a million of them; but that never made no difference to Aunt Sally, she despised snakes, be the breed what they might, and she couldn't stand them no way you could fix it; and every time one of them flopped down on her, it didn't make no difference what she was doing, she would just lay that work down and light out. I never see such a woman. And you could hear her whoop to Jericho. You couldn't get her to take aholt of one of them with the tongs. And if she turned over and found one in bed, she would scramble out and lift a howl that you would think the house was afire. She

disturbed the old man so, that he said he could most wish there hadn't ever been no snakes created. Why, after every last snake had been gone clear out of the house for as much as a week, Aunt Sally warn't over it yet; she warn't near over it; when she was setting thinking about something, you could touch her on the back of her neck with a feather and she would jump right out of her stockings. It was very curious. But Tom said all women was just so. He said they was made that way; for some reason or other.

allycumpain: elecampane, a medicinal herb

We got a licking every time one of our snakes come in her way; and she allowed these lickings warn't nothing to what she would do if we ever loaded up the place again with them. I didn't mind the lickings, because they didn't amount to nothing; but I minded the trouble we had, to lay in another lot. But we got them laid in, and all the other things; and you never see a cabin as blithe-some* as Jim's was when they'd all swarm out for music and go for him. Jim didn't like the spiders, and the spiders didn't like Jim; and so they'd lay for him and make it mighty warm for him. And he said that between the rats, and the snakes, and the grindstone, there warn't no room in bed for him skasely; and when there was, a body couldn't sleep, it was so lively, and it was always lively, he said, because *they* never all slept at one time, but took turn about, so when the snakes was asleep the rats was on deck, and when the rats turned in the snakes come on watch, so he always had one gang under him, in his way, and t'other gang having a circus over him, and if he got up to hunt a new place, the spiders would take a chance at him as he crossed over. He said if he ever got out, this time, he wouldn't ever be a prisoner again, not for a salary.

blithesome: merry

Well, by the end of three weeks, everything was in pretty good shape. The shirt was sent in early, in a pie, and every time a rat bit Jim he

"Warnings to the people that something is up. Sometimes it's done one way, sometimes another. But there's always somebody spying around, that gives notice to the governor of the castle. When Louis XVI was going to light out of the Tooleries,* a servant girl done it. It's a very good way, and so is the nonnamous letters. We'll use them both. And it's usual for the prisoner's mother to change clothes with him, and she stays in, and he slides out in her clothes. We'll do that too."

Tooleries: Tuileries: royal residence in Paris, 1564-1871

"But looky here, Tom, what do we want to *warn* anybody for, that something's up? Let them find it out for themselves—it's their lookout."

"Yes, I know; but you can't depend on them. It's the way they've acted from the very start—left us to do *everything*. They're so confiding and mullet-headed they don't take notice of nothing at all. So if we don't *give* them notice, there won't be nobody nor nothing to interfere with us, and so after all our hard work and trouble this escape'll go off perfectly flat: won't amount to nothing—won't be nothing *to* it."

"Well, as for me, Tom, that's the way I'd like."

"Shucks," he says, and looked disgusted. So I says:

"But I ain't going to make no complaint. Anyway that suits you suits me. What you going to do about the servant-girl?"

"You'll be her. You slide in, in the middle of the night, and hook that yaller girl's frock."

"Why, Tom, that'll make trouble next morning; because of course she prob'ly hain't got any but that one."

"I know; but you don't want it but fifteen minutes, to carry the nonnamous letter and shove it under the front door."

"All right, then, I'll do it; but I could carry it just as handy in my own togs."

"You wouldn't look like a servant-girl *then*, would you?"

would get up and write a little in his journal whilst the ink was fresh; the pens was made, the inscriptions and so on was all carved on the grindstone; the bed-leg was sawed in two, and we had et up the sawdust, and it give us a most amazing stomach-ache. We reckoned we was all going to die, but didn't. It was the most undigestible sawdust I ever see; and Tom said the same. But as I was saying, we'd got all the work done, now, at last; and we was all pretty much fagged out, too, but mainly Jim. The old man had wrote a couple of times to the plantation below Orleans to come and get their runaway nigger, but hadn't got no answer, because there warn't no such plantation; so he allowed he would advertise Jim in the St. Louis and New Orleans papers; and when he mentioned the St. Louis ones, it give me the cold shivers, and I see we hadn't no time to lose. So Tom said, now for the nonnamous* letters.

nonnamous: anonymous

"What's them?" I says.

"No, but there won't be nobody to see what I look like, *anyway.*"

"That ain't got nothing to do with it. The thing for us to do is just do our *duty,* and not worry about whether anybody *sees* us do it or not. Hain't you got no principle at all?"

"All right, I ain't saying nothing; I'm the servant-girl. Who's Jim mother?"

"I'm his mother. I'll hook a gown from Aunt Sally."

"Well, then, you'll have to stay in the cabin when me and Jim leaves."

"Not much. I'll stuff Jim's clothes full of straw and lay it on his bed to represent his mother in disguise, and Jim'll take the nigger woman's gown off of me and wear it, and we'll all evade together. When a prisoner of style escapes, it's called an evasion. It's always called so when a king escapes, f'rinstance. And the same with a king's son; it don't make no difference whether he's a natural one or an unnatural one."

So Tom he wrote the nonnamous letter, and I smouched the yaller wench's frock, that night, and put it on, and shoved it under the front door, the way Tom told me to. It said:

Beware. Trouble is brewing. Keep a sharp lookout.

Unknown Friend.

Next night we stuck a picture which Tom drawed in blood, of a skull and crossbones, on the front door; and the next night another one of a coffin, on the back door. I never see a family in such a sweat. They couldn't a been worse scared if the place had a been full of ghosts laying for them behind everything and under the beds and shivering through the air. If a door banged, Aunt Sally she jumped, and said "ouch!" if anything fell, she jumped and said "ouch!" if you happened to touch her, when she warn't noticing, she done the same; she couldn't face noway and be satisfied, because she allowed there was something behind her every time–so she was always a whirling around, sudden, and saying "ouch," and before she'd get two-thirds around, she'd whirl back again, and say it again; and she was afraid to go to bed, but she dasn't set up. So the thing was working very well, Tom said; he said he never see a thing work more satisfactory. He said it showed it was done right.

So he said, now for the grand bulge! So the very next morning at the streak of dawn we got another letter ready, and was wondering what we better do with it, because we heard them say at supper they was going to have a nigger on watch at both doors all night. Tom he went down the lightning-rod to spy around; and the nigger at the back door was asleep, and he stuck it in the back of his neck and come back. This letter said:

Don't betray me, I wish to be your friend. There is a desperate gang of cutthroats from over in the Ingean Territory* going to steal your runaway nigger to-night, and they have been trying to scare you so as you will stay in the house and not bother them. I am one of the gang, but have got relligion and wish to quit it and lead a honest life again, and will betray the helish design. They will sneak down from northards, along the fence, at midnight exact, with a false key, and go in the nigger's cabin to get him. I am to be off a piece and blow a tin horn if I see any danger; but stead of that I will *BA* like a sheep soon as they get in and not blow at all; then whilst they are getting his chains loose, you slip there and lock them in, and can kill them at your leasure. Don't do anything but just the way I am telling you, if you do they will suspicion something and raise whoopjamboreehoo. I do not wish any reward but to know I have done the right thing.

Unknown Friend.

Ingean Territory: From 1834 to 1890, present-day Oklahoma was designated Indian Territory. During those years it was frequently used by outlaws as a refuge from state and federal authorities.

For Thought and Discussion

1. In what ways is the initiation experience of the narrator of *Life on the Mississippi* similar to that of Christopher Newman in *The American?* What specifically does the narrator gain and lose by learning his trade in *Life on the Mississippi?* Point out the passage in Chapter 6 in which the narrator is first faced with the reality of his job. What point does he make at the end of Chapter 9 by comparing his profession with the medical profession?

2. Twain is considered to be one of America's greatest humorists. What particular incidents in *Life on the Mississippi* and *Huckleberry Finn* do you find humorous? What makes the incidents humorous? Find specific sentences in both selections that show Twain's skill in using both exaggeration and understatement to create humor. How do the roles of the cub pilot and Huck Finn as naive narrators add to the humor of both selections?

3. As a satirist, Twain criticizes what he considers to be human weaknesses. How does he satirize romanticism in Chapter 4 of *Life on the Mississippi* and Chapters 17 and 38 of *Huckleberry Finn?*

4. Although a skilled humorist and satirist, Twain at times uses humor as a cloak for bitter cynicism. His total disdain for God and organized religion is apparent throughout his writing. Find examples from Chapter 4 of *Life on the Mississippi* which illustrate Twain's blasphemous attitude. In Chapter 31 of *Huckleberry Finn,* how does the moral dilemma in which the author places Huck serve to sway the reader toward a positive reaction to Huck's decision to ''go to hell?'' Is Twain's ''either-or'' proposition (i.e., the reader must choose Huck's view or society's view) a valid one? Why or why not?

5. Compare and contrast the characters of Tom Sawyer and Huck Finn as they appear in the escape attempt of Chapter 7 and the imprisonment and escape attempt of Chapters 38 and 39. Which character is a realist and which is a romantic? How does Twain show the superiority of realism over romanticism in these episodes?

10 Naturalists

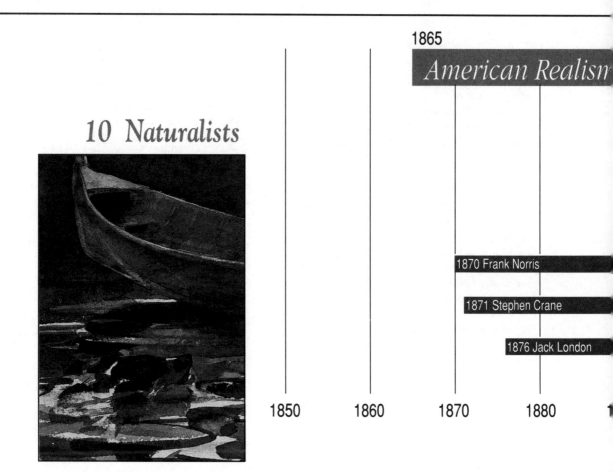

1865

American Realism

1870 Frank Norris

1871 Stephen Crane

1876 Jack London

1850   1860   1870   1880

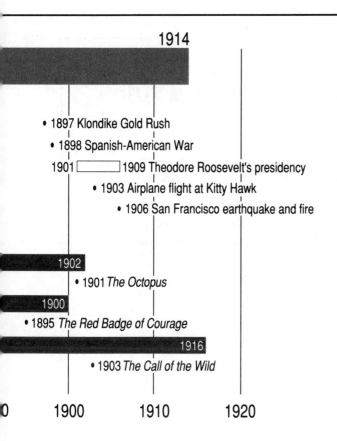

1914

- 1897 Klondike Gold Rush
- 1898 Spanish-American War

1901 ⬜ 1909 Theodore Roosevelt's presidency

- 1903 Airplane flight at Kitty Hawk
- 1906 San Francisco earthquake and fire

1902

- 1901 *The Octopus*

1900

- 1895 *The Red Badge of Courage*

1916

- 1903 *The Call of the Wild*

0   1900   1910   1920

Stephen Crane   1871-1900

"Modern American literature," one critic claims, "may be said . . . to have begun with Stephen Crane." Crane's poetry has encouraged modern poets to experiment widely in subject matter and verse form. Crane's naturalistic themes have anticipated the dark pessimism of much modern fiction. In fact, both in his life and in his writing, Crane represents the broad religious and literary rebellion characteristic of modern literature.

Stephen Crane was born in Newark, New Jersey, on November 1, 1871, the fourteenth and youngest child of a Methodist minister. Both parents were college graduates and authors whose devout Methodism appeared everywhere in their lives and writing. Stephen Crane, however, very early questioned and then rejected his parents' religious beliefs. In 1888, eight years after his father's death, Crane entered a journalistic career. He began writing for his brother's news agency in Asbury Park, New Jersey. After briefly attending Lafayette College (1890) and Syracuse University (1891), Crane moved to New York City where he became a reporter. While in New York, he immersed himself in the life of the Bowery, the sordid section of lower Manhattan and the setting for several of his early pieces.

In 1893 Crane began his literary career by privately publishing his first novel, *Maggie: A Girl of the Streets,* under the pen name of "Johnston Smith." Although the book was admired by Hamlin Garland and promoted by William Dean Howells, most readers ignored it. The novel's emphasis upon the role of environment made it one of the earliest literary expressions of naturalism in America. Crane remained detached from the characters and their problems as he told a story of the sordid Bowery life. His central character is a girl who having "blossomed in a mud-puddle" loses her virtue, becomes a prostitute, and finally commits suicide. Crane attributes Maggie's downfall to her environment in the Bowery, not to any moral weakness within her.

Maggie is also one of the earliest American works to focus attention on city life, particularly its less savory parts. The language is that of the "modern slum-world," writes one critic, "ferocious and sordid."

"I met a chump deh odder day way up in deh city. . . . When I was a-crossin' deh street deh chump runned plump inteh me, an' den he turns aroun' an' says, 'Yer insolen' ruffin!' he says, like dat. 'Oh, gee!' I says, 'Oh, gee! git off d' eart'!' I says, like dat. See? 'Git off d' eart'!' like dat. Den deh blokie he got wild. He says I was a contempt'ble scoun'el, er somethin' like dat, an' he says I was doom, teh everlastin' pe'dition, er somethin' like dat. 'Gee!' I says, 'gee! Yer joshin' me,' I says. 'Yer joshin' me.' An' den I slugged 'im. See?''

In 1895 Crane published *The Red Badge of Courage,* the novel that brought its twenty-four-year-old author international fame. In this initiation story set during the Civil War, Crane, who had not experienced war personally, nevertheless probes with clinical objectivity the workings of a young man's mind. Crane suggests that Henry Fleming's acts of heroism are not expressions of noble principles and self-sacrificing courage. They are rather the result of war-induced insanity or of certain external conditions that activate the character's natural instincts of survival and pride. Crane thus implies that man's heroism has the same basis as man's cowardice. Like most of Crane's other works, this novel describes the condition of loneliness, a major theme of modern writers.

Crane transformed a near disaster he experienced in January 1897 into the basis of his best-known short story, "The Open Boat." This story recounts his thirty-hour experience in a ten-foot dinghy off the coast of Florida after the *Commodore* (on a gun-running expedition to the rebels in Cuba) had developed a leak and sunk. In this story nature appears totally indifferent to the shipwrecked men. A tower on the Florida coast symbolizes nature's relationship to mankind:

This tower was a giant, standing with its back to the plight of the ants. It represented in a degree, to the correspondent [the character representing Crane himself], the serenity of nature amid the struggles of the individual–nature in the wind, and nature in the vision of men. She did not seem cruel to him then, nor beneficent, nor treacherous, nor wise. But she was indifferent, flatly indifferent.

Realizing their insignificance in the universe, the men can do nothing but curse the way things are and draw together in brotherhood. The bond of brotherhood, however, is broken because the strongest and ablest of the four men in the lifeboat–Billie Higgins, the oiler–dies in the surf, his head crushed by a timber. Ironically, the other three men live: the weak and overweight cook, the inexperienced and exhausted correspondent, and the injured captain. Crane implies, first, that man's natural condition is one of helplessness and, second, that man's survival in the world is merely accidental. There is no force at all kindly disposed toward him. Human beings, like the survivors, are "all in the same boat," and it is an open boat–exposed to the whimsical, terrifying actions of nature.

Crane's first book of poetry, *The Black Riders and Other Lines,* appeared in 1895. This volume supposedly owed its birth to William Dean Howells's reading aloud to Crane selections from Emily Dickinson's poetry. *The Black Riders* was not well received, however, because its form and ideas were too unconventional. Many of the poems, for instance, show their author's quarrel with God. Men appear as gnatlike creatures, subject to forces they cannot understand or control. Like Ambrose Bierce, Crane evokes a nightmarish world of "menace, violence, and isolation."

In 1897 Crane reported on the Cuban and Greek wars of independence. Also in 1897 he settled in an English manor house with his common-law wife, Cora Taylor. By this time Crane was a respected author enjoying the friendship of such important writers as Henry James, Joseph Conrad, and H. G. Wells. The late 1890s, however, saw a decline in Crane's writing. He had already written his memorable works in the period from 1893 to 1897. After 1897 his health, which had been declining for years, rapidly failed him. On June 5, 1900, while in Germany, he died at the age of twenty-eight of tuberculosis.

Crane's works reveal the main tenets of naturalism. They emphasize the shaping role of environment and heredity. In his inscription in several copies of *Maggie,* Crane wrote that he had tried "to show that environment is a tremendous thing in the world, and frequently shapes lives regardless. If one proves that theory, one makes room in Heaven for all sorts of souls, notably an occasional street girl, who are not confidently expected to be there by many excellent people." His works portray men caught in an indifferent and puzzling universe, the victims of fate. "The Blue Hotel," a short story set out West, describes men as "lice which were caused to cling to a whirling, fire-smitten, ice-locked, disease-stricken, space-lost bulb." He places the blame for the wretchedness of most men's lives not on their sin and rebellion, but on blind fate, which he believes has determined their course for them. Against the power of fate, man is helpless. Like the "injured and rebellious" cowboy in this story, man can only exclaim "blindly into this fog of mysterious theory: 'Well, I didn't do anythin', did I?' "

With this defiant cry Crane voiced modern thought. In his rebellion man finds the universe bewildering, for apart from God's truth there is no satisfying explanation for man's state. Confused, man thinks he has been cheated and victimized. He cries out, "It's not my fault!" Like other writers of his time and later, Crane recognized man's problems. But he could not offer solutions because he did not understand the root of man's plight–sin. Crane's work shows as a whole a deliberate rejection of orthodox religious views. His poetry, to which we will turn first, shows in particular the pessimism man sinks into when he denies the Biblical view of God.

A Man Said to the Universe

This short poem is typical of Crane's poetry. It is starkly simple in form. It is also bitter in tone. Notice that in some ways it very much resembles a Dickinson poem. Like Emily Dickinson, Crane often communicates his meaning indirectly. But whereas Dickinson's poems are generally lyric, Crane's are usually narrative. They often turn out to be parables making pessimistic points about man's relation to the universe and God.

A man said to the universe:
"Sir, I exist!"
"However," replied the universe,
"The fact has not created in me
A sense of obligation."

I Saw a Man Pursuing the Horizon

I saw a man pursuing the horizon;
Round and round they sped.
I was disturbed at this;
I accosted* the man.
"It is futile,"* I said,
"You can never–"

"You lie," he cried
And ran on.

accosted: approached
to speak to
futile: useless

5

Snow Flurries; Andrew N. Wyeth; National Gallery of Art, Washington; Gift of Dr. Margaret I. Handy.

(handwritten notes)
* Realism, Regionalism, and Naturalism Notes

"An Occurence @ Owl Creek Bridge"
"Desiree's Baby"
"Notorious Jumping Frog"
"Yellow Wallpaper"
* 3 Stephen Crane Poems

God Fashioned the Ship of the World Carefully

God fashioned the ship of the world carefully.
With the infinite skill of an all-master
Made He the hull* and the sails,
Held He the rudder*
Ready for adjustment.   5
Erect stood He, scanning His work proudly.
Then—at fateful time—a wrong called,
And God turned, heeding.
Lo, the ship, at this opportunity, slipped slyly,
Making cunning* noiseless travel down the ways.   10
So that, forever rudderless, it went upon the seas
Going ridiculous voyages,
Making quaint* progress,
Turning as with serious purpose
Before stupid winds.   15
And there were many in the sky
Who laughed at this thing.

hull: the main body of
the ship

rudder: the steering
mechanism of the
ship

cunning: crafty

quaint: strange

Should the Wide World Roll Away

Should the wide world roll away,

Leaving black terror,

Limitless night,

Nor God, nor man, nor place to stand

Would be to me essential,

If thou and thy white arms were there,

And the fall to doom a long way.

The Bride Comes to Yellow Sky

*This 1898 short story lacks the naturalistic thrust of most of Crane's fiction and poetry. Instead, it is a realistic picture of the closing of the Old West. Such battles as the one between the sheriff (Jack Potter) and the drunken, armed desperado (Scratchy Wilson) were in the 1890s already passing into Western folklore. What signals the historical change in the story is Potter's arrival with his new bride, the symbol of domesticity and civilization. The story thus becomes a historical **allegory** of the taming of the Old West.*

Notice Crane's skillful characterization: the bashful new bride, the self-conscious groom, the drummer (traveling salesman), and even Scratchy himself. All of the characters exist as clearly defined figures because of Crane's careful and accurate description. In this story, as in others, Crane explores with great care the behavior of a man faced by a crisis.

1

The great Pullman* was whirling onward with such dignity of motion that a glance from the window seemed simply to prove that the plains of Texas were pouring eastward. Vast flats of green grass, dull-hued spaces of mesquit* and cactus, little groups of frame houses, woods of light and tender trees, all were sweeping into the east, sweeping over the horizon, a precipice.

Pullman: a parlor or sleeping car on a train
mesquit: a shrub of the Southwest

A newly married pair had boarded this coach at San Antonio. The man's face was reddened from many days in the wind and sun, and a direct result of his new black clothes was that his brick-coloured hands were constantly performing in a most conscious fashion. From time to time he looked down respectfully at his attire. He sat with a hand on each knee, like a man waiting in a barber's shop. The glances he devoted to other passengers were furtive* and shy.

---

furtive: secret

The bride was not pretty, nor was she very young. She wore a dress of blue cashmere, with small reservations of velvet here and there, and with steel buttons abounding. She continually twisted her head to regard her puff sleeves, very stiff, straight, and high. They embarrassed her. It was quite apparent that she had cooked, and that she expected to cook, dutifully. The blushes caused by the careless scrutiny* of some passengers as she had entered the car were strange to see upon this plain, under-class countenance, which was drawn in placid,* almost emotionless lines.

---

scrutiny: a critical observation
placid: peaceful

They were evidently very happy. "Ever been in a parlour-car before?" he asked, smiling with delight.

"No," she answered; "I never was. It's fine, ain't it?"

"Great! And then after a while we'll go forward to the diner, and get a big lay-out, finest meal in the world. Charge a dollar."

"Oh, do they?" cried the bride. "Charge a dollar? Why, that's too much–for us–ain't it, Jack?"

"Not this trip, anyhow," he answered bravely. "We're going to go the whole thing."

Later he explained to her about the trains. "You see, it's a thousand miles from one end of Texas to the other; and this train runs right across it, and never stops but four times." He had the pride of an owner. He pointed out to her the dazzling fittings of the coach; and in truth her eyes opened wider as she contemplated the sea-green figured velvet, the shining brass, silver, and glass, the wood that gleamed as darkly brilliant as the surface of a pool of oil. At one end a bronze figure sturdily held a support for a separated chamber, and at convenient places on the ceiling were frescos* in olive and silver.

frescos: paintings on plaster

To the minds of the pair, their surroundings reflected the glory of their marriage that morning in San Antonio; this was the environment of their new estate; and the man's face in particular beamed with an elation* that made him appear ridiculous to the negro porter. This individual at times surveyed them from afar with an amused and superior grin. On other occasions he bullied them with skill in ways that did not make it exactly plain to them that they were being bullied. He subtly used all the manners of the most unconquerable kind of snobbery. He oppressed them; but of the oppression they had small knowledge, and they speedily forgot that infrequently a number of travellers covered them with stares of derisive* enjoyment. Historically there was sup-

posed to be something infinitely humorous in their situation.

elation: happiness, high spirits
derisive: mocking

"We are due in Yellow Sky at 3:42," he said, looking tenderly into her eyes.

"Oh, are we?" she said, as if she had not been aware of it. To evince* surprise at her husband's statement was part of her wifely amiability.* She took from a pocket a little silver watch; and as she held it before her, and stared at it with a frown of attention, the new husband's face shone.

evince: show
amiability: pleasantness

"I bought it in San Anton' from a friend of mine," he told her gleefully.

"It's seventeen minutes past twelve," she said, looking up at him with a kind of shy and clumsy coquetry.* A passenger, noting this play, grew excessively sardonic,* and winked at himself in one of the numerous mirrors.

coquetry: flirtation
sardonic: scornful

At last they went to the dining-car. Two rows of negro waiters, in glowing white suits, surveyed their entrance with the interest, and also the equanimity,* of men who had been forewarned. The pair fell to the lot of a waiter who happened to feel pleasure in steering them through their meal. He viewed them with the manner of a fatherly pilot, his countenance radiant with benevolence.* The patronage,* entwined* with the ordinary deference,* was not plain to them. And yet, as they returned to their coach, they showed in their faces a sense of escape.

equanimity: calmness
benevolence: kindness
patronage: treatment given with an air of superiority
entwined: combined
deference: courteous respect

To the left, miles down a long purple slope, was a little ribbon of mist where moved the Rio

Grande. The train was approaching it at an angle, and the apex* was Yellow Sky. Presently it was apparent that, as the distance from Yellow Sky grew shorter, the husband became commensurately* restless. His brick-red hands were more insistent in their prominence. Occasionally he was even rather absent-minded and far-away when the bride leaned forward and addressed him.

apex: meeting point
commensurately: to the same extent

As a matter of truth, Jack Potter was beginning to find the shadow of a deed weigh upon him like a leaden slab. He, the town marshal of Yellow Sky, a man known, liked, and feared in his corner, a prominent person, had gone to San Antonio to meet a girl he believed he loved, and there, after the usual prayers, had actually induced her to marry him, without consulting Yellow Sky for any part of the transaction. He was now bringing his bride before an innocent and unsuspecting community.

Of course people in Yellow Sky married as it pleased them, in accordance with a general custom; but such was Potter's thought of his duty to his friends, or of their idea of his duty, or of an unspoken form which does not control men in these matters, that he felt he was heinous.* He had committed an extraordinary crime. Face to face with this girl in San Antonio, and spurred by his sharp impulse, he had gone headlong over all the social hedges. At San Antonio he was like a man hidden in the dark. A knife to sever any friendly duty, any form, was easy to his hand in that remote city. But the hour of Yellow Sky—the hour of daylight—was approaching.

heinous: wicked

He knew full well that his marriage was an important thing to his town. It could only be exceeded by the burning of the new hotel. His friends could not forgive him. Frequently he had reflected on the advisability of telling them by telegraph, but a new cowardice had been upon him. He feared to do it. And now the train was hurrying him toward a scene of amazement, glee, and reproach. He glanced out of the window at the line of haze swinging slowly in toward the train.

Yellow Sky had a kind of brass band, which played painfully, to the delight of the populace. He laughed without heart as he thought of it. If the citizens could dream of his prospective arrival with his bride, they would parade the band at the station and escort them, amid cheers and laughing congratulations, to his adobe home.

He resolved that he would use all the devices of speed and plainscraft in making the journey from the station to his house. Once within that safe citadel,* he could issue some sort of vocal bulletin, and then not go among the citizens until they had time to wear off a little of their enthusiasm.

citadel: a place of defense

The bride looked anxiously at him. "What's worrying you, Jack?"

He laughed again. "I'm not worrying, girl; I'm only thinking of Yellow Sky."

She flushed in comprehension.

A sense of mutual guilt invaded their minds and developed a finer tenderness. They looked at each other with eyes softly aglow. But Potter often laughed the same nervous laugh; the flush upon the bride's face seemed quite permanent.

The traitor to the feelings of Yellow Sky narrowly watched the speeding landscape. "We're nearly there," he said.

Presently the porter came and announced the proximity of Potter's home. He held a brush in his hand, and, with all his airy superiority gone, he brushed Potter's new clothes as the latter slowly turned this way and that way. Potter fumbled out a coin and gave it to the porter, as he had seen others do. It was a heavy and muscle-bound business, as that of a man shoeing his first horse.

The porter took their bag, and as the train began to slow they moved forward to the hooded platform of the car. Presently the two engines and their long string of coaches rushed into the station of Yellow Sky.

"They have to take water here," said Potter, from a constricted* throat and in mournful cadence,* as one announcing death. Before the train stopped his eye had swept the length of the platform, and he was glad and astonished to see there was none upon it but the station-agent, who, with a slightly hurried and anxious air, was walking toward the water-tanks. When the train had halted, the porter alighted first, and placed in position a little temporary step.

constricted: tightened
cadence: rhythmic flow of speech or music

"Come on, girl," said Potter, hoarsely. As he helped her down they each laughed on a false note. He took the bag from the negro, and bade his wife cling to his arm. As they slunk rapidly away, his hang-dog glance perceived that they were unloading the two trunks, and also that the station-agent, far ahead near the baggage-car, had turned and was running toward him, making gestures. He laughed, and groaned as he laughed, when he noted the first effect of his marital bliss upon Yellow Sky. He gripped his wife's arm firmly to his side, and they fled. Behind them the porter stood, chuckling fatuously.*

fatuously: foolishly

2

The California express on the Southern Railway was due at Yellow Sky in twenty-one minutes. There were six men at the bar of the Weary Gentleman saloon. One was a drummer who talked a great deal and rapidly; three were Texans who did not care to talk at that time; and two were Mexican sheepherders, who did not talk as a general practice in the Weary Gentleman saloon. The barkeeper's dog lay on the board walk that crossed in front of the door. His head was on his paws, and he glanced drowsily here and there with the constant vigilance of a dog that is kicked on occasion. Across the sandy street were some vivid green grass-plots, so wonderful in appearance, amid the sands that burned near them in a blazing sun, that they caused a doubt in the mind. They exactly resembled the grass mats used to represent lawns on the stage. At the cooler end of the railway station, a man without a coat sat in a tilted chair and smoked his pipe. The fresh-cut bank of the Rio Grande circled near the town, and there could be seen beyond it a great plum-coloured plain of mesquit.

Save for the busy drummer and his companions in the saloon, Yellow Sky was dozing. The new-comer leaned gracefully upon the bar, and recited many tales with the confidence of a bard who has come upon a new field.

"—and at the moment the old man fell downstairs with the bureau in his arms, the old woman was coming up with two scuttles* of coal, and of course—"

scuttles: pails

The drummer's tale was interrupted by a young man who suddenly appeared in the open door. He cried: "Scratchy Wilson's drunk, and has turned loose with both hands." The two Mex-

icans at once set down their glasses and faded out of the rear entrance of the saloon.

The drummer, innocent and jocular,* answered: "All right, old man. S'pose he has? Come in and have a drink, anyhow."

jocular: jolly

But the information had made such an obvious cleft in every skull in the room that the drummer was obliged to see its importance. All had become instantly solemn. "Say," said he, mystified, "what is this?" His three companions made the introductory gesture of eloquent speech; but the young man at the door forestalled* them.

forestalled: prevented

"It means, my friend," he answered, as he came into the saloon, "that for the next two hours this town won't be a health resort."

The barkeeper went to the door, and locked and barred it; reaching out of the window, he pulled in heavy wooden shutters, and barred them. Immediately a solemn, chapel-like gloom was upon the place. The drummer was looking from one to another.

"But say," he cried, "what is this, anyhow? You don't mean there is going to be a gunfight?"

"Don't know whether there'll be a fight or not," answered one man, grimly; "but there'll be some shootin'—some good shootin'."

The young man who had warned them waved his hand. "Oh, there'll be a fight fast enough, if any one wants it. Anybody can get a fight out there in the street. There's a fight just waiting."

The drummer seemed to be swayed between the interest of a foreigner and a perception of personal danger.

"What did you say his name was?" he asked.

"Scratchy Wilson," they answered in chorus.

"And will he kill anybody? What are you going to do? Does this happen often? Does he rampage* around like this once a week or so? Can he break in that door?"

rampage: run wild

"No; he can't break down that door," replied the barkeeper. "He's tried it three times. But when he comes you'd better lay down on the floor, stranger. He's dead sure to shoot at it, and a bullet may come through."

Thereafter the drummer kept a strict eye on the door. The time had not yet been called for him to hug the floor, but, as a minor precaution, he sidled near to the wall. "Will he kill anybody?" he said again.

The men laughed low and scornfully at the question.

"He's out to shoot, and he's out for trouble. Don't see any good in experimentin' with him."

"But what do you do in a case like this? What do you do?"

A man responded; "Why, he and Jack Potter–"

"But," in chorus the other men interrupted, "Jack Potter's in San Anton'."

"Well, who is he? What's he got to do with it?"

"Oh, he's the town marshal. He goes out and fights Scratchy when he gets on one of these tears."

"Wow!" said the drummer, mopping his brow. "Nice job he's got."

The voices had toned away to mere whisperings. The drummer wished to ask further questions, which were born of an increasing anxiety and bewilderment; but when he attempted them, the men merely looked at him in irritation and motioned him to remain silent. A tense waiting hush was upon them. In the deep shadows of the room their eyes shone as they listened for sounds from the street. One man made three gestures at the barkeeper; and the latter, moving like a ghost, handed him a glass and a bottle. The man poured a full glass of whisky, and set down the bottle noiselessly. He gulped the whisky in a swallow, and turned again toward the door in immovable silence. The drummer saw that the barkeeper, without a sound, had taken a Winchester* from beneath the bar. Later he saw this individual beckoning to him, so he tiptoed across the room.

Winchester: rifle

"You better come with me back of the bar."

"No, thanks," said the drummer, perspiring; "I'd rather be where I can make a break for the back door."

Whereupon the man of bottles made a kindly but peremptory* gesture. The drummer obeyed it, and, finding himself seated on a box with his head below the level of the bar, balm was laid upon his soul at the sight of various zinc and copper fittings that bore a resemblance to armour-plate. The barkeeper took a seat comfortably upon an adjacent* box.

peremptory: commanding
adjacent: nearby

"You see," he whispered, "this here Scratchy Wilson is a wonder with a gun–a perfect wonder; and when he goes on the war-trail, we hunt our holes–naturally. He's about the last one of the old gang that used to hang out along the river here. He's a terror when he's drunk. When he's sober he's all right–kind of simple–wouldn't hurt a fly–nicest fellow in town. But when he's drunk–whoo!"

There were periods of stillness. "I wish Jack Potter was back from San Anton'," said the barkeeper. "He shot Wilson up once–in the leg–and would sail in and pull the kinks in this thing."*

pull . . . thing: i.e., straighten things out

Presently they heard from a distance the sound of a shot, followed by three wild yowls. It instantly removed a bond from the men in the darkened saloon. There was a shuffling of feet. They looked at each other. "Here he comes," they said.

3

A man in a maroon-coloured flannel shirt, which had been purchased for purposes of decoration, and made principally by some Jewish women on the East Side of New York, rounded a corner and walked into the middle of the main street of Yellow Sky. In either hand the man held a long, heavy, blue-black revolver. Often he yelled, and these cries rang through a semblance of a deserted village, shrilly flying over the roofs in a volume that seemed to have no relation to the ordinary vocal strength of a man. It was as if the surrounding stillness formed the arch of a tomb over him. These cries of ferocious challenge rang against walls of silence. And his boots had red tops with gilded imprints, of the kind beloved in winter by little sledding boys on the hillsides of New England.

The man's face flamed in a rage begot of whisky. His eyes, rolling, and yet keen for ambush, hunted the still doorways and windows. He walked with the creeping movement of the midnight cat. As it occurred to him, he roared menacing* information. The long revolvers in his hands were as easy as straws; they were moved with an electric swiftness. The little fingers of each hand played sometimes in a musician's way. Plain from the low collar of the shirt, the cords of his neck straightened and sank, straightened and sank, as passion moved him. The only sounds were his terrible invitations. The calm adobes preserved their demeanour* at the passing of the small thing in the middle of the street.

menacing: threatening
demeanour: outward manner

There was no offer of fight—no offer of fight. The man called to the sky. There were no attractions. He bellowed and fumed and swayed his revolvers here and everywhere.

The dog of the barkeeper of the Weary Gentleman saloon had not appreciated the advance of events. He yet lay dozing in front of his master's door. At sight of the dog, the man paused and raised his revolver humorously. At sight of the man, the dog sprang up and walked diagonally away, with a sullen head, and growling. The man yelled, and the dog broke into a gallop. As it was

about to enter an alley, there was a loud noise, a whistling, and something spat the ground directly before it. The dog screamed, and, wheeling in terror, galloped headlong in a new direction. Again there was a noise, a whistling, and sand was kicked viciously before it. Fear-stricken, the dog turned and flurried like an animal in a pen. The man stood laughing, his weapons at his hips.

Ultimately the man was attracted by the closed door of the Weary Gentleman saloon. He went to it and, hammering with a revolver, demanded drink.

The door remaining imperturbable,* he picked a bit of paper from the walk, and nailed it to the framework with a knife. He then turned his back contemptuously upon this popular resort and, walking to the opposite side of the street and spinning there on his heel quickly and lithely,* fired at the bit of paper. He missed it by a half-inch. He swore at himself, and went away. Later he comfortably fusilladed* the windows of his most intimate friend. The man was playing with this town; it was a toy for him.

imperturbable: incapable of being disturbed
lithely: gracefully
fusilladed: shot with a rapid succession of shots

But still there was no offer of fight. The name of Jack Potter, his ancient antagonist, entered his mind, and he concluded that it would be a glad thing if he should go to Potter's house, and by bombardment induce him to come out and fight. He moved in the direction of his desire, chanting Apache scalp-music.

When he arrived at it, Potter's house presented the same still front as had the other adobes. Taking up a strategic position, the man howled a challenge. But this house regarded him as might a great stone god. It gave no sign. After a decent wait, the man howled further challenges, mingling with them wonderful epithets.*

epithets: insulting names

Presently there came the spectacle of a man churning himself into deepest rage over the immobility of a house. He fumed at it as the winter wind attacks a prairie cabin in the North. To the distance there should have gone the sound of a tumult like the fighting of two hundred Mexicans. As necessity bade him, he paused for breath or to reload his revolvers.

4

Potter and his bride walked sheepishly and with speed. Sometimes they laughed together shamefacedly and low.

"Next corner, dear," he said finally.

They put forth the efforts of a pair walking bowed against a strong wind. Potter was about to raise a finger to point the first appearance of the new home when, as they circled the corner, they came face to face with a man in a maroon-coloured shirt, who was feverishly pushing cartridges into a large revolver. Upon the instant the man dropped his revolver to the ground and, like lightning, whipped another from its holster. The second weapon was aimed at the bridegroom's chest.

There was a silence. Potter's mouth seemed to be merely a grave for his tongue. He exhibited an instinct to at once loosen his arm from the woman's grip, and he dropped the bag to the sand. As for the bride, her face had gone as yellow as old cloth. She was a slave to hideous rites, gazing at the apparitional* snake.

apparitional: ghostlike

The two men faced each other at a distance of three paces. He of the revolver smiled with a new and quiet ferocity.

"Tried to sneak up on me," he said. "Tried to sneak up on me!" His eyes grew more baleful.* As Potter made a slight movement, the man thrust his revolver venomously* forward. "No; don't you do it, Jack Potter. Don't you move a finger toward a gun just yet. Don't you move an eyelash. The time has come for me to settle with you, and I'm goin' to do it my own way, and loaf along with no interferin'. So if you don't want a gun bent on you, just mind what I tell you."

baleful: threatening evil
venomously: dangerously

Potter looked at his enemy. "I ain't got a gun on me, Scratchy," he said. "Honest, I ain't." He was stiffening and steadying, but yet somewhere at the back of his mind a vision of the Pullman floated; the sea-green figured velvet, the shining brass, silver, glass, the wood that gleamed as darkly brilliant as the surface of a pool of oil—all the glory of the marriage, the environment of the new estate. "You know I fight when it comes to fighting, Scratchy Wilson; but I ain't got a gun on me. You'll have to do all the shootin' yourself."

His enemy's face went livid.* He stepped forward, and lashed his weapon to and fro before Potter's chest. "Don't you tell me you ain't got no gun on you, you whelp.* Don't tell me no lie like that. There ain't a man in Texas ever seen you without no gun. Don't take me for no kid." His eyes blazed with light, and his throat worked like a pump.

livid: pale with rage
whelp: scoundrel

"I ain't takin' you for no kid," answered Potter. His heels had not moved an inch backward. "I'm takin' you for a fool. I tell you I ain't got a gun, and I ain't. If you're goin' to shoot me up, you better begin now; you'll never get a chance like this again."

So much enforced reasoning had told on Wilson's rage; he was calmer. "If you ain't got a gun, why ain't you got a gun?" he sneered. "Been to Sunday-school?"

"I ain't got a gun because I've just come from San Anton' with my wife. I'm married," said Potter. "And if I'd thought there was going to be any galoots* like you prowling around when I brought my wife home, I'd had a gun, and don't you forget it."

galoots: rude, clumsy persons

"Married?" said Scratchy, not at all comprehending.

"Yes, married. I'm married," said Potter, distinctly.

"Married!" said Scratchy. Seemingly for the first time, he saw the drooping, drowning woman at the other man's side. "No!" he said. He was like a creature allowed a glimpse of another world. He moved a pace backward, and his arm, with the revolver, dropped to his side. "Is this the lady?" he asked.

"Yes; this is the lady," answered Potter.

There was another period of silence.

"Well," said Wilson at last, slowly, "I s'pose it's all off now."

"It's all off if you say so, Scratchy. You know I didn't make the trouble." Potter lifted his valise.*

valise: small traveling bag

"Well, I 'low it's off, Jack," said Wilson. He was looking at the ground. "Married!" He was not a student of chivalry;* it was merely that in the presence of this foreign condition he was a simple child of the earlier plains. He picked up his starboard* revolver, and, placing both weapons in their holsters, he went away. His feet made funnel-shaped tracks in the heavy sand.

chivalry: courtesy
starboard: i.e., right-handed

For Thought and Discussion

1. State in a sentence each the themes of the first and third poems of Crane. Show how their messages challenge Biblical revelation concerning the existence and nature of God and His relationship to mankind.

2. Explain what Crane meant by "a man pursuing the horizon." What kind of false hopes and goals may he have had in mind?

3. Who of the characters in "A Bride Comes to Yellow Sky" is the most complex? How does the conflict within him relate to the conflict he will be drawn into outside him? How are both conflicts emblematic of the clash of forces determining the destiny of the West? Which side in these conflicts has won or will win?

4. Why should Potter regard himself as "a traitor to the feelings of Yellow Sky"? What are the "social hedges" of Yellow Sky he overleaped in pursuing marriage? Why should the town feel any involvement in such a personal decision as his marriage?

5. Are there symbolic aspects in the geography—of the railroad intersecting the Rio Grande at Yellow Sky? of the opposite directions, east and west, from which the trains arrive?

6. Why do you think the story refers to Jack Potter as "the ancient antagonist" of Scratchy Wilson?

7. What is the narrative function of the drummer?

8. Do the numbered parts reflect the story's organization?

Jack London   1876-1916

Jack London is remembered by most readers for his adventure stories about dogs. At the heart of his fiction, however, is a set of ideas distinguishing his works from those of other adventure writers striving for popularity. In the fifty books London wrote from 1900 to his death in 1916, he illustrated many of the beliefs central to the socialistic and evolutionary doctrines he had accepted from his wide reading. Although not considered a major writer by some critics, London nevertheless contributed significantly to popularizing American naturalism.

Born in California on January 12, 1876, John Griffith (Jack) London came from a background that today would cause people to label him as underprivileged and a juvenile delinquent. He was an illegitimate child reared in the San Francisco slums. He was forced by poverty to drop out of school after finishing the eighth grade. In his early teens he had to help support his family. Since London found crime financially more profitable than legitimate work, he became an oyster pirate, robbing privately owned oyster beds during the night. His sailing skills were the envy of many an older sailor in the bay. After a time, however, he unexpectedly changed sides and began working with the State Fish Patrol to catch the oyster pirates he had formerly assisted. During this period he began drinking heavily, nearly killing himself with alcohol. He was not yet seventeen.

On his seventeenth birthday he signed on a sealing schooner. Upon his return from the seven-month voyage, he worked in a cannery and at other jobs. In 1894 he joined a march on Washington to demand government aid for the unemployed. Quitting the protest in Iowa, he traveled to the major Midwestern and Eastern cities as a hobo. A three-month prison sentence for vagrancy encouraged his socialist leanings. When he returned to California after a year of tramping, the nineteen-year-old youth enrolled in high school to prepare for college. In 1896, after two years of cramming, he passed the entrance examination of the University of California. But he stayed only one semester, leaving to help support his parents. London tried at first to make money by writing, but all his manuscripts were rejected. He soon returned to physical labor that left him no energy for writing.

In the late 1890s London, like Samuel Clemens years earlier, struck a rich vein of material for writing. In March 1897, he left California to search for gold in the Klondike. He came back the following year not with gold but with story nuggets. He then turned furiously to writing, producing scores of stories, essays, jokes, and poems. In 1899 his stories and articles began appearing in leading magazines. London's career rapidly shot upward. In 1900, the year of his marriage to Bessie Maddern, he published his first novel, *A Daughter of the Snows.* In 1903 he published what has become his most famous tale, *The Call of the Wild.*

Ten years later London was the highest-paid and best-known writer in the world. Mixed with his success, however, were several less fortunate experiences. He was divorced from his first wife in 1905 and married Charmian Kittredge the same year. In 1907 he began an around-the-world cruise in the *Snark,* a forty-five-foot boat he had built himself. Two years later he had to abandon this cruise in Polynesia because of illness. All the time he kept writing. In 1913 his fortunes turned dramatically downward. Wolf House, a dream house he had been building for four years and into which he had poured a fortune, was destroyed by fire before he could move into it. The fire was apparently set deliberately. London's debts piled up, the crops on his farm were ruined, his drinking increased, his health failed, and his second marriage went sour. He even became disillusioned with the socialistic ideas he had earlier embraced. In 1916–alcoholic, in debt, and weary of life itself–the forty-year-old author died, quite possibly by suicide.

London laced his writings with ideas that reveal his enthusiasm for socialist and Darwinian thought. *The Call of the Wild,* for instance, demonstrates London's deep interest in evolution. The novel tells the story of Buck (half St. Bernard, half Scotch shepherd), who is stolen from a wealthy California farmer and sent to become a sled dog during the Klondike gold rush. Even before he enters the wilderness, Buck quickly learns the laws of survival. London writes that after Buck witnesses the death of another dog under the rush of a pack of huskies, "the scene often came back to Buck to trouble him in his sleep. So that was the way. No fair play. Once down, that was the end of you." Later, after Buck cleverly steals a chunk of bacon from his owners, London comments: "This first theft marked Buck as fit to survive in the hostile Northland environment. It marked his adaptability, his capacity to adjust himself to changing conditions, the lack of which would have meant swift and terrible death." London adds that this theft "marked, further, the decay or going to pieces of his [Buck's] moral nature, a vain thing and a handicap in the ruthless struggle for existence." According to London, morality has no place in the real world.

The Call of the Wild ends with Buck's succumbing to the voice of his ancestors calling him back to savagery. After a marauding band of Yeehats murder his beloved master, John Thornton, Buck joins a wolfpack and becomes its leader.

The years were not many when the Yeehats noted a change in the breed of timber wolves; for some were seen with splashes of brown on head and muzzle, and with a rift of white centering down the chest. But more remarkable than this, the Yeehats tell of a Ghost Dog that runs at the head of the pack. They are afraid of this Ghost Dog, for it has cunning greater than they, stealing from their camps in fierce winters, robbing their traps, slaying their dogs, and defying their bravest hunters.

Buck thus enacts his revenge against those who had killed his master. The dog, however, returns yearly to the scene of the murder, to pay tribute to the man that he had loved above all others. "Here he muses for a time," writes London, "howling once, long and mournfully, ere he departs."

London's Darwinian views also appear in his treatment of man. According to one critic, London "wrote of animals as if they were people—and of people as if they were animals, recognizing no essential difference between human and animal societies." London's short story "The Law of Life" makes the point that the same laws apply to animal and human existence. In this story Koskoosh, an old man no longer able to keep up with his tribe, is left behind to die. Like animals the old and the weak of the tribe must fall prey to the ravages of nature. Koskoosh does not object.

It was the way of life, and it was just. He had been born close to the earth, close to the earth had he lived, and the law thereof was not new to him. It was the law of all flesh. Nature was not kindly to the flesh. She had no concern for that concrete thing called the individual. Her interest lay in the species, the race.

As a spokesman for literary naturalism, London clearly illustrates how strongly the theory of evolution affected the imagination of the naturalists. Perhaps without intention, he illustrates something else: that when men form an idea of themselves as mere animals, they begin to act as animals. And as London himself finally had to acknowledge, brute instincts, no matter how romantically portrayed, do not lead men to happiness.

The Law of Life

This 1901 short story, more clearly than most, shows the extent to which the theory of evolution influenced London's imagination. The constant linking of the old man's death to the laws of nature reveals that London's primary concern is the illustration of ideas rather than the creation of adventure. The story seems secondary, the thesis primary.

Old Koskoosh listened greedily. Though his sight had long since faded, his hearing was still acute, and the slightest sound penetrated to the glimmering* intelligence which yet abode behind the withered forehead, but which no longer gazed forth upon the things of the world. Ah! that was Sit-cum-to-ha, shrilly anathematizing* the dogs as she cuffed* and beat them into the harnesses. Sit-cum-to-ha was his daughter's daughter, but she was too busy to waste a thought upon her broken grandfather, sitting alone there in the snow, forlorn and helpless. Camp must be broken. The long trail waited while the short day refused to linger. Life called her, and the duties of life, not death. And he was very close to death now.

glimmering: shining faintly
anathematizing: cursing
cuffed: struck

The thought made the old man panicky for the moment, and he stretched forth a palsied* hand which wandered tremblingly over the small heap of dry wood beside him. Reassured that it was indeed there, his hand returned to the shelter of his mangy* furs, and he again fell to listening. The sulky* crackling of half-frozen hides told him that the chief's moose-skin lodge had been struck,* and even then was being rammed and jammed into portable compass.* The chief was his son, stalwart* and strong, head man of the tribesmen, and a mighty hunter. As the women toiled with the camp luggage, his voice rose, chiding them for their slowness. Old Koskoosh strained his ears. It was the last time he would hear that voice. There went Greehow's lodge! And Tusken's! Seven, eight, nine; only the Shaman's could be still standing. There! They were at work upon it now. He could hear the Shaman grunt as he piled it on the sled. A child whimpered, and a woman soothed it with soft, crooning gutturals.* Little Koo-tee, the old man thought, a fretful child, and not over strong. It would die soon, perhaps, and they would burn a hole through the frozen tundra* and pile rocks above to keep the wolverines away. Well, what did it matter? A few years at best, and as many an empty belly as a full one. And in the end, Death waited, ever-hungry and hungriest of them all.

palsied: uncontrolled shaking
mangy: having worn and bare spots
sulky: gloomy
struck: i.e., taken down
portable compass: i.e., size capable of being carried
stalwart: sturdy
gutturals: noises made in the throat
tundra: frozen arctic ground

What was that? Oh, the men lashing the sleds and drawing tight the thongs. He listened, who would listen no more. The whip-lashes snarled and bit among the dogs. Hear them whine! How

they hated the work and the trail! They were off! Sled after sled churned slowly away into the silence. They were gone. They had passed out of his life, and he faced the last bitter hour alone. No. The snow crunched beneath a moccasin; a man stood beside him; upon his head a hand rested gently. His son was good to do this thing. He remembered other old men whose sons had not waited after the tribe. But his son had. He wandered away into the past, till the young man's voice brought him back.

"Is it well with you?" he asked.

And the old man answered, "It is well."

"There be wood beside you," the younger man continued, "and the fire burns bright. The morning is gray, and the cold has broken. It will snow presently. Even now is it snowing."

"Ay, even now is it snowing."

"The tribesmen hurry. The bales are heavy, and their bellies flat with lack of feasting. The trail is long and they travel fast. I go now. It is well?"

"It is well. I am as a last year's leaf, clinging lightly to the stem. The first breath that blows, and I fall. My voice is become like an old woman's. My eyes no longer show me the way of my feet, and my feet are heavy, and I am tired. It is well."

He bowed his head in content till the last noise of the complaining snow had died away, and he knew his son was beyond recall. Then his hand crept out in haste to the wood. It alone stood betwixt him and the eternity which yawned* in upon him. At last the measure of his life was a handful of faggots.* One by one they would go to feed the fire, and just so, step by step, death would creep upon him. When the last stick had surrendered up its heat, the frost would begin to gather strength. First his feet would yield, then his hands; and the numbness would travel, slowly, from the extremities* to the body. His head would fall forward upon his knees, and he would rest. It was easy. All men must die.

yawned: opened wide
faggots: sticks
extremities: the hands and feet

He did not complain. It was the way of life, and it was just. He had been born close to the earth, close to the earth he lived, and the law thereof was not new to him. It was the law of all flesh. Nature was not kindly to the flesh. She had no concern for that concrete thing called the individual. Her interest lay in the species, the race. This was the deepest abstraction* old Koskoosh's barbaric* mind was capable of, but he grasped it firmly. He saw it exemplified in all life. The rise of the sap, the bursting greenness of the willow bud, the fall of the yellow leaf—in this alone was told the whole history. But one task did nature set the individual. Did he not perform it, he died. Did he perform it, it was all the same, he died. Nature did not care; there were plenty who were obedient, and it was only the obedience in this matter, not the obedient, which lived and lived always. The tribe of Koskoosh was very old. The old men he had known when a boy, had known old men before them. Therefore it was true that the tribe lived, that it stood for the obedience of all its members, way down into the forgotten past, whose very resting places were unremembered. They did not count; they were episodes.* They had passed away like clouds from a summer sky. He also was an episode, and would pass away. Nature did not care. To life she set one task, gave one law. To perpetuate* was the task of life, its law was death. A maiden was a good creature to look upon, . . . with spring to her step and light in her eyes. But her task was yet before her. The light in her eyes brightened, her step quickened, she was now bold with the young men, now timid, and she gave them of her own unrest. And ever she grew fairer and yet fairer to look upon, till some hunter, able no longer to withhold himself, took her to his lodge to cook and toil for him and to become the mother of his children. And with the coming of her offspring her looks left her. Her limbs dragged and shuffled, her eyes dimmed and bleared,* and only the little children found joy against the withered cheek of the old squaw by the fire. Her task was done. But a little while, on the first pinch of famine or the first long trail, and she would be left, even as he had been left, in the snow, with a little pile of wood. Such was the law.

abstraction: a general idea arrived at by mental action
barbaric: crude, uneducated
episodes: incidents
perpetuate: prolong the existence of
bleared: blurred

He placed a stick carefully upon the fire and resumed his meditations. It was the same everywhere, with all things. The mosquitos vanished with the first frost. The little tree-squirrel crawled away to die. When age settled upon the rabbit it became slow and heavy, and could no longer outfoot its enemies. Even the big bald-face grew clumsy and blind and quarrelsome, in the end to be dragged down by a handful of yelping huskies. He remembered how he had abandoned his own father on an upper reach of the Klondike one winter, the winter before the missionary came with his talk-books and his box of medicines. Many a time had Koskoosh smacked his lips over the recollection of that box, though now this mouth refused to moisten. The "painkiller" had been especially good. But the missionary was a bother after all, for he brought no meat into the camp, and he ate heartily, and the hunters grumbled. But he chilled his lungs on the divide by the Mayo, and the dogs afterwards nosed the stones away and fought over his bones.

Koskoosh placed another stick on the fire and harked back* deeper into the past. There was the time of the Great Famine, when the old men crouched empty-bellied to the fire, and from their lips fell dim traditions of the ancient day when the Yukon* ran wide open for three winters, and then lay frozen for three summers. He had lost his mother in that famine. In the summer the salmon run had failed, and the tribe looked forward to the winter and the coming of the caribou.*

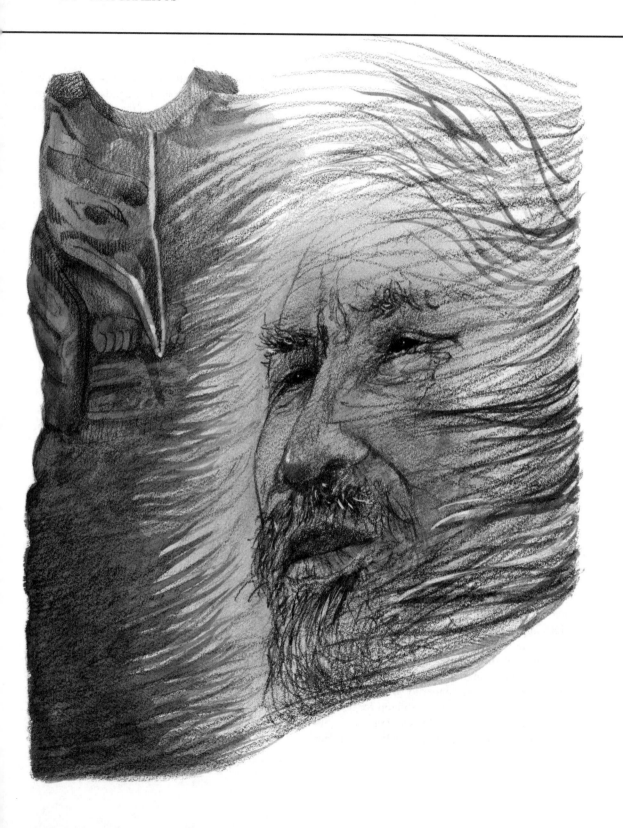

Then the winter came, but with it there were no caribou. Never had the like been known, not even in the lives of the old men. But the caribou did not come, and it was the seventh year, and the rabbits had not replenished, and the dogs were naught but bundles of bones. And through the long darkness the children wailed and died, and the women, and the old men; and not one in ten of the tribe lived to meet the sun when it came back in the spring. That *was* a famine!

harked back: returned
Yukon: river flowing through Canada and Alaska
caribou: a deer of the arctic regions

But he had seen times of plenty, too, when the meat spoiled on their hands, and the dogs were fat and worthless with over-eating–times when they let the game go unkilled, and the women were fertile, and the lodges were cluttered with sprawling men-children and women-children. Then it was the men became high-stomached, and revived ancient quarrels, and crossed the divides to the south to kill the Pellys, and to the west that they might sit by the dead fires of the Tananas. He remembered, when a boy, during a time of plenty, when he saw a moose pulled down by the wolves. Zing-ha lay with him in the snow and watched–Zing-ha, who later became the craftiest of hunters, and who, in the end, fell through an air-hole on the Yukon. They found him, a month afterward, just as he had crawled halfway out and frozen stiff to the ice.

But the moose. Zing-ha and he had gone out that day to play at hunting after the manner of their fathers. On the bed of the creek they struck the fresh track of a moose, and with it the tracks of many wolves. "An old one," Zing-ha, who was quicker at reading the sign, said–"an old one who cannot keep up with the herd. The wolves have cut him out from his brothers, and they will never leave him." And it was so. It was their way. By day and by night, never resting, snarling on his heels, snapping at his nose, they would stay by him to the end. How Zing-ha and he felt the blood-lust quicken! The finish would be a sight to see!

Eager-footed, they took the trail, and even he, Koskoosh, slow of sight and an unversed* tracker, could have followed it blind, it was so wide. Hot were they on the heels of the chase, reading the grim tragedy, fresh-written, at every step. Now they came to where the moose had made a stand. Thrice the length of a grown man's body, in every direction, had the snow been stamped about and uptossed. In the midst were the deep impressions of the splay-hoofed game, and all about, everywhere, were the lighter footmarks of the wolves. Some, while their brothers harried* the kill, had lain to one side and rested. The full-stretched impress of their bodies in the snow was as perfect as though made the moment before. One wolf had been caught in a wild lunge* of the maddened victim and trampled to death. A few bones, well picked, bore witness.

unversed: inexperienced
harried: annoyed by constant attacks
lunge: sudden forward movement

Again, they ceased the uplift of their snow-shoes at a second stand. Here the great animal had fought desperately. Twice had he been dragged down, as the snow attested, and twice had he shaken his assailants clear and gained footing once more. He had done his task long since, but none the less was life dear to him. Zing-ha said it was a strange thing, a moose once down to get free again; but this one certainly had. The Shaman would see signs and wonders in this when they told him.

And yet again, they came to where the moose had made to mount the bank and gain the timber. But his foes had laid on from behind, till he reared and fell back upon them, crushing two deep into the snow. It was plain the kill was at hand, for their brothers had left them untouched. Two more stands were hurried past, brief in time-length and very close together. The trail was red now, and the clean stride of the great beast had grown short and slovenly.* Then they heard the first sounds of the battle—not the full-throated chorus of the chase, but the short, snappy bark which spoke of close quarters and teeth to flesh. Crawling up the wind, Zing-ha bellied it through the snow, and with him crept he, Koskoosh, who was to be chief of the tribesmen in the years to come. Together they shoved aside the under branches of a young spruce and peered forth. It was the end they saw.

---

slovenly: i.e., clumsy

The picture, like all of youth's impressions, was still strong with him, and his dim eyes watched the end played out as vividly as in that far-off time. Koskoosh marveled at this, for in the days which followed, when he was a leader of men and a head of councilors, he had done great deeds and made his name a curse in the mouths of the Pellys, to say naught of the strange white man he had killed, knife to knife, in open fight.

For long he pondered on the days of his youth, till the fire died down and the frost bit deeper. He replenished it with two sticks this time, and gauged* his grip on life by what remained. If Sit-cum-to-ha had only remembered her grandfather, and gathered a larger armful, his hours would have been longer. It would have been easy. But she was ever a careless child, and honored not her ancestors from the time the Beaver, son of the son of Zing-ha, first cast eyes upon her. Well, what mattered it? Had he not done likewise in his own quick youth? For a while he listened to the silence. Perhaps the heart of his son might soften, and he would come back with the dogs to take his old father on with the tribe to where the caribou ran thick and the fat hung heavy upon them.

---

gauged: measured

He strained his ears, his restless brain for the moment stilled. Not a stir, nothing. He alone took breath in the midst of the great silence. It was very lonely. Hark! What was that? A chill passed over his body. The familiar, long-drawn howl broke the void,* and it was close at hand. Then

on his darkened eyes was projected* the vision of the moose—the old bull moose—the torn flanks* and bloody sides, the riddled* mane, and the great branching horns, down low and tossing to the last. He saw the flashing forms of gray, the gleaming eyes, the lolling* tongues, the slavered* fangs. And he saw the inexorable* circle close in till it became a dark point in the midst of the stamped snow.

---

void: emptiness
projected: thrown forward
flanks: part of the animal between the last rib and hip
riddled: pierced with holes
lolling: hanging loosely
slavered: slobbering
inexorable: unyielding

A cold muzzle* thrust against his cheek, and at its touch his soul leaped back to the present. His hand shot into the fire and dragged out a burning faggot. Overcome for the nonce* by his hereditary fear of man, the brute retreated, raising a prolonged call to his brothers; and greedily they answered, till a ring of crouching, jaw-slobbered gray was stretched round about. The old man listened to the drawing in of this circle. He waved his brand wildly, and sniffs turned to snarls; but the panting brutes refused to scatter. Now one wormed his chest forward, dragging his haunches after, now a second, now a third; but never a one drew back. Why should he cling to life? he asked, and dropped the blazing stick into the snow. It sizzled and went out. Again he saw the last stand of the old bull moose, and Koskoosh dropped his head wearily upon his knees. What did it matter after all? Was it not the law of life?

---

muzzle: the jaws and nose of an animal
nonce: the present

For Thought and Discussion

1. Through what incident, witnessed in youth, does Koskoosh visualize his death? Point out the details of the parallelism. What naturalistic assumption does this parallelism express?

2. Why is Koskoosh not angry with his son or with the rest of the tribe for abandoning him? What view of death does this attitude express?

3. What is the one task of life given by nature? Does nature care whether this task is carried out by a particular individual? Why or why not?

4. Life in almost all primitive tribal communities is tied to religious observances and dominated by awe of the supernatural. Are Koskoosh and his fellow tribesmen religious? Where is religion mentioned? Does it seem relevant to their tribal existence? What would happen to London's naturalistic thesis were this a typical tribe?

5. In Koskoosh's life have ethical principles mattered? Has Koskoosh followed any rule of conduct other than "blood-lust" and survival?

Frank Norris   1870-1902

Along with Stephen Crane and Theodore Dreiser, Frank Norris is recognized as one of the three major naturalists in American literature. Yet, as biographer W. M. Frohock points out, the name *Frank Norris* "is much better known today than anything he ever wrote." Norris's work, which drew heavily on the work of Émile Zola, seems tame to modern readers but shocked his contemporaries. Where London's works stress the role of the law of nature, Norris's works stress the role of social and economic forces. The novels of Frank Norris thus tend to portray large forces at work on numerous characters drawn from various levels of society.

Born to well-to-do parents in Chicago in 1870, Benjamin Franklin Norris enjoyed many advantages of wealth. His family moved to San Francisco when he was fourteen and then sent him to Paris at seventeen to study art. His father called him home, however, when he learned that his son was writing romantic stories about the days of chivalry rather than studying art. Norris then spent four years at the University of California (leaving without a degree) and one at Harvard (as a special student in English). While an undergraduate at California, he published at his mother's expense his first work, a long narrative poem entitled *Yvernelle: A Legend of Feudal France* (1892). Also while in college, he began writing two novels, *McTeague* (1899) and *Vandover and the Brute* (1914). Both of these novels reflect his sympathetic reading of Zola's works.

In 1895, when Norris returned to California from Harvard, he became a journalist in San Francisco. Not content to stay in California, he traveled to Africa, where he fought in the Boer War, and to Cuba, where–like Stephen Crane–he reported on the Spanish-American War. During this time, he continued writing essays, short stories, and novels. In 1898 he began working for the publishing firm of Doubleday,

McClure, and Company. While there, he discovered and drew attention to the work of another but more important naturalist, Theodore Dreiser.

In 1899 Norris began to write a gigantic work he thought worthy of the American West. He called the projected trilogy an "Epic of the Wheat." His plan was to write three novels that told the story of the production, distribution, and consumption of American wheat. The first novel, *The Octopus* (1901), portrays the struggle of the California wheat growers against the railroad. The second, *The Pit* (1903), depicts the buying and selling of wheat in Chicago, where the Board of Trade helped manipulate the market. The third, *The Wolf,* was to develop the distribution of American wheat in Europe. This part of the trilogy was never written because in October 1902 the thirty-two-year-old Norris died suddenly after an operation for appendicitis.

Norris's novels embody Zola's pattern of naturalistic fiction. They overflow with documented, detailed facts; their characters are drawn primarily from the working class; and their author maintains a detached, scientific attitude toward his material. While writing *McTeague,* Norris commented on the role of violence in his fiction: "Terrible things must happen to characters of the naturalistic tale. They must be twisted from the ordinary, wrenched from the quiet, uneventful round of everyday life and flung into the throes of a vast and terrible drama that works itself out in unleashed passions, in blood, and in sudden death."

Everywhere in Norris's works the reader sees the author's belief in evolution and determinism. In the title character of *McTeague,* for instance, Norris portrays a person with unusual strength (an unlicensed dentist who pulls teeth with his fingers) but with a weak mind. As McTeague degenerates in the last section of the novel, he reveals himself to be just a brute animal driven by his instincts. In *The Octopus* Norris shows the might of strong, impersonal powers like the railroad and the wheat itself. His characters are helpless pawns. They are caught up in the movement of uncontrollable economic and social forces that remain indifferent to the havoc they cause in human lives. Norris reveals through his novels the pessimistic theme that nothing can withstand the destructive forces that originate from inside a human being or that oppose him from the world around him. Apparently Norris never knew the liberating power of the truth of God's Word.

The Octopus

The first excerpt portrays a key event from one of the four plots running through The Octopus. *Norris illustrates in this subplot his ability to create reader sympathy for those caught in the power of an inexorable force.*

Once one of the railroad's best and most loyal employees, Dyke loses his job when the railroad cuts back everyone's wages. When he protests that his loyalty and service ought to count for something, Dyke finds himself out of a job. Deciding to join his brother in raising hops (a plant used in manufacturing malt liquors), Dyke confidently expects to make a good profit from his farming. Dreams of materialistic success and of educating his daughter run through his mind. The railroad, however, raises its shipping rates and thus destroys all Dyke's hopes for success by eliminating his chance to make a profit. When bankruptcy forces Dyke from his farm, he robs a train, kills a man, and is hunted down as a criminal.

The second excerpt depicts the death of S. Behrman, the grotesque representative of the railroad. Since the railroad destroys all who oppose it, the wheat fittingly destroys Behrman. Notice that Norris uses strongly naturalistic phrases like "the Fear of the Trap" and "terrible dance of death" in this selection.

Although the overriding tone of The Octopus *is pessimistic, Norris ends the novel with a rather optimistic view of the world. All the deaths and the corruption caused by the railroad vanish in a view that encompasses the whole. "The larger view always and through all shams, all wickedness, discovers the Truth that will, in the end, prevail," writes Norris, "and all things, surely, inevitably, resistlessly work together for good." In spite of the Biblical allusion in this quotation, Norris replaces God with the natural forces he believed are the true controlling forces in the world.*

Book Two, Chapter Two

The ex-engineer reached the Post Office in Bonneville* towards eleven o'clock, but he did not at once present his notice of the arrival of his consignment* at Ruggles's office. It entertained him to indulge in an hour's lounging about the streets. It was seldom he got to town, and when he did he permitted himself the luxury of enjoying his evident popularity. He met friends everywhere, in the Post Office, in the drug store, in the barber shop and around the court-house. With each one he held a moment's conversation; almost invariably this ended in the same way:

Bonneville: a town in California
consignment: goods committed to someone else for sale

"Come on 'n have a drink."

"Well, I don't care if I do."

And the friends proceeded to the Yosemite bar, pledging each other with punctilious* ceremony. Dyke, however, was a strictly temperate man. His life on the engine had trained him well. Alcohol he never touched, drinking instead ginger ale, sarsaparilla-and-iron*–soft drinks.

---

punctilious: showing close attention to detail
sarsaparilla-and-iron: a soft drink flavored with the root of a tropical American plant

---

At the drug store, which also kept a stock of miscellaneous stationery, his eye was caught by a "transparent slate," a child's toy, where upon a little pane of frosted glass one could trace with considerable elaboration outline figures of cows, ploughs, bunches of fruit and even rural water

mills that were printed on slips of paper underneath.

"Now, there's an idea, Jim," he observed to the boy behind the soda-water fountain: "I know a little tad* that would just about jump out of her skin for that. Think I'll have to take it with me."

---

tad: a small child: i.e., Dyke's daughter

"How's Sidney getting along?" the other asked, while wrapping up the package.

Dyke's enthusiasm had made of his little girl a celebrity throughout Bonneville.

The ex-engineer promptly became voluble,* assertive, doggedly emphatic.

---

voluble: talkative

"Smartest little tad in all Tulare County, and more fun! A regular whole show in herself."

"And the hops?" inquired the other.

"Bully,"* declared Dyke, with the good-natured man's readiness to talk of his private affairs to anyone who would listen. "Bully. I'm dead sure of a bonanza* crop by now. The rain came *just* right. I actually don't know that I can store the crop in those barns I built, it's going to be so big. That foreman of mine was a daisy. Jim, I'm going to make money in that deal. After I've paid off the mortgage*–you know I had to mortgage, yes, crop and homestead, both, but I can pay it off and all the interest to boot, lovely,–well, as I was saying, after all expenses are paid off I'll clear big money, m'son. Yes, sir. I knew there was boodle* in hops. You know the crop is contracted for already. Sure, the foreman managed that. He's a daisy. Chap in San Francisco will take it all and at the advance price. I wanted to hang on, to see if it wouldn't go to six cents, but the foreman said, 'No, that's good enough.' So I signed. Ain't it bully, hey?"

Bully: excellent
bonanza: a source of great wealth
mortgage: a pledge of one's property in exchange for a loan of money
boodle: money

"Then what'll you do?"

"Well, I don't know. I'll have a lay-off for a month or so and take the little tad and mother up and show 'em the city–'Frisco–until it's time for the schools to open, and then we'll put Sid in the seminary at Marysville. Catch on?''

''I suppose you'll stay right by hops now?''

''Right you are, m'son. I know a good thing when I see it. There's plenty of others going into hops next season—I set 'em the example. Wouldn't be surprised if it came to be a regular industry hereabouts. I'm planning ahead for next year already. I can let the foreman go, now that I've learned the game myself, and I think I'll buy a piece of land off Quien Sabe and get a bigger crop, and build a couple more barns, and, by George, in about five years' time I'll have things humming. I'm going to make *money,* Jim.'' . . .

The chronometer* in the window of the jewelry store warned him that time was passing. He turned about, and, crossing the street, took his way to Ruggles's office, which was the freight as well as the land office of the P. and S. W.* Railroad.

chronometer: a very precise clock
P. and S. W.: Pacific and South West

As he stood for a moment at the counter in front of the wire partition, waiting for the clerk to make out the order for the freight agent at the depot,* Dyke was surprised to see a familiar figure in conference with Ruggles himself, by a desk inside the railing.

depot: railroad station

The figure was that of a middle-aged man, fat, with a great stomach, which he stroked from time to time. As he turned about, addressing a remark to the clerk, Dyke recognized S. Behrman. The banker, railroad agent, and political manipulator* seemed to the ex-engineer's eyes to be more gross than ever. His smooth-shaven jowl* stood out big and tremulous* on either side of his face; the roll of fat on the nape* of his neck, sprinkled with sparse, stiff hairs, bulged out with greater prominence. His great stomach, covered with a light brown linen vest, stamped with innumerable interlocked horseshoes, protruded far in advance,

enormous, aggressive. He wore his inevitable round-topped hat of stiff brown straw, varnished so bright that it reflected the light of the office windows like a helmet, and even from where he stood Dyke could hear his loud breathing and the clink of the hollow links of his watch chain upon the vest buttons of imitation pearl, as his stomach rose and fell.

manipulator: one who influences in an underhanded manner
jowl: flesh under the lower jaw
tremulous: trembling, quivering
nape: the back of the neck

Dyke looked at him with attention. There was the enemy, the representative of the Trust with which Derrick's League was locking horns. The great struggle had begun to invest* the combatants with interest. Daily, almost hourly, Dyke was in touch with the ranchers, the wheat-growers; he heard their denunciations,* their growls of exasperation and defiance. Here was the other side—this placid,* fat man, with a stiff straw hat and linen vest, who never lost his temper, who smiled affably* upon his enemies, giving them good advice, commiserating with them in one defeat after another, never ruffled, never excited, sure of his power, conscious that back of him was the Machine, the colossal force, the inexhaustible coffers* of a mighty organization, vomiting millions to the League's thousands.

invest: to provide with something
denunciations: hostile criticism
placid: unhurried, calm
affably: pleasantly
coffers: treasury

The League was clamorous,* ubiquitous,* its objects known to every urchin* on the streets, but the Trust was silent, its ways inscrutable,* the public saw only the results. It worked on in the dark—calm, disciplined, irresistible. Abruptly Dyke received the impression of the multitudinous* ramifications* of the colossus. Under his feet the ground seemed mined; down there below him in the dark the huge tentacles were silently twisting and advancing, spreading out in every direction, sapping the strength of all opposition, quiet, gradual, biding the time to reach up and out and grip with a sudden unleashing of gigantic strength.

---

clamorous: noisy
ubiquitous: existing or seeming to exist everywhere at the same time
urchin: a boy, youngster
inscrutable: not able to be understood
multitudinous: very numerous
ramifications: consequences

"I'll be wanting some cars* of you people before the summer is out," observed Dyke to the clerk as he folded up and put away the order that the other had handed him. He remembered perfectly well that he had arranged the matter of transporting his crop some months before, but his role of proprietor* amused him and he liked to busy himself again and again with the details of his undertaking.

---

cars: i.e., railroad cars
proprietor: owner

"I suppose," he added, "you'll be able to give 'em to me. There'll be a big wheat crop to move this year and I don't want to be caught in any car famine."

"Oh, you'll get your cars," murmured the other.

"I'll be the means of bringing business your way." Dyke went on; "I've done so well with my hops that there are a lot of others going into the business next season. Suppose," he continued, struck with an idea, "suppose we went into some sort of pool, a sort of shippers' organization, could you give us special rates, cheaper rates—say a cent and a half?"

The other looked up.

"A cent and a half! Say *four* cents and a half and maybe I'll talk business with you."

"Four cents and a half," returned Dyke. "I don't see it. Why, the regular rate is only two cents."

"No, it isn't," answered the clerk, looking him gravely in the eye; "it's five cents."

"Well, there's where you are wrong, m'son," Dyke retorted, genially.* "You look it up. You'll find the freight on hops from Bonneville to 'Frisco is two cents a pound for car load lots. You told me that yourself last fall."

---

genially: good-naturedly

"That was last fall," observed the clerk. There was a silence. Dyke shot a glance of suspicion at the other. Then, reassured, he remarked: "You look it up. You'll see I'm right."

S. Behrman came forward and shook hands politely with the ex-engineer.

"Anything I can do for you, Mr. Dyke?"

Dyke explained. When he had done speaking, the clerk turned to S. Behrman and observed, respectfully:

"Our regular rate on hops is five cents."

"Yes," answered S. Behrman, pausing to reflect; "yes, Mr. Dyke, that's right—five cents."

The clerk brought forward a folder of yellow paper and handed it to Dyke. It was inscribed at the top "Tariff Schedule No. 8," and underneath these words, in brackets, was a smaller inscription, *"Supersedes No. 7 of Aug. 1."*

"See for yourself," said S. Behrman. He indicated an item under the head of "Miscellany."

"The following rates for carriage of hops in car load lots," read Dyke, "take effect June 1, and will remain in force until superseded* by a later tariff. Those quoted beyond Stockton are subject to changes in traffic arrangements with carriers by water from that point."

---

superseded: replaced

In the list that was printed below, Dyke saw that the rate for hops between Bonneville and Guadalajara and San Francisco was five cents.

For a moment Dyke was confused. Then swiftly the matter became clear in his mind. The Railroad had raised the rate on hops from two cents to five.

All his calculations as to a profit on his little investment he had based on a freight rate of two cents a pound. He was under contract to deliver his crop. He could not draw back. The new rate ate up every cent of his gains. He stood there ruined.

"Why, what do you mean?" he burst out. "You promised me a rate of two cents and I went ahead with my business with that understanding. What do you mean?"

S. Behrman and the clerk watched him from the other side of the counter.

"The rate is five cents," declared the clerk doggedly.

"Well, that ruins me," shouted Dyke. "Do you understand? I won't make fifty cents. *Make?* Why, I will *owe,*–I'll be–be–That ruins me, do you understand?"

The other raised a shoulder.

"We don't force you to ship. You can do as you like. The rate is five cents."

"Well–but– . . . I'm under contract to deliver. What am I going to do? Why, you told me–you promised me a two-cent rate."

"I don't remember it," said the clerk. "I don't know anything about that. But I know this; I know that hops have gone up. I know the German crop was a failure and that the crop in New York wasn't worth the hauling. Hops have gone up to nearly a dollar. You don't suppose we don't know that, do you. Mr. Dyke?"

"What's the price of hops got to do with you?"

"It's got *this* to do with us," returned the other with sudden aggressiveness, "that the freight rate has gone up to meet the price. We're not doing business for our health. My orders are to raise your rate to five cents, and I think you are getting off easy."

Dyke stared in blank astonishment. For the moment, the audacity* of the affair was what most appealed to him. He forgot its personal application.

audacity: brashness

"What will you people do next?" he murmured. "Look here. What's your basis of applying freight rate, anyhow?" he suddenly vociferated* with furious sarcasm. "What's your rule? What are you guided by?"

vociferated: shouted

But at the words, S. Behrman, who had kept silent during the heat of the discussion, leaned abruptly forward. For the only time in his knowledge, Dyke saw his face inflamed with anger and with the enmity* and contempt of all this farming element with whom he was contending.

enmity: hatred

"Yes, what's your rule? What's your basis?" demanded Dyke turning swiftly to him.

S. Behrman emphasized each word of his reply with a tap of the one forefinger on the counter before him:

"All–the–traffic–will–bear."

Book Two, Chapter Nine

S. Behrman went forward to the hatch that opened down into the vast hold of the ship. A great iron chute connected this hatch with the elevator,* and through it was rushing a veritable* cataract* of wheat.

elevator: storehouse of grain
veritable: actual
cataract: a downpour like a waterfall

It came from some gigantic bin within the elevator itself, rushing down the confines of the chute to plunge into the roomy, gloomy interior of the hold with an incessant,* metallic roar, persistent, steady, inevitable. No men were in sight. The place was deserted. No human agency seemed to be back of the movement of the wheat. Rather, the grain seemed impelled* with a force of its own, a resistless, huge force, eager, vivid, impatient for the sea.

incessant: continuous
impelled: urged forward

S. Behrman stood watching, his ears deafened with the roar of the hard grains against the metallic lining of the chute. He put his hand once into the rushing tide, and the contact rasped the flesh of his fingers and, like an undertow, drew his hand after it in its impetuous* dash.

impetuous: marked by force, haste

Cautiously he peered down into the hold. A musty odor rose to his nostrils, the vigorous, pungent* aroma of the raw cereal. It was dark. He could see nothing; but all about and over the opening of the hatch the air was full of a fine, impalpable* dust that blinded the eyes and choked the throat and nostrils.

pungent: sharp or bitter
impalpable: finely divided: i.e., powdery

As his eyes became used to the shadows of the cavern below him, he began to distinguish the gray mass of the wheat, a great expanse, almost liquid in its texture, which, as the cataract from above plunged into it, moved and shifted in long, slow eddies.* As he stood there, this cataract on a sudden increased in volume. He turned about, casting his eyes upward toward the elevator to discover the cause. His foot caught in a coil of rope, and he fell head foremost into the hold.

eddies: currents

The fall was a long one, and he struck the surface of the wheat with the sodden* impact of a bundle of damp clothes. For the moment he was stunned. All the breath was driven from his body. He could neither move nor cry out. But, by degrees, his wits steadied themselves and his breath returned to him. He looked about and above him. The daylight in the hold was dimmed and clouded by the thick chaff-dust thrown off by the pour of grain, and even this dimness dwindled to twilight at a short distance from the opening of the hatch, while the remotest quarters were lost in impenetrable blackness. He got upon his feet, only to find that he sunk ankle-deep in the loose-packed mass underfoot.

sodden: heavy with moisture, soggy

"Here's a fix." he muttered.

Directly underneath the chute, the wheat, as it poured in, raised itself in a conical* mound, but from the sides of this mound it shunted* away incessantly in thick layers, flowing in all directions with the nimbleness of water. Even as S. Behrman spoke, a wave of grain poured around his legs and rose rapidly to the level of his knees. He stepped quickly back. To stay near the chute would soon bury him to the waist.

conical: in the shape of a cone
shunted: moved aside

No doubt there was some other exit from the hold, some companion-ladder that led up to the deck. He scuffled and waded across the wheat, groping in the dark with outstretched hands. With every inhalation he choked, filling his mouth and nostrils more with dust than with air. At times he could not breathe at all, but gagged and gasped, his lips distended.* But search as he would, he could find no outlet to the hold, no stairway, no companion-ladder. Again and again, staggering along in the black darkness, he bruised his knuckles and forehead against the iron sides of the ship. He gave up the attempt to find any interior means of escape and returned laboriously to the space under the open hatchway. Already he could see that the level of the wheat was raised.

distended: swollen

"This isn't going to do at all." He uttered a great shout. "Hello, on deck there, somebody."

The steady, metallic roar of the pouring wheat drowned out his voice. He could scarcely hear it himself above the rush of the cataract. Besides this, he found it impossible to stay under the hatch. The flying grains of wheat, spattering as they fell, stung his face like wind-driven particles of ice. It was a veritable torture; his hands smarted

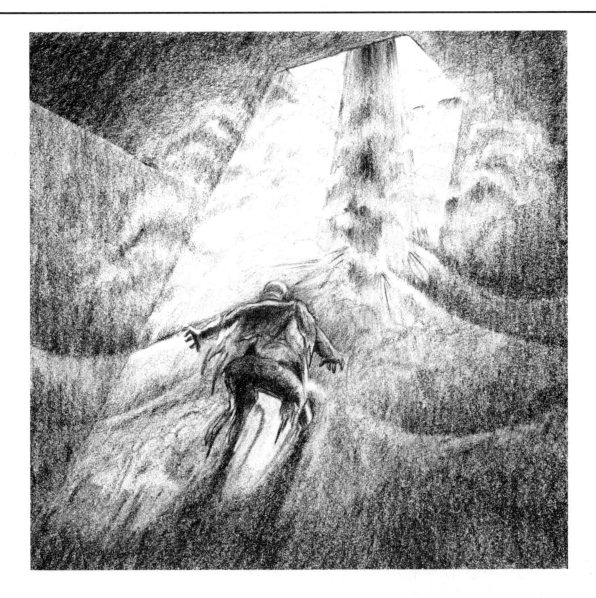

with it. Once he was all but blinded. Furthermore, the succeeding waves of wheat, rolling from the mound under the chute, beat him back, swirling and dashing against his legs and knees, mounting swiftly higher, carrying him off his feet.

Once more he retreated, drawing back from beneath the hatch. He stood still for a moment and shouted again. It was in vain. His voice re-turned upon him, unable to penetrate the thunder of the chute, and horrified, he discovered that so soon as he stood motionless upon the wheat, he sank into it. Before he knew it, he was knee-deep again, and a long swirl of grain sweeping outward from the everbreaking, ever-reforming pyramid below the chute poured around his thighs, im-mobilizing him.

A frenzy of terror suddenly leaped to life within him. The horror of death, the Fear of the Trap, shook him like a dry reed. Shouting, he tore himself free of the wheat and once more scrambled and struggled toward the hatchway. He stumbled as he reached it and fell directly beneath the pour. Like a storm of small shot, mercilessly, pitilessly, the unnumbered multitude of hurtling grains flagellated* and beat and tore his flesh. Blood streamed from his forehead and, thickening with the powder-like chaff-dust, blinded his eyes. He struggled to his feet once more. An avalanche from the cone of wheat buried him to his thighs. He was forced back and back and back, beating the air, falling, rising, howling for aid. He could no longer see; his eyes, crammed with dust, smarted as if transfixed* with needles whenever he opened them. His mouth was full of the dust, his lips were dry with it; thirst tortured him, while his outcries choked and gagged in his rasped throat.

flagellated: whipped
transfixed: pierced

And all the while, without stop, incessantly, inexorable, the wheat, as if moving with a force all its own, shot downward in a prolonged roar, persistent, steady, inevitable.

He retreated to a far corner of the hold and sat down with his back against the iron hull of the ship, and tried to collect his thoughts, to calm himself. Surely there must be some way of escape; surely he was not to die like this, die in this dreadful substance that was neither solid nor fluid. What was he to do? How make himself heard?

But even as he thought about this, the cone under the chute broke again and sent a great layer of grain rippling and tumbling toward him. It reached him where he sat and buried his hand and one foot.

He sprang up trembling and made for another corner.

Once more the level of the wheat rose and the grains began piling deeper about him. Once more

he retreated. Once more he crawled staggering to the foot of the cataract, screaming till his ears sang and his eyeballs strained in their sockets, and once more the relentless tide drove him back.

Then began the terrible dance of death; the man dodging, doubling, squirming, hunted from one corner to another, the wheat slowly, inexorably flowing, rising, spreading to every angle, to every nook and cranny. It reached his middle. Furious and with bleeding hands and broken nails, he dug his way out to fall backward, all but exhausted, gasping for breath in the dust-thickened air. Roused again by the slow advance of the tide, he leaped up and stumbled away, blinded with the agony in his eyes, only to crash against the metal hull of the vessel. He turned about, the blood streaming from his face, and paused to collect his senses, and with a rush, another wave swirled about his ankles and knees. Exhaustion grew upon him. To stand still meant to sink; to lie or sit meant to be buried the quicker; and all this in the dark, all this in an air that could scarcely be breathed, all this while he fought an enemy that could not be gripped, toiling in a sea that could not be stayed.

Guided by the sound of the falling wheat, S. Behrman crawled on hands and knees toward the hatchway. Once more he raised his voice in a shout for help. His bleeding throat and raw, parched lips refused to utter but a wheezing moan. Once more he tried to look toward the one patch of faint light above him. His eyelids, clogged with chaff, could no longer open. The wheat poured about his waist as he raised himself upon his knees.

Reason fled. Deafened with the roar of the grain, blinded and made dumb with its chaff, he threw himself forward with clutching fingers, rolling upon his back, and lay there, moving feebly, the head rolling from side to side. The wheat, leaping continuously from the chute, poured around him. It filled the pockets of the coat, it crept up the sleeves and trouser legs, it covered the great, protuberant stomach, it ran at last in rivulets* into the distended gasping mouth. It covered the face.

rivulets: small streams

Upon the surface of the wheat, under the chute, nothing moved but the wheat itself. There was no sign of life. Then, for an instant, the surface stirred. A hand, fat with short fingers and swollen veins, reached up, clutching, then fell limp and prone. In another instant it was covered. In the hold of the *Swanhilda* there was no movement but the widening ripples that spread flowing from the ever-breaking, ever-reforming cone; no sound, but the rushing of the wheat that continued to plunge incessantly from the iron chute in a prolonged roar, persistent, steady, inevitable.

For Thought and Discussion

1. Does self-seeking opportunism appear in Dyke as well as in S. Behrman? Can a writer be consistently naturalistic and show moral disapproval of a selfish character or institution?

2. What is the octopus of the novel? What else is it called? What is its prey? Where does the imagery appear in the first selection?

3. How does S. Behrman's answer to Dyke's question "What's your rule?" support the naturalistic view of life?

4. What parallelism can you see between S. Behrman's futile struggling in the hold—his "dance of death" and "Fear of the Trap"—and that of his victims such as Dyke? What tentaclelike object dragged him down?

5. Look up the term *poetic justice.* Does it seem that Norris is portraying S. Behrman's death as moral requital for the suffering he has caused as administrator of the railroad? If so, is Norris in this incident relaxing his naturalistic, amoral world view? Is he fictionally acknowledging a moral order that he elsewhere has denied?

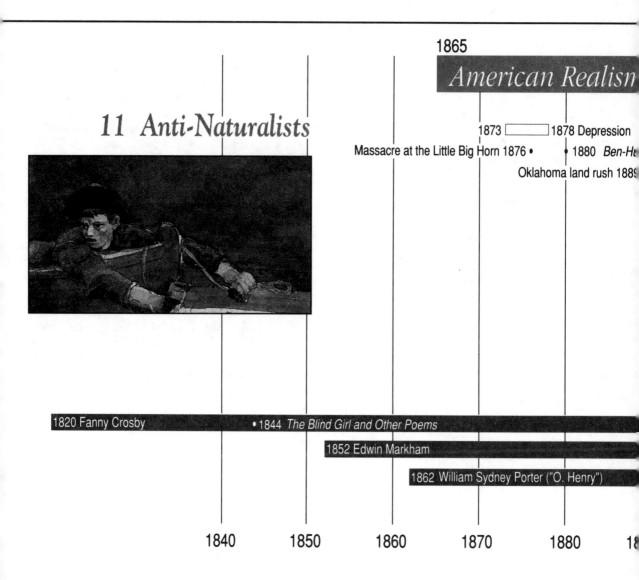

1865

American Realism

11 Anti-Naturalists

1873 ☐ 1878 Depression

Massacre at the Little Big Horn 1876 •   • 1880 *Ben-Hu*

Oklahoma land rush 1889

1820 Fanny Crosby   • 1844 *The Blind Girl and Other Poems*

1852 Edwin Markham

1862 William Sydney Porter ("O. Henry")

1840   1850   1860   1870   1880   18

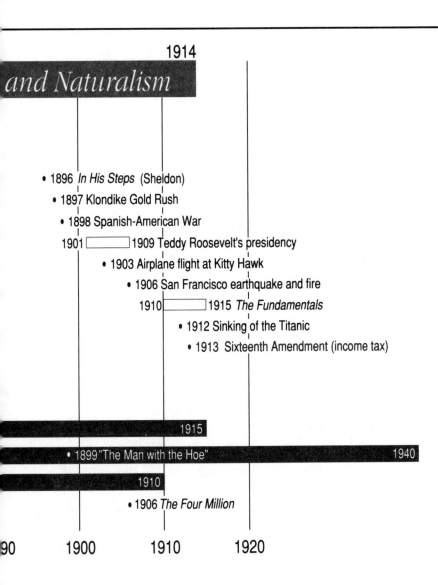

and Naturalism

1914

- 1896 *In His Steps* (Sheldon)
- 1897 Klondike Gold Rush
- 1898 Spanish-American War
- 1901 ☐ 1909 Teddy Roosevelt's presidency
- 1903 Airplane flight at Kitty Hawk
- 1906 San Francisco earthquake and fire
- 1910 ☐ 1915 *The Fundamentals*
- 1912 Sinking of the Titanic
- 1913 Sixteenth Amendment (income tax)

1915

- 1899 "The Man with the Hoe"   1940

1910

- 1906 *The Four Million*

90   1900   1910   1920

Edwin Markham
1852-1940

Edwin Markham's popularity rests almost completely on one poem published at the end of the 1890s. Through it Markham implied a belief in the possibility of mankind's solving its great social and economic problems. Markham's optimistic theme thus runs counter to the pessimism of most of the American naturalists.

Markham was born in 1852 to pioneer parents in Oregon City, Oregon. While still a boy, Markham moved to California, where he received relatively little education because the nearest school was open only three months a year. Markham learned early to love books and eventually completed a hard-earned degree although discouraged by his mother from studying. He graduated from the State Normal School (a teachers' college) in San Jose and attended Christian College in Santa Rosa. He then entered public education, becoming first a teacher, then a principal. While a principal in Oakland, California, he wrote "The Man with the Hoe." As a result of its publication, he became wealthy and world famous.

Markham said that he had wanted "to write a poem that should cry the lost rights of the toiling multitude in the abyss of civilization." His concern for the plight of exploited peoples became a common theme in his poetry. Although writing during a period of literary pessimism, Markham proclaimed a steadfast romantic belief in man's potential to help himself, even through rebellion and revolution. His works thus opposed naturalism from a romantic, humanistic perspective. By the time he died in 1940 at the age of eighty-eight, he had written enough poetry to fill ten volumes.

The Man with the Hoe

In 1886 Markham saw in Scribner's *magazine a black-and-white reproduction of a painting by the French pastoral landscapist Jean François Millet (1814-75). Markham wrote later that this painting, entitled* The Man with the Hoe, *held his soul "as one is held by some object of menace and terror." Although he immediately jotted down what became the first draft of the poem, he did not finish it until twelve years later. Then, having the opportunity to see Millet's original painting, he spent three days reworking his rough draft and published the poem on January 15, 1899, in a San Francisco newspaper. It became immediately popular and was reprinted all over the world. Nothing Markham wrote afterwards ever achieved the success of "The Man with the Hoe."*

Bowed by the weight of centuries he leans
Upon his hoe and gazes on the ground,
The emptiness of ages in his face,
And on his back the burden of the world.
Who made him dead to rapture and despair,   5
A thing that grieves not and that never hopes,
Stolid* and stunned, a brother to the ox?
Who loosened and let down this brutal jaw?
Whose was the hand that slanted back this brow?
Whose breath blew out the light within this brain?   10

Is this the Thing the Lord God made and gave
To have dominion over sea and land;
To trace the stars and search the heavens for power;
To feel the passion of Eternity?
Is this the dream He dreamed who shaped the suns   15
And marked their ways upon the ancient deep?
Down all the caverns of Hell to their last gulf

Stolid: showing little emotion

There is no shape more terrible than this—
More tongued with censure of the world's blind greed—*
More filled with signs and portents* for the soul—
More packt with danger to the universe.

What gulfs between him and the seraphim!*
Slave of the wheel of labor, what to him
Are Plato and the swing of Pleiades?*
What the long reaches of the peaks of song,
The rift of dawn, the reddening of the rose?
Through this dread shape the suffering ages look;
Time's tragedy is in that aching stoop;
Through this dread shape humanity betrayed,
Plundered, profaned,* and disinherited,
Cries protest to the Judges of the World,
A protest that is also prophesy.

O masters, lords and rulers in all lands,
Is this the handiwork you give to God,
This monstrous thing distorted and soul-quenched?
How will you ever straighten up this shape;
Touch it again with immortality;
Give back the upward looking and the light;
Rebuild in it the music and the dream;
Make right the immemorial infamies,*
Perfidious* wrongs, immedicable* woes?

O masters, lords and rulers in all lands,
How will the Future reckon with this man?
How answer his brute question in that hour
When whirlwinds of rebellion shake all shores?
How will it be with kingdoms and with kings—
With those who shaped him to the thing he is—
When this dumb terror shall rise to judge the world,
After the silence of the centuries?

20

25

30

35

40

45

More . . . greed: i.e.,
The figure eloquently
condemns the greed-
iness of the world.
portents: forewarnings
indicating a soon-to-
come calamity
seraphim: the highest
order of angels (see
Isa. 6:2)
Pleiades: a cluster of
stars

profaned: treated with
contempt or
irreverence

infamies: public
disgraces

Perfidious: treacherous
immedicable:
incurable

For Thought and Discussion

1. Who are responsible for the condition of the man with the hoe, according to the poem? Where is this question asked? Where is it answered?
2. Is the man with the hoe an individual or a representative figure? If the latter, of whom is he representative?
3. How has the man with the hoe been oppressed? What human capacities has he lost? What does the world have to fear of him?

4. Look up the term *rhetorical question*. What rhetorical questions appear in the poem?

5. What Biblical allusions appear in the poem? Do they imply a Christian view of mankind and the world? Comment on the poem's message in the light of Genesis 3:17-19.

William Sidney Porter
1862-1910

The author known as "O. Henry" (the most famous American pen name next to "Mark Twain") became an extremely popular writer during the first decades of the twentieth century. In fact, even today his work remains a favorite with many readers. His thoroughly American stories have been admired by French and English readers but especially by the Russians, who issued a commemorative stamp in 1962 on the centennial of his birth. The humor and compassion, mixed with the delightful surprise of his endings, make his work a sharp artistic contrast to the pessimistic works of the naturalists.

O. Henry was born William Sydney (later Sidney) Porter on September 11, 1862, in Greensboro, North Carolina. When fifteen, he left school to work with his pharmacist uncle and eventually became a licensed pharmacist himself. In 1882, because of ill health, Porter moved from North Carolina to Texas, where for two years he lived on a cattle ranch. Then for fours years he worked as a bookkeeper in Austin, Texas. In 1887 he married Athol Estes. Before his marriage Porter had been somewhat unsettled and apparently had felt little shame living off the generosity of friends, whom he charmed with his humor, sketching, and writing. After his marriage he settled down first as a draftsman in the Texas Land Office, then as a teller in the First National Bank of Austin.

Porter soon ran into financial trouble. His young wife became seriously ill after the difficult birth of a daughter in 1889. *The Rolling Stone,* a humorous weekly newspaper he had published for a year, failed. In 1894 Porter was accused of stealing bank funds. Although his friends posted bond and proclaimed his innocence, Porter's actions suggested otherwise. Two years later, when several indictments were issued against him, he skipped bond and fled to Honduras and then wandered through South America and Mexico. After several months he returned to Austin only when it became clear that his wife was soon going to die. Following her death, he was tried, found guilty, and sentenced to five years' imprisonment in the federal penitentiary in Columbus, Ohio.

While Porter awaited trial, he received word that his first story, "The Miracle of Lava Canyon," had been accepted for publication. During the next three years (he was released early for good behavior), he wrote more than a dozen stories published by national magazines. When he emerged from prison in 1901, he was a professional writer. He moved to New York City, where he quickly gained fame under the pseudonym "O. Henry," a name he supposedly borrowed from a guard at the Ohio Penitentiary, Orrin Henry. Editors were soon bidding for his stories, and Porter found himself busily writing to meet their demands. At his peak he produced an average of one story a week, writing quickly and revising little. His first book, *Cabbages and Kings* (1904), was a collection of short stories tied together to resemble a novel. In 1906 he published his most famous collection, *The Four Million,* whose title indicates the population of New York City at the time. These collections were followed by a dozen more.

Porter's last years were sad ones. Although he married his childhood sweetheart in 1907, the marriage was a failure. He had no close friends and, according to one biographer, died at the age of forty-eight, "a gentle, alienated, and lonely alcoholic."

Unlike much of the serious literature of the day, Porter's stories are not naturalistic. In fact, they refute many of the naturalists' pessimistic assumptions about life. While the naturalists insisted on revealing the "stark reality" that they believed defined life, Porter "lifted the veil from stark reality and showed the romance beneath it." In his well-known story "The Gift of the Magi," Porter details the poverty of a young couple. Only through costly sacrifice are the two able to give a gift to each other. Porter, however, does not stop with this couple's hardships but shows the beauty of their self-sacrificing love. Their positive, humane values thus shine out through the "stark reality" of their lives.

Porter's trademark is the surprise ending. Donald Heiney explains the way Porter used this device: "The trick in a typical O. Henry story consists in withholding an important piece of information from the readers as long as possible, so that only as he finishes the story does he fully understand the significance of the previous action." Both "The Gift of the Magi" and "The Ransom of Red Chief" illustrate Porter's talent in employing this literary device.

Porter's place in American literary history, it is true, is a relatively minor one. Critics list sentimentality, contrived endings, exaggerated characters, and shallowness among his artistic shortcomings. Oftentimes, Porter's stories only amuse. Nevertheless, as one critic remarks, Porter "knew precisely how much of the sugar of sentimentality the great average reading public must have, and how much of the pepper of sensation, and the salt of facts, and the salad dressing of romance." Further, Porter's stories convey many parts of reality that escape the naturalists: the

> humor, the incongruities, the possibility for success, the inviting reality of human life. Unfortunately they do not give insight into human life as it is described in God's Word.

The Gift of the Magi

This is one of the four million stories Porter thought could be written about the inhabitants of New York City. The story is also one of his most ingenious tales. Notice that he concentrates primarily on the development of the **plot.**

One dollar and eighty-seven cents. That was all. And sixty cents of it was in pennies. Pennies saved one and two at a time by bulldozing* the grocer and the vegetable man and the butcher until one's cheek burned with silent imputation* of parsimony* that such close dealing implied. Three times Della counted it. One dollar and eighty-seven cents. And the next day would be Christmas.

bulldozing: pressuring
imputation: the laying of guilt or fault: i.e., accusation
parsimony: stinginess

There was clearly nothing to do but flop down on the shabby little couch and howl. So Della did it. Which instigates* the moral reflection that life is made up of sobs, sniffles, and smiles with sniffles predominating.

instigates: urges to action

While the mistress of the home is gradually subsiding from the first stage to the second, take a look at the home. A furnished flat at eight dollars per week. It did not exactly beggar* description, but it certainly had that word on the lookout for the mendicancy squad.*

beggar: to make seem useless
mendicancy squad: police that pick up beggars

In the vestibule* below was a letter box into which no letter would go, and an electric button from which no mortal finger could coax a ring.

Also appertaining* thereunto was a card bearing the name "Mr. James Dillingham Young."

vestibule: lobby
appertaining: being part of

The "Dillingham" had been flung to the breeze during a former period of prosperity when its possessor was being paid thirty dollars per week. Now, when the income was shrunk to twenty dollars, the letters of "Dillingham" looked blurred, as though they were thinking seriously of contracting* to a modest and unassuming D. But whenever Mr. James Dillingham Young came home and reached his flat above he was called "Jim" and greatly hugged by Mrs. James Dillingham Young, already introduced to you as Della. Which is all very good.

contracting: shrinking

Della finished her cry and attended to her cheeks with the powder rag. She stood by the window and looked out dully at a gray cat walking a gray fence in a gray backyard. Tomorrow would be Christmas Day, and she had only one dollar and eighty-seven cents with which to buy Jim a present. She had been saving every penny she could for months, with this result. Twenty dollars a week doesn't go far. Expenses had been greater than she had calculated. They always are. Only one dollar and eighty-seven cents to buy a present for Jim. Her Jim. Many a happy hour she had spent planning for something nice for him. Something fine and rare and sterling*–something just a little bit near to being worthy of the honor of being owned by Jim.

---

sterling: of high quality

There was a pier glass* between the windows of the room. Perhaps you have seen a pier glass in an eight-dollar flat. A very thin and very agile* person may, by observing his reflection in a rapid sequence of longitudinal strips, obtain a fairly accurate conception of his looks. Della, being slender, had mastered the art.

---

pier glass: a long mirror
agile: quick of movement

Suddenly she whirled from the window and stood before the glass. Her eyes were shining brilliantly, but her face had lost its color within twenty seconds. Rapidly she pulled down her hair and let it fall to its full length.

Now there were two possessions of the James Dillingham Youngs in which they both took a mighty pride. One was Jim's gold watch that had been his father's and his grandfather's. The other was Della's hair. Had the Queen of Sheba* lived in the flat across the air shaft, Della would have let her hair hang out the window someday to dry, just to depreciate Her Majesty's jewels and gifts. Had King Solomon been the janitor, with all his treasures piled up in the basement, Jim would have pulled out his watch every time he passed, just to see him pluck at his beard from envy.

Queen of Sheba: the wealthy and beautiful queen who admired Solomon's wisdom and riches; see I Kings 10

So now Della's beautiful hair fell about her, rippling and shining like a cascade of brown waters. It reached below her knee and made itself almost a garment for her. And then she did it up again nervously and quickly. Once she faltered for a minute and stood still while a tear or two splashed on the worn red carpet.

On went her old brown jacket; on went her old brown hat. With a whirl of skirts and with the brilliant sparkle still in her eyes, she fluttered out the door and down the stairs to the street.

Where she stopped the sign read: "Mme. Sofronie. Hair Goods of All Kinds." One flight up Della ran–and collected herself, panting. Madame, large, too white, chilly, hardly looked the "Sofronie."

"Will you buy my hair?" asked Della.

"I buy hair," said Madame. "Take yer hat off and let's have a sight at the looks of it."

Down rippled the brown cascade.

"Twenty dollars," said Madame, lifting the mass with a practiced hand.

"Give it to me quick," said Della.

Oh, and the next two hours tripped by on rosy wings. Forget the hashed* metaphor. She was ransacking* the stores for Jim's present.

---

hashed: jumbled
ransacking: searching thoroughly

She found it at last. It surely had been made for Jim and no one else. There was no other like it in any of the stores, and she had turned all of them inside out. It was a platinum fob* chain simple and chaste* in design, properly proclaiming its value by substance alone and not by meretricious* ornamentation–as all good things should do. It was even worthy of The Watch. As soon as she saw it she knew that it must be Jim's. It was like him. Quietness and value–the description applied to both. Twenty-one dollars they took from her for it, and she hurried home with the eighty-seven cents. With that chain on his watch Jim might be properly anxious about the time in any company. Grand as the watch was, he sometimes looked at it on the sly on account of the old leather strap that he used in place of a chain.

---

fob: short chain for a pocket watch
chaste: plain
meretricious: gaudy, cheap

When Della reached home her intoxication* gave way a little to prudence* and reason. She got out her curling irons and lighted the gas and went to work repairing the ravages made by generosity added to love. Which is always a tremendous task, dear friends–a mammoth task.

intoxication: excitement
prudence: good judgment

Within forty minutes her head was covered with tiny, close-lying curls that made her look wonderfully like a truant* schoolboy. She looked at her reflection in the mirror long, carefully, and critically.

truant: absent from school without permission

"If Jim doesn't kill me," she said to herself, "before he takes a second look at me, he'll say I look like a Coney Island* chorus girl. But what could I do–oh! what could I do with a dollar and eighty-seven cents?"

Coney Island: an amusement park in New York

At seven o'clock the coffee was made and the frying pan was on the back of the stove hot and ready to cook chops.

Jim was never late. Della doubled the fob chain in her hand and sat on the corner of the table near the door that he always entered. Then she heard his step on the stair away down on the first flight, and she turned white for just a moment. She had a habit of saying little silent prayers about the simplest everyday things, and now she whispered, "Please, God, make him think I am still pretty."

The door opened and Jim stepped in and closed it. He looked thin and very serious. Poor fellow, he was only twenty-two–and to be burdened with a family! He needed a new overcoat and he was without gloves.

Jim stopped inside the door, as immovable as a setter at the scent of quail. His eyes were fixed upon Della; and there was an expression in them that she could not read, and it terrified her. It was not anger, nor surprise, nor disapproval, nor horror, nor any of the sentiments that she had been prepared for. He simply stared at her fixedly with that peculiar expression on his face.

Della wriggled off the table and went to him.

"Jim, darling," she cried, "don't look at me that way. I had my hair cut off and sold it because I couldn't have lived through Christmas without giving you a present. It'll grow out again–you won't mind, will you? I just had to do it. My hair grows awfully fast. Say 'Merry Christmas!' Jim, and let's be happy. You don't know what a nice–what a beautiful, nice gift I've got for you."

"You've cut off your hair?" asked Jim laboriously,* as if he had not arrived at that patent* fact yet even after the hardest mental labor.

laboriously: with great effort
patent: obvious

"Cut it off and sold it," said Della. "Don't you like me just as well, anyhow? I'm me without my hair, ain't I?"

Jim looked about the room curiously.

"You say your hair is gone?" he said with an air almost of idiocy.

"You needn't look for it," said Della. "It's sold, I tell you–sold and gone, too. It's Christmas Eve, boy. Be good to me, for it went for you. Maybe the hairs of my head were numbered," she went on with a sudden serious sweetness, "but nobody could ever count my love for you. Shall I put the chops on, Jim?"

Out of his trance Jim seemed quickly to wake. He enfolded his Della. For ten seconds let us regard with discreet* scrutiny some inconsequential object in the other direction. Eight dollars a week or a million a year–what is the difference? A mathematician or a wit would give you the wrong answer. The Magi* brought valuable gifts, but that was not among them. This dark assertion will be illuminated later on.

discreet: respectful, modest
Magi: the Wise Men

Jim drew a package from his overcoat pocket and threw it upon the table.

"Don't make any mistake, Dell," he said, "about me. I don't think there's anything in the way of a haircut or a shave or a shampoo that could make me like my girl any less. But if you'll unwrap that package you may see why you had me going awhile at first.''

White fingers and nimble tore at the string and paper. And then an ecstatic scream of joy; and then, alas! a quick feminine change to hysterical tears and wails, necessitating the immediate employment of all the comforting powers of the lord of the flat.

For there lay The Combs—the set of combs, side and back, that Della had worshiped for long in a Broadway window. Beautiful combs, pure tortoise shell, with jeweled rims—just the shade to wear in the beautiful vanished hair. They were expensive combs, she knew, and her heart had simply craved and yearned over them without the least hope of possession. And now they were hers, but the tresses that should have adorned the coveted adornments were gone.

But she hugged them to her bosom, and at length she was able to look up with dim eyes and a smile and say, ''My hair grows so fast, Jim!''

And then Della leaped up like a little singed* cat and cried, ''Oh, oh!''

singed: lightly burned

Jim had not yet seen his beautiful present. She held it out to him eagerly upon her open palm. The dull precious metal seemed to flash with a reflection of her bright and ardent* spirit.

ardent: enthusiastic

''Isn't it a dandy, Jim? I hunted all over town to find it. You'll have to look at the time a hundred times a day now. Give me your watch. I want to see how it looks on it.''

Instead of obeying, Jim tumbled down on the couch and put his hands under the back of his head and smiled.

''Della,'' said he, ''let's put our Christmas presents away and keep 'em awhile. They're too nice to use just at present. I sold the watch to get the money to buy your combs. And now suppose you put the chops on.''

The Magi, as you know, were wise men—wonderfully wise men—who brought gifts to the Babe in the manger. They invented the art of giving Christmas presents. Being wise, their gifts were no doubt wise ones, possibly bearing the privilege of exchange in case of duplication. And here I have lamely* related to you the uneventful chronicle of two foolish children in a flat who most unwisely sacrificed for each other the greatest treasures of their house. But in a last word to the wise of these days let it be said that of all who give gifts these two were the wisest. Of all who give and receive gifts, such as they are wisest. Everywhere they are wisest. They are the Magi.

lamely: weakly

For Thought and Discussion

1. What kind of irony is exemplified by the outcome? Explain.
2. Compare O. Henry's handling of the Youngs' disillusionment with what a naturalistic writer like Crane would have done with it.
3. The story reveals Della's plan while withholding information about the parallel plan of Jim. The story could just as well have been told in the reverse, with our knowing of Jim's intentions and not knowing Della's. If the story were written thus, would the conclusion have been as striking? Why or why not?

4. O. Henry's stories are generally considered only entertainment pieces. Is this story an exception? Does it make a moral point for the reader? If so, is the point stated and where does it appear?

5. What is the allusion in the title of the story?

Where is it mentioned in the story? What is the season of the year? Explain what the author means in the last two sentences. Do you agree?

6. Is there significance in the couple's surname? Is their behavior suitable to it and, if so, in a positive or negative way?

Fanny Crosby   1820-1915

The poems of Fanny Crosby are probably more familiar to Christians than poems of writers with more secure places in the American literary tradition. Called ''the mother of modern congregational singing,'' Mrs. Crosby (as she was popularly known) penned over eight thousand hymns as well as more than a thousand secular poems. For a hundred years songs like ''Pass Me Not,'' ''Rescue the Perishing,'' and ''Safe in the Arms of Jesus'' have been bringing the lost to Christ and comforting the saints. Her poems of joy and faith offer the strongest of all refutations to the bleak pessimism of the American naturalists.

Frances Jane Crosby was born March 24, 1820, to John and Mercy Crosby in a country community in New York. When she was only six weeks old, treatment for an eye infection scarred the corneas of her eyes and left her blind. Shortly thereafter her father died, and her mother began working to support the family. Her grandmother, determined to be eyes for the child, spent hours with her. She described to her the physical world and taught her to distinguish birds by their calls and trees by the feel of their leaves. Her grandmother also thoroughly trained the child in the Bible, helping her memorize many passages.

When five, the young girl learned from medical experts that she would be blind for the rest of her life. She never, however, thought of her blindness as a handicap. An active child, she climbed trees, rode horses bareback, and developed a reputation as a mischief-maker. When only eight, she composed her first poem, a short one on her blindness:

> Oh, what a happy child I am,
>   Although I cannot see!
> I am resolved that in this world
>   Contented I will be!
>
> How many blessings I enjoy
>   That other people don't!
> So weep or sigh because I'm blind
>   I cannot and I won't!

In the late 1820s she and her mother moved from New York to Connecticut. While her mother worked, the child was kept by Mrs. Hawley, their childless landlady, who took a special interest in the girl. Mrs. Hawley started teaching her to memorize large sections of the Bible, and within two years she had memorized the first five books of the Old Testament, the four Gospels, many of the Psalms, and all of Proverbs, Ruth, and the Song of Solomon.

By the time she entered her teen-age years, Fanny Crosby was well known for her musical talent (she sang and played the guitar), her horsemanship, her story-telling, and her poetry. At fifteen she entered New York City Institution for the Blind, where she remained for over twenty years, first as a student, then as a faculty member. She left in 1857 when she married Alexander Van Alstyne, another blind instructor and a brilliant musician.

While at this school, she first received recognition as "the blind poetess." From time to time students from the Institution toured the country to demonstrate their training and to raise support for the school. Besides singing and performing on the piano, organ, and harp (she was considered one of the best harpists of her time), she amazed audiences on these tours by reciting original poems composed just for the occasion.

In 1844 she published her first volume of poetry, *The Blind Girl and Other Poems*. Soon her poems were appearing regularly in publications like the *New York Herald* and the *Saturday Evening Post*. Although well known during her lifetime for these secular poems, Crosby did not begin the work for which she is remembered today until 1864, when she started writing hymns for William B. Bradbury and Company.

The religious environment of the post-Civil War years called for new qualities in congregational singing. During the revival of the late 1850s, the traditional somber, formal hymns had begun giving way to lighter, more melodic gospel songs. Since few song books were available, congregations needed songs more easily sung and remembered. William Bradbury soon discovered Crosby and asked her to compose words for his tunes. This association opened a new and rich means of service for her and led later to her working with other important hymn-writers like William H. Doane and Ira Sankey (Dwight L. Moody's song leader). Once she had begun writing hymns, she continued until her death in 1915 at the age of ninety-four.

Crosby composed her hymns in various ways. Sometimes she wrote a poem from a title or subject or even a phrase given to her. At other times she wrote a poem to fit a tune. Such was the case with one of her best-known hymns. When a friend, Mrs. Phoebe Knapp, played a hymn tune she had just composed, Crosby exclaimed, ''Why, that says 'Blessed Assurance'!'' The poet created her verses in her head, usually in the quiet of the night. She then dictated them the next day to a secretary. Her memory was phenomenal, for at least twice she mentally composed groups of forty poems before dictating them to her secretary.

Because of her enormous output, Fanny Crosby's poems sometimes lack high literary quality. One hymnologist describes her hymns as, ''with a few exceptions, very weak and poor, their simplicity and earnestness being their redeeming features.'' Her work undoubtedly suffered because she wrote so many hymns so quickly. She had little time for revision. Although she could have written poems of high literary worth, she likely chose to write simply for the sake of her audience. Her frequent allusions to Scripture, her use of both repetition and familiar phrases, and her appeals to the emotions were designed to speak to the hearts and minds of even the humblest singer or listener. Instead of seeking literary acclaim, she sought to serve the Lord by ministering to people's needs. George C. Stebbins, for whom she wrote many hymns, said, ''There was probably no writer in her day who appealed more to the varied experiences of the Christian life or who expressed more sympathetically the deep longings of the human heart than Fanny Crosby.''

Her life and goals thus dramatically differed from those of other American writers of this period. Although she had reason to be bitter and rebellious, she recognized her blindness as a blessing. ''I believe the greatest blessing the Creator ever bestowed on me,'' she said later in life, ''was when He permitted my external vision to be closed.'' Her wholehearted acceptance and joy had already been expressed in hymns such as ''All the Way My Saviour Leads Me,'' ''To God Be the Glory,'' and ''Praise Him! Praise Him!'' No one knows how many persons have experienced similar comfort and peace from these hymns. Fanny Crosby's poetry, it is true, does not receive high praise from literary critics. Worldly acclaim, however, mattered little to her, for her intention was never to receive the praise of men but to give praise to the Lord she unquestionably loved.

Pass Me Not

Pass me not, O gentle Saviour,
Hear my humble cry;
While on others Thou art calling,
Do not pass me by.

Let me at Thy throne of mercy   5
Find a sweet relief;
Kneeling there in deep contrition,
Help my unbelief.

Trusting only in Thy merit,
Would I seek Thy face;   10
Heal my wounded, broken spirit,
Save me by Thy grace.

Thou the Spring of all my comfort,
More than life to me;
Whom have I on earth beside Thee?   15
Whom in heaven but Thee?

Refrain:

Saviour, Saviour, hear my humble cry,
While on others Thou art calling,
Do not pass me by.

Draw Me Nearer

I am Thine, O Lord, I have heard Thy voice,
And it told Thy love to me;
But I long to rise in the arms of faith,
And be closer drawn to Thee.

Consecrate me now to Thy service, Lord,   5
By the pow'r of grace divine;
Let my soul look up with a steadfast hope,
And my will be lost in Thine.

O the pure delight of a single hour
That before Thy throne I spend;   10
When I kneel in pray'r, and with Thee, my God,
I commune as friend with friend!

There are depths of love that I cannot know
Till I cross the narrow sea;
There are heights of joy that I may not reach   15
Till I rest in peace with Thee.

Refrain:

Draw me nearer, nearer, blessed Lord,
To the cross where Thou hast died;
Draw me nearer, nearer, nearer, blessed Lord,
To Thy precious, bleeding side.

More like Jesus Would I Be

More like Jesus would I be,
Let my Saviour dwell in me;
Fill my soul with peace and love,
Make me gentle as a dove;
More like Jesus, while I go,   5
Pilgrim in this world below;
Poor in spirit would I be;
Let my Saviour dwell in me.

If He hears the raven's cry,
If His ever-watchful eye   10
Marks the sparrows when they fall,
Surely He will hear my call:
He will teach me how to live,

All my sinful thoughts forgive;
Pure in heart I still would be;   15
Let my Saviour dwell in me.

More like Jesus when I pray,
More like Jesus day by day;
May I rest me by His side,
Where the tranquil waters glide: 20
Born of Him, through grace renewed,
By His love my will subdued,
Rich in faith I still would be;
Let my Saviour dwell in me.

Christ Seats the Child in the Midst of the Disciples by Mattia Preti, called Il Cavaliere Calabrese From the Bob Jones University Collection

God of Eternity

God of eternity,
Saviour and King,
Help us to honor Thee,
Help while we sing;
Now may the clouds of night   5
Break into splendor bright
Jesus, our life and light,
Our Lord and King!

God of eternity,
Ancient of Days,   10
Glorious in majesty,
Author of Praise;
Hear Thou our earnest call,
While at Thy feet we fall,
Jesus, our all in all,   15
Our Lord and King!

God of eternity,
Ruler divine,
Strength of the mighty hills,
All power is Thine;   20
Boundless Thy reign shall be,
Wondrous Thy victory,
Earth shall be fill'd with Thee,
Our Lord and King!

God of eternity,   25
Love is thy name,
God of the earth and sea,
Thee we proclaim;
Love, thro' Thine only Son,
Thy work of grace hath done;   30
O blessed Three in One,
Our Lord and King!

All the Way My Saviour Leads Me

All the way my Saviour leads me;
What have I to ask beside?
Can I doubt His tender mercy,
Who thro' life has been my guide?
Heav'nly peace, divinest comfort,   5
Here by faith in Him to dwell!
For I know whate'er befall me,
Jesus doeth all things well.

All the way my Saviour leads me,
Cheers each winding path I tread,   10
Gives me grace for ev'ry trial,
Feeds me with the living bread:

Tho' my weary steps may falter,
And my soul athirst may be,
Gushing from the Rock before me,   15
Lo! a spring of joy I see.

All the way my Saviour leads me;
Oh, the fulness of His love!
Perfect rest to me is promis'd
In my Father's house above: 20
When my spirit, cloth'd immortal,
Wings its flight to realms of day,
This my song thro' endless ages:
Jesus led me all the way.

For Thought and Discussion

1. Explain the connection of Matthew 20:29-34 with "Pass Me Not." What other Biblical contexts might apply?
2. Which of Crosby's poems are prayers? Should they be sung as prayers? Is there Biblical support for using composed prayers? See Hosea 14:2 and Luke 11:1-4.
3. Notice the density of Biblical allusions and quoted phrases in "More Like Jesus Would I Be." Identify some of them.
4. To what extent is the order of the stanzas important in these poems? Are the stanzas interdependent? Is the next-to-last stanza always able to be omitted?
5. Notice the conversational simplicity of the poems. Would their impact have been greater had they used striking metaphors and fancy diction?

PART FOUR

Modern American Literature

An Era of Pessimism

For all practical purposes the modern period in American literature was born in a cold-blooded murder in central Europe. On June 28, 1914, a Serbian fanatic in Sarajevo, Yugoslavia, assassinated the crown prince of Austria. This act set in motion a series of political actions that plunged all Europe into war. The Central Powers (led by Austria-Hungary and Germany) were militarily eager and prepared for war. The Allies (notably Great Britain, France, and Russia) were reluctant to fight, however, and quite unprepared for military action. For three years, while the outcome of the conflict hung in the balances, the United States stayed out of the war.

In January 1917, however, Germany announced that its U-boats would begin unrestricted submarine attacks against all ships in the Atlantic. Faced with heavy losses of its unarmed merchant ships, a possible invasion from Mexico, and widespread German spy activity within the country, the United States could no longer remain neutral. On April 6, 1917, the nation declared war against Germany. From then until a truce was signed on November 11, 1918, American men and supplies poured overseas to aid the Allies. Although the country returned to an official policy of isolation after the war, it could not escape the effects of the Great War. In fact, this so-called "war to end all wars" started a flurry of events that have generated in most Americans, especially writers, a mood of deep-seated pessimism.

POST-WAR UPHEAVALS

The United States after World War I entered a period of social upheaval. The war itself was one of the most important agents of change. Another, according to numerous historians, was the increased mobility of Americans, a condition caused largely by the automobile. A third contributing cause has been the rise of modern communication, especially radio and television.

The Roaring Twenties

The first full decade after World War I–the decade known as the Roaring Twenties or the Jazz Age–brought widespread popularity to silent movies, radio, and the automobile. It also brought a period of grave political, moral, and economic irresponsibility. Although the United States had just fought a war to save the world for democracy, it now chose to ignore that world. National leaders pursued a policy of political isolationism. Americans, it seemed, wanted to forget the lesson of the recent war: that America's interests extend beyond American shores.

In a misguided search for freedom, Americans during the 1920s threw aside the moral guidelines of previous generations. The wild abandon of the decade's most popular dance, the Charleston, symbolized the behavior of many people. The national pastime became the pursuit of pleasure and wealth. The nation's shifting values appeared in the rising popularity of the flapper (a young woman who behaved and dressed unconventionally) and the bootlegger. Illegal liquor was manufactured and sold in open disregard of Prohibition, which had outlawed the manufacture, sale, and transportation of alcoholic liquors. As a result, the 1920s became a period of undisguised lawlessness. Gang leaders like Chicago's Al Capone ruled the big cities, raking in millions from liquor, prostitution, and extortion. Americans chose all too often to wink at police graft and political corruption. Not surprisingly, during this decade's pursuit of pleasure, church attendance fell to a low level.

The 1920s also featured a headlong rush by Americans to gain personal wealth. Caught up in the frantic Wall Street speculation, millions gambled their life savings on the stock market. A few made legitimate fortunes. Whereas in 1914 the nation had 4,500 millionaires, by 1926 it had 11,000. Land sales in Florida and California experienced spectacular booms. Like the rich farmer of Luke 12:16-20, the country was enjoying unprecedented prosperity.

The Depression Thirties

But with the suddenness of God's judgment against the rich fool, the frenzied upward economic spiral of the 1920s abruptly ended. On "Black Tuesday" (October 29, 1929) the bottom dropped out of the stock market. Frantic selling sent the stocks to new lows. Although the market attempted a feeble comeback in 1930, by the middle of 1932 even the most stable stocks had dropped to their lowest levels ever.

As the economy worsened, banks and businesses failed, and unemployment dramatically rose. Millions of people lost both their savings and their jobs. During the middle of the Depression, bread and soup lines stretched for blocks, armies of the unemployed insisted on having jobs, the New Deal programs which were put into operation by President Franklin Delano Roosevelt (1933-45) created huge relief agencies, and profound uneasiness about the American business system replaced the nation's earlier unbounded confidence. For many Americans the title of the popular Depression song "Brother, Can You Spare a Dime?" told the whole story.

Although the Depression was worldwide, Americans felt conditions especially keenly because of the prosperity of the previous decade. By 1935 one out of every six or seven Americans was on relief. The average annual income for a third of the American families was less than five hundred dollars (two hundred of which went for food). Annual income for the upper third in the nation averaged only slightly more than two thousand dollars. Even low prices were too steep for most Americans (a Plymouth automobile, for example, cost just over five hundred dollars in 1935). A Pittsburgh housewife at this time could buy a loaf of bread for ten cents, a pound of round steak for twenty-five, a quart of milk for twelve, and a pound of apples for five. Although the nation had experienced several depressions before, this one was unquestionably the worst. Only as the decade of the 1940s began did Americans see the return of prosperity.

World War II

Preoccupied with their economic woes, Americans in the 1930s ignored ominous events abroad. In 1931, for example, Japan invaded Manchuria. In 1935 Italy invaded Ethiopia. In 1936 Germany occupied the Rhineland. In 1937 Japan invaded China. In 1938 Germany seized Austria. In 1939 Germany seized Czechoslovakia and Italy seized Albania. Finally, on September 1, Germany invaded Poland. Two days later, because of treaty obligations to Poland, Great Britain and France declared war on Germany. Hitler's war machine, however, was not to be stopped. In a *blitzkrieg* (lightning war) the German army overran western Poland while the Russians (who had shortly before signed a nonaggression pact with Germany) attacked Poland from the east. In just four weeks Poland fell to these two aggressors.

After a six-month period called the "phony war," Germany opened war again in April 1940 by sweeping into Denmark and Norway. One month later Germany invaded the Lowlands. By late June, France also had fallen, but the Free French government had fled to North Africa and England. Hitler then launched a massive air attack against Great Britain, preparatory to invasion. Winston Churchill, the newly elected prime minister, expressed the courage and hope of the only unconquered nation in western Europe:

> We shall not flag or fail, we shall go on to the end, we shall fight in France, we shall fight on the seas and oceans, . . . we shall fight on the landing grounds, we shall fight in the fields and in the streets, we shall fight in the hills; we shall never surrender. And even if . . . this island . . . were subjugated and starving, then our Empire beyond the seas, armed and guarded by the British Fleet, would carry on the struggle, until, in God's good time, the new world, with all its power and might, steps forth to the rescue and liberation of the old.

The most important nation in "the new world," however, was still sharply divided over entering the war. Nevertheless, it served as the arsenal of democracy by sending planes, guns, ammunition, and vast quantities of supplies to war-torn Great Britain and other allies. As Italy and Japan also expanded their war fronts, the free world seemed in grave danger of falling captive to the totalitarian governments of Germany, Italy, and Japan. (In September 1940 these three nations had signed the Tripartite Pact, pledging all of them to declare war against nations attacking any one of the three.) By the end of June 1941 Russia was no longer allied with Germany, who in deliberate violation of the nonaggression pact had invaded the Soviet Union.

On December 7, 1941, all American debate over the involvement in the war suddenly ceased. Japan's attack against Pearl Harbor (which killed 2,403 and wounded 1,178) first stunned, then electrified America. As the United States entered the war, most of Europe and North Africa lay in the hands of the Germans and Italians while the Pacific was controlled by the Japanese. American men and arms, however, gradually changed the course of the war. While American servicemen distinguished themselves in some of the bloodiest battles of the war, American industry rose to the challenge of swiftly producing mountains of war materials.

By the time the fiercely waged war ended in 1945, it had cost the United States over three hundred billion dollars. Its cost in human lives was also staggering. Estimates place the total number of dead at twenty-two million and the wounded at thirty-four million. After the war the United States generously helped its former enemies to their feet. It poured money and materials into Germany and Japan, which have since become two of America's most important allies. But national leaders both during and immediately after the war made a monumental error in judgment: they trusted the Russians who eventually proved their desire not only to protect but to extend their communistic influence. In the resulting conflicts the United States assumed the role of protector of the free world.

Aftermath of World War II

Never again would the American attitude toward itself or the rest of the world be quite the same. Events within the United States have reflected a virtual social revolution in progress. World War II is largely responsible for introducing women into the work force, for stimulating the civil rights struggles by various minority groups, and for encouraging the moral revolution sweeping across the nation. What has especially affected the heart of the nation, however, is the fear of nuclear war. The A-bombs dropped in the final days of World War II released forces so devastating that the world has yet to lose its fear that this weapon might again be used. For nuclear warfare not only kills and maims its immediate victims but threatens generations yet unborn.

Since the dropping of the A-bomb in 1945, two events have tremendously complicated the world picture. First, the A-bomb has been replaced by the even more powerful H-bomb. Second, the United States no longer holds a monopoly on these weapons. As other nations have gained possession of nuclear secrets, the world has moved steadily nearer the brink of catastrophe. Many fear that the action of just one madman might trigger a nuclear holocaust.

Although the two decades immediately following the war brought prosperity to the American people, a deep uneasiness settled over the nation. Although man believed he controlled events, the war confirmed that he could not control himself. Despite the United Nations, man has remained powerless to bring world peace. The wars in Korea and Vietnam are only two of a number of regional conflicts that have broken out since World War II. Having abandoned belief in the Bible, modern man has often yielded to pessimism or embraced irrational hope. The pessimists, on the one hand, say that events have no meaning, that the world is simply chaotic, and therefore attempts to change things for the better are futile. The optimists, on the other hand, have frantically undertaken the burden of solving all mankind's problems. Their lack of success has seemed only to justify the pessimists' cynicism. Many Americans who do not know Christ have lost their traditional optimism and idealism, turned pessimistic, and given themselves over to despair.

INTELLECTUAL AGITATION

These political, economic, and social events have strongly affected American thought since World War I. At the root of modern American thought is the un-Biblical view of man's nature and calling. The Bible teaches that God made man "a little lower than the angels," "crowned him with glory and honour," gave him "dominion over" His creation, and "put all things under his feet" (Ps. 8:5-6). The Bible also teaches that because of man's sin all human righteousness is, in God's eyes, nothing more than "filthy rags" (Isa. 64:6). Thus man is not only the apex of God's creation but also a creature thoroughly depraved by his sinful nature and totally dependent on divine grace for his salvation. Leading American thinkers, rejecting the Biblical view of man, adopted either of two distortions. Some regarded man as merely an animal. Others reverenced him as God.

Debasement of Man

The modern debasement of man is largely due to the influence of Charles Darwin's *Origin of Species*. The theory of evolution, to which Darwin supposedly gave scientific support, portrays man as merely a higher form of animal. As a result, the evolutionist believes that man lacks an eternal soul desiring fellowship with God and needing salvation. The evolutionist also believes that immortality exists only in earthly accomplishments and in earthly descendants left after death. He thus denies man's hope of a future life. This pessimism about human nature and immortality, which underlies most post-World War I thought, has been furthered in the twentieth century by two evolutionary systems that profoundly debase the Biblical view of man.

Freudianism The theories of Sigmund Freud (1856-1939) became popular in the United States during the morally irresponsible 1920s. Since then Freudianism has shaped virtually all of the psychoanalytic theories about the human mind. What Freud taught grew out of Darwinian theory that man is merely an animal. Freudianism assumes that mankind's behavior is motivated almost solely by sexual desire. It declares that people should not deny their sexual urges if they wish to remain normal. Conscience, it says, is merely the result of social conditioning. As a result, Freudianism has encouraged people to throw off all moral restraint and free their inhibitions. It has made them believe that they are all right as they are and that their desires are acceptable. In essence, Freudianism debases human nature by portraying the subconscious (irrational human desire) as more powerful than the conscious (the rational). In Freudian thought man is merely an animal enslaved by animalistic urges. Since he can do no better, he is not responsible for his behavior and has no need to seek forgiveness from an almighty, holy God. Freudianism is obviously and thoroughly in conflict with Christian thought. Where the Bible counsels man to resist his evil desires, Freudianism counsels man to yield. This movement unquestionably contradicts the Bible's teaching about man's sinfulness (see Gen. 6:5; Jer. 23:17; Matt. 15:18-19; II Cor. 10:5).

As a result of its widespread acceptance, Freudianism has stimulated writers to study their characters' thoughts, dreams, and suppressed desires as a key to motivation. Modern stream-of-consciousness fiction (which consists of the random sequence of thoughts and sensations within the mind of the central character) is particularly indebted to Freudianism, for free association is a technique used by Freudian psychologists. This movement has also encouraged writers to emphasize sexual motivation in their characters. Consequently, modern writers often include

frankly sexual materials in their works, sometimes even glorifying the perverted.

Marxism While Freudianism dominated the 1920s, Marxism dominated the Depression years of the 1930s. During this decade Marxist thought became popular, even fashionable, among American writers. It also appealed to the more radical members of the working class (especially those in unions), to some of the nation's intellectuals, and even to leading liberal preachers who naively saw communism as an application of practical Christianity. Although few American writers remained true Marxists, most were strongly influenced by the dire economic conditions of the decade to accept the theory. What later disillusioned many of the Marxists is that under any brand of Marxism the individual loses his personal liberty. A Marxist society is inevitably a slave state. Clearly this brand of atheistic, evolutionary thought–despite its lofty claims of providing equality for the sexes and destroying class distinctions–reduces man to the status of a brute beast.

Marxism originated in the work of nineteenth-century German philosopher Karl Marx, the ''Father of Communism.'' According to Marx, history is a series of class struggles, the last stage of which is capitalism. Marx predicted that once capitalism toppled, an ideal classless society would emerge. Marx's predictions proved as inept as his historical observations. Throughout Eastern Europe and the Soviet Union, the Bolshevik brand of Marxism produced only tyranny and long bread lines. The popular revolutions in Eastern Europe in 1989 which overthrew long-standing communist regimes demonstrated that the Marxist system is economically, politically, and morally bankrupt.

Deification of Man

While Freudianism and Marxism, the offspring of evolution, were debasing the Biblical conception of man, the secularization of American society, fostered by industrial and technological progress, was encouraging Americans to think they did not need God. In particular, a modern movement called secular humanism has tried to replace God with man. This movement claims that because man actually directs the world, he has no need of God. Secular humanism is, in fact, a substitute religion, glorifying the creation rather than the Creator. Many developments in American education and society are directly traceable to the influence of this movement, whose beliefs have been publicly stated in two major documents.

Humanist Manifesto I The Humanist Manifesto of 1933, signed by thirty-four influential people in various fields, declares that ''science and economic change have disrupted the old beliefs.'' It adds that these beliefs ''have lost their significance and . . . are powerless to solve the problem of humans living in the Twentieth Century." According to this document, the world needs a new religion, one more responsive to the needs of modern man.

Its fifteen articles reveal its anti-Biblical bias. Among its declarations are these: (1) the universe is "self-existing and not created," (2) man is part of the evolutionary process, (3) man's nature is entirely physical, not separable into body and mind, (4) man is the product solely of his culture, (5) modern science has shown that there are no supernatural and no heaven or hell, (6) "religion consists of those actions, purposes, and experiences which are humanly significant," (7) the purpose for living is to help oneself achieve his full potential, (8) man should work toward improving society rather than preparing for heaven, (9) socialism is superior to capitalism, and (10) man should "endeavor to establish the conditions of a satisfactory life for all, not merely for the few." This document flaunts its rejection of the Bible and its foolish faith in man's ability to create a new world.

Humanist Manifesto II Forty years after the appearance of the first manifesto, another group of humanists issued Humanist Manifesto II. This document, they believed, more accurately speaks to modern society. Like the first manifesto, it deifies man in its rejection of Biblical truth and traditional Christianity: "While there is much that we do not know, humans are responsible for what we are or will become. No deity will save us; we must save ourselves." This document also argues that because of the "preciousness and dignity of the individual person," abortion, divorce, sexual perversion, and promiscuity should not be condemned. The signers imagine a world community with "a system of world law and a world order based on transnational [i.e., worldwide] federal government." They appeal for "men and women of good will" throughout the world to join them. They close with the call for "each person to become, in ideal as well as practice, a citizen of the world community."

This secular faith of the humanists has greatly affected modern thought. Their faith underlies the actions of social engineers in the federal government seeking to control American life and make a unified society. It prevails in the thoughts of most writers and other national spokesmen, especially those of the public media. It permeates the nation's textbooks and educational philosophy, particularly through the influence of John Dewey (1859-1952)—a signer of Humanist Manifesto I and the greatest single contributor to modern educational theory. It promotes the various economic, political, and religious attempts to solve international problems through the One-World movement. In short, like Satan's deception of Eve (Gen. 3:5), secular humanism has tempted modern man with the false promise of becoming like God.

RELIGIOUS TURMOIL

At the beginning of the post-World War I period, organized religion still exerted considerable influence on American society. It was, for instance, largely because of pressure by churches and various religious groups that Congress enacted Prohibition. The movement for prohibiting the sale of liquor had begun almost immediately after the Civil War. With the formation of the Anti-Saloon League in 1895 (the National Temperance Society had begun in 1865, the Women's Crusade in 1873, and the Women's Christian Temperance Union in 1874), the movement gained enough power to make Prohibition a national law.

In 1917, the same year that the United States entered World War I, Congress passed the Eighteenth Amendment, which prohibited the manufacture, sale, and transportation of alcoholic liquors. This amendment, after ratification by the required number of states, took effect in January 1920. For a short while it dramatically reduced national consumption of alcohol. But skillful propagandizing by the liquor industry and growing disregard of Prohibition by millions of Americans made the law ineffective. Smugglers carried contraband liquor into the country from Mexico, Canada, and Cuba. Rumrunners in fast boats brought it in from ships anchored just beyond the country's three-mile territorial limits. Moonshiners manufactured home-made brew in stills located in the Appalachian Mountains as well as in attics and basements from New York City to San Francisco. Americans not wishing to encourage the growth of organized crime even made "bathtub" gin in their own homes. When the nation's unhappiness with the Eighteenth Amendment finally forced its repeal in 1933, those religious organizations that earlier had pushed for Prohibition suffered a considerable loss of influence.

Forces Outside Protestantism

The fate of Prohibition was only one symptom of the nation's weakening religious life. Other forces both during Prohibition and afterwards have affected religious attitudes in the United States. Certainly the false view of man taught by Freudians, Marxists, and secular humanists has contributed to the decline of religious belief, a decline further encouraged by the nation's deepening unconcern about spiritual matters and the people's increasing hunger for wealth. Assisting these secular forces have been two major *religious* forces, both of which strongly oppose the nation's Protestant beliefs.

Roman Catholicism During the early twentieth century, the Roman Catholic church greatly increased in power in the United States. Before immigration laws in the 1920s began limiting the "new immigration," millions of Catholics from Mediterranean countries had poured into the country, especially into the large Eastern and Midwestern cities. As the number of Catholics grew, the church gained more influence and prestige. In 1928 the stigma of being a Roman Catholic denied the presidency to Al Smith, the Democratic four-term governor of New York. But in 1960 the stigma was gone, for Americans elected John F. Kennedy as their first Catholic president. With its new respectability Roman Catholicism has become an important influence in education through its extensive private school system. On the religious scene its influence has been felt in the ecumenical movement. Since Vatican Council II (1962-64) Roman Catholic leaders have opened dialogue with liberal Protestants in the hopes of undoing the work of the Protestant Reformation. Through its influence in politics and the media, modern Roman Catholicism has

MORMON TEMPLE

become, in fact, the nation's most powerful religious force.

Cults Many Americans, disillusioned with traditional organized religion, have turned to other forms of belief to fill their spiritual void. The Mormons (Church of Jesus Christ of Latter-day Saints) and Jehovah's Witnesses have staked out considerable territory especially in the western United States and in the lower economic brackets respectively. Sun Myung Moon's Unification Church has also attracted a large following. Religions such as these deny the Christian doctrines necessary for salvation but still claim to give inner peace and a purpose for living. Interest among Americans in nontraditional religions has, in addition, stimulated the growth of radical sects. The development of the New Age movement is one example. Another example is the development of certain communes where drug-induced hallucinations become a counterfeit way to God. This interest has also enticed Americans to worship cultic leaders like Jim Jones, who in 1979 compelled nearly one thousand of his followers to commit mass suicide in Guyana. All these false versions of true religion and worship contribute to the growing theological anarchy of a nation whose people do merely what seems right in their own eyes (see Judges 17:6; 21:25).

Forces Within Protestantism

Liberalism Within American Protestantism, theological liberalism has steadily undermined the nation's religious inheritance. By definition liberalism is ''the opinion that an individual, or a new generation, ought to have liberty to question and reject orthodox doctrines and dogmas if these seem contrary to reason or morality . . . and to apply ordinary historical methods to the Bible.'' Liberalism claims the right to distinguish ''the permanent and central values of inherited orthodoxy'' from its outmoded beliefs and to use these values ''in meeting the needs of a modern world.'' Liberalism thus attempts to accommodate traditional Christianity to a godless, modern view of the world. In fact, it deliberately elevates man's mind over God's. For whenever a conflict arises between the modern mind and the Bible, the Bible, in liberal thinking, always bows to the modern mind.

The most popular liberal preacher of the twentieth century was Harry Emerson Fosdick (1878-1969). This Baptist minister exerted great influence on the nation through his preaching (at New York City's prestigious Riverside Church), his professorship at Union Theological Seminary, and his extensive writing (especially in his notorious *The Modern Use of the Bible*). Because of the false teaching of this man and others, thousands of Americans have accepted liberalism's version of Christianity.

The spiritual deadness of liberalism has contributed to the rise of two counter-movements since the early 1920s. One of these is Neo-Orthodoxy, which was strongly influential in the 1930s. This movement began in Europe as a theological reaction by Karl Barth (1886-1986) against the spiritual coldness of liberalism. Neo-Orthodoxy emphasizes "the transcendence of God . . . but with a new conviction that God's self-revelation must be interpreted afresh." In other words, where liberalism reduces the Bible to just another religious book and through disbelief tears page after page from it, Neo-Orthodoxy acknowledges the Bible to be God's Word—when it speaks to the reader! This view, of course, falls short of God's view of His Word. For the Bible is God's message to mankind regardless of whether the reader accepts the message.

Another significant movement within liberalism is the heretical death-of-God school. Active since the early 1960s, the death-of-God theologians have tried to retain the values of Christianity while accepting atheism and agnosticism as valid beliefs too. These theologians, in fact, have established a theology for a God that they believe either does not exist or is unknowable. They have thus a secular theology. This movement systematizes the practical atheism of many Americans who live as though they do not believe in the existence of God anyway.

Fundamentalism Yet, in spite of the power of American liberalism, there has remained a remnant that believes in God's Word and fights for its truth. Often accused of being unscientific, unscholarly, and even unloving, this remnant has, since the end of World War I, found itself locked in an open battle against the various forms of liberalism. As conservatives within the major denominations battled during the 1920s for the fundamental truths of God's Word, they became known as fundamentalists. Their battle within the denominations was virtually over before it began. The liberals controlled the denominational machinery, the colleges and seminaries, the mission boards, and the publishing houses. The only course of action left for fundamentalists was separation from their denominations even though withdrawal meant for many preachers the loss of pensions and prestige.

During the 1920s and 1930s, the most scholarly spokesman for fundamentalism was J. Gresham Machen (1881-1937), a Presbyterian who taught at Princeton Seminary for twenty-three years. Machen, who became the leading defender of the conservative position lays bare the nature of liberalism in his book *Christianity and Liberalism* (1923). Machen describes it as both "un-Christian" and "unscientific." He explains that "the liberal attempt at reconciling Christianity with modern science has really relinquished everything distinctive of Christianity, so that what remains is . . . only that same indefinite type of religious aspiration which was in the world before Christianity came upon the scene." In other words, liberalism is only a modern form of the paganism of Christ's day.

Machen was only one of several major fundamentalists of the early modern period. Noted preachers like T. T. Shields (1873-1955), W. B. Riley (1891-1947), and J. Frank Norris (1877-1952) were important leaders of the movement. Since the 1920s, fundamentalist churches and pastors have banded together in organizations like the Baptist Bible Fellowship (BBF), the General Association of Regular Baptists (GARB), and the Independent Fundamental Churches of America (IFCA). Others have created new denominations like the Bible Presbyterians. In 1927 evangelist Bob Jones (1883-1968) founded what has become the country's most famous fundamentalist institution of higher learning, Bob Jones University. This school has consistently stood for the tenets of fundamentalism, strengthening the faith of students rather than stripping it from them.

As fundamentalists have turned to the task of evangelizing the nation, their ranks have repeatedly been thinned by compromise and broken by peripheral issues. The temptations to ignore necessary distinctions and to make unnecessary ones have threatened the movement's strength and unity of purpose. As the nation has turned further and further away from God's truth, faithful fundamentalists have become more conspicuous. For when everyone else bows to the ground, those left standing appear in stark contrast to those surrounding them (see Dan. 3:8-12).

Representation Within Religious Fiction

Popular modern fiction treating religious matters reflects the nation's attitude toward Christianity. Although religious novels have ignored the religious controversies, they have absorbed the spirit of the age. During the period from 1931 to 1943, the yearly best-seller lists invariably included at least one religious work. Some of these advance purely rationalistic explanations for Biblical miracles. For instance, one best seller describes Paul's blindness (Acts 9:3,8) as temporarily caused by the unusually bright sunshine reflected from the golden dome of the temple of Damascus.

The Robe, one of the most popular religious novels of the twentieth century, portrays several key liberal notions. In this novel Lloyd Douglas (1877-1951), a former Lutheran clergyman, tells the story of the Roman soldier Marcellus and his Greek slave Demetrius. The robe to which the title refers is the one Jesus wore, the one gambled for at the foot of the cross (John 19:23-24). This robe, possessing mysterious powers, nearly destroys Marcellus's sanity when this drunken soldier puts it on. Later it heals his troubled mind and changes his life. Inspired by the robe, he then helps transform a village of surly melon pickers to warm, loving people. None of these villagers, however, experience the Bible's picture of salvation, the new birth. At the end of the novel, Marcellus and his new bride, Diana, go bravely to martyrdom at the hands of the cruel Roman emperor Caligula. In this final scene Marcellus envisions a new kingdom on earth where humans are in right relation to each other, a kingdom of love and peace—in short, merely the earthly kingdom sought by those preaching the social gospel.

Quite different is the satirical novel *Elmer Gantry,* whose author, Sinclair Lewis (1885-1951), became in 1930 the first American to receive the Nobel Prize in literature. In *Elmer Gantry* Lewis launches a biting attack against American religion, finding it shot through and through with hypocrisy. The protagonist of this novel, for instance, gets ahead religiously through deceit and sensationalist tactics. His lying, adulteries, drinking, and con artistry help him advance in the various organizations for which he preaches.

Even more damaging to the religious establishment it attacks is the story of its composition. Lewis, while researching organized religion firsthand, met weekly in Kansas City with a group of the city's prominent liberal ministers. This group included a Roman Catholic priest, a rabbi, and the city's chief agnostic. Lewis preached in local churches and carefully investigated both the public and private lives of all the local clergymen. In his weekly meetings, publicized as "Sinclair Lewis's Sunday School Class," he listened to the ministers talk, argued theological points with them, and deliberately baited them with questions. He also provided liquor to loosen their tongues. Although these ministers were greatly angered by their fictional representation, Lewis apparently pictured accurately what he saw. The result is a novel that savagely denounces conditions within American religion, for Lewis portrays atheistic churchmen on all ecclesiastical levels serving only themselves and their earthly ambitions.

LITERARY FERMENT

It is not surprising that the modern writer has been affected by the spirit of his age. He typically does not hold anything to be absolute, that is, unconditional or certain. He questions all philosophical and religious beliefs, even the validity of his own experience. Furthermore, he has little respect for traditional literary forms. Few modern writers have remained traditional in both form and theme. Most have borrowed freely from various literary experiments of their time. Such short-lived experimental groups as the imagists of the 1910s and the Beat Poets of the 1950s have influenced contemporary poetry. The popularity of the narrative technique known as stream-of-consciousness and the vogue of the antihero have altered modern fiction.

While almost all literature mirrors human life, the modern writer so rigorously imitates life that he rejects virtually all restrictions. Reasoning that he should fully record what people actually do and think, he tends to portray all actions no matter how vile and all words and thoughts no matter how crude or blasphemous. It is not uncommon for writers of serious literature to challenge moral conventions by including in their work elements of the pornographic (from Gk. *pornographos,* writing about prostitutes: i.e., writing intended to excite lustful feelings). The spirit of the age–especially disbelief in God, cynical pessimism, and the resulting despair–dominates modern literature. Perhaps no other period in history has laid so bare the soul of men deliberately cut off from God.

Crisis of Belief

The moral and religious attitude underlying modern literature is rebellion. By rebelling against past values and beliefs but particularly against the God of their fathers, modern American writers have experienced a "crisis of belief." A recent critic identifies basic categories in literary responses to this modern crisis: (1) "Despair," (2) "Escapism" (into either primitivism or aestheticism), (3) the adopting of "Substitute religions" such as humanism or the "worship of the Life Force, whether in Earth, Sea, or Woman," (4) a "Retreat into the Self," and (5) an "Open Door Policy" that rejects absolute knowledge in favor of mere belief. As a consequence of their rebellion, modern writers attempt to find meaning for human existence in their own or in others' subjective interpretations of life.

The modern literary spirit grew out of the influence exercised by writers maturing during World War I. This generation of American authors eagerly entered the war, motivated by high ideals. Some volunteered for service with Italian or French units before the United States declared war. Others enlisted immediately after the nation entered the war in 1917. Their experiences during World War I, especially their nearness to death, caused them to re-examine the beliefs and values taught them by their parents and society. Their contact with like-minded writers and with European literary attitudes also forced them to re-evaluate their own literary principles. As a result, modern American literature differs in form and content from the mainstream of earlier American writing. It also differs in philosophical assumptions and literary attitudes. The most important decades for shaping this modern spirit were the 1920s and 1930s.

The Lost Generation

Many American writers in the 1920s chose the life of an expatriate (lit., one not living in his native land). Most settled in France, where their attitudes and activities earned them the name "the lost generation." Others lived in Italy, Germany, England, and even Mexico. These writers fled their homeland because they believed that the American spirit was destructive to the creative imagination. They particularly disliked the nation's materialism. They also disliked what they called its "puritanism," a term that came to describe anything they objected to, especially in moral or social attitudes and in literary criticism.

The outspoken leader of the attack against the so-called puritanism was H. L. Mencken (1880-1956), a Baltimore journalist and historian of the English language. Called the most influential private citizen in the United States, Mencken savagely caricatured puritanism as "the haunting fear that somewhere, somebody might be happy." He fiercely attacked anyone who advocated traditional moral restraints. Mencken's belief in total freedom of thought and expression led him to ridicule the 1925 Scopes Trial in Tennessee. In this trial a high-school science teacher was found guilty of defying state law against the teaching of evolution and was given a token fine. Thus Mencken (to whom Sinclair Lewis dedicated *Elmer Gantry*), speaking for many Americans in his time, openly repudiated the nation's inherited system of values and beliefs.

Writers of the 1920s expressed their revolt in two basic ways. One form was *bohemianism*, an indulgence in unconventional lifestyles. The center for this expression of their rebellion was New York City's Greenwich Village. Here writers, artists, and others displayed the intensity of their hatred for traditional morality by experimenting with various forms of moral license. Writers of the 1920s also revolted against the status quo by their political *radicalism*, the result of their special revulsion for American capitalism, which they believed responsible for all the ills of American business and society. Many of the radicals went beyond socialism to become Communists. The destruction of private ownership, many of them naively believed, would actually cure the problem caused in reality by man's depraved nature.

This open rebellion by writers of the twenties set an example for later American writers, who in turn have helped shape the attitudes of the public. Having rebelled against Christianity and its promise of heaven or hell, writers lived only for the fleeting moment. They therefore had to live intensely. Embracing the myth of experience, some writers believed that they had to experience in person whatever they wrote about. Moreover, writers of this decade rejected the past. Many revolted against family and church, some against small-town life and its traditional values, others against conventional forms (although E. A. Robinson and Robert Frost both resisted this trend), a few even against life itself by choosing suicide as preferable to living.

The literary work of the 1920s that most precisely and memorably defines the spirit of the decade is an experimental poem entitled "The Waste Land." In this work T. S. Eliot (1888-1965), an American expatriate in London, used images of dryness, brokenness, and desolation to portray the spiritual sterility of modern Western life. Eliot describes modern society as both a physical and spiritual wasteland. Unlike his fellow writers, Eliot came to accept Christianity as the only answer to the spiritual vacuum in modern life. In fact, his drama and poetry following "The Waste Land" are dominated by religious symbols. Most other American writers, however, made art their religion. To them only the aesthetic held eternal value.

The Social Idealists

Like most writers, those of the 1930s turned a critical eye on their age. They concentrated, however, on current social issues. They looked for what they believed should characterize American life and could not find it. They contrasted what seemed to them the realities of American society with what seemed to them the ideal. As a result, they became social activists in their writings. Some approached social problems as naturalists, emphasizing strong deterministic forces within society. Others approached problems in Marxist terms, prescribing the removal of the conflicts between the economic classes. Few American Marxist writers, however, remained enchanted with Communist thought after the decade ended.

Perhaps one of the thirties' most representative novels of social awareness is *The Grapes of Wrath* (1939). Its author, John Steinbeck (1902-68), received a Pulitzer Prize in 1940 for the novel and the Nobel Prize in 1962 for his entire body of work. Steinbeck's *Grapes of Wrath* grew out of the agricultural disaster in the 1930s known as the Dust Bowl. From 1933 to 1939 an area comprised of southwestern Kansas, southeastern Colorado, northeastern New Mexico, and the panhandles of Texas and Oklahoma experienced severe drought. Wind whipped up dry soil, creating sand dunes thirty feet high in places and burying roads, fences, and even houses. Parts of the Dust Bowl suffered a sixty per cent loss of population in the late 1930s.

The Grapes of Wrath tells the story of the Joad family, Oklahoma sharecroppers forced to flee the Dust Bowl because of the drought and increased mechanization of farming. Accompanied by Jim Casy (an ex-preacher who spreads his own brand of humanistic religion), the Joads head in their somewhat dilapidated truck for California. Along the road they experience the fierce hatred of others for being displaced, poverty-stricken Okies. They also direct their own fierce hatred toward the representatives of the middle class who pass them on the highway. Among the narrative chapters of this panoramic novel, Steinbeck inserts essays on the changes sweeping over the country. He thus connects the Joad story with national change. Steinbeck's moral view appears in words uttered by Jim Casy: "There ain't no sin and there ain't no virtue. There's just stuff people do. It's all part of the same thing. And some of the things folks do is nice, and some ain't nice, but that's as far as any man got a right to say." This passage fittingly summarizes the subjective morality of the whole modern age.

Caught up in struggles they only faintly understand, various members of the Joad family fall away. Once in California, the family unit, which has been held together by Ma Joad, seems about to disintegrate. Near the end of the novel, Tom Joad (an ex-convict who earlier had served a term for murder) kills the deputy sheriff who had killed Jim Casy as he led a group of striking farm workers in California. When Ma Joad worries aloud to her son Tom that he will likely be killed in return, Tom says: "Then it don't matter. Then I'll be aroun' in the dark. I'll be ever'where—wherever you look. Whenever they's a fight so hungry people can eat, I'll be there. Wherever they's a cop beating up a guy, I'll be there. If Casy knowed, why, I'll be in the way guys yell when they're mad an'—I'll be in the way kids laugh when they're hungry an' know supper's ready. An' when our folks eat the stuff they raise an' live in the houses they build—why I'll be there." Tom's reply defines not just the crusading spirit of *The Grapes of Wrath* but also that of the 1930s, a decade preoccupied with social issues.

Clearly the foundation of modern American literature lies in the 1920s and 1930s. Since then Americans, losing much of their former confidence, have learned fear. Two forms of futility appear in the literature since World War I. One has been a withdrawal into a fearful pessimism aggravated by threats of communistic infiltration, economic collapse, and unstable political conditions abroad. The other reaction has been an abandonment to living just for the moment, taking no thought of the past or of the future. American writers of the latter sort, reflecting the values of most Americans, echo the age-old cry of foolish man: "Let's eat, drink, and be merry, for tomorrow we may die."

The book of Judges seems all too prophetic of the United States in the post-World War I period. If any one passage speaks of the nation's plight, it is this: "They chose new gods; then was war in the gates" (Judges 5:8). Americans have taken "new gods" in their pursuit of modern answers to life's age-old problems. They have followed new religions like Freudianism, Marxism, secular humanism, or the purely private secular and religious ideas of the day. The resulting war within the American spirit—restless, rebellious, self-betrayed—is likely only the first stage of "war at the gates." Christians, however, need not fear. For they can enjoy the peace that comes from a personal knowledge of the Creator and faith in His Word, which is "for ever . . . settled in heaven" (Ps. 119:89).

12 Modern American Poetry

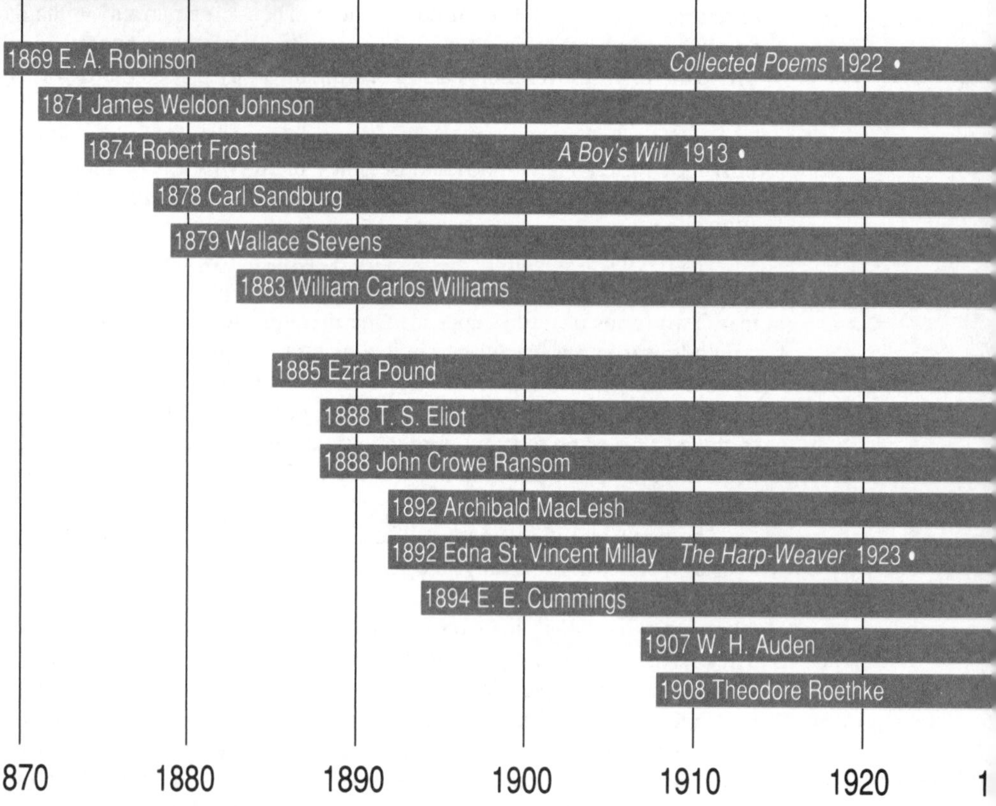

1914

World War I 1914 ☐ 1918

United States' entrance into World War I 1917 •

Prohibition 1919 ☐

Nineteenth Amendment (women's suffrage) 1920 •

Scopes Trial 1925 •

Lindbergh's historic flight from New York to Paris 1927 •

Stock market crash 19

1869 E. A. Robinson   *Collected Poems* 1922 •

1871 James Weldon Johnson

1874 Robert Frost   *A Boy's Will* 1913 •

1878 Carl Sandburg

1879 Wallace Stevens

1883 William Carlos Williams

1885 Ezra Pound

1888 T. S. Eliot

1888 John Crowe Ransom

1892 Archibald MacLeish

1892 Edna St. Vincent Millay   *The Harp-Weaver* 1923 •

1894 E. E. Cummings

1907 W. H. Auden

1908 Theodore Roethke

1870   1880   1890   1900   1910   1920   1

The Present

Modern American Literature

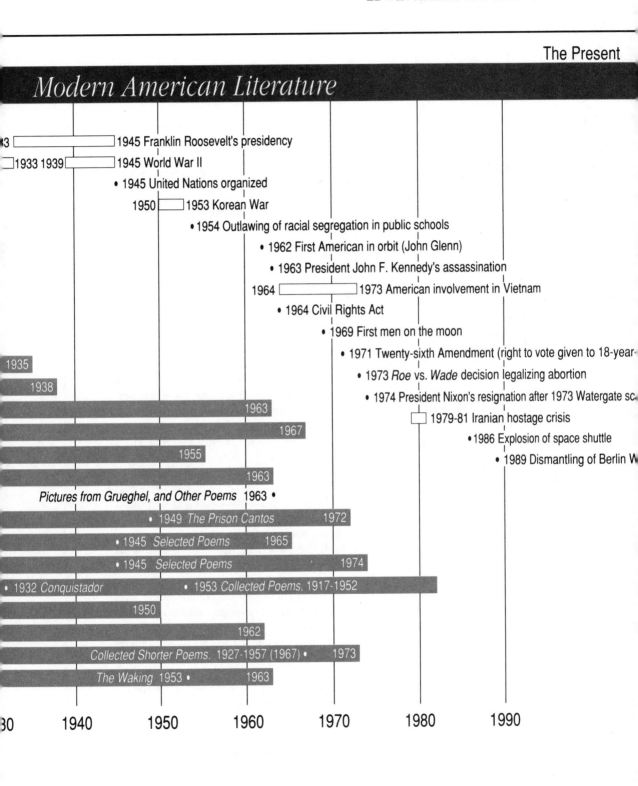

43 ☐ 1945 Franklin Roosevelt's presidency

☐ 1933 1939 ☐ 1945 World War II

• 1945 United Nations organized

1950 ☐ 1953 Korean War

• 1954 Outlawing of racial segregation in public schools

• 1962 First American in orbit (John Glenn)

• 1963 President John F. Kennedy's assassination

1964 ☐ 1973 American involvement in Vietnam

• 1964 Civil Rights Act

• 1969 First men on the moon

• 1971 Twenty-sixth Amendment (right to vote given to 18-year-

• 1973 *Roe* vs. *Wade* decision legalizing abortion

• 1974 President Nixon's resignation after 1973 Watergate sc

☐ 1979-81 Iranian hostage crisis

• 1986 Explosion of space shuttle

• 1989 Dismantling of Berlin W

1935

1938

1963

1967

1955

1963

Pictures from Grueghel, and Other Poems 1963 •

• 1949 *The Prison Cantos* 1972

• 1945 *Selected Poems* 1965

• 1945 *Selected Poems* 1974

• 1932 *Conquistador* • 1953 *Collected Poems, 1917-1952*

1950

1962

Collected Shorter Poems, 1927-1957 (1967) • 1973

The Waking 1953 • 1963

30 1940 1950 1960 1970 1980 1990

Traditionalists

Edwin Arlington Robinson
1869-1935

The poetry of Edwin Arlington Robinson is representative of both the nineteenth and the twentieth centuries. Robert Frost, his New England countryman, summarized Robinson's poetic career by stating that ''Robinson stayed content with the old-fashioned way to be new.'' Uneasy in either century, Robinson combined traditional form with modern themes.

Born just four years after the Civil War, Robinson was distantly related to the first American poet, Anne Bradstreet. Early in life he sensed that his destiny was to write poetry. His feelings toward becoming a poet, however, were mixed. He recalled later that in 1890, when twenty-one, ''I realized finally . . . that I was doomed, or elected, or sentenced for life, to the writing of poetry. . . . I kept the grisly secret to myself. . . . My father died–two years later–without suspecting it.''

The sense of tragedy that darkens many of Robinson's poems was born in his youthful experience in Gardiner, Maine (the model for his fictional Tilbury Town). Like his characters, the poet suffered from family problems and personal frustration. His parents, who apparently favored his two older brothers, gave him little encouragement to enter a writing profession. A local doctor, however, taught him meter and, with others, served as a sympathetic audience for Robinson's early work.

After two years at Harvard as a special student (1891-93) and four more back in Gardiner, Robinson moved to New York City, where he lived for the rest of his life. In 1896 he published at his own expense his first volume of poetry, *The Torrent and the Night Before*. During the next year appeared his second, *The Children of the Night,* also published at his own expense. These two collections along with *Captain Craig* (1902) so impressed Theodore Roosevelt that (unlike any other president) he wrote an article on the poet and (like other presidents) arranged a governmental position for him. But Robinson found himself unable to write under the requirements of a regular job. After working from 1905 to 1910 in the New York Custom House, he gave up the position. Until the mid-1920s, when the sale of his poetry finally began supporting him, he lived off the generosity of friends.

From 1911 on, Robinson spent his summers at the MacDowell Colony in Peterborough, New Hampshire. Surrounded by writers, artists, and musicians, he wrote most of his poetry here. During the other months of the year, the unmarried poet tried to relieve the poverty and barrenness of his life by heavy drinking. After the early 1920s he produced mostly long narratives in **blank verse.** Some of the most popular of these were written about members of King Arthur's famed Round Table.

In the last years of his life, Robinson reaped numerous honors. He received, for instance, three Pulitzer Prizes (1922, 1925, 1928). His book-length poem *Tristram* (1927) became a best seller. All together, he published over a dozen volumes of poetry, a total of fifteen hundred pages. Shortly before his death in 1935, Robinson declared to a friend: "I could never have done *anything* but write poetry."

According to most critics, Robinson's best work is the short, revealing sketches of painfully isolated people. In writing these sketches, Robinson turned to traditional forms. Unlike most modern poets, he wrote in **rhyme** and **meter** and depended on the **sonnet** and **quatrain.** Yet, like most modern poets, Robinson wrote of human failure. He portrayed his characters as victims of a narrow, repressive environment. His poems explore what goes on inside the characters, who invariably are failures. Some, like Miniver Cheevy, experience neither outward nor inward success. Others, like Richard Cory, enjoy outward success but are inwardly empty and hopeless. Still others appear outwardly as failures but are inwardly successful.

Stung by a critic's description of Robinson's early poetic world as a "prison house," the poet replied that he wrote of a world that is "a kind of spiritual kindergarten where bewildered infants are trying to spell God with the wrong blocks." Robinson sometimes softened his description of the human condition by implying the coming of some type of redeeming "Light." This light was his only answer to the question "What is the meaning of life?" In his verse he defined the light variously as the Grail or as love itself or as "the light behind the stars." This visionary notion associates Robinson with the twentieth-century rejection of "the true Light, which lighteth every man that cometh into the world" (John 1:9).

Like his New England predecessor Sarah Orne Jewett, Robinson drew on childhood experience for his setting and characters. Unlike Jewett, he concentrated on the negative side of human existence. Robinson peered into the human soul and found darkness, not light. Although his verse yields truths about modern man, it offers little guidance for modern life.

Miniver Cheevy

Miniver Cheevy is a failure in his own eyes as well as in the eyes of others. A romantic dreamer, he is a misfit in Tilbury Town. Although he lives in an imaginary world of the past, his motives and values are closely tied to the present.

Miniver Cheevy, child of scorn,
    Grew lean while he assailed* the seasons;
He wept that he was ever born,
    And he had reasons.

Miniver loved the days of old   5
    When swords were bright and steeds were prancing;
The vision of a warrior bold
    Would set him dancing.

Miniver sighed for what was not,
    And dreamed, and rested from his labors;   10
He dreamed of Thebes* and Camelot,*
    And Priam's* neighbors.

Miniver mourned the ripe renown*
    That made so many a name so fragrant;
He mourned Romance, now on the town,*   15
    And Art, a vagrant.*

Miniver loved the Medici,*
    Albeit* he had never seen one;
He would have sinned incessantly*
    Could he have been one.   20

Miniver cursed the commonplace
    And eyed a khaki suit* with loathing;
He missed the mediaeval grace
    Of iron clothing.*

Miniver scorned the gold he sought,   25
    But sore annoyed was he without it;
Miniver thought, and thought, and thought,
    And thought about it.

assailed: attacked verbally

Thebes: an ancient Greek city / *Camelot:* the legendary town where King Arthur had his court
Priam's: the King of Troy in Greek mythology
renown: fame
on . . . town: i.e., on public assistance or welfare
vagrant: tramp
Medici: a powerful Italian family that dominated Florence during the Renaissance
Albeit: even though
incessantly: unceasingly: i.e., he would have constantly sinned by participating in the debauchery of this notorious family.
khaki suit: the uniform of modern soldiers
iron clothing: armor worn by medieval knights

Miniver Cheevy, born too late,
    Scratched his head and kept on thinking;   30
Miniver coughed, and called it fate,
    And kept on drinking.

Richard Cory

"Richard Cory," one of Robinson's best-known poems, is the story of a Tilbury man who seems to have everything but inward happiness. The poet deliberately keeps the ending a surprise until the last line. Notice that the expository pattern does not change throughout the poem: namely, the use of and *to add details about Richard Cory. Notice also that the "people on the pavement" play an important role in this poem.*

Whenever Richard Cory went down town,
We people on the pavement looked at him:
He was a gentleman from sole to crown,
Clean favored, and imperially* slim.

imperially: majestically, regally

And he was always quietly arrayed,*   5
And he was always human when he talked;
But still he fluttered pulses when he said,
'Good-morning,' and he glittered when he walked.

arrayed: dressed in finery

And he was rich—yes, richer than a king—
And admirably schooled in every grace: 10
In fine,* we thought that he was everything
To make us wish that we were in his place.

In fine: in summation

So on we worked, and waited for the light,
And went without the meat, and cursed the bread;
And Richard Cory, one calm summer night,   15
Went home and put a bullet through his head.

Cliff Klingenhagen

Cliff Klingenhagen is unlike most of Robinson's characters because he is happy. Notice that the poem gives in parable form the cause of the character's happiness. (Wormwood [l. 5], a very bitter drink, likely symbolizes the disappointments and hardships of life.) Notice also that the point of the poem develops from the **irony** *of the situation.*

Cliff Klingenhagen had me in to dine
With him one day; and after soup and meat,
And all the other things there were to eat,
Cliff took two glasses and filled one with wine
And one with wormwood. Then, without a sign   5
For me to choose at all, he took the draught*   *draught:* drink
Of bitterness himself, and lightly quaffed*   *quaffed:* drank
It off, and said the other one was mine.

And when I asked him what the deuce* he meant   *deuce:* devil (i.e., an
By doing that, he only looked at me   10   oath)
And smiled, and said it was a way of his.
And though I know the fellow, I have spent
Long time a-wondering when I shall be
As happy as Cliff Klingenhagen is.

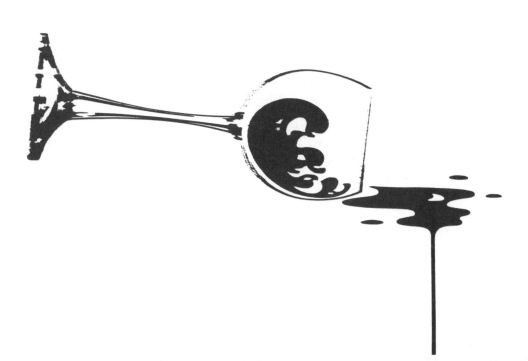

Cassandra

*The Cassandra of Greek mythology was the daughter of Priam, king of Troy.
The gods gave her the gift of prophecy, but because she offended Apollo, she was
cursed so that no one would believe her prophecies.*

I heard one who said: "Verily,
    What word have I for children here?
Your Dollar is your only Word.
    The wrath of it your only fear.

"You build it altars tall enough   5
    To make you see, but you are blind;
You cannot leave it long enough
    To look before you or behind.

"When Reason beckons you to pause,
    You laugh and say that you know best;   10
But what it is you know, you keep
    As dark as ingots* in a chest.

"You laugh and answer, 'We are young;
    O leave us now, and let us grow.'—
Not asking how much more of this   15
    Will Time endure or Fate bestow.

"Because a few complacent* years
    Have made your peril of your pride,
Think you that you are to go on
    Forever pampered and untried?   20

"What lost eclipse* of history,
    What bivouac* of the marching stars,
Has given the sign for you to see
    Millenniums* and last great wars?

"What unrecorded overthrow   25
    Of all the world has ever known,
Or ever been, has made itself
    So plain to you, and you alone?

ingots: metal molded into shapes convenient for storage

complacent: self-satisfied

eclipse: the obscuring of one celestial body by another
bivouac: a temporary encampment of soldiers in the field
Millenniums: cf. "millennium," a thousand years

"Your Dollar, Dove* and Eagle* make
    A Trinity that even you   30
Rate higher than you rate yourselves;
    It pays, it flatters, and it's new.

"And though your very flesh and blood
    Be what your Eagle eats and drinks,
You'll praise him for the best of birds,   35
    Not knowing, what the Eagle thinks.

"The power is yours, but not the sight;
    You see not upon what you tread;
You have the ages for your guide,
    But not the wisdom to be led.   40

"Think you to tread forever down
    The merciless old verities?*
And are you never to have eyes
    To see the world for what it is?

"Are you to pay for what you have   45
    With all you are?"–No other word
We caught, but with a laughing crowd
    Moved on. None heeded, and few heard.

Dove: symbol of peace/*Eagle:* the emblem of the United States

verities: established truths

Credo

The title of this poem published in 1897 means literally "I believe." Robinson portrays human existence as bleak and confusing, "the black and awful chaos of the night" (l. 11). Nevertheless, he senses the coming of some special, positive force, "the coming glory of the Light" (l. 14). This light, however, is not the Biblical light described in John 1:4-9, even though Robinson includes Biblical allusions that remind the reader of the passage in John. It is merely the symbol of his own religious invention.

Notice that although the traditional form of the poem is that of the Italian **sonnet,** *its bleak account of life is thoroughly modern.*

I cannot find my way: there is no star
In all the shrouded* heavens anywhere;
And there is not a whisper in the air
Of any living voice but one so far
That I can hear it only as a bar*   5
Of lost, imperial* music, played when fair
And angel fingers wove, and unaware,
Dead leaves to garlands where no roses are.

No, there is not a glimmer, nor a call,
For one that welcomes, welcomes when he fears,   10
The black and awful chaos of the night;
For through it all–above, beyond it all–
I know the far-sent message of the years,
I feel the coming glory of the Light.

shrouded: i.e., hidden (as though wrapped in burial clothing)

bar: a measure in musical notation
imperial: majestic, regal

For Thought and Discussion

1. Much of Robinson's poetry deals with characters who are misfits of society or are in some way isolated from their contemporaries. How do you know from reading "Miniver Cheevy" that Cheevy is a failure in his own eyes as well as in the eyes of others? What type of person do you think he represents? How does the poet reveal his attitude toward him in lines 23-24?

2. At what point in "Richard Cory" do you realize Cory has a problem? Who are the "people on the pavement" in line 2, and why does the speaker include himself by using the pronoun *we?* What qualities do the townspeople admire in Cory? What does the poet indicate about the attitude of the townspeople in lines 13-14? Were you prepared at all for the last line? Do you think the poem would be more or less effective if the poet had revealed a reason for Cory's final act?

3. Robinson uses irony of situation in "Cliff Klingenhagen" to present a man who is happy despite adverse circumstances. What does the poet use to symbolize the disappointments and hardships of Klingenhagen's life? How does Klingenhagen respond to his companion's question regarding his reason for drinking the bitter draught? What do you think he meant by this response? Are there also examples of irony in "Miniver Cheevy" and "Richard Cory"?

4. What warning does the modern prophet give in "Cassandra"? How does the poet make Cassandra's words sound prophetic in the opening stanza? What does Cassandra mean when she says, "Your Dollar is your only Word"? What new "Trinity" does she suggest Americans have accepted? What does she mean when she says, "You have the ages for your guide,/But not the wisdom to be led" and "Are you to pay for what you have/With all you are?"

5. How is the Cassandra of the last line similar to the Cassandra of Greek mythology? In what ways do you think Cassandra's prophecy is as relevant today as it was when Robinson wrote the poem?

6. One of the most obvious of Robinson's characteristics is his pessimism. How does he express this pessimism in "Credo"? Why do you think the poet chose "Credo" for the title of his poem? Is there at least a hint of optimism in the poem? Are the other Robinson poems totally pessimistic? As a Christian, what do you see as the root cause of Robinson's pessimism? Do you see any similarity between the actions of Robinson's fictional characters and the actions of people in today's society?

7. Robinson is considered a transitional poet because he uses traditional forms to present modern ideas. Identify the rhyme scheme and meter in the first quatrain of "Richard Cory" and in the Italian sonnet "Credo." Into what two parts is the sonnet divided? Although these two poems use traditional forms, what modern ideas are presented in each?

Robert Frost   1874-1963

Robert Frost, America's most popular modern poet, is a poet of contradictions. His works, while distinctively regional in setting, character, and language, are strikingly universal. His poems, while following traditional forms like the **sonnet, blank verse,** and rhymed **quatrains,** are permeated by the modern spirit of skepticism. Deceptively simple on the surface, Frost's poetry communicates complex attitudes and meanings. Like the man himself, the poems are often more than they seem.

Though a New Englander by ancestry and choice, Frost was born in San Francisco (March 26, 1874) and spent his first ten years there. His father, of New Hampshire birth, had sympathized with the Confederacy during the Civil War and named his son after the Southern general Robert E. Lee. After Frost's father died of tuberculosis, the family moved to New England, where Frost's mother supported them by teaching. In 1890, when fifteen, Frost published his first poem in his high school newspaper.

Following his high school graduation in 1892, Frost entered Dartmouth but returned home after only two months to take his mother's place teaching school at

Methuen, Massachusetts. Two years later the poet saw for the first time one of his poems (''My Butterfly'') published in a national publication. In 1895 he married Elinor White, his covaledictorian in high school. Then for two years he attended Harvard as a special student, and in 1900 he moved to a farm in Derry, New Hampshire. For the next decade or so, Frost farmed and, after 1906, also taught school, continuing to write poetry but having no success in publishing any of it. In 1912 Frost decided to devote himself exclusively to poetry and moved his wife and children to England, where they could live more inexpensively. There, almost twenty years after ''My Butterfly'' had appeared in print in 1894, he published two volumes of poetry: *A Boy's Will* (1913) and *North of Boston* (1914).

In 1915 Frost returned to the States with his family and found himself famous. During the nearly fifty years left of his life, his fame continued to grow. He frequently served at prominent colleges and universities (including Amherst, Harvard, and the University of Michigan) as poet in residence and as a special professor. He also published ten more volumes of poetry, four of which earned a Pulitzer Prize as the best book of poetry published during the year. (Frost is the only American poet ever to earn *four* Pulitzers.) He received honorary degrees from Oxford and Cambridge as well as from nearly forty American colleges and universities. The honor that he seemed most to appreciate was the invitation to participate in the presidential inauguration of 1961. Frost believed that the invitation marked an important event in American letters and politics. He wrote to President-elect John F. Kennedy that ''the arts, poetry, now for the first time [are] taken into the affairs of statesmen.''

With a career stretching over five decades, Robert Frost became a beloved and familiar figure to a very large but somewhat undiscerning American audience. Recent biographies have revealed that Frost's public image, which attracted numerous Americans even among the working class, was not the real Frost at all. Like Samuel Clemens, he consciously created a role for himself that was practically as much a part of his art as was the poetry itself. His pose as a folksy, homey patriarch of country wit and ancient wisdom contrasted sharply with the real-life ambitious and often embittered writer. Among Frost's interests late in life was the Biblical character of Job, with whom he felt special sympathy because of his own misfortunes: the deaths of three children, the death of his wife (1938), the suicide of a son (1940), the mental illness of a daughter, and the denial of a Nobel Prize in literature and other real and imagined slights. In spite of Frost's personal deficiencies, his poetry captures something essential in the American experience and expresses it in a way comprehensible to his countrymen. The whole nation mourned his death on January 29, 1963. In ''The Lesson for Today'' (1942) he had already written his epitaph: ''I would have written of me on my stone:/I had a lover's quarrel with the world.''

Frost's poetry at first glance appears to be nature poetry. Almost every work details physical features of the New England countryside. Indeed, titles like ''The Pasture,'' ''Birches,'' and ''Desert Places'' seem to indicate that the poet's primary concern is nature. Nevertheless, in each of these poems—as well as in virtually all his others—Frost focuses on man. The details of nature function, in fact, as a backdrop for human thought and action. Frost also used nature in explaining his aesthetic views. Concerning realism, he once said: "There are two types of realists. There is the one who offers a good deal of dirt with his potato to show that it is a real potato. And there is the one who is satisfied with the potato brushed clean. I'm inclined to be the second kind. To me, the thing that art does for life is to clean it, to strip it to form."

Frost's verse often contains subtle didacticism. Unlike the poetry of his contemporaries, Frost's poems typically unfold a lesson to be learned or an insight to be perceived. In a 1930 address Frost defended poetic indirectness: "poetry begins in trivial metaphors, pretty metaphors, 'grace' metaphors, and goes on to the profoundest thinking that we have. Poetry provides the one permissible way of saying one thing and meaning another. People say, 'Why don't you say what you mean?' We never do that, do we, being all of us too much poets. We like to talk in parables and in hints and in indirections—whether from diffidence or some other instinct." Frost wrote in "The Figure a Poem Makes," his preface to the 1939 edition of his *Collected Works,* that a poem "begins in delight and ends in wisdom" or, as he added three sentences later, "ends in a clarification of life." Indeed, most of Frost's poems begin with the "delight" raised through a concrete recollection by the poet and end with an observation on human experience.

Though sometimes valuable for their practical wisdom, Frost's poetic observations seldom show a sympathy for and understanding of the Bible. Although attracted at times to Biblical themes and stories, Frost remained modern in the subjectivity of his belief and his religious doubt. If he did not go to the extremes of his fellow moderns, he did nevertheless remain thoroughly skeptical. He tried, as it were, to walk a middle course between faith and denial. His keeping to a middle way would perhaps seem reasonable if there were no right way. But since God reveals a right way to mankind, Frost's middle way misses the mark as surely as does the way of his more radical contemporaries. Frost's poetry proposes a humanistic answer to man's problems, an answer that finds values solely in human relationships. Unfortunately, it leaves virtually no place for God.

The Pasture

This short poem, published in Frost's first book of verse, is an invitation to the reader to come away with the poet. Like most of Frost's poetry, it is written in first person, the poet speaking directly to his reader; its language is colloquial and idiomatic; and it is filled with homey details of the rural New England life.

I'm going out to clean the pasture spring;
I'll only stop to rake the leaves away
(And wait to watch the water clear, I may):
I shan't be gone long.–You come too.

I'm going out to fetch the little calf   5
That's standing by the mother. It's so young
It totters when she licks it with her tongue.
I shan't be gone long.–You come too.

The Gift Outright

Frost was much in demand as a reader of his own poetry. Probably his most memorable recitation occurred at the inauguration of President Kennedy in January 1961. The brisk wind and bright sunlight of the winter day made it too difficult for Frost to read the seventy-seven-line rhymed history he had prepared. And so the eighty-six-year-old poet recited this poem from memory.

Frost first published "The Gift Outright" in 1942. He once called it "a history of the United States in a dozen lines of blank verse."

The land was ours before we were the land's.
She was our land more than a hundred years
Before we were her people. She was ours
In Massachusetts, in Virginia,
But we were England's, still colonials,   5
Possessing what we still were unpossessed by,
Possessed by what we now no more possessed.
Something we were withholding made us weak
Until we found out that it was ourselves
We were withholding from our land of living,   10
And forthwith found salvation in surrender.
Such as we were we gave ourselves outright

(The deed of gift was many deeds of war)
To the land vaguely realizing westward,
But still unstoried, artless,* unenhanced,*
Such as she was, such as she would become.

15 *artless:* natural, uncelebrated in art/*unenhanced:* not made more attractive

Eve; Billy Morrow Jackson; National Gallery of Art, Washington; Gift of the artist.

The Road Not Taken

"The Road Not Taken" is symbolic. It presents a universal situation all men face many times in their lives when they must choose between two alternatives. But it is not more specific than that. The responses of the speaker are those experienced by us all whether our choice involves a vocation, salvation, or marriage. The responses described in the poem may legitimately be applied to particular situations by the reader, but he must be careful to remember that the poem itself (and the poet) does not make that application.

Two roads diverged in a yellow wood,
And sorry I could not travel both
And be one traveler, long I stood
And looked down one as far as I could
To where it bent in the undergrowth;   5

Then took the other, as just as fair,
And having perhaps the better claim,
Because it was grassy and wanted wear;
Though as for that the passing there
Had worn them really about the same,   10

And both that morning equally lay
In leaves no step had trodden black.
Oh, I kept the first for another day!
Yet knowing how way leads on to way,
I doubted if I should ever come back.   15

I shall be telling this with a sigh
Somewhere ages and ages hence:
Two roads diverged in a wood, and I—
I took the one less traveled by,
And that has made all the difference.   20

The Death of the Hired Man

"The Death of the Hired Man" is one of Frost's most famous poems. Louis Untermeyer finds that it is, in fact, "many kinds of poem. It is a narrative, a dialogue, a drama; it has been successfully acted as a one-act play. Three people are portrayed: the farmer, his wife, and an old incompetent hired hand, shiftless and proud—and the character most fully revealed is the one who never appears."

Mary sat musing on the lamp-flame at the table,
Waiting for Warren. When she heard his step,
She ran on tiptoe down the darkened passage
To meet him in the doorway with the news
And put him on his guard. "Silas is back."   5
She pushed him outward with her through the door
And shut it after her. "Be kind," she said.
She took the market things from Warren's arms
And set them on the porch, then drew him down
To sit beside her on the wooden steps.   10

"When was I ever anything but kind to him?
But I'll not have the fellow back," he said.
"I told him so last haying, didn't I?
If he left then, I said, that ended it.
What good is he? Who else will harbor him   15
At his age for the little he can do?
What help he is there's no depending on.
Off he goes always when I need him most.
He thinks he ought to earn a little pay,
Enough at least to buy tobacco with,   20
So he won't have to beg and be beholden.
'All right,' I say, 'I can't afford to pay
Any fixed wages, though I wish I could.'
'Someone else can.' 'Then someone else will have to.'
I shouldn't mind his bettering himself   25
If that was what it was. You can be certain,
When he begins like that, there's someone at him
Trying to coax him off with pocket money—
In haying time, when any help is scarce.
In winter he comes back to us. I'm done."   30

"Sh! not so loud: he'll hear you," Mary said.

"I want him to: he'll have to soon or late."

"He's worn out. He's asleep beside the stove.
When I came up from Rowe's I found him here,
Huddled against the barn door fast asleep,   35
A miserable sight, and frightening, too–
You needn't smile–I didn't recognize him–
I wasn't looking for him–and he's changed.
Wait till you see."

            "Where did you say he'd been?"

"He didn't say. I dragged him to the house,   40
And gave him tea and tried to make him smoke.
I tried to make him talk about his travels.
Nothing would do: he just kept nodding off."

"What did he say? Did he say anything?"

"But little."

            "Anything? Mary, confess   45
He said he'd come to ditch the meadow for me."

"Warren!"

            "But did he? I just want to know."

"Of course he did. What would you have him say?

Surely you wouldn't grudge* the poor old man   grudge: to be reluctant
Some humble way to save his self-respect.   50   to give or admit
He added, if you really care to know,
He meant to clear the upper pasture, too.
That sounds like something you have heard before?
Warren, I wish you could have heard the way
He jumbled everything. I stopped to look   55
Two or three times–he made me feel so queer–
To see if he was talking in his sleep.
He ran on Harold Wilson–you remember–
The boy you had in haying four years since.
He's finished school, and teaching in his college.   60
Silas declares you'll have to get him back.
He says they two will make a team for work:

Between them they will lay this farm as smooth!
The way he mixed that in with other things.
He thinks young Wilson a likely lad, though daft*   65   *daft:* crazy
On education–you know how they fought
All through July under the blazing sun,
Silas up on the cart to build the load,
Harold along beside to pitch it on.''

''Yes, I took care to keep well out of earshot.''   70

''Well, those days trouble Silas like a dream.
You wouldn't think they would. How some things linger!
Harold's young college-boy's assurance piqued* him.   *piqued:* vexed,
After so many years he still keeps finding   provoked
Good arguments he sees he might have used.   75
I sympathize. I know just how it feels
To think of the right thing to say too late.
Harold's associated in his mind with Latin.
He asked me what I thought of Harold's saying
He studied Latin like the violin,   80
Because he liked it–that an argument!
He said he couldn't make the boy believe
He could find water with a hazel prong–*   *hazel prong:* a forked
Which showed how much good school had ever done him.   stick
He wanted to go over that. But most of all   85
He thinks if he could have another chance
To teach him how to build a load of hay–''

''I know, that's Silas' one accomplishment.
He bundles every forkful in its place,
And tags and numbers it for future reference,   90
So he can find and easily dislodge it
In the unloading. Silas does that well.
He takes it out in bunches like big birds' nests.
You never see him standing on the hay
He's trying to lift, straining to lift himself.''   95

''He thinks if he could teach him that, he'd be
Some good perhaps to someone in the world.
He hates to see a boy the fool of books.
Poor Silas, so concerned for other folk,
And nothing to look backward to with pride,   100
And nothing to look forward to with hope,
So now and never any different.''

Part of a moon was falling down the west,
Dragging the whole sky with it to the hills.
Its light poured softly in her lap. She saw it   105
And spread her apron to it. She put out her hand
Among the harplike morning-glory strings,
Taut with the dew from garden bed to eaves,
As if she played unheard some tenderness
That wrought on him beside her in the night.   110
"Warren," she said, "he has come home to die:
You needn't be afraid he'll leave you this time."

"Home," he mocked gently.

          "Yes, what else but home?
It all depends on what you mean by home.
Of course he's nothing to us, any more   115
Than was the hound that came a stranger to us
Out of the woods, worn out upon the trail."

"Home is the place where, when you have to go there,
They have to take you in."

          "I should have called it
Something you somehow haven't to deserve."   120

Warren leaned out and took a step or two,
Picked up a little stick, and brought it back
And broke it in his hand and tossed it by.
"Silas has better claim on us you think
Than on his brother? Thirteen little miles   125
As the road winds would bring him to his door.
Silas has walked that far no doubt today.
Why doesn't he go there? His brother's rich,
A somebody—director in the bank."

"He never told us that."

          "We know it, though."   130

"I think his brother ought to help, of course.
I'll see to that if there is need. He ought of right
To take him in, and might be willing to—
He may be better than appearances.
But have some pity on Silas. Do you think   135

If he had any pride in claiming kin
Or anything he looked for from his brother,
He'd keep so still about him all this time?''

"I wonder what's between them.''

        "I can tell you.
Silas is what he is—we wouldn't mind him—   140
But just the kind that kinsfolk can't abide.
He never did a thing so very bad.
He don't know why he isn't quite as good
As anybody. Worthless though he is,
He won't be made ashamed to please his brother.''   145

"*I* can't think Si ever hurt anyone.''

"No, but he hurt my heart the way he lay
And rolled his old head on that sharp-edged chair-back.
He wouldn't let me put him on the lounge.
You must go in and see what you can do.   150
I made the bed up for him there tonight.
You'll be surprised at him—how much he's broken.
His working days are done; I'm sure of it.''

"I'd not be in a hurry to say that.''

"I haven't been. Go, look, see for yourself.   155
But, Warren, please remember how it is:
He's come to help you ditch the meadow.
He has a plan. You mustn't laugh at him.
He may not speak of it, and then he may.
I'll sit and see if that small sailing cloud   160
Will hit or miss the moon.''

        It hit the moon.
Then there were three there, making a dim row,
The moon, the little silver cloud, and she.

Warren returned—too soon, it seemed to her—
Slipped to her side, caught up her hand and waited.   165

"Warren?'' she questioned.

        "Dead,'' was all he answered.

Stopping by Woods on a Snowy Evening

Like "The Road Not Taken" this poem has also suffered at the hands of readers trying to make it into something it is not. As you read, enjoy the poet's deft use of imaginative comparisions and images; be careful, however, to interpret these details in light of the text itself.

Whose woods these are I think I know.
His house is in the village, though;
He will not see me stopping here
To watch his woods fill up with snow.

My little horse must think it queer   5
To stop without a farmhouse near
Between the woods and frozen lake
The darkest evening of the year.

He gives his harness bells a shake
To ask if there is some mistake.   10
The only other sound's the sweep
Of easy wind and downy flake.

The woods are lovely, dark, and deep,
But I have promises to keep,
And miles to go before I sleep,   15
And miles to go before I sleep.

Mending Wall

Farmers in New England often made fences from the stones they collected in their fields. Frost pictures such fences as walls and develops the poem by describing two New Englanders' efforts to repair them. As the poem unfolds, the word "wall" comes to represent something much more important than a fence.

Something there is that doesn't love a wall,
That sends the frozen-ground-swell under it
And spills the upper boulders in the sun,
And makes gaps even two can pass abreast.
The work of hunters is another thing: 5
I have come after them and made repair
Where they have left not one stone on a stone,
But they would have the rabbit out of hiding,
To please the yelping dogs. The gaps I mean,
No one has seen them made or heard them made,   10
But at spring mending-time we find them there.
I let my neighbor know beyond the hill;
And on a day we meet to walk the line
And set the wall between us once again.
We keep the wall between us as we go.   15
To each the boulders that have fallen to each.
And some are loaves and some so nearly balls
We have to use a spell to make them balance:
"Stay where you are until our backs are turned!"
We wear our fingers rough with handling them.   20
Oh, just another kind of outdoor game,
One on a side. It comes to little more:
There where it is we do not need the wall:
He is all pine and I am apple orchard.
My apple trees will never get across   25
And eat the cones under his pines, I tell him.
He only says, "Good fences make good neighbors."
Spring is the mischief in me, and I wonder
If I could put a notion in his head:
"*Why* do they make good neighbors. Isn't it   30
Where there are cows? But here there are no cows.
Before I built a wall I'd ask to know
What I was walling in or walling out,
And to whom I was like to give offense.
Something there is that doesn't love a wall,   35

That wants it down." I could say "Elves" to him,
But it's not elves exactly, and I'd rather
He said it for himself. I see him there,
Bringing a stone grasped firmly by the top
In each hand, like an old-stone savage armed.   40
He moves in darkness as it seems to me,
Not of woods only and the shade of trees.
He will not go behind his father's saying,
And he likes having thought of it so well
He says again, "Good fences make good neighbors."   45

Birches

*"Birches," like Frost's ideal poem, "begins in delight and ends in wisdom."
In fact, the three sections of the poem (ll. 1-20, 21-40, 41-59) show a steady
progression toward the "wisdom" of the final lines.*

When I see birches bend to left and right
Across the lines of straighter darker trees,
I like to think some boy's been swinging them.
But swinging doesn't bend them down to stay
As ice storms do. Often you must have seen them   5
Loaded with ice a sunny winter morning
After a rain. They click upon themselves
As the breeze rises, and turn many-colored
As the stir cracks and crazes* their enamel.
Soon the sun's warmth makes them shed crystal shells   10
Shattering and avalanching* on the snow crust—
Such heaps of broken glass to sweep away
You'd think the inner dome of heaven had fallen.
They are dragged to the withered bracken* by the load,
And they seem not to break; though once they are bowed   15
So low for long, they never right themselves:
You may see their trunks arching in the woods
Years afterwards, trailing their leaves on the ground
Like girls on hands and knees that throw their hair
Before them over their heads to dry in the sun.   20
But I was going to say when Truth broke in
With all her matter of fact about the ice storm,
I should prefer to have some boy bend them
As he went out and in to fetch the cows–
Some boy too far from town to learn baseball,   25

crazes: produces a
pattern of fine cracks

avalanching: sliding
rapidly in a large
mass

bracken: ferns

Whose only play was what he found himself,
Summer or winter, and could play alone.
One by one he subdued his father's trees
By riding them down over and over again
Until he took the stiffness out of them,   30
And not one but hung limp, not one was left
For him to conquer. He learned all there was
To learn about not launching out too soon
And so not carrying the tree away
Clear to the ground. He always kept his poise   35
To the top branches, climbing carefully
With the same pains you use to fill a cup
Up to the brim, and even above the brim.
Then he flung outward, feet first, with a swish,
Kicking his way down through the air to the ground.   40
So was I once myself a swinger of birches.
And so I dream of going back to be.
It's when I'm weary of considerations,
And life is too much like a pathless wood
Where your face burns and tickles with the cobwebs   45
Broken across it, and one eye is weeping
From a twig's having lashed across it open.
I'd like to get away from earth awhile
And then come back to it and begin over.
May no fate willfully misunderstand me   50
And half grant what I wish and snatch me away
Not to return. Earth's the right place for love:
I don't know where it's likely to go better.
I'd like to go by climbing a birch tree,
And climb black branches up a snow-white trunk   55
Toward heaven, till the tree could bear no more,
But dipped its top and set me down again.
That would be good both going and coming back.
One could do worse than be a swinger of birches.

Desert Places

"Desert Places" seems to be a simple description of nature but is, in reality, a description of man.

Snow falling and night falling fast, oh, fast
In a field I looked into going past,
And the ground almost covered smooth in snow,
But a few weeds and stubble showing last.

The woods around it have it—it is theirs.   5
All animals are smothered in their lairs.*
I am too absent-spirited to count;
The loneliness includes me unawares.

lairs: the dens of wild animals

And lonely as it is, that loneliness
Will be more lonely ere it will be less—   10
A blanker whiteness of benighted* snow
With no expression, nothing to express.

benighted: darkened, overtaken by night

They* cannot scare me with their empty spaces
Between stars—on stars where no human race is.
I have it in me so much nearer home   15
To scare myself with my own desert* places.

They: the scientists making startling discoveries about the vastness of space

desert: deserted, empty

For Thought and Discussion

1. In "The Pasture" what two activities does the speaker describe? What colloquial, idiomatic expressions and homey details of rural New England life does he use in describing the activities? What do you think the activities symbolize? How does he involve the reader, and why do you think he does so? What does he achieve by using repetition in lines 1 and 5 and lines 4 and 8?

2. What examples of paradox do you find in "The Gift Outright"? How does the poem explain the paradoxes? In what lines does the poet indicate that the sacrifice involved was worthwhile?

3. In "The Road Not Taken" the poet uses simple rural images to achieve his goal of "saying one thing in terms of another." How do you know that the poet is talking about more than just roads? Since the speaker gives no indication that the roads represent anything specific, in general terms what might the roads symbolize? How do you know that one road is not necessarily superior to the other? How does the poet reveal the tone of the poem through the title?

4. "The Death of the Hired Man," one of Frost's longer narratives, is characterized by the realistic dialogue between Mary and Warren as they discuss Silas. What does the dialogue reveal about the characters of Mary and Warren? What kind of relationship do they have? Point out specific lines which show how Mary wins her husband over to her point of view. What kind of person is Silas? Why has he returned to the farm? What are the two definitions of "home" which are given in the poem, and which definition do you think is more accu-

rate? How is the ending of the poem ironic? What verse form did Frost use, and how does the form reinforce the content of the poem?

5. In "Stopping by Woods on a Snowy Evening," what visual images does the poet present in the first two stanzas? What sounds does he describe in the third stanza? What do you think the woods, promises, and sleep represent in the last stanza? Identify the meter and rhyme scheme of the poem, and discuss how the stanzas are linked together through the rhyme scheme. How is the last stanza different? What effect does the repetition of the last two lines have in bringing the poem to a satisfactory conclusion?

6. What do the first and last lines of "Mending Wall" reveal about the attitudes of the speaker and his neighbor? Which of the two characters is more dogmatic? What reason is given for this dogmatism? What literal hinderances to a wall does the poet mention? Does the poet indicate that there may be reasons other than physical forces which would discourage the building of walls? What do you think he means by "elves"? What types of barriers is the speaker denouncing? With whose opinion of walls do you agree–the speaker's or the neighbor's? What is the significance of the poet's closing with the neighbor's statement?

Minor Traditionalists

John Crowe Ransom
1888-1974

John Crowe Ransom was an important twentieth-century literary critic and poet. He was closely associated at Vanderbilt University (Tennessee) with a group of Southern poets called the Fugitives, or Southern Agrarians. This group, of which Ransom was the leader, regularly met to discuss philosophy and to read their own verse. In a prose volume entitled *I'll Take My Stand* (1930), the Fugitives defended the Southern way of life and thought. They fervently called for an agrarian South rather than an industrialized one. As a literary critic Ransom became the chief spokesman for a set of critical attitudes called the New Criticism. Active since the 1920s (although declining in importance after the 1950s), this movement stressed intensive study of a literary work through close reading and detailed analysis. The New Critics rejected earlier critics' "interest in the mind and personality of the poet, sources, the history of ideas, and political and social implication.'' In 1939, two years after joining the faculty of Kenyon College (Ohio), Ransom founded the *Kenyon Review,* one of this century's most influential critical magazines. As a poet Ransom often combined serious content with wit and irony. His themes frequently include death (as in ''Bells for John Whiteside's Daughter''), the decline of the South after the Civil War, and the contrast between rural and urban life, between chivalry and commercialism. His verse has been called ''unsentimental,'' ''tough-minded,'' and ''penetrating.'' Nevertheless, it examines the modern world through traditional metrics and other poetic conventions inherited from the past.

Bells for John Whiteside's Daughter

This poem, published in 1924, illustrates clearly the unsentimentality of Ransom's verse. The poet, holding his emotions in check, contrasts the stillness of the girl as she is now and as she was formerly.

There was such speed in her little body,
And such lightness in her footfall,
It is no wonder her brown study*
Astonishes us all.

study: a state of deep thought, reverie

Her wars were bruited* in our high window.   5
We looked among orchard trees and beyond,
Where she took arms against her shadow,
Or harried* unto the pond

bruited: reported, noised

harried: chased

The lazy geese, like a snow cloud
Dripping their snow on the green grass,   10
Tricking and stopping, sleepy and proud,
Who cried in goose, Alas,

For the tireless heart within the little
Lady with rod that made them rise
From their noon apple-dreams and scuttle*   15
Goose-fashion under the skies!

scuttle: run hastily

But now go the bells, and we are ready,
In one house we are sternly stopped
To say we are vexed* at her brown study,
Lying so primly* propped.   20

vexed: dismayed; also angered (cf. ''astonished,'' l. 4)
primly: formally

Theodore Roethke
1903-1963

Theodore Roethke was born in Saginaw, Michigan, to a family of German florists. After earning two degrees from the University of Michigan, he became an English teacher at Pennsylvania State University and the University of Washington. An outstanding teacher of poetry and a careful craftsman, he advised students not to follow the path of "undisciplined self-expression" but to "write like someone else"–that is, to study carefully and imitate the work of another poet. His poems fall generally into two groups: those that are "orthodox in form, rational in theme, ironic in tone"; and those that are free in form, sometimes bordering on the irrational and surrealistic. Roethke's verse is also traditional in the sense that his themes and forms are heavily dependent at times on those of two American predecessors, Ralph Waldo Emerson and Walt Whitman. Before his sudden death from a heart attack in 1963, Roethke had been awarded the Pulitzer and the Bollingen prizes in poetry. Some critics place him "among the foremost American poets of his generation."

Dolor

This poem, published in 1948, describes a type of sadness or grief. Roethke once explained to a group of students that the poem "is an exposition of one of the modern hells: the institution that overwhelms the individual man. The 'order,' the trivia of the institution, is, in human terms, a disorder, and as such, must be resisted."

I have known the inexorable* sadness of pencils,
Neat in their boxes, dolor of pad and paper-weight,
All the misery of manila folders and mucilage,*
Desolation* in immaculate public places,
Lonely reception room, lavatory, switchboard,   5
The unalterable pathos* of basin and pitcher,
Ritual* of multigraph,* paper-clip, comma,
Endless duplication of lives and objects.
And I have seen dust from the walls of institutions,
Finer than flour, alive, more dangerous than silica,*   10
Sift, almost invisible, through long afternoons of tedium,*
Dripping a fine film on nails and delicate eyebrows,
Glazing the pale hair, the duplicate gray standard faces.

inexorable: unyielding

mucilage: glue
Desolation: barrenness

pathos: a quality that arouses sadness
Ritual: formality/*multigraph:* an office machine for printing
silica: a white or colorless compound used in manufacturing glass or concrete
tedium: boredom

Edna St. Vincent Millay
1892-1950

Edna St. Vincent Millay began writing poetry in her childhood. Her mother–a strong, independent woman who reared her three daughters alone after separation from her husband–taught "Vincent" to rhyme when the girl was only four years old. Her first published poem, "Renascence," brought its twenty-year-old author national attention when it won fourth place in a prestigious poetry contest. After graduation from Vassar (1917), Millay moved to Greenwich Village, where she adopted a bohemian lifestyle. Her lifestyle, along with her lyrics, caused her to symbolize for many the liberated woman of the 1920s. Her spirit of rebellion suited the times. After leaving Greenwich Village, Millay traveled in the States and in Europe, giving readings of her poetry. She married a Dutch importer, Eugen Boissevain, who gave up his business in order to manage her poetic career. By the time she died of a heart attack in 1950, her poetic reputation had declined. Although a romantic rebel in her life, Millay remained very much a traditionalist in a great part of her poetry. Typically traditional in vocabulary and verse form (Millay is, for instance, a master of the **sonnet**), her work is nevertheless thoroughly modern in **theme** and **tone**. One prominent critic observes that Millay "has been from the beginning the one poet of our time who has successfully stood athwart two ages," the nineteenth and twentieth centuries.

Sonnet XXVI

*This **sonnet** is one of a sequence of sonnets appearing in Millay's Pulitzer Prize-winning collection,* The Harp-Weaver and Other Poems *(1923). Like most sonnets, this one treats the subject of love. Notice, however, that Millay's viewpoint is not conventional but similar to that of Shakespeare's sonnet "My mistress' eyes are nothing like the sun," which attacks the foolish statements made by sonneteers. Notice also that this technically flawless poem expresses a complex view of the "I." The poet seems to be looking into a mirror or at a picture as she comments on her features. Rather than directly addressing her lover, she instead seems at times to adopt his perspective on her. The poem becomes, in fact, a miniature drama, moving from the reworked cliché of line 1 to the understated wisdom of line 14.*

Love is not blind. I see with single eye*
Your ugliness and other women's grace.
I know the imperfection of your face,—
The eyes too wide apart, the brow too high
For beauty. Learned from earliest youth am I   5
In loveliness, and cannot so erase
Its letters from my mind, that I may trace
You faultless, I must love until I die.
More subtle* is the sovereignty* of love:
So am I caught that when I say, "Not fair,"   10
'Tis but as if I said, "Not here—not there—
Not risen—not writing letters." Well I know
What is this beauty men are babbling of;
I wonder only why they prize it so.

single eye: cf. Matthew 6:22; Luke 11:34

subtle: clever, devious/*sovereignty:* supremacy, power

W. H. Auden   1907-1973

Like Henry James and T. S. Eliot, W. H. Auden is claimed by both England and the United States. Although born in England, Auden settled in the States in 1939 and became a naturalized citizen in 1946. Auden's move to the United States marked a major shift in his thought. Before 1939 his thinking was predominantly Marxist. He often satirized social problems and expressed his belief in the collapse of the British middle class and in the coming of revolution. After 1939 his thought became predominantly religious. Always concerned with the disintegration of modern life, Auden suggested in his later poetry that the solution to social ills may lie in religion (although he does not specify the religion of the Bible). Auden is a traditional poet not just in his return to religion but also in his adaptation of earlier poetic styles and techniques. For example, his use of **alliteration, assonance,** and **internal rhyme** reveals the influence of Anglo-Saxon poetry on his work. His poem ''The Unknown Citizen'' incorporates satiric techniques used by the great English satirists of the eighteenth century: Jonathan Swift (1667-1745) and Alexander Pope (1688-1744). Like the other American traditionalists, Auden used conventional literary forms to analyze modern problems and attitudes.

The Unknown Citizen

This poem, published in 1940, satirizes the modern welfare state—the earthly paradise conceived by modern political and social scientists. It does so by mock praise of a model citizen of such a society. A special element in this poem's satire is the **burlesque** *of the type of poetry that bureaucratic agencies might produce. Notice that lines 6-7 are* **doggerel** *(verse of a poorly executed type, usually monotonous in* **rhyme** *and* **meter** *and trivial in subject matter). Lines 17-19 are simply prose. This poem is also an example of irony.*

(To JS/07/M/378 This Marble Monument Is Erected by the State)

He was found by the Bureau of Statistics to be
One against whom there was no official complaint,
And all the reports on his conduct agree
That, in the modern sense of an old-fashioned word, he was a saint,
For in everything he did he served the Greater Community.   5

Except for the War till the day he retired
He worked in a factory and never got fired,
But satisfied his employers, Fudge Motors Inc.
Yet he wasn't a scab* or odd in his views,
For his Union reports that he paid his dues,   10
(Our report on his Union shows it was sound)
And our Social Psychology workers found
That he was popular with his mates and liked a drink.
The Press are convinced he bought a paper every day
And that his reactions to advertisements were normal in every way.   15
Policies taken out in his name prove that he was fully insured,
And his Health-card shows he was once in hospital but left it cured.
Both Producers Research and High-Grade Living declare
He was fully sensible to the advantages of the Instalment Plan
And had everything necessary to the Modern Man,   20
A phonograph, a radio, a car, and a frigidaire.*
Our researchers into Public Opinion are content
That he held the proper opinions for the time of year;
When there was peace, he was for peace; when there was war, he went.
He was married and added five children to the population,   25
Which our Eugenist* says was the right number for a parent of his generation,
And our teachers report that he never interfered with their education.
Was he free? Was he happy? The question is absurd:*
Had anything been wrong, we should certainly have heard.

scab: a strikebreaker

frigidaire: refrigerator

Eugenist: one who studies human improvement through control of heredity
absurd: ridiculously unreasonable

For Thought and Discussion

1. What words does the speaker use in Ransom's "Bells for John Whiteside's Daughter" to create the poem's central contrast between the living child and the child as she appears in death? What does he mean by the girl's "brown study"? Why does this study "astonish" and "vex" the speaker and others with him? What examples of alliteration do you find in the last stanza, and how do these alliterative phrases contribute to the overall effect of the poem? Why do you think the poet concentrates more on the living girl than on her death? Do you think the poem would have been more effective if the speaker had reacted more emotionally? Why or why not?

2. What is the reason for the speaker's grief in Theodore Roethke's poem "Dolor"? What unlikely images does the poet use to sustain the melancholy mood? In your answer point out examples of his use of general terms for sadness to describe specific concrete images or objects. According to the last two lines of the poem, what is the ultimate result of the situations or institutions he is lamenting?

3. Identify the meter and rhyme scheme in Millay's "Sonnet XXVI." Using the interpretation given in the headnote, tell what relationship the speaker of the poem sees between love and beauty. In what way is the speaker's viewpoint unconventional?

4. What aspects of the welfare state does Auden satirize in "The Unknown Citizen"? How does the modern definition of "saint" mentioned in line 4 differ from the traditional definition? How is the irony of the title heightened by the details given in the poem? In what way is the overall tone of the poem ironic? How do you think the poet's answer to the two questions asked in line 28 would differ from the answer given by the speaker of the poem? In what ways do you think the theme of the poem is relevant to American society today?

5. Most of the traditionalists presented modern themes while retaining conventions such as rhyme. In "Bells for John Whiteside's Daughter," what basic rhyme scheme does the poet use? What examples throughout the poem do you find of approximate rhyme rather than exact rhyme? In W. H. Auden's "The Unknown Citizen," notice the monotony of the rhyme. How does this monotony reinforce the content of the poem? How does even the subtitle illustrate traditional rhyme?

Experimentalists

Ezra Pound   1885-1972

Ezra Pound, who spent most of his adult life in Europe, was one of the most influential experimentalists among modern American poets. After leaving the United States in 1908, Pound joined other American expatriates in London, where he soon established himself as their leader and gained a considerable reputation as a translator and literary scholar. He became for a short time the moving force behind the short-lived (1909-17) but influential imagist movement.

The imagist writers revolted against most poetic forms developed in the past. Their experimentation was strongly influenced by aesthetic principles drawn from Oriental poetry (especially the Japanese *haiku*, classical Greek verse, and contemporary French symbolism). In 1913 Pound edited the movement's first volume of poems, *Des Imagistes* (1913), a collection that helped define and give direction to the movement. Their poetic creed, comprised in 1915, was stated in six rules: (1) "to use the language of common speech, but to employ always the *exact* word," (2) "to create new rhythms" through the use of free verse, (3) "to allow absolute freedom in the choice of subject," (4) "to present an image" through the use of particular details, (5) "to produce poetry that is hard and clear, never blurred nor indefinite," and (6) to concentrate as much as possible into the fewest words possible. By following these rules, imagists like Pound produced gemlike bits of verse that had little or nothing to say. Their message, if any, is that poetry should have no message.

After 1920 Pound lived in Paris for four years and then in Italy. While in Italy, he became an outspoken supporter of Fascism and anti-Semitism. Although still a United States citizen, he made anti-American propaganda broadcasts during World War II. As a result, he was charged with treason and returned to the States after the war. The charges were dropped, however, when he was declared insane by a board of medical examiners. He was then confined for twelve years in a federal hospital in Washington, D.C., before efforts led by his lawyers, several congressmen, and Archibald MacLeish gained his release in 1958. Pound spent the remaining years of his life in Italy, where he died in 1972.

Pound's poetics are best expressed by his own statement shortly before his death: "When I talk it is like an explosion in an art museum, you have to hunt around for the pieces." His highly allusive, "open" form has helped bring about a revolution in poetic taste and standards in modern English-language poetry. W. H. Auden aptly summarized Pound's effect on modern poetry: "There are few living poets . . . who could say, 'My work would be exactly the same if Mr. Pound had never lived.' "

In a Station of the Metro

This poem of only two lines is one of the shortest yet one of the most famous imagist productions. The "metro" is the Paris subway, the setting for a scene that Pound imaginatively captures through a sharply focused metaphor.

The apparition of these faces in the crowd;
Petals on a wet, black bough.

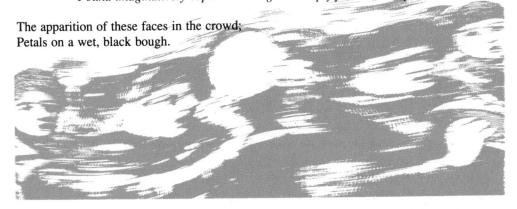

William Carlos Williams
1883-1963

William Carlos Williams was both a pediatrician and (in the moments he could spare at night and between professional appointments) a writer. While studying medicine at the University of Pennsylvania, he met Ezra Pound and Hilda Doolittle, both of whom strongly influenced his verse. Although he spent time in Europe, Williams did not settle there but returned to his hometown (Rutherford, New Jersey), where he spent the rest of his life. Williams attacked conventional forms of poetic expression throughout his long career. He consciously strove to represent actual American speech in his verse. His greatest poetic affinity lay with Walt Whitman (1819-92), the first major poetic experimentalist in American literature. During the 1930s Williams wrote that his interest in imagism was a passing interest. "Yet," observes critic John Brinnin, "no other American poet—with perhaps the exception of H. D. [Hilda Doolittle]—has written so many poems that can serve as models illustrating the imagist canon."

Williams, who often used the phrase "no ideas but in things," believed that meaning could be found only in actual objects. As a result, his imagist poems focus on lowly, familiar subjects. The following two fulfill the essential goals of the imagists.

Poem

As the cat
climbed over
the top of

the jamcloset
first the right   5
forefoot

carefully
then the hind
stepped down

into the pit of   10
the empty
flowerpot

The Red Wheelbarrow

So much depends
upon

a red wheel
barrow

glazed with rain
water

beside the white
chickens

Archibald MacLeish
1892-1982

Archibald MacLeish is a somewhat unusual representative of American imagism. Like many of his fellow poets, he outgrew the artistic creed of imagism. Unlike many of his fellow poets, he held important public positions. After graduation from Yale (1915) and then Harvard Law School (1919), MacLeish practiced law in Boston for a short time (1920-23). In 1923, having published his first book of poetry six years earlier, MacLeish moved his family to Paris in order to devote himself totally to writing. While there, he became good friends with American expatriates like Ernest Hemingway, F. Scott Fitzgerald, and Ezra Pound. After five years in Paris, MacLeish deliberately rejected the life of an expatriate to return to the States. Here he entered the second phase of his career by writing poetry that showed a growing awareness of his national, social, and cultural heritage. After the mid-1930s, when he entered the final phase of his career, he called attention to the nation's pressing social issues. He held a number of public offices (Librarian of Congress, 1939-44, for instance, and assistant secretary of state, 1944-45) and won several major literary prizes. He also enjoyed an academic career as a professor at Harvard. Although MacLeish drew from the imagist movement, he was not limited by it.

Ars Poetica

In "Ars Poetica" (1926), whose Latin title means, "the art of poetry," MacLeish aptly defines and expresses the imagists' theory of poetry. This poem, which has been called a fitting epitaph for the movement, particularly illustrates the modern misconception that poetry should not include didactic elements but exist solely as an art object.

A poem should be palpable* and mute*
As a globed fruit

palpable: capable of being touched, tangible/*mute:* silent

Dumb*
As old medallions* to the thumb

Dumb: without speech

medallions: large medals or coins

Silent as the sleeve-worn stone   5
Of casement* ledges where the moss has grown–

casement: window

A poem should be wordless
As the flight of birds

A poem should be motionless in time
As the moon climbs   10

Leaving, as the moon releases
Twig by twig the night-entangled trees,

Leaving, as the moon behind the winter leaves,
Memory by memory the mind–

A poem should be motionless in time   15
As the moon climbs

A poem should be equal to:
Not true

For all the history of grief
An empty doorway and a maple leaf   20

For love
The leaning grasses and two lights above the sea–

A poem should not mean
But be

For Thought and Discussion

1. How well does Pound's "In a Station of the Metro" fulfill the rules announced by the imagists and their nondidactic concept of poetry?

2. Though "In a Station of the Metro" uses neither rhyme nor meter, it employs sound patterning in such a way as to give an impression of poetic "shape." What instances of sound repetition, or near repetition, can you detect? Is there some rhythmical parallelism?

3. The two lines of Pound's poem form an elliptical sentence. What words would need to be added to fill out the statement? What figurative expression would the poem then exemplify?

4. What word in Pound's poem has multiple meaning? What less ambiguous, one-dimensional word might have been used in its place? How does the additional meaning add impact to the imagery?

5. The two poems of Williams capture an action and an object respectively. Show how they satisfy the imagist rules for poetry.

6. Write out Williams's poems in normal sentence form. How much of their poetic effect depends upon their segmentation in lines and stanzas? Does modern poetry typically depend less on oral and more on visual effects than earlier poetry?

7. Taking what the world considers trivial and raising it to a level of momentousness ("So much depends upon") is a hallmark of imagism as well as of aestheticism. It challenges conventional notions of what is important and lay attitudes toward "pure art." Is such a challenge implicit in Williams's poems, particularly the second–an indictment of those who will see no poetry in the motion (admittedly a highly poetic one) of a cat stepping into a pot or in a backyard tableau of red wheelbarrow plus rain plus white chickens? Is there a worthwhile point being made?

8. MacLeish's "Ars Poetica" can be considered a poetic manifesto of the imagist movement. To what extent does it exemplify its thesis–that "A poem should not mean/But be"? Can a poem with a thesis rightly be called an imagist poem?

9. Examine some of the similes in "Ars Poetica." Are they logical? Can a poem strictly be silent, wordless, and movementless and still use language and have something going on within it? Is MacLeish insisting that genuine poetry has nothing to communicate but pictures and feelings?

Carl Sandburg   1878-1967

Although Carl Sandburg became a noted biographer of his Illinois hero (Abraham Lincoln) and a famous historian of American folk music, he influenced American literature most strongly through his poetry. From 1916 to 1922 he published four volumes of experimental poetry that established his reputation as a spokesman for the American workingman. In fact, in all modern poetry, Sandburg's voice has been probably the most truly representative of the American worker.

Sandburg was born in 1878 in Galesburg, Illinois, to Swedish immigrants. His somewhat irregular education stopped in the eighth grade, when he had to begin working at a regular job. During the next half dozen years, Sandburg roamed throughout the Midwest working at whatever jobs he could find. He was, for instance, a dishwasher, newspaper boy, milkman, wheat harvester, salesman, janitor, house painter, and stagehand. These jobs gave him a firsthand knowledge of the common people he later wrote about in his verse.

While still a teen-ager, Sandburg decided to become a writer. He prophesied to his sister: "I'm going to be a writer. And if I find I can't be a writer, I'll be a hobo." Ironically, he had already been a hobo but would later become a writer. After serving eight months in Puerto Rico during the Spanish-American War (1898), Sandburg entered Lombard College in his hometown of Galesburg, supporting himself by working in the local fire department. Although he attended college for four years (1898-1902), he did not receive a degree. A college professor (Phillip Green Wright) privately published in 1904 the young poet's first book of verse, *In Reckless Ecstasy.*

During the next decade Sandburg worked as a political organizer, a minor city official, and a journalist. He also continued writing poetry, particularly about Chicago, the bustling city that seemed to him to represent what was essential about the United States. In 1914 the influential magazine *Poetry* published several of his poems about Chicago. These poems exemplified a new and very unconventional style. They showed no regard for **rhyme** and **meter.** They also shocked readers by their free use of slang and their uninhibited content. Although **free verse** was not new to American poetry (Walt Whitman had used it extensively before the Civil War), Sandburg made it more popular with the general public. Some readers praised Sandburg's bold originality; others were shocked and angry that he dared to call his works poetry.

During the 1920s Sandburg began turning from poetry toward biography and folk literature. Like his poetic ancestor Whitman, Sandburg intensely admired Abraham Lincoln. Both poets saw Lincoln as the supreme example of the common man's opportunities in a democracy. Both also saw Lincoln's rise from obscurity to the presidency as a heroic inspiration for all Americans. While Whitman honored Lincoln in poetry, Sandburg celebrated him in a six-volume biography published in two parts: *The Prairie Years* (two volumes, 1926) and *The War Years* (four volumes, 1939). Sandburg studied Lincoln's life for over thirty years and spent eight years writing the biography that still remains a classic account of our sixteenth president.

By the time Sandburg published the last volume of the Lincoln biography, he had become a familiar and well-loved public figure. He was a popular platform performer who gave readings of his poems in a peculiarly personal manner, often to the accompaniment of his guitar. The image Sandburg projected was that of a rather shaggy, homespun, folksy man who lived close to the earth and to the common people. His collections of folk tales and songs as well as his children's stories further endeared him to large segments of the American people. When Sandburg died in 1967, President Lyndon Johnson spoke for a large portion of the American public: "Carl Sandburg was more than the voice of America, more than the poet of its strength and genius. He was America."

Sandburg's poetry has created sharp divisions among its critics. Some readers flatly reject the free verse of his poetry. Two of his contemporaries had rather sharp comments to make about the verse form Sandburg and other modern poets were using. When asked why he did not experiment with free verse, E. A. Robinson replied: "I write badly enough as it is." And Robert Frost, who called Sandburg a fraud, declared that "for my pleasure I had as soon write free verse as play tennis with the net down." Because free verse does not depend on the traditional patterns of rhyme and meter, it often seems unpoetic, a mere exercise in prose. In reality, the rhythmic patterns in free verse create a poetic effect (an effect, incidentally, produced by the Psalms in the King James Version of the Bible).

In recent years Sandburg's poetic reputation has declined. For one thing, the work of more recent poets has made Sandburg's experimentation seem outdated. For another, Sandburg's works often lack careful craftsmanship. One reason is that they generally served as vehicles for his socialistic views. The concern of the propagandist overshadowed the concern of the artist. Sandburg's propagandism certainly does not recommend him to Christians or to conservatives generally. In one poem he attacked the evangelist Billy Sunday; in another he defended the anarchists Sacco and Vanzetti.

In spite of his deficiencies, Sandburg contributed importantly to the poetic experimentation of the early modern period. His voice was a representative one for his day. Called the "laureate of industrial America," Sandburg praised the strength and vitality of the American way of life. His moral values and view of man, unfortunately, are not those of the Word of God. In fact, Sandburg's work consistently shows sympathy with forces denying Biblical truth.

Chicago

This poem, first published in 1914, perhaps more than any other illustrates Sandburg's contributions to American poetry. Notice that Sandburg breaks with poetic tradition in choice of words ("Hog Butcher for the World" seems unpoetic), in subject matter, and in metrics. Sandburg felt a special attraction to the Chicago of the early twentieth century. In a letter to a friend, he wrote on July 30, 1913: "The truth is it [Chicago] is a good place for a poet to get his head knocked when he needs it. In fact, it is so good a place for a healthy man who wants to watch the biggest, most intense, brutal and complicated game in the world–the game by which the world gets fed and clothed–the method of control–the economics and waste–so good a place is it from this viewpoint that I think you will like it." Sandburg's reasons for liking it appear particularly in the second half of the poem.

Hog Butcher for the World,
Tool Maker, Stacker of Wheat,
Player with Railroads and the Nation's Freight Handler;
Stormy, husky, brawling,
City of the Big Shoulders: 5

They tell me you are wicked and I believe them, for I have seen your painted women
    under the gas lamps luring the farm boys.
And they tell me you are crooked and I answer: Yes, it is true I have seen the
    gunman kill and go free to kill again.
And they tell me you are brutal and my reply is: On the faces of women and children
    I have seen the marks of wanton hunger.
And having answered so I turn once more to those who sneer at this my city, and I
    give them back the sneer and say to them:
Come and show me another city with lifted head singing so proud to be alive and
    coarse and strong and cunning.   10

Flinging magnetic curses amid the toil of piling job on job, here is a tall bold slugger
    set vivid against the little soft cities;
Fierce as a dog with tongue lapping for action, cunning as a savage pitted against
    the wilderness,
        Bareheaded,
        Shoveling,
        Wrecking,   15
        Planning,
        Building, breaking, rebuilding,

Under the smoke, dust all over his mouth, laughing with white teeth,

Under the terrible burden of destiny laughing as a young man laughs,
Laughing even as an ignorant fighter laughs who has never lost a battle,   20
Bragging and laughing that under his wrist is the pulse, and under his ribs the heart
    of the people,
                Laughing!
Laughing the stormy, husky, brawling laughter of Youth, half-naked, sweating,
    proud to be Hog Butcher, Tool Maker, Stacker of Wheat, Player with Railroads
    and Freight Handler to the Nation.

Fog

Whereas "Chicago" shows Sandburg's indebtedness to Walt Whitman's verse, "Fog" (1916) shows Sandburg's debt to imagistic theory.

The fog comes
on little cat feet.

It sits looking
over harbor and city
on silent haunches   5
and then moves on.

Grass

"Grass" (1918) is a highly allusive poem. Austerlitz (l. 1) was the Czechoslo- vakian setting, in 1805, of one of Napoleon's greatest victories. Waterloo (l. 1) was the location in Belgium where Napoleon met his final defeat in 1815. At Gettysburg (l. 4), Pennsylvania, the Confederate army suffered a major defeat in 1863. Ypres and Verdun (l. 5), in Belgium and France respectively, were the battlefields for some of the fiercest fighting during World War I. At Verdun, for instance, nearly a million troops died; at Ypres some 300,000 Allied soldiers died. All of these battle- fields have huge cemeteries. Notice that Sandburg represents both the work of nature and the attitude of humans in this short lyric.

Pile the bodies high at Austerlitz and Waterloo.
Shovel them under and let me work–
        I am the grass; I cover all.

And pile them high at Gettysburg
And pile them high at Ypres and Verdun.   5

Shovel them under and let me work.
Two years, ten years, and passengers ask the conductor:
        What place is this?
        Where are we now?

        I am the grass.   10
        Let me work.

For Thought and Discussion

1. What characteristics of Chicago does Sandburg celebrate? Translate his imagistic account into a list of descriptive qualities. Compare the result with the Puritan ideal of a godly community as "a city set on a hill."
2. If Chicago is Sandburg's essential America, who is Sandburg's essential American? From what level of society does he come? What is his vocation? His temperament? His age? What figurative expression does the poem as a whole exemplify?
3. At first glance "Chicago" seems shapeless—a free-verse collage of images and colorful phrases. Look closely at the first and last four lines. Do they connect in such a way as to give the poem a distinct beginning and end? What is the relationship of the second and third sections?
4. Obviously, some qualities of cats are not applicable to fog, and some qualities of fog could not pertain to cats. What shared qualities enable this comparison to succeed? What figurative comparison is exemplified by the poem?
5. What does the poem convey by "silent haunches"? Look up the term *catachresis*. What can poetry gain by the use of nonlogical modes of expression?
6. Consider the order of the allusions to battles in "Grass." What about them determines the sequence? How does it suggest the action of grass, and of time?
7. What is included in the word "all" in line 3?
8. In the wars in which these battles occurred, were the victors those whose causes Sandburg would have thought just? Would the tone of the poem be less neutral if otherwise?
9. What figurative expression does the poem embody? Describe the personality of the grass as it is revealed through its spoken words. How is this personality appropriate to the thought of the poem?

E. E. Cummings 1894-1962

E. E. Cummings was a painter, poet, novelist, and playwright, but above all he was an individualist. His poetic experimentation with capitalization, punctuation, coined words, syntax, and typography identified him as a member of the *avant-garde* (Fr. "advance guard": i.e., something new or ahead of its time). Indeed, no other poet has yet successfully imitated his work. Through his attempts to exploit the full potential of language and to help his readers see their world in a new way, Cummings has significantly influenced modern American poetry.

Born in 1894 in Cambridge, Massachusetts, Cummings was the son of a Harvard professor of English and social ethics who later became a Unitarian minister in

Boston. Following graduation from Harvard in 1916 with a master's degree in English and classical studies, he sailed for France. Arriving in the midst of World War I, he promptly joined the Ambulance Corps of the American Red Cross. Soon, however, a misunderstanding with French authorities (who thought from his letters that Cummings was guilty of treason) landed the young man in a detention camp for three months. This experience later provided Cummings with material for a novel, *The Enormous Room,* published in 1922.

After the war Cummings lived in Paris, studying art. He became friends with the painter Pablo Picasso and with poets Archibald MacLeish and Ezra Pound. These men importantly influenced Cummings's own works. When the poet returned to the States in 1924, he found himself already famous for *The Enormous Room* and for his first book of poetry, *Tulips and Chimneys* (1923).

Throughout the rest of his life, Cummings divided his time—when not in Paris—between his Greenwich Village apartment in New York City and his New Hampshire farm. He painted in the afternoons and wrote in the evenings. Before his death from a stroke in 1962, he produced several more volumes of poetry. These volumes bore such unusual titles as *&* (1925), *XLI Poems* (1925), *is 5* (1926), *ViVa* (1931), *1/20 Poems* (1936), and *I x I* (1944). Cummings also wrote a play, *Him* (1927), which is a forerunner of the theater of the absurd; a ballet, *Tom* (1935), which is based on *Uncle Tom's Cabin;* and *i: six nonlectures* (1953), which is the text of his Harvard lectures on poetry.

Most of Cummings's poems are either lyrics (celebrating love, freedom, sensual pleasure, or spring) or satiric pieces (ridiculing materialism, social institutions like marriage, or anything that threatens individuality). Cummings described contemporary life as a ''pseudoworld'' made up of ''mostpeople'' playing ''impotent nongames of wrongright and rightwrong.'' His philosophy is summed up well in this statement: ''Mostpeople are frozen into conventional death, the individual alone is alive . . .[;] life is freshened by love.'' Cummings ''found modern conveniences contemptible,'' writes one critic; ''he shunned electricity in his home, hated radio and television, and called packaged food 'Battle Creek seaweed.' Above all he loved poetry. Reading to an indifferent audience in 1950, he finally grew angry and stormed out, shouting at his listeners, 'Well, write poetry. . . ; it's the only thing that matters.' ''

Although Cummings was admired from the beginning by poetic innovators like Ezra Pound and T. S. Eliot, others reacted unfavorably to his work. Those who reacted negatively were offended by his poems that did not look like poems, his strange use of capital letters, his habit of using verbs as nouns and adverbs as adjectives, and his creation of new words. Eventually, though, he won the esteem of most critics as they learned to understand what he was attempting to do. Cummings's verse tries to shock readers into seeing the familiar in a new way. By breaking the traditional rules of grammar, mechanics, and typography, it makes readers explore new possibilities of meaning. By presenting them with the unexpected, it catches their attention and focuses it where the poet wished it to be. In his best poems Cummings achieves his desired effect; in his worst his verse degenerates into cuteness and sensationalism.

More than anything else, Cummings elevated the individual. He advocated complete freedom for people and gloried in the sensual. While we can appreciate the role he played in shaping modern poetry and can enjoy selections from his work, we cannot condone his view of the world. In fact, Cummings's view of life is incompatible with a Christian philosophy.

when serpents bargain for the right to squirm

This poem is surprisingly traditional in its form, although the omission of capitalization and punctuation makes it appear otherwise. Notice that it follows the form of a **sonnet.** *It uses a special form of rhyme called* **slant rhyme,** *which only approximates the rhyming sounds. Notice also that the poem is a series of absurdities, all of which draw attention to the greatest absurdity, according to Cummings: belief in mankind.*

when serpents bargain for the right to squirm
and the sun strikes to gain a living wage—
when thorns regard their roses with alarm
and rainbows are insured against old age

when every thrush may sing no new moon in   5
if all screech-owls have not okayed his voice
—and any wave signs on the dotted line
or else an ocean is compelled to close*

when the oak begs permission of the birch
to make an acorn—valleys accuse their   10
mountains of having altitude*—and march
denounces april as a saboteur*

then we'll believe in that incredible*
unanimal mankind (and not until)

close: i.e., foreclose (to seize the property that a debtor has failed to make payments for)

altitude: height

saboteur: one who obstructs normal functioning, as an enemy agent might

incredible: unbelievable

somewhere i have never travelled

Although the capitalization, spacing, and punctuation of this poem are unconventional, it is very much a love poem. Notice how the "I" of the poem describes the effect that the one he loves has on him.

somewhere i have never travelled,gladly beyond
any experience,your eyes have their silence:
in your most frail gesture are things which enclose me,
or which i cannot touch because they are too near

your slightest look easily will unclose me   5
though i have closed myself as fingers,
you open always petal by petal myself as Spring opens
(touching skilfully,mysteriously)her first rose

or if your wish be to close me,i and
my life will shut very beautifully,suddenly,   10
as when the heart of this flower imagines
the snow carefully everywhere descending;

nothing which we are to perceive in this world equals
the power of your intense fragility:whose texture
compels me with the colour of its countries,   15
rendering death and forever with each breathing

(i do not know what it is about you that closes
and opens;only something in me understands
the voice of your eyes is deeper than all roses)
nobody,not even the rain,has such small hands   20

in Just-

This poem, which appeared in 1923 in Cummings's first book of poetry, is a tribute to spring. The strange description of the balloonman as ''goat-footed'' (l. 20) takes on meaning when the reader recognizes the term as an allusion to the Greek god Pan. According to Greek mythology, Pan was the god of woods, fields, and flocks. He was described as having a human torso with goat's legs, horns, and ears.

in Just-
spring   when the world is mud-
luscious the little
lame balloonman

whistles   far   and wee   5

and eddieandbill come
running from marbles and
piracies and it's
spring

when the world is puddle-wonderful   10

the queer
old balloonman whistles
far   and   wee
and bettyandisbel come dancing

from hop-scotch and jump-rope and   15

it's
spring
and
      the
         goat-footed   20

balloonMan   whistles
far
and
wee

r-p-o-p-h-e-s-s-a-g-r

This poem, published in 1935 in no thanks, *is initially the most difficult of Cummings's poems in this text. Yet, with rearrangement, the poem becomes easily decipherable. By ignoring the parentheses, except in line 14, and by unscrambling the letters in lines 1, 5, and 12, the reader can unravel the poem. Notice that the reader is forced to become something of a grasshopper himself.*

r-p-o-p-h-e-s-s-a-g-r

who

a)s w(e loo)k
upnowgath

PPEGORHRASS

eringint(o-
aThe):l
         e A
          !p:
S   a
              (r
r!v!nG   .gRrEaPsPhOs)
                                     to
rea(be)rran(com)gi(e)ngly
,grass hopper;

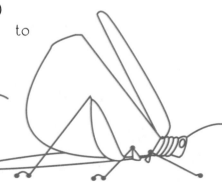

For Thought and Discussion

1. What continuity is there in the impossibilities listed as conditions for believing in mankind in "when serpents bargain"? Do they amount to a favorable or an unfavorable view of human behavior? Should we be grateful that nature cannot act like man?

2. What metaphor runs through "somewhere i have never travelled"? What does it convey about how the subject of the poem affects the speaker? How does the comparison in the last line connect with this central metaphor?

3. The first three lines of the last stanza of "somewhere i have never travelled" repeats elements from the first three stanzas. What are these elements and in what order are they repeated? Does this repetition help to give the poem shape?

4. Notice the parallelism within "in Just-" and the way repetition divides the poem into units. What are these units? Why do you suppose the poem breaks off abruptly in the middle of the third unit? Is there a meaningful progression in the adjectives describing the balloon man?

5. The last of the Cummings selections uses anagrams to designate the subject of the poem. The letters of the subject's name have been scrambled in the title and in lines 1, 5, and 12. Unscramble them and read the poem, omitting the second and third occurrences of the name and all parenthesis marks other than those in line 14. Do the mental contortions required for reading the poem reflect the physical ungainliness of the poem's subject in the action described?

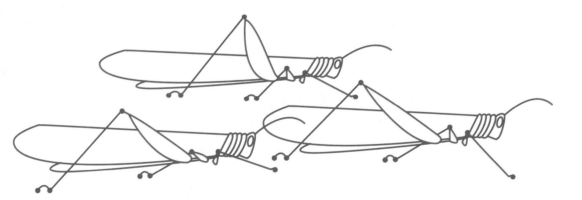

Poets and Religious Issues

Wallace Stevens   1879-1955

For most of his adult life, Wallace Stevens was part of the legal department of the Hartford Accident and Indemnity Company of Hartford, Connecticut. Although his fellow workers and for a time even his wife did not know it, he was also a poet whose work was being widely discussed and acclaimed. Although Stevens began writing poetry early in his adult life, he did not receive public recognition until 1914, when his first poems appeared in *Poetry* magazine. His first volume of poems, *Harmonium,* was published in 1923 but remained relatively unnoticed because of the furor over T. S. Eliot's "The Waste Land," which had been published a year earlier. During the rest of his life, Stevens published several more volumes of poetry, winning both Bollingen (1950) and Pulitzer (1955) prizes. In his work Stevens particularly focused on the nature and function of poetry, the role of the poet, and the power of the imagination. In his search to find meaning in the universe, Stevens found art, which became to him a virtual religion. He believed that man is surrounded by chaos, which is unrelieved by divine purpose. In order to help man survive in the world in which he finds himself, the creative imagination must impose order on experience so as to make sense out of the confusion. In "Sunday Morning" Stevens gives probably the clearest statement of his religious beliefs. He rejects outright the Word of God, choosing to turn to nature for his answer to the meaning of life. Although a representative modern poet, Stevens ironically re-creates in this poem only the ancient pagan view of man and the world.

Sunday Morning

"Sunday Morning," first published in 1915, is thoroughly modern in its form and attitude. The difficulty of its vocabulary, allusions, and dramatized argument is characteristic of modern poetry. Its rejection of Christ's incarnation and the soul's immortality is typical of modern religious unbelief. It sets aside Biblical answers to age-old questions about death and life after death, substituting a neo-pagan religious view of the world.

I

This first stanza establishes the setting, situation, and central question of the poem. An apparently wealthy woman with an active imagination is basking in the sun on a pleasant Sunday morning. As she leisurely enjoys a late breakfast and the pleasant surroundings, her thoughts turn to what Sunday actually commemorates. It is the first day of the week, the day upon which Christ rose from the dead. She feels uneasy as she thinks of Christ's death, the sacrifice that took place centuries before in Palestine.

Complacencies* of the peignoir,* and late
Coffee and oranges in a sunny chair,
And the green freedom of a cockatoo*
Upon a rug mingle to dissipate*
The holy hush of ancient sacrifice.*   5
She dreams a little, and she feels the dark
Encroachment* of that old catastrophe,*
As a calm darkens among water-lights.
The pungent* oranges and bright, green wings*
Seem things in some procession of the dead,   10
Winding across wide water, without sound.
The day is like wide water, without sound,
Stilled for the passing of her dreaming feet
Over the seas, to silent Palestine,
Dominion of the blood and sepulchre.*   15

Complacencies: i.e., a scene of contentment/*peignoir:* a woman's dressing gown
cockatoo: a parrot with a long crest (perhaps a figure in the rug)
dissipate: drive away
ancient sacrifice: i.e., Christ's death on the cross
Encroachment: a gradual intrusion or wrongful entering/*catastrophe:* Christ's crucifixion
pungent: having a biting smell or taste/*green wings:* part of the cockatoo
blood and sepulchre: Christ's blood and His tomb

II

In this stanza the woman questions her need to give her life ("her bounty," l. 16) to Christ. She wants, instead, to find comfort in nature. She believes that its pleasures and sympathetic response to her emotions are the key to life's meaning and destiny. She also expresses the heretical, romantic notion that mankind is divine (l. 23).

Why should she give her bounty* to the dead?
What is divinity if it can come
Only in silent shadows and in dreams?*
Shall she not find in comforts of the sun,
In pungent fruit and bright, green wings, or else   20
In any balm* or beauty of the earth,
Things to be cherished like the thought of heaven?*
Divinity must live within herself;*
Passions of rain, or moods in falling snow;
Grievings in loneliness, or unsubdued   25
Elations* when the forest blooms; gusty
Emotions on wet roads on autumn nights;
All pleasures and all pains, remembering
The bough of summer and the winter branch.
These are the measures* destined* for her soul.*   30

bounty: payment, offering

silent . . . dreams: in mystical contemplations and visions

balm: something that heals or soothes

Things . . . heaven: i.e., nature is as much to be cherished as thoughts of immortality or heaven

Divinity . . . herself: the notion that God lives within everyone

Elations: exalted feelings

measures: limits/*destined:* determined/*her soul:* i.e., her sympathetic bond to nature is what life intended for her

III

The first part of this stanza describes Jove, or Jupiter, and links the supreme god of Roman mythology (a human invention) to the God of the Bible, whose nature "commingling" with human nature "virginal" in the incarnation fulfilled human desire. Both myths, it implies, are mere wish fulfillment. The woman then ponders immortality (ll. 39-41). If there is no immortality (i.e., "shall the earth/Seem all of paradise that we shall know?"), then the sky will be a friendly place, not merely the division between the earth and paradise (i.e., heaven).

Jove* in the clouds had his inhuman birth.*
No mother suckled him, no sweet land gave
Large-mannered motions to his mythy mind.
He moved among us, as a muttering king,
Magnificent, would move among his hinds,*   35
Until our blood, commingling,* virginal,*
With heaven, brought such requital* to desire
The very hinds discerned it, in a star.*
Shall our blood fail? Or shall it come to be
The blood of paradise? And shall the earth   40
Seem all of paradise that we shall know?
The sky will be much friendlier then than now,
A part of labor and a part of pain,
And next in glory to enduring love,
Not this dividing and indifferent blue.*   45

Jove: the supreme god in Roman mythology, also called Jupiter/*inhuman birth:* i.e., he was supposedly divine, not of human birth

hinds: servants

commingling: lit., mingling together/*virginal:* chaste, pure

requital: a return, as in repayment

The . . . star: perhaps the Magi from the East (see Matt. 2:2)

indifferent blue: i.e., heaven lies beyond the sky

IV

In this stanza the woman questions whether earth is really the paradise mankind has longed for. The poetic speaker, who has already made his presence felt in the poem, now directly answers the woman's question. He says that immortality is a vain delusion. According to him, permanence lies only in the cycle of nature (the seasons of the year) and mankind's memories of nature.

She says, "I am content when wakened birds,
Before they fly, test the reality
Of misty fields, by their sweet questionings;*
But when the birds are gone, and their warm fields
Return no more, where, then, is paradise?"   50
There is not any haunt* of prophecy,
Nor any old chimera* of the grave,
Neither the golden underground, nor isle
Melodious, where spirits gat* them home,
Nor visionary south,* nor cloudy palm   55
Remote on heaven's hill, that has endured
As April's green endures; or will endure
Like her* remembrance of awakened birds,
Or her desire for June and evening, tipped
By the consummation* of the swallow's wings.   60

sweet questionings:
    i.e., songs

haunt: i.e., heaven

chimera: a foolish
    fancy

gat: archaic for *got*

visionary south: allu-
    sions (ll. 53-55) to
    various non-Biblical
    conceptions of
    paradise

her: the woman in the
    poem

consummation:
    fulfillment

V

The woman states that she still feels a need for some type of "imperishable bliss" (l. 62). The speaker responds that an awareness of death heightens one's appreciation of life and thus replaces one's dream of and desire for an eternal state.

She says, "But in contentment I still feel
The need of some imperishable bliss."
Death is the mother of beauty; hence from her,
Alone, shall come fulfillment to our dreams
And our desires. Although she strews* the leaves   65
Of sure obliteration* on our paths,
The path sick sorrow took, the many paths
Where triumph rang its brassy phrase,* or love
Whispered a little out of tenderness,
She makes the willow shiver in the sun   70
For maidens who were wont* to sit and gaze
Upon the grass, relinquished* to their feet.
She causes boys to pile new plums and pears
On disregarded plate. The maidens taste
And stray impassioned* in the littering leaves.*   75

strews: scatters
obliteration: destruc-
    tion without even a
    trace remaining
brassy phrase: i.e., the
    ringing of bells to
    celebrate victory

wont: accustomed

relinquished:
    abandoned

impassioned: filled
    with passion
And . . . leaves: cf.
    lines 65-66

VI

In this stanza the speaker caricatures paradise as a static place where nothing happens because of the absence of death. He again returns to the theme that "Death is the mother of beauty" (l. 88).

There is no change of death in paradise?
Does ripe fruit never fall? Or do the boughs
Hang always heavy in that perfect sky,
Unchanging, yet so like our perishing earth,
With rivers like our own that seek for seas   80
They never find, the same receding* shores
That never touch with inarticulate* pang?
Why set the pear upon those river-banks
Or spice the shores with odors of the plum?
Alas, that they should wear our colors there,   85
The silken weavings of our afternoons,
And pick the strings of our insipid* lutes!*
Death is the mother of beauty, mystical,*
Within whose burning bosom* we devise*
Our earthly mothers waiting, sleeplessly.   90

receding: lit., going back

inarticulate: speechless

insipid: lacking interest/*lutes:* guitarlike instruments
mystical: spiritually symbolic
bosom: center/*devise:* archaic for *imagine*

VII

This stanza depicts the pagan rites of sun-worshipers who chant the praises of nature, not of God. The last two lines are particularly significant. Mankind, stresses the poetic speaker, has only a natural origin (not a God-created one) and a natural destiny to molder in the tomb (rather than an eternal life in heaven or hell). The fact that the men walk only upon the dew sharply contrasts with Christ's walking on the water.

Supple* and turbulent,* a ring of men
Shall chant in orgy* on a summer morn
Their boisterous devotion to the sun,
Not as a god, but as a god might be,
Naked among them, like a savage source.   95
Their chant shall be a chant of paradise,
Out of their blood, returning to the sky;
And in their chant shall enter, voice by voice,
The windy lake wherein their lord delights,
The trees, like serafin,* and echoing hills,   100
That choir* among themselves long afterward.
They shall know well the heavenly fellowship
Of men that perish and of summer morn.
And whence they came and whither they shall go
The dew upon their feet shall manifest.   105

Supple: limber/*turbulent:* violently active
orgy: a secret rite in cults

serafin: angels
choir: sing in chorus

VIII

In the poem's final stanza the poet brings his argument against Christianity to a close. The woman hears a voice saying that Christ did not rise from the dead. (Notice that the poet uses in line 109 the human name of Jesus to imply that Christ was not the divine Son of God.) The poem then develops the notion that mankind lives without any support by God. The earth is merely an island in space, not created by the divine act of God and not subject to His laws. The stanza closes with a series of images from nature. The final lines introduce a movement toward darkness, a universal **metaphor** *for death. According to the poet, death is all mankind can look forward to. In this poem Stevens thus embodies the view of the modern man who has renounced the truth of God's Word.*

She hears, upon that water without sound,
A voice that cries, "The tomb in Palestine
Is not the porch of spirits lingering.*   *lingering:* cf. Matthew
It is the grave of Jesus, where he lay."   28:1-7
We live in an old chaos of the sun,   110
Or old dependency* of day and night,   *old dependency:* de-
Or island solitude,* unsponsored,* free,   tached territory
Of that wide water, inescapable.   *solitude:* the earth as
Deer walk upon our mountains,* and the quail   alone in space/*un-*
Whistle about us their spontaneous cries;   115   *sponsored:* without
Sweet berries ripen in the wilderness: God's providential
And, in the isolation of the sky,   direction
At evening, casual flocks of pigeons make   *Deer . . . mountain:* cf.
Ambiguous* undulations* as they sink,   Matthew 17:1-5
Downward to darkness, on extended wings.   120

Ambiguous: uncertain/
undulations: wave-
like movements

For Thought and Discussion

1. The woman, having drifted from Christianity, enjoys her new freedom of life–represented in her self-indulgent languor on Sunday morning when others are in church; but she misses the promise of heaven where beauty and goodness do not fade. The arguments of the poem's speaker (perhaps the voice of her reason) are designed to reassure her–and, of course, the reader. Does she seem reconciled to the loss of Christian immortality by the end of the poem? Is the closing image reassuring?

2. Stanza VII provides for a paganistic worship of nature in the secular world view being advocated. Is this worship supernatural, otherworldly? Could an agnostic scientist participate? Is modern secularism opposed to all religion?

3. What arguments for the goodness of death are advanced in the poem? Are they convincing? Compare them to the comforting explanations of Scripture.

4. Consider the idea of stanza VI that if there were no end to pleasures we could not greatly enjoy them: that the passing of a pleasure gives it a delight that

would not be experienced otherwise. Are there pleasures that do not wear out with time?

5. Compare the imagery of the last stanza to similar imagery earlier in the poem. What Biblical incidents are echoed? Show how the stanza clinches the meaning of the poem.

James Weldon Johnson
1871-1938

James Weldon Johnson was an unusually gifted man. He was the first black after Reconstruction to be admitted to the bar (i.e., licensed to practice law) in his home state, Florida. He was the author of the Negro national hymn, "Lift Ev'ry Voice and Sing." In collaboration with his brother, he wrote numerous songs and contributed to several musical comedies. From 1906 to 1913 he served as the United States consul first in Venezuela and then in Nicaragua. He was field secretary (1916-20) and general secretary (1920-30) of the National Association for the Advancement of Colored People (NAACP). From 1931 until his death in 1938 from an automobile accident, he was professor of creative literature at Fisk University. Johnson was also a critic and novelist (*The Autobiography of an Ex-Colored Man,* published anonymously in 1912). But he was especially a poet, and his work helped lay a foundation for the Harlem Renaissance of the 1920s. This movement, which was centered in the Harlem section of New York City, was the first major literary outpouring from black American writers. Johnson was regarded as an elder statesman to the group of writers that included Langston Hughes, Jean Toomer, and Countee Cullen. Johnson's best-known work is *God's Trombones* (1927). In this series of seven Negro sermons in verse (beginning with "The Creation" and ending with "The Judgment Day"), Johnson captures the style and imagination of the old-time black preachers he had heard in his youth.

The Creation

"The Creation," in particular, achieves grandeur by uniting a reverent but humanlike view of the Creator and His actions with a serious, dignified style. Although God's Trombones *uses Biblical material, the poet's real interest is the black heritage of religious expression, not the Biblical material itself. In fact, Johnson regarded his material as mere legend or myth, a view with which modern liberalism is altogether sympathetic.*

And God stepped out on space,
And he looked around and said:
I'm lonely–
I'll make me a world.

And far as the eye of God could see   5
Darkness covered everything,
Blacker than a hundred midnights
Down in a cypress swamp.

Then God smiled,
And the light broke,   10
And the darkness rolled up on one side,
And the light stood shining on the other,
And God said: That's good!

Then God reached out and took the light in his hands,
And God rolled the light around in his hands   15
Until he made the sun;
And he set that sun a-blazing in the heavens.
And the light that was left from making the sun
God gathered it up in a shining ball
And flung it against the darkness,   20
Spangling the night with the moon and stars.
Then down between
The darkness and the light
He hurled the world;
And God said: That's good!   25

Then God himself stepped down–
And the sun was on his right hand,
And the moon was on his left;
The stars were clustered about his head,

God the Father by Cristoforo Scacco From the Bob Jones University Collection

And the earth was under his feet.   30
And God walked, and where he trod
His footsteps hollowed the valleys out
And bulged the mountains up.

Then he stopped and looked and saw
That the earth was hot and barren.   35
So God stepped over the edge of the world
And he spat out the seven seas—
He batted his eyes, and the lightnings flashed—
He clapped his hands, and the thunders rolled—
And the waters above the earth came down,   40
The cooling waters came down.

Then the green grass sprouted,
And the little red flowers blossomed,
The pine tree pointed his finger to the sky,
And the oak spread out his arms,   45
The lakes cuddled down in the hollows of the ground,
And the rivers ran down to the sea;

And God smiled again,
And the rainbow appeared,
And curled itself around his shoulder.   50

Then God raised his arm and he waved his hand
Over the sea and over the land,
And he said: Bring forth! Bring forth!
And quicker than God could drop his hand,
Fishes and fowls   55
And beasts and birds
Swam the rivers and the seas,
Roamed the forests and the woods,
And split the air with their wings.
And God said: That's good!   60

Then God walked around,
And God looked around
On all that he had made.
He looked at his sun,
And he looked at his moon,   65
And he looked at his little stars;
He looked on his world
With all its living things,
And God said: I'm lonely still.

Then God sat down—   70
On the side of a hill where he could think;
By a deep, wide river he sat down;
With his head in his hands,
God thought and thought,
Till he thought: I'll make me a man!   75

Up from the bed of the river
God scooped the clay;
And by the bank of the river
He kneeled him down;
And there the great God Almighty   80
Who lit the sun and fixed it in the sky,
Who flung the stars to the most far corner of the night,
Who rounded the earth in the middle of his hand;
This Great God,
Like a mammy bending over her baby,   85
Kneeled down in the dust

Toiling over a lump of clay
Till he shaped it in his own image;

Then into it he blew the breath of life,
And man became a living soul.
Amen. Amen.

For Thought and Discussion

1. Compare the events of creation as Johnson presents them with the narrative in Genesis 1-2. Is the order the same? Is anything added?
2. There is of course a danger of irreverence in anthropomorphism: in assigning human behavior to the Creator and ascribing to Him human feelings and thought processes. Is there, however, justification in Scripture for speaking of God in human terms–for referring to His eyes, ears, hands, voice, wrath, love, etc.? In your opinion, does the poem stay within reverent limits in its depiction of the Creator?
3. Does the style of the poem encourage an acceptance of the details of its narrative as true on the one hand, a dismissal of the entire content as fantasy on the other, or something in between? Is the idea of God that it projects one that orthodox Christians should accept and appreciate? What Biblical characteristics of God appear through the description?
4. Notice the high degree of concreteness in Johnson's narrative as well as in Genesis. Point out a few of the more striking images, and list some of the more vivid verbs. As writers what can we learn from Johnson's example?
5. Where in the poem does Johnson's language come closest to the language of Genesis? What significance can you see in this fact?

T. S. Eliot   1888-1965

Thomas Stearns Eliot dominated the English and American literary scene during the middle third of the twentieth century. His influence affected modern poetry, drama, and criticism. Eliot's earlier years, however, were unspectacular. His broad education included periods at Harvard, the Sorbonne (in Paris), and Oxford. He then taught school in England for two years (1915-17) and from 1918 to 1924 served in various capacities at Lloyd's Bank in London. In 1925 he became a member of the British publishing firm Faber and Faber, where he remained until his death in 1965. Although Eliot's roots were unquestionably American, he felt more at home in England. In fact, in 1927 he became a British subject. The following year, in a statement declaring his conservatism, he described himself as "a royalist in politics, a classicist in literature, and an Anglo-Catholic in religion." In his most important early productions, "The Love Song of J. Alfred Prufrock" (1917) and "The Waste Land" (1922), Eliot starkly portrayed the sterility of modern life. For this purpose he forged a new form of poetry that incorporates irony, abrupt shifts, wide variation in diction, and countless allusions. Meanwhile his literary criticism was shaping the tastes of a whole generation of poets and critics. The year 1927 marked a major shift in Eliot's life and work. After this point his works became more religious. The "Journey of the Magi" (1927), which appeared during this time of transition, describes the poet's conversion to Christianity. Although Eliot's interest in traditional Christianity alienated some of his following, his influence remained considerable. He received numerous honors, including the Nobel Prize for literature and Great Britain's highest award, the Order of Merit. Eliot's speaking tours of the United States became popular events. Indeed, no other modern poet has written difficult verse that stirred such an enthusiastic response from the general readers. And yet Eliot's conservatism places him in a dwindling minority among modern writers. Like many of them he records modern ills, but unlike them he diagnoses these ills and prescribes a remedy. That remedy is a return to tradition, particularly to traditional religion.

Journey of the Magi

"Journey of the Magi," first published in 1927, came as an abrupt contrast to Eliot's earlier poems describing the sterility and materialism of modern life. This later poem provides meaning on at least three levels. It is, first, a **dramatic monologue** *spoken by one of the Biblical wise men who came to see the Christ Child.*

It is, second, according to many critics, a symbolic account of Eliot's own conversion to Christianity. It is, third, an imaginative portrayal of the journey of a soul from doubt and despair to spiritual life.

"A cold coming we had of it,
Just the worst time of the year
For a journey, and such a long journey:
The ways deep and the weather sharp,
The very dead of winter."*   5
And the camels galled,* sore-footed, refractory,*
Lying down in the melting snow.
There were times we regretted*
The summer palaces on slopes, the terraces,
And the silken girls bringing sherbet.   10
Then the camel men cursing and grumbling
And running away, and wanting their liquor and women,
And the night-fires going out, and the lack of shelters,
And the cities hostile and the towns unfriendly
And the villages dirty and charging high prices: 15
A hard time we had of it.
At the end we preferred to travel all night,
Sleeping in snatches,
With the voices singing in our ears, saying
That this was all folly.   20

Then at dawn we came down to a temperate* valley,
Wet, below the snow line, smelling of vegetation,
With a running stream and a water-mill beating the darkness,
And three trees on the low sky.*
And an old white horse* galloped away in the meadow.   25
Then we came to a tavern with vine-leaves over the lintel,*
Six hands at an open door dicing for pieces of silver,*
And feet kicking the empty wine-skins.
But there was no information, and so we continued
And arrived at evening, not a moment too soon   30
Finding the place; it was (you may say) satisfactory.

All this was a long time ago, I remember,
And I would do it again, but set down
This set down
This: were we led all that way for   35
Birth or Death? There was a Birth, certainly,
We had evidence and no doubt. I had seen birth and death,

The . . . winter: This passage (ll. 1-5) appears in a sermon by Lancelot Andrewes (1555-1626).
galled: gall: a skin sore/*refractory:* unmanageable
regretted: i.e., felt sorry for leaving

temperate: having a mild climate

three . . . sky: cf. Matthew 27:38, 45
white horse: cf. Revelation 19:11
lintel: cf. Exodus 12:7-13
Six . . . silver: cf. Matthew 27:3

But had thought they were different; this Birth was
Hard and bitter agony for us, like Death, our death.
We returned to our places, these Kingdoms,   40
But no longer at ease here, in the old dispensation,*
With an alien* people clutching their gods.
I should be glad of another death.

old dispensation: the dispensation of law (while the speaker is under the dispensation of grace)
alien: strange

For Thought and Discussion

1. "Tell all the truth, but tell it slant," wrote Emily Dickinson in one of her poems. There is no question that Eliot told it "slant"–that is, indirectly. Did he tell "all the truth" clearly enough to be recognizable? Why do you suppose he chose in this poem to reveal his beliefs obliquely through the words of a character and by means of a difficult style?

2. What is the dominant impression of the phase of the journey summarized in stanza 1 (ll. 1-20)? What does this characteristic suggest about the experience of a person seeking salvation? What quality of character does it require of him?

3. What must the traveler overcome in the phase of the journey described in stanza 2 (ll. 21-31)? What might the momentary delay of the Magi in the poem correspond to in the Biblical account of the Wise Men? In the experience of the modern seeker?

4. What two interpretations might be given for the last statement in stanza 2? Which of them do you think is better warranted from the facts of the poem?

5. Explain the paradoxical statements about birth and death in the last stanza. In how many senses are birth and death referred to? In what way did the travelers' sight of the divine Child produce in them a birth and a death? How has this death continued to affect them and their relationships with others? Why should the poem's speaker "be glad of another death"?

13 Modern American Prose

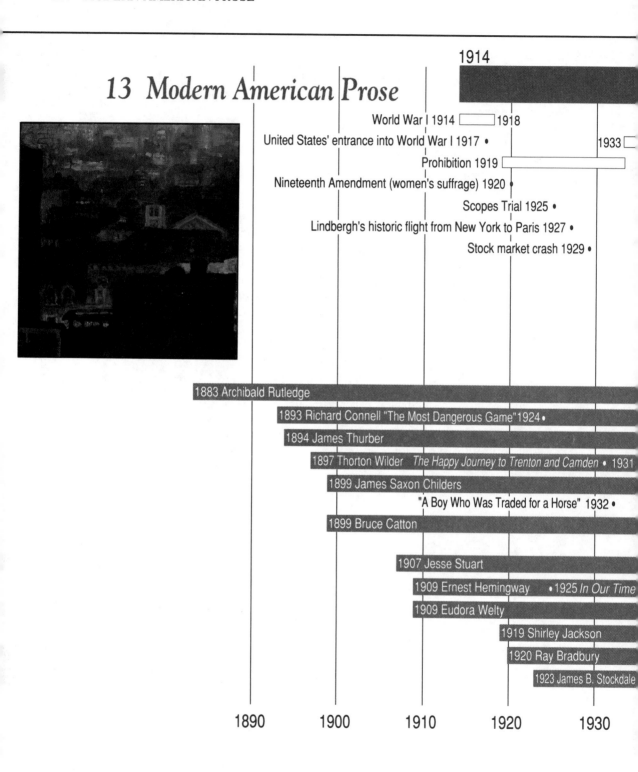

1914

World War I 1914 ☐ 1918

United States' entrance into World War I 1917 •

1933 ☐

Prohibition 1919 ☐

Nineteenth Amendment (women's suffrage) 1920 •

Scopes Trial 1925 •

Lindbergh's historic flight from New York to Paris 1927 •

Stock market crash 1929 •

1883 Archibald Rutledge

1893 Richard Connell "The Most Dangerous Game"1924 •

1894 James Thurber

1897 Thorton Wilder *The Happy Journey to Trenton and Camden* • 1931

1899 James Saxon Childers

"A Boy Who Was Traded for a Horse" 1932 •

1899 Bruce Catton

1907 Jesse Stuart

1909 Ernest Hemingway • 1925 *In Our Time*

1909 Eudora Welty

1919 Shirley Jackson

1920 Ray Bradbury

1923 James B. Stockdale

1890   1900   1910   1920   1930

The Present

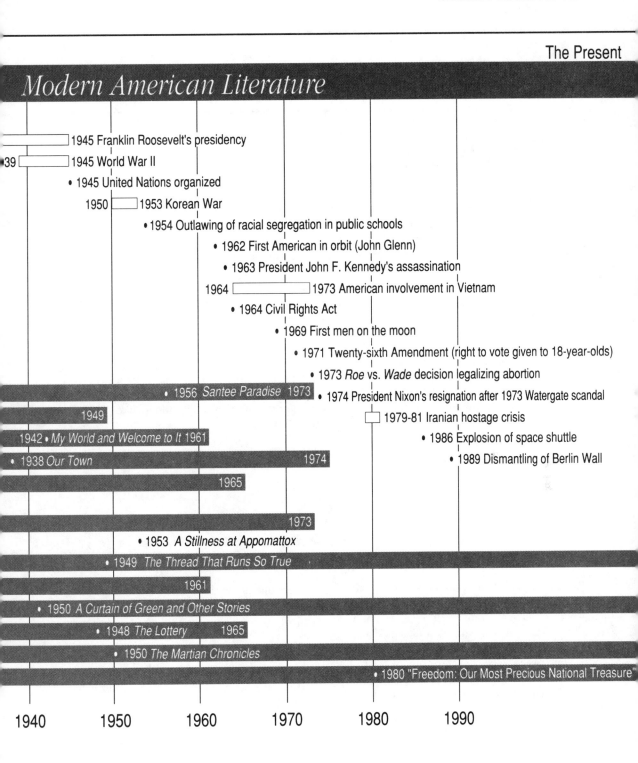

Modern American Literature

1945 Franklin Roosevelt's presidency

39 1945 World War II

• 1945 United Nations organized

1950 1953 Korean War

• 1954 Outlawing of racial segregation in public schools

• 1962 First American in orbit (John Glenn)

• 1963 President John F. Kennedy's assassination

1964 1973 American involvement in Vietnam

• 1964 Civil Rights Act

• 1969 First men on the moon

• 1971 Twenty-sixth Amendment (right to vote given to 18-year-olds)

• 1973 *Roe* vs. *Wade* decision legalizing abortion

• 1956 *Santee Paradise* 1973

• 1974 President Nixon's resignation after 1973 Watergate scandal

1949

1979-81 Iranian hostage crisis

1942 • *My World and Welcome to It* 1961

• 1986 Explosion of space shuttle

• 1938 *Our Town* 1974

• 1989 Dismantling of Berlin Wall

1965

1973

• 1953 *A Stillness at Appomattox*

• 1949 *The Thread That Runs So True*

1961

• 1950 *A Curtain of Green and Other Stories*

• 1948 *The Lottery* 1965

• 1950 *The Martian Chronicles*

• 1980 "Freedom: Our Most Precious National Treasure"

1940   1950   1960   1970   1980   1990

Developers of Plot and Conflict

Shirley Jackson   1919-1965

Although born in San Francisco, Shirley Jackson (1919-1965) spent all but the first fourteen years of her life in the East. By the time she was fourteen, she was already actively writing. During her college years at Syracuse University, she published her work in student publications and founded and edited a campus literary magazine. After graduation and marriage, she combined writing for national publications with rearing a family of four children. In 1948 her first novel and several of her most memorable stories appeared. As interest in her writing grew, she received invitations to speak at writers' conferences and universities around the country. In 1965, while in her forty-sixth year, she died of heart failure.

Jackson wrote primarily to entertain. A born storyteller, she combined humor, mystery, and **suspense** to create stories whose endings often surprise their readers. Her fiction falls generally into one of two categories. One group is the bizarre stories that detail the horror arising from the supernatural or from emotional and mental disturbance. Her attraction to demonology and abnormality in these stories, however, mars them for Christian readers. The other category is the humorous stories, like ''Charles,'' that were suggested by her family experiences.

Charles

''Charles,'' which first appeared in 1948, is an entertaining story in which appearances are deceptive.

The day my son Laurie started kindergarten, he renounced corduroy overalls with bibs and began wearing blue jeans with a belt; I watched him go off the first morning with the older girl next door, seeing clearly that an era of my life was ended, my sweet-voiced, nursery-school tot replaced by a long-trousered, swaggering* character who forgot to stop at the corner and wave good-by to me.

swaggering: walking with a self-important air

He came home the same way, the front door slamming open, his cap on the floor, and the voice suddenly become raucous* shouting, ''Isn't anybody *here?*''

raucous: rough-sounding, harsh

At lunch he spoke insolently* to his father, spilled his baby sister's milk, and remarked that his teacher said we were not to take the name of the Lord in vain.

insolently: impudently, insultingly

"How *was* school today?" I asked, elaborately casual.

"All right," he said.

"Did you learn anything?" his father asked.

Laurie regarded his father coldly. "I didn't learn nothing," he said.

"Anything," I said. "Didn't learn anything."

"The teacher spanked a boy, though," Laurie said, addressing his bread and butter. "For being fresh," he added, with this mouth full.

"What did he do?" I asked. "Who was it?"

Laurie thought. "It was Charles," he said. "He was fresh. The teacher spanked him and made him stand in a corner. He was awfully fresh."

"What did he do?" I asked again, but Laurie slid off his chair, took a cookie, and left, while his father was still saying, "See here, young man."

The next day Laurie remarked at lunch, as soon as he sat down, "Well, Charles was bad again today." He grinned enormously and said, "Today Charles hit the teacher."

"Good heavens," I said, mindful of the Lord's name, "I suppose he got spanked again?"

"He sure did," Laurie said. "Look up," he said to his father.

"What?" his father said, looking up.

"Look down," Laurie said. "Look at my thumb. Gee, you're dumb." He began to laugh insanely.

"Why did Charles hit the teacher?" I asked quickly.

"Because she tried to make him color with red crayons," Laurie said. "Charles wanted to color with green crayons so he hit the teacher and she spanked him and said nobody play with Charles but everybody did."

The third day—it was Wednesday of the first week—Charles bounced a seesaw onto the head of a little girl and made her bleed, and the teacher made him stay inside all during recess. Thursday Charles had to stand in a corner during story time because he kept pounding his feet on the floor. Friday Charles was deprived of blackboard privileges because he threw chalk.

On Saturday I remarked to my husband, "Do you think kindergarten is too unsettling for Laurie? All this toughness, and bad grammar, and this Charles boy sounds like such a bad influence."

"It'll be all right," my husband said reassuringly. "Bound to be people like Charles in the world. Might as well meet them now as later."

On Monday Laurie came home late, full of news. "Charles," he shouted as he came up the hill; I was waiting anxiously on the front steps. "Charles," Laurie yelled all the way up the hill, "Charles was bad again."

"Come right in," I said, as soon as he came close enough. "Lunch is waiting."

"You know what Charles did?" he demanded, following me through the door. "Charles yelled so in school they sent a boy in from first grade to tell the teacher she had to make Charles keep quiet, and so Charles had to stay after school. And so all the children stayed to watch him.''

"What did he do?" I asked.

"He just sat there," Laurie said, climbing into his chair at the table. "Hi, Pop, y'old dust mop."

"Charles had to stay after school today," I told my husband. "Everybody stayed with him."

"What does Charles look like?" my husband asked Laurie. "What's his other name?"

"He's bigger than me," Laurie said. "And he doesn't have any rubbers and he doesn't ever wear a jacket."

Monday night was the first Parent-Teachers meeting, and only the fact that the baby had a cold kept me from going; I wanted passionately to meet Charles's mother. On Tuesday Laurie remarked suddenly, "Our teacher had a friend come to see her in school today."

"Charles's mother?" my husband and I asked simultaneously.

"Naaah," Laurie said scornfully. "It was a man who came and made us do exercises; we had to touch our toes. Look." He climbed down from his chair and squatted down and touched his toes. "Like this," he said. He got solemnly back into his chair and said, picking up his fork, "Charles didn't even *do* exercises."

"That's fine," I said heartily. "Didn't Charles want to do exercises?"

"Naaah," Laurie said. "Charles was so fresh to the teacher's friend he wasn't *let* do exercises."

"Fresh again?" I said.

"He kicked the teacher's friend," Laurie said. "The teacher's friend told Charles to touch his toes like I just did and Charles kicked him."

"What are they going to do about Charles, do you suppose?" Laurie's father asked him.

Laurie shrugged elaborately. "Throw him out of school, I guess," he said.

Wednesday and Thursday were routine; Charles yelled during story hour and hit a boy in the stomach and made him cry. On Friday Charles stayed after school again, and so did all the other children.

With the third week of kindergarten, Charles was an institution in our family; the baby was being a Charles when she cried all afternoon; Laurie did a Charles when he filled his wagon full of mud and pulled it through the kitchen; even my husband, when he caught his elbow in the telephone cord and pulled telephone, ash tray, and bowl of flowers off the table, said, after the first minute, "Looks like Charles."

During the third and fourth weeks it looked like a reformation in Charles; Laurie reported grimly at lunch on Thursday of the third week, "Charles was so good today the teacher gave him an apple."

"What?" I said, and my husband added warily,* "You mean Charles?"

---
warily: cautiously

"Charles," Laurie said. "He gave the crayons around and he picked up the books afterwards and the teacher said he was her helper."

"What happened?" I asked incredulously.*

---
incredulously: i.e., with complete disbelief

"He was her helper, that's all," Laurie said, and shrugged.

"Can this be true about Charles?" I asked my husband that night. "Can something like this happen?"

"Wait and see," my husband said cynically. "When you've got a Charles to deal with, this may mean he's only plotting."

He seemed to be wrong. For over a week Charles was the teacher's helper; each day he handed things out and he picked things up; no one had to stay after school.

"The P.T.A. meeting's next week again," I told my husband one evening. "I'm going to find Charles's mother there."

"Ask her what happened to Charles," my husband said. "I'd like to know."

"I'd like to know myself," I said.

On Friday of that week, things were back to normal, "You know what Charles did today?" Laurie demanded at the lunch table in a voice slightly awed. "He told a little girl to say a word and she said it and the teacher washed her mouth out with soap and Charles laughed."

"What word?" his father asked unwisely, and Laurie said, "I'll have to whisper it to you, it's so bad." He got down off his chair and went around to his father. His father bent his head down, and Laurie whispered joyfully. His father's eyes widened.

"Did Charles tell the little girl to say *that?*" he asked respectfully.

"She said it *twice,*" Laurie said. "Charles told her to say it *twice.*"

"What happened to Charles?" my husband asked.

"Nothing," Laurie said. "He was passing out crayons."

Monday morning Charles abandoned the little girl and said the evil word himself three or four times, getting his mouth washed out with soap each time. He also threw chalk.

My husband came to the door with me that evening as I set out for the P.T.A. meeting. "Invite her over for a cup of tea after the meeting," he said. "I want to get a look at her."

"If only she's there," I said prayerfully.

"She'll be there," my husband said. "I don't see how they could hold a P.T.A. meeting without Charles's mother."

At the meeting I sat restlessly, scanning each comfortable matronly face, trying to determine which one hid the secret of Charles. None of them looked to me haggard* enough. No one stood up in the meeting and apologized for the way her son had been acting. No one mentioned Charles.

---

haggard: worn and exhausted

After the meeting I identified and sought out Laurie's kindergarten teacher. She had a plate with a cup of tea and a piece of chocolate cake;

I had a plate with a cup of tea and a piece of marshmallow cake. We maneuvered up to one another cautiously and smiled.

"I've been so anxious to meet you," I said. "I'm Laurie's mother."

"We're so interested in Laurie," she said.

"Well, he certainly likes kindergarten," I said. "He talks about it all the time."

"We had a little trouble adjusting, the first week or so," she said primly, "but now he's a fine little helper. With occasional lapses, of course.''

"Laurie usually adjusts very quickly," I said. "I suppose this time it's Charles's influence."

"Charles?"

"Yes," I said, laughing, "you must have your hands full in that kindergarten with Charles."

"Charles?" she said. "We don't have any Charles in the kindergarten."

For Thought and Discussion

1. In "Charles" the conflict is actually two-fold. What is the most obvious conflict, and how do the main parties in this conflict respond to one another? What other conflict becomes apparent at the conclusion of the story?

2. How would you describe Laurie, the main character of the story? How do you find out about him? How does he change after he begins kindergarten and throughout the course of the story? In what ways is he a realistic character?

3. How does Jackson develop the plot in "Charles"? From whose point of view is the story told? How does the author build suspense? What period of time does the story cover? Do you think the surprise ending is effective and consistent with the rest of the story?

4. Were you as surprised as Laurie's mother was when she discovered who Charles really was? Point out several examples of foreshadowing that Jackson provides for the careful reader to prepare him for the surprise. Do you think Laurie's parents should have realized what was happening? Why or why not?

5. How does Jackson create a humorous tone in the story? Are there any elements which the author treats humorously that are troublesome to you as a Christian? What is the basis for your objections?

Richard Connell 1893-1949

Born in Poughkeepsie, New York, Richard Connell became a professional writer while still a child. When ten, he began reporting on baseball games for his father's newspaper. At sixteen he was the paper's editor. While a student at Harvard, he wrote for two campus publications. In the army during World War I, he edited an army-camp newspaper called *Gas Attack*. After the war he became a free-lance writer working primarily in the short-story **genre.** By the time of his death in 1949, he had published over three hundred short stories.

Probably Connell's most famous story is "The Most Dangerous Game." This tale contains a highly original **plot** based upon the universal predicament of the hunted. It is a masterpiece of **suspense.** As in the stories of Edgar Allan Poe (1809-49), the outcome is not determined until the final paragraph. Although primarily a romantic thriller, this story implies a serious **theme:** the conflict between the morality of the Old World and that of the New. You will find it significant to note whether the American, the "good" man, emerges triumphant at the end.

The Most Dangerous Game

"Off there to the right–somewhere–is a large island," said Whitney. "It's rather a mystery–"

"What island is it?" Rainsford asked.

"The old charts call it 'Ship-Trap Island,' " Whitney replied. "A suggestive name, isn't it? Sailors have a curious dread of the place. I don't know why. Some superstition–"

"Can't see it," remarked Rainsford, trying to peer through the dank* tropical night that was palpable* as it pressed its thick warm blackness in upon the yacht.

---

dank: uncomfortably damp
palpable: able to be touched

"You've good eyes," said Whitney, with a laugh, "and I've seen you pick off a moose moving in the brown fall bush at four hundred yards, but even you can't see four miles or so through a moonless Caribbean night."

"Nor four yards," admitted Rainsford. "Ugh! It's like moist black velvet."

"It will be light enough in Rio," promised Whitney. "We should make it in a few days. I hope the jaguar guns have come from Purdey's. We should have some good hunting up the Amazon. Great sport, hunting."

"The best sport in the world," agreed Rainsford.

"For the hunter," amended* Whitney. "Not for the jaguar."

---

amended: corrected

"Don't talk rot, Whitney," said Rainsford. "You're a big-game hunter, not a philosopher. Who cares how a jaguar feels?"

"Perhaps the jaguar does," observed Whitney.

"Bah! They've no understanding."

"Even so, I rather think they understand one thing–fear. The fear of pain and the fear of death."

"Nonsense," laughed Rainsford. "This hot weather is making you soft, Whitney. Be a realist. The world is made up of two classes–the hunters and the huntees. Luckily, you and I are the hunters. Do you think we've passed that island yet?"

"I can't tell in the dark. I hope so."

"Why?" asked Rainsford.

"The place has a reputation–a bad one."

"Cannibals?" suggested Rainsford.

"Hardly. Even cannibals wouldn't live in such a place. But it's got into sailor lore,* somehow. Didn't you notice that the crew's nerves seemed a bit jumpy today?"

---

lore: traditional knowledge

"They were a bit strange, now you mention it. Even Captain Nielsen–"

"Yes, even that tough-minded old Swede. . . . Those fishy blue eyes held a look I never saw there before. All I could get out of him was: 'This place has an evil name among seafaring men, sir.' Then he said to me, very gravely: 'don't you feel anything?'–as if the air about us was actually poisonous. Now, you mustn't laugh when I tell you this–I did feel something like a sudden chill.

"There was no breeze. The sea was as flat as a plate-glass window. We were drawing near the island then. What I felt was a–a mental chill; a sort of sudden dread."

"Pure imagination," said Rainsford. "One superstitious sailor can taint* the whole ship's company with his fear."

---

taint: affect with something bad

"Maybe. But sometimes I think sailors have an extra sense that tells them when they are in danger. Sometimes I think evil is a tangible* thing–with wave lengths, just as sound and light have. An evil place can, so to speak, broadcast vibrations of evil. Anyhow, I'm glad we're getting out of this zone. Well, I think I'll turn in now, Rainsford.''

---

tangible: able to be felt or touched

''I'm not sleepy,'' said Rainsford. ''I'm going to smoke another pipe up on the after deck.''

''Good night, then, Rainsford. See you at breakfast.''

There was no sound in the night as Rainsford sat there but the muffled throb of the engine that drove the yacht swiftly through the darkness, and the swish and ripple of the wash of the propeller.

Rainsford, reclining in a streamer chair, indolently* puffed on his favorite brier. The sensuous* drowsiness of the night was on him. ''It's so dark,'' he thought, ''that I could sleep without closing my eyes; the night would be my eyelids–''

---

indolently: lazily
sensuous: appealing to the senses

An abrupt sound startled him. Off to the right he heard it, and his ears, expert in such matters, could not be mistaken. Again he heard the sound, and again. Somewhere, off in the blackness, someone had fired a gun three times.

Rainsford sprang up and moved quickly to the rail, mystified. He strained his eyes in the direction from which the reports had come, but it was like trying to see through a blanket. He leaped upon the rail and balanced himself there, to get greater elevation; his pipe, striking a rope, was knocked from his mouth. He lunged for it; a short, hoarse cry came from his lips as he realized he had reached too far and lost his balance. The cry was pinched off short as the blood-warm waters of the Caribbean Sea closed over his head.

He struggled up to the surface and tried to cry out, but the wash from the speeding yacht slapped him in the face and the salt water in his open mouth made him gag and strangle. Desperately he struck out with strong strokes after the receding lights of the yacht, but he stopped before he had swum fifty feet. A certain coolheadedness had come to him; it was not the first time he had been in a tight place. There was a chance that his cries could be heard by someone aboard the yacht, but that chance was slender, and grew more slender as the yacht raced on. He wrestled himself out of his clothes, and shouted with all his power. The lights of the yacht became faint and ever-vanishing fireflies; then they were blotted out entirely by the night.

Rainsford remembered the shots. They had come from the right, and doggedly he swam in that direction, swimming with slow, deliberate strokes, conserving his strength. For a seemingly endless time he fought the sea. He began to count his strokes; he could do possibly a hundred more and then–

Rainsford heard a sound. It came out of the darkness, a high screaming sound, the sound of an animal in an extremity of anguish and terror.

He did not recognize the animal that made the sound; he did not try to; with fresh vitality he swam toward the sound. He heard it again; then it was cut short by another noise, crisp, staccato.

''Pistol shot,'' muttered Rainsford, swimming on.

Ten minutes of determined effort brought another sound to his ears–the most welcome he had ever heard–the muttering and growling of the sea breaking on a rocky shore. He was almost on the rocks before he saw them; on a night less calm he would have been shattered against them. With his remaining strength he dragged himself from the swirling waters. Jagged crags appeared to jut up into the opaqueness;* he forced himself upward, hand over hand. Gasping, his hand raw, he reached a flat place at the top. Dense jungle came down to the very edge of the cliffs. What perils that tangle of trees and underbrush might hold for him did not concern Rainsford just then. All he knew was that he was safe from his enemy, the sea, and that utter weariness was on him. He flung himself down at the jungle edge and tumbled into the deepest sleep of his life.

opaqueness: darkness

When he opened his eyes he knew from the position of the sun that it was late in the afternoon. Sleep had given him new vigor; a sharp hunger was picking at him. He looked about, almost cheerfully.

"Where there are pistol shots, there are men. Where there are men, there is food," he thought. But what kind of men, he wondered, in so forbidding a place? An unbroken front of snarled and ragged jungle fringed the shore.

He saw no sign of a trail through the closely knit web of weeds and trees; it was easier to go along the shore, and Rainsford floundered along by the water. Not far from where he had landed, he stopped.

Some wounded thing, by the evidence, a large animal, had thrashed about in the underbrush; the jungle weeds were crushed down and the moss was lacerated; one patch of weed was stained crimson. A small, glittering object not far away caught Rainsford's eye and he picked it up. It was an empty cartridge.

"A twenty-two," he remarked. "That's odd. It must have been a fairly large animal too. The hunter had his nerve with him to tackle it with a light gun. It's clear that the brute put up a fight. I suppose the first three shots I heard was when the hunter flushed* his quarry* and wounded it. The last shot was when he trailed it here and finished it."

flushed: drove from hiding
quarry: that which is hunted

He examined the ground closely and found what he had hoped to find—the print of hunting boots. They pointed along the cliff in the direction he had been going. Eagerly he hurried along, now slipping on a rotten log or a loose stone, but making headway; night was beginning to settle down on the island.

Bleak darkness was blacking out the sea and the jungle when Rainsford sighted the lights. He came upon them as he turned a crook in the coast line, and his first thought was that he had come upon a village, for there were many lights. But as he forged along he saw to his great astonishment that all the lights were in one enormous building—a lofty structure with pointed towers plunging upward into the gloom. His eyes made out the shadowy outlines of a palatial* château;* it was set on a high bluff, and on three sides of it cliffs dived down to where the sea licked greedy lips in the shadows.

palatial: like a palace
château: a large French country house

"Mirage," thought Rainsford. But it was no mirage, he found, when he opened the tall spiked iron gate. The stone steps were real enough; the massive door with a leering gargoyle for a knocker was real enough; yet above it all hung an air of unreality.

He lifted the knocker, and it creaked up stiffly, as if it had never before been used. He let it fall, and it startled him with its booming loudness. He thought he heard steps within; the door remained closed. Again Rainsford lifted the heavy knocker, and let it fall. The door opened then, opened suddenly as if it were on a spring, and Rainsford stood blinking in the river of glaring gold light that poured out. The first thing Rainsford's eyes discerned was the largest man Rainsford had ever seen—a gigantic creature, solidly made and black-bearded to the waist. In his hand the man held a long-barreled revolver, and he was pointing it straight at Rainsford's heart.

Out of the snarl of beard two small eyes regarded Rainsford.

"Don't be alarmed," said Rainsford, with a smile which he hoped was disarming.* "I'm no robber. I fell off a yacht. My name is Sanger Rainsford of New York City."

disarming: removing suspicion or fear

The menacing look in the eyes did not change. The revolver pointed as rigidly as if the giant were a statue. He gave no sign that he understood Rainsford's words, or that he had even heard them. He was dressed in uniform, a black uniform trimmed with gray asktrakhan.*

asktrakhan: curled fur

"I'm Sanger Rainsford of New York," Rainsford began again. "I fell off a yacht. I am hungry."

The man's only answer was to raise with his thumb the hammer of his revolver. Then Rains-ford saw the man's free hand go to his forehead in a military salute, and he saw him click his heels together and stand at attention. Another man was coming down the broad marble steps, an erect, slender man in evening clothes. He advanced to Rainsford and held out his hand.

In a cultivated voice marked by a slight accent that gave it added precision and deliberateness, he said: "It is a very great pleasure and honor to welcome Mr. Sanger Rainsford, the celebrated hunter, to my home."

Automatically Rainsford shook the man's hand.

"I've read your book about hunting snow leopards in Tibet, you see," explained the man. "I am General Zaroff."

Rainsford's first impression was that the man was singularly handsome; his second was that there was an original, almost bizarre quality about the general's face. He was a tall man past the middle age, for his hair was a vivid white; but his thick eyebrows and pointed military mustache were as black as the night from which Rainsford had come. His eyes, too, were black and very bright. He had high cheek bones, a sharp-cut nose, a spare, dark face, the face of a man used to giving orders, the face of an aristocrat. Turning to the giant in uniform, the general made a sign. The giant put away his pistol, saluted, withdrew.

"Ivan is an incredibly strong fellow," remarked the general, "but he has the misfortune to be deaf and dumb. A simple fellow, but, I'm afraid, like all his race, a bit of a savage."

"Is he Russian?"

"He is Cossack,"* said the general, and his smile showed red lips and pointed teeth. "So am I."

Cossack: i.e., from southern Russia

"Come," he said, "we shouldn't be chatting here. We can talk later. Now you want clothes, food, rest. You shall have them. This is a most restful spot."

Ivan had reappeared, and the general spoke to him with lips that moved but gave forth no sound.

"Follow Ivan, if you please, Mr. Rainsford," said the general. "I was about to have my dinner when you came. I'll wait for you. You'll find that my clothes will fit you, I think."

It was to a huge, beam-ceilinged bedroom with a canopied bed big enough for six men that Rainsford followed the silent giant. Ivan laid out an evening suit, and Rainsford, as he put it on, noticed that it came from a London tailor who ordinarily cut and sewed for none below the rank of a duke.

The dining room to which Ivan conducted him was in many ways remarkable. There was a medieval magnificence about it; it suggested a baronial* hall of feudal times with its oaken panels, its high ceiling, its vast refectory* tables where twoscore men could sit down to eat. About the hall were the mounted heads of many animals—lions, tigers, elephants, moose, bears; larger or more perfect specimens Rainsford had never seen. At the great table the general was sitting, alone.

baronial: belonging to a nobleman
refectory: long, narrow dining table

"You'll have a cocktail, Mr. Rainsford," he suggested. The cocktail was surpassingly good; and, Rainsford noted, the table appointments* were of the finest—the linen, the crystal, the silver, the china.

appointments: furnishings

They were eating borsch, the rich red soup with whipped cream so dear to Russian palates. Half apologetically General Zaroff said: "We do our best to preserve the amenities* of civilization here. Please forgive any lapses.* We are well off the beaten track, you know. Do you think the champagne has suffered from its long ocean trip?"

amenities: social courtesies
lapses: fallings away from a standard

"Not in the least," declared Rainsford. He was finding the general a most thoughtful and affable* host, a true cosmopolite.* But there was one small trait of the general's that made Rainsford uncomfortable. Whenever he looked up from his plate he found the general studying him, appraising* him narrowly.

affable: pleasant
cosmopolite: one who is at home everywhere
appraising: judging the quality of

"Perhaps," said General Zaroff, "you were surprised that I recognized your name. You see, I read all the books on hunting published in English, French, and Russian. I have but one passion in my life, Mr. Rainsford, and it is the hunt."

"You have some wonderful heads here," said Rainsford as he ate a particularly well cooked *filet mignon.* "That Cape buffalo is the largest I ever saw."

"Oh, that fellow. Yes, he was a monster."

"Did he charge you?"

"Hurled me against a tree," said the general. "Fractured my skull. But I got the brute."

"I've always thought," said Rainsford, "that the Cape buffalo is the most dangerous of all big game."

For a moment the general did not reply; he was smiling his curious, red-lipped smile. Then he said slowly: "No. You are wrong, sir. The Cape buffalo is not the most dangerous big game." He sipped his wine. "Here in my preserve on this island," he said in the same slow tone, "I hunt more dangerous game."

Rainsford expressed his surprise. "Is there big game on this island?"

The general nodded. "The biggest."

"Really?"

"Oh, it isn't here naturally, of course. I have to stock the island."

"What have you imported, general?" Rainsford asked. "Tigers?"

The general smiled. "No," he said. "Hunting tigers ceased to interest me some years ago. I exhausted their possibilities, you see. No thrill left in tigers, no real danger. I live for danger, Mr. Rainsford."

The general took from his pocket a gold cigarette case and offered his guest a long black cigarette with a silver tip; it was perfumed and gave off a smell like incense.

"We will have some capital* hunting, you and I," said the general. "I shall be most glad to have your society."

capital: first-rate

"But what game—" began Rainsford.

"I'll tell you," said the general. "You will be amused, I know. I think I may say, in all modesty, that I have done a rare thing. I have invented a new sensation. May I pour you another glass of port?"

"Thank you, general."

The general filled both glasses, and said: "God makes some men poets. Some He makes kings, some beggars. Me He made a hunter. My hand was made for the trigger, my father said. He was a very rich man with a quarter of a million acres in the Crimea, and he was an ardent* sportsman. When I was only five years old he gave me a little gun, specially made in Moscow for me, to shoot sparrows with. When I shot some of his prize turkeys with it, he did not punish me; he complimented me on my marksmanship. I killed my first bear in the Caucasus when I was ten. My whole life has been one prolonged hunt. I went into the army—it was expected of noblemen's sons—and for a time commanded a division of Cossack cavalry, but my real interest was always the hunt. I have hunted every kind of game in every land. It would be impossible for me to tell you how many animals I have killed."

ardent: zealous, intense

The general puffed at his cigarette.

"After the debacle* in Russia I left the country, for it was imprudent for an officer of the Tsar to stay there. Many noble Russians lost everything. I, luckily, had invested heavily in American securities,* so I shall never have to open a tea room in Monte Carlo or drive a taxi in Paris. Naturally, I continued to hunt—grizzlies in your Rockies, crocodile in the Ganges, rhinoceroses in East Africa. It was in Africa that the Cape buffalo hit me and laid me up for six months. As soon as

I recovered I started for the Amazon to hunt jaguars, for I had heard they were unusually cunning. They weren't.'' The Cossack sighed. ''They were no match at all for a hunter with his wits about him, and a high-powered rifle. I was bitterly disappointed. I was lying in my tent with a splitting headache one night when a terrible thought pushed its way into my mind. Hunting was beginning to bore me! And hunting, remember, had been my life. I have heard that in America businessmen often go to pieces when they give up the business that has been their life.''

debacle: i.e., the 1917 Bolshevik Revolution
securities: stocks, bonds, etc.

''Yes, that's so,'' said Rainsford.

The general smiled. ''I had no wish to go to pieces,'' he said. ''I must do something. Now, mine is an analytical* mind, Mr. Rainsford. Doubtless that is why I enjoy the problems of the chase.''

analytical: skilled in reasoning

''No doubt, General Zaroff.''

''So,'' continued the general, ''I asked myself why the hunt no longer fascinated me. You are much younger than I am, Mr. Rainsford, and have not hunted as much, but you perhaps can guess the answer.''

''What was it?''

''Simply this: hunting had ceased to be what you call 'a sporting proposition.' It had become too easy. I always got my quarry. Always. There is no greater bore than perfection.''

The general lit a fresh cigarette.

''No animal had a chance with me any more. That is no boast; it is mathematical certainty. The animal had nothing but his legs and his instinct. Instinct is no match for reason. When I thought of this it was a tragic moment for me, I can tell you.''

Rainsford leaned across the table, absorbed in what his host was saying.

''It came to me as an inspiration what I must do,'' the general went on.

''And that was?''

The general smiled the quiet smile of one who has faced an obstacle and surmounted* it with success. ''I had to invent a new animal to hunt,'' he said.

surmounted: overcome

''A new animal? You're joking.''

''Not at all,'' said the general. ''I never joke about hunting. I needed a new animal. I found one. So I bought this island, built this house, and here I do my hunting. The island is perfect for my purposes–there are jungles with a maze of trails in them, hills, swamps–''

''But the animal, General Zaroff?''

''Oh,'' said the general, ''it supplies me with the most exciting hunting in the world. No other hunting compares with it for an instant. Every day I hunt, and I never grow bored now, for I have quarry with which I can match my wits.''

Rainsford's bewilderment showed in his face.

''I wanted the ideal animal to hunt,'' explained the general. ''So, I said: 'What are the attributes of an ideal quarry?' And the answer was, of course; 'It must have courage, cunning, and above all, it must be able to reason.' ''

''But no animal can reason,'' objected Rainsford.

''My dear fellow,'' said the general, ''there is one that can.''

''But you can't mean–'' gasped Rainsford.

''And why not?''

''I can't believe you are serious, General Zaroff. This is a grisly* joke.''

grisly: horrible

''Why should I not be serious? I am speaking of hunting.''

''Hunting? Hunting? General Zaroff, what you speak of is murder.''

The general laughed with entire good nature. He regarded Rainsford quizzically. ''I refuse to believe that so modern and civilized a young man as you seem to be harbors romantic ideas about the value of human life. Surely your experiences in the war–''

''Did not make me condone cold-blooded murder,'' finished Rainsford stiffly.

Laughter shook the general. ''How extraordinarily droll* you are!'' he said. ''One does not expect nowadays to find a young man of the educated class, even in America, with such a naïve,* and if I may say so, Mid-Victorian point of view. It's like finding a snuffbox in a limousine. Ah, well, doubtless you had Puritan ancestors. So many Americans appear to have had. I'll wager you'll forget your notions when you go hunting with me. You've a genuine new thrill in store for you, Mr. Rainsford.''

droll: amusing
naïve: foolishly simple

''Thank you, I'm a hunter, not a murderer.''

''Dear me,'' said the general, quite unruffled, ''again that unpleasant word. But I think I can show you that your scruples* are quite ill-founded.''

scruples: objection to something one thinks is wrong

''Yes?''

''Life is for the strong, to be lived by the strong, and, if need be, taken by the strong. The weak of the world were put here to give the strong pleasure. I am strong. Why should I not use my gift? If I wish to hunt, why should I not? I hunt the scum of the earth–sailors from tramp ships–lascars,* blacks, Chinese, whites, mongrels*–a thoroughbred horse or hound is worth more than a score of them.''

lascars: sailors of east India
mongrels: of mixed or unknown ancestry

''But they are men,'' said Rainsford hotly.

''Precisely,'' said the general. ''That is why I use them. It gives me pleasure. They can reason, after a fashion. So they are dangerous.''

''But where do you get them?''

The general's left eyelid fluttered down in a wink. ''This island is called Ship Trap,'' he answered. ''Sometimes an angry god of the high seas sends them to me. Sometimes, when Providence is not so kind, I help Providence a bit. Come to the window with me.''

Rainsford went to the window and looked out toward the sea.

''Watch! Out there!'' exclaimed the general, pointing into the night. Rainsford's eyes saw only blackness, and then as the general pressed a button, far out to sea Rainsford saw the flash of lights.

The general chuckled. ''They indicate a channel,'' he said, ''where there's none; giant rocks with razor edges crush like a sea monster with wide-open jaws. They can crush a ship as easily as I crush this nut.'' He dropped a walnut onto the hardwood floor and brought his heel grinding down on it. ''Oh, yes,'' he said, casually, as if in answer to a question, ''I have electricity. We try to be civilized here.''

''Civilized? And you shoot down men?''

A trace of anger was in the general's black eyes, but it was there for but a second, and he said, in his most pleasant manner: ''Dear me, what a righteous young man you are! I assure you I do not do the thing you suggest. That would be barbarous. I treat these visitors with every consideration. They get plenty of good food and exercise. They get into splendid physical condition. You shall see for yourself tomorrow.''

''What do you mean?''

''We'll visit my training school,'' smiled the general. ''It's in the cellar. I have about a dozen pupils down there now. They're from the Spanish bark *San Lucar* that had the bad luck to go on the rocks out there. A very inferior lot, I regret to say. Poor specimens and more accustomed to the deck than to the jungle.''

He raised his hand, and Ivan, who served as waiter, brought thick Turkish coffee. Rainsford, with an effort, held his tongue in check.

"It's a game, you see," pursued the general blandly.* "I suggest to one of them that we go hunting. I give him a supply of food and an excellent hunting knife. I give him three hours' start. I am to follow, armed only with a pistol of the smallest caliber and range. If my quarry eludes* me for three whole days, he wins the game. If I find him"–the general smiled–"he loses."

---
blandly: mildly
eludes: avoids

"Suppose he refuses to be hunted?"

"Oh," said the general, "I give him his option, of course. He need not play that game if he doesn't wish to. If he does not wish to hunt, I turn him over to Ivan. Ivan once had the honor of serving as official knouter* to the Great White Tsar, and he has his own ideas of sport. Invariably, Mr. Rainsford, invariably they choose the hunt."

---
knouter: one who flogged criminals with a Russian whip called a knout

---

"And if they win?"

The smile on the general's face widened. "To date I have not lost," he said. Then he added, hastily: "I don't wish you to think me a braggart, Mr. Rainsford. Many of them afford only the most elementary sort of problem. Occasionally I strike a tartar.* One almost did win. I eventually had to use the dogs."

---
tartar: an especially formidable opponent

The general steered Rainsford to a window. The lights from the windows sent a flickering illumination that made grotesque patterns on the courtyard below, and Rainsford could see moving about there a dozen or so huge black shapes; as they turned toward him, their eyes glittered greenly.

"A rather good lot, I think," observed the general. "They are let out at seven every night. If anyone should try to get into my house–or out of it–something extremely regrettable would oc-cur to him." He hummed a snatch of song from the *Folies Bergères.*

"And now," said the general, "I want to show you my new collection of heads. Will you come with me to the library?"

"I hope," said Rainsford, "that you will excuse me tonight, General Zaroff. I'm really not feeling well."

"Ah, indeed?" the general inquired solicitously.* "Well, I suppose that's only natural, after your long swim. You need a good, restful night's sleep. Tomorrow you'll feel like a new man, I'll wager.* Then we'll hunt, eh? I've one rather promising prospect–" Rainsford was hurrying from the room.

---
solicitously: showing attentive care or attention
wager: bet

"Sorry you can't go with me tonight," called the general. "I expect rather fair sport–a big, strong black. He looks resourceful–Well, good night, Mr. Rainsford; I hope you have a good night's rest."

The bed was good, and the pajamas of the softest silk, and he was tired in every fiber of his being, but nevertheless Rainsford could not quiet his brain with the opiate* of sleep. He lay, eyes wide open. Once he thought he heard stealthy* steps in the corridor outside his room. He sought to throw open the door; it would not open. He went to the window and looked out. His room was high up in one of the towers. The lights of the château were out now, and it was dark and silent, but there was a fragment of sallow* moon, and by its wan* light he could see, dimly, the courtyard; there weaving in and out in the pattern of shadow, were black, noiseless forms; the hounds heard him at the window and looked up, expectantly, with their green eyes. Rainsford went back to the bed and lay down. By many methods he tried to put himself to sleep. He had achieved a doze when, just as morning began to come, he heard, far off in the jungle, the faint report of a pistol.

opiate: something that quiets or soothes
stealthy: slow, deliberately secret
sallow: of a pale yellow color
wan: faint

General Zaroff did not appear until luncheon. He was dressed faultlessly in the tweeds of a country squire. He was solicitous about the state of Rainsford's health.

"As for me," sighed the general, "I do not feel so well. I am worried, Mr. Rainsford. Last night I detected traces of my old complaint."

To Rainsford's questioning glance the general said: "Ennui.* Boredom."

Ennui: a feeling of weariness and dissatisfaction

Then, taking a second helping of crêpes suzette,* the general explained: "The hunting was not good last night. The fellow lost his head. He made a straight trail that offered no problems at all. That's the trouble with these sailors; they have dull brains to begin with, and they do not know how to get about in the woods. They do excessively stupid and obvious things. It's most annoying. Will you have another glass of Chablis, Mr. Rainsford?"

crêpes suzette: very thin pancakes rolled in a hot orange sauce

"General," said Rainsford firmly, "I wish to leave this island at once."

The general raised his thickets of eyebrows; he seemed hurt. "But my dear fellow," the general protested, "you've only just come. You've had no hunting—"

"I wish to go today," said Rainsford. He saw the dead black eyes of the general on him, studying him. General Zaroff's face suddenly brightened.

He filled Rainsford's glass with venerable* Chablis from a dusty bottle.

venerable: old

"Tonight," said the general, "we will hunt—you and I."

Rainsford shook his head. "No, general," he said. "I will not hunt."

The general shrugged his shoulders and delicately ate a hothouse grape. "As you wish, my friend," he said. "The choice rests entirely with you. But may I not venture to suggest that you will find my idea of sport more diverting than Ivan's?"

He nodded toward the corner to where the giant stood scowling, his thick arms crossed on his hogshead* of chest.

hogshead: large barrel

"You don't mean—" cried Rainsford.

"My dear fellow," said the general, "have I not told you I always mean what I say about hunting? This is really an inspiration. I drink to a foeman worthy of my steel—at last." The general raised his glass, but Rainsford sat staring at him.

"You'll find this game worth playing," the general said enthusiastically. "Your brain against mine. Your woodcraft against mine. Your strength and stamina against mine. Outdoor chess! And the stake* is not without value, eh?"

stake: that which is given the winner

"And if I win—" began Rainsford huskily.

"I'll cheerfully acknowledge myself defeated if I do not find you by midnight of the third day," said General Zaroff. "My sloop* will place you on the mainland near a town." The general read what Rainsford was thinking.

sloop: a single-masted sailing vessel

"Oh, you can trust me," said the Cossack. "I will give you my word as a gentleman and a sportsman. Of course you, in turn, must agree to say nothing of your visit here."

"I'll agree to nothing of the kind," said Rainsford.

"Oh," said the general, "in that case—But why discuss that now? Three days hence we can discuss it over a bottle of *Veuve Cliquot,* unless—"

The general sipped his wine.

Then a businesslike air animated* him. "Ivan," he said to Rainsford, "will supply you with hunting clothes, food, a knife. I suggest you wear moccasins; they leave a poorer trail. I suggest, too, that you avoid the big swamp in the southeast corner of the island. We call it Death Swamp. There's quicksand there. One foolish fellow tried it. The deplorable* part of it was that Lazarus followed him. You can imagine my feelings, Mr. Rainsford. I loved Lazarus; he was the finest hound in my pack. Well, I must beg you to excuse me now. I always take a siesta after lunch. You'll hardly have time for a nap, I fear. You'll want to start, no doubt. I shall not follow till dusk. Hunting at night is so much more exciting than by day, don't you think? Au revoir, Mr. Rainsford, au revoir." General Zaroff, with a deep, courtly bow, strolled from the room.

animated: enlivened
deplorable: regrettable

From another door came Ivan. Under one arm he carried khaki hunting clothes, a haversack of food, a leather sheath containing a long-bladed hunting knife; his right hand rested on a cocked revolver thrust in the crimson sash about his waist.

Rainsford had fought his way through the bush for two hours. "I must keep my nerve. I must keep my nerve," he said through tight teeth.

He had not been entirely clearheaded when the château gates snapped shut behind him. His whole idea at first was to put distance between himself and General Zaroff, and, to this end, he had plunged along, spurred on by the sharp rowels* of something very like panic. Now he had got a grip on himself, had stopped, and was taking stock of himself and the situation. He saw that straight flight was futile;* inevitably it would bring him face to face with the sea. He was in a picture with a frame of water, and his operations, clearly, must take place within that frame.

rowels: pricks like spurs
futile: useless

"I'll give him a trail to follow," muttered Rainsford, and he struck off from the rude path he had been following into the trackless wilderness. He executed a series of intricate loops; he doubled on his trail again and again, recalling all the lore of the fox hunt, and all the dodges of the fox. Night found him leg-weary, with hands and

face lashed by the branches, on a thickly wooded ridge. He knew it would be insane to blunder on through the dark, even if he had the strength. His need for rest was imperative* and he thought: "I have played the fox, now I must play the cat of the fable." A big tree with a thick trunk and outspread branches was nearby, and, taking care to leave not the slightest mark, he climbed up into the crotch, and stretching out on one of the broad limbs, after a fashion, rested. Rest brought him new confidence and almost a feeling of security. Even so zealous a hunter as General Zaroff could not trace him there, he told himself; only the devil himself could follow that complicated trail through the jungle after dark. But, perhaps the general was a devil—

imperative: absolutely necessary

An apprehensive night crawled slowly by like a wounded snake, and sleep did not visit Rainsford, although the silence of a dead world was on the jungle. Toward morning when a dingy gray was varnishing* the sky, the cry of some startled bird focused Rainsford's attention in that direction. Something was coming through the bush, coming slowly, carefully, coming by the same winding way Rainsford had come. He flattened himself down on the limb, and through a screen of leaves almost as thick as tapestry,* he watched. . . . That which was approaching was a man.

varnishing: brightening
tapestry: a heavy cloth woven with designs

It was General Zaroff. He made his way along with his eyes fixed in utmost concentration on the ground before him. He paused, almost beneath the tree, dropped to his knees and studied the ground. Rainsford's impulse was to hurl himself down like a panther, but he saw that the general's right hand held something metallic–a small automatic pistol.

The hunter shook his head several times, as if he were puzzled. Then he straightened up and took from his case one of his black cigarettes; its pungent* incenselike smoke floated up to Rainsford's nostrils.

pungent: sharp

Rainsford held his breath. The general's eyes had left the ground and were traveling inch by inch up the tree. Rainsford froze there, every muscle tensed for a spring. But the sharp eyes of the hunter stopped before they reached the limb where Rainsford lay; a smile spread over his brown face. Very deliberately he blew a smoke ring into the air; then he turned his back on the tree and walked carelessly away, back along the trail he had come. The swish of the underbrush against his hunting boots grew fainter and fainter.

The pent-up air burst hotly from Rainsford's lungs. His first thought made him feel sick and numb. The general could follow a trail through the woods at night; he could follow an extremely difficult trail; he must have uncanny powers; only by the merest chance had the Cossack failed to see his quarry.

Rainsford's second thought was even more terrible. It sent a shudder of cold horror through his whole being. Why had the general smiled? Why had he turned back?

Rainsford did not want to believe what his reason told him was true, but the truth was as evident as the sun that had by now pushed through the morning mists. The general was playing with him! The general was saving him for another day's sport! The Cossack was the cat; he was the mouse. Then it was that Rainsford knew the full meaning of terror.

"I will not lose my nerve. I will not." He slid down from the tree, and struck off again into the woods. His face was set and he forced the machinery of his mind to function. Three hundred yards from his hiding place he stopped where a huge dead tree leaned precariously* on a smaller, living one. Throwing off his sack of food, Rainsford took his knife from its sheath and began to work with all his energy.

precariously: dangerously unstable

The job was finished at last, and he threw himself down behind a fallen log a hundred feet away. He did not have to wait long. The cat was coming again to play with the mouse.

Following the trail with the sureness of a bloodhound came General Zaroff. Nothing escaped those searching black eyes, no crushed blade of grass, no bent twig, no mark, no matter how faint, in the moss. So intent was the Cossack on his stalking that he was upon the thing Rainsford had made before he saw it. His foot touched the protruding* bough that was the trigger. Even as he touched it, the general sensed his danger and leaped back with the agility* of an ape. But he was not quite quick enough; the dead tree, delicately adjusted to rest on the cut living one, crashed down and struck the general a glancing blow on the shoulder as it fell; but for his alertness, he must have been smashed beneath it. He staggered, but he did not fall; nor did he drop his revolver. He stood there, rubbing his injured shoulder, and Rainsford, with fear again gripping at his heart, heard the general's mocking laugh ring through the jungle.

protruding: sticking out
agility: ease and quickness of movement

"Rainsford," called the general, "if you are within sound of my voice, as I suppose you are, let me congratulate you. Not many men know how to make a Malay man-catcher. Luckily, for me, I too have hunted in Malacca. You are proving interesting, Mr. Rainsford. I am going now to have my wound dressed; it's only a slight one. But I shall be back. I shall be back."

When the general, nursing his bruised shoulder, had gone, Rainsford took up his flight again. It was flight now, a desperate, hopeless flight, that carried him on for some hours. Dusk came, then darkness, and still he pressed on. The ground grew softer under his moccasins; the vegetation grew ranker, denser; insects bit him savagely.

Then, as he stepped forward, his foot sank into the ooze. He tried to wrench it back, but the muck sucked viciously at his foot as if it were a giant leech. With a violent effort, he tore his feet loose. He knew where he was now. Death Swamp and its quicksand.

His hands were tight closed as if his nerve were something tangible that someone in the darkness was trying to tear from his grip. The softness of the earth had given him an idea. He stepped back from the quicksand a dozen feet or so and, like some huge prehistoric beaver, he began to dig.

Rainsford had dug himself in in France when a second's delay meant death. That had been a placid pastime compared to his digging now. The pit grew deeper; when it was above his shoulders, he climbed out and from some hard saplings cut stakes and sharpened them to a fine point. These stakes he planted in the bottom of the pit with the points sticking up. With flying fingers he wove a rough carpet of weeds and branches and with it he covered the mouth of the pit. Then wet with sweat and aching with tiredness, he crouched behind the stump of a lightning-charred tree.

He knew his pursuer was coming; he heard the padding sound of feet on the soft earth, and the night breeze brought him the perfume of the general's cigarette. It seemed to Rainsford that the general was coming with unusual swiftness; he was not feeling his way along, foot by foot. Rainsford, crouching there, could not see the general, nor could he see the pit. He lived a year in a minute. Then he felt an impulse to cry aloud with joy, for he heard the sharp crackle of the breaking branches as the cover of the pit gave way; he heard the sharp scream of pain as the pointed stakes found their mark. He leaped up from his place of concealment. Then he cowered back. Three feet from the pit a man was standing, with an electric torch in his hand.

"You've done well, Rainsford," the voice of the general called. "Your Burmese tiger pit has claimed one of my best dogs. Again you score. I think, Mr. Rainsford, I'll see what you can do against my whole pack. I'm going home for a rest now. Thank you for a most amusing evening."

At daybreak Rainsford, lying near the swamp, was awakened by a sound that made him know that he had new things to learn about fear. It was a distant sound, faint and wavering, but he knew it. It was the baying of a pack of hounds.

Rainsford knew he could do one of two things. He could stay where he was and wait. That was suicide. He could flee. That was postponing the inevitable. For a moment he stood there, thinking. An idea that held a wild chance came to him, and, tightening his belt, he headed away from the swamp.

The baying of the hounds drew nearer, then still nearer, nearer, ever nearer. On a ridge Rainsford climbed a tree. Down a water-course, not a quarter of mile away, he could see the bush mov-

ing. Straining his eyes, he saw the lean figure of General Zaroff; just ahead of him Rainsford made out another figure whose wide shoulder surged* through the tall jungle weeds; it was the giant Ivan, and he seemed pulled forward by some unseen force; Rainsford knew Ivan must be holding the pack in leash.

surged: moved with strong, forceful motion

They would be on him any minute now. His mind worked frantically. He thought of a native trick he had learned in Uganda. He slid down the tree. He caught hold of a springy young sapling and to it he fastened his hunting knife, with the blade pointing down the trail; with a bit of wild grapevine he tied back the sapling. Then he ran for his life. The hounds raised their voices as they hit the fresh scent. Rainsford knew now how an animal at bay feels.

He had to stop to get his breath. The baying of the hounds stopped abruptly, and Rainsford's heart stopped too. They must have reached the knife.

He shinned* excitedly up a tree and looked back. His pursuers had stopped. But the hope that was in Rainsford's brain when he climbed died, for he saw in the shallow valley that General Zaroff was still on his feet. But Ivan was not. The knife, driven by the recoil of the springing tree, had not wholly failed.

shinned: climbed, using hands and legs for gripping

Rainsford had hardly tumbled to the ground when the pack took up the cry again.

"Nerve, nerve, nerve!" he panted, as he dashed along. A blue gap showed between the trees dead ahead. Ever nearer drew the hounds. Rainsford forced himself on toward that gap. He reached it. It was the shore of the sea. Across a cove he could see the gloomy gray stone of the château. Twenty feet below him the sea rumbled and hissed. Rainsford hesitated. He heard the hounds. Then he leaped far out into the sea. . . .

When the general and his pack reached the place by the sea, the Cossack stopped. For minutes he stood regarding the blue-green expanse of water. He shrugged his shoulders. Then he sat down, took a drink of brandy from a silver flask, lit a cigarette and hummed a bit from *Madame Butterfly*.

General Zaroff had an exceedingly good dinner in his great paneled dining hall that evening. With it he had a bottle of Pol Roger and half a bottle of Chambertin. Two slight annoyances kept him from perfect enjoyment. One was the thought that it would be difficult to replace Ivan; the other was that his quarry had escaped him; of course the American hadn't played the game—so thought the general as he tasted his after-dinner liqueur. In his library he read, to soothe himself, from the works of Marcus Aurelius. At ten he went up to his bedroom. He was deliciously tired, he said to himself, as he locked himself in. There was a little moonlight, so, before turning on his light, he went to the window and looked down at the courtyard. He could see the great hounds, and he called, "Better luck another time," to them. Then he switched on the light.

A man, who had been hiding in the curtains of the bed, was standing there.

"Rainsford!" screamed the general. "How is it possible that you got here?"

"Swam," said Rainsford. "I found it quicker than walking through the jungle."

The general sucked in his breath and smiled. "I congratulate you," he said. "You have won the game."

Rainsford did not smile. "I am still a beast at bay," he said, in a low, hoarse voice. "Get ready, General Zaroff."

The general made one of his deepest bows. "I see," he said. "Splendid! One of us is to furnish a repast* for the hounds. The other will sleep in this very excellent bed. On guard, Rainsford."

---

repast: meal

He had never slept in a better bed, Rainsford decided.

For Thought and Discussion

1. What ironic reversals occur in this story? In what respects does the hunter become the hunted? What surprise (for the reader as well as for Zaroff) is reserved for the end?

2. Rainsford's behavior in the jungle seems imitative of what animals?

3. Where do animallike screams appear in the story? Do they serve a narrative function?

4. Notice the references to civilization. What differences appear between Zaroff's and Rainsford's concepts of civilized behavior? Is the nature of civilization a theme in the story?

5. Is there narrative logic in the sequence of the traps laid by Rainsford? What plan of Rainsford is not enacted in the forest?

6. What animal was the last animal to be hunted by Zaroff before he turned to more challenging prey? What animal is Rainsford planning to hunt before he falls overboard? Are these facts only coincidental in the story?

7. Are the characters of Rainsford and Zaroff flat or round, static or developing? Are they adequately drawn for the purposes of the story?

8. Would the impact of the conclusion have been greater had Connell provided a detailed account of the struggle in the bedroom rather than simply indicating the outcome in the ironic summarizing statement that ends the story? Support your answer.

James Thurber   1894-1961

Although partially blind from a childhood accident, James Thurber saw clearly the fear and pretense of modern man. Thurber began writing seriously while a student at Ohio State University. After his college years (he did not graduate), he became a newspaper reporter for a time, then a free-lance writer. In 1927 his career took a successful turn when he joined the staff of the *New Yorker,* one of the most prestigious national magazines. His first book appeared two years later. It was followed in 1931 by his first book of cartoons. In spite of the loss of his remaining sight, Thurber continued writing. In fact, he wrote more books in the last ten years of his life than in any other decade. He died in 1961 after emergency surgery for a blood clot on the brain.

Thurber was predominantly a humorist. Both his cartoons and his fiction often provoke laughter. Thurber's humor is not always gentle. Like Ambrose Bierce and Samuel Clemens, Thurber at times became bitterly critical of mankind. In one piece, for instance, a lemming complains to a scientist that men are ''murderous, maladjusted, maleficent, malicious, and muffleheaded.'' The animal continues, ''You kill, you mangle, you torture, you imprison, you starve each other.'' The scientist agrees that the description is true. But, puzzled about the behavior of lemmings, he asks why they all rush down to the sea and drown themselves. ''How curious,'' replies the lemming. ''The one thing I don't understand is why you humans don't.''

In a typical story by Thurber, the chief character is baffled or even terrified by life. In his stories depicting unhappy marriages, overbearing women invariably dominate weak men. In ''The Secret Life of Walter Mitty,'' one of Thurber's most popular stories, the chief character retreats into an imaginative, romantic world of daydreams in order to make his real world more tolerable. Only occasionally in Thurber's work does a timid and seemingly ineffective man like Walter Mitty triumph over his circumstances. In ''The Catbird Seat,'' however, just such a man maintains his position against the challenge of a loud and domineering woman.

The Catbird Seat

The humor of ''The Catbird Seat'' grows out of the absurd contrast between what Mr. Martin habitually does and what he contemplates doing. Yet beneath the humor of the situation is a certain wistfulness. Doubtlessly, many a modern reader, feeling himself unable to control the circumstances affecting his own life, participates vicariously in Mr. Martin's amoral triumph.

Mr. Martin bought the pack of Camels on Monday night in the most crowded cigar store on Broadway. It was theater time and seven or eight men were buying cigarettes. The clerk didn't even glance at Mr. Martin, who put the pack in his overcoat pocket and went out. If any of the staff at F & S had seen him buy the cigarettes, they would have been astonished, for it was generally known that Mr. Martin did not smoke, and never had. No one saw him.

It was just a week to the day since Mr. Martin had decided to rub out Mrs. Ulgine Barrows. The term "rub out" pleased him because it suggested nothing more than the correction of an error–in this case an error of Mr. Fitweiler. Mr. Martin had spent each night of the past week working out his plan and examining it. As he walked home now he went over it again. For the hundredth time he resented the element of imprecision,* the margin of guesswork that entered into the business. The project as he had worked it out was casual and bold, the risks were considerable. Something might go wrong anywhere along the line. And therein lay the cunning* of his scheme. No one would ever see in it the cautious, painstaking hand of Erwin Martin, head of the filing department at F & S, of whom Mr. Fitweiler had once said, "Man is fallible* but Martin isn't." No one would see his hand, that is, unless it were caught in the act.

imprecision: lack of exactness
cunning: shrewdness
fallible: capable of erring

Sitting in his apartment, drinking a glass of milk, Mr. Martin reviewed his case against Mrs. Ulgine Barrows, as he had every night for seven nights. He began at the beginning. Her quacking voice and braying* laugh had first profaned* the halls of F & S on March 7, 1941 (Mr. Martin had a head for dates). Old Roberts, the personnel chief, had introduced her as the newly appointed special adviser to the president of the firm, Mr. Fitweiler. The woman had appalled Mr. Martin

instantly, but he hadn't shown it. He had given her his dry hand, a look of studious* concentration, and a faint smile. "Well," she had said, looking at the papers on his desk, "are you lifting the oxcart out of the ditch?" As Mr. Martin recalled that moment, over his milk, he squirmed slightly. He must keep his mind on her crimes as a special adviser, not on her peccadillos* as a personality. This he found difficult to do, in spite of entering an objection and sustaining it. The faults of the woman as a woman kept chattering on in his mind like an unruly witness. She had, for almost two years now, baited* him. In the halls, in the elevator, even in his own office, into which she romped now and then like a circus horse, she was constantly shouting these silly questions at him. "Are you lifting the oxcart out of the ditch? Are you tearing up the pea patch? Are you hollering down the rain barrel? Are you scraping around the bottom of the pickle barrel? Are you sitting in the catbird seat?"

braying: making a loud, harsh sound, as a donkey
profaned: violated the sanctity or sacredness of
studious: diligent
peccadillos: small sins
baited: tormented

It was Joey Hart, one of Mr. Martin's two assistants, who had explained what the gibberish* meant. "She must be a Dodger fan," he had said. "Red Barber announces the Dodger games over the radio and he uses those expressions–picked 'em up down South." Joey had gone on to explain one or two. "Tearing up the pea patch" meant going on a rampage; "sitting in the catbird seat" meant sitting pretty, like a batter with three balls and no strikes on him. Mr. Martin dismissed all this with an effort. It had been annoying, it had driven him near to distraction, but he was too solid a man to be moved to murder by anything so childish. It was fortunate, he reflected as he passed on to the important charges against Mrs. Barrows, that he had stood up under it so well. He had maintained always an outward appearance of polite tolerance. "Why, I even believe you like the woman," Miss Paird, his other assistant, had once said to him. He had simply smiled.

gibberish: meaningless talk

A gavel* rapped in Mr. Martin's mind and the case proper was resumed. Mrs. Ulgine Barrows stood charged with willful, blatant,* and persistent attempts to destroy the efficiency and system of F & S. It was competent, material,* and relevant to review her advent* and rise to power. Mr. Martin had got the story from Miss Paird, who seemed always able to find things out. According to her, Mrs. Barrows had met Mr. Fitweiler at a party, where she had rescued him from the embrace of a powerfully built drunken man who had mistaken the president of F & S for a famous retired Middle Western football coach. She had led him to a sofa and somehow worked upon him a monstrous magic. The aging gentleman had jumped to the conclusion there and then that this was a woman of singular attainments, equipped to bring out the best in him and in the firm. A week later he had introduced her into F & S as his special adviser. On that day confusion got its foot in the door. After Miss Tyson, Mr. Brundage, and Mr. Bartlett had been fired and Mr. Munson had taken his hat and stalked out, mailing in his resignation later, old Roberts had been emboldened to speak to Mr. Fitweiler. He mentioned that Mr. Munson's department had been "a little disrupted" and hadn't they perhaps better resume the old system there? Mr. Fitweiler had said certainly not. He had the greatest faith in Mrs. Barrows' ideas. "They require a little seasoning, a little seasoning, is all," he had added. Mr. Roberts had given it up. Mr. Martin reviewed in detail all the changes wrought by Mrs. Barrows. She had begun chipping at the cornices* of the firm's edifice* and now she was swinging at the foundation stones with a pickaxe.

gavel: hammer used by a judge to call for attention in a courtroom
blatant: offensively obvious
material: having importance
advent: arrival
cornices: moldings at the top of the building
edifice: i.e., the building itself

Mr. Martin came now, in his summing up, to the afternoon of Monday, November 2, 1942—just one week ago. On that day, at 3 P.M., Mrs. Barrows had bounced into his office. "Boo!" she had yelled. "Are you scraping around the bottom of the pickle barrel?" Mr. Martin had looked at her from under his green eyeshade, saying nothing. She had begun to wander about the office, taking it in with her great, popping eyes. "Do you really need *all* these filing cabinets?" she had demanded suddenly. Mr. Martin's heart had jumped. "Each of these files," he had said, keeping his voice even, "plays an indispensable* part in the system of F & S." She had brayed at him, "Well, don't tear up the pea patch!" and gone to the door. From there she had bawled, "But you sure have got a lot of fine scrap in here!" Mr. Martin could no longer doubt that the finger was on his beloved department. Her pickaxe was on the upswing, poised for the first blow. It had not come yet; he had received no blue memo from the enchanted Mr. Fitweiler bearing nonsensical instructions deriving from the obscene* woman. But there was no doubt in Mr. Martin's mind that one would be forthcoming. He must act quickly. Already a precious week had gone by. Mr. Martin stood up in his living room, still holding his milk glass. "Gentleman of the jury," he said to himself, "I demand the death penalty for this horrible person."

indispensable: essential, required
obscene: offensive, repulsive

The next day Mr. Martin followed his routine, as usual. He polished his glasses more often and once sharpened an already sharp pencil, but not even Miss Paird noticed. Only once did he catch sight of his victim; she swept past him in the hall with a patronizing* "Hi!" At five-thirty he walked home, as usual, and had a glass of milk, as usual. He had never drunk anything stronger in his life—unless you could count ginger ale. The late Sam Schlosser, the S of F & S, had praised Mr. Martin at a staff meeting several years before for his temperate habits. "Our most efficient worker neither drinks nor smokes," he had said. "The results speak for themselves." Mr. Fitweiler had sat by, nodding approval.

patronizing: i.e., speaking to him as an inferior

Mr. Martin was still thinking about that red-letter day as he walked over to the Schrafft's on Fifth Avenue near Forty-sixth Street. He got there as he always did, at eight o'clock. He finished his dinner and the financial page of the *Sun* at a quarter to nine, as he always did. It was his custom after dinner to take a walk. This time he walked down Fifth Avenue at a casual pace. His gloved hands felt moist and warm, his forehead cold. He transferred the Camels from his overcoat to a jacket pocket. He wondered, as he did so, if they did not represent an unnecessary note of strain. Mrs. Barrows smoked only Luckies. It was his idea to puff a few puffs on a Camel (after the rubbing-out), stub* it out in the ashtray holding her lipstick-stained Luckies, and thus drag a small red herring* across the trail. Perhaps it was not a good idea. It would take time. He might even choke, too loudly.

stub: to crush in order to snuff out
red herring: something that draws attention from the matter at hand. Originally, farmers dragged a strong-smelling fish across the trail of a hunted animal to confuse hunting dogs and thus frustrate the hunt.

Mr. Martin had never seen the house on West Twelfth Street where Mrs. Barrows lived, but he had a clear enough picture of it. Fortunately, she had bragged to everybody about her ducky* first-floor apartment in the perfectly darling three-story red-brick. There would be no doorman or other attendants; just the tenants of the second and third floors. As he walked along, Mr. Martin realized that he would get there before nine-thirty. He had considered walking north on Fifth Avenue from Schrafft's to a point from which it would take him until ten o'clock to reach the house. At that hour people were less likely to be coming in or going out. But the procedure would have made

an awkward loop in the straight thread of his causalness,* and he had abandoned it. It was impossible to figure when people would be entering or leaving the house, anyway. There was a great risk at any hour. If he ran into anybody, he would simply have to place the rubbing-out of Ulgine Barrows in the inactive file forever. The same thing would hold true if there were someone in her apartment. In that case he would just say that he had been passing by, recognized her charming house and thought to drop in.

ducky: slang for excellent
causalness: cause-effect reasoning

It was eighteen minutes after nine when Mr. Martin turned into Twelfth Street. A man passed him, and a man and a woman talking. There was no one within fifty paces when he came to the house, halfway down the block. He was up the steps and in the small vestibule in no time, pressing the bell under the card that said "Mrs. Ulgine Barrows." When the clicking in the lock started, he jumped forward against the door. He got inside fast, closing the door behind him. A bulb in a lantern hung from the hall ceiling on a chain seemed to give a monstrously bright light. There was nobody on the stair, which went up ahead of him along the left wall. A door opened down the hall in the wall on the right. He went toward it swiftly, on tiptoe.

"Well . . . look who's here!" bawled Mrs. Barrows, and her braying laugh rang out like the report of a shotgun. He rushed past her like a football tackle, bumping her. "Hey, quit shoving!" she said, closing the door behind them. They were in her living room, which seemed to Mr. Martin to be lighted by a hundred lamps. "What's after you?" she said. "You're as jumpy as a goat." He found he was unable to speak. His heart was wheezing in his throat. "I–yes," he finally brought out. She was jabbering and laughing as she started to help him off with his coat. "No, no," he said. "I'll put it here." He took it off and put it on a chair near the door. "Your hat and gloves, too,'' she said. ''You're in a lady's house.'' He put his hat on top of the coat. Mrs. Barrows seemed larger than he had thought. He kept his gloves on. ''I was passing by,'' he said. ''I recognized–is there anyone here?'' She laughed louder than ever. ''No,'' she said, ''We're all alone. You're white as a sheet, you funny man. What ever *has* come over you? I'll mix you a toddy.''* She started toward a door across the room. ''Scotch-and-soda be all right? But say, you don't drink, do you?'' She turned and gave him her amused look. Mr. Martin pulled himself together. ''Scotch-and-soda will be all right,'' he heard himself say. He could hear her laughing in the kitchen.

toddy: a hot alcoholic drink

Mr. Martin looked quickly around the living room for the weapon. He had counted on finding one there. There were andirons* and a poker and something in a corner that looked like an Indian club. None of them would do. It couldn't be that way. He began to pace around. He came to a desk. On it lay a metal paper knife with an ornate handle. Would it be sharp enough? He reached for it and knocked over a small brass jar. Stamps spilled out of it and it fell to the floor with a clatter. ''Hey,'' Mrs. Barrows yelled from the kitchen, ''are you tearing up the pea patch?'' Mr. Martin gave a strange laugh. Picking up the knife, he tried its point against his left wrist. It was blunt. It wouldn't do.

andirons: metal supports for holding logs in a fireplace

When Mrs. Barrows reappeared, carrying two highballs,* Mr. Martin, standing there with his gloves on, became acutely conscious of the fantasy he had wrought.* Cigarettes in his pocket, a drink prepared for him–it was all too grossly improbable. It was more than that. It was impossible. Somewhere in the back of his mind a vague idea stirred, sprouted. ''For heaven's sake, take off those gloves,'' said Mrs. Barrows. ''I always wear them in the house,'' said Mr. Martin. The

idea began to bloom, strange and wonderful. She put the glasses on a coffee table in front of a sofa and sat on the sofa. ''Come over here, you odd little man,'' she said. Mr. Martin went over and sat beside her. It was difficult getting a cigarette out of the pack of Camels, but he managed it. She held a match for him, laughing. ''Well,'' she said, handing him his drink, ''this is perfectly marvelous. You with a drink and a cigarette.''

highballs: alcoholic drinks
wrought: made, created

Mr. Martin puffed, not too awkwardly, and took a gulp of the highball. ''I drink and smoke all the time,'' he said. He clinked his glass against hers. ''Here's nuts to that old windbag, Fitweiler,'' he said, and gulped again. The stuff tasted awful, but he made no grimace. ''Really, Mr. Martin,'' she said, her voice and posture changing, ''you are insulting our employer.'' Mrs. Barrows was now all special adviser to the president. ''I am preparing a bomb,'' said Mr. Martin, ''which will blow [up] the old goat. . . .'' He had only had a little of the drink, which was not strong. It couldn't be that. ''Do you take dope or something?'' Mrs. Barrows asked coldly. ''Heroin,'' said Mr. Martin. ''I'll be coked to the gills when I bump that old buzzard off.'' ''Mr. Martin!'' she shouted, getting to her feet. ''That will be all of that. You must go at once.'' Mr. Martin took another swallow of his drink. He tapped his cigarette out in the ashtray and put the pack of Camels on the coffee table. He walked over and put on his hat and coat. ''Not a word about this,'' he said, and laid an index finger against his lips. All Mrs. Barrows could bring out was ''Really!'' Mr. Martin put his hand on the doorknob. ''I'm sitting in the catbird seat,'' he said. He stuck his tongue out at her and left. Nobody saw him go.

Mr. Martin got to his apartment, walking, well before eleven. No one saw him go in. He had two glasses of milk after brushing his teeth, and he felt elated. It wasn't tipsiness, because he hadn't been tipsy. Anyway, the walk had worn off all effects of the whiskey. He got in bed and read a magazine for a while. He was asleep before midnight.

Mr. Martin got to the office at eight-thirty next morning, as usual. At a quarter to nine, Ulgine Barrows, who had never before arrived at work before ten, swept into his office. "I'm reporting to Mr. Fitweiler now!" she shouted. "If he turns you over to the police, it's no more than you deserve!" Mr. Martin gave her a look of shocked surprise. "I beg your pardon?" he said. Mrs. Barrows snorted and bounced out of the room, leaving Miss Paird and Joey Hart staring at her. "What's the matter with that old ogre now?" asked Miss Paird. "I have no idea," said Mr. Martin, resuming his work. The other two looked at him and then at each other. Miss Paird got up and went out. She walked slowly past the closed door of Mr. Fitweiler's office. Mrs. Barrows was yelling inside, but she was not braying. Miss Paird could not hear what the woman was saying. She went back to her desk.

Forty-five minutes later, Mrs. Barrows left the president's office and went into her own, shutting the door. It wasn't until half an hour later that Mr. Fitweiler sent for Mr. Martin. The head of the filing department, neat, quiet, attentive, stood in front of the old man's desk. Mr. Fitweiler was pale and nervous. He took his glasses off and twiddled them. He made a small, bruffing sound in his throat. "Martin," he said, "you have been with us more than twenty years." "Twenty-two, sir," said Mr. Martin. "In that time," pursued the president, "your work and your–uh–manner have been exemplary." "I trust so, sir," said Mr. Martin. "I have understood, Martin," said Mr. Fitweiler, "that you have never taken a drink or smoked." "That is correct, sir," said Mr. Martin. "Ah, yes." Mr. Fitweiler polished his glasses. "You may describe what you did after leaving the office yesterday, Martin," he said. Mr. Martin allowed less than a second for his bewildered pause. "Certainly, sir," he said. "I walked home.

Then I went to Schrafft's for dinner. Afterward I walked home again. I went to bed early, sir, and read a magazine for a while. I was asleep before eleven." "Ah, yes," said Mr. Fitweiler again. He was silent for a moment, searching for the proper words to say to the head of the filing department. "Mrs. Barrows," he said finally, "Mrs. Barrows has worked hard, Martin, very hard. It grieves me to report that she has suffered a severe breakdown. It has taken the form of a persecution complex accompanied by distressing hallucinations." "I am very sorry, sir," said Mr. Martin. "Mrs. Barrows is under the delusion," continued Mr. Fitweiler, "that you visited her last evening and behaved yourself in an–ah–unseemly* manner. He raised his hand to silence Mr. Martin's little pained outcry. "It is the nature of these psychological diseases," Mr. Fitweiler said, "to fix upon the least likely and most innocent party as the–uh–source of persecution. These matters are not for the lay mind to grasp, Martin. I've just had my psychiatrist, Dr. Fitch, on the phone. He would not, of course, commit himself, but he made enough generalizations to substantiate my suspicions. I suggested to Mrs. Barrows when she had completed her–uh–story to me this morning, that she visit Dr. Fitch, for I suspected a condition at once. She flew, I regret to say, into a rage, and demanded–uh–requested that I call you on the carpet. You may not know, Martin, but Mrs. Barrows had planned a reorganization of your department–subject to my approval, of course, subject to my approval. This brought you, rather than anyone else, to her mind–but again that is a phenomenon for Dr. Fitch and not for us. So, Martin, I am afraid Mrs. Barrows' usefulness here is at an end." "I am dreadfully sorry, sir," said Mr. Martin.

unseemly: improper

It was at this point that the door to the office blew open with the suddenness of a gas-main explosion and Mrs. Barrows catapulted* through it. "Is the little rat denying it?" she screamed. "He can't get away with that!" Mr. Martin got up and moved discreetly to a point beside Mr. Fitweiler's chair. "You drank and smoked at my apartment," she bawled at Mr. Martin, "and you know it! You called Mr. Fitweiler an old windbag and said you were going to blow him up when you got coked to the gills on your heroin!" She stopped yelling to catch her breath and a new glint came into her popping eyes. "If you weren't such a drab, ordinary little man," she said, "I'd think you'd planned it all. Sticking your tongue out, saying you were sitting in the catbird seat, because you thought no one would believe me when I told it! It's really too perfect!" She brayed loudly and hysterically, and the fury was on her again. She glared at Mr. Fitweiler. "Can't you see how he has tricked us, you old fool? Can't you see his little game?" But Mr. Fitweiler had been surreptitiously* pressing all the buttons under the top of his desk and employees of F & S began pouring into the room. "Stockton," said Mr. Fitweiler, "you and Fishbein will take Mrs. Barrows to her home. Mrs. Powell, you will go with them." Stockton, who had played a little football in high school, blocked Mrs. Barrows as she made for

Mr. Martin. It took him and Fishbein together to force her out of the door into the hall, crowded with stenographers and office boys. She was still screaming imprecations* at Mr. Martin, tangled and contradictory imprecations. The hubbub finally died out down the corridor.

catapulted: sprang abruptly
surreptitiously: secretly
imprecations: curses

"I regret that this has happened," said Mr. Fitweiler. "I shall ask you to dismiss it from your mind, Martin." "Yes, sir," said Mr. Martin, anticipating his chief's "That will be all" by moving to the door. "I will dismiss it." He went out and shut the door, and his step was light and quick in the hall. When he entered his department he had slowed down to his customary gait, and he walked quietly across the room to the W20 file, wearing a look of studious concentration.

For Thought and Discussion

1. What is the most obvious conflict in the story? How do the differences in Mr. Martin's and Mrs. Barrows's personalities make this conflict inevitable? What other conflicts do you find in the story?

2. Much of Thurber's humor is a result of his exaggerated characterization. What adjectives does he use to describe Mr. Martin? What verbs does he use to describe Mrs. Barrows? How are these terms appropriate to the characters? What trite expressions does Mrs. Barrows use, and how do these expressions add to the humor of the story? What aspects of Miss Paird's and Mr. Fitweiler's characterizations do you find most amusing? In what ways are all of these exaggerated characterizations realistic?

3. From whose point of view is the story told? How does the use of this viewpoint contribute to plot development? Describe the trial scene that takes place in Mr. Martin's mind. Why is this scene necessary? At what point in the encounter in Mrs. Barrows's apart-

ment does Thurber cease to let the reader know what is going on in Mr. Martin's mind? What effect does he create by this change in viewpoint?

4. The central irony in the story is the apparent incongruity of Mr. Martin's character with his bizarre plan. Discuss the details of his first scheme, and tell how he plans to divert suspicion from himself. Why does he change his mind after he is in Mrs. Barrows's apartment? What does his new plan turn out to be? How is he able to succeed? How does the title of the story reinforce the irony of the plot?

5. As a humorist writing a farcical tale, Thurber offers no moral judgment on the acts planned and perpetrated by Mr. Martin. Is Mr. Martin a sympathetic character? Why or why not? Although Mr. Martin does not commit murder, what crime is he guilty of committing? Are his actions justified? Do you think that your judgment of Mr. Martin's actions would be what Thurber intended? Explain your answer.

Archibald Rutledge
1883-1973

The roots of Archibald Rutledge—like those of a giant live oak along the Santee River—reach deep into the South Carolina delta country northeast of Charleston. He was born at Hampton Plantation, in a house built in 1730 on property owned by the family since 1686. In 1904 Rutledge left South Carolina, and for a short while he worked as a newspaperman in Washington, D.C. Then for thirty-three years he taught English at the famed Mercersburg Academy (Pennsylvania). In 1931, while still teaching in the North, he was appointed poet laureate of his native state by its governor. Six years later Rutledge returned to Hampton and began the difficult task of restoring the famous plantation house. Until his death in 1973 he continued writing of the South he had known and deeply loved.

Both in his poetry and in his fiction and essays, Rutledge wrote about the beauty and tradition, the men and animals of the delta country. Oftentimes, as in this passage from *Santee Paradise* (1956), his tone is nostalgic:

Once stately white plantation homes stood on the banks of my Santee, and in the huge rice fields Negroes toiled and sang. But now all is changed. The homes have, almost without exception, been destroyed by fire. The intricate system of ditches and dikes has almost disappeared. The Negroes are but a handful of what they were. A whole civilization has vanished. But the country and the wildlife are there. Hundreds of plantations have reverted to their wild state. With a semitropical fecundity of growth, bushes and vines run riot over the young trees, falling in vast emerald tapestries to the ground where they form incredible green carpets clothing the very earth.

The Tomb of Raven McCloud

A keen observer of nature and mankind, Rutledge weaves in "The Tomb of Raven McCloud" a story of the conflict between two blacks, one good and the other evil. The victory of the one is made possible by the awesome "Thing" that lives in the tomb of Raven McCloud.

When you pass out of the peach and tobacco country of North Carolina and come to the moss-hung live-oaks, the towering yellow pines, the supine* Negroes, and the dreamy waters of the coastal country between Wilmington and Charleston, the strange spell of that lonely land begins to take hold of you–if anything can. And when you drive slowly over the great three-mile bridge spanning the mighty delta* of the Santee,* a bridge over a shimmering wilderness of greenery starred with aquatic wild flowers, you come to the locality where old Isaac McCoy and Dandy Davis had their deadly and memorable encounter, which ended more strangely than anyone, however inventive, could have planned.

supine: lazy
delta: a deposit of sediment at the mouth of a river
Santee: a river in eastern South Carolina

From the moment you quit the main artery of traffic to Florida, with its ceaseless roar, its general odor of whiskey, gasoline, and oil, its trump-

ery* of flaring* signs, all is green, hushed, dewy, in the hale* fragrance of the wilderness. Bearing westward, you will be on a road that winds between ranks of great yellow pines–a road bedded with pinestraw, that, for the most part, lies high and level but now and then dips into the aromatic* gloom of a watery glade. On either hand, far as eye can see, the forest withdraws in dim fabulous aisles; and besides the pine-land road, as in the long savannas* that mistily retire from it, are the vivid green of flytraps,* the late daisies, stargrass,* the snowy orchids, wild asters, tawny goldenrod.

trumpery: showiness
flaring: flaming: i.e., signs that light up
hale: healthy
aromatic: fragrant
savannas: grassy flatlands
flytraps: plants that catch insects
stargrass: a plant with grasslike leaves and star-shaped flowers

Soon you will come to the King's Highway. Turn southward on it. This is the ancient road connecting Georgetown and Charleston. It is the road that Washington travelled, and Lafayette, Lord Rawdon, Tarleton, and Marion.* But the new concrete highway having been laid over an entirely new route, traffic has almost ceased on the old. In a little while, you will come to St. James, Santee, parish church, quaint and beautiful, built in 1760, of English brick and native black cypress.* It would have been utterly out of place beside a modern highway; but here in the old days it was where it belonged, in this far back country, and here it belongs now, here where Yesterday is not too much desecrated by the clangor* of Today and by the onrush of Tomorrow.

Washington . . . Marion: All these were important leaders during the War of Independence: for the American colonists–George Washington (1732–99), Marquis de Lafayette (1757-1834), and "the Swamp Fox," Francis Marion (1732?-95): for the British–Francis Rawdon (1754-1826), an officer who defeated colonial forces in South Carolina, and Banastre Tarleton (1754-1833), an officer defeated by the colonists in South Carolina.
cypress: an evergreen that grows in warm climates
clangor: loud ringing

The spell of beauty and of ancient peace is upon the place. Although you may not know it, you are miles from any human habitation, save only the little shack where old Isaac McCoy lives. That is a half-mile down the road. About the church is an enclosed yard some two acres in extent, forever being encroached* upon by the fecund* growths of the wilderness.

encroached: intruded
fecund: fruitful

Isaac worked among the tombs of the churchyard. Once or twice a week this old Negro walked the half-mile from his staggering* cabin among the pines to the church–ostensibly to keep the yard clean; but most of his time was spent musing on the old days, when regular services had been held there, and when he had been the sexton,* or, as the plantation Negroes said, "the section." His sole duty now in relation to the deserted shrine was to keep its enclosure from looking too much like the surrounding wilderness. Only once a year, on Palm Sunday, did the far-scattered parishioners gather here for worship. For the rest of the time, this wayside church, which was built before our nation came into being, slept placidly* in the lonely pinelands, now shimmering in the sunlight, now dark with sweeping rains, now silvered in moonlight. The church slept; and those in the churchyard slept: old rice planters of the Santee country; old indigo-growing French Huguenots;* Revolutionary patriots; women who in their day had been the belles of the parish; men who had been the hard riders, the duellists, the great lovers of their time. All these slumbered now, in a little dust quiescent.*

staggering: tottering
sexton: caretaker
placidly: calmly
Huguenots: French Protestants who immigrated to America to avoid persecution
quiescent: at rest

Any visitor to that church is sure to be attracted by one of the moldering tombs: a huge affair it is, of English brick, shaped like a vast hogshead,* half buried on its side in the ground. A careful observer will notice a hole in its side flush with the ground, an aperture* large enough to admit the body of a small man; and he may muse how, in the general mutability* of things, even our tombs decay! He may further notice how little wildwood shrubs and streamers of ivy grow out of the chinks between the bricks, almost covering with a green mantle the sacred place. And if he reads the lichened inscription* on the marble slab that covers the top of the grave, he will discover that within this vault lie the mortal remains of one Raven McCloud, "who was drowned at Murphy's Island, at the mouth of the South Santee River, in the great gale of 1822."

hogshead: large barrel
aperture: opening
mutability: i.e., frequent change
lichened inscription: i.e., covered with a crust of fungi and algae

For reasons that he kept to himself, old Isaac would never let a visitor to the church go near the McCloud tomb. If asked his reason, he would merely shake his head and look inscrutably* away through the forest. Nor could this visitor fail to feel about this old pinewoods Negro something as unfathomable* as the stillness, the air of eternal spiritual autumn over the church and its dead.

inscrutably: i.e., mysteriously
unfathomable: unable to be understood

Old Isaac alone knew that a Thing lived in the dark and haunted depths of the tomb of Raven McCloud–a Thing incredibly beautiful, graceful, terrible, and deadly.

One day, a visitor out of the busy world, struck by the dreaming quietude of the church, said, smiling, to its keeper, "I guess nothing ever happens here, does it?"

Isaac had been trained in a school that had taught him to agree with everything a white man ever said. It was the safe and easy way through life.

"No, sah," he answered, "nothin' doan ever happen here."

But Isaac did not smile as his guest drove away. He did not exactly know what this visitor from the mysterious outer world meant by things happening, but as far as he was concerned, life was strenuous, even hectic. For the moment, he had on him the problem of Dandy Davis, probably the worst Negro that the Santee country had ever known. Just what to do about Dandy and his wickedness kept Isaac's mind in a turmoil. He had, like many people who lived close to the soil, to the trees, to the wind and the rain, a certain dim infallible wisdom; and this now seemed to tell him that the day of his final reckoning with Dandy was close at hand.

When Isaac had returned home, only the church and the dead remained; the church and the dead, and those living things in the wilderness that, when night falls over the world, come forth from their dens and their other day-time fastnesses to seek their meat from God. Had you been there, you would have seen what Isaac had several times seen: you would have seen a living Thing steal from the McCloud tomb–a thing of sinister beauty and of primeval might. And if you had asked Isaac about it, he could have told you that, at least in that stretch of coastal country, the most attractive place in all the world as a home for this formidable* chimera* was a moldering tomb. But he never mentioned this Presence to anyone; and he never molested it, knowing it to be an old resident, indigenous* to the churchyard, and to his dim mind, somehow related to the awful enigma* of the grave and to his own solemn guardianship of the church.

formidable: fearful
chimera: fantastic monster
indigenous: native or belonging to a certain place
enigma: puzzle

Dandy Davis, that weasel of a man, that yellow weasel, had, not many months before, drifted into the Santee country out of the region near Florence and Lake City–a very modern and civilized country compared to Santee, and therefore, Isaac thought, calculated to produce Negroes of his type: furtive,* sly, treacherous. A high mulatto,* he could read and write, he was a flashy dresser, had five times served terms on the chain gang,* had killed a man in a brawl over a crap game,* would try to steal anything he wanted, had had at least six wives. He had a great way with women, especially with plantation Negro women, who sensed in Dandy a breath of the great world of glamour, society, fashion, and high romance. It was even rumored that he had been as far north as Richmond. To those who admired him for his travels Dandy did not supply the detail that while in Richmond he had spent his time in a public building at the expense of the State of Virginia. Isaac mistrusted and hated him as he mistrusted all things modern and hated all people of Dandy's kind, and he knew that this flamboyant* visitor was corrupting the manners and the morals of the people of his own Johnson Hill Church. He had been especially disgusted to hear that some of the younger set had managed to get Dandy invited to preach to them. Isaac's comment on hearing this news was: "Those young people don't want to hear religion. What they want is to hear somebody who can tell them how they can sin and be happy."

furtive: shifty
mulatto: a person of mixed white and Negro blood
chain gang: convicts chained together to do outside work
crap game: gambling game
flamboyant: showy

Of the Johnson Hill Church Isaac was accounted the most important and trusted member; for he had been, for many years, the treasurer of the Skyrocket Resurrection Burial Society, the greatest organization in the church. In the case of all other burial societies in the Santee country, the treasurer kept the cash box, and some other member of the congregation kept the key; but in this case, he was allowed to keep both. And Isaac had never had any apprehension concerning the money entrusted to his care until Dandy Davis had come into the Santee country; of him alone Isaac had a haunting premonition* of fear. It is human nature that a native usually has far more dread of a foreigner than he ever has of another native. In this case you could hardly imagine two people more different, even in appearance.

premonition: forewarning

Walking down a pineland road at dusk, Isaac might easily have been taken for a prehistoric man—with his ragged shirt open, showing the black and hairy arch of his mighty chest, his prodigious* arms and his huge hands, with palms turned forward, hanging below his knees and swinging back and forth as he walked, his short, burly neck that had the effect of burying his chin in his bosom, and a certain shambling yet easy gait which gave the impression that he walked with his feet rather than his legs. He might have startled you into a feeling that you were in Gabon or in the Belgian Congo.*

prodigious: enormous
Gabon . . . Congo: countries in Africa

It was not only in a general moral way that Isaac disliked Dandy Davis. He had a premonition that this suave* mulatto might have designs on the moneys of the Skyrocket Society, moneys entrusted to him. Even now, in the little battered tin box hidden behind one of the big beams in the loft of his cabin he had the savings of forty-one families—money that would in time afford all those who had contributed to the fund some measure of decent burial. Next Sunday the quarterly payments were to be made, and Isaac would have more responsibility on him than ever. And, all the while, the conviction was growing on him that Dandy was taking a sinister interest in his cash box. How to meet this crisis, he did not know.

suave: outwardly polished and gracious

Isaac finally came to two decisions: he could cut for himself and would travel with a much larger hickory stick than had been his wont; and he would no longer keep the money in his house. He believed that somewhere in the churchyard would be a far safer place to hide it until Dandy left the country. For he was sure that Dandy's bubble would soon burst.

"Dat kind," he used to say, "can't last." But he might last long enough to do irretrievable* damage.

irretrievable: incapable of being recovered

Back on the edge of Wildcat Branch, Isaac cut for his own personal use a hickory club of imposing proportions, with a gnarled root for the handle. Thus armed, he set out on that Sunday night for the Negro church. It was the night when the collections would be made. Alone he walked through the moonlight, his precious box tucked under his arm. Every few hundred yards he would pause to look about him and listen; but silence slept over the dreaming forest, and the wide sandy road was deserted. All was well.

After the service, which nearly every member of the Johnson Hill community attended, the payoff was made in a dingy little back room. The

pennies and nickels and dimes poured in apace.*
Once Isaac saw the leering face of Dandy Davis
at the open window. The sight made him come to
another decision. When all the payments were in,
he asked Ben Vandross to walk home with him.
Ben was the strongest Negro in the Santee country; courageous, too, except when it came to matters of superstition.

apace: rapidly

It must have been eleven o'clock, with the full
moon riding almost overhead, when Isaac and
Ben set out for Isaac's lonely little cabin in the

pinelands. Nothing happened. They walked safely
and securely until they came within sight of St.
James Church, glimmering eerily in the forest.

"Well," said Ben, "I think I will leave you
here. You is almost home. You ain't got so far to
go on as what I got to go back."

But distance was not the thing on Ben's mind.
He did not so much mind passing the old church
in Isaac's company, but he did not intend to return
by it alone. What business had he, a self-respect-
ing Negro, to prowl by churchyards in the deep
and dead of night?

"Thank you for comin', Ben," Isaac said. "I
think I will be all right now."

On the back-track, Ben travelled rather fast;
so that he was a long way from Isaac when the
treasurer of the Skyrocket Society reached the
church. Isaac was not afraid of the church or of
the churchyard; not even of the tomb of Raven
McCloud. All he was afraid of was Dandy Davis;
and he now felt in his old bones that Dandy was
near. He was. Indeed, there he stood by the road
just beyond the church. There was no mistaking
that slim and cocky figure. He must have taken
the short-cut by Elmwood to get here before Isaac
did. At any rate, Ben was gone; and physically,
even with his huge hickory stick, the old man was
no match for Dandy–no match for him even if
Dandy had no gun. But he did have one. In the
moonlight the barrel of a short pistol gleamed
dully.

Making sure of his quarry, Dandy sauntered
forward. "Old man," he said with easy insolence,
"don't make me no trouble. I got to have the box
what you got. Gimme dat box, and you can go
home."

Isaac was too busy thinking to answer him.
Through his mind rushed the series of places in
the churchyard where he had considered hiding
his trust funds. If he made a run for the enclosure,
he might hide the box before Dandy laid his yellow hands on it.

With a speed surprising for his age, Isaac
dashed across the road, jammed open the gate

and ran in among the tombs. But Dandy Davis was hot after him. He had clubbed his pistol, ready to deal his victim a lethal* blow. Isaac ran around the McCloud tomb. Black in the moonlight yawned the singular opening at its base. Should he throw the box in there? He swung it in his right hand to do so; there was no mistaking the purpose of his movement. But in that second the butt of the pistol crashed on the back of his head, and he sprawled forward. He fell beyond the opening; and under him lay the treasury of the Skyrocket Resurrection Burial Society.

lethal: deadly

But Dandy Davis thought he had thrown the box into the tomb of Raven McCloud; and being a man with no respect for anybody, he did not even respect the dead. Also, having consumed a pint of moonshine liquor to nerve him for this especial event, he had no sense and no fear left.

"Ah, hah," he said. "You t'ink you would fool me, eh? Well, I gwine after dat money."

On all fours he backed towards the opening in the tomb. Being of slight build, he forced his body in. He let himself down into that ancient darkness. When he was once in, all he had to do, he might have thought, was to strike some matches and recover the treasure. But the tomb was deep, and he was short of stature. He let himself down to arm's length, and still found no footing. At last he dropped into the noisome* depths.

noisome: foul, dangerous

If Isaac had seen what Dandy was doing, much as he hated him, he would have warned him. But he fell into a daze, and by the time he regained his senses, whatever commotion there had been was over. All was still. Isaac called, but there was no answer. And he well knew then there would never be one.

Slowly the old Negro rose to his feet, clutching with joy the treasury of his congregation. And with prayers of thanksgiving on his lips and in his heart he passed unmolested toward his home.

An hour later, he began to think of the Thing, and he thought he could see, as clearly as if he were still there, what was happening in the silent moonlight, by the ancient tomb. Out of it came that which, long before, the Seminoles* had called the Great King, of which they always went in reverent dread. As became such majesty, he advanced slowly. And, for all the horror of his wide unlidded eyes of bloodshot topaz, the sullen droop, almost human in its malice, at the corners of his mouth, the pallor* of thin contemptuous lips, the powerful jaws, articulated with the strength of steel, the Banded Death was beautiful in his regal black-and-gold coloring. A savage yet graceful strength made all his movements rhythmic and flowing; a spirit of power went with him, and a spirit of awe went before him. Once clear of the den, he lay at full length, wary and still as old Isaac had so often seen him—this great diamond-back rattlesnake, more than nine feet long and as large around as a strong man's thigh, the serpent terror of the Santee world.

Seminoles: Indians who originally lived in Alabama
pallor: unnatural paleness

Since Dandy Davis had been regarded as a "floater," it was some days before anyone particularly noticed his absence. Then the gossips began, directing their remarks towards those members of the church who were suspected of having yielded their charms to him: "Ah, hah! Ain't I done tole you so? I bet you he done gone back where he done come from."

It was some time after his mysterious disappearance, when things in the Santee country had settled back to normal, that one of the Negro girls who was especially concerned over his abandonment of her asked old Isaac what he thought of the chances of Dandy's return.

"Katie, chile," he said gently, "I think Dandy is gone to come no mo'. You must git you another man. Where Dandy is now, I 'spect he don't eber eben think of you." The finality of Isaac's opinion ended Katie's suspense, and in that way brought her comfort; and she at once energetically proceeded to the business of seeking out another lover.

A few days after he had given Katie this advice, Isaac again met at the old church the same white man who had asked him if anything ever happened there.

"Nothing happened here yet, old man?" he asked smiling.

"No, sah; nothing yet," answered Isaac. But his eyes had in them an inscrutable look.

For Thought and Discussion

1. What aspects of Rutledge's work link him to the early regionalists? Give specific examples from the story that illustrate his use of regionalism.

2. Rutledge, like Thurber in "The Catbird Seat," develops his conflict through his portrayal of contrasting characters. How are the protagonist and antagonist of this story completely different from one another both in appearance and moral character? What aspects of society does each character symbolize? How does Rutledge, unlike Thurber, offer a moral judgment through the outcome of his plot?

3. To which characters do the following lines refer, and what do the lines reveal about the characters?

    a. "In the case of all other burial societies in the Santee country, the treasurer kept the cash box, and some other member of the congregation kept the key; but in this case, he was allowed to keep both."

    b. "While in Richmond he had spent his time in a public building at the expense of the State of Virginia."

    c. "He did not so much mind passing the old church in Isaac's company, but he did not intend to return by it alone."

    d. "Ah, hah," he said. "You t'ink you would fool me, eh? Well, I gwine after dat money."

    e. "If [he] had seen what Dandy was doing, much as he hated him, he would have warned him."

4. Discuss the relationship of the following objects to the plot of the story: a cash box, a hickory club, a pistol, the tomb of Raven McCloud, the Thing. What examples of foreshadowing does Rutledge provide for the reader? What is the climax of the story? Discuss the dénouement and tell how the white man's question and Isaac's answer at the end of the story are ironic. Point out any other ironic elements you can discover in the plot.

5. Discuss how Rutledge creates a specific atmosphere for his story by the use of descriptive language. Point out specific images that he uses to describe the delta country, the churchyard, and the mysterious Thing in Raven McCloud's tomb. Do you consider these images effective? Why or why not?

Developers of Character

Eudora Welty   1909-2001

In much of her fiction, Eudora Welty carefully examines her native region of the South, the Mississippi delta country. Born in Jackson, Mississippi, Welty came to national attention in 1936 with the appearance of her first short story, "Death of a Traveling Salesman." Five years later she published her first collection of stories, *A Curtain of Green* (1941). Since then her short stories have regularly appeared in major national magazines. Also a novelist, Welty won a Pulitzer Prize in 1973 for her novel *The Optimist's Daughter* (1972). Although she received numerous national honors and prizes, she chose to remain in southern Mississippi, the locale that dominates her fiction. A versatile and gifted writer, she is regarded as one of the modern masters of the short-story form.

Welty's stories and novels communicate a powerful sense of place, particularly of local tradition and culture. Her characters–sometimes attractive, sometimes repulsive–are delicate studies of strength and weakness, of pettiness and magnanimity. They unquestionably are individuals, not types.

A Worn Path

In "A Worn Path" nothing happens that would make the front page, or even the last page, of the Natchez Democrat. *The walk to town has happened before and often: "as regularly as clockwork." It will happen again, until the close of "the whole enduring time" of Phoenix Jackson's life. The only witnesses of her "trip" take little note of it. But something about it, Welty would have us believe, is deeply meaningful. Though not strictly allegorical, many of its details, as well as its title, are symbolically suggestive. Perhaps there is more than one species of heroism. In an essay Welty explained the story's subject as "the deep-grained habit of love."*

It was December—a bright frozen day in the early morning. Far out in the country there was an old Negro woman with her head tied in a red rag, coming along a path through the pinewoods. Her name was Phoenix Jackson. She was very old and small and she walked slowly in the dark pine shadows, moving a little from side to side in her steps, with the balanced heaviness and lightness of a pendulum in a grandfather clock. She carried a thin, small cane made from an umbrella, and with this she kept tapping the frozen earth in front of her. This made a grave and persistent noise in the still air, that seemed meditative like the chirping of a solitary little bird.

She wore a dark striped dress reaching down to her shoe tops, and an equally long apron of bleached sugar sacks, with a full pocket: all neat and tidy, but every time she took a step she might have fallen over her shoelaces, which dragged from her unlaced shoes. She looked straight ahead. Her eyes were blue with age. Her skin had a pattern all its own of numberless branching wrinkles and as though a whole little tree stood in the middle of her forehead, but a golden color ran underneath, and the two knobs of her cheeks were illumined by a yellow burning under the dark. Under the rag her hair came down on her neck in the frailest of ringlets, still black, and with an odor like copper.

Now and then there was a quivering in the thicket. Old Phoenix said, "Out of my way, all you foxes, owls, beetles, jack rabbits, coons and wild animals! . . . Keep out from under these feet, little bob-whites. . . . Keep the big wild hogs out of my path. Don't let none of those come running my direction. I got a long way." Under her small black-freckled hand her cane, limber as a buggy whip, would switch at the brush as if to rouse up any hiding things.

On she went. The woods were deep and still. The sun made the pine needles almost too bright to look at, up where the wind rocked. The cones dropped as light as feathers. Down in the hollow was the mourning dove—it was not too late for him.

The path ran up a hill. "Seem like there is chains about my feet, time I get this far," she said, in the voice of argument old people keep to use with themselves. "Something always take a hold of me on this hill—pleads I should stay."

After she got to the top she turned and gave a full, severe look behind her where she had come. "Up through pines," she said at length. "Now down through oaks."

Her eyes opened their widest, and she started down gently. But before she got to the bottom of the hill a bush caught her dress.

Her fingers were busy and intent, but her skirts were full and long, so that before she could pull them free in one place they were caught in another. It was not possible to allow the dress to tear. "I in the thorny bush," she said. "Thorns, you doing your appointed work. Never want to let folks pass, no sir. Old eyes thought you was a pretty little *green* bush."

Finally, trembling all over, she stood free, and after a moment dared to stoop for her cane.

"Sun so high!" she cried, leaning back and looking, while the thick tears went over her eyes. "The time getting all gone here."

At the foot of this hill was a place where a log was laid across the creek.

"Now comes the trial," said Phoenix.

Putting her right foot out, she mounted the log and shut her eyes. Lifting her skirt, leveling her cane fiercely before her, like a festival in some parade, she began to march across. Then she opened her eyes and she was safe on the other side.

"I wasn't as old as I thought," she said.

But she sat down to rest. She spread her skirts on the bank around her and folded her hands over her knees. Up above her was a tree in a pearly cloud of mistletoe. She did not dare to close her eyes, and when a little boy brought her a plate with a slice of marble-cake on it she spoke to him. "That would be acceptable," she said. But when she went to take it there was just her own hand in the air.

So she left that tree, and had to go through a barbed-wire fence. There she had to creep and crawl, speading her knees and stretching her fingers like a baby trying to climb the steps. But she talked loudly to herself: she could not let her dress be torn now, so late in the day, and she could not pay for having her arm or her leg sawed off if she got caught fast where she was.

As last she was safe through the fence and risen up out in the clearing. Big dead trees, like black men with one arm, were standing in the purple stalks of the withered cotton field. There sat a buzzard.

"Who you watching?"

In the furrow she made her way along.

"Glad this not the season for bulls," she said, looking sideways, "and the good Lord made his snakes to curl up and sleep in the winter. A pleasure I don't see no two-headed snake coming around that tree, where it come once. It took a while to get by him, back in the summer."

She passed through the old cotton and went into a field of dead corn. It whispered and shook and was taller than her head. "Through the maze now," she said, for there was no path.

Then there was something tall, black, and skinny there, moving before her.

At first she took it for a man. It could have been a man dancing in the field. But she stood still and listened, and it did not make a sound. It was as silent as a ghost.

"Ghost," she said sharply, "who be you the ghost of? For I have heard of nary death close by."

But there was no answer—only the ragged dancing in the wind.

She shut her eyes, reached out her hand, and touched a sleeve. She found a coat and inside that an emptiness, cold as ice.

"You scarecrow," she said. Her face lighted. "I ought to be shut up for good," she said with laughter. "My senses is gone. I too old. I the oldest people I ever know. Dance, old scarecrow," she said, "while I dancing with you."

She kicked her foot over the furrow, and with mouth drawn down, shook her head once or twice in a little strutting way. Some husks blew down and whirled in streamers about her skirts.

Then she went on, parting her way from side to side with the cane, through the whispering field. At last she came to the end, to a wagon track where the silver grass blew between the red ruts. The quail were walking around like pullets, seeming all dainty and unseen.

"Walk pretty," she said. "This is the easy place. This the easy going."

She followed the track, swaying through the quiet bare fields, through the little strings of trees silver in their dead leaves, past cabins silver from weather, with the doors and windows boarded shut, all like old women under a spell sitting there. "I walking in their sleep," she said, nodding her head vigorously.

In a ravine she went where a spring was silently flowing through a hollow log. Old Phoenix bent and drank. "Sweet-gum makes the water sweet," she said, and drank more. "Nobody know who made this well, for it was here when I was born."

The track crossed a swampy part where the moss hung as white as lace from every limb. "Sleep on, alligators, and blow your bubbles." Then the track went into the road.

Deep, deep the road went down between the high green-colored banks. Overhead the live-oaks met, and it was as dark as a cave.

A black dog with a lolling tongue came up out of the weeds by the ditch. She was meditating, and not ready, and when he came at her she only hit him a little with her cane. Over she went in the ditch, like a little puff of milkweed.

Down there, her senses drifted away. A dream visited her, and she reached her hand up, but nothing reached down and gave her a pull. So she lay there and presently went to talking. "Old woman," she said to herself, "that black dog come up out of the weeds to stall you off, and now there he sitting on his fine tail smiling at you."

A white man finally came along and found her–a hunter, a young man, with his dog on a chain.

"Well, Granny!" he laughed. "What are you doing there?"

"Lying on my back like a June-bug waiting to be turned over, mister," she said, reaching up her hand.

He lifted her up, gave her a swing in the air, and set her down. "Anything broken, Granny?"

"No sir, them old dead weeds is springy enough," said Phoenix, when she had got her breath. "I thank you for your trouble."

"Where do you live, Granny?" he asked, while the two dogs were growling at each other.

"Away back yonder, sir, behind the ridge. You can't even see it from here."

"On your way home?"

"No sir, I going to town."

"Why, that's too far! That's as far as I walk when I come out myself, and I get something for my trouble." He patted the stuffed bag he carried, and there hung down a little closed claw. It was one of the bob-whites, with its beak hooked bitterly to show it was dead. "Now you go on home, Granny!"

"I bound to go to town, mister," said Phoenix. "The time come around."

He gave another laugh, filling the whole landscape. "I know you old colored people! Wouldn't miss going to town to see Santa Claus!"

But something held old Phoenix very still. The deep lines in her face went into a fierce and different radiation. Without warning, she had seen with her own eyes a flashing nickel fall out of the man's pocket onto the ground.

"How old are you, Granny?" he was saying.

"There is no telling, mister," she said, "no telling."

Then she gave a little cry and clapped her hands and said, "Git on away from here, dog! Look! Look at that dog!" She laughed as if in admiration. "He ain't scared of nobody. He a big black dog." She whispered, "Sic him!"

"Watch me get rid of that cur," said the man. "Sic him, Pete! Sic him!"

Phoenix heard the dogs fighting, and heard the man running and throwing sticks. She even heard a gunshot. But she was slowly bending forward by that time, further and further forward, the lids stretched down over her eyes, as if she were doing this in her sleep. Her chin was lowered almost to her knees. The yellow palm of her hand came out from the fold of her apron. Her fingers slid down and along the ground under the piece of money with the grace and care they would have in lifting an egg from under a setting hen. Then she slowly straightened up, she stood erect, and the nickel was in her apron pocket. A bird flew by. Her lips moved. "God watching me the whole time. I come to stealing."

The man came back, and his own dog panted about them. "Well, I scared him off that time," he said, and then he laughed and lifted his gun and pointed it at Phoenix.

She stood straight and faced him.

"Doesn't the gun scare you?" he said, still pointing it.

"No, sir, I seen plenty go off closer by, in my day, and for less than what I done," she said, holding utterly still.

He smiled, and shouldered the gun. "Well, Granny," he said, "you must be a hundred years old, and scared of nothing. I'd give you a dime if I had any money with me. But you take my advice and stay home, and nothing will happen to you."

"I bound to go on my way, mister," said Phoenix. She inclined her head in the red rag. Then they went in different directions, but she could hear the gun shooting again and again over the hill.

She walked on. The shadows hung from the oak trees to the road like curtains. Then she smelled wood-smoke, and smelled the river, and she saw a steeple and the cabins on their steep steps. Dozens of little black children whirled around her. There ahead was Natchez shining. Bells were ringing. She walked on.

In the paved city it was Christmas time. There were red and green electric lights strung and crisscrossed everywhere, and all turned on in the daytime. Old Phoenix would have been lost if she had not distrusted her eyesight and depended on her feet to know where to take her.

She paused quietly on the sidewalk where people were passing by. A lady came along in the crowd, carrying an armful of red-, green- and silver-wrapped presents; she gave off perfume like the red roses in hot summer, and Phoenix stopped her.

"Please, missy, will you lace up my shoe?" She held up her foot.

"What do you want, Grandma?"

"See my shoe," said Phoenix. "Do all right for out in the country, but wouldn't look right to go in a big building."

"Stand still then, Grandma," said the lady. She put her packages down on the sidewalk beside her and laced and tied both shoes tightly.

"Can't lace 'em with a cane," said Phoenix. "Thank you, missy. I doesn't mind asking a nice lady to tie up my shoe, when I gets out on the street."

Moving slowly and from side to side, she went into the big building, and into a tower of steps, where she walked up and around and around until her feet knew to stop.

She entered a door, and there she saw nailed up on the wall the document that had been stamped with the gold seal and framed in the gold frame, which matched the dream that was hung up in her head.

"Here I be," she said. There was a fixed and ceremonial stiffness over her body.

"A charity case, I suppose," said an attendant who sat at the desk before her.

But Phoenix only looked above her head. There was sweat on her face, the wrinkles in her skin shone like a bright net.

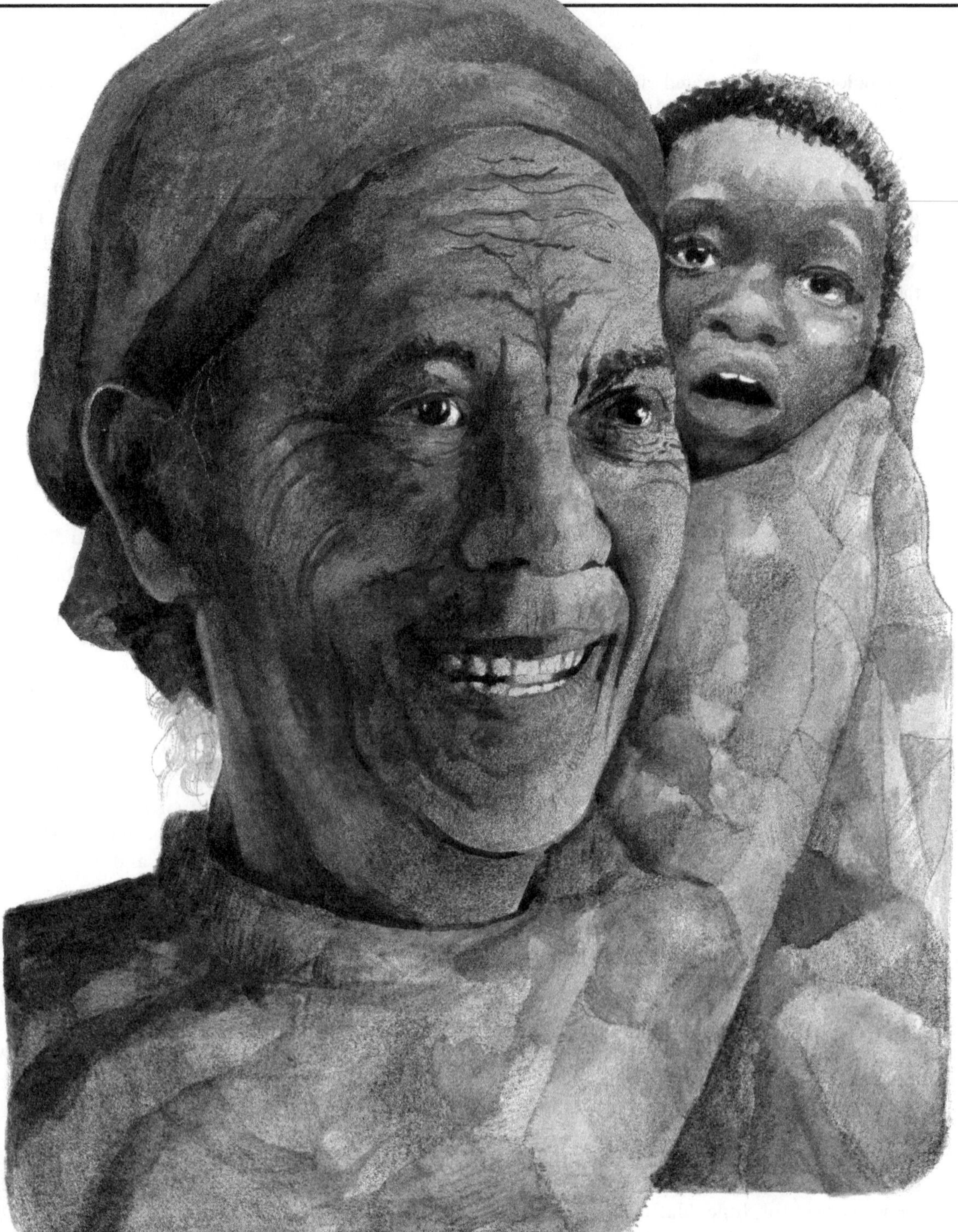

"Speak up, Grandma," the woman said. "What's your name? We must have your history, you know. Have you been here before? What seems to be the trouble with you?"

Old Phoenix only gave a twitch to her face as if a fly were bothering her.

"Are you deaf?" cried the attendant.

But then the nurse came in.

"Oh, that's just old Aunt Phoenix," she said. "She doesn't come for herself–she has a little grandson. She makes these trips just as regular as clockwork. She lives away back off the Old Natchez Trace." She bent down. "Well, Aunt Phoenix, why don't you just take a seat? We won't keep you standing after your long trip." She pointed.

The old woman sat down, bolt upright in the chair.

"Now, how is the boy?" asked the nurse.

Old Phoenix did not speak.

"I said, how is the boy?"

But Phoenix only waited and stared straight ahead, her face very solemn and withdrawn into rigidity.

"Is his throat any better?" asked the nurse. "Aunt Phoenix, don't you hear me? Is your grandson's throat any better since the last time you came for the medicine?"

With her hands on her knees, the old woman waited, silent, erect and motionless, just as if she were in armor.

"You mustn't take up our time this way, Aunt Phoenix," the nurse said. "Tell us quickly about your grandson, and get it over. He isn't dead, is he?"

At last there came a flicker and then a flame of comprehension across her face, and she spoke.

"My grandson. It was my memory had left me. There I sat and forgot why I made my long trip."

"Forgot?" the nurse frowned. "After you came so far?"

Then Phoenix was like an old woman begging a dignified forgiveness for waking up frightened in the night. "I never did go to school, I was too old at the Surrender," she said in a soft voice. "I'm an old woman without an education. It was my memory fail me. My little grandson, he is just the same, and I forgot it in the coming."

"Throat never heals, does it?" said the nurse, speaking in a loud, sure voice to old Phoenix. By now she had a card with something written on it, a little list. "Yes. Swallowed lye. When was it–January–two, three years ago–"

Phoenix spoke unasked now. "No, missy, he not dead, he just the same. Every little while his throat begin to close up again, and he not able to swallow. He not get his breath. He not able to help himself. So the time come around, and I go on another trip for the soothing medicine."

"All right. The doctor said as long as you came to get it, you could have it," said the nurse. "But it's an obstinate case."

"My little grandson, he sit up there in the house all wrapped up, waiting by himself," Phoenix went on. "We is the only two left in the world. He suffer and it don't seem to put him back at all. He got a sweet look. He going to last. He wear a little patch quilt and peep out holding his mouth open like a little bird. I remembers so plain now. I not going to forget him again, no, the whole enduring time. I could tell him from all the others in creation."

"All right." The nurse was trying to hush her now. She brought her a bottle of medicine. "Charity," she said, making a check mark in a book.

Old Phoenix held the bottle close to her eyes, and then carefully put it into her pocket.

"I thank you," she said.

"It's Christmas time, Grandma," said the attendant. "Could I give you a few pennies out of my purse?"

"Five pennies is a nickel," said Phoenix stiffly.

"Here's a nickel," said the attendant.

Phoenix rose carefully and held out her hand. She received the nickel and then fished the other nickel out of her pocket and laid it beside the new one. She stared at her palm closely, with her head on one side.

Then she gave a tap with her cane on the floor.

"This is what come to me to do," she said. "I going to the store and buy my child a little windmill they sells, made out of paper. He going to find it hard to believe there such a thing in the world. I'll march myself back where he waiting, holding it straight up in this hand."

She lifted her free hand, gave a little nod, turned around, and walked out of the doctor's office. Then her slow step began on the stairs, going down.

For Thought and Discussion

1. Using an encyclopedia or a college dictionary, what can you discover about Phoenix Jackson's name that would make it appropriate to the personality and behavior of the central character in this story?

2. Notice details that are repeated (motifs). Do you find meaning in the birds, in black things, and in the uplifted hand or arm?

3. At what point in the story do we learn the purpose of Phoenix's journey? What does the story gain by delaying this information? Why do you think Phoenix momentarily forgets, or seems to forget, the purpose of her journey?

4. Explain the irony in the words of the hunter, "I know you old colored people! Wouldn't miss going to town to see Santa Claus!"

5. What is the "worn path" of the title? Can it have more than one meaning?

Developers of Theme

Ernest Hemingway
1899-1961

Ernest Hemingway is one of the most controversial and highly publicized writers of modern times. Although he was born and reared in a prosperous Chicago suburb (Oak Park, Illinois), he frequently fished and hunted in the wilds of northern Michigan and participated in sports like football and boxing. From these activities he gained an appetite for bullfighting and big game hunting, the dangerous sports he admired as an adult. After his high-school graduation in 1917, he tried to enlist in the army but was turned down because of an eye injury received while boxing. He then became a reporter for the *Kansas City Star,* where he learned to follow what he called "the best rules . . . for writing": "avoid the use of adjectives," write "short sentences" and "short first paragraphs," and use "vigorous English."

In 1918 Hemingway joined the Red Cross ambulance corps and was sent to Europe. In Italy, after only three weeks of duty, he was seriously wounded by shrapnel. He managed, however, to carry a fatally wounded Italian soldier back to a first-aid station, an act which prompted the Italian government to award him a medal for valor and to allow him to fight as an infantryman in the Italian army for the remainder of the war. His experiences in Italy became the basis for one of his most successful novels, *A Farewell to Arms* (1929).

Returning to Illinois after the war, he remained unsettled for a time before becoming a newspaperman again. In 1921 he married Hadley Richardson, the first of four wives. In December they moved to Paris so that he could serve as a foreign correspondent for the *Toronto Daily Star*. In Paris he joined the American expatriates and came under the influence of writers like Ezra Pound and Gertrude Stein (she gave the title the "lost generation" to Hemingway and the other American writers in Paris during the 1920s). His first published book, *Three Stories and Ten Poems*, was privately printed in 1923. Two years later appeared the American edition of *In Our Time*, a collection of sketches and stories centered on a semiautobiographical character, Nick Adams. Hemingway's first major novel, *The Sun Also Rises*, was published the next year, became a best seller, and established his reputation as an important new writer. These Paris years ended on a sour note, however, for Hemingway divorced his wife. After marrying Pauline Pfeiffer in 1927, he moved to Key West, Florida, where he spent most mornings writing and most afternoons fishing.

In the following three decades Hemingway traveled widely, enjoying big game hunting in Africa and working as a war correspondent in the Spanish Civil War (1936-39) and in World War II. He lived in Key West for ten years and then in Cuba for twenty. He was twice again divorced and remarried. He also continued writing, publishing nearly a dozen books and collections of short stories in this period.

In 1954 Hemingway received the Nobel Prize for literature. The citation spoke specifically of his "forceful and . . . style-making mastery" as it had appeared particularly in his most recent novel, *The Old Man and the Sea* (1952). Because of injuries received in a plane crash while on a hunting expedition in Africa, Hemingway could not attend the ceremonies in Stockholm. In his acceptance speech, read by the U. S. ambassador to Sweden, Hemingway declared that "for a true writer each book should be a new beginning where he tries again for something that is beyond attainment. He should always try for something that has never been done or that others have tried and failed. Then sometimes, with great luck he will succeed." His short address ended abruptly: "I have spoken too long for a writer. A writer should write what he has to say and not speak it."

The remaining seven years of Hemingway's life were difficult ones. His heavy drinking, indulgent lifestyle, and numerous injuries sustained throughout his lifetime had left him both physically and mentally weakened. Moreover, he found himself unable to write as he once had. In 1960 he left Cuba because of Castro's anti-American stance and moved to Ketchum, Idaho. At times he distrusted everyone, fearing that the government and even his most trusted friends were trying to trick him. Hemingway also began seriously considering suicide. In *For Whom the Bell Tolls,* he had had his hero soundly condemn suicide as a way of resolving personal problems. Hemingway himself had always believed that his father's suicide in 1928 was an indefensible act of weakness. Yet on the morning of July 2, 1961, Ernest Hemingway took his own life. And thus ended the career of one of the most controversial American writers.

Perhaps the most distinctive feature of Hemingway's work is the style. The sentences are usually short and simple, composed largely of common nouns and verbs uncluttered with adjectives and adverbs. Although his writing is sometimes choppy, it achieves the effect he wanted: crispness and clarity. Hemingway's words, said a contemporary novelist, "strike you, each one, as if they were pebbles fetched fresh from a brook." Hemingway said that he wished "to strip language clean, to lay it bare down to the bone."

Another characteristic feature of Hemingway's fiction is the hero. Set in a world that seems meaningless, the characters must find a way to make their peace with it. Hemingway, writes Robert E. Spiller, "had but a single theme—how man may meet death in a world stripped of all values except that of intensity." As spokesman for the Lost Generation, Hemingway wrote of men and women who had thrown aside all values inherited from the past. His notorious definition of morality became the generation's creed: "I know only that what is moral is what you feel good after and what is immoral is what you feel bad after." This subjective definition, of course, totally ignores God's moral laws. It is no wonder then that those who hold this view of life can only, like Hemingway, come to despair.

Big Two-Hearted River

This short story shows Hemingway's own strong love for the outdoors. In places it even functions as a masterfully written guide to the intricacies of trout fishing and camping, two activities that Hemingway enjoyed in his youth.

Although the story bears the name of an actual river in northern Michigan, the meaning of the name is puzzling. Some critics believe that it implies two "hearts": one of light (the sunny meadow and pines) and one of darkness (the forbidding swamp).

This story will seem plotless and pointless to most readers unless they are aware of the background to the work. Hemingway placed it at the end of In Our Time *(1925), his collection of sketches and tales that develop the story of Nick Adams. A semiautobiographical hero, Nick had fought in World War I and has returned home to recuperate from the physical and emotional injuries he has received in battle. His return, alone, to the Upper Peninsula is a return to an important site from his childhood. Like the story itself, Nick seems to be empty. He performs one task after another, methodically and unthinkingly. His careful attention to detail seems to be the means of healing the mental wounds he still bears from the war. According to several critics, Nick is searching for sanity.*

Hemingway divided "Big Two-Hearted River" into two parts. In part I Nick arrives at the burned-over town of Seney. Both the town and the forest have disappeared. Nick walks across the blackened plain to the river and sets up camp. As part II opens, Nick is ready for his first day of solitary fishing.

Notice that the story is "full of rituals," as one of Hemingway's best critics, Carlos Baker, observes. The ritualistic actions of catching grasshoppers (the bait), of baiting the hook, of playing the hooked trout, of releasing the undersized fish, even of cleaning those he keeps become the means of keeping his mind from dwelling on the past he wishes to forget. The swamp that lies downstream and that sinisterly attracts him implies an encounter that Nick is not yet ready to face.

Part II

In the morning the sun was up and the tent was starting to get hot. Nick crawled out under the mosquito netting stretched across the mouth of the tent, to look at the morning. The grass was wet on his hands as he came out. He held his trousers and his shoes in his hands. The sun was just up over the hill. There was the meadow, the river and the swamp. There were birch trees in the green of the swamp on the other side of the river.

The river was clear and smoothly fast in the early morning. Down about two hundred yards were three logs all the way across the stream. They made the water smooth and deep above them. As Nick watched, a mink crossed the river on the logs and went into the swamp. Nick was excited. He was excited by the early morning and the river. He was really too hurried to eat breakfast, but he knew he must. He built a little fire and put on the coffee pot. While the water was heating in the pot he took an empty bottle and went down over the edge of the high ground to the meadow. The meadow was wet with dew and Nick wanted to catch grasshoppers for bait before the sun dried the grass. He found plenty of good grasshoppers. They were at the base of the grass stems. Sometimes they clung to a grass stem. They were cold and wet with the dew, and could

not jump until the sun warmed them. Nick picked them up, taking only the medium sized brown ones and put them into the bottle. He turned over a log and just under the shelter of the edge were several hundred hoppers. It was a grasshopper lodging house. Nick put about fifty of the medium browns into the bottle. While he was picking up the hoppers the others warmed in the sun and commenced to hop away. They flew when they hopped. At first they made one flight and stayed stiff when they landed, as though they were dead.

Nick knew that by the time he was through with breakfast they would be as lively as ever. Without dew in the grass it would take him all day to catch a bottle full of good grasshoppers and he would have to crush many of them, slamming at them with his hat. He washed his hands at the stream. He was excited to be near it. Then he walked up to the tent. The hoppers were already jumping stiffly in the grass. In the bottle, warmed by the sun, they were jumping in a mass. Nick put in a pine stick as a cork. It plugged the mouth of the bottle enough, so the hoppers could not get out and left plenty of air passage.

He had rolled the log back and knew he could get grasshoppers there every morning.

Nick laid the bottle full of jumping grasshoppers against a pine trunk. Rapidly he mixed some buckwheat flour with water and stirred it smooth, one cup of flour, one cup of water. He put a

handful of coffee in the pot and dipped a lump of grease out of a can and slid it sputtering across the hot skillet. On the smoking skillet he poured smoothly the buckwheat batter. It spread like lava, the grease spitting sharply. Around the edges the buckwheat cake began to firm, then brown, then crisp. The surface was bubbling slowly to porousness*. Nick pushed under the browned under surface with a fresh pine chip. He shook the skillet sideways and the cake was loose on the surface. I won't try and flop it, he thought. He slid the chip of clean wood all the way under the cake, and flopped it over onto its face. It sputtered in the pan.

porousness: lit., full of pores

When it was cooked Nick regreased the skillet. He used all the batter. It made another big flapjack and one smaller one.

Nick ate a big flapjack and a smaller one, covered with apple butter. He put apple butter on the third cake, folded it over twice, wrapped it in oiled paper and put it in his shirt pocket. He put the apple butter jar back in the pack and cut bread for two sandwiches.

In the pack he found a big onion. He sliced it in two and peeled the silky outer skin. Then he cut one half into slices and made onion sandwiches. He wrapped them in oiled paper and buttoned them in the other pocket of his khaki shirt. He turned the skillet upside down on the grill, drank the coffee, sweetened and yellow brown with the condensed milk in it, and tidied up the camp. It was a nice little camp.

Nick took his fly rod out of the leather rod-case, jointed it, and shoved the rod-case back into the tent. He put on the reel and threaded the line through the guides. He had to hold it from hand to hand, as he threaded it, or it would slip back through its own weight. It was a heavy, double tapered fly line. Nick had paid eight dollars for it a long time ago. It was made heavy to lift back in the air and come forward flat and heavy and straight to make it possible to cast a fly which has no weight. Nick opened the aluminum leader box. The leaders were coiled between the damp flannel pads. Nick had wet the pads at the water cooler on the train up to St. Ignace.* In the damp pads the gut leaders had softened and Nick unrolled one and tied it by a loop at the end to the fly line. He fastened a hook on the end of the leader. It was a small hook; very thin and springy.

St. Ignace: a city in the southernmost part of Michigan's Upper Peninsula

Nick took it from his hook book, sitting with the rod across his lap. He tested the knot and spring of the rod by pulling the line taut.* It was a good feeling. He was careful not to let the hook bite into his finger.

taut: tight

He started down to the stream, holding his rod, the bottle of grasshoppers hung from his neck by a thong tied in half hitches* around the neck of the bottle. His landing net hung by a hook from his belt. Over his shoulder was a long flour sack tied at each corner into an ear. The cord went over his shoulder. The sack flapped against his legs.

hitches: a type of knot

Nick felt awkward and professionally happy with all his equipment hanging from him. The grasshopper bottle swung against his chest. In his shirt the breast pockets bulged against him with the lunch and his fly book.

He stepped into the stream. It was a shock. His trousers clung tight to his legs. His shoes felt the gravel. The water was a rising cold shock.

Rushing, the current sucked against his legs. Where he stepped in, the water was over his knees. He waded with the current. The gravel slid under his shoes. He looked down at the swirl of water below each leg and tipped up the bottle to get a grasshopper.

The first grasshopper gave a jump in the neck of the bottle and went out into the water. He was sucked under in the whirl by Nick's right leg and came to the surface a little way down stream. He floated rapidly, kicking. In a quick circle, breaking the smooth surface of the water, he disappeared. A trout had taken him.

Another hopper poked his face out of the bottle. His antennae wavered. He was getting his front legs out of the bottle to jump. Nick took him by the head and held him while he threaded the slim hook under his chin, down through his thorax and into the last segments of his abdomen. The grasshopper took hold of the hook with his front feet, spitting tobacco juice on it. Nick dropped him into the water.

Holding the rod in his right hand he let out line against the pull of the grasshopper in the current. He stripped off line from the reel with his left hand and let it run free. He could see the hopper in the little waves of the current. It went out of sight.

There was a tug on the line. Nick pulled against the taut line. It was his first strike. Holding the now living rod across the current, he brought in the line with his left hand. The rod bent in jerks, the trout pumping against the current. Nick knew it was a small one. He lifted the rod straight up in the air. It bowed with the pull.

He saw the trout in the water jerking with his head and body against the shifting tangent of the line in the stream.

Nick took the line in his left hand and pulled the trout, thumping tiredly against the current, to the surface. His back was mottled* the clear, water-over-gravel color, his side flashing in the sun. The rod under his right arm, Nick stooped, dipping his right hand into the current. He held the trout, never still, with his moist right hand, while he unhooked the barb from his mouth, then dropped him back into the stream.

mottled: covered with spots or streaks of different shades or colors

He hung unsteadily in the current, then settled to the bottom beside a stone. Nick reached down his hand to touch him, his arm to the elbow under water. The trout was steady in the moving stream, resting on the gravel, beside a stone. As Nick's fingers touched him, touched his smooth, cool, underwater feeling he was gone, gone in a shadow across the bottom of the stream.

He's all right, Nick thought. He was only tired.

He had wet his hand before he touched the trout, so he would not disturb the delicate mucus* that covered him. If a trout was touched with a dry hand, a white fungus attacked the unprotected spot. Years before when he had fished crowded streams, with fly fishermen ahead of him and behind him, Nick had again and again come on dead trout, furry with white fungus, drifted against a rock, or floating belly up in some pool. Nick did not like to fish with other men on the river. Unless they were of your party, they spoiled it.

mucus: protective, lubricant coating

He wallowed down the stream, above his knees in the current, through the fifty yards of shallow water above the pile of logs that crossed the stream. He did not rebait his hook and held it in his hand as he waded. He was certain he could catch small trout in the shallows, but he did not want them. There would be no big trout in the shallows this time of day.

Now the water deepened up his thighs sharply and coldly. Ahead was the smooth dammed-back flood water above the logs. The water was smooth and dark; on the left, the lower edge of the meadow; on the right the swamp.

Nick leaned back against the current and took a hopper from the bottle. He threaded the hopper on the hook and spat on him for good luck. Then he pulled several yards of line from the reel and tossed the hopper out ahead onto the fast, dark water. It floated down towards the logs, then the weight of the line pulled the bait under the surface. Nick held the rod in his right hand, letting the line run out through his fingers.

There was a long tug. Nick struck and the rod came alive and dangerous, bent double, the line tightening, coming out of water, tightening, all in a heavy, dangerous, steady pull. Nick felt the moment when the leader would break if the strain increased and let the line go.

The reel ratcheted* into a mechanical shriek as the line went out in a rush. Too fast, Nick could not check it, the line rushing out, the reel note rising as the line ran out.

---

ratcheted: produced a clicking sound from the action of a ratchet, which is a mechanism that engages the sloping teeth of a wheel so as to permit motion in only one direction

---

With the core of the reel showing, his heart feeling stopped with the excitement, leaning back against the current that mounted icily his thighs, Nick thumbed the reel hard with his left hand. It was awkward getting his thumb inside the fly reel frame.

As he put on pressure the line tightened into sudden hardness and beyond the logs a huge trout went high out of water. As he jumped, Nick lowered the tip of the rod. But he felt, as he dropped the tip to ease the strain, the moment when the strain was too great; the hardness too tight. Of course, the leader had broken. There was no mis-

taking the feeling when all spring left the line and it became dry and hard. Then it went slack.

His mouth dry, his heart down, Nick reeled in. He had never seen so big a trout. There was a heaviness, a power not to be held, and then the bulk of him, as he jumped. He looked as broad as a salmon.

Nick's hand was shaky. He reeled in slowly. The thrill had been too much. He felt, vaguely, a little sick, as though it would be better to sit down.

The leader had broken where the hook was tied to it. Nick took it in his hand. He thought of the trout somewhere on the bottom, holding himself steady over the gravel, far down below the light, under the logs, with the hook in his jaw. Nick knew the trout's teeth would cut through the snell* of the hook. The hook would imbed itself in his jaw. He'd bet the trout was angry. Anything that size would be angry. That was a trout. He had been solidly hooked. Solid as a rock. He felt like a rock, too, before he started off. . . . He was a big one. . . . He was the biggest one I ever heard of.

---

snell: a short length of monofilament or gut used to attach a fishhook to a heavier line

---

Nick climbed out onto the meadow and stood, water running down his trousers and out of his shoes, his shoes squelchy.* He went over and sat on the logs. He did not want to rush his sensations any.

---

squelchy: i.e., water-soaked

He wriggled his toes in the water, in his shoes, and got out a cigarette from his breast pocket. He lit it and tossed the match into the fast water below the logs. A tiny trout rose at the match, as it swung around in the fast current. Nick laughed. He would finish the cigarette.

He sat on the logs, smoking, drying in the sun, the sun warm on his back, the river shallow ahead entering the woods, curving into the woods, shallows, light glittering, big water-smooth rocks, cedars along the bank and white birches, the logs warm in the sun, smooth to sit on, without bark, gray to the touch; slowly the feeling of disappointment left him. It went away slowly, the feeling of disappointment that came sharply after the thrill that made his shoulders ache. It was all right now. His rod lying out on the logs, Nick tied a new hook on the leader, pulling the gut tight until it grimped* into itself in a hard knot.

grimped: i.e., tightened

He baited up, then picked up the rod and walked to the far end of the logs to get into the water, where it was not too deep. Under and beyond the logs was a deep pool. Nick walked around the shallow shelf near the swamp shore until he came out on the shallow bed of the stream.

On the left, where the meadow ended and the woods began, a great elm tree was uprooted. Gone over in a storm, it lay back into the woods, its roots clotted with dirt, grass growing in them rising a solid bank beside the stream. The river cut to the edge of the uprooted tree. From where Nick stood he could see deep channels, like ruts, cut in the shallow bed of the stream by the flow of the current. Pebbly where he stood and pebbly and full of boulders beyond; where it curved near the tree roots, the bed of the stream was marly* and between the ruts of deep water green weed fronds* swung in the current.

marly: i.e., soft and streaked
fronds: leaves of water weeds

Nick swung the rod back over his shoulder and forward, and the line, curving forward, laid the grasshopper down on one of the deep channels in the weeds. A trout struck and Nick hooked him.

Holding the rod far out toward the uprooted tree and sloshing backward in the current, Nick worked the trout, plunging, the rod bending alive, out of the danger of the weeds into the open river. Holding the rod, pumping alive against the current, Nick brought the trout in. He rushed, but always came, the spring of the rod yielding to the

rushes, sometimes jerking under water, but always bringing him in. Nick eased downstream with the rushes. The rod above his head he led the trout over the net, then lifted.

The trout hung heavy in the net, mottled trout back and silver sides in the meshes. Nick unhooked him; heavy sides, good to hold, big undershot jaw, and slipped him, heaving and big sliding, into the long sack that hung from his shoulders in the water.

Nick spread the mouth of the sack against the current and it filled, heavy with water. He held it up, the bottom in the stream, and the water poured out through the sides. Inside at the bottom was the big trout, alive in the water.

Nick moved downstream. The sack out ahead of him sunk heavy in the water, pulling from his shoulders.

It was getting hot, the sun hot on the back of his neck.

Nick had one good trout. He did not care about getting many trout. Now the stream was shallow and wide. There were trees along both banks. The trees of the left bank made short shadows on the current in the forenoon sun. Nick knew there were trout in each shadow. In the afternoon, after the sun had crossed toward the hills, the trout would be in the cool shadows on the other side of the stream.

The very biggest ones would lie up close to the bank. You could always pick them up there on the Black. When the sun was down they all moved out into the current. Just when the sun made the water blinding in the glare before it went down, you were liable to strike a big trout anywhere in the current. It was almost impossible to fish then, the surface of the water was blinding as a mirror in the sun. Of course, you could fish upstream, but in a stream like the Black, or this, you had to wallow against the current and in a deep place, the water piled up on you. It was not fun to fish upstream with this much current.

Nick moved along through the shallow stretch watching the banks for deep holes. A beech tree

grew close beside the river, so that the branches hung down into the water. The stream went back in under the leaves. There were always trout in a place like that.

Nick did not care about fishing that hole. He was sure he would get hooked in the branches.

It looked deep though. He dropped the grasshopper so the current took it under water, back in under the overhanging branch. The line pulled hard and Nick struck. The trout threshed heavily, half out of water in the leaves and branches. The line was caught. Nick pulled hard and the trout was off. He reeled in and holding the hook in his hand, walked down the stream.

Ahead, close to the left bank, was a big log. Nick saw it was hollow; pointing up river the current entered it smoothly, only a little ripple spread each side of the log. The water was deepening. The top of the hollow log was gray and dry. It was partly in the shadow.

Nick took the cork out of the grasshopper bottle and a hopper clung to it. He picked him off, hooked him and tossed him out. He held the rod far out so that the hopper on the water moved into the current flowing into the hollow log. Nick lowered the rod and the hopper floated in. There was a heavy strike. Nick swung the rod against the pull. It felt as though he were hooked into the log itself, except for the live feeling.

He tried to force the fish out into the current. It came, heavily.

The line went slack and Nick thought the trout was gone. Then he saw him, very near, in the current, shaking his head, trying to get the hook out. His mouth was clamped shut. He was fighting the hook in the clear flowing current.

Looping in the line with his left hand, Nick swung the rod to make the line taut and tried to lead the trout toward the net, but he was gone, out of sight, the line pumping. Nick fought him against the current, letting him thump in the water against the spring of the rod. He shifted the rod to his left hand, worked the trout upstream, holding his weight, fighting on the rod, and then let him down into the net. He lifted him clear of the water, a heavy half circle in the net, the net dripping, unhooked him and slid him into the sack.

He spread the mouth of the sack and looked down in at the two big trout alive in the water.

Through the deepening water, Nick waded over to the hollow log. He took the sack off, over his head, the trout flopping as it came out of water, and hung it so the trout were deep in the water. Then he pulled himself up on the log and sat, the water from his trousers and boots running down into the stream. He laid his rod down, moved along to the shady end of the log and took the sandwiches out of his pocket. He dipped the sandwiches in the cold water. The current carried away the crumbs. He ate the sandwiches and dipped his hat full of water to drink, the water running out through his hat just ahead of his drinking.

It was cool in the shade, sitting on the log. He took a cigarette out and struck a match to light it. The match sunk into the gray wood, making a tiny furrow. Nick leaned over the side of the log, found a hard place and lit the match. He sat smoking and watching the river.

Ahead the river narrowed and went into a swamp. The river became smooth and deep and the swamp looked solid with cedar trees, their trunks close together, their branches solid. It would not be possible to walk through a swamp like that. The branches grew so low. You would have to keep almost level with the ground to move at all. You could not crash through the branches. That must be why the animals that live in swamps were built the way they were, Nick thought.

He wished he had brought something to read. He felt like reading. He did not feel like going on into the swamp. He looked down the river. A big cedar slanted all the way across the stream. Beyond that the river went into the swamp.

Nick did not want to go in there now. He felt a reaction against deep wading with the water deepening up under his armpits, to hook big trout in places impossible to land them. In the swamp the banks were bare, the big cedars came together overhead, the sun did not come through, except in patches; in the fast deep water, in the half light, the fishing would be tragic. In the swamp fishing was a tragic adventure. Nick did not want it. He did not want to go down the stream any further today.

He took out his knife, opened it and stuck it in the log. Then he pulled up the sack, reached into it and brought out one of the trout. Holding him near the tail, hard to hold, alive, in his hand, he whacked him against the log. The trout quivered, rigid. Nick laid him on the log in the shade and broke the neck of the other fish the same way. He laid them side by side on the log. They were fine trout.

Nick cleaned them, slitting them from the vent to the tip of the jaw. All the insides and the gills and tongue came out in one piece. They were both males; long gray-white strips of milt* smooth and clean. All the insides clean and compact, coming out all together. Nick tossed the offal* ashore for the minks to find.

milt: fish sperm
offal: waste parts, especially of a butchered animal

He washed the trout in the stream. When he held them back up in the water they looked like live fish. Their color was not gone yet. He washed his hands and dried them on the log. Then he laid the trout on the sack spread out on the log, rolled them up in it, tied the bundle and put it in the landing net. His knife was still standing, blade stuck in the log. He cleaned it on the wood and put it in his pocket.

Nick stood up on the log, holding his rod, the landing net hanging heavy, then stepped into the water and splashed ashore. He climbed the bank and cut up into the woods, toward the high ground. He was going back to camp. He looked back. The river just showed through the trees. There were plenty of days coming when he could fish the swamp.

For Thought and Discussion

1. Find examples from the first paragraph of the story that illustrate the crisp, clear style for which Hemingway is famous. Notice particularly his choice of words and the length of the sentences and paragraphs.

2. The introduction to part II reveals that Nick has returned home to recuperate both emotionally and physically from injuries he has received in battle. How is the setting of the story similar to the setting Nick has just left? In what ways is it different? Discuss the significance of the town itself, the river, the swamp, and the fish.

3. Throughout the story Nick forces himself to be aware of only the physical sensations which surround him. In what specific passages in the story are you able to experience with Nick exactly how something looks or feels? What do these passages reveal about Hemingway's skill as a writer?

4. What theme concerning a person's ability to deal with life's difficulties do you find in the story's implications? Consider the importance of Nick's return to nature, his concentration on dealing only with the present, his performance of routine tasks, and his refusal to go into the swamp. What is your personal evaluation of Hemingway's theme?

5. What physical barriers to fishing in the swamp does Nick observe? How would fishing there be a "tragic experience"? Find a sentence which indicates Nick's intention to fish there in the future. Do you think he will ever do so? Base your answer on the insight that Hemingway gives into Nick's character in this selection.

Ray Bradbury   1920-

Born in Waukegan, Illinois, Ray Bradbury actually began his writing career in high school in Los Angeles. There he founded and edited a small mimeographed quarterly, *Futura Fantasia*. Following graduation from high school in 1938, Bradbury joined a local theater group but dropped out after a year because writing had become his main interest. In fact, for four years he worked as a newsboy in order to support himself while writing. In 1941 he sold his first science fiction short story. Two years later he became a full-time writer producing not only short stories but also novels, plays, film and television scripts, and books for children. He is now known for his fantasy and science fiction, both of which have brought him several national prizes and a considerable international reputation.

Bradbury's work oftentimes expresses his fears for the world's future. His writing therefore tends to be didactic. He represents himself as a "moral fablist, a teller of cautionary tales, someone who looks at the machines we have now and says if this is true, ten years from now that will be true, and thirty years from now the other thing will be true." Bradbury finds science fiction to be a "wonderful shorthand way of telling us the truth about the thing that is right in front of us."

Bradbury's view of "truth," however, is often pessimistic. Donald A. Wolfheim states that "Ray Bradbury is essentially a doomsman where the future is concerned. He distrusts science, distrusts technology, fears the complexity of a world deriving its substance from these things." "August 2026: There Will Come Soft Rains" expresses the pessimism that is characteristic of the attitudes and literature of many Americans of the twentieth century.

August 2026: There Will Come Soft Rains

In The Martian Chronicles *(1950), which contains "August 2026: There Will Come Soft Rains," Bradbury gives a fictional account of the colonization of Mars. He chronicles the arrival of the Earthmen, the resulting destruction of the Martians, and the destruction of life on Earth. At the end of the novel (the story below is the next to the last chapter in the book), only a few isolated Earthmen are alive, all on Mars. Atomic warfare has destroyed all life on Earth.*

In the living room the voice-clock sang, *Tick-tock, seven o'clock, time to get up, time to get up, seven o'clock!* as if it were afraid that nobody would. The morning house lay empty. The clock ticked on, repeating and repeating its sounds into the emptiness. *Seven-nine, breakfast time, seven-nine!*

In the kitchen the breakfast stove gave a hissing sigh and ejected from its warm interior eight pieces of perfectly browned toast, eight eggs sunnyside up, sixteen slices of bacon, two coffees, and two cool glasses of milk.

"Today is August 4, 2026," said a second voice from the kitchen ceiling, "in the city of Allendale, California." It repeated the date three times for memory's sake. "Today is Mr. Featherstone's birthday. Today is the anniversary of Tilita's marriage. Insurance is payable, as are the water, gas, and light bills."

Somewhere in the walls, relays* clicked, memory tapes glided under electric eyes.

relays: electronic devices

Eight-one, tick tock, eight-one o'clock, off to school, off to work, run, run, eight-one! But no doors slammed, no carpets took the soft tread of rubber heels. It was raining outside. The weather box on the front door sang quietly: "Rain, rain, go away; rubbers, raincoats for today. . . ." And the rain tapped on the empty house, echoing.

Outside, the garage chimed and lifted its door to reveal the waiting car. After a long wait the door swung down again.

At eight-thirty the eggs were shriveled and the toast was like stone. An aluminum wedge scraped them into the sink, where hot water

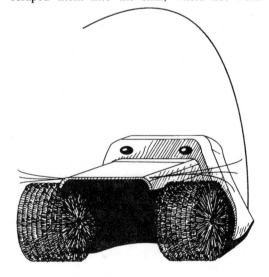

whirled them down a metal throat which digested and flushed them away to the distant sea. The dirty dishes were dropped into a hot washer and emerged twinkling dry.

Nine-fifteen, sang the clock, *time to clean.*

Out of warrens* in the walls, tiny robot mice darted. The rooms were acrawl with the small cleaning animals, all rubber and metal. They thudded against chairs, whirling their mustached runners, kneading the rug nap, sucking gently at hidden dust. Then, like mysterious invaders, they popped into their burrows. Their pink electric eyes faded. The house was clean.

warrens: enclosures for small animals

Ten o'clock. The sun came out from behind the rain. The house stood alone in a city of rubble and ashes. This was the one house left standing. At night the ruined city gave off a radioactive glow which could be seen for miles.

Ten-fifteen. The garden sprinklers whirled up in golden founts, filling the soft morning air with scatterings of brightness. The water pelted windowpanes, running down the charred west side where the house had been burned evenly free of its white paint. The entire west face of the house was black, save for five places. Here the silhouette* in paint of a man mowing a lawn. Here, as in a photograph, a woman bent to pick flowers. Still farther over, their images burned on wood in one titanic* instant, a small boy, hands flung into the air; higher up, the image of a thrown ball, and opposite him a girl, hands raised to catch a ball which never came down.

silhouette: a likeness represented by an outline
titanic: of enormous power

The five spots of paint—the man, the woman, the children, the ball—remained. The rest was a thin charcoaled layer.

The gentle sprinkler rain filled the garden with falling light.

Until this day, how well the house had kept its peace. How carefully it had inquired, ''Who

goes there? What's the password?'' and, getting no answer from lonely foxes and whining cats, it had shut up its windows and drawn shades in an oldmaidenly preoccupation with self-protection which bordered on a mechanical paranoia.*

paranoia: a mental disorder characterized by delusions of
  persecution

It quivered at each sound, the house did. If a sparrow brushed a window, the shade snapped up. The bird, startled, flew off! No, not even a bird must touch the house!

The house was an altar with ten thousand attendants, big, small, servicing, attending in choirs. But the gods had gone away, and the ritual of the religion continued senselessly, uselessly.

Twelve noon.

A dog whined, shivering, on the front porch.

The front door recognized the dog voice and opened. The dog, once huge and fleshy, but now gone to bone and covered with sores, moved in and through the house, tracking mud. Behind it whirred angry mice, angry at having to pick up mud, angry at inconvenience.

For not a leaf fragment blew under the door but what wall panels flipped open and the copper scrap rats flashed swiftly out. The offending dust, hair, or paper, seized in miniature steel jaws, was raced back to the burrows. There, down tubes which fed into the cellar, it was dropped into the sighing vent of an incinerator* which sat like evil Baal* in a dark corner.

incinerator: a furnace for burning waste
Baal: an idol to which burnt offerings were made during Old Testament times

The dog ran upstairs, hysterically yelping to each door, at last realizing, as the house realized, that only silence was here.

It sniffed the air and scratched the kitchen door. Behind the door, the stove was making pancakes which filled the house with a rich baked odor and the scent of maple syrup.

The dog frothed at the mouth, lying at the door, sniffing, its eyes turned to fire. It ran wildly in circles, biting at its tail, spun in a frenzy, and died. It lay in the parlor for an hour.

Two o'clock, sang a voice.

Delicately sensing decay at last, the regiments of mice hummed out as softly as blown gray leaves in an electrical wind.

Two-fifteen.

The dog was gone.

In the cellar, the incinerator glowed suddenly and a whirl of sparks leaped up the chimney.

Two thirty-five.

Bridge tables sprouted from patio walls. Playing cards fluttered onto pads in a shower of pips.* Martinis manifested on an oaken bench with egg-salad sandwiches. Music played.

---

pips: the marks on the cards which indicate numerical value

But the tables were silent and the cards untouched.

At four o'clock the tables folded like great butterflies back through the paneled walls.

Four-thirty.

The nursery walls glowed.

Animals took shape: yellow giraffes, blue lions, pink antelopes, lilac panthers cavorting* in crystal substance. The walls were glass. They looked out upon color and fantasy. Hidden films clocked through well-oiled sprockets,* and the walls lived. The nursery floor was woven to resemble a crisp, cereal* meadow. Over this ran aluminum roaches and iron crickets, and in the hot still air butterflies of delicate red tissue wavered among the sharp aroma of animal spoors!* There was the sound like a great matted yellow hive of bees within a dark bellows, the lazy bumble of a purring lion. And there was the patter of okapi* feet and the murmur of a fresh jungle rain, like other hoofs, falling upon the summer-starched grass. Now the walls dissolved into distances of parched weed, mile on mile, and warm endless sky. The animals drew away into thorn brakes* and water holes.

---

cavorting: bounding about
sprockets: teeth on the rim of a wheel
cereal: adj., grassy
spoors: animal tracks
okapi: an animal similar to the giraffe but having a short neck
brakes: overgrown areas

It was the children's hour.

Five o'clock. The bath filled with clear hot water.

Six, seven, eight o'clock. The dinner dishes manipulated like magic tricks, and in the study a *click.* In the metal stand opposite the hearth where a fire now blazed up warmly, a cigar popped out, half an inch of soft gray ash on it, smoking, waiting.

Nine o'clock. The beds warmed their hidden circuits, for nights were cool here.

Nine-five. A voice spoke from the study ceiling:

"Mrs. McClellan, which poem would you like this evening?"

The house was silent.

The voice said at last, "Since you express no preference, I shall select a poem at random." Quiet music rose to back the voice. "Sara Teasdale. As I recall, your favorite. . . .

"There will come soft rains and the smell
  of the ground,
And swallows circling with their shimmering sound;

And frogs in the pools singing at the night,
And wild plum trees in tremulous white;

Robins will wear their feathery fire,
Whistling their whims on a low fence-wire;

And not one will know of the war, not one
Will care at last when it is done.

Not one would mind, neither bird nor tree,
If mankind perished utterly;

And Spring herself, when she woke at dawn
Would scarcely know that we were gone."

The fire burned on the stone hearth and the cigar fell away into a mound of quiet ash on its tray. The empty chairs faced each other between the silent walls, and the music played.

At ten o'clock the house began to die.

The wind blew. A falling tree bough crashed through the kitchen window. Cleaning solvent,* bottled, shattered over the stove. The room was ablaze in an instant!

---

solvent: a liquid that dissolves other substances

"Fire!" screamed a voice. The house lights flashed, water pumps shot water from the ceilings. But the solvent spread on the linoleum, licking, eating, under the kitchen door, while the voice took it up in chorus: "Fire, fire, fire!"

The house tried to save itself. Doors sprang tightly shut, but the windows were broken by the heat and the wind blew and sucked upon the fire.

The house gave ground as the fire in ten billion angry sparks moved with flaming ease from room to room and then up the stairs. While scurrying water rats squeaked from the walls, pistoled* their water, and ran for more. And the wall sprays let down showers of mechanical rain.

---

pistoled: i.e., shot

But too late. Somewhere, sighing, a pump shrugged to a stop. The quenching rain ceased. The reserve water supply which had filled baths and washed dishes for many quiet days was gone.

The fire crackled up the stairs. It fed upon Picassos and Matisses* in the upper halls, like delicacies, baking off the oily flesh, tenderly crisping the canvases into black shavings.

Picassos and Matisses: works of modern art

Now the fire lay in beds, stood in windows, changed the colors of drapes!

And then, reinforcements.

From attic trapdoors, blind robot faces peered down with faucet mouths gushing green chemical.

The fire backed off, as even an elephant must at the sight of a dead snake. Now there were twenty snakes whipping over the floor, killing the fire with a clear cold venom of green froth.

But the fire was clever. It had sent flames outside the house, up through the attic to the pumps there. An explosion! The attic brain which directed the pumps was shattered into bronze shrapnel* on the beams.

---

shrapnel: fragments from an exploded shell

The fire rushed back into every closet and felt of the clothes hung there.

The house shuddered, oak bone on bone, its bared skeleton cringing from the heat, its wire, its nerves revealed as if a surgeon had torn the skin off to let the red veins and capillaries quiver in the scalded air. Help, help! Fire! Run, run! Heat snapped mirrors like the brittle winter ice. And the voices wailed Fire, fire, run, run, like a tragic nursery rhyme, a dozen voices, high, low, like children dying in the forest, alone, alone. And the voices fading as the wires popped their sheathings* like hot chestnuts. One, two, three, four, five voices died.

---
sheathings: coverings

In the nursery the jungle burned. Blue lions roared, purple giraffes bounded off. The panthers ran in circles, changing color, and ten million animals, running before the fire, vanished off toward a distant steaming river. . . .

Ten more voices died. In the last instant under the fire avalanche, other choruses, oblivious,* could be heard announcing the time, playing music, cutting the lawn by remote-control mower, or setting an umbrella frantically out and in the slamming and opening front door, a thousand things happening, like a clock shop when each clock strikes the hour insanely before or after the other, a scene of maniac confusion, yet unity; singing, screaming, a few last cleaning mice darting bravely out to carry the horrid ashes away! and one voice, with sublime disregard for the situation, read poetry aloud in the fiery study, until all the film spools burned, until all the wires withered and the circuits cracked.

---
oblivious: unaware

The fire burst the house and let it slam flat down, puffing out skirts of spark and smoke.

In the kitchen, an instant before the rain of fire and timber, the stove could be seen making breakfast at a psychopathic* rate, ten dozen eggs, six loaves of toast, twenty dozen bacon strips, which, eaten by fire, started the stove working again, hysterically hissing!

---
psychopathic: i.e., mad, insane

The crash. The attic smashing into kitchen and parlor. The parlor into cellar, cellar into sub-cellar. Deep freeze, armchair, film tapes, circuits, beds, and all like skeletons thrown in a cluttered mound deep under.

Smoke and silence. A great quantity of smoke.

Dawn showed faintly in the east. Among the ruins, one wall stood alone. Within the wall, a last voice said, over and over again and again, even as the sun rose to shine upon the heaped rubble and steam:

"Today is August 5, 2026, today is August 5, 2026, today is. . . . "

For Thought and Discussion

1. The plot of Bradbury's story covers the events that take place during how many hours? What mechanical device signals the beginning and ending of the story? What other mechanical devices did you find interesting? What is the climax of the story and what causes the climactic event?

2. Because this story is science fiction, the setting is a fantastic one. Bradbury succeeds, however, in making the story realistic. Give specific examples from the story to show how he achieves this realism.

3. What didactic theme does Bradbury set forth in his story? What tone, characteristic of modern writers, supports this theme?

4. What is the significance of the poem by Sara Teasdale? Why do you think that Bradbury's choice of this poem is appropriate?

5. Is there anything at all remaining at the end of the story? Do you think Bradbury's description of the world's destruction could be accurate? Why or why not? How does a Christian perspective toward future events differ from Bradbury's outlook?

Modern Drama

Thornton Wilder 1897-1975

Thornton Wilder was the son of a consular officer who was a devout Congregationalist. The writer's education was exceptionally diverse. He not only earned degrees from Yale and Princeton but also studied in the Orient and Rome. From 1921 to 1937, he was an English teacher, first on the high school and then on the college level. He served his country in the artillery during World War I and as an intelligence officer during World War II.

Wilder's first published works were novels, and for the second of them, *The Bridge of San Luis Rey,* he won a Pulitzer Prize in 1928. Set in Peru, the novel is a depiction of the lives of five quite different characters, all of whom suffer the same tragic end as the result of the collapse of a bridge.

Although a skillful craftsman of the novel, Wilder's greatest success was as a playwright. He began writing plays during his undergraduate years at Yale. *Our Town,* produced in 1938, brought him a second Pulitzer Price, and he received yet another in 1943 for *The Skin of Our Teeth.* His most popular drama with the American public, however, is *The Matchmaker,* a farce which originally appeared as *The Merchant of Yonkers* in 1938. Another American favorite and one which is most like *Our Town* in form is *The Happy Journey to Trenton and Camden.* The popularity of this play is due at least in part to the ease with which it can be produced. The script, which calls for no scenery, is set in a small New Hampshire town, where the characters carry on their everyday lives in a simple manner familiar to most Americans of recent generations.

Plays like *The Happy Journey to Trenton and Camden* and *Our Town* are presentational, or nonillusionistic, dramas. Such plays call for no curtains or sets and few stage props, and the playwright makes no attempt to conceal the theatrical devices he employs. In the case of Wilder's plays, an actor in the role of the Stage Manager directly comments to the audience on the action, reminding them that they are witnessing a play, not reality. Wilder himself played this role in early productions to the high acclaim of reviewers. For his other works, Wilder employed a variety of settings, including ancient Greece and modern Rome as well as midwestern America. In each, however, he depicts the human experience as much the same, regardless of time and place. His characters are ordinary, sympathetic human beings who, all alike, experience sadness and failure.

Wilder was a skillful craftsman and a sensitive, imaginative dramatist. Beneath the surface simplicity of his works, the discerning reader discovers a probing treatment of complex issues. Although the context and philosophy are traditional rather than explicitly Christian, Wilder's works include values such as honesty, love, and faith in the providence of God which the Christian reader can appreciate.

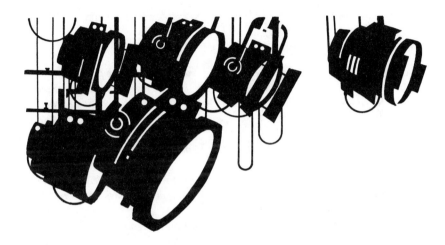

The Happy Journey to Trenton and Camden

Wilder has referred to this play, published in 1931, as his own favorite. It represents an early experiment by the playwright in the nonrealistic staging technique for which he was to become widely known. The setting is designated by the title of the play, but the drama ultimately transcends localization in its portrayal of the universal conflict of man with sorrow and death. Wilder's serious theme, however, is balanced by his humorous treatment of the daily problems of family life. This humor adds a refreshing and entertaining element to the well-structured plot, which is divided into three episodes: the family preparations for the journey, the journey itself, and the arrival at Camden.

Characters

Ma Kirby, *The Mother*
Elmer Kirby, *The Father*
Beulah Kirby, *The Older Daughter*
Caroline Kirby, *The Younger Daughter*
Arthur Kirby, *The Son*
The Stage Manager

No scenery is required for this play. Perhaps a few dusty flats may be seen leaning against the brick wall at the back of the stage.

The five members of the Kirby family and THE STAGE MANAGER *compose the cast.*

THE STAGE MANAGER *not only moves forward and withdraws the few properties that are required, but he reads from a typescript the lines of all the minor characters. He reads them clearly, but with little attempt at characterization, scarcely troubling himself to alter his voice, even when he responds in the person of a child or a woman.*

As the curtain rises THE STAGE MANAGER *is leaning lazily against the proscenium pillar at the audience's left. He is smoking.*

ARTHUR *is playing marbles in the center of the stage.*

CAROLINE *is at the remote back right talking to some girls who are invisible to us.*

MA KIRBY *is anxiously putting on her hat before an imaginary mirror.*

MA	Where's your pa? Why isn't he here? I declare we'll never get started.
ARTHUR	Ma, where's my hat? I guess I don't go if I can't find my hat.
MA	Go out into the hall and see if it isn't there. Where's Caroline gone to now, the plagued child?
ARTHUR	She's out waitin' in the street talkin' to the Jones girls.–I just looked in the hall a thousand times, ma, and it isn't there. [*He spits for good luck before a difficult shot and mutters:*] Come on, baby.
MA	Go and look again, I say. Look carefully.

[ARTHUR *rises, runs to the right, turns around swiftly, returns to his game, flinging himself on the floor with a terrible impact and starts shooting an aggie.*]

ARTHUR	No, ma, it's not there.
MA	[*Serenely.*] Well, you don't leave Newark without that hat, make up your mind to that. I don't go no journeys with a hoodlum.

ARTHUR	Aw, ma!

[*MA comes down to the footlights and talks toward the audience as through a window.*]

MA	Oh, Mrs. Schwartz!
THE STAGE MANAGER	[*Consulting his script.*] Here I am, Mrs. Kirby. Are you going yet?
MA	I guess we're going in just a minute. How's the baby?
THE STAGE MANAGER	She's all right now. We slapped her on the back and she spat it up.
MA	Isn't that fine!—Well now, if you'll be good enough to give the cat a saucer of milk in the morning and the evening, Mrs. Schwartz, I'll be ever so grateful to you.—Oh, good afternoon, Mrs. Hobmeyer!
THE STAGE MANAGER	Good afternoon, Mrs. Kirby, I hear you're going away.
MA	[*Modest.*] Oh, just for three days, Mrs. Hobmeyer, to see my married daughter, Beulah, in Camden. Elmer's got his vacation week from the laundry early this year, and he's just the best driver in the world.

[*CAROLINE comes "into the house" and stands by her mother.*]

THE STAGE MANAGER	Is the whole family going?
MA	Yes, all four of us that's here. The change ought to be good for the children. My married daughter was downright sick a while ago—
THE STAGE MANAGER	Tchk–Tchk–Tchk! Yes. I remember you tellin' us.
MA	And I just want to go down and see the child. I ain't seen her since then. I just won't rest easy in my mind without I see her. [*To CAROLINE.*] Can't you say good afternoon to Mrs. Hobmeyer?
CAROLINE	[*Blushes and lowers her eyes and says woodenly.*] Good afternoon, Mrs. Hobmeyer.
THE STAGE MANAGER	Good afternoon, dear.—Well, I'll wait and beat these rugs until after you're gone, because I don't want to choke you. I hope you have a good time and find everything all right.
MA	Thank you, Mrs. Hobmeyer, I hope I will.—Well, I guess that milk for the cat is all, Mrs. Schwartz, if you're sure you don't mind. If anything should come up, the key to the back door is hanging by the ice box.
ARTHUR AND CAROLINE	Ma! Not so loud. Everybody can hear yuh.
MA	Stop pullin' my dress, children. [*In a loud whisper.*] The key to the back door I'll leave hangin' by the ice box and I'll leave the screen door unhooked.

THE STAGE MANAGER	Now have a good trip, dear, and give my love to Loolie.
MA	I will, and thank you a thousand times. [*She returns "into the room."*] What can be keeping your pa?
ARTHUR	I can't find my hat, ma.

[*Enter ELMER holding a hat.*]

ELMER	Here's Arthur's hat. He musta left it in the car Sunday.
MA	That's a mercy. Now we can start.–Caroline Kirby, what you done to your cheeks?
CAROLINE	[*Defiant-abashed.*] Nothin'.
MA	If you've put anything on 'em, I'll slap you.
CAROLINE	No, ma, of course I haven't. [*Hanging her head.*] I just rubbed'm to make'm red. All the girls do that at High School when they're goin' places.
MA	Such silliness I never saw. Elmer, what kep' you?
ELMER	[*Always even-voiced and always looking out a little anxiously through his spectacles.*] I just went to the garage and had Charlie give a last look at it, Kate.
MA	I'm glad you did. I wouldn't like to have no breakdown miles from anywhere. Now we can start. Arthur, put those marbles away. Anybody'd think you didn't want to go on a journey, to look at yuh.

[*They go out through the "hall," take the short steps that denote going downstairs, and find themselves in the street.*]

ELMER	Here, you boys, you keep away from that car.
MA	Those Sullivan boys put their heads into everything.

[*THE STAGE MANAGER has moved forward four chairs and a low platform. This is the automobile. It is in the center of the stage and faces the audience. The platform slightly raises the two chairs in the rear. PA'S hands hold an imaginary steering wheel and continually shift gears. CAROLINE sits beside him. ARTHUR is behind him and MA behind CAROLINE.*]

CAROLINE	[*Self-consciously.*] Goodbye, Mildred. Goodbye, Helen.
THE STAGE MANAGER	Goodbye, Caroline. Goodbye, Mrs. Kirby. I hope y'have a good time.
MA	Goodbye, girls.
THE STAGE MANAGER	Goodbye, Kate. The car looks fine.
MA	[*Looking upward toward a window.*] Oh, goodbye, Emma! [*Modestly.*] We think it's the best little Chevrolet in the world.– Oh, goodbye, Mrs. Alder!

THE STAGE MANAGER	What, are you going away, Mrs. Kirby?
MA	Just for three days, Mrs. Alder, to see my married daughter in Camden.
THE STAGE MANAGER	Have a good time.

[*Now* MA, CAROLINE, *and* THE STAGE MANAGER *break out into a tremendous chorus of goodbyes. The whole street is saying goodbye.* ARTHUR *takes out his pea shooter and lets fly happily into the air. There is a lurch or two and they are off.*]

ARTHUR	[*In sudden fright.*] Pa! Pa! Don't go by the school. Mr. Biedenbach might see us!
MA	I don't care if he does see us. I guess I can take my children out of school for one day without having to hide down back streets about it. [ELMER *nods to a passerby.* MA *asks without sharpness:*] Who was that you spoke to, Elmer?
ELMER	That was the fellow who arranges our banquets down to the Lodge, Kate.
MA	Is he the one who had to buy four hundred steaks? [PA *nods.*] I declare, I'm glad I'm not him.
ELMER	The air's getting better already. Take deep breaths, children.

[*They inhale noisily.*]

ARTHUR	Gee, it's almost open fields already. "*Weber and Heilbronner Suits for Well-dressed Men.*" Ma, can I have one of them some day?
MA	If you graduate with good marks perhaps your father'll let you have one for graduation.
CAROLINE	[*Whining.*] Oh, Pa! do we have to wait while that whole funeral goes by? [PA *takes off his hat.* MA *cranes forward with absorbed curiosity.*]
MA	Take off your hat, Arthur. Look at your father.–Why, Elmer, I do believe that's a lodge-brother of yours. See the banner? I suppose this is the Elizabeth branch. [ELMER *nods.* MA *sighs: Tchk–tchk–tchk. They all lean forward and watch the funeral in silence, growing momentarily more solemnized. After a pause,* MA *continues almost dreamily:*] Well, we haven't forgotten the one that we went on, have we? We haven't forgotten our good Harold. He gave his life for his country, we mustn't forget that. [*She passes her finger from the corner of her eye across her cheek. There is another pause.*] Well, we'll all hold up the traffic for a few minutes some day.

THE CHILDREN   [*Very uncomfortable.*] Ma!

MA   [*Without self-pity.*] Well I'm "ready," children. I hope everybody in this car is "ready." [*She puts her hand on PA'S shoulder.*] And I pray to go first, Elmer. Yes. [*PA touches her hand.*]

THE CHILDREN   Ma, everybody's looking at you. Everybody's laughing at you.

MA   Oh, hold your tongues! I don't care what a lot of silly people in Elizabeth, New Jersey, think of me.–Now we can go on. That's the last.

[*There is another lurch and the car goes on.*]

CAROLINE   "*Fit-Rite Suspenders. The Working Man's Choice.*" Pa, why do they spell Rite that way?

ELMER   So that it'll make you stop and ask about it, Missy.

CAROLINE   Papa, you're teasing me.–Ma, why do they say "*Three Hundred Rooms Three Hundred Baths?*"

ARTHUR   "*Miller's Spaghetti: The Family's Favorite Dish.*" Ma, why don't you ever have spaghetti?

MA   Go along, you'd never eat it.

ARTHUR   Ma, I like it now.

CAROLINE   [*With gesture.*] Yum-yum. It looks wonderful up there. Ma, make some when we get home?

MA   [*Dryly.*] "The management is always happy to receive suggestions. We aim to please."

[*The whole family finds this exquisitely funny. The CHILDREN scream with laughter. Even ELMER smiles. MA remains modest.*]

ELMER   Well, I guess no one's complaining, Kate. Everybody knows you're a good cook.

MA   I don't know whether I'm a good cook or not, but I know I've had practice. At least I've cooked three meals a day for twenty-five years.

ARTHUR   Aw, ma, you went out to eat once in a while.

MA   Yes. That made it a leap year.

[*This joke is no less successful than its predecessor. When the laughter dies down, CAROLINE turns around in an ecstasy of well-being and kneeling on the cushions says:*]

CAROLINE   Ma, I love going out in the country like this. Let's do it often, ma.

MA   Goodness, smell that air will you! It's got the whole ocean in it.–Elmer, drive careful over that bridge. This must be New Brunswick we're coming to.

ARTHUR   [*Jealous of his mother's success.*] Ma, when is the next comfort station?

MA   [*Unruffled.*] You don't want one. You just said that to be awful.

CAROLINE   [*Shrilly.*] Yes, he did ma. He's terrible. He says that kind of thing right out in school and I want to sink through the floor, ma. He's terrible.

MA   Oh, don't get so excited about nothing, Miss Proper! I guess we're all yewman-beings in this car, at least as far as I know. And, Arthur, you try and be a gentleman.–Elmer, don't run over that collie dog. [*She follows the dog with her eyes.*] Looked kinda peakèd to me. Needs a good honest bowl of leavings. Pretty dog, too. [*Her eyes fall on a billboard.*] That's a pretty advertisement for Chesterfield cigarettes, isn't it? Looks like Beulah, a little.

ARTHUR   Ma?

MA   Yes.

ARTHUR   [*"Route" rhymes with "out."*] Can't I take a paper route with the Newark *Daily Post?*

MA   No, you cannot. No, sir. I hear they make the paper boys get up at four-thirty in the morning. No son of mine is going to get up at four-thirty every morning, not if it's to make a million dollars. Your *Saturday Evening Post* route on Thursday mornings is enough.

ARTHUR   Aw, ma.

MA   No, sir. No son of mine is going to get up at four-thirty and miss the sleep God meant him to have.

ARTHUR   [*Sullenly.*] Hhm! Ma's always talking about God. I guess she got a letter from him this morning. [*MA rises, outraged.*]

MA   Elmer, stop that automobile this minute. I don't go another step with anybody that says things like that. Arthur, you get out of this car. Elmer, you give him another dollar bill. He can go back to Newark, by himself. I don't want him.

ARTHUR   What did I say? There wasn't anything terrible about that.

ELMER   I didn't hear what he said, Kate.

MA   God has done a lot of things for me and I won't have him made fun of by anybody. Go away. Go away from me.

CAROLINE   Aw, Ma,–don't spoil the ride.

MA   No.

ELMER   We might as well go on, Kate, since we've got started. I'll talk to the boy tonight.

MA   [*Slowly conceding.*] All right, if you say so, Elmer. But I won't sit beside him. Caroline, you come, and sit by me.

ARTHUR	[*Frightened.*] Aw, ma, that wasn't so terrible.
MA	I don't want to talk about it. I hope your father washes your mouth out with soap and water.–Where'd we all be if I started talking about God like that, I'd like to know! We'd be in the speak-easies and night-clubs and places like that, that's where we'd be.–All right, Elmer, you can go on now.
CAROLINE	What did he say, ma? I didn't hear what he said.
MA	I don't want to talk about it.

[*They drive on in silence for a moment, the shocked silence after a scandal.*]

ELMER	I'm going to stop and give the car a little water, I guess.
MA	All right, Elmer. You know best.
ELMER	[*To a garage hand.*] Could I have a little water in the radiator–to make sure?
THE STAGE MANAGER	[*In this scene alone he lays aside his script and enters into a rôle seriously.*] You sure can. [*He punches the tires.*] Air, all right? Do you need any oil or gas?
ELMER	No, I think not. I just got fixed up in Newark.
MA	We're on the right road for Camden, are we?
THE STAGE MANAGER	Yes, keep straight ahead. You can't miss it. You'll be in Trenton in a few minutes. [*He carefully pours some water into the hood.*] Camden's a great town, lady, believe me.
MA	My daughter likes it fine,–my married daughter.
THE STAGE MANAGER	Ye'? It's a great burg all right. I guess I think so because I was born near there.
MA	Well, well. Your folks still live there?
THE STAGE MANAGER	No, my old man sold the farm and they built a factory on it. So the folks moved to Philadelphia.
MA	My married daughter Beulah lives there because her husband works in the telephone company.–Stop pokin' me, Caroline!–We're all going down to see her for a few days.
THE STAGE MANAGER	Ye'?
MA	She's been sick, you see, and I just felt I had to go and see her. My husband and my boy are going to stay at the Y.M.C.A. I hear they've got a dormitory on the top floor that's real clean and comfortable. Had you ever been there?
THE STAGE MANAGER	No. I'm Knights of Columbus myself.
MA	Oh.
THE STAGE MANAGER	I used to play basketball at the Y though. It looked all right to me. [*He has been standing with one foot on the rung of MA'S chair. They have taken a great fancy to one another. He reluctantly shakes himself out of it and pretends to examine the car*

	again, whistling.] Well, I guess you're all set now, lady. I hope you have a good trip; you can't miss it.
EVERYBODY	Thanks. Thanks a lot. Good luck to you *[Jolts and lurches.]*
MA	*[With a sigh.]* The world's full of nice people.–That's what I call a nice young man.
CAROLINE	*[Earnestly.]* Ma, you oughtn't to tell'm all everything about yourself.
MA	Well, Caroline, you do your way and I'll do mine.–He looked kinda thin to me. I'd like to feed him up for a few days. His mother lives in Philadelphia and I expect he eats at those dreadful Greek places.
CAROLINE	I'm hungry. Pa, there's a hot dog stand. K'n I have one?
ELMER	We'll all have one, eh, Kate? We had such an early lunch.
MA	Just as you think best, Elmer.
ELMER	Arthur, here's half a dollar.–Run over and see what they have. Not too much mustard either. *[ARTHUR descends from the car and goes off stage right. MA and CAROLINE get out and walk a bit.]*
MA	What's that flower over there?–I'll take some of those to Beulah.
CAROLINE	It's just a weed, ma.
MA	I like it.–My, look at the sky, wouldya! I'm glad I was born in New Jersey. I've always said it was the best state in the Union. Every state has something no other state has got.

[They stroll about humming. Presently ARTHUR returns with his hands full of imaginary hot dogs which he distributes. He is still very much cast down by the recent scandal. He finally approaches his mother and says falteringly:]

ARTHUR	Ma, I'm sorry. I'm sorry for what I said.

[He bursts into tears and puts his forehead against her elbow.]

| MA | There. There. We all say wicked things at times. I know you didn't mean it like it sounded. *[He weeps still more violently than before.]* Why, now, now! I forgive you, Arthur, and tonight before you go to bed you . . . *[She whispers.]* You're a good boy at heart, Arthur, and we all know it. *[CAROLINE starts to cry too. MA is suddenly joyously alive and happy.]* Sakes alive, it's too nice a day for us all to be cryin'. Come now, get in. You go up in front with your father, Caroline. Ma wants to sit with her beau. I never saw such children. Your hot dogs are all getting wet. Now chew them fine, everybody.–All right, Elmer, forward march.–Caroline, whatever are you doing? |

CAROLINE	I'm spitting out the leather, ma.
MA	Then say: Excuse me.
CAROLINE	Excuse me, please.
MA	What's this place? Arthur, did you see the post office?
ARTHUR	It said Lawrenceville.
MA	Hhn. School kinda. Nice. I wonder what that big yellow house set back was.—Now it's beginning to be Trenton.
CAROLINE	Papa, it was near here that George Washington crossed the Delaware. It was near Trenton, mama. He was first in war and first in peace, and first in the hearts of his countrymen.
MA	[*Surveying the passing world, serene and didactic.*] Well, the thing I like about him best was that he never told a lie. [*The* CHILDREN *are duly cast down. There is a pause.*] There's a sunset for you. There's nothing like a good sunset.
ARTHUR	There's an Ohio license in front of us. Ma, have you ever been to Ohio?
MA	No.

[*A dreamy silence descends upon them.* CAROLINE *sits closer to her father.* MA *puts her arm around* ARTHUR.]

ARTHUR	Ma, what a lotta people there are in the world, ma. There must be thousands and thousands in the United States. Ma, how many are there?
MA	I don't know. Ask your father.
ARTHUR	Pa, how many are there?
ELMER	There are a hundred and twenty-six million, Kate.
MA	[*Giving a pressure about* ARTHUR'S *shoulder.*] And they all like to drive out in the evening with their children beside'm. [*Another pause.*] Why doesn't somebody sing something? Arthur, you're always singing something; what's the matter with you?
ARTHUR	All right. What'll we sing? [*He sketches:*]

    "In the Blue Ridge mountains of Virginia,
    On the trail of the lonesome pine . . . "
No, I don't like that any more. Let's do:
    "I been workin' on de railroad
    All de liblong day.
    I been workin' on de railroad
    Just to pass de time away."

[CAROLINE *joins in at once. Finally even* MA *is singing. Even* PA *is singing.* MA *suddenly jumps up with a wild cry:*]

MA	Elmer, that signpost said Camden, I saw it.

ELMER   All right, Kate, if you're sure.

[*Much shifting of gears, backing, and jolting.*]

MA   Yes, there it is. Camden–five miles. Dear old Beulah.–Now, children you be good and quiet during dinner. She's just got out of bed after a big sorta operation, and we must all move around kinda quiet. First you drop me and Caroline at the door and just say hello, and then you men-folk go over to the Y.M.C.A. and come back for dinner in about an hour.

CAROLINE   [*Shutting her eyes and pressing her fists passionately against her nose.*] I see the first star. Everybody make a wish.

    Star light, star bright,
    First star I seen tonight.
    I wish I may, I wish I might
    Have the wish I wish tonight.

[*Then solemnly.*] Pins. Mama, you say "needles."

[*She interlocks little fingers with her mother.*]

MA   Needles.
CAROLINE   Shakespeare. Ma, you say "Longfellow."
MA   Longfellow.
CAROLINE   Now it's a secret and I can't tell it to anybody. Ma, you make a wish.
MA   [*With almost grim humor.*] No, I can make wishes without waiting for no star. And I can tell my wishes right out loud too. Do you want to hear them?
CAROLINE   [*Resignedly.*] No, ma, we know'm already. We've heard'm. [*She hangs her head affectedly on her left shoulder and says with unmalicious mimicry:*] You want me to be a good girl and you want Arthur to be honest-in-word-and-deed.
MA   [*Majestically.*] Yes. So mind yourself.
ELMER   Caroline, take out that letter from Beulah in my coat pocket by you and read aloud the places I marked with red pencil.
CAROLINE   [*Working.*] "*A few blocks after you pass the two big oil tanks on your left . . .*"
EVERYBODY   [*Pointing backward.*] There they are!
CAROLINE   "*. . . you come to a corner where there's an A and P store on the left and a firehouse kitty-corner to it . . .*" [*They all jubilantly identify these landmarks.*] "*. . . turn right, go two blocks, and our house is Weyerhauser St. Number 471.*"
MA   It's an even nicer street than they used to live in. And right handy to an A and P.

CAROLINE   [*Whispering.*] Ma, it's better than our street. It's richer than our street.–Ma, isn't Beulah richer than we are?

MA   [*Looking at her with a firm and glassy eye.*] Mind yourself, missy. I don't want to hear anybody talking about rich or not rich when I'm around. If people aren't nice I don't care how rich they are. I live in the best street in the world because my husband and children live there. [*She glares impressively at* CAROLINE *a moment to let this lesson sink in, then looks up, sees* BEULAH *and waves.*] There's Beulah standing on the steps lookin' for us.

[BEULAH *has appeared and is waving. They all call out:*] Hello, Beulah–Hello. [*Presently they are all getting out of the car.* BEULAH *kisses her father long and affectionately.*]

BEULAH   Hello, papa. Good old papa. You look tired, pa.–Hello, mama.–Lookit how Arthur and Caroline are growing!

MA   They're bursting all their clothes!–Yes, your pa needs a rest. Thank Heaven, his vacation has come just now. We'll feed him up and let him sleep late. Pa has a present for you, Loolie. He would go and buy it.

BEULAH   Why, pa, you're terrible to go and buy anything for me. Isn't he terrible?

MA   Well, it's a secret. You can open it at dinner.

ELMER   Where's Horace, Loolie?

BEULAH   He was kep' over a little at the office. He'll be here any minute. He's crazy to see you all.

MA   All right. You men go over to the Y and come back in about an hour.

BEULAH   [*As her father returns to the wheel, stands out in the street beside him.*] Go straight along, pa, you can't miss it. It just stares at yuh. [*She puts her arm around his neck and rubs her nose against his temple.*] Crazy old pa, goin' buyin' things! It's me that ought to be buyin' things for you, pa.

ELMER   Oh, no! There's only one Loolie in the world.

BEULAH   [*Whispering, as her eyes fill with tears.*] Are you glad I'm still alive, pa? [*She kisses him abruptly and goes back to the house steps.* THE STAGE MANAGER *removes the automobile with the help of* ELMER *and* ARTHUR *who go off waving their goodbyes.*] Well, come on upstairs, ma, and take off your things. Caroline, there's a surprise for you in the back yard.

CAROLINE   Rabbits?

BEULAH   No.

CAROLINE   Chickins?

BEULAH No. Go and see. [CAROLINE runs off stage. BEULAH and MA gradually go upstairs.] There are two new puppies. You be thinking over whether you can keep one in Newark.

MA I guess we can. It's a nice house, Beulah. You just got a *lovely* home.

BEULAH When I got back from the hospital, Horace had moved everything into it, and there wasn't anything for me to do.

MA It's lovely.

[THE STAGE MANAGER pushes out a bed from the left. Its foot is toward the right. BEULAH sits on it, testing the springs.]

BEULAH I think you'll find the bed comfortable, ma.

MA [Taking off her hat.] Oh, I could sleep on a heapa shoes, Loolie! I don't have no trouble sleepin'. [She sits down beside her.] Now let me look at my girl. Well, well, when I last saw you, you didn't know me. You kep' saying: *When's mama comin'? When's mama comin'?* But the doctor sent me away.

BEULAH [Puts her head on her mother's shoulder and weeps.] It was awful, mama. It was awful. She didn't even live a few minutes, mama. It was awful.

MA [Looking far away.] God thought best, dear. God thought best. We don't understand why. We just go on, honey, doin' our business. [Then almost abruptly–passing the back of her hand across her cheek.] Well, now, what are we giving the men to eat tonight?

BEULAH There's a chicken in the oven.

MA What time didya put it in?

BEULAH [Restraining her.] Aw, ma, don't go yet. I like to sit here with you this way. You always get the fidgets when we try and pet yuh, mama.

MA [Ruefully, laughing.] Yes, it's kinda foolish. I'm just an old Newark bag-a-bones.

[She glances at the backs of her hands.]

BEULAH [Indignantly.] Why, ma, you're good-lookin'! We always said you were good-lookin'.–And besides, you're the best ma we could ever have.

MA [Uncomfortable.] Well, I hope you like me. There's nothin' like being liked by your family.–Now I'm going downstairs to look at the chicken. You stretch out here for a minute and shut your eyes.–Have you got everything laid in for breakfast before the shops close?

BEULAH   Oh, you know! Ham and eggs.

[*They both laugh.*]

MA   I declare I never could understand what men see in ham and eggs. I think they're horrible.–What time did you put the chicken in?

BEULAH   Five o'clock.

MA   Well, now, you shut your eyes for ten minutes. [*BEULAH stretches out and shuts her eyes. MA descends the stairs absentmindedly singing:*]

"There were ninety and nine that safely lay
In the shelter of the fold,
But one was out on the hills away,
Far off from the gates of gold. . . ."

AND THE CURTAIN FALLS

For Thought and Discussion

1. Discuss the central symbol of the journey in *The Happy Journey to Trenton and Camden*. What does a journey usually symbolize in literature? What literal journey does the Kirby family make? (Where do they begin their journey and what is their destination?) Who keeps the family on the right road during the journey? What is the occasion and purpose of the journey? Is this purpose accomplished? How? Why does Wilder describe such a journey as "happy"? Is he merely being ironic? What kind of spiritual journey does the action of the play symbolize?

2. Discuss the purpose of Arthur's argument with Ma. What is its significance in the plot of the play? How does it serve Wilder's characterization of both Arthur and Ma? How does it relate to the major theme of the play? What does it foreshadow?

3. Is Wilder's depiction of family life realistic? Support your answer with specific incidents from the text. Who is the dominant member of the Kirby family? What kind of person is Elmer Kirby? How do you react to this feature of Wilder's depiction of the family?

4. Discuss Wilder's depiction of sorrow and death in the play. How does he manage to provide suspense while conveying this theme? By what earlier plot events does Wilder foreshadow the climactic revelation by Beulah? How is the penultimate conflict of the plot resolved? What dominant feature of Ma's character allows her to resolve this conflict? What has Ma done and said earlier in the plot that prepares the audience for her final display of strength? In Wilder's context, what is the meaning of Ma's final song? Why do the stage directions state that she sings it "absentmindedly"? Apart from Wilder's play, what does the song mean?

5. Discuss Wilder's depiction of traditional American values in the play. What

symbols and allusions to the founding of America and the American way of life does he employ? Which character has material aspirations? How does Ma react to these aspirations? What does this reaction reveal about Ma's attitude toward materialism? What is Ma's reaction to Caroline's references to making a wish on a star? How do Ma's values compare to those which we call ''traditional American values''? Using Psalm 1 as a guide, formulate a Christian description of ''the good life.''

Modern Essay

Jesse Stuart   1907-1984

Jesse Stuart was born in the Kentucky mountains to a very poor, uneducated family of pioneer English and Scottish stock. His education in the local one-room schoolhouse was sketchy at best. He was never able to attend classes for a full term because he had to help on the family farm. He did, however, manage to attend high school; he was the first one in his family to do so. He later graduated from Lincoln Memorial University in Harrogate, Tennessee, with a teacher's degree. A firm believer in the potential of education, Stuart became an enthusiastic teacher, principal, and county school administrator in the mountainous sections of southern Ohio and northern Kentucky. His crusades for better educational opportunities for young people in these regions involved him in over thirty lawsuits. He left teaching, he writes, ''because I thought I couldn't make enough to live. I raised sheep, lectured, wrote novels, and made money, but my heart was always in the schoolroom.''

The Thread That Runs So True

Stuart's most popular book is The Thread That Runs So True, *an autobiographical account of his teaching experiences. Like the author's other works, it gives ''a voice to the far and lost land of the Appalachians, a voice which calls us ever and delightedly into the outdoor world.'' Moreover, it illustrates a fundamental principle of his teaching: ''One thing I have learned in my contacts with youth and older people as well is that when I am enthusiastic about my teaching, they are enthusiastic. When I am depressed, they seem to be that way too. Their feelings seem to rise as high as my feelings are high or as low as mine are low. Therefore I have tried to be as enthusiastic as I can about any subject I teach.''*

Winslow Homer, *Snap the Whip,* 1872. Oil on canvas, 22 x 36". Courtesy The Butler Institute of American Art, Youngstown, Ohio.

Often I walked alone beside the Tiber in autumn. For there was a somberness that put me in a mood that was akin to poetry. I'd watch the big sycamore leaves zigzag from the interlocking branches above to the clear blue Tiber water and drift away like tiny golden ships. I'd find the farewell-to-summer* in bloom along this river. Then a great idea occurred to me. It wasn't about poetry. It was about schools.

---

farewell-to-summer: an aster that blooms in late summer

I thought if every teacher in every school in America—rural, village, city, township, church, public, or private—could inspire his pupils with all the power he had, if he could teach them as they had never been taught before to live, to work, to play, and to share, if he could put ambition into their brains and hearts, that would be a great way to make a generation of the greatest citizenry America had ever had. All of this had to begin with the little unit. Each teacher had to do his share. Each teacher was responsible for the destiny of America, because the pupils came under his influence. The teacher held the destiny of a great country in his hand as no member of any other profession could hold it. All other professions stemmed from the products of his profession.

Within this great profession, I thought, lay the solution of most of the cities', counties', states', and the nation's troubles. It was within the teacher's province to solve most of these things. He could put inspiration in the hearts and brains of his pupils to do greater things upon this earth. The schoolroom was the gateway to all the problems of humanity. It was the gateway to the correcting of evils. It was the gateway to inspire the nation's succeeding generations to greater and more beautiful living with each other; to happiness, to health, to brotherhood, to everything!

I thought these things as I walked in the somber autumn beside this river and watched the leaves fall from the tall bankside trees to the blue swirling water. And I believed deep in my heart that I was a member of the greatest profession of mankind, even if I couldn't make as much salary shaping the destinies of fourteen future citizens of America as I could if I were a blacksmith with little education at the Auckland Steel Mills. . . .

When I told my pupils about a scholastic contest with Landsburgh High School, I watched their expressions. They were willing and ready for the challenge. The competitive spirit was in them.

"We must review everything we have covered in our textbooks," I told them. "We must cover more territory in our textbooks too. Hold up your right hand if you are willing!"

Every pupil raised his hand.

Right then we started to work. In addition to regular assignments, my pupils began reviewing all of the old assignments we had covered.

Despite the challenge ahead and all the reviewing and study we planned to do, we never stopped play. The Tiber River was frozen over. The ring of skates and merry laughter broke the stillness of the winter nights. We skated on the white winding ribbon of ice beneath the high, cold winter moon. . . .

Over the weekends we'd go to the Tiber, where we'd cut holes in the ice and gig* fish. The boys and I would rabbit-hunt up and down the Tiber Valley in the old stubble fields now covered with snow and swept by wind. . . . When we hunted, the girls didn't go with us, but when we skated, fished, and rode sleighs, they went along.

There was a long gentle slope not far from the schoolhouse, we found ideal for our sleighs. It was almost a mile to the end of our sleigh run. We went over the river bank and downstream for many yards on the Tiber ice. We rode sleighs during the noon hour, before and after school.

gig: spear

On winter days when the snow had melted, leaving the dark earth a sea of sloppy mud, we designed floor games for our little one-room school. They were simple games such as throwing bolts in small boxes. And we played darts. We also played a game called "fox and goose." We made our fox-and-goose boards and we played with white, yellow, and red grains of corn. We had to make our own recreation. I never saw a distracted look on a pupil's face. I never heard one complain that the short, dark winter days were boresome because there wasn't anything to do. I think each pupil silently prayed for the days to be longer. We were a united little group. We were small, but we were powerful. We played hard, and we studied hard. We studied and played while the December days passed.

That day in early January, we dismissed school. . . . This was the big day for us. It was too bad that another blizzard had swept our rugged land and that a stinging wind was smiting the valleys and the hills. But this didn't stop the boys and me from going. Leona Maddox, my best Latin pupil, couldn't go along. Her father, Alex Maddox, wouldn't let her ride a mule seventeen miles to Landsburgh to compete in a contest on a day like this. I couldn't persuade him to let her go.

On that cold blizzardy morning, Budge Waters rode his mule to school very early and built a fire in the potbellied stove. When the rest of us arrived on our mules at approximately seven o'clock, Budge had the schoolroom warm. We tied our mules to the fence, stood before the fire, and warmed ourselves before we started on our journey. Then we unhitched our mules from the fence and climbed into the saddles. Little clouds of frozen snow in powdery puffs arose from the mules' hoofs as six pupils and their teacher rode down the road.

Though the force of wind in the Tiber Valley was powerful, it was at our backs. The wind was strong enough to give our mules more momentum. We made good time until we left the valley and climbed the big hill. Here, we faced the wind. It was a whipping wind–stinging, biting wind on this mountain–that made the water run from our eyes and our mules' eyes, but for us there was no turning back. We were going to Landsburgh High School. That was that. We were determined to meet this big school–big to us, for they out-numbered us twenty-six to one. Soon we were down in Hinton Valley. Then we rode to the top of Raccoon Hill. . . .

"Mr. Stuart, I have been thinking," Budge Waters said, as we rode along together, "if you can sleep in a fodder shock* when it's twelve degrees below zero, we can take this contest from Landsburgh High School! I've not forgotten how you walked seventeen miles to carry us books. All of your pupils remember. We'll never let you down!"

---

fodder shock: a tepee-shaped stack of cornstalks

Budge Waters thought of this because we were riding down the mountain where I had slept that night. Then we rode down into the Raccoon Valley, and Billie Leonard, only thirteen years old, complained of numbness in his hands, feet, and lips. He said he felt as if he was going to sleep. . . . We stopped at a home, tied our mules to the fence, and went in and asked to warm. Bert Patton, a stranger to us, piled more wood on the open fire until we were as warm as when we had left the schoolhouse. We told him who we were and where we were going.

"On a day like this!" he said, shaking his head sadly.

We climbed into the saddles again. We were over halfway now. The second hitch would put us at Landsburgh High School. We had valley all

the way to Landsburgh, with walls of rugged hills on each side for windbreaks.

At eleven o'clock we rode across the Landsburgh High School yard, and hitched our mules to the fence around the athletic field. There were faces against the window-panes watching us. Then we walked inside the high school, where Principal Ernest Charters met and welcomed us. He told us that he was surprised we had come on a day like this and that we had been able to arrive so soon.

In the principal's office my pupils and I huddled around the gas stove while we heard much laughter in the high-school corridors. The Landsburgh High School pupils thought we were a strange-looking lot. Many came inside their principal's office to take a look at us. We were regarded with curiosity, strangeness, and wonder. Never before had these pupils seen seven mules hitched to their schoolyard fence. Never before had they competed scholastically with so few in number–competitors who had reached them by muleback. The Landsburgh High School principal didn't feel about the contest the way we felt. To him, this was just a "setup" to test his pupils for the district contest which would soon be held. He told me this when he went after the sealed envelopes that held the questions. We warmed before the gas stove while he made arrangements for the contest.

"These questions were made out by the state department of education," he said when he returned. "I don't know how hard they are."

My pupils stood silently by the stove and looked at each other. We were asked to go to one of the largest classrooms. A Landsburgh High School teacher had charge of giving the test. When the Landsburgh High School pupils came through the door to compete against my pupils, we knew why Principal Charters had selected this large classroom. My pupils looked at each other, then at their competitors.

I entered redheaded Jesse Jarvis to compete with ten of their plane-geometry pupils. I entered

Billie Leonard against twenty-one of their selected algebra pupils.

"Budge, you'll have to represent us in grammar, English literature, and history," I said. "And I believe I'll put you in civil government. Is that all right?"

"Yes," he agreed. Budge had never had a course in civil government. All he knew about it was what he had read in connection with history.

"Robert Batson, you enter in history and grammar.

"Robin Baylor, you enter in algebra.

"Snookie Baylor, you enter in algebra and plane geometry.

"Sorry, Mr. Charters," I said, "we don't have anyone to enter in Latin. My best Latin pupil, Leona Maddox, couldn't make this trip."

After the contest had begun, I left the room. Miss Bertha Madden was in charge. I took our mules to Walter Scott's barn on the east end of Landsburgh, where I fed and watered them.

With the exception of an interval when the contestants ate a quick lunch, the contest lasted until 2:30 P. M. I had one pupil, Budge Waters, in four contests. I had planned to enter him in two. Just as soon as Budge had finished with civil government, we started grading the papers. All the pupils were requested to leave the room.

We graded the papers with keys. Mr. Charters, Miss Madden, and two other teachers and I did the grading. Mr. Charters read the answers on the keys, and we checked the answers. Once or twice we stopped long enough to discuss what stiff questions these were. We wondered how far we would have gotten if we–all of us, college graduates–had taken the same test. One of the teachers asked me, while we graded these papers, if Budge Waters had ever seen these questions.

When we were through grading the papers, Mr. Charters called the contestants into the classroom.

"I want to read you the scores of this contest," he said. His voice was nervous.

"Budge Waters, winner in English literature.

"Budge Waters, winner in grammar.

"Budge Waters, winner in history with almost a perfect score.

"Budge Waters, winner in civil government.

"Why didn't you bring just this one boy?" Principal Charters asked me.

"Because I've got other good pupils," I quickly retorted.

"Billie Leonard, winner in algebra, with plenty of points to spare.

"Jesse Jarvis, second in plane geometry.

"Snookie Baylor and Robin Baylor tied for second place in algebra.

"Congratulations," said Principal Charters, "to your pupils and to you, on your success. It looks as though Winston High will represent this county in the district scholastic contest. I've never heard of such a remarkable thing."

When we left the Landsburgh High School we heard defeated pupils crying because "a little mud-hole in the road like Winston beat us."

In a few minutes our mule cavalcade passed the Landsburgh High School. Faces were against the windowpanes and many pupils waved jubilantly to us as we rode by, our coattails riding the wind behind our saddles, and the ends of our scarfs bright banners on the wind. We rode victoriously down the main street of Landsburgh on our way home.

For Thought and Discussion

1. Why does Stuart consider teaching the most important and honorable of the professions? Do you think that teaching gets the public recognition it deserves?

2. What qualities of a good teacher appear in Stuart's account of his experiences at Winston High? Was his involvement with the students limited to the classroom?

3. Which student seems most sensitive to the sacrifices of his teacher? Which student distinguishes himself and his school most brilliantly at the contest?

4. Compare the responses of the Landsburgh

students to the arrival and to the departure of the Winston students. What similar contrasts give irony to the outcome?

5. Why, other than the fact that it is autobiographical, may this narrative be considered an essay rather than a short story? What point is it illustrating?

6. Narratives gain realism and generate reader interest by specific detail. Point out places where a lesser writer might simply have condensed the action through generalizations.

James Saxon Childers
1899-1965

Born in Birmingham, Alabama, James Saxon Childers became a critic, author, publisher, and teacher. His student days were spent at Oberlin College (Ohio) and later as a Rhodes Scholar at Oxford University. Although he worked for a time as the literary editor of the *Birmingham News,* he devoted most of his time to teaching English at Birmingham Southern College.

A Boy Who Was Traded for a Horse

Childer's biographical sketch of the famous scientist George Washington Carver (c. 1864-1943) illustrates the author's lasting interest in the South and its people.

The stooped old Negro shuffled along through the dust of an Alabama road at a curiously rapid rate. He was carrying an armful of sticks and wild flowers.

The sticks I could understand–he would use them for kindling–but I had never before seen an old black man ambling* along a road at nine o'clock in the morning with swamp roses, wild geranium, and creeping buttercups mingled with a lot of dry sticks.

ambling: walking slowly

When I got a little closer to him I saw that he was wearing a saggy coat which originally might have been a green alpaca,* but which the sun had faded until I couldn't be sure about the color; there were so many patches that I couldn't even be certain about the material.

alpaca: a fabric made from the wool of an animal related to the llama

The old man was walking toward a large brick building, one of the buildings of Tuskegee Institute, the famous school for Negroes at Tuskegee, Alabama. His thin body bent by the years, his hair white beneath a ragged cap, he seemed pathetically lost on the campus of a great modern educational institution.

At the entrance of the building toward which we were both walking, the old Negro turned in. "He's probably the janitor," I told myself, "and I'm sincerely glad that they've given him a job of some kind."

I stepped into the hallway. I saw a trim little secretary hurry toward the bent old Negro. I heard her say to him, "That delegation from Washington is waiting for you, Dr. Carver."

Dr. George Washington Carver, the very man I had come to see! Fantastic and unbelievable as it seemed, this old man with his armful of sticks and wild flowers was none other than the distinguished Negro scientist of Tuskegee Institute—a discoverer renowned far and wide for his chemical wizardry in creating useful new products from such stuff as peanut shells and fallen leaves, which most of us waste and throw away.

That saggy alpaca coat covered a Bachelor of Science, Master of Science, Honorary Doctor of Science; winner of the Spingarn Medal for Negro achievement; member of the Royal Society for the Encouragement of Arts, Manufactures, and Commerce of Great Britain.

Yet as I looked at him, studied his kindly face, and recalled what I had heard of the story of his life, I saw that the figure of the man himself was not half so fantastic or unbelievable as is the record of his achievement.

Dr. George Washington Carver started with nothing. He never had anything. Yet out of nothing he had created inestimable* wealth for fellow human beings, to whom he has devoted his life.

inestimable: not capable of being calculated

Born a slave child, he began life without even so much as a name. He never knew his father. He never knew his mother. To this day* he doesn't know just when he was born, though he figures his age at somewhere close to seventy. Without a red cent he worked out his own early schooling, then his higher college education, then the postgraduate work for his Master of Science degree. All his life he has been joyously at work with common, everyday things, making something out of nothing or next to nothing. During the thirty-six years in which he has been director of agricultural research at Tuskegee Institute, that has been his work. And out of it have come scientific marvels:

To this day: 1934

From wood shavings he has made synthetic marble.

From peanut shells he has made insulating walls for houses.

From the muck of swamps and the leaves of the forest floor he has made valuable fertilizers.

From cow dung he has made paint.

From the common, ordinary peanut he has made 285 useful products, including milk, butter, cheese, candies, instant coffee, pickles, sauces, oils, shaving lotion, wood stains, dyes, lard, linoleum, flour, breakfast foods, soap, stock foods, face powder, tan remover, shampoo, printer's ink, and even axle grease!

From the lowly sweet potato he has made 118 products, among them flour, meal, starch, library paste, vinegar, shoe blacking, ginger, ink, rubber compound, chocolate compound, dyes, molasses, wood filler, caramels.

From clays of the earth he has made non-fading paints and pigments.

From worn-out, sandy soil he has produced paying crops.

Something from nothing. And this is only a portion of his work. Experts say that he has probably done more than any other living man to rehabilitate* agriculture in the South.

rehabilitate: restore

And more still. Dr. Carver is also an artist, especially skilled in painting flowers. His paintings have been exhibited at world fairs, and at least one is going to the Luxembourg Gallery in Paris after his death. He makes all his own paints, using Alabama clays. The paper he paints on he makes from peanut shells, and the frames for his

pictures he makes out of cornhusks. His work in embroidery and crochet has won prizes in various exhibits. He has woven gorgeous rugs with fibers he had made from cotton stalks. He is a skilled musician, too—once he toured the Middle West as a concert pianist. And last, but not least, he is an expert cook. His recipes are used today in some of the leading hotels in the country.

All this does sound a bit incredible, doesn't it? I confess that when I set out for Tuskegee to see and talk with Dr. Carver I was more than skeptical of many of the stories I had heard about him. And so, after he had entertained the visiting delegations from Washington, I returned to see him, in his office in the big brick building, with many doubts lingering in my mind.

He was sitting behind a desk cluttered inches high with letters and papers. On top of the papers were the sticks and wild flowers that I had seen him carrying that morning. As I went in, he was looking through a microscope at the stem of a wild rose.

"I beg your pardon," I said.

The old man raised his head and looked at me; then, taking hold of the edge of the desk to steady himself, he pushed himself up from his squeaky swivel chair. He wore a long canvas apron that was splotched and stained. His gold-rimmed spectacles rested far down on his nose. Standing there so tall despite his noticeable stoop, he peered over the tops of his spectacles and smiled at me.

"Good morning," he said, and the quiet tone of his voice blended with the gentle sincerity of his smile.

In slight confusion, then, I explained why I had called on him.

"Do you mind if I stay here awhile?" I asked. "I'd like to very much—that is, if I won't trouble you."

"It will be a pleasure, sir, a very great pleasure to me."

I was touched by his gentleness, and by an unmistakable spiritual quality in the glow of his face. Frankly, I was confused. To open the conversation, I remarked on the numerous Maxfield Parrish paintings that hang on his office walls. "Somehow they seem a little out of place in the office of a scientist," I said lamely.

"But can't a scientist be a lover of the beautiful?" he asked. "There is not one of the moderns who uses blue half so well as Maxfield Parrish uses it.''

And then he was off. For forty-five minutes he shuffled about his office, showing me how Maxfield Parrish uses blue, and telling how the ancients used the color. Quietly, even humbly, he told how the Egyptians loved it, how they had adorned their homes and tombs with it.

Then he led me from his office across the hall into his laboratory, a room about thirty by twenty feet. It was filled with racks and shelves and tables, bottles and tubes and retorts.* He picked up a jar and carried it to the window. "See"—and he held it to the sun.

---

retorts: vessels in which substances are distilled or decomposed by heat

---

And I saw the richest, the purest blue that I have ever seen.

Dr. Carver was talking quietly as he tilted the jar one way and the other, giving the sun its full chance to mate with the glorious color. "I believe," he went on, "that it's a rediscovery of the old Egyptian blue. A number of chemists have come to see it, and they agree with me. At present I'm working on the Egyptian purple; I believe that soon we shall have that too.

"I get my dyes," the old man continued, "from Alabama clays. You remember what the Bible says"—Dr. Carver has built his life on what the Bible says—"you remember that the Bible says, 'Look to the hills from whence cometh your help.' I did it; I looked to these Alabama hills, and I made these dyes from the clays that I found there. All these dyes and paints"—he waved toward thirty-six boards, each of which was colored differently—"all of them were made from Alabama clay—all," he added, "except this one; it was made from rotten sweet potatoes; and this one, which was made from cow dung; and this one, a much finer paint, was made from horse dung."

After I had been an hour in Dr. Carver's laboratory, after I had seen rope made from okra fiber; baskets from wistaria; and dyes from the dandelion, black oak, wood ashes, sweet gum, swamp maple, sweet potato, pomegranate, peanut, Osage orange, muscadine grape, onion, velvet bean, and tomato vine—after I had seen those discoveries, among a few hundred others, I was willing to believe almost anything possible to this kindly man to whom apparently bricks without straw* would be a simple problem.

---

bricks . . . straw: cf. Exodus 5:6-19

"When you do the common things of life in an uncommon way," Dr. Carver once said to his students, "you will command the attention of the world." In that sentence lies the secret of his own achievement.

He was born in a rude slave cabin on the farm of Moses Carver near Diamond Grove, Missouri. Moses Carver owned his mother, and a neighbor owned his father. When he was a baby six months old, night riders swooped down on his master's plantation and carried away a number of slaves, among them the baby and his mother.

In their flight, the raiders took no care of the child; he developed whooping cough and was dying when emissaries* sent out by Moses Carver arrived from Missouri to buy back the stolen slaves.

---

emissaries: messengers

But the mother had already been disposed of; no one ever learned what became of her. Indeed, there is only one thing of hers that is left: in Dr. Carver's room in one of the dormitories at Tuskegee is a battered old spinning wheel on which his mother spun flax when she was a slave. A friend of Dr. Carver's said to me, "I've seen him touch that wheel; he touches it like a priest reverently touching an altar. I sometimes feel that if I could be in his room when he retires, I should hear the old man say 'Good night' to that wheel."

The emissaries sent to ransom the stolen slaves finally struck a bargain with the night riders. The baby was evaluated and traded back to his owner; he was traded for a broken-down race horse worth about $300!

For Thought and Discussion

1. What does the essay gain by delaying the identification of the old man shuffling along the dusty Alabama road?
2. What is gained by the author's initial skepticism concerning the accomplishments of Carver?
3. What nonscientific interests did Carver pursue and excel in? In what object held up to view in the lab do Carver's scientific, practical, and aesthetic interests converge?
4. What admirable human qualities of Carver are highlighted in this incident? Where are we made to feel we have been introduced not only to a great scientist but also to a great man?
5. What is the irony of the final sentence? How does it connect with the irony of the opening scene?
6. Is there a lesson intended for the reader in the example of this one who did so much with so little?

Bruce Catton   1899-1978

A newspaperman, government official, and historian originally from Michigan, Bruce Catton enjoyed a distinguished career. He worked as a journalist in Cleveland, Boston, and Washington for twenty years or more before entering government service in 1942. During his years in Washington, Catton contributed book reviews and a regular column to *The Nation*. From his boyhood days he had had a keen interest in the Civil War. In 1952 he finally turned his hobby into a vocation and began devoting his time to writing a history of the Civil War. *A Stillness at Appomattox* (1953), the third book in his Civil War series, won the Pulitzer Prize for history in 1954. In that same year he became one of the editors of the *American Heritage* magazine. Five years later he became its senior editor, a position he held until his death in 1978.

The Great American Game

"The Great American Game," which first appeared in 1959 in the American Heritage, *shows Catton's ability to see the ways in which baseball reflects American society. This essay is thus both a history of the sport and a study of American society.*

By the carefully repeated definition of men who stand to make money out of its acceptance, baseball is the Great American Game. The expression was invented long ago and it has been rammed home by talented press agents ever since, even in times when most Americans seemed to be interested very largely in something else. But what has given the phrase its sticking power is not the fact that a big industry has kept plugging it, or the allied fact that unceasing repetition has dinned it into an unreflecting public's ears for generations, but simply the fact that in its underlying essence it is perfectly true.

Baseball is the American game, great or otherwise, because it reflects so perfectly certain aspects of the American character that no other sport portrays.

It has few of the elements of pure sportsmanship, as that dubious word is commonly accepted, and it is not notably a game for gentlemen. But it does embody certain native-born fundamentals, including above all others the notion that the big thing about any contest is to win it. It also is built upon the idea that anything you can get away with is permissible, and it is the only sport (at least the only one since the Roman populace sat in the thumbsdown section* at the gladiatorial games) that puts an invitation to homicide in one of its enduring sayings: ''Kill the umpire!'' (The thing has actually been attempted, too, more than once.) It is pre-eminently the sport for the professional rather than the amateur, the sport in which the well-intentioned duffer* neither is given nor especially wants a part.

thumbsdown section: By turning their thumbs down, spectators in ancient Rome indicated their wish that the victor kill the loser.
duffer: an incompetent, unskilled person

Almost everyone in the country has played it at one time or another, but almost nobody except the professional dreams of going on playing it once full manhood has come. It is a spectator sport in which each spectator has had just enough personal experience to count himself an expert,

and it is the only pastime on earth that leans heavily on the accumulation of page upon page of inherently dry statistics. It is also an unchanging pageant and a ritualized drama, as completely formalized as the Spanish bullfight, and although it is wholly urbanized it still speaks of the small town and the simple, rural era that lived before the automobile came in to blight the landscape. One reason for this is that in a land of unending change, baseball changes very little. There has been no important modification of its rules for well over half a century. The ball in use now will go farther when properly hit, and the gloves worn on defense are designed to do automatically what personal skill once had to do, but aside from these things the game is as it was in the early 1900's. Even the advent of night baseball, which seemed like pure sacrilege when it was introduced two decades ago, has made little difference; the pictorial aspect of the game—which is one of its most important features—has perhaps even gained thereby. The neat green field looks greener and cleaner under the lights, the moving players are silhouetted more sharply, and the enduring visual fascination of the game—the immobile pattern of nine men, grouped according to ancient formula and then, suddenly, to the sound of a wooden bat whacking a round ball, breaking into swift ritualized movement, movement so standardized that even the tyro* in the bleachers can tell when someone goes off in the wrong direction—this is as it was in the old days. A gaffer* from the era of William McKinley, abruptly brought back to the second half of the twentieth century, would find very little in modern life that would not seem new, strange, and rather bewildering, but put in a good grandstand seat back of first base he would see nothing that was not completely familiar.

tyro: beginner
gaffer: old man

But that is only the surface part of it. Baseball, highly organized, professionalized within an inch of its life, and conducted by men who like dollars better than they like sport, still speaks for the old days when nine young men in an open park somehow expressed the hot competitive instincts of everybody and spoke of home-town pride.

And perhaps the central part of all of this is the fact that in its essence baseball is still faintly disreputable and rowdy. Its players chew tobbaco, or at least look as if they were chewing it; many of them do not shave every day; and they argue bitterly with each other, with their opponents, and with the umpires just as they did when John McGraw and Ed Delehanty were popular idols. They have borrowed nothing from the ''sportsmanship'' of more sedate countries; they believe that when you get into a fight you had better win, and the method by which you win does not matter very much. Anything goes; victory is what counts.

This John McGraw, for example. When he was playing third base and there was a runner there, and someone hit a fly to the outfield, McGraw would unobtrusively hook his fingers in the player's belt so that the take-off for the plate, once the ball was caught, would be delayed by half a second or so. He got away with it, too, and no one thought the worse of him, until one day a baserunner unbuckled his belt in this situation and, legging it for home, left the belt dangling in McGraw's hand, tangible evidence of crime. Note, also, that baseball knows about the bean ball—the ball thrown at the batter's head to drive him away

from the plate and hamper his hitting process. A big leaguer was once killed by such a pitch; it has been condemned by everyone ever since then, and it is still a regular feature of the game.

In its essentials, then, baseball is plebeian, down-to-earth, and robustious. Even half a century ago it was dwindling to the rank of secondary sport in the colleges. Professors who have adjusted themselves to the presence on the campus of *soi-disant** students who are paid to attend college so that they may play football have a way of considering the football player one cut above the baseball player. The former may be a hulking behemoth of pure muscle, wholly incapable of differentiating between Virgil's *Eclogues** and Boyle's law,* but he does not seem quite as uncouth as the baseball player—who, in his own turn, may also be on the campus as a paid hand, the difference being that his is being paid by some major-league team that wants to see his athletic skills developed, while the football player gets his from ardent alumni who want to see the college team beat State on Homecoming Day next fall. There has never been any social cachet* attached to skill on the diamond.

soi-disant: so-called
Eclogues: Latin poetry
Boyle's law: in physics, a law of gases
cachet: distinction

The reason, obviously, is that baseball came up from the sand lots—the small town, the city slum, and the like. It had a rowdy air because rowdies played it. One of the stock tableaux* in American sports history is the aggrieved* baseball player jawing with the umpire. In all our games, this tableau is unique; it belongs to baseball, from the earliest days it has been an integral part of the game, and even in the carefully policed major leagues today it remains unchanged. Baseball never developed any of the social niceties.

tableaux: scenes or pictures consisting of a striking or artistic grouping
aggrieved: treated unjustly

In the old days, when (as we suppose, anyway) most of us lived in small towns, or at least in fairly small cities, the local baseball team represented civic pride, to say nothing of representing at the same time the dreams of a great many young men who wished to be much more athletic than they actually were. In very small towns, its games were usually held in Farmer Jones's pasture, where the difficulty, in a hot moment of split-second play, of distinguishing between third base and some natural cow-pasture obstacle sometimes led to odd happenings; and in slightly larger places the county fairground or a recreational park at the end of the streetcar line provided the arena. In any case, muscular young men, wearing the singularly unbecoming uniforms that were standardized seventy-five years ago, presently took their positions on the grass, and the game was on.

It was, and still is, hotly competitive, and within reasonable limits anything goes. If the umpire (there was just one, in the old days) could be suborned* to give all vital judgments in favor of the home side, all well and good; no one ever blushed to accept a victory that derived from an umpire's bias. If he could be intimidated, so that close decisions would go as the spectators wanted them to go, that also was good. This often happened; an umpire who decided a crucial play against the home team was quite likely to be mobbed, and few pictures from the old-time sports album are more authentic or more enduring than the vision of an umpire frantically legging it for the train, pursued by irate citizens who wished to do him great bodily harm. It took physical courage to render impartial judgments in old-time small-town baseball, and not all umpires were quite up to it.

suborned: induced to commit a wrong act

If the umpire could be deceived while the game was on, that also was good. A man running from first to third on a base hit would cut twenty feet short of second base if he thought he could get away with it, and no one dreamed of censuring* him for it. If an opposing player could be intimidated, so that he shirked his task, that was good, too. Not for nothing was the greatest baseball player who ever lived, Ty Cobb, famous for sitting on the bench just before the game sharpening his spikes with a file. An infielder, witnessing this, and knowing that Cobb was practically certain to ram those spikes into his calf or thigh in a close play, was apt to flinch just a little at the moment of contact, and out of that split second of withdrawal Cobb would gain the hair's edge of advantage that he needed. It was considered fair, too, to denounce an opponent verbally, with any sort of profane, personal objurgation* that came to mind, on the off-chance that he might become unsettled and do less than his best. (This still goes on, like practically all of the other traditional things in baseball, and the "bench jockey"–the man who will say anything at all if he thinks it will upset an enemy's poise–can be a prized member of a big-league team even now.)

censuring: blaming
objurgation: scolding or rebuke

Baseball is conservative. What was good enough in Cap Anson's day is good enough now, and a populace that could stand unmoved while the federal Constitution was amended would protest with vehemence at any tampering with the formalities of baseball. It looks as it used to look; the batter still grabs a handful of dust between swings, the catcher still slams the ball over to third base after a strike-out, and the umpire still jerks thumb over right shoulder to indicate a put-out. (Dismayingly enough, some umpires now grossly exaggerate this gesture, using an elaborate full-swing, but possibly the point is a minor one.)

An inning begins; the pitcher takes his warm-up tosses, now as in the days half a century ago, and after three, four, or five of these he steps aside and the catcher whips the ball down to second base. The second baseman tosses it to the shortstop, two yards away, and the shortstop throws it to the third baseman, who is standing halfway between his own base and the pitcher's box; the third baseman, in turn, tosses it over to the pitcher, and the inning can get started. To vary from this formula is unthinkable; from the little leaguers up to Yankee Stadium, it is as one with the laws of the Medes and the Persians.*

laws . . . Persians: i.e., unchanging: See Esther 8:8

Then action: players shifting about, pounding their gloves, uttering cries of encouragement (which, like all the rest, are verbatim out of the script of 1900); and the batter approaches the plate, swinging two bats (another ironclad requirement), tossing one aside, planting his feet in the batter's box, and then swinging his single bat in determined menace. The fielders slowly freeze into fixed positions; for a moment no one anywhere moves, except that the pitcher goes into his stretch, takes a last look around, and then delivers–and then the frozen pattern breaks, the ball streaks off, men move deftly from here to there, and the quick moments of action are on.

In all of this there is unending fascination, coupled with the knowledge that wholly fantastic athletic feats may at any moment be displayed by any one of the players. Even an easy fly ball to the outfield or a simple grounder to short can call forth a nonchalant, effortless expertness that a man from another land would find quite incredible. (I once took an Englishman to see his first baseball game, and he was dumbfounded by the simplest plays, marveling at what all the rest of us took for automatic outs.) In no contest can the split second be so important. A routine double play can make both outs with no more than half a second to spare, and if the half second is lost anywhere, the player who lost it will be derided for a clumsy oaf.

Primarily a team game, baseball is also the game for the individualist. The team play is essential, and when you watch closely you can see it, but the focus is usually on one man. A base runner streaks for second with the pitch, falls

away while in full stride, and slides in in a cloud of dust, baseman stabbing at him with gloved hand, umpire bending to peer through the murk and call the play; an outfielder runs deep and far, arching ball coming down–apparently–just out of his reach, trajectories of fielder and baseball coming miraculously together at the last, gloved hand going out incredibly to pick the ball out of the air; a pitcher who has been getting his lumps looks about at filled bases, glowers at the batter, and then sends one in that is struck at and missed . . . always, some individual is trying for an astounding feat of athletic prowess and, now and then, actually accomplishing it.

Hence baseball celebrates the vicarious* triumph. The spectator can identify himself completely with the player, and the epochal* feat becomes, somehow, an achievement of his own. Babe Ruth, mocking the Chicago Cubs, pointing to the distant bleachers and then calmly hitting the ball into those bleachers, took a host of Walter Mittys with him when he jogged around the bases.

(There is some dispute about this, to be sure; he was jawing with the Cubs, but purists say he did not actually call his shot. This makes no difference whatever.) It was the same when old Grover Cleveland Alexander, the all-but-washed-up veteran of many baseball wars, came into the seventh inning of a decisive World Series game, found the bases filled with Yankees, and struck out Tony Lazzeri, going on to win game and Series; and this was after a wearing night on the tiles,* Alexander having supposed that his work was over until next spring. Many an aging fan shared in Old Alex's triumph.

vicarious: substituted
ephocal: history-making
on the tiles: i.e., on the town, partying

These things are part of baseball's legend, for the game never forgets its gallery of immortals. That it actually has a tangible Hall of Fame, with bronze plaques to commemorate the greatest, is only part of the story; the noble deeds of the super-players are handed down in bar-side stories, year after year, losing nothing in the telling. Some of the heroes have been supermen, in a way, at that. There was, for instance, Shoeless Joe Jackson, barred from baseball in mid-career because he let himself be bribed to help lose a World Series. (He did not do very well at losing; even under a bribe, he batted .375 in that Series—a natural hitter who just couldn't make himself miss even when paid to do so.) A sand-lot pitcher tells of a day, a whole generation later, when, pitching for a textile-mill team in the Carolinas, he found on the opposing team none other than Jackson—a pathetic, fat, doddering* wreck in his late fifties, with a monstrous belly like some disreputable* Santa Claus, still picking up a few odd bucks playing semi-pro ball under an assumed name. The young pitcher figured Jackson would be easy; a low inside curve, coming in close to the overhang of that prodigious* paunch, was obviously the thing to throw. He threw, Jackson swung, and swung as he used to thirty years earlier, and the ball went far

out of the park, one of the most authoritative home runs the young pitcher ever witnessed. Old Jackson lumbered heavily around the bases, and halfway between third and home he turned to accost* the young pitcher. "Son," he said, "I always could hit them low inside curves."

doddering: moving about feebly
disreputable: not respectable
prodigious: huge
accost: approach and speak first

There were others cast in similar molds. . . . Rube Waddell, the wholly legendary character who, when cold sober, which was not often, may have been the greatest pitcher of them all: the man who now and then, on a whim, would gesture the entire outfield off the premises and then retire the side without visible means of support; Walter Johnson, who once pitched fifty-odd consecutive scoreless innings, and who to the end of his days had nothing much in his repertoire except an unhittable fast ball; Tris Speaker, who played such a short center field that he often threw a batter out at first on what ought to have been a legitimate down-the-middle base hit; and lean Satchel Paige, who in his great days in the Negro leagues had a way of pointing to the shortstop and then throwing something which the batter must hit to short, and who then would go on around the infield in the same way, compelling the opposition to hit precisely where he wanted it to hit. The legends are, in some ways, the most enduring part of the game. Baseball has even more of them than the Civil War, and its fans prize them highly.

Under the surface, baseball is always played to a subdued but inescapable tension, because at any second one of these utterly fabulous events may take place. The game may be distressingly one-sided, and the home team may come up in the ninth inning five runs behind, and in a clock game like football or basketball the margin would be physically unbeatable; but in baseball anything can happen, and the tiniest fluke* can change everything. (Remember the World Series game the Yankees won when a Brooklyn catcher dropped a third strike with two men out in the ninth?) A com-mon-place game can turn into a hair-raiser at any moment, and things do not actually need to happen to create the suspense. A free-hitting, high-scoring game may be most eventful, but few strains are greater than the strain of watching a pitcher pro-tect a 1-0 lead in the late innings of a routine game. Nothing, perhaps, actually happens—but every time the ball is thrown the game may turn upside down, and nobody ever forgets it.

fluke: an accidental stroke of good fortune

All of this is built in, for the spectator. Built in, as well, is the close attention to records and statis-tics. Batting averages and pitchers' records are all-important; to know that a Rogers Hornsby, for in-stance, could bat more than .400 in three different years—that is, could average getting two hits for every five times he came to the plate, 154 games a year, for three years—is important. It has been sug-gested, now and then, that big league playing schedules be reduced from 154 games to some smaller figure, and the suggestion has always been howled down: it would upset all the averages. Un-thinkable; how do you compare today's pitcher with Walter Johnson or Lefty Grove if today's pitcher plays in fewer games every year?

The circumstances under which baseball is played nowadays have changed greatly, to be sure. Less than half a century ago, every town that amounted to anything at all was represented in some league of professional players, and these leagues—the minor leagues, of hallowed memo-ry—have been dissolving and vanishing, as more and more spectators get their games by television or by radio and ignore the local ball park. The Little Leagues have come up, and semi-subsi-dized sand-lot leagues, and even college baseball is here and there enjoying a new lease on life—after all, the new players in the big leagues have to come from somewhere, and, besides, young Americans still like to play baseball; but

the old pattern is gone, and even the major leagues themselves have undergone profound changes and, to a purist from the old days, are all but unrecognizable. Where are the St. Louis Browns, or the Philadelphia Athletics, or the Boston Braves—or, for the matter of that, even the mag-nificent New York Giants, and Brooklyn Dodg-ers? Gone forever, to be sure, with new cities taking over, and with a few old-timers muttering that the last days are at hand.

Actually, the last days are probably a long, long way off, for baseball even in its modern guise has not changed in its essentials. It is a rough, tough game, encased by rules that were made to be broken if the breaking can be accom-plished smoothly enough, a game that never quite became entirely respectable, a game in which no-body wants to do anything but win. It will un-doubtedly be around for a good time to come, and it will continue, in spite of its own press agents, to be in truth the great American game.

Or so, at least, believes one old-time fan.

For Thought and Discussion

1. Catton's essay first appeared more than three decades ago. If Catton were revising his es-say today, what statements might he wish to alter?

2. Do you agree that baseball is still "The Great American Game"? Why or why not?

3. Examine the first paragraph. In what part of the essay is the thesis fully revealed? Explain the value of this paragraph strategy.

4. Which paragraph provides a concluding summary of the essay's argument? Why is it not the last paragraph?

5. What is the function of the third paragraph from the end? Does it contradict the thesis?

6. Most of Catton's examples come from an era of baseball unknown to his readers ex-cept by report. Why did Catton not make fuller use of contemporary happenings?

James B. Stockdale   1923-

James B. Stockdale is a genuine hero of modern America. After graduation in 1946 from the U.S. Naval Academy, Stockdale became a career officer in the navy. In 1962 he received a master's degree from Stanford University. For nearly eight years (1965-73) he was a prisoner of war (POW) in Vietnam. Rising to the rank of vice admiral in 1977, Stockdale has served as president of the Naval War College (1977-79) and The Citadel, the Military College of South Carolina (1979-80). Although not a professional writer, this highly decorated military figure of modern times writes with clarity and conviction about an issue that touches all Americans: their freedom.

Freedom: Our Most Precious National Treasure

Stockdale's essay "Freedom: Our Most Precious National Treasure," originally published in the June 29, 1980, issue of Parade, *reveals many of the details of his imprisonment.*

Before the big iron gates slammed behind me as I entered the Hanoi prison, I found it hard to think of freedom as something other than an abstraction that's used in songs, Supreme Court debates and political speeches. In this respect I was like many Americans today who take freedom for granted. By the time I was released to come home nearly eight years later, freedom had long since ceased to be an abstraction to me.

To those of us who have served time in Communist jails, freedom has a delicious, tangible meaning. It has become something we can figuratively reach out and touch. Such feelings are likely understandable in men who have spent years shackled and manacled in isolation. But my love of freedom is not just a reaction to cruelty; my appreciation of its preciousness stems from a first-hand understanding of its rarity. The void of freedom in other parts of the world–and particularly the passivity with which this lack is accepted–is staggering to a man who is born and raised free. In my Hanoi cell, I found myself daily picking up shocking signals in that milieu* of deadened sensitivities. Like these:

milieu: environment

The routine feedlot attitude of the simple peasant guards who delivered daily food rations down the line to cooped-up humans, fowl and livestock, with expressionless unconcern for the continual darkness, suffocating closeness, and isolation in which the chickens, pigs and men were confined.

The continuous barking of loudspeakers on the street telling the people of Hanoi what to think.

The pathetic ignorance behind the outburst of a prominent political cadre* who shouted to me in a moment of exasperation: "We may not have freedom, but after 400 years we have order, and we will settle for that."

---

cadre: i.e., a trained communist official

These and countless other impressions drive home to me the fact that human freedom is not the way of the world. To be free to come and go, to choose your life's work, to go for the big bucks or selfless service, or to hit the road as a drifter—these are not open choices to most of the 4.5 billion souls on this planet. Human freedom as we Americans know it is available only to a steadily shrinking minority of people.

You don't know what freedom is until, for a starter, you live for several years in a box-cell 10 feet long and 4 feet wide. I was crouched in the corner of that cell when my guards caught me writing a note to one of my fellow POWs. They were very mad about that note, so they took me from that box-cell to an even smaller, low-ceiling outbuilding, a place we called "Calcutta," and laid me on the floor in squeeze irons. Fetters and jail take away your external freedom; you can't get up and go. But what about the freedom of your will and spirit? Our captors wanted to get at that more than anything. Not by brainwashing—I don't believe there is any such thing—it's a journalist's word. The real answer is simpler: it's pain. They tied your arms behind your back with ropes, shutting off circulation, and then violently and methodically tightened those ropes further, forcing your head down between your legs to produce claustrophobia.* Death was not an option; there was only one way to stop it, and that was to say, "I submit."

---

claustrophobia: extreme fear of confined places

In his *Nicomachean Ethics,* Aristotle points out the difference between acts done voluntarily and those under compulsion.* But he adds that a measure of free choice may remain even in the severest extortion* situations. We had many ways of clinging to that tiny residue of freedom in Hanoi. One way was the tap code. Although we were in solitary confinement we could surreptitiously* communicate with one another, set up a chain of command, encourage the doubtful, console the depressed, comfort the hurt.

---

compulsion: force or constraint
extortion: act of forcing information or some such thing from someone
surreptitiously: secretly

We figured out ways to prevent our captors from manipulating us into making photo and television propaganda for them. One way was to assume a character like an actor—a personality of unpredictability. Our captors did not hold with our unpredictability. When they put an American pilot before the cameras they wanted to be sure of his total submission. For that they had to be sure that his behavior was predictable. To sabotage* that, when put under stress you could stage random scenes of emotional instability. You could throw chairs around. . . . You had to be a good actor. If they thought you had not lost control of yourself but were putting them on, within minutes you could be back in the ropes sobbing like a baby. When you pulled off the act convincingly, they didn't like it. For then you were not useful as propaganda. They'd say, "This guy is not what we want to take downtown."

---

sabotage: to deliberately attempt to defeat an endeavor

People have said to me, "I couldn't take a prison experience like you guys. You all must have had a tremendously high threshold of pain." But it was not a question of a high or low threshold of pain; it was a question of endurance. It didn't matter so much if you submitted under pain one day so long as you made them start all over again the next day. They didn't like to do that.

So the thing was to cling to that tiny vestige* of freedom it was in your power to hold.

vestige: small remaining part

That word freedom is crucial. Freedom does not exist because our Constitution says it should. Over the course of our country's history, people have constantly labored to keep freedom and have paid dearly for it.

Our Declaration of Independence of 204 years ago this week remains one of the most stirring documents in history, signaling a commitment to bear the responsibilities of protecting a way of life. After our bitter struggle for independence, brave and earnest men stepped forward to write our Constitution and formally frame the reasons for which we had fought that unpopular war against the British. No one had to remind our Founding Fathers of the cost. Fifty-six of them knowingly laid their lives, liberty and honor on the line when they signed that Declaration of Independence. And they paid their dues. In the ensuing war, nine were killed in action, five died as prisoners of war, 12 had their homes burned, several lost sons, one man's wife died in prison, and 17 (including Thomas Jefferson) went broke. The legacy of these men was summed up very simply by Tom Paine: "Those who expect to reap the blessings of freedom must, like men, undergo the fatigue of supporting it."

This nation has come a long way since the drafting of the Constitution, and the milestones are littered with human sacrifice. We've fought wars around the globe in freedom's name and have paid a terrible price for our most fundamental national belief. Today, there are men and women who may lay down their lives for this country and the freedom for which it stands.

We all bear the painful cost of freedom. As we formally celebrate the commitment to break from England and to protect our natural rights, let's hug to our breast our freedom–our most precious national treasure–knowing that it, like a child, is imperfect and demanding but undeniably good. Let's keep our centuries-old habit of protecting that child of America, that freedom. She's getting more rare and precious every day.

For Thought and Discussion

1. Does Stockdale regard his suffering in the Vietnam War as a worthwhile sacrifice? Was the United States participation in the war an honorable action, in his view? What, does he assume, was the purpose of the war?

2. What kind of freedom did many of the Hanoi captives find ways to preserve? What were some of the ways in which they retained and expressed it?

3. Is freedom a normal condition of humanity, according to Stockdale?

4. In the last sentence of paragraph one, Stockdale says that during his eight years of confinement freedom ceased to be merely an abstraction. What does he mean? Does this statement suggest his purpose in the essay? If so, how does he carry it out?

5. In Stockdale's account of his imprisonment, who seem to be more intelligent and resourceful, the captors or their captives? Why do you think this is so?

6. Of what commodities other than freedom might it be said that we tend not to value until we are without them? Is this tendency especially true with regard to abstractions?

Glossary

allegory A story with a literal and an implied level of meaning. The implied level of meaning may suggest actual persons, places, events, and situations (as in historical allegory) or a set of ideas (as in conceptual allegory). A **parable** is a form of allegory.

alliteration See **figures of sound.**

allusion A reference within a work of literature to something outside it. Literary allusions refer to other works of literature. Classical and Biblical allusions are types of literary allusions. Historical allusions refer to persons, places, events, and situations in history.

ambiguity Doubleness or inconclusiveness of meaning in a work of literature. Ambiguity may reflect an author's pessimism about the possibility of reaching certainty of knowledge in this world. If so, it expresses a non-Christian view of the world. Sometimes ambiguity is used to refer generally to all multiple meaning. In this sense it denotes something that is essential to all imaginative writing and figurative expression. It is more precise, however, to restrict its meaning to the narrower sense of unresolved contradictions in a work of literature.

anapest See **meter.**

antagonist See **character.**

antihero The central figure of a narrative who is the opposite of the traditional hero. The antihero is usually weak, bumbling, thoughtless, and dishonest. This type of **protagonist** reflects the modern age's disbelief in ideal virtue and in the possibility of heroic action.

apostrophe See **figures of thought.**

assonance See **figures of sound.**

atmosphere See **setting.**

avant-garde Writing that is revolutionary in style, form, and subject matter. The term derives from a French word meaning "advance guard," the troops advancing farthest forward. The term implies hostility toward the prevailing literary spirit of the day.

ballad A short, simple narrative song. Folk ballads are characteristically impersonal, compressed, dramatic (in use of dialogue and absence of transitions), ritualistic in effect (through the use of various devices of repetition), and simple in stanza form. Common ballad stanza consists of four lines, of which the first and third have four stresses and the second and fourth have three stresses and rhyme.

Beat Poets A group of experimental poets of the 1950s and 1960s who openly rebelled against American cultural and moral values.

black humor A form of humor whose grotesque and morbid situations reveal the bitter disillusionment of its author. Life appears as a cruel joke played upon man by an impersonal or malevolent force. Black humor reflects a cynical view of human existence.

blank verse Unrhymed **iambic pentameter.** See also **meter** and **rhyme.**

burlesque See **satire.**

cadence See **rhythm.**

caesura See **meter.**

catalog A formal list of persons, objects, or attributes in poetry. Such lists are associated with primitive oral poetry and give a ritualistic effect to the passages in which they appear. See especially Sandburg's "Chicago."

character Representations of persons in literature. Main characters are more fully treated than lesser characters. The chief or main character is known as the **protagonist** (lit., first character). His opponent (whether a person, force, or situation) is the **antagonist. Flat characters** have little individuality (few distinguishing physical or psychological details). **Round characters** are distinguished physically and psychologically as individuals.

conceit An unusually striking comparison carried out in considerable detail.

conflict The heart of plot. Conflict may be external (between characters or between a character and his environment, whether society or nature) or internal (between a character's emotions or duties or both). A story may include more than one conflict; in Hemingway's "Big Two-Hearted River," the obvious conflict between the **protagonist** and nature (specifically the trout) is actually not as important as the less obvious one within the character himself.

consonance See **figures of sound.**

couplet A pair of rhymed lines. **Heroic couplets** are couplets of **iambic pentameter.**

dactyl See **meter.**

dialect The manner of speech characteristic of a certain area or class. Dialectal differences may appear in vocabulary, grammatical constructions, and pronunciation.

didacticism Instruction in literature. Since ancient times writers and critics have believed that imaginative literature has two purposes: to delight and to teach. That is, literature should give both pleasure and wisdom. Christian moral critics have held that literature delights in order to teach. Modern writers and critics have generally denied the teaching function of literature and stressed exclusively its purpose to give aesthetic pleasure. However, literature that contains no message has never been taken very seriously. Didacticism is essential to the highest literary achievement.

dirge See **elegy.**

doggerel Poorly written verse. Doggerel is characterized by monotonous **rhyme** and **rhythm,** trite or trivial subject matter, and shallowness of emotion.

dramatic irony. See **irony.**

dramatic monologue A poem consisting of a speech by a character (who is not the author) addressing an audience at a critical moment in his life. The poem focuses on the character of the speaker, which is revealed entirely and unintentionally by what he says. Other kinds of monologue are the soliloquy (a speech addressed to an audience by an actor alone on stage) and monodrama (a dramatic situation in which there is only one character).

elegy Originally any poem of solemn meditation. Now a formal poem lamenting the death of a particular person or meditating on the subject of death itself. The **dirge** is also a poem expressing lament or mourning but is shorter, less formalized, and usually intended as a song.

end-stopped line See **meter.**

enjambment See **meter.**

fable A brief tale with a moral point and generally with nonhuman characters. The beast fable since ancient times has satirized human follies.

figure An artful deviation from the usual way of saying something. **Figures of thought** (sometimes called **figures of speech**) use normal arrangements of words but produce changes in their meanings (e.g., **metaphor, apostrophe, verbal irony**). **Figures of sound** select and arrange words for their sound values (e.g., **alliteration, assonance, onomatopoeia**).

figures of sound:

    alliteration The recurrence of consonant sounds at the beginning of nearby stressed syllables, as in "*l*ively *l*ads and *l*asses."

    assonance The recurrence of vowel sounds in nearby stressed syllables, as in "her f*ears* and t*ears*."

    consonance The recurrence of consonant sounds in nearby stressed syllables, as in "my lo*v*e doth li*v*e."

    onomatopoeia The use of words that sound like what they mean (e.g., *boom, hiss, moan, murmur*).

figures of thought:

    apostrophe The address of some nonpersonal (or absent) object as if it were able to reply (e.g., "O death, where is thy sting?").

    hyperbole See **irony.**

metaphor Broadly, the expression of one thing in terms of another. In stricter usage, the stated or implied equivalence of two things (e.g., "I am the bread of life").

paradox A seeming contradiction (e.g., "Death, thou shalt die").

personification The giving of personal characteristics to something that is not a person. See also **apostrophe.**

simile A stated comparison of two things using a linking word or phrase (e.g., *like, as, as if*): "my luve is like a red, red rose."

symbol An object that stands for something else as well as for itself. It thus points to a meaning beyond itself. Unlike a metaphor it has a number of related meanings and exists on the literal level of a work. See also **image** and **metaphor.**

flat character See **character.**

foot See **meter.**

free association The literary technique of arranging words or ideas in nonlogical sequence to suggest the random associations of a character's mind. The term derives from the commonly used psychological practice of having a patient state what he associates with a particular object without censoring or arranging his thoughts.

free verse Poetry without **rhyme** or **meter.** It is printed in lines (usually irregular in length) and often has some rhythmical patterning.

genre A standard or category of literature.

haiku A Japanese poetic form consisting of three lines containing seventeen syllables (5/7/5). It delineates a sharp visual image designed to arouse a distinct emotion in the reader.

hyperbole See **irony.**

iamb See **meter.**

iambic pentameter See **meter** and **blank verse.**

image A word or phrase that conveys an impression appealing to one of the five senses (hearing, sight, smell, touch, and taste).

irony A **figure of thought** that contrasts appearance and reality. There are two main types of irony: verbal and situational. In **verbal irony** a contrast exists between the literal and implied levels of meaning of an expression or statement. The literal level gives only the apparent meaning while the implied level carries the actual meaning. The expression "A likely story!" implies the opposite of what it states literally, and the implied meaning is the real meaning, the one intended. Some special types of verbal irony are hyperbole, understatement, and sarcasm. **Hyperbole**–i.e., exaggeration–implies less than what is said: "Then did I beat them small as the dust before the wind" (David speaking of his destruction of his enemies, Ps. 18:42). **Understatement** implies more than what is said: "Fear ye not therefore, ye are of more value than many sparrows" (Matt. 10:31; cf. Mark 8:36, which states more directly the value of the soul). **Sarcasm** is often loosely applied to all scornful wit but is best restricted to mock praise or mock assent: "No doubt but ye are the people, and wisdom shall die with you" (Job 12:2). Sarcasm seems similar to hyperbole but is actually different; its literal meaning is a contradiction rather than an exaggeration of its implied meaning. Verbal irony sustained throughout an entire work is known as structural irony. The second major type of irony, **situational irony,** presents a contrast between supposition and reality. We say that Peter's inability to gain entrance to the house where the believers were praying for his release (they did not believe it was he) is ironic, because one would suppose they would pray with faith that their prayers could be answered (Acts 12:12-16). A literary application of situational irony is **dramatic irony,** in which the reader or audience is put in touch with the reality of a situation to create a contrast between the knowledge of the reader or audience and the ignorance of the characters. The book of Esther creates reader interest through dramatic irony: the reader's prior knowledge of what Mordecai and Esther are planning for Haman puts his ignorant actions and boasting in an absurd light.

metaphor See **figures of thought.**

meter The regular recurrence of accented syllables in a line of poetry. The meter of a poem is the meter of its normal lines (lines often contain metrical irregularities). In English meter, accent is produced by the force and pitch with which syllables are pronounced (rather than, as in classical languages, from the duration of syllables). Accented syllables are voiced more loudly or with a higher pitch than unaccented syllables. The accent of a syllable is relative to that of adjacent syllables, rather than to a general implied norm for the line. Just as the trough between two waves in a swell may be higher than the crest of a wavelet between swells, so an unaccented syllable in one part of a line may be stressed more heavily than an accented syllable elsewhere. In the line "Before it can put forth its blossoming," the *-ing* in *blossoming* is accented in relation to the adjacent syllable *-som-* though it is less heavily stressed than *it,* which is however unaccented in relation to the heavily stressed *fore* and *can.* The factors determining the placing of stresses in a line are three: (1) normal word accent in polysyllabic words (*blos* som ing); (2) the grammatical function of monosyllabic words (nouns, verbs, adjectives, and adverbs usually are more heavily stressed than articles, coordinating conjunctions, and prepositions); and (3) the previously established metrical pattern (responsible for the accenting of "it *can* put *forth*" above).

In analyzing the meter of a line of poetry (called **scansion**), we are concerned with syllables rather than with words and with sounds rather than with letters. A line must be divided into its component syllables, and its metrical units may divide a polysyllabic word (e.g., "Be *fore/* it *can/* put *forth/* its *blos/* som *ing*"). The syllables that seem to require a greater vocal emphasis are identified here by italics rather than by accent marks. In a normal line that is analyzed correctly, the accented syllables appear evenly spaced among the unaccented ones. The next step is to identify the repetitive unit in the line, called a **foot.** A foot consisting of two syllables, the second of which is accented, is called **iambic** (or an **iamb**). The opposite of an iambic foot–one containing an accented syllable followed by an unaccented–is a **trochaic** foot (or **trochee**). A three-syllable foot consisting of two unaccented syllables followed by an accented is an **anapestic** foot (or **anapest**). The opposite of an anapestic foot–a three-syllable foot beginning with an accented syllable–is a **dactylic** foot (or **dactyl**). The standard feet thus consist of one or more unaccented syllables preceding or following an accented syllable:

iamb: be *ware*
trochee: *hap* py
anapest: un der *stand*
dactyl: *love* li ness

Poets, for variety or emphasis, may use **substitute feet.** A substitute foot may be a standard foot that occurs in a poem in which another foot is normal. For example, iambic lines often begin with trochaic feet: *"Cour* age/ he *said/* and *poin/* ted *to/* the *land."* (It is important not to assume that the meter of a line is determined by its first foot.) The substitute foot may be one of two specialized feet employed exclusively for that purpose. The **spondaic** foot (or **spondee**) consists of two stressed syllables: *"Fire-wing'd/* and *make/* a *morn/* ing in/ his *mirth"* (*"Fire-wing'd"* is a spondee). The **pyrrhic** foot consists of two unstressed syllables. Some metricists deny the existence of the pyrrhic foot, insisting that in every pair of lightly stressed syllables one is stressed slightly more heavily than the other. In the following example, which comes from

"To Spenser," a **sonnet** by John Keats, what might be considered a pyrrhic foot precedes a substitute trochaic foot in a predominantly iambic line: "A *for/* es ter/ *deep* in/ thy *mid/* most *trees.*" Notice, however, that the pyrrhic foot could also be scanned as a weak iambic: "es *ter.*" The scansion of a given line can vary somewhat according to the reader's interpretation of it. Nevertheless, many lines admit only one justifiable scansion, and even the lines that allow more than one proper scansion can be scanned improperly.

Describing the meter of a line requires two terms: (1) the name of the dominant foot and (2) an indication of the number of feet. Meter of only one foot per line (quite rare) is called **monometer;** two feet, **dimeter;** three feet, **trimeter;** four feet, **tetrameter;** five feet, **pentameter;** six feet, **hexameter;** seven feet, **heptameter;** and eight feet, **octameter.** The line "Be *fore/* it *can/* put *forth/* its *blos/* some *ing*" thus exemplifies **iambic pentameter,** one of the most common meters in English poetry.

A complete metrical analysis of a poem also includes both the identification of a major pause within its lines (such a pause is called a **caesura** and is marked by a double bar: //) and the distinguishing of **end-stopped lines**–lines that end with a natural break in the syntax (the pause that follows a phrase, clause, or sentence)–from **enjambed** lines–lines whose end breaks up a grammatical unity such as subject and verb or verb and object. The following pair of lines contains a **caesura** and exemplifies **enjambment:**

Be *with/* me *in/* the *sum/* mer *days,//* and *I*
Will *for/* thine *hon/* or *and/* his *pleas/* ure *try.*

mock heroic See **satire.**
mood The emotional atmosphere of a work. The feeling the reader is meant to share with the characters (e.g., uneasiness, horror, exhilaration, sadness).

narration The telling of a story by a character or directly by the author himself. See also **point of view.**

occasional verse Poetry written to enhance or make memorable a particular occasion, normally public and contemporary.
octave See **sonnet.**
onomatopoeia See **figures of sound.**

parable See **allegory.**
paradox See **figures of thought.**
parody See **satire.**
personification See **figures of thought.**
plot A connected series of incidents. The connecting principle is not chronological but causal. That is, the incidents of a standard plot are not necessarily arranged in the order in which they supposedly occur. Often an author will begin his narrative *in medias res* ("in the middle of things") with an incident of high inherent interest or of central significance to the story and fill in the antecedent action by having it reported or re-enacted in the mind of one of the characters. In serious writing, the order of incidents is determined by considerations such as characterization, emotional impact, aesthetic effect, or theme.
point of view Narrative perspective. The way a story is told (whether by a voice representing the author or by a major or minor character or whether by one who knows all or by one whose knowledge is limited) is its point of view.
prosody The study of **meter.**
protagonist See **character.**
pun The creation of a double meaning by the use of homonyms (words that sound alike with differences in meaning). A pun may be humorous (e.g., Joseph's use of "lift up thine head" in Gen. 40:13, 19-20, 22) or entirely serious (e.g., the Lord's use of *house* in II Sam. 7:5, 7, 11).
pyrrhic See **meter.**

quatrain A four-line **stanza,** one of the most common stanzas in English poetry.

rhyme Identical sound in corresponding words or phrases. **Perfect rhyme** requires agreement of sounds from the last stressed vowel sound onward, with a difference in the immediately preceding consonant sounds. For example, in "A Ballad of Trees and the Master" by Sidney Lanier, the final syllables of lines 3 and 4 exemplify perfect rhyme: "came," "shame." There is agreement between the sounds of the last stressed vowels in the line and the succeeding sounds. When the rhyming sounds consist of only one syllable (as above), the rhyme is known as **masculine**. When the rhyming sounds include more than one syllable, the rhyme is called **feminine:** "hiring," "firing." **Imperfect rhyme** includes partial rhyme and eye rhyme. **Partial (or slant) rhyme** usually shows agreement in terminal consonant sounds (see **consonance**) but disagreement in the preceding vowel sounds: "held," "build." Partial rhyme may, on the other hand, show agreement in the vowel sounds (see **assonance**) but disagreement in the succeeding consonant sounds: "in," "trim." **Eye rhyme,** which is not as respectable a type of imperfect rhyme, is based on the similarity of sight rather than sound. The "rhyme" consists of identical spelling: "laughter," "daughter." Though eye rhyme may be similar in the nature of its sounds to partial rhyme, the identical spelling implies that the poet does not understand the nature of the rhyme, confusing sounds with letters.

Rhyme is distinguished also by its location: **end rhyme** refers to rhymes at the ends of lines, **internal rhyme** to rhymes within a line. In the famous opening lines of Poe's "The Raven," "dreary" and "weary," "napping" and "tapping," exemplify internal rhyme:"Once upon a midnight dreary, while I pondered, weak and weary,/Over many a quaint and curious volume of forgotten lore–/While I nodded, nearly napping, suddenly there came a tapping,/As of some one gently rapping, rapping at my chamber door." The patterning of end rhymes in a poem or stanza forms its rhyme scheme.

The **rhyme scheme** is described by assigning to each rhyme sound successive letters of the alphabet. In Lanier's first stanza of "A Ballad of Trees and the Master," "went" and "–spent" are designated by the letter *a,* "came," "shame," and "came" by *b,* and the three words "Him" by *c.* This stanza is said to rhyme *aabbcccb.* Rhyme, though a valuable resource for poets, is not essential to poetry (see **blank verse, free verse**).

rhythm A more or less regular recurrence of stressed syllables in written or spoken utterance. As rhythm approaches regularity in poetry, it becomes **meter**. Such regularity is rare in prose (cf. "*Bless* ed are *they* which do *hun*ger and *thirst* after *right*eousness," Matt. 5:6). Prose rhythm is usually a looser sort, involving syllable groups of varying length and patterning and occurring sporadically. The spacing of stressed syllables in rhythmical prose is more often according to time intervals than according to numbers of syllables, and this spacing is constantly fluctuating according to meaning, pacing, and emphasis (e.g., "Though I *speak* with the *tongues* of *men* and of *an*gels, and *have* not *char*ity, *I* am be*come* as *sound*ing *brass,* or a *tink*ling *cym*bal," I Cor. 13:1). Prose with a high degree of rhythm–including a pleasurable sensation of rise and fall–is said to possess **cadence** (e.g., Paine's "*These* are the *times* that *try* men's *souls*"). This satisfaction of reader (or listener) expectations by a patterned recurrence of sound, whether in verse or in highly stylized prose, is a universally pleasurable experience.

romanticism European and American reaction to the cultural climate and values of neoclassicism. Romanticism insisted on the greater importance of (1) individual than group perceptions, (2) imagination and feeling than reason, and (3) the natural than the artificial. In literature romanticism stressed the importance of originality and therefore abhorred slavish imitation by one author of another and conforming to conventional social proprieties. It preferred the emotionally dynamic to the rationally controlled (denying the possibility of their coexistence). Romantic writers widened the subject matter of poetry to include mundane experiences ignored by neoclassical writers and thus anticipated the later nineteenth-century movements called realism and naturalism (though realism is itself a reaction against romantic idealism). In its exaltation of man in nature over man in society (where the individual is subject to the influence of corrupt institutions), romanticism shows a primitivistic character. Romantic primitivism was congenial to the literary nationalism of nineteenth-century American writers, who set out to create a uniquely American literature from native materials. Romantic primitivism, along with romantic individualism, gave expression to the values of the frontier. Such figures as the noble savage and the high-principled, resourceful backwoodsman are products of American romantic idealism. The period of American Romanticism is 1820-65, though some of its elements (antiauthoritarianism, antiintellectualism, subjectivism) are still dominant today.

round character See **character.**

run-on line (also **enjambment**) See **meter.**

sarcasm See **irony.**

satire Corrective ridicule in literature, or a work that is designed to correct an evil by means of ridicule. Satire should not be confused with **verbal irony,** a common ingredient of satire, or with **sarcasm,** a common type of verbal irony. A special form of satire is **burlesque,** which mocks its subject by incongruous imitation either of its style (**parody**) or content (**travesty**) or by incongruous representation in terms of high seriousness (e.g., **mock heroic**).

scansion See **meter.**

sestet See **sonnet.**

setting The time and place in which a narrative (whether poetic or prose-fictional) takes place, or in which an incident within a narrative takes place. Setting contributes to **atmosphere,** the emotion pervading a work (i.e., the emotion that the reader shares with the characters). Some romantic writing treats setting almost as a character; Nature is a brooding presence communicating wisdom to man through his physical surroundings.

simile See **figures of thought.**

situational irony See **irony.**

slant rhyme See **rhyme.**

sonnet A lyric poem of fourteen **iambic-pentameter** lines conventionally rhyming according to one of two patterns. The **Italian** (or **Petrarchan**) **sonnet** consists of two parts. The first eight lines, called the **octave,** rhyme *abbaabba.* The last six lines, called the **sestet,** may use any combination of two or three new rhymes: for example, *cdcdcd, cdecde, cdedce.* The Italian sonnet, popularized by the Italian poet Petrarch (1304-74), was introduced into England by Sir Thomas Wyatt (1503-54) and widely cultivated in England during the Renaissance. Another version of the sonnet, the **English** (or **Shakespearean**), was improvised by Wyatt's younger contemporary, the Earl of Surrey (1517?-47), and splendidly refined by Shakespeare (1564-1616). The English sonnet consists of three **quatrains** and a closing **couplet** and rhymes *ababcdcdefefgg.* The sonnet has been a popular **genre** in America as well as in England and continental Europe. Though originally treating almost exclusively disappointed love (often in connected series called **sonnet sequences**), the sonnet soon became the vehicle for a variety of **themes,** public as well as private, religious as well as secular. Sonnets deviating from the conventional **rhyme schemes** are common.

spondee See **meter.**

stanza A group of lines constituting a section of

a poem and usually distinguished in print by spacing. Stanzas normally divide rhymed poems into sections of identical length and rhyme scheme. However, stanzas may vary in structure within a poem, and stanza divisions may occur even in unrhymed verse (in which case they serve the function of paragraphs in prose). The description of a stanza must indicate its **meter** (the number and predominant type of feet) and its **rhyme scheme,** or the lack of either or both. See also **meter** and **rhyme.**

stream-of-consciousness Random sequence of thoughts and sensations within the mind of the central character. See **free association.**

style The manner of expression in prose or verse, in written or oral discourse. Style may be **plain** (simple, direct, unadorned) or **ornate** (elevated in diction, complicated in structure, figuratively embellished). The Puritans cultivated the plain style in prose and verse, though their style, by modern standards, appears ornate. Style varies according to historical fashion, among particular writers, and even within individual practice (according to formality of the occasion and according to the degree to which the writer wishes to let his personality show).

surprise The violation of the reader's expectations.

suspense The anticipation created in the reader because of the author's withholding information about the nature or outcome of a situation while raising the reader's curiosity or anxiety. Suspense may exist in the reader's lack of knowledge about who or what or how; or, when the reader knows these, it may exist solely in the reader's lack of knowledge about when.

symbol See **figures of thought.**

theme A recurring or emerging idea in a work of literature. A work may have many themes. Its major theme is its main point, similar to the thesis of an essay. A theme may be **explicit** (a moral stated by a character or by the author in his own voice) or **implicit** (a conception that must be inferred). Theme serves the didactic purpose of a work by embodying and emphasizing its message. Theme serves the aesthetic aim of a work by providing coherence.

tone The attitude of a work toward its subject. Tone is the emotional view of the subject (indignation, awe, compassion, derision, etc.) the reader is meant to share with the author. Interpretation of tone is crucial in determining and evaluating meaning.

travesty See **satire.**

trochee See **meter.**

understatement See **irony.**

verbal irony See **irony.**

voice The reader's sense of the author's personality behind the features of his work. In considering the characters, incidents, style, and particularly tone, the reader forms an impression of the creator of the work, of the puppet master pulling the strings behind the scenes. Voice is to some extent controlled by an author and may vary to a degree from work to work. Nevertheless, the voice of an author is the unique imprint of his personality on his works.

Index

Photo Credits

Acknowledgments

Barnett, Elizabeth "Love is not blind. I see with single eye" by Edna St. Vincent Millay. From *Collected Poems,* HarperCollins. Copyright 1923, 1951 by Edna St. Vincent Millay and Norma Millay Ellis. All rights reserved. Reprinted by permission of Elizabeth Barnett, Literary Executor.

Blackwell Publishing "The Tomb of Raven McCloud" by Archibald Rutledge. *The Yale Review.* Copyright 1947 Yale University.

Brandt & Hoehman Literary Agents, Inc. "The Most Dangerous Game" by Richard Connell. Copyright ©1924 by Richard Connell. Copyright renewed ©1952 by Louise Fox Connell. Reprinted by permission of Brandt & Hoehman Literary Agents, Inc.

Don Congdon Associates, Inc. "There Will Come Soft Rains" by Ray Bradbury. Reprinted by permission of Don Congdon Associates, Inc. Copyright © 1950 by the Crowell Collier Publishing Co., renewed 1977 by Ray Bradbury.

Doubleday "Dolor," Copyright 1943 by Modern Poetry Association, Inc. From *Collected Poems of Theodore Roethke* by Theodore Roethke. Used by permission of Doubleday, a division of Random House, Inc. for U.S., Canada, Philippines, and Open Market. **Faber and Faber Limited** granted permission for non-exclusive United Kingdom rights.

Farrar, Straus and Giroux, Inc. "Charles" from *The Lottery and Other Stories* by Shirley Jackson. Copyright © 1948, 1949 by Shirley Jackson. Copyright renewed 1976, 1977 by Laurence Hyman, Barry Hyman, Mrs. Sarah Webster and Mrs. Joanne Schnurer. Reprinted by permission of Farrar, Straus and Giroux, Inc. **Linda Allen Literary Agency** granted permission for non-exclusive United Kingdom rights.

Forbes "The Great American Game" by Bruce Catton. Reprinted by Permission of AMERICAN HERITAGE INC. 1959.

Harcourt, Inc. "Chicago," "Grass," and "Fog" from *Chicago Poems* by Carl Sandburg, copyright 1916 by Holt, Rinehart and Winston and renewed 1944 by Carl Sandburg, reprinted by permission of Harcourt, Inc.

"The Journey of the Magi" from *Collected Poems 1909-1962* by T. S. Eliot, copyright 1936 by Harcourt, Inc., copyright © 1964, 1963 by T. S. Eliot, reprinted by permission of the publisher for U.S. and its territories and the Philippine Republic. Non-exclusive world rights granted by **Faber and Faber Limited.**

"A Worn Path" from *A Curtain of Green and Other Stories,* copyright 1941 and renewed 1969 by Eudora Welty, reprinted by permission of Harcourt, Inc. for world rights. Reprinted by the permission of **Russell & Volkening, Inc.,** as agents for the author. Copyright © 1941 by Eudora Welty, renewed in 1969 by Eudora Welty for British Commonwealth rights.

Harold Matson Company, Inc. "A Boy Who Was Traded for a Horse" by James Saxon Childers. Copyright © 1932 by James Saxon Childers, Harold Matson Company, Inc.

Harvard University Press Poems 49, 67, 219, 254, 288, 435, 441, 585, 764, 986, 1052, 1078, 1176, 1212, 1263, 1510, 1755 by Emily Dickinson. Reprinted by permission of the publishers and the Trustees of Amherst College from *The Poems of Emily Dickinson,* Thomas H. Johnson, ed., Cambridge, Mass.: The Belknap Press of Harvard University Press, Copyright © 1951, 1955, 1979 by the President and Fellows of Harvard College.

Henry Holt and Company "Birches," "The Death of the Hired Man," "Desert Places," "The Gift Outright," "Mending Wall," "The Pasture," "The Road Not Taken," and "Stopping by Woods on a Snowy Evening" by Robert Frost. From *The Poetry of Robert Frost* edited by Edward Connery Lathem. Copyright 1923, 1930, © 1967, 1969 by Henry Holt and Co., copyright 1942, 1944, 1951 by Robert Frost, copyright © 1970 by Lesley Frost Ballantine. Reprinted by permission of Henry Holt and Company, LLC.

Houghton Mifflin Company "Ars Poetica" from *Collected Poems* by Archibald MacLeish. Copyright © 1985 by the Estate of Archibald MacLeish. Reprinted by permission of Houghton Mifflin Company. All rights reserved.

Liveright Publishing Corporation "somewhere i have never travelled,gladly beyond," Copyright 1931, © 1959, 1991 by the Trustees for the E. E. Cummings Trust. Copyright © 1979 by George James Firmage.

"in Just-" Copyright 1923, 1951, © 1991 by the Trustees for the E. E. Cummings Trust. Copyright © 1976 by George James Firmage.